P9-BZW-035

# John Willis

# Screen World

## Volume 53
### 2002

Associate Editor
Barry Monush

APPLAUSE
THEATRE & CINEMA BOOKS

# Screen World
Volume 53

Copyright © 2002 by John Willis
All rights reserved

Printed in Canada

No part of this publication may be reproduced or transmitted in any form or by any means, electronic or mechanical, including photocopy, recording, or any other information storage or retrieval system now known or to be invented, without permission in writing from the publisher, except by a reviewer who wishes to quote brief passages in connection with a review written for inclusion in a magazine, newspaper, or broadcast.

Library of Congress Card No. 50-3023

ISBN: 1-55783-598-5 (hardcover)
ISBN: 1-55783-599-3 (paperback)

Applause Theatre & Cinema Books
151 West 46th Street, 8th Floor
New York, NY 10036
Phone: (212) 575-9265
Fax: (646) 562-5852
Email: info@applausepub.com
Internet: www.applausepub.com

## SALES & DISTRIBUTION

North America:
HAL LEONARD CORP.
7777 West Bluemound Road
P. O. Box 13819
Milwaukee, WI 53213
Phone: (414) 774-3630
Fax: (414) 774-3259
Email: halinfo@halleonard.com
Internet: www.halleonard.com

UK:
COMBINED BOOK SERVICES LTD.
Units I/K, Paddock Wood Distribution Centre
Paddock Wood, Tonbridge, Kent TN12 6UU
Phone: (44) 01892 837171
Fax: (44) 01892 837272
United Kingdom

# Table of Contents

**EDITOR:** JOHN WILLIS

**ASSOCIATE EDITOR:** BARRY MONUSH

*Acknowledgements:* Anthology Film Archives, Artistic License, Jenna Bagnini, Castle Hill, Samantha Dean, DreamWorks, Brian Durnin, The Film Forum, First Look, First Run Features, Fox Searchlight, Kino International, Leisure Time Features, Tom Lynch, Mike Maggiore, Miramax Films, New Line Cinema/Fine Line Features, New Yorker Films, October Films, Paramount Pictures, Kristen Schilo, 7th Art Releasing, Sony Pictures Entertainment, Sheldon Stone, Strand Releasing, Twentieth Century Fox, Universal Pictures, Walt Disney Pictures, Zeitgeist Films

*Walk on the Wild Side*

*Period of Adjustment*

*Barefoot in the Park*

*They Shoot Horses, Don't They?*

*Klute*

*Steelyard Blues*

*Fun with Dick and Jane*

*Julia*

*Coming Home*

# TO
# JANE FONDA

**A magnetic and influential talent whose impact reached beyond motion pictures to make her one of the most thought-provoking, outspoken, and unforgettable figures of our time.**

**FILMS:** *Tall Story* (1960); *Walk on the Wild Side* (1962), *The Chapman Report* (1962), *Period of Adjustment* (1962); *In the Cool of the Day* (1963); *Sunday in New York* (1964), *Joy House* (1964); *Cat Ballou* (1965), *Circle of Love* (1965); *The Chase* (1966), *The Game Is Over* (1967), *Hurry Sundown* (1967), *Barefoot in the Park* (1967); *Barbarella* (1968); *Spirits of the Dead* (1969), *They Shoot Horses, Don't They?* (Academy Award nomination, 1969); *Klute* (Academy Award for Best Actress, 1971); *F.T.A.* (also producer, 1972); *Steelyard Blues* (1973), *Tout va Bien* (1973), *A Doll's House* (1973); *Introduction to the Enemy* (1974); *The Blue Bird* (1976); *Fun With Dick and Jane* (1977), *Julia* (Academy Award nomination, 1977); *Coming Home* (Academy Award for Best Actress, 1978), *Comes a Horseman* (1978), *California Suite* (1978); *The China Syndrome* (Academy Award nomination, 1979), *An Almost Perfect Affair* (1979), *The Electric Horseman* (1979); *No Nukes* (1980), *Nine to Five* (1980); *On Golden Pond* (Academy Award nomination, 1981), *Rollover* (1981); *Agnes of God* (1985); *The Morning After* (Academy Award nomination, 1986); *Leonard Part 6* (1987); *Old Gringo* (1989); *Stanley & Iris* (1990).

*The China Syndrome*

*Nine to Five*

*The Morning After*

# TOP BOX OFFICE STARS
## OF 2001

1. Tom Cruise

2. George Clooney

3. Julia Roberts

4. Russell Crowe

5. Nicole Kidman

6. Denzel Washington

7. Will Smith

8. Brad Pitt

9. Ben Affleck

10. Jackie Chan

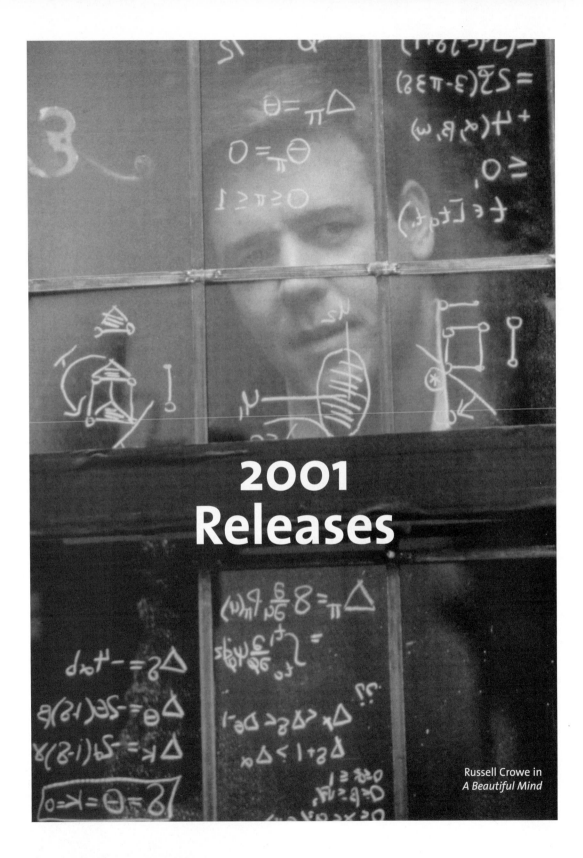

# 2001
# Releases

Russell Crowe in
*A Beautiful Mind*

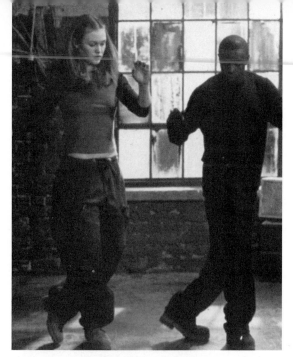

Julia Stiles, Sean Patrick Thomas

Kerry Washington, Sean Patrick Thomas

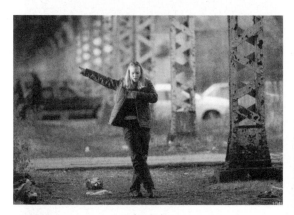

Julia Stiles

# SAVE THE LAST DANCE

**(PARAMOUNT)** Producers, Robert W. Cort, David Madden; Director, Thomas Carter; Screenplay, Duane Adler, Cheryl Edwards; Story, Duane Adler; Photography, Robbie Greenberg; Designer, Paul Eads; Editor, Peter E. Berger; Costumes, Sandra Hernandez; Co-Producer, Marie Cantin; Music, Mark Isham; Music Supervisor, Michael McQuarn; Choreographer, Fatima; Ballet Choreographer, Randy Duncan; Casting, Avy Kaufman; a Cort/Madden production, presented in association with MTV Films; Dolby; Deluxe color; Rated PG-13; 105 minutes; Release date: January 12, 2001

## CAST

Sara . . . . . . . . . . . . . . . . . . . . . . . . . . . . . . . . . . . . . . . . . Julia Stiles
Derek . . . . . . . . . . . . . . . . . . . . . . . . . .Sean Patrick Thomas
Chenille . . . . . . . . . . . . . . . . . . . . . . . . . . . . .Kerry Washington
Malakai . . . . . . . . . . . . . . . . . . . . . . . . . . . . . . . . . . .Fredro Starr
Roy . . . . . . . . . . . . . . . . . . . . . . . . . . . . . . . . . . .Terry Kinney
Nikki . . . . . . . . . . . . . . . . . . . . . . . . . . . . . . . . . .Bianca Lawson
Snookie . . . . . . . . . . . . . . . . . . . . . . . . . . . . . . . .Vince Green
Kenny . . . . . . . . . . . . . . . . . . . . . . . . . . . . . . . .Garland Whitt
Diggy . . . . . . . . . . . . . . . . . . . . . . . . . . . . . . . . .Elisabeth Oas
Arvel . . . . . . . . . . . . . . . . . . . . . . . . . . . . . .Artel Jarod Walker
Lip . . . . . . . . . . . . . . . . . . . . . . . . . . . . . . . . . .Cory Stewart
Glynn . . . . . . . . . . . . . . . . . . . . . . . . . . . . . .Jennifer Anglin
Momma Dean . . . . . . . . . . . . . . . . . . . . . . .Dorothy Martin
Lindsay . . . . . . . . . . . . . . . . . . . . . . . . . . . . . . . . .Kim Tlusty
Woman on Train . . . . . . . . . . . . . . . . . . . . . . . . . .Felicia Fields
Mrs. Gwynn . . . . . . . . . . . . . . . . . . . . . . . . . . . . . .Ora Jones
Mr. Campbell . . . . . . . . . . . . . . . . . . . . . . . . . . . . . . .Tab Baker
and Kevin Reid (Wonk), Andrew Rothenberg (Stern Judge), Mekdes Bruk (Lakisha), Ronald Ray (Stepps Slacker), Tai'isha Davis (Tiffnee), Karimah Westbrook (Alyssa), Eric Hubbard (Jasmine), Richmond Talauega (Stepps Dancer), Whitney Powell (Toni), Brenda Pickleman (Older Disgusted Woman), Julie Greenberg (Gymnastics Teacher), Anna Paskeveska (Ballet Instructor), Malaika Paul (Basketball Player), Jennifer Echols (Lavatory Girl), Ellie Weingardt (Ballet Judge's Assistant), Earl Manning, Latisha Oliver, Nefertiti Robinson, Roland "Ro Ro" Tabor, Anthony Talauega, Richard Whitebear, Earl Wright (Hip-Hop Dancers), Ariane Dolan, Chryssie Whitehead, Sarita Smith Childs, Trinity Hamilton, Randy Herrera, Audrey Leung, Katrina Oeffling, Joanna Wozniak (Ballet Dancers), Maia Wilkins, Davis C. Robertson (Sea Shadow Dancers), Michael Anderson, Deanne Brown, Deborah Dawn, Nicole Marie Duffy, Sam Franke, Jennifer Goodman, Taryn Kaschock, Stacy Joy Keller, Calvin Kitten, Michael Levine, Pierre Lockett, Suzanne Lopez, Brian McSween, Jeremiah O'Connor, Emily Patterson, Domingo Rubio, Tracy Shields, Patrick Simonello, Guoping Wang, Teanna Zarro (Les Presages Dancers)

*Having given up her dreams of training for ballet at Juilliard, Sara moves in with her father in Chicago's South Side, where she finds romance with hip-hop dancer Derek.*

© Paramount Pictures

**Julia Stiles, Terry Kinney**

8

Claire Forlani, Ryan Phillippe

# ANTITRUST

**(MGM)** Producers, Nick Wechsler, Keith Addis, David Nicksay; Executive Producers, David Hoberman, Ashok Amritraj, C. E. Erickson, Julia Chasman; Director, Peter Howitt; Screenplay, Howard Franklin; Photography, John Bailey; Designer, Catherine Hardwicke; Editor, Zach Staenberg; Costumes, Maya Mani; Music, Don Davis; Casting, Amanda Mackey Johnson, Cathy Sandrich; an Industry Entertainment production, presented in association with Hyde Park Entertainment; Dolby; Panavision; Color; Rated PG-13; 108 minutes; Release date: January 12, 2001

### CAST

| | |
|---|---|
| Milo Hoffman | Ryan Phillippe |
| Lisa Calighan | Rachael Leigh Cook |
| Alice Poulson | Claire Forlani |
| Gary Winston | Tim Robbins |
| Bob Shrot | Douglas McFerran |
| Lyle Barton | Richard Roundtree |
| Larry Banks | Tygh Runyan |
| Teddy Chin | Yee Jee Tso |
| Brian Bissel | Nate Dushku |
| Phil Grimes | Ned Bellamy |

and Tyler Labine (Redmond), Scott Bellis (Randy), David Lovgren (Danny), Zahf Hajee (Desi), Jonathon Young (Stinky), Rick Worthy (Shrot's Assistant), Nathaniel Deveaux, Ian Robison (Lawyers), Linda Ko (Gary's Secretary), Ed Beechner (Ken Cosgrove), Bobby Stewart, Eric Breker, Colin Cunningham (Building 20 Guards), J. R. Bourne (Building 21 Guard), Eric Keenleyside (Coffee Guard), Dayna Devon (TV Interviewer), Ron Halder (Houseman), Sarah Deakins (DOJ Receptionist), Daniel McKellar (Co-Worker), Howard Storey (Rent-a-Guard), Elizabeth Carol Savenkoff (Clarissa Winston), Ingelise Nherlan (Yoga Woman), Peter New, Blaine Perrin (Skinheads), Colin Foo (Grocer), Helena Yea (Grocer's Wife), Kevin Hayes (News Anchor), Claire Riley, Patti Vieta, Rob Court, Scott Fee, Norma Wick, Tamara Taggart, Linden Banks (Reporters), Benita Ha (Party Reporter), Justin Sain, Ricardo Scarabelli, Ian Bliss (Reporters), Peter Goudie, Anees Peterman (Senators), Gregor Trpin (Computer Guy), Peter Howitt (Homeless Man), Julie McDowell (Concerned Guest), Miguel de Icaza, Scott McNealy (Themselves), Brian Walley (Press Photographer), Robert J. Halas (Cameraman), Daniel Cruz, Dino Pallome, Tyson Holmes, Paresh Ramji, Rachel McGinnis, Jason Singer, Francisco Ortiz, Simon Wong, Greg Armstrong-Morris (Geeks), David Clennon (Barry Linder)

*Computer genius Milo Hoffman is recruited to join software millionaire Gary Winston's corporation, N.U.R.V., where he begins to suspect illegal and dangerous motives behind his boss's pet project, Synapse, a digital convergence system.*

© Metro-Goldwyn-Mayer Pictures, Inc.

# DOUBLE TAKE

**(TOUCHSTONE)** Producers, David Permut, Brett Ratner; Executive Producers, Barry Bernardi, Michael Rotenberg; Director/Screenplay, George Gallo; Photography, Theo Van De Sande; Designer, Stephen Lineweaver; Editor, Malcolm Campbell; Costumes, Sharen Davis; Co-Producers, Steven A. Longi, Frank Pesce; Music, Graeme Revell; Music Supervisors, Gary Jones, Happy Walters; Casting, Marcia Ross, Donna Morong, Gail Goldberg; a Permut Presentations/Rat Entertainment production; Dolby; Panavision; Technicolor; Rated PG-13; 88 minutes; Release date: January 12, 2001

### CAST

| | |
|---|---|
| Daryl Chase | Orlando Jones |
| Freddy Tiffany | Eddie Griffin |
| Timothy Jarrett McCready | Gary Grubbs |
| Agent Norville | Daniel Roebuck |
| Agent Gradney | Sterling Macer |
| Agent Martinez | Benny Nieves |
| Chloe | Garcelle Beauvais |
| Maque Sanchez | Andrea Navedo |
| Charles Allsworth | Edward Herrmann |
| Thomas Chela/Minty Gutierrez | Shawn Elliot |
| Junior Barnes | Brent Briscoe |

and Donna Eskra (Kiki Barnes), Carlos Carrasco (Captain Garcia), Frank Pesce (Vito), Julie Lott (Julie), Robby Robinson (Man in Suit), John M. Seiber (Security Guard), Jeff Griggs (Fashion Show Security Guard), James Gregory, Ted White (Troopers), Tony Genaro (Governor Quintana), Martin Morales (Border Guard), Jimmy Evangelatos (Border Patrol Agent), Raul Julia-Levy (Quintana Driver), George Sharperson (Thug), Joe Gironda (Doorman Joe), Joe Basile, Mark Chalant Phifer (Cops), Brent Sexton, Kevin Will (NYPD Cops), Richard Miro (Federale), Alexander Folk (Amtrak Waiter), Annie O'Donnell, Pamela Kosh (Nuns), Frank Gallegos (Shoeshine Guy), Tom Adams (FBI Agent), Johanna Cypis (Screaming Woman), Shirley Thomas (Lady by Phone), Norm Compton (Mexican Thug), George Czarnecki (Bar Patron #1), Xanthia Decaux (Fiona), Robert Harvey (McCready's Agent), Ana Bianco (Latino Crying Woman), Juan Soto, Jr. (Grieving Boy), Loran Taylor (Charles Allsworth's Wife), Chelsea Bond (Waitress at Malibu), Lisa Zee (Flight Attendant), Willow (Delores), Vivica A. Fox

*A New York investment banker, fleeing from the FBI because he's been framed for laundering money for a Mexican drug cartel, switches identity with a petty thief.*

© Touchstone Pictures

Orlando Jones, Eddie Griffin

Robin Wright Penn, Jack Nicholson

# THE PLEDGE

(**WARNER BROS.**) Producers, Michael Fitzgerald, Sean Penn, Elie Samaha; Executive Producer, Andrew Stevens; Director, Sean Penn; Screenplay, Jerzy Kromolowski, Mary Olson-Kromolowski; Based on the novel *Versprechen* by Friedrich Dürrenmatt; Photography, Chris Menges; Designer, Bill Groom; Editor, Jay Cassidy; Music, Hans Zimmer, Klaus Badelt; Costumes, Jill Ohanneson; Casting, Don Phillips; a Morgan Creek Productions, Inc. and Franchise Pictures presentation of a Clyde Is Hungry Films production; Dolby; Panavision; Color; Rated R; 124 minutes; Release date: January 19, 2001

Jack Nicholson

## CAST

| | |
|---|---|
| Jerry Black | Jack Nicholson |
| Lori | Robin Wright Penn |
| Erick Pollack | Sam Shepard |
| Stan Krolak | Aaron Eckhart |
| Annalise Hansen | Vanessa Redgrave |
| Duane Larsen | Michael O'Keefe |
| Toby Jay Wadenah | Benicio Del Toro |
| Jim Olstand | Mickey Rourke |
| Floyd Cage | Harry Dean Stanton |
| Doctor | Helen Mirren |
| Gary Jackson | Tom Noonan |
| Helen Jackson | Lois Smith |
| Chrissy | Pauline Roberts |
| Margaret Larsen | Patricia Clarkson |
| Strom | Dale Dickey |
| Monash Deputy | Costas Mandylor |
| Rudy | Beau Daniels |
| Resort Owner | Wendy Morrow Donaldson |
| Sheriff | P. Adrien Dorval |
| Bus Driver | Shawn Henter |

Jack Nicholson, Aaron Eckhart, Sam Shepard

and Kathy Jensen (Store Clerk), Taryn Knowles (Ginny Larsen), Nels Lennarson (Hank), J. J. McColl (Real Estate Agent), Gordon May (Criminologist #1), Adam Nelson, Gardinar Millar (Deputies), Tony Parsons (TV Anchorman), Robert Popoff (Prisoner), Nicole Robert (Flea Market Saleslady), Eileen Ryan (Jean), Lucy Schmidt (Alma Cage), John R. Taylor (Grey-Haired Man), Theodore Thomas (Rest Home Resident), Brittany Tiplady (Becky Fiske), Mavourneen Varcoe-Ryan (Crime Scene Reporter), Françoise Yip (Bartender at Airport)

*Jerry Black, a recently retired homicide detective, refuses to believe that a case involving the rape and murder of several little girls has been solved and settles down with a young single mother and her daughter with the intention of continuing his quest for the real criminal.*

© Franchise Pictures, LLC

Patricia Clarkson, Michael O'Keefe, Jack Nicholson

# THE WEDDING PLANNER

(COLUMBIA) Producers, Peter Abrams, Robert L. Levy, Gigi Pritzker, Deborah Del Prete, Jennifer Gibgot; Executive Producers, Nina R. Sadowsky, Moritz Borman, Chris Sievernich, Guy East, Nigel Sinclair; Director, Adam Shankman; Screenplay, Pamela Falk, Michael Ellis; Photography, Julio Macat; Designer, Bob Ziembicki; Costumes, Pamela Withers; Editor, Lisa Zeno Churgin; Co-Producer, Carrie Morrow; Music, Mervyn Warren; Music Supervisors, Mary Ramos, Michelle Kuznetsky; Casting, Mary Gail Artz, Barbara Cohen; an Intermedia Films presentation of a Tapestry Films/Dee Gee Entertainment/IMF Production in association with Prufrock Pictures; Dolby; Panavision; Deluxe color; Rated PG-13; 102 minutes; Release date: January 26, 2001

Matthew McConaughey, Jennifer Lopez, Bridgette Wilson-Sampras

## CAST

| | |
|---|---|
| Mary Fiore | Jennifer Lopez |
| Steve Edison | Matthew McConaughey |
| Fran Donolly | Bridgette Wilson-Sampras |
| Massimo | Justin Chambers |
| Penny | Judy Greer |
| Salvatore | Alex Rocco |
| Mrs. Donolly | Joanna Gleason |
| Mr. Donolly | Charles Kimbrough |
| Dr. John Dojny | Kevin Pollak |
| Basil St. Mosely | Fred Willard |
| Burt Weinberg | Lou Myers |
| Dottie | Frances Bay |
| Geri | Kathy Najimy |
| Mary Fiore (7 years old) | Cortney Shounia |
| Benton | Philip Pavel |
| Crying Bride | Natalie Jaroszyk |

and F. William Parker (Father of the Bride, Mr. Bartlett), Caisha Williams (Self-Conscious Bridesmaid), Dan Finnerty (Best Man), Fabiana Udenio (Anna Bosco), Bree Turner (Tracy, Bride), Don West (Bernard), Susan Mosher (Frieda), Peter Brown (Justice), Adam Loeffler (Boy in Hospital), Chelsea Hollingsworth, Bianca Brockl (Girls in Hospital), Karon Bihari, Nikki Arlyn (Guests), Seth Howard (Bellhop), Greg Lauren (Keith), Magali Amadei (Wendy), Phil Chong (Taxi Driver), Lydell Cheshier (Guard in Statue Park), Dee Dee Weathers (Bride, Copeland Wedding), Harry Danner (Wedding Minister), Anthony Katala (Wedding Photographer), Betsy Brockhurst (Sister Elizabeth Scrabble), Huntley Ritter (Groom), Joan Del Mar (Renee), Raphaela Kleiman (Flower Girl), Rocco Vienhage (Man)

Jennifer Lopez, Matthew McConaughey

Matthew McConaughey, Jennifer Lopez

*After a chance encounter with Dr. Steve Edison, wedding planner Mary Fiore finds herself falling in love, only to discover that Steve is the groom-to-be of her newest and most lucrative account.*

© Columbia Pictures Industries Inc.

Justin Chambers, Matthew McConaughey

Marley Shelton, Melissa George, Mena Suvari,
Sara Marsh, Rachel Blanchard, Alexandra Holden

# SUGAR AND SPICE

**(NEW LINE CINEMA)** Producer, Wendy Finerman; Executive Producers, Claire Rudnick Polstein, Matt Moore, Greg Mooradian; Director, Francine McDougall; Screenplay, Mandy Nelson; Co-Producer, Michael Nelson; Photography, Robert Brinkmann; Designer, Jeff Knipp; Editor, Sloane Klevin; Music, Mark Mothersbaugh; Costumes, Wendy Chuck; Cheerleading Consultant, Beth Knutson; Choreographer, Amber Struzyk; Casting, Juel Bestrop, Jeanne McCarthy; a Wendy Finermann production; Dolby; Super 35 Widescreen; Color; Rated PG-13; 81 minutes; Release date: January 26, 2001

## CAST

| | |
|---|---|
| Lisa | Marla Sokoloff |
| Diane | Marley Shelton |
| Cleo | Melissa George |
| Kansas | Mena Suvari |
| Hannah | Rachel Blanchard |
| Fern | Alexandra Holden |
| Lucy | Sara Marsh |
| Jack | James Marsden |
| Mrs. Hill | Sean Young |
| Hank | W. Earl Brown |
| Geeky Guy | Adam Busch |
| Ted | Jake Hoffman |
| Chris | Nate Maher |
| Bruce | David Belenky |
| Factory Worker | Kevin Kling |
| Apartment Manager | Dave Quimby |
| Food Valley Cashier | Jacy Dumermuth |
| Principal Smith | Wiley Harker |

and Stevie Ray Rentfrow (Diane's Dad—Dennis), Kirsten Frantzich (Diane's Mom—DeeDee), Christopher Denton (Jack's Dad—Ed), Jan Puffer (Jack's Mom—Edna), Claudia Wilkens (Grandmother), Jeff Hopkins (Police Officer), Kevin Joseph Klein (FBI Agent), Jeremy Kent Jackson, Jamison Haase (Football Players), Jessie Schoen (Butch Girl), Susan Fuller (Bank Loan Officer), Andy Hubbell (Husband), Katie Kelly (Nurse), Ann Kellog (Mink), Isabell Monk, Miriam Must, Jenner Snell (Inmates), Andrea Guilford (Lamaze Instructor)

*When pregnant teenager Diane finds herself in deep financial trouble, she convinces her fellow cheerleaders to help her rob a bank.*

© New Line Cinema Inc.

James Marsden

Amanda Peet, Jack Black, Steve Zahn

Jack Black, Steve Zahn

Neil Diamond, Jason Biggs, Jack Black, Steve Zahn

Jason Biggs, Amanda Detmer

# SAVING SILVERMAN

(COLUMBIA) Producer, Neal H. Moritz; Executive Producers, Bruce Berman, Bernie Goldmann, Brad Luff, Peter Ziegler; Director, Dennis Dugan; Screenplay, Greg DePaul, Hank Nelken; Photography, Arthur Albert; Designer, Michael Bolton; Editor, Debra Neil-Fisher; Music, Mike Simpson; Music Supervisors, Michelle Silverman, Mary Ramos; Co-Producer, Warren Carr; Costumes, Melissa Toth; Casting, Mary Vernieu, Anne McCarthy, Felicia Fasano; a Village Roadshow Pictures presentation in association with NPV Entertainment, of an Original Film production; Dolby; Super 35 Widescreen; Deluxe color; Rated PG-13; 91 minutes; Release date: February 9, 2001

## CAST

| | |
|---|---|
| Wayne Le Fessier | Steve Zahn |
| J. D. McNugent | Jack Black |
| Darren Silverman | Jason Biggs |
| Judith | Amanda Peet |
| Sandy | Amanda Detmer |
| Coach | R. Lee Ermey |
| Himself | Neil Diamond |
| Bar Dude | Kyle Gass |
| Minister | Norman Armour |
| Old Man | Colin Foo |
| Vageet | Chris Logan |

and Esme Lambert (Raccoon Woman), Max Fomitchev (Mime), Tony Parsons (Newscaster), Brett Armstrong (Brett), Patrick Pfrimmer (Clayton), Frank Frazier (Bouncer), Andrew McIlroy (Waiter), Oscar Goncalves (Man), Lillian Carlson (Mother Superior), Eli Ranger (Young Darren), Ivan Jurcev (Young J. D.), Devin Douglas Drewitz (Young Wayne), Carly McKillip (Cute Girl), Carla Boudreau (Beautiful Woman), Phil Trasolini (Referee on Sideline), David Neale, Mary Ann Skoll (Cops at Police Station), Biski Gugushe (Cop at Darren's House), Gus Lynch (Security Guard), Mark Wagner (Luigi), Steven McMichael (Josh), Larry Lam (Thai Kickboxer), Stephen Chang (Thai Referee), Eliza Murbach (Wayne's Mom), Blake Stovin (Wayne's Dad), Brittany Moldowan, Katlyn Ducharme (Little Girls), Michael Roberts (Doctor), Frank Hache (Abe), Odessa Munroe, Tracy Trueman (Hookers), Nicole Robert (Nun), Nancy J. Lilley (Bearded Lady), David Mylrea (Dogfaced Boy), Dario De Iaco (Strong Man), Eleana Johnson, Margaret Ryan (Old Ladies), Lowela Jotie, Shannon Bennett, Theresa Coombe, Leigh Hilary-Lakin, Jennifer Armstrong, Linda Bernath (Cheerleaders), Dennis Dugan (Ref)

*After their best friend Darren takes up with a pretentious woman who forbids him to see his pals, Wayne and J. D. formulate a plan to reunite Darren with his high-school sweetheart.*

© Columbia Pictures Industries Inc.

Anthony Hopkins, Julianne Moore

Francesca Neri, Giancarlo Giannini

Anthony Hopkins (in hospital)

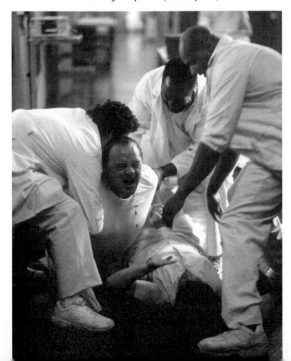

# HANNIBAL

(MGM/UNIVERSAL) Producers, Dino De Laurentiis, Martha De Laurentiis, Ridley Scott; Executive Producer, Branko Lustig; Director, Ridley Scott; Screenplay, David Mamet, Steven Zaillian; Based upon the novel by Thomas Harris; Photography, John Mathieson; Designer, Norris Spencer; Editor, Pietro Scalia; Music, Hans Zimmer; Costumes, Janty Yates; Casting, Louis DiGiaimo; a Scott Free production, presented in association with Dino De Laurentiis; Dolby; Technicolor; Rated R; 131 minutes; Release date: February 9, 2001

## CAST

Hannibal Lecter..............................................................Anthony Hopkins
Clarice Starling....................................................................Julianne Moore
Mason Verger .......................................................................Gary Oldman
Paul Krendler ..........................................................................Ray Liotta
Barney..............................................................................Frankie R. Faison
Pazzi..............................................................................Giancarlo Giannini
Allegra Pazzi ........................................................................Francesca Neri
Dr. Cordell Doemling ...............................................................Zeljko Ivanek
Evelda Drumgo ................................................................Hazelle Goodman
FBI Agent Pearsall....................................................................David Andrews
FBI Director Noonan ..............................................................Francis Guinan
DEA Agent Eldridge................................................................James Opher
Gnocco..............................................................................Enrico Lo Verso
Carlo .................................................................................Ivano Marescotti
Matteo ................................................................................Fabrizio Gifuni
Piero ....................................................................................Alex Corrado
Tommaso.............................................................................Marco Greco
Sogliato ................................................................................Robert Rietti
Officer Bolton .......................................................................Terry Serpico
Special Agent Burke ...............................................................Boyd Kestner
Special Agent Brigham ...............................................................Peter Shaw
FBI Mail Boy .........................................................................Kent Linville
Asst. Mayor Benny Holcombe.............................................Don McManus
Larkin Wayne ...........................................................................Harold Ginn
BATF Agent Sneed ....................................................................Ted Koch
FBI Agent .....................................................................Wm. Powell Blair II
"Il Mostro" Detective ...............................................................Aaron Craig
Agent Benetti.................................................................Andrea Piedimonte
Ricci .................................................................................Ennio Coltorti
Young Boy in Plane ..................................................................Ian Iwataki
Perfume Experts...........................Mark Margolis, Ajay Naidu, Kelly Piper
FBI Tech (Lecter's Letter) ...................................................Bruce MacVittie
Verger's Fingerprint Technician ...........................................Giannina Facio
Police Officer...................................................................Andrew C. Boothby
Police Sergeant .............................................................Kenneth W. Smith
Theatergoer ...........................................................................Roberta Armani
Mr. Konie...................................................................Johannes Kiebranz
Dante.............................................................................Bruno Lazzaretti
Beatrice ...........................................................................Danielle de Niese
and Judie Aronson, Tom Trigo, Sam Wells, Ric Young, Joseph M. West, Jr. (News Reporters)

*A millionaire who was hideously deformed during an encounter with Dr. Hannibal Lecter, swears revenge on his assailant, who has managed to elude the FBI for ten years by living undercover in Venice. This is the third film to feature the character of Dr. Hannibal Lecter, who was first played by Brian Cox in the 1986 DeLaurentiis Films release* Manhunter *and then by Anthony Hopkins in the 1991 Orion release* The Silence of the Lambs. *Hopkins and Frankie Faison repeat their roles from the latter film.*

© Metro-Goldwyn-Mayer Pictures, Inc.

Julianne Moore,
Anthony Hopkins

(Below) Anthony Hopkins, Giancarlo Giannini

(Below) Anthony Hopkins, Julianne Moore

(Below) Ray Liotta, Julianne Moore

(Below) Anthony Hopkins, Ray Liotta

## RECESS: SCHOOL'S OUT

(**WALT DISNEY PICTURES**) Producers, Paul Germain, Joe Ansolabehere, Stephen Swofford; Director, Chuck Sheetz; Creators, Paul Germain, Joe Ansolabehere; Story, Joe Ansolabehere, Paul Germain, Jonathan Greenberg; Screenplay, Jonathan Greenberg; Music Score, Denis M. Hannigan; Dialogue Director, Paul Germain; Voice Casting, Allyson Bosch; Supervising Film Editor, Nancy Frazen; Art Director/Lead Character Designer, Eric Keyes; Original Character Design, David Shannon; Visual Development, Plamen Christov, Bob Schaefer, Jose Zelaya; Technical Director, Glo Minaya; Storyboard Supervisors, David Knott, Brad Vandergrift; Associate Producer, Michael Tyau; Song: "Green Tambourine" by Shelley Pinz and Paul Leka/Performed by Robert Goulet; Dolby; Color; Rated G; 84 minutes; Release date: February 16, 2001.

### VOICE CAST

| | |
|---|---|
| Vince | Rickey D'Shon Collins |
| Mikey | Jason Davis |
| Gretchen | Ashley Johnson |
| T. J | Andy Lawrence |
| Gus | Courtland Mead |
| Spinelli | Pamela Segall |
| Principal Peter Prickly | Dabney Coleman |
| Mikey's Singing Voice | Robert Goulet |
| Becky | Melissa Joan Hart |
| Fenwick | Peter MacNicol |
| Ms. Finster/Mrs. Detweiler | April Winchell |
| Benedict | James Woods |

and Dan Castellaneta, Diedrich Bader (Guards), Allyce Beasley (Miss Grotke), Gregg Berger (Tech #1), Klee Bragger (Digger Sam), Clancy Brown (Bald Guy), Toran Caudell (King Bob), Rachel Crane (Ashley Q), E. G. Daily (Cap'n Sticky), R. Lee Ermey (Colonel O'Malley), Ron Glass (Dr. Lazenby/Tech #2), Tony Jay (Dr. Rosenthal), Clyde Kusatsu (Mr. Yamashiro), Charles Kimbrough (Mort Chalk), Tress MacNeille (Lunch Lady #2/Opera Director/Dr. Steinheimer), Andrea Martin (Lunch Lady #1), Anndi McAfee (Ashley A), Mark Robert Myers (Technician), Ryan O'Donohue (Digger Dave/Randall), Phil Proctor (Golfer #2/Scientist #2), Patrick Renna (Jordan), Nick Turturro, Kevin Michael Richardson (Cops), Jack Riley (Golfer #1), Justin Shenkarow (Soldier Kid/Wrestler Kid), Michael Shulman (Hustler Kid), Francesca Marie Smith (Ashley B/Swinger Girl/Upside-Down Girl), Kath Soucie (Counselor), Robert Stack (Superintendent), Ken Swofford (Coach), Erik Von Detten (Captain Brad/Lawson), Paul Willson (Coach Kloogie/Mr. Detweiler)

*T. J. Detweiler summons his friends back from summer camp when he suspects mysterious doings at their supposedly empty school. Based on the ABC series Recess that debuted in 1997.*

© Disney Enterprises, Inc.

(Below) Charlize Theron, Keanu Reeves

Vince, T.J., Spinelli, Gretchen, Gus, Mike

## SWEET NOVEMBER

(**WARNER BROS.**) Producers, Erwin Stoff, Deborah Aal, Steven Reuther, Elliott Kastner; Executive Producer, Wendy Wanderman; Co-Producer, Marty Ewing; Director, Pat O'Connor; Screenplay, Kurt Voelker; Story, Paul Yurick, Kurt Voelker; Based on a screenplay by Herman Raucher; Photography, Edward Lachman; Editor, Anne V. Coates; Music, Christopher Young; Music Supervisor, G. Marq Roswell; Designer, Naomi Shohan; Costumes, Shay Cunliffe; Associate Producer, Jodi Ehrlich; Casting, Risa Bramon Garcia, Randi Hiller; a 3 Arts Entertainment production, presented in association with Bel-Air Entertainment; Dolby; Technicolor; Rated PG-13; 119 minutes; Release date: February 16, 2001.

### CAST

| | |
|---|---|
| Nelson Moss | Keanu Reeves |
| Sara Deever | Charlize Theron |
| Chaz | Jason Isaacs |
| Vince | Greg Germann |
| Abner | Liam Aiken |
| Raeford Dunne | Robert Joy |
| Angelica | Lauren Graham |
| Brandon | Michael Rosenbaum |
| Edgar Price | Frank Langella |
| Manny | Jason Kravits |
| Buddy Leach | Ray Baker |
| Al | Tom Bullock |
| Osiris | Adele Proom |
| DMV Doctor | L. Peter Callender |
| Beatrice | June Lomena |
| Burly Man | Kelvin Han Yee |
| Homeless Man | David Fine |
| Lexy | Elizabeth Weber |
| Chinese Woman | Doreen Croft |
| Waitress | Susan Zelinsky |

and Kathy Garver (Nurse), Chuck Isen (Bald Man), Igor Hiller, Chase Oliver, Nathan McAlone (Kids), Garth Kravits (Techie Nerd), Karina Andrews (Office Manager), Sanford Marshall (Clown on Train), Tessa Koning-Martinez (Marie), Diane Amos (Coffee Shop Waitress), Jeffrey Patrick Dean, Diana C. Weng, Milo Young, Meghan Marx, Reuben Grundy (Art Department Coordinators), Raquel Aurillia (Cute Cashier), Kaliopi Eleni (Woman on Train), Eric Kouba (Big Brother Organizer), Kathy McGraw (Billy Boy's Mother), Tyler Bell (Billy Boy), Ann W. Leon (Hospital Administrator), John Lewis (Jack the Barman)

*Sara Deever invites uptight advertising executive Nelson Moss to move in with her for the month of November, intending to make him into a more caring individual. Remake of the 1968 Warner Bros. film that starred Sandy Dennis and Anthony Newley.*

© Warner Bros. Pictures and Bel-Air Pictures, LLC.

Eugene Levy, Chris Rock, Chazz Palminteri

Chris Rock, Regina King

Chris Rock, Greg Germann, Jennifer Coolidge

# DOWN TO EARTH

(PARAMOUNT) Producers, Sean Daniel, Michael Rotenberg, James Jacks; Executive Producers, Chris Rock, Barry Berg; Directors, Chris Weitz, Paul Weitz; Screenplay, Chris Rock, Lance Crouther, Ali LeRoi, Louis CK; Based on the film *Heaven Can Wait*, screenplay by Elaine May and Warren Beatty, from the film *Here Comes Mr. Jordan*, screenplay by Sidney Buchman and Seton I. Miller, from the play *Heaven Can Wait* by Harry Segall; Photography, Richard Crudo; Designer, Paul Peters; Editor, Priscilla Nedd Friendly; Music, Jamshied Sharifi; Executive Music Producers, Ken Kushnick, Bill Stephney, Matt Walden; Costumes, Debrae Little; a Village Roadshow Pictures presentation in association with NPV Entertainment of an Alphaville 3 Arts Entertainment production; Dolby; Deluxe color; Rated PG-13; 87 minutes; Release date: February 16, 2001

## CAST

| | |
|---|---|
| Lance Barton | Chris Rock |
| Sontee | Regina King |
| King | Chazz Palminteri |
| Keyes | Eugene Levy |
| Whitney Daniels | Frankie Faison |
| Cisco | Mark Addy |
| Sklar | Greg Germann |
| Mrs. Wellington | Jennifer Coolidge |
| Wanda | Wanda Sykes |
| Phil Quon | John Cho |
| Apollo MC | Mario Joyner |
| Gospel Singer | Bryetta Calloway |
| Rosa | Martha Chaves |
| Charles Wellington | Brian Rhodes |
| Trashman | Herb Lovelle |
| Heckler | Kedar |
| Doorman | Adam Dannheiser |
| Singers | Malcolm Devine, Colette Wilson, Maiesha McQueen |
| Women in Balcony. | Robin Montague, Hollie Harper |
| Bouncer | Scott Wickware |
| Middle-Aged Guy (Bob Krantz) | Jack Newman |
| Elderly Man | William Lynn |
| Party Girl (Tina Lovette) | Leah Miller |

and David Huband (Maitre D' Serge), Woodrow W. Asai (Asian Man), Laz Alonzo (BET Announcer), Dennis Pressey (MC at Comedy Shack), Arnold Pinnock (Joe Guy), David M. Rodriguez (Flower Delivery Man), Linda Sithole, Gwen Stewart, Chris Ausnit (Protesters), Mary Burton (Reporter Outside Hospital), Jernard Burks (Man in Wheelchair), Clement Moorman (Patient), Hollis Granville (Sick Person), Mung Ling Tsui (Reporter Inside Hospital), Paulette Sinclair (Blanche), Ali LeRoi (Crazy Hostile Dreadlock Guy), Reginald Footman (Dreadlock's Buddy), Michael Port (Mugger), Colin Fox, Paul Hecht, Jack Jessop (Directors), Kenny Robinson (Club MC), Mary Kate Law (Fur Protester), Roger Kugler (Hit Man), Roma Torre (Portraying Herself), Harlin Kearsley (Mike Green), Dan Duran (Reporter)

*After comedian Lance Barton is prematurely sent to heaven, he is allowed to return to earth where he is given a new body, that of a millionaire who has just been bumped off by his scheming wife. Remake of* Heaven Can Wait *(Paramount, 1978), which starred Warren Beatty, and of* Here Comes Mr. Jordan *(Columbia, 1941), which starred Robert Montgomery.*

© Paramount Pictures

Monkeybone, Brendan Fraser

Chris Kattan

(Below) Citizens of Downtown

(Below) Bridget Fonda, Brendan Fraser

# MONKEYBONE

(20TH CENTURY FOX) Producers, Michael Barnathan, Mark Radcliffe; Executive Producers, Lata Ryan, Henry Selick, Sam Hamm, Chris Columbus; Director, Henry Selick; Screenplay, Sam Hamm; Based on the graphic novel *Dark Town* by Kaja Blackley; Photography, Andrew Dunn; Designer, Bill Boes; Editors, Mark Warner, Jon Poll, Nicholas C. Smith; Costumes, Beatrix Aruna Pasztor; Music, Anne Dudley; Music Supervisor, Dawn Solér; Visual Effects Producer, Terry Clotiaux; a 1492 Production; Dolby; Deluxe color; Rated PG-13; 92 minutes; Release date: February 23, 2001

## CAST

| | |
|---|---|
| Stu Miley | Brendan Fraser |
| Julie McElroy | Bridget Fonda |
| Organ Donor Stu | Chris Kattan |
| Voice of Monkeybone | John Turturro |
| Hypnos | Giancarlo Esposito |
| Kitty | Rose McGowan |
| Herb | Dave Foley |
| Kimmy | Megan Mullally |
| Head Surgeon | Bob Odenkirk |
| Burger God Representative | Pat Kilbane |
| Medusa | Lisa Zane |
| Death | Whoopi Goldberg |
| Alice | Sandra Thigpen |
| Hutch | Wayne Wilderson |
| Clarissa | Amy Higgins |
| Dr. Edelstein | Alan Gelfant |
| Nurse | Kristin Norton |
| Bazoom Toy Representative | Chris Hogan |
| Beautiful Fan | Wendy Fowler |

and Jamie Donovan, Paul Guiles (Reporters), Skyler Marshall (Janitor), Brendan Burns (Detective #1), Jason Kravitz, Lucy Butler (Guests), John Sylvain (Driver), Lou Romano (Cop), Leon Laderach (Surgeon in Nightmare), Scott Rogers, Chris Thomas Palomino, Tony Pantera (Surgeons), Ted Rooney (Grim Reaper), Christopher Franciosa (Reaper Who Takes Lulu), Mary Stein (Lulu), Randall Bosley (Fred), Fred Pierce (Reaper in Death's Office), Harper Roisman (Earl Biegler), Kristopher Logan (Patron), Scott Workman (Arnold the Super Reaper), Shawnee Free Jones (Lizzie Borden), Ilia Volok (Rasputin), Edgar Allan Poe IV (Edgar Allan Poe), Claudette Mink (Typhoid Mary), Jon Bruno (Man in the Dungeon), Owen Masterson (Jack the Ripper), Jen Sung Outerbridge (Attila the Hun), Mike Mitchell (George), Tracy Zahoryn, Sunshine Deia Tutt, Jo Haugen Gash, Lindsay Bryan, Brooke Boisse, Meron Abebe, Mie Kringelbach (Models), Sybil Azur, Anne Fletcher, Diane Mizota (Museum Dancers), Etty Lau (Sax—All-Girl Band), Latonya Holmes (Percussion—All-Girl Band), Leslee Jean Matta (Drummer—All-Girl Band), Rachen Assapimonwait (Korean Father), Veena Bishasha (Statue Woman), M. Anthony Jackson (Bug Man), Doug Jones (Yeti), Arturo Gil (Rat Guard), Jody St. Michael (Centaur), Frit Fuller, Frat Fuller (3-Headed Devil), Brian Steele (Elephant God), Leif Tilden (Cyclops), Tom Fisher (Community Service Cigarette Sweeper), Joseph Griffo (BBQ Pig), Kim Timbers Patteri (Wasp Woman), Lisa Ebeyer (Betty the Bovine), Wayne D. Doba (Scorpion), Mark Viniello (Ass Backward), Nathan Stein (Sea Monster), Ed Holmes (Buffalo Kachina), Erica Gudis, Melinda Milton., Caroline A. Rice (Party-Babe Hybrids), Michael MacFarlane (Bull Double), Michael Hammond (Reaper Performer); Character Voices: Joe Ranft (Streetsquash Rabbit), Bruce Lanoil (Streetsquash Racoon), Debi Durst (Streetsquash Snake), Phil Brotherton (Subramansa), Roger Jackson (Arnold the Super Reaper), Jym Dingler (Community-Service Cigarette Sweeper), Toby Gleason (Buffalo Kachina)

*After an accident puts him in a coma, Stu Miley, creator of a popular comic strip called Monkeybone, finds his conscious spirit transported to a carnival-like purgatory called Downtown, while his simian creation takes over his earthly form.*

© Twentieth Century Fox

Arquette, Russell, Costner, Slater, Woodbine

Kurt Russell, Courteney Cox

Kurt Russell, Kevin Costner

Kevin Costner, Courteney Cox

# 3000 MILES TO GRACELAND

(WARNER BROS.) Producers, Demian Lichtenstein, Richard Spero, Eric Manes, Elie Samaha, Andrew Stevens; Executive Producers, Don Carmody, Tracee Stanley; Director, Demian Lichtenstein; Screenplay, Richard Recco, Demian Lichtenstein; Photography, David Franco; Designer, Robert DeVico; Costumes, Mary McLeod; Editors, Michael Duthie, Miklos Wright; Music, George S. Clinton; Casting, Pam Dixon Mickelson; a Morgan Creek and Franchise Pictures production in association with Lightstone Entertainment; Dolby; Super 35 Widescreen; Color; Rated R; 125 minutes; Release date: February 23, 20001

## CAST

| | |
|---|---|
| Michael Zane | Kurt Russell |
| Murphy | Kevin Costner |
| Cybil Waingrow | Courteney Cox |
| Hanson | Christian Slater |
| Damitry | Kevin Pollak |
| Gus | David Arquette |
| Jay Peterson | Jon Lovitz |
| Jack | Howie Long |
| Quigley | Thomas Haden Church |
| Franklin | Bokeem Woodbine |
| Hamilton | Ice-T |
| Jesse Waingrow | David Kaye |
| Otto Sinclair | Louis Lombardi |

and Shawn Michael Howard (Roller Elvis), Michael Kopsa (Jefferson), Daisy McCrackin (Megan), Sharron Leigh (Naomi), J. W. Carroll (Captain Vanucci), Paul Anka, Eric James, Tim Misney (Pitt Bosses), Kim Hawthorne (Panel Operator), Craig March (Supervisor), Rod Lake (Mack), Norma Campbell (Elevator Old Lady), Gianni Russo (Money Cart Guard), John Casino (Federal Marshal), Hamilton von Watts (Announcer), Lorraine Cote (Slot Old Woman), David Meeker (Security Guard), Kenneth Anderson (Old Indian), Morgan H. Margolis, Aubrey Jordan, Terry Chen (Policemen), 'r' Nelson Brown (Motor Inn Clerk), Luis Moro (FBI Man), Ross Haines (Gas Station Dad), Christine Chatelain (Sexy Waitress), Michael Busswood (Tourist), Charles Andre (Big Trucker), Campbell Lane (Billy), Raoul Ganeev (Taxi Driver), Mark Acheson (Dockmaster), Peter Bryant (Tom Matthews), John Destrey (Marcus Tittlebaum), Mike St. John Smith (Eugene Gribbs), Scott Swanson (Greg Forester), Doug Abrahams (Det. Steve Finn), Mary Ann Skoll (Paramedic), Dave Babych (Mt. Vernon Cop), Mark Gibbon (Boise Cop), Frank C. Turner (Impound Shop Man), Don MacKay (Judge Carmody), Demian Lichtenstein (Shoplifter), Susse Budde (News Reporter), Colm O'Faolain, Max Goldblatt (Impersonators), Tom Heaton (Captain Elden), Ralph Alderman (Holding Tank Officer), Brian Drummond (Washington State Trooper), Larry Holdridge, Robert "Bobby Z" Zajonc (Helicopter Pilots), Peter Kent (Swat Leader), Greg Miller, Michael Conti, Eddie Powers, Steve Connolly, Tim Welch, Jim Leboeuf, Lawrence McMurray, Johnny Edwards (Dancing Elvises), Jennifer Gagliano, Yvonne Grace, Jill Landess, Georgie Bernasek, Angelina McCoy, Laura Lago, Jamie Preston, Melinda Harambasic, Daniella Murray, Terri Gomez (Viva Las Vegas Showgirls), Rice Honeywell (Swat Member), Kevin Mundy (Station Clerk), Renee Cherrier (Cashier), Shelly Lien (Vegas Babe), Marci Lake, Kelly Carlson, Rob Lake, Dante D'Ambruoso, Tim Hoctor, Kerry Puccio, Eric Arlt, Robert Martin, Tony Alves, Jeanette Lee, Bart Dorsa, Stephanie Swinney, Dave Dunlap, Alberto Mastrangelo, Wayne Harter, "J. G." Jim Grant, Duncan Keller, Skylark, Staz (Motocycle Gang)

*A group of criminals arrives in Las Vegas during an Elvis Presley impersonation convention to rob a casino.*

© 3000 Miles Productions, Inc.

Aunjanue Ellis, Samuel L. Jackson

## THE CAVEMAN'S VALENTINE

**(UNIVERSAL FOCUS)** Producers, Danny DeVito, Michael Shamberg, Stacey Sher, Scott Frank, Elie Samaha, Andrew Stevens; Executive Producers, Samuel L. Jackson, Julie Yorn, Eli Selden, Nicolas Clermont; Co-Producers, Michael Bennett, James Holt, Pamela Abdy; Director, Kasi Lemmons; Screenplay, George Dawes Green, based on his novel; Photography, Amelia Vincent; Designer, Robin Standefer; Editor, Terilyn A. Shropshire; Co-Executive Producers, Stephanie Davis, Jonathan Weisgal; Associate Producers, Michael Drake, Tracee Stanley; Music, Terence Blanchard; a Franchise Pictures presentation of a Jersey Shore production in association with Arroyo Pictures; Dolby; Color; Rated R; 105 minutes; Release date: March 2, 2001

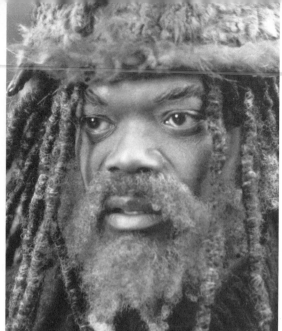

Samuel L. Jackson

### CAST

| | |
|---|---|
| Romulus Ledbetter | Samuel L. Jackson |
| David Leppenraub | Colm Feore |
| Moira Leppenraub | Ann Magnuson |
| Arnold | Damir Andrei |
| Lulu | Aunjanue Ellis |
| Sheila | Tamara Tunie |
| Cork | Peter MacNeill |
| Joey/No Face | Jay Rodan |
| Matthew | Rodney Eastman |
| Bob | Anthony Michael Hall |
| Betty | Kate McNeil |
| Shake/Greater No Face | Leonard Thomas |
| Boy Toy/Andy | Joris Jorsky |
| Toupee | Pierre Alcide |
| Walter | Richard Fitzpatrick |
| Scotty Gates | Sean MacMahon |
| Penny | Vija Brigita Grosgalvis |
| Chore | Phillip Jarrett |
| Manuel | Cecil Phillips |

and Henry Stram (Social Worker), Carla Collins (First Reporter), Deborah Lobban (Librarian), Erik Laray Harvey (Young Rom), Mica Le John (Young Lulu), Joanne Jang (Beauty/Cassandra), Alex Karzis (Byzantine Emperor/Dan), Val Boyle (Lucinda); Andre Matthews, Horace Abel, Phillip Harding, Dave Smith, Warren Belle, Lyriq Bent, Robert Warner, Richard Fagon, Julian Adigun, Ken Sylvan, Chad Keens-Douglas, Barrington Bignall, Blair Liburd, Glen Miller, Junior Brown (Seraph Dancers), John Strong, Lowell Hall, Nicholas Shand, Fern Bellavance (Seraph Musicians)

*A former classical musician, now living as a vagrant in Manhattan, begins to snap out of his mentally unhinged state after he discovers the corpse of a young drifter outside of his cave-like dwelling.*

Samuel L. Jackson, Anthony Michael Hall

Ann Magnuson, Samuel L. Jackson

© Universal Studios, Inc.

Julia Roberts, Brad Pitt

Brad Pitt

James Gandolfini, Julia Roberts

Brad Pitt, Julia Roberts

# THE MEXICAN

**(DREAMWORKS)** Producers, Lawrence Bender, John Baldecchi; Executive Producers, William Tyrer, Chris J. Ball, Aaron Ryder, J. H. Wyman; Director, Gore Verbinski; Screenplay, J. H. Wyman; Photography, Dariusz Wolski; Designer, Cecilia Montiel; Editor, Craig Wood; Costumes, Colleen Atwood; Co-Producer, William S. Beasley; Music, Alan Silvestri; Casting, Denise Chamian; Presented in association with Newmarket; Dolby; Panavision; Technicolor; Rated R; 123 minutes; Release date: March 2, 2001

## CAST

| | |
|---|---|
| Jerry Welbach | Brad Pitt |
| Samantha Barzell | Julia Roberts |
| Leroy | James Gandolfini |
| Ted | J. K. Simmons |
| Nayman | Bob Balaban |
| Well-Dressed Black Man | Sherman Augustus |
| Frank | Michael Cerveris |
| Car Thief | Richard Coca |
| Beck | David Krumholtz |
| Joe the Pawnshop Owner | Castulo Guerra |
| Arnold Margolese | Gene Hackman |
| Emanuelle | Maira Serbulo |
| Gunsmith | Salvador Sanchez |
| Gunsmith's Assistant | Alan Cianguerotti |
| Gunsmith's Daughter | Melisa Romero |
| Tropillo | Ernesto Gomez Cruz |
| Raoul | Daniel Escobar |
| Estelle | Dale Raoul |
| Bobby Victory | Jeremy Roberts |

and Jorge Malpica (Mexican Gas Station Clerk), Pedro Armendariz (Mexican Policeman), Steve Rossi (Vegas M.C.), Clint Curtis (Vegas Busboy), Lawrence Bender (Vegas Onlooker), Ariane Pellicer (Mexican Ticket Agent), Carlos LaCamara (Car Rental Rep), Daniel Zacapa (Bartender), Alfredo Escobar, Luis Artagnan (Car Thieves), Fermin Martinez (Chicken Farmer), Jose Carlos Rodriguez (Hotel Clark), Gustavo Aguilar (Junk Yard Proprietor), Lucia Pailles (Mexican Woman—Phone), Gilberto Barraza (2nd Man with Gun), Humberto Fernandez Tristan (Nobleman), Luis Felipe Tovar (Nobleman's Son), Fausta Torres (Elderly Mexican Lady), Lolo Navarro (Chosen Grandmother), Emiliano Guerra (Small Boy with Flashlight), Miguel Angel Fuentes (Big Thief #4), Angelina Pelaez (Mother), Harrison Fuller (Big Tom), Gerardo Taracena (Reveler to Fire Gun), John Pisci, Rudy Aikels, Ronald Simone (Musicians)

*Despite his promise to girlfriend Samantha that he will sever his ties with the mob, two-bit bagman Jerry Welbach agrees to one last job, to drive down to Mexico to retrieve a priceless antique pistol.*

© DreamWorks LLC and Pistolero Productions LLC

## SERIES 7: THE CONTENDERS

(USA FILMS) Producers, Jason Kliot, Joana Vicente, Christine Vachon, Katie Roumel; Executive Producer, Charles J. Rusbasan; Director/Screenplay, Daniel Minahan; Co-Executive Producers, Judith Zarin, Tom Brown, Mike Escott, Evan T. Cohen, Gretchen McGowan; Associate Producer, Pamela Koffler; Line Producer, Libby Richman; Photography, Randy Drummond; Designer, Gideon Ponte; Editor, Malcolm Jamieson; Music, Girls Against Boys; Music Supervisor, Julie Panebianco; Costumes, Christine Bieselin; Casting, Susan Shopmaker; a Blow Up Pictures presentation of a Killer Films/Open City Films production; Dolby; DuArt color; Rated R; 88 minutes; Release date: March 2, 2001

### CAST

| | |
|---|---|
| Dawn | Brooke Smith |
| Connie | Marylouise Burke |
| Jeff | Glenn Fitzgerald |
| Tony | Michael Kaycheck |
| Franklin | Richard Venture |
| Lindsay | Merritt Wever |
| Sheila | Donna Hanover |
| Doria | Angelina Phillips |

and Mark Woodbury (Dairy Mart Clerk), Tom Gilroy (Dawn's Cameraman), Nada Despotovich (Michelle), Stephen Michael Rinaldi (Craig), Alex Yershov (Nathan), Danton Stone (Bob), Joseph Barrett (Doctor), Shawna Moore (Nurse), Jennifer Van Dyck (Laura), Tanny McDonald (Dawn's Mother), Caitlin Bateman (Colby), Robin Borden, Lauren Ward (Doria Look-Alikes), Aydin Bengisu, Josh Mosby (Jeff Look-Alikes), Babo Harrison (Dawn Look-Alike), Will Arnett (Narrator), Adena Shea Loomis (Ultra Sound Baby), Pamela Wehner (Dispatch Operator), Kirsten Krohn, William Graves (Promo Voices)

*Dawn, the reigning champion of* The Contenders, *a reality television show in which six random people are selected to kill one another, hopes to win the final round and end her obligation to the series.*

© USA Films

Brooke Smith

(Below) Glenn Fitzgerald, Brooke Smith

Bob, Michael Clarke Duncan

## SEE SPOT RUN

(WARNER BROS.) Producers, Robert Simonds, Tracey Trench, Andrew Deane; Executive Producers, Michael Alexander Miller, Bruce Berman; Co-Producers, John Peters Kousakis, Ira Shuman; Director, John Whitesell; Screenplay, George Gallo, Gregory Poirier, Danny Baron, Chris Faber; Story, Andrew Deane, Michael Alexander Miller, George Gallo; Adaptation, Stuart Gibbs, Craig Titley; Photography, John Bartley; Editor, Cara Silverman; Designer, Mark Freeborn; Costumes, Diane M. Widas; Music, John Debney; Visual Effects, Perpetual Motion Pictures; Casting, Roger Mussenden; a Village Roadshow Pictures and NPV Entertainment presentation of a Roger Simonds production; Dolby; Technicolor; Rated PG; 94 minutes; Release date: March 2, 2001

### CAST

| | |
|---|---|
| Gordon Smith | David Arquette |
| Agent Murdoch | Michael Clarke Duncan |
| Stephanie | Leslie Bibb |
| Gino Valente | Joe Viterelli |
| James | Angus T. Jones |
| Benny | Anthony Anderson |
| Sonny Talia | Paul Sorvino |
| Arliss Santino | Steven R. Schirripa |
| Agent Cassavettes | Kim Hawthorne |
| Ricky | Kavan Smith |

and Peter Bryant, Fiona Hogan (Cops), Roger Haskett (Michaels), Fulvio Cecere (Lawyer), Stephen E. Miller (Danvers), Darcy Laurie (Perierra), Sara-Jane Redmond (Agent Sharp), Rachel McGinnis (Starchild), J. B. Bivens (Desk Sgt.), Tom Shorthouse (Elderly Van Driver), Jason Low (FBI Agent), Farrell Spence (Petting Zoo Driver), Irene Karas (Neighbor), Brena James (Woman at Park), Colin Foo (Shuttler Van Driver), Michael Stunczyk (Tommy), Bill Dow (Doctor), Marcus Hondro (Inmate), Pat Waldron, Rick Tae (Dog Owners), Sadie Lawrence, Lisa Benner (Signing Women), Maria J. Cruz (Woman Watching), Kandyse McClure (Attractive Woman), Dan O'Connell (Voice of Spot)

*Stephanie, desperate for a baby-sitter, leaves her six-year-old son with Gordon, an inept mailman in whose van an FBI bull mastiff, wanted by the Mafia, has taken refuge.*

© Warner Bros.

# 15 MINUTES

**(NEW LINE CINEMA)** Producers, David Blocker, John Herzfeld, Keith Addis, Nick Wechsler; Executive Producer, Claire Rudnick Polstein; Director/Screenplay, John Herzfeld; Photography, Jean Yves Escoffier; Designer, Mayne Berke; Editor, Steve Cohen; Music, Anthony Marinelli, J. Peter Robinson; Costumes, April Ferry; Associate Producers, David Gaines, James M. Freitag; Casting, Mindy Marin; an Industry Entertainment/Tribeca production; Dolby; Super 35 Widescreen; Deluxe color; Rated R; 120 minutes; Release date: March 9, 2001

## CAST

| | |
|---|---|
| Eddie Flemming | Robert De Niro |
| Jordy Warsaw | Edward Burns |
| Robert Hawkins | Kelsey Grammer |
| Leon Jackson | Avery Brooks |
| Nicolette Karas | Melina Kanakaredes |
| Emil Slovak | Karel Roden |
| Oleg Razgul | Oleg Taktarov |
| Daphne Handlova | Vera Farmiga |
| Bobby Korfin | John DiResta |
| Captain Duffy | James Handy |
| Tommy Cullen | Darius McCrary |
| Himself | Bruce Cutler |
| Rose Hearn | Charlize Theron |
| Cassandra | Kim Cattrall |
| Mugger | David Alan Grier |
| Milos | Vladimir Mashkov |

and Arina Gasanova (Tamina), Noelle Evans (Honey), Mindy Marin (Maggie), Christine Claibourne (Maggie's Assistant), Paul Herman (Paulie), Gabriel Casseus (Unique), Joe Lisi (Police Captain), Stephen Davis (Murphy), Bill Stanton (Garcia), Louis F. Garcia (Fire Chief), Mike Camello (Fireman Camello), Tygh Runyan (Stephen Geller), Barry Blueian (Immigration Supervisor), Ritchie Coster (News Stand Vendor), Roseanne, Peter Arnett (Themselves), Ashton Dane (Talk Show Father), Gail Greaves (Talk Show Wife), Bobby Fields (Talk Show Son), Anton Yelchin (Boy in Burning Building), Lynette Ruiz (Sketch Artist), Kurt Andon (Pizza Man), Rikki J. Klieman (Daphne's Lawyer), Sebastian Roche (Ludwig), Kata Dobo (Red Head at Ludwig's), Elma Vann (Linda), Olga Morgounova, Dorit Sauer (Escort Service Women), Haik Garibyan, Marco Kahn (Emigrants), Toni Kalem (Woman at Planet Hollywood), Jorge H. Guzman (Bouncer), Lennox Brown (Lookout Guy), George Poulos (Greek Waiter), Sylvia Lopez Ferullo, Jane Velez Mitchell (Newscasters), Bryan Foster (Hawkins' Cameraman), Alan Cohen (Hawkins' Sound Man), Spiros Stamboulis (Nicolette's Cameraman), Joseph Alfieri (Reporter), Barry Primus (Cab Driver), Julieta Espinoza (Unique's Girlfriend), Brantley Bush (Fireman), Macy Merced, Tracey Mulqueen (Paramedics), Scotty Dillin (Battery Park Policeman), Dominic Maylione, Ron Wall (Police Officers)

*An arson investigator and a media-hungry homicide detective team up to stop a pair of killers who have been videotaping their crimes.*

© New Line Cinema Inc.

Oleg Taktarov

Edward Burns

(Below) Melina Kanakaredes, Robert De Niro

Kelsey Grammer

Ben Foster, Colin Hanks, Sisqó

Shane West, Melissa Sagemiller, Ben Foster

Kirsten Dunst, Mila Kunis

# GET OVER IT

(MIRAMAX) Producers, Michael Burns, Marc Butan, Paul Feldsher; Executive Producers, Jill Sobel Messick, Jeremy Kramer; Director, Tommy O'Haver; Screenplay, R. Lee Fleming, Jr.; Co-Producer, Louise Rosner, Richard Hull, Leanna Creel; Photography, Maryse Alberti; Designer, Robin Standefer; Editor, Jeff Betancourt; Music, Steve Bartek; Music Supervisors, Elliot Lurie, Randy Spendlove; Songs, Marc Shaiman, Scott Wittman; Costumes, Mary Jane Fort; Casting, Kim Davis-Wagner, Justine Baddeley; an Ignite Entertainment and a Morpheus production; Dolby; Super 35 Widescreen; Color; Rated PG-13; 86 minutes; Release date: March 9, 2001

## CAST

| | |
|---|---|
| Kelly | Kirsten Dunst |
| Berke Landers | Ben Foster |
| Allison | Melissa Sagemiller |
| Dennis | Sisqó |
| Striker | Shane West |
| Felix | Colin Hanks |
| Maggie | Zoë Saldana |
| Basin | Mila Kunis |
| Beverly Landers | Swoosie Kurtz |
| Frank Landers | Ed Begley, Jr. |
| Dr. Desmond Forrest Oates | Martin Short |
| Mistress Moira | Carmen Electra |
| Themselves | Vitamin C, Coolio |
| Peter Wong | Christopher Jacot |
| Dora Lynn | Kylie Bax |
| Little Steve | Dov Tiefenbach |
| Jessica | Jeanie Calleja |
| Chook | Park Bench |
| Grendan | Daniel Enright |
| Hugh | Andrew McGillivray |
| Shirin | Megan Fahlenboch |
| Coach Hibble | Jonathan Whittaker |

and Shawn Roberts (Colin), Sadie LaBlanc (Jamilla), Jodan Madley (Corrine), Ravi Steve Khajuria (Del Molden, Jr.), Tommy O'Haver ("Love Matters" Director), Reuben Thompson (EMT), Roger McKeen, Chris Benson (Cops), Albert Chung (Trombonist), Antoinette Delond, Krista Leis, Judy Stoimenov, Larissa Gomes (Strippers), Jeffrey Wong, Shawn Fernandez, Catherine Hernandez (Attendants/Fairies), Lindsay Cole (Hippolyta), Dolores Ettienne (Sweet Old Lady), Michael Kremko (Guy in Restaurant), Danny Truelove (Little Boy in Restaurant), Jack Babock, Michael Coristine (Boy Band Members), Christine Nowland, Brent Bushnell, Amy Todd, Troy P. Liddell, Joshua Feldman, Louis Paquette, Jesse Robb, Jenn Butler, Mario Castillo, Michael Boisvert, Krista Martins, Patrick Patterson, Chloe Randel Reis, Diane Fabian, Bradley Garrick, Jamie Holmes (Dancers)

*Dumped by the girl he's dated for years, Berke Landers turns to his best friend's sister, Kelly, for love advice.*

© Miramax Films

**(Below) Kirsten Dunst, Martin Short**

Anthony LaPaglia, Douglas McGrath

Alan Cumming

# COMPANY MAN

**(PARAMOUNT CLASSICS)** Producers, John Penotti, James W. Scotchdopole, Rick Leed, Guy East; Co-Executive Producers, Nigel Sinclair, Matt Williams, Susan Cartsonis, Jon Ein, Robert Greenhut; Directors/Screenplay, Douglas McGrath, Peter Askin; Photography, Russell Boyd; Designer, Jane Musky; Costumes, Ruth Myers; Editor, Camilla Toniolo; Music, David Nessim Lawrence; Casting, Ellen Lewis; an Intermedia Films presentation in association with Foundry Film Partners of a Wind Dancer Films/GreeneStreet Films production; Dolby; Color; Rated PG-13; 86 minutes; Release date: March 9, 2001

## CAST

Allen Quimp........................................................Douglas McGrath
Daisy Quimp ........................................................Sigourney Weaver
Crocker Johnson........................................................John Turturro
General Batista........................................................Alan Cumming
Fidel Castro ........................................................Anthony LaPaglia
Rudolph Petrov ........................................................Ryan Phillippe
Nora ........................................................Heather Matarazzo
Officer Fry........................................................Denis Leary
Ms. Judge........................................................Terry Beaver
Mother Quimp........................................................Kathleen Chalfant
Officer Hickle........................................................Paul Guilfoyle
Senator Biggs........................................................Jeffrey Jones
Danny........................................................Matt Ross
Lowther........................................................Woody Allen
and Reathel Bean (Senator Farwood), Harriet Koppel (Stenographer), Sean Dugan (Skull and Bones Waiter), Grant Walden (Older Man), Nathan Dean (Younger Man), John Randolph Jones (Fobbs), Kim Merrill (Woman in Line), Merwin Goldsmith (Mr. Brisk), Larry Clarke (Fred Quimp), Sandy McGrath (Tom Quimp), Frank Brosens (Chuck Quimp), Luis Placer (Man on the Beach), Norberto Kerner (Cuban Waiter), Jane Reed Martin (Betty Crichton), Liz Welch Tirrell (Sally Smith), Octavio Gómez (Field Worker), Darlene Tejeiro (Rosa), Raul Aranas (Guard #1), José Ramón Rosario (Audience Member), Andrew Driscoll, Bill Greenlee, David McKinley, Brian Nelson (The Lifeguards), Matteo Gómez (Aide), John McDonnell (Emissary), Pablo Cunquiero (Cuban Man), Tuck Milligan (President Kennedy), Susanna Hobrath, Lisa Ganz, Susan Stout (JFK Women), Steven Banks (Officer Emmons)

*In order to impress his social-climbing wife, mild-mannered grammar teacher Allen Quimp pretends to be a CIA agent, a fib that ultimately gets him mixed up in real spy work in Cuba, where he is asked to depose Fidel Castro.*

© Paramount Classics

John Turturro, Sigourney Weaver

Ryan Phillippe

Guy Pearce

Carrie-Anne Moss

Guy Pearce

# MEMENTO

(NEWMARKET) Producers, Jennifer Todd, Suzanne Todd; Executive Producer, Aaron Ryder; Co-Executive Producers, William Tyrer, Chris Ball; Co-Producer, Elaine Dysinger; Director/Screenplay, Christopher Nolan; Based on the short story by Jonathan Nolan; Photography, Wally Pfister; Designer, Patti Podesta; Costumes, Cindy Evans; Editor, Dody Dorn; Music, David Julyan; Casting, John Papsidera; a Team Todd production, presented in association with Summit Entertainment; Dolby; Panavision; Fotokem color; Rated R; 116 minutes; Release date: March 16, 2001

## CAST

Leonard Shelby ........................................................................Guy Pearce
Natalie ...........................................................................Carrie-Anne Moss
Teddy ...................................................................................Joe Pantoliano
Burt ............................................................................Mark Boone Junior
Waiter......................................................................................Russ Fega
Leonard's Wife.............................................................................Jorja Fox
Sammy ...........................................................................Stephen Tobolowsky
Mrs. Jankis...............................................................Harriet Sansom Harris
Doctor...............................................................................Thomas Lennon
Dodd....................................................................Callum Keith Rennie
Blonde...........................................................................Kimberly Campbell
Tattooist...............................................................Marianne Muellerleile
Jimmy ..............................................................................Larry Holden

*Leonard Shelby, suffering from the inability to form any new memories, chases after the murderer of his wife, a person whose identity he cannot possibly know for sure.*

*This film received Oscar nominations for original screenplay and editing.*

© Newmarket

Joe Pantoliano, Guy Pearce

Guy Pearce,
Carrie-Anne Moss

# EXIT WOUNDS

(WARNER BROS.) Producers, Joel Silver, Dan Cracchiolo; Executive Producer, Bruce Berman; Co-Producer, John M. Eckert; Director, Andrzej Bartkowiak; Screenplay, Ed Horowitz, Richard D'Ovidio; Based on the novel by John Westermann; Photography, Glen MacPherson; Designers, Paul Denham Austerberry; Editor, Derek G. Brechin; Music, Jeff Rona, Damon "Grease" Blackman; Costumes, Jennifer Bryan; Casting, Rick Pagano, Diane Kerbel; a Silver Pictures production, presented in association with Village Roadshow Pictures and NPV Entertainment; Dolby; Super 35 Widescreen; Technicolor; Rated R; 117 minutes; Release date: March 16, 2001

Anthony Anderson, Steven Seagal

DMX

## CAST

| | |
|---|---|
| Orin Boyd | Steven Seagal |
| Latrell Walker | DMX |
| George Clark | Isaiah Washington |
| T. K. | Anthony Anderson |
| Strutt | Michael Jai White |
| Hinges | Bill Duke |
| Annette Mulcahy | Jill Hennessy |
| Henry Wayne | Tom Arnold |
| Daniels | Bruce McGill |
| Montini | David Vadim |
| Trish | Eva Mendes |
| Useldinger | Matthew G. Taylor |
| Parker | Paolo Mastropietro |
| Fitz | Shane Daly |
| Shaun | Drago-On |
| Linda | Jennifer Irwin |
| Rory | Daniel Kash |
| Housewife | Quancetia Hamilton |
| Jail Guard | Rick Dennis |

and Jason Stephens, Peter Kosaka (Lab Technicians), Chris Lawford (Vice President), Noah Danby (Terrorist Leader), Shakira Harper (Static Waitress), Eduardo Gómez (Father), Yanina Contreras (Mother), Mario Torres (José), Jenny Celly (Maria), Rothaford Gray (Norris), Dean Monroe McKenzie (Carlson), Tom Seniuk, Bobby Johnston, Neville Edwards (Secret Service Agents), Arnold Pinnock (Morris), Gregory Vitale (Car Salesman), Shawn Lawrence (O'Malley), John Ralston (Mulcahy's Date), Simon "Tiger Twins" Kim, James "Tiger Twins" Kim, Shekib Ahmad Foroughi, Ekundayo Odesanyo, Christopher Oster (Thugs), Naomi Gaskin (George's Wife), Phillip Jarrett, Michael Boisvert, John McConnach, Moses Nyarko, Eldridge Hyndman (SWAT Guys), Elio Campbell, Mark Williams (Cops), Stromm Bradshaw (Stormy), Shannon Jobe, Kym Krystalie (Strippers), Peter Walsh (Ducati Guy), Gary Johnston, Joe Alberico, Stone Conway, Barrington Bignall, Greg Zajac, Ed Semenuk, David Boyce, Jaime Estrada (Anger Management Group)

*A Detroit police officer is transferred to the tough 15th District where he investigates Latrell Walker, a mysterious drug dealer, whose actions are not what they seem.*

© Warner Bros.

Morris Chestnut, D.L. Hughley, Bill Bellamy, Shemar Moore

# THE BROTHERS

(SCREEN GEMS) Producers, Darin Scott, Paddy Cullen; Executive Producer, Doug McHenry; Director/Screenplay, Gary Hardwick; Photography, Alexander Gruszynski; Designer, Amy Ancona; Editor, Earl Watson; Costumes, Debraé Little; Music Supervisor, Melodee Sutton; Casting, Reuben Cannon; Dolby; Deluxe color; Rated R; 106 minutes; Release date: March 23, 2001

## CAST

| | |
|---|---|
| Jackson Smith | Morris Chestnut |
| Brian Palmer | Bill Bellamy |
| Derrick West | D. L. Hughley |
| Terry White | Shemar Moore |
| Denise Johnson | Gabrielle Union |
| Louise Smith | Jenifer Lewis |
| Cheré Smith | Tatyana Ali |
| Sheila West | Tamala Jones |
| Fred Smith | Clifton Powell |
| Ursula | Nadege Auguste |
| Jesse Caldwell | Julie Benz |
| Spurned Woman | Redena Bivins |
| Judge Carla Williams | Angelle Brooks |
| Dr. Thelma Woolridge | Vanessa Bell Calloway |
| Bailiff | Nicole Cummins |
| BeBe Fales | Susan Dalian |
| Sista at Wedding | Marie Frazier |
| Mary West | Marla Gibbs |
| T-Boy | Gary Hardwick |
| Ceyno, the Multi-Ethnic Lover | Henry Kingi, Jr. |
| Steve on the Strip | Roland "Buddy" Lewis |
| Sandra the Temp | Kim Porter |

and Darin Scott (Derrick's Attorney), Nikki Thompson (Bartender), Nayo Wallace (Red the Stripper), Aloma Wright (Helen Palmer), Tanya Wright (LaMuzindah), Sean P. Young (Tyrel Palmer)

*A group of friends are shocked to find out that one of their own is getting married, a decision that causes each of them to try to work out their own romantic problems.*

© Screen Gems

# HEARTBREAKERS

(MGM) Producers, John Davis, Irving Ong; Executive Producers, Clayton Townsend, Gary Smith, Hadeel Reda; Director, David Mirkin; Screenplay, Robert Dunn, Paul Guay, Stephen Mazur; Photography, Dean Semler; Designer, Lilly Kilvert; Editor, William Steinkamp; Costumes, Gary Jones, Ann Roth; Music, John Debney; Heartbreakers Theme, Danny Elfman; Music Supervisor, Maureen Crowe; Casting, Juel Bestrop, Jeanne McCarthy; a Davis Entertainment Company/Irving Ong production; Dolby; Panavision; Deluxe color; Rated PG-13; 123 minutes; Release date: March 23, 2001

## CAST

| | |
|---|---|
| Max Conners (Angela Nardino/Ulga Yevanova) | Sigourney Weaver |
| Page Conners (Wendy/Jane Helstrom) | Jennifer Love Hewitt |
| Dean Cumanno (Vinny Staggliano) | Ray Liotta |
| Jack Withrowe | Jason Lee |
| Gloria Vogal (Barbara) | Anne Bancroft |
| Mr. Appel | Jeffrey Jones |
| William B. Tensy | Gene Hackman |
| Miss Madress | Nora Dunn |
| Leo | Julio Oscar Mechoso |
| Dawson's Auctioneer | Ricky Jay |
| Linda | Sarah Silverman |
| Bill | Zach Galifianakis |
| Davis | Michael Hitchcock |
| Priest at First Wedding | Pierre Gonneau |
| Minister at Second Wedding | Shawn Colvin |
| Wedding Band Singer | Michael Andrew |
| Busboy | Andy Brewster |
| Ray | Gonzo Raymond |
| Ms. Surpin | Carrie Fisher |
| Mr. Gruber | Jack Shearer |
| Man in Gas Station | Alan Blumenfeld |
| Waiter | Adam Novicki |
| Maitre D' | Robert Alan Beuth |
| Philip Tinker | Steve Mellor |
| Davis Mom | Janni Brenn |

and Jackie O'Brien (Woman at Dawson's), Denalda Williams (David Maid), Haresh Raval (Man in Auction), Jack Douglas Cooper (Other Man at Auction), Peter Spellos (Dawson's Workman), Elya Baskin (Vladimir), Oleg Stefan (Kremlin Band Leader), Ken Magee (Police Sergeant), Geremy Dingle (Breakers Waiter), Patricia Belcher (Hotel Housekeeping Maid), Moné Walton (Bank Teller), Bernadette Birkett (Jack's Mother), David Mirkin (Jack's Lawyer), Catherine Butterfield (Bridal Shop Saleslady), Lawrence Sacco (Man at Banquet), Jennifer Genco (Waitress)

*A mother-daughter con artist team sets out to swindle cigarette tycoon William B. Tensy.*

© Metro-Goldwyn-Mayer Pictures, Inc.

Gene Hackman, Sigourney Weaver

Jason Lee, Jennifer Love Hewitt

Ray Liotta, Jennifer Love Hewitt, Jason Lee

Anne Bancroft, Sigourney Weaver

Carla Gugino, Daryl Sabara, Antonio Banderas, Alexa Vega

Alan Cumming

Daryl Sabara, Alexa Vega

Teri Hatcher, Alexa Vega

# SPY KIDS

**(DIMENSION)** Producers, Elizabeth Avellan, Robert Rodriguez; Executive Producers, Bob Weinstein, Harvey Weinstein, Cary Granat; Director/Screenplay/Editor, Robert Rodriguez; Photography, Guillermo Navarro; Designer, Cary White; Floop's Song and Spy Kids Theme, Danny Elfman; Costumes, Deborah Everton; Line Producer, Bill Scott; Co-Producer, Tamee Smith-Zimmerman; Special Makeup Effects, Robert Kurtzman, Gregory Nicotero, Howard Berger; Stunts, Jeff Dashnaw; Digital Visual Effects, Hyrbride Technologies, Digital.Art.Media; Casting, Mary Vernieu, Anne McCarthy; a Troublemaker Studios production ; Distributed by Miramax Films; Dolby; Color; Rated PG; 86 minutes; Release date: March 30, 2001

## CAST

| | |
|---|---|
| Gregorio Cortez | Antonio Banderas |
| Ingrid Cortez | Carla Gugino |
| Carmen Cortez | Alexa Vega |
| Juni Cortez | Daryl Sabara |
| Fegan Floop | Alan Cumming |
| Alexander Minion | Tony Shalhoub |
| Ms. Gradenko | Teri Hatcher |
| Felix Gumm | Cheech Marin |
| Mr. Lisp | Robert Patrick |
| Machete | Danny Trejo |
| Donnagon/Donnamight | Mike Judge |
| Cool Spy | Richard Linklater |
| Pastor | Guillermo Navarro |
| Agent Johnny | Johnny Reno |
| FoOglie #1/Flower | Shannon Shea |
| FoOglie #2/Tall & Skinny | Norman Cabrera |
| FoOglie #3/Too Too | Trant Batey |
| Brat | Andy W. Bossley |
| Brat's Dad | Jeff Dashnaw |
| Carmen's Friend | Kara Slack |
| Cab Driver | Ermahn Ospina |

and Emilio Navarro Mackissack (Excited Kid at Playground), Evan Sabara ("Intruder" Spy Kid), Rachel Duhame (President's Robot Daughter), Houston Hooker (Lisp's Robot Son), Louis Black, Charles Ramirez-Berg, Dick Clark, Steve Havens, Roberto Santibanez (Financiers), Julio Villarreal (Spy Driver), Becca Rodriguez, Patricia Vonne (Spy Bridesmaids), Angela Lanza (Newscaster), George Clooney (Devlin)

*Young Carmen and Juni Cortez find out that their parents are former international spies after the two adults are kidnapped, prompting the kids to spring into action to save them from an evil mastermind determined to take over the world. This film was also reissued in August of 2001 with an additional three minutes of footage.*

© Dimension Films

(Below) Daryl Sabara, Alexa Vega

Carla Gugino, Antonio Banderas

Daryl Sabara, Alan Cumming, Alexa Vega

Daryl Sabara, Alexa Vega

Ashley Judd, Greg Kinnear

# SOMEONE LIKE YOU

**(20TH CENTURY FOX)** Producer, Lynda Obst; Executive Producer, Jim Chory; Director, Tony Goldwyn; Screenplay, Elizabeth Chandler; Based upon the novel *Animal Husbandry* by Laura Zigman; Photography, Anthony B. Richmond; Designer, Dan Leigh; Editor, Dana Congdon; Costumes, Ann Roth, Michelle Maitlin; Music, Rolfe Kent; Music Supervisor, Dana Millman-DuFine; Casting, Billy Hopkins, Suzanne Smith, Kerry Barden; a Fox 2000 Pictures presentation of a Lynda Obst production; Dolby; Deluxe color; Rated PG-13; 97 minutes; Release date: March 30, 2001

## CAST

| | |
|---|---|
| Jane Goodale | Ashley Judd |
| Ray Brown | Greg Kinnear |
| Eddie Alden | Hugh Jackman |
| Liz | Marisa Tomei |
| Diane Roberts | Ellen Barkin |
| Evelyn | Laura Regan |
| Alice | Catherine Dent |
| Stephen | Peter Friedman |
| Mary Lou Corkle | Donna Hanover |
| Staff Member | Matthew Coyle |
| Chinese Vendor | Pon Yang |
| Realtor | Colleen Camp |
| Girl in Bar | Sabine Singh |
| Young Intern | Nicole Leach |
| Isabel | Murielle Arden |

and Jess Platt (Dr. Krane), Shuler Hensley (Hick Farmer), Joe J. Mosso (Technician), AJ Ekoku (Jane's Assistant), Sue Jin Song, Keith Reddin (Scientists), Derick Karlton Grant (Flower Delivery Man), Bear Jackson (Street Vendor), David Kener (Stage Manager), Leanna Croom (Rebecca), Mireille Enos, Adrienne Burke (Instructors), Veronica Webb (Herself), Naomi Judd (Makeup Artist)

*Recently dumped by her boyfriend, Jane Goodale reluctantly moves in with her womanizing co-worker, Eddie Alden, and begins formulating a theory that the behavior of men is akin to that of animals, an idea that spins into an anonymous sex column.*

© Twentieth Century Fox

Marissa Tomei

Ellen Barkin

Ashley Judd, Hugh Jackman

Jamie Lee Curtis, Pierce Brosnan

# THE TAILOR OF PANAMA

(COLUMBIA) Producer/Director, John Boorman; Executive Producer, John Le Carré; Screenplay, Andrew Davies, John Le Carré, based on the novel by John Le Carré; Photography, Philippe Rousselot; Designer, Derek Wallace; Editor, Ron Davis; Costumes, Maeve Paterson; Music, Shaun Davey; Co-Producer, Kevan Barker; Casting, Mary Gail Artz, Barbara Cohen, Jina Jay; a Merlin Films production; U.S.-Irish; Dolby; Panavision; Color; Rated R; 109 minutes; Release date: March 30, 2001

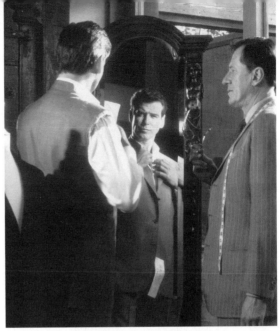

Pierce Brosnan, Geoffrey Rush

## CAST

| | |
|---|---|
| Andy Osnard | Pierce Brosnan |
| Harry Pendel | Geoffrey Rush |
| Louisa Pendel | Jamie Lee Curtis |
| Marta | Leonor Varela |
| Mickie Abraxas | Brendan Gleeson |
| Uncle Benny | Harold Pinter |
| Francesca | Catherine McCormack |
| Mark Pendel | Daniel Radcliffe |
| Sarah Pendel | Lola Boorman |
| Luxmore | David Hayman |
| Rafi Domingo | Mark Margolis |
| Teddy | Martin Ferrero |
| Maltby | John Fortune |
| Stormont | Martin Savage |
| Juan-David | Edgardo Molino |
| Ramon Rudd | Jon Polito |
| Cavendish | Jonathan Hyde |
| Dusenbaker | Dylan Baker |
| Joe | Paul Birchard |
| Elliot | Harry Ditson |
| Morecombe | Ken Jenkins |
| President | Adolfo Arias Espinosa |
| Marco | Juan Carlos Adames |
| Ernesto Delgado | Luis A. Goti |
| Customer | Vladimir Vega |
| Palace Secretary | Cesar Sanjur |

Lola Boorman, Daniel Radcliffe

and Heather Emmanuel (Angelo the Manager), Diomara De Ruiz (Mrs. Delgado), Doug Cockle (Pentagon Aide), Patrick Poletti, Andrew French (Officers), Frank Melia, Siraj Zaidi (Officials), Lisa Dwan (Stewardess), Paolo Tulio (Panamanian Businessman)

*A ruthless spy, banished to Panama for his sexual indiscretions, blackmails ex-con-turned-tailor Harry Pendel into finding information about the future ownership of the Panama Canal.*

© Columbia Pictures Industries Inc.

Pierce Brosnan, Martin Savage, Catherine McCormack, John Fortune

Johnny Depp

Penélope Cruz, Johnny Depp

Franka Potente, Rachel Griffiths

# BLOW

(NEW LINE CINEMA) Producers, Ted Demme, Joel Stillerman, Denis Leary; Executive Producers, Georgia Kacandes, Michael De Luca; Director, Ted Demme; Screenplay, David McKenna, Nick Cassavetes; Photography, Ellen Kuras; Designer, Michael Hanan; Editor, Kevin Tent; Music, Graeme Revell; Music Supervisor, Amanda Scheer Demme; Costumes, Mark Bridges; Casting, Avy Kaufman; a Spanky Pictures/Apostle production; Dolby; Panavision; Deluxe color; Rated R; 124 minutes; Release date: April 6, 2001

## CAST

| | |
|---|---|
| George Jung | Johnny Depp |
| Mirtha Jung | Penélope Cruz |
| Barbara Buckley | Franka Potente |
| Ermine Jung | Rachel Griffiths |
| Derek Foreal | Paul Reubens |
| Diego Delgado | Jordi Mollà |
| Escobar | Cliff Curtis |
| Augusto Oliveras | Miguel Sandoval |
| Tuna | Ethan Suplee |
| Fred Jung | Ray Liotta |
| Leon Minghella | Kevin Gage |
| Kevin Dulli | Max Perlich |
| Young Georg | Jesse James |
| Alessandro | Miguel Perez |
| Cesar Toban | Dan Ferro |
| Sanchez | Tony Amendola |
| Mr. T | Bobcat Goldthwait |
| Dr. Bay | Michael Tucci |
| Maria | Monet Mazur |
| Rada | Lola Glaudini |
| Inez | Jennifer Gimenez |
| Young Kristina Jung | Emma Roberts |
| Jack Stevens | Charles Noland |

and Genevieve Maylem, Tracy Falco, Pamela Abdy, Sophie Tsimel, Kathleen Mullan (Beach Women), John Harrington Bland, Dale Snowberger, Brantley Bush, Jimmy Burke, Pamela Walker (FBI Waiters), Kevin H. Chapman (DEA Eastham), The Dawk (Guard, Visit Area #2), Edward Demme (Archie Zigmond), Crystal Erickson, Elif Guertin, Vanessa Greyson, Meriah Nelson, Leslie Schirrmacher, Faith Hoover (Stewardesses), Daniel Escobar (Emilio Ochoa), Jean-Carlos Felix (Prison Guard—Warden's Office), Lazaro Galarraga (Band Singer), Brian Goodman (Guard Gus), Josh Herman, Richard LaGravenese (Detectives), Brad Hunt (GG), Patrick Husted (Bank Manager—Mass.), Kristina Jung (Clerk), Ralph Kampshoff (Guard—Visit Area #1), Ajgie Kirkland (James Trout), Skip O'Brien (Customs Agent), Roberto Lopez (Guard—Danbury), Matt Robinson, Raoul Rizik, Lydell M. Cheshier (Inmates), Dorothy Lyman (Judge—Chicago), Jodie Mann (Nurse—Cape Cod), Charles Martinez (Bank Employee), Gonzalo Mendoza (Ramon Ochoa), Alan James Morgan (Young Tuna), Randy Mulkey (Employee #1), Tony Perez (Bank President), Jack Polick (Ben), Elizabeth Rodriguez (Martha Oliveras), Bert Rosario (Bank President—Panama), Julia Vera (Clara Blanca), Santiago Verdu (Juan Carlos)

*The true story of how George Jung became one of the top cocaine dealers in the country during the 1970s.*

© New Line Cinema Inc.

(Below) Johnny Depp

Franka Potente, Johnny Depp

Paul Reubens

Johnny Depp, Ray Liotta

Johnny Depp, Jordi Mollà

Morgan Freeman

Morgan Freeman

Craig March, Kim Hawthorne, Charles Andison,
Morgan Freeman, Dylan Baker, Monica Potter

Morgan Freeman, Monica Potter

# ALONG CAME A SPIDER

**(PARAMOUNT)** Producers, David Brown, Joe Wizan; Executive Producers, Morgan Freeman, Marty Hornstein; Director, Lee Tamahori; Screenplay, Marc Moss; Based on the novel by James Patterson; Photography, Matthew F. Leonetti; Designer, Ida Random; Editor, Neil Travis; Music, Jerry Goldsmith; Costumes, Sanja Milkovic Hays; Casting, Denise Chamian, Stuart Aikins; a David Brown/Phase 1 production in association with Revelations Entertainment in association with MFP Munich Film Partners GmbH & Co., AZL Productions KG; U.S.-German; Dolby; Panavision; Deluxe color; Rated R; 104 minutes; Release date: April 6, 2001

## CAST

| | |
|---|---|
| Alex Cross | Morgan Freeman |
| Jezzie Flannigan | Monica Potter |
| Gary Soneji/Jonathan Mercurio | Michael Wincott |
| Elizabeth Rose | Penelope Ann Miller |
| Senator Hank Rose | Michael Moriarty |
| Special Agent Oliver "Ollie" McArthur | Dylan Baker |
| Megan Rose | Mika Boorem |
| Dimitri Starodubov | Anton Yelchin |
| Agent Hickley | Kim Hawthorne |
| FBI Special Agent Kyle Craig | Jay O. Sanders |
| Secret Service Agent Ben Devine | Billy Burke |
| Floyd the Fisherman | Scott Heindl |
| Jim | Christopher Shyer |
| Tracie | Jill Teed |
| Sam | Ian Marsh |
| Bodyguard | Raoul Ganeev |
| Mrs. Hume | Samantha Ferris |
| Amy Masterson | Ocean Hellman |
| County Chief Cabell | Tom McBeath |

and Tamara Taggart, Suzette Meyers, Brian Arnold, Chris Robson, Jonathan Walker, Debra Donahue (Reporters), Mila Dobrozdravich (Hannah), Aaron Joseph (Kennedy), Ravil Isyanov (Leromontov), Ronin Wong (Medical Examiner), Campbell Lane (Mathias), Charles André (Diplomatic Patrol Officer), Claire Riley, Paul Carson, Donna Lysell (News Anchors), Kevin Hayes, Steve Makaj (News Co-Anchors), Anna Maria Horsford (Vickie), Nathaniel Deveuax (Coast Guard Captain), Nguyen Hall (Watergate Employee), Charles Andison, Tarie Tennessey, Darryl Scheelar, Craig March (McArthur Entourages), Darryl Dillard (D.C. Policeman), Carter Jahncke (Man Who Can't Answer Phone), Jim Hild (Potentially Evil Guy on Train)

*Detective Alex Cross teams with Secret Service Agent Jezzie Flannigan to save a senator's daughter, who has been kidnapped by the psychopathic Gary Soneji. Morgan Freeman returns as Alex Cross, the character he played in the 1997 film* Kiss the Girls.

© Paramount Pictures

(Clockwise from bottom center): Alan Cumming, Seth Green, Donald Faison, Alex Martin, Breckin Meyer

# JOSIE AND THE PUSSYCATS

(UNIVERSAL/MGM) Producers, Marc Platt, Tracey E. Edmonds, Chuck Grimes, Tony DeRosa-Grund; Executive Producers, Kenneth Edmonds, Michael Silberkleit, Richard Goldwater; Directors/Screenplay, Deborah Kaplan, Harry Elfont; Based on characters appearing in Archie comics and the Hanna-Barbera cartoon series; Photography, Matthew Libatique; Designer, Jasna Stefanovich; Editor, Peter Teschner; Co-Producer, Grace Gilroy; Music, John Frizzell; Music Supervisors, Tracey E. Edmonds, Michael McQuarn; Choreographer, Viktoria Langton; a Marc Platt/Riverdale production; Dolby; Color; Rated PG-13; 95 minutes; Release date: April 11, 2001

Rosario Dawson, Tara Reid, Rachael Leigh Cook, Parker Posey

## CAST

Josie McCoy ...................................................Rachael Leigh Cook
Melody Valentine ...........................................................Tara Reid
Valerie Brown ...................................................Rosario Dawson
Wyatt Frame ...................................................Alan Cumming
Fiona...........................................................Parker Posey
Alan M...........................................................Gabriel Mann
Alexander Cabot ...........................................Paulo Costanzo
Alexandra Cabot...........................................Missi Pyle
Agent Kelly...........................................................Tom Butler
Les ...........................................................Alex Martin
Teenage Fans ............Faedragh Carpenter, Justin Chatwin, Marites Pineda
Wedding Dress Girl ...........................................Kimberly Rimer
Aquarium Tour Guide...........................................Corinne Reilly
and Marnie Alton, Katharine Isabelle, Aeja Goldsmith (Laughing Girls), Nicole Fraissinet, Jessica Murdoch, Juliana Wimbles (Megastore Girls), Zak Alam (Megastore DJ), David Kopp, Sean J. Dory (College Dudes), Heather Robertson (Unstylish Girl), Hiro Kanagawa (Japanese Delegate), Kurt Max Runte (German Delegate), Claude De Martino (French Delegate), Colin Foo (Chinese Delegate), Balinder Johal (Sri-Lankan Delegate), Enuka Okuma, Clay St. Thomas (Fashion Team), Erin Fitzgerald, Linda Ko (Slang Team), Serena Altschul, Mark Seliger, Sally Hershberger, Jann T. Carl, Carson Daly (Themselves), Stuart Lilley, Chris Lovick, Natalye Vivian (New Josie Fans), Karalee Paterson (Pointing Fan), Aries Spears (The Other Carson Daly), Dion Johnstone (Federal Agent), Harry Elfont (Pilot), Tamara Taggart (TV Reporter), Anthony Creery (Incompetent Techie), JR Bourne (Shop Owner), Shayn Solberg (Geek Guy), Harmoni Everett (Josie's Manicurist), Kris Pope (Gregor), Kevin Bergsman, Todd Talbot, Craig Taylor, Paul Becker, Jay Williams (Fiona's Dancers), Russ Leatherman (Mr. Moviefone). Breckin Meyer, Seth Green, Donald Faison, Eugene Levy

Rosario Dawson, Tara Reid, Gabrielle Mann, Rachael Leigh Cook

*Aspiring rock musicians Josie and the Pussycats get their big break when they are signed up by MegaRecords, only to find out that their manager is plotting to control the youth of America through subliminal messages contained in the Pussycats' songs. Based on the Hanna-Barbera animated series, which ran on CBS from 1970–1972.*

© Universal Studios

Tara Reid, Rachael Leigh Cook, Rosario Dawson

# KINGDOM COME

**(FOX SEARCHLIGHT)** Producers, John Morrissey, Edward Bates; Executive Producers, Rochelle Bates, Lawrence Turman; Director, Doug McHenry; Screenplay, David Dean Bottrell, Jessie Jones, based on their play *Dearly Departed*; Photography, Francis Kenny; Designer, Simon Dobbin; Costumes, Francine Jamison-Tanchuck; Editor, Richard Halsey; Co-Producer, Hester Hargett; Music, Tyler Bates; Original Songs, Kirk Franklin; Music Supervisor, Derrick L. Wade; Casting, Robi Reed-Humes; a Bates Entertainment/The Turman-Morrissey Company production; Dolby; Super 35 Widescreen; Color; Rated PG; 92 minutes; Release date: April 11, 2001

## CAST

| | |
|---|---|
| Ray Bud Slocumb | LL Cool J |
| Charisse Slocumb | Jada Pinkett Smith |
| Lucille Slocumb | Vivica A. Fox |
| Marguerite | Loretta Devine |
| Junior Slocumb | Anthony Anderson |
| Juanita Slocumb | Toni Braxton |
| Reverend Hooker | Cedric the Entertainer |
| Royce | Darius McCrary |
| Clyde | Richard Gant |
| Raynelle Slocumb | Whoopi Goldberg |
| Delightful | Masasa |
| Antoine Depew | Dominic Hoffman |
| Merline Depew | Patrice Moncell |
| Charles Winslow | Clifton Davis |
| Bernice | Kellita Smith |
| Veda | Aloma Wright |
| Nadine | Tamala Jones |

and Ellen L. Cleghorne, Tamela J. Mann, Natalie D. Wilson, Sandrina Nicole Shepherd (Ladies), Tony Paul (Tiny), Chuck Campbell (Pedal Steel Player)

*Members of the dysfunctional Slocumb family come together for the funeral of patriarch Bud Slocumb, bringing forth a great deal of tension and squabbling.*

© Twentieth Century Fox

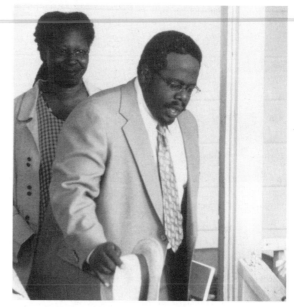

Whoopi Goldberg, Cedric the Entertainer

Jada Pinkett Smith

LL Cool J

Darius McCrary, Loretta Devine

# JOE DIRT

(COLUMBIA) Producer, Robert Simonds; Executive Producers, Adam Sandler, Jack Giarraputo; Director, Dennie Gordon; Screenplay, David Spade, Fred Wolf; Co-Producer, Ira Shuman; Photography, John R. Leonetti; Designer, Perry Andelin Blake; Editor, Peck Prior; Music, Waddy Wachtel; Music Supervisor, Michael Dilbeck; Costumes, Alexandra Welker; Casting, Roger Mussenden; a Happy Madison/Robert Simonds production; Dolby; Deluxe color; Rated PG-13; 91 minutes; Release date: April 11, 2001

## CAST

| | |
|---|---|
| Joe Dirt | David Spade |
| Brandy | Brittany Daniel |
| Zander Kelly | Dennis Miller |
| Kicking Wing | Adam Beach |
| Clem | Christopher Walken |
| Jill | Jaime Pressly |
| Robby | Kid Rock |
| Little Joe Dirt | Erik Per Sullivan |
| Joe's Little Sister | Megan Taylor Harvey |
| Joe's Mom | Caroline Aaron |
| Joe's Dad | Fred Ward |

and John Farley (Security Guard), Bob Zany, Bean Miller (Men), Fred Wolf (Producer Fred), Lee Walker (Zeke), Que Kelly, Kathleen Lambert, Liz Torres, Elisa Leonetti (Beauty College Women), Chris Wylde, Justin Staffer, Justin Kupanoff (Railroad Boys), Hamilton Camp (Meteor Bert), Tom McGillen, John Kirk, Anthony Mastrimauro (Painters), Greg M. Martin (Dude), Angela Paton (Woman with Roadrunner), Robb Skyler (Man at Dental Clinic), Tyler Mane (Bondi), Gordon Michaels (Oil Rig Boss), Lenny Schmidt (Bill/Co-Worker), Rance Howard (Bomb Squad Cop), Erin Murphy, Bree Turner, Natalia Cigliuti (Sorority Girls), Avery Rosin (Kid at Carnival), Brian Thompson (Buffalo Bob), Steven Brill (Cop at Crime Scene), Mitzi Martin (Miss Clipper), Mark Abney, Ian Falk, Matthew Siemonsma, Joshua Farrell, Alexandra Amoscato, Brian Chiesa (Cafeteria Kids), Eric Marquette (Chemistry Student), Fred Stoller (Chemistry Teacher), Steven Schirripa (Hood), Kevin Farley (Cop at Clem's), Richard Riehle (Car Dealer), Blake Clark (Old Cajun Man), Hal Fishman (Newscaster), Eddie Money (Himself), David Garry (Joe's Fan), Jourdan Fremin (Reporter at Parent's House), Kristina Simonds (Newswoman on the Bridge), Karl Makinen, James Tupper (Cops at Bridge), Jana Sandler (Woman on Bridge), Joe Don Baker, Rosanna Arquette, Kevin Nealon, Carson Daly

*A grubby, white-trash janitor, abandoned by his family when he was a child, hits the road in hopes of finding his parents.*

© Columbia Pictures

David Spade, Jaime Pressly

David Spade, Kid Rock

Peter Falk, Charles Durning

George Wendt, Robert Forster

# LAKEBOAT

(PANORAMA) Producers, Eric R. Epperson, Tony Mamet, Morris Ruskin; Executive Producer, Alan James; Director/Producer, Joe Mantegna; Screenplay, David Mamet, based on his play; Photography, Paul Sarossy; Designer, Thomas Carnegie; Editor, Christopher Cibelli; Music, Bob Mamet; Co-Producers, Stacia Sekuler Miehe, Andrea Hecht Endewardt; Costumes, Margaret Mohr; Presented in association with Oregon Trail Films and One Vibe Entertainment; Color; Rated R; 98 minutes; Release date: April 13, 2001

## CAST

| | |
|---|---|
| Skippy | Charles Durning |
| Pierman | Peter Falk |
| Joe | Robert Forster |
| Stan | J. J. Johnston |
| Fireman | Denis Leary |
| Dale Katzman | Tony Mamet |
| Fred | Jack Wallace |
| Collins | George Wendt |
| Cuthman | Saul Rubinek |
| Guigliani | Andy Garcia |

and Roberta Angelica (Prostitute), Diane Fabian (Janice, 50 years old), Lori Gordon (Janice), Steven Grayhm (Fred, 18 years old), Jason Jazrawy (Joe Litko, 20 years old), Patrick Patterson (Janice's Husband), Charles Seixas (Fred's Uncle)

*A young man looking to pick up a few bucks joins the crew of a steel freighter where he becomes engrossed in the lives of the ship's tough-talking but unfulfilled crew members.*

© Lakeboat Productions LLC

Renée Zellweger, Colin Firth

Hugh Grant

Renée Zellweger

Shirley Henderson, Sally Phillips, James Callis

# BRIDGET JONES'S DIARY

**(MIRAMAX/UNIVERSAL)** Producers, Tim Bevan, Eric Fellner, Jonathan Cavendish; Director, Sharon Maguire; Screenplay, Helen Fielding, Andrew Davies, Richard Curtis; Based on the novel by Helen Fielding; Executive Producer, Helen Fielding; Photography, Stuart Dryburgh; Designer, Gemma Jackson; Editor, Martin Walsh; Line Producer, Peter McAleese; Costumes, Rachael Fleming; Music, Patrick Doyle; Music Supervisor, Nick Angel; Co-Producers, Debra Hayward, Liza Chasin; Casting, Michelle Guish; a Working Title production; Dolby; Technicolor; Rated R; 97 minutes; Release date: April 13, 2001

Colin Firth, Embeth Davidtz

## CAST

| | |
|---|---|
| Bridget Jones | Renée Zellweger |
| Mark Darcy | Colin Firth |
| Daniel Cleaver | Hugh Grant |
| Bridget's Dad | Jim Broadbent |
| Mother | Gemma Jones |
| Shazza | Sally Phillips |
| Jude | Shirley Henderson |
| Tom | James Callis |
| Natasha | Embeth Davidtz |
| Una Alconbury | Celia Imrie |
| Penny Bosworth-Husbands | Honor Blackman |
| Uncle Geoffrey | James Faulkner |
| Mrs. Darcy | Charmian May |
| Mr. Fitzherbert | Paul Brooke |
| Perpetua | Felicity Montague |
| Handsome Stranger | Charlie Caine |
| Simon in Marketing | Gareth Marks |
| Elderly Man | John Clegg |
| Themselves | Salman Rushdie, Jeffrey Archer |
| Kafka Author | Matthew Bates |
| Julian | Patrick Barlow |
| Receptionist | Rebecca Charles |
| Bernard | Dominic McHale |
| Shirley | Joan Blackman |
| Lara | Lisa Barbuscia |
| Interviewers | Joseph Alessi, Rhydian Jai-Persad |
| Richard Finch | Neil Pearson |
| Mr. Sit Up Britain | Paul Ross |
| Stage Manager | Stewart Wright |
| Magda | Claire Skinner |
| Woney | Dolly Wells |
| Cosmo | Mark Lingwood |
| Alastair | Toby Whithouse |
| Cameraman | David Cann |
| Eleanor Ross Heaney | Lisa Kay |
| Kafit Aghani | Sulayman Al-Bassam |
| The Musicians | Millennia Strings |
| Mr. Darcy | Donald Douglas |
| Mr. Ramdas | Renu Setna |
| Pauline | Emma Amos |
| Melinda | Sarah Stockbridge |

Renée Zellweger

Renée Zellweger, Hugh Grant

Colin Firth, Hugh Grant

*Thirty-two years old and single, Bridget Jones finds herself indulging in an affair with her self-centered boss, all the while finding herself being drawn back into the orbit of family friend Mark Darcy, whom she believes she despises.*

*This film received an Oscar nomination for actress (Renée Zellweger).*

© Miramax Films

# THE CENTER OF THE WORLD

(ARTISAN) Producers, Peter Newman, Wayne Wang; Director, Wayne Wang; Screenplay, Ellen Benjamin Wong; Story, Wayne Wang, Miranda July, Paul Auster, Siri Hustvedt; Photography, Mauro Fiore; Designer, Donald Graham Burt; Line Producer, Andrew Loo; Co-Producer, Francey Grace; Editor, Lee Percy; Costumes, Sophie de Rakoff Carbonell; Music Supervisor, Deva Anderson; Casting, Heidi Levitt; a Redeemable Features production; Dolby; Color; Not rated; 86 minutes; Release date: April 18, 2001

## CAST

| | |
|---|---|
| Florence | Molly Parker |
| Richard Longman | Peter Sarsgaard |
| Jerri | Carla Gugino |
| Brian Pivano | Balthazar Getty |
| Porter | Shane Edelman |
| Lap Dancer | Karry Brown |
| Pandora Stripper | Alisha Klass |
| Roxanne | Mel Gorham |
| Porn Site Woman | Lisa Newlan |
| Pete | Jason McCabe Calacanis |
| Dog Owner | Travis Miljan |

and Jerry Sherman (Old Man), Pat Morita (Taxi Driver), Robert Lefkowitz (Motel Manager), John Lombardo (Gondolier), Kathy Florez (Maid), Barbara Ann (Flo's Band), Ian Gomez (Delivery Man)

*Richard, a wealthy computer engineer who longs to make human contact, meets Florence, an aspiring musician who moonlights as a stripper. She agrees to accompany him in Las Vegas but only on the condition that the two do not engage in any sexual activity.*

© Artisan Entertainment Inc.

Peter Sarsgaard, Molly Parker

Molly Parker, Carla Gugino

Michael Douglas, Matt Dillon

John Goodman, Liv Tyler

# ONE NIGHT AT McCOOL'S

(USA FILMS) Producers, Michael Douglas, Allison Lyon Segan; Executive Producer, Whitney Green; Director, Harald Zwart; Screenplay, Stan Seidel; Photography, Karl Walter Lindenlaub; Designer, Jon Gary Steele; Editor, Bruce Cannon; Costumes, Ellen Mirojnick; Music, Marc Shaiman; Music Supervisor, Peter Afterman; Casting, Juel Bestrop, Jeanne McCarthy; an October Films presentation of a Furthur Films production; Dolby; Deluxe color; Rated R; 100 minutes; Release date: April 27, 2001

## CAST

| | |
|---|---|
| Jewel | Liv Tyler |
| Randy | Matt Dillon |
| Detective Dehling | John Goodman |
| Carl | Paul Reiser |
| Mr. Burmeister | Michael Douglas |
| Dr. Green | Reba McEntire |
| Utah/Elmo | Andrew Silverstein |
| Father Jimmy | Richard Jenkins |
| Bingo Caller | Mary Jo Smith |
| Uniformed Cop at Bar | Ric Sarabia |
| Detective Ertagian | Tim DeZarn |
| Joey Dinardo | Leo Rossi |

and Rob Neukirch (Deliveryman), Andrea Bendewald (Karen), Anthony Winsick (Ethan), David Kronenberg, Michael Kronenberg (Baby Tom), Roscoe DeSpain, Earl Carroll (Bingo Player), Eric Schaeffer (Greg Spalding), Eric Ware, Gary Brussell (Uniformed Cops at House), Donielle Artese (Carl's Assistant), Rad Milo (State Trooper), Veslemoey Ruud Zwart (Clinique Counter Saleswoman), Harry Van Gorkum (Psychic Guru), Jeanne McCarthy (Psychic), Kelly Slater (Jeep Owner)

*Three different men take up with a callous, hell-raising woman, prompting one of them to hire a hit man to do away with her.*

© USA Films

# TOWN & COUNTRY

(NEW LINE CINEMA) Producers, Andrew Karsch, Fred Roos, Simon Fields; Executive Producers, Sidney Kimmel, Michael DeLuca, Lynn Harris; Director, Peter Chelsom; Screenplay, Michael Laughlin, Buck Henry; Co-Producer, Cyrus Yavneh; Photography, William A. Fraker; Designer, Caroline Hanania; Editors, David Moritz, Claire Simpson; Music, Rolfe Kent; Costumes, Molly Maginnis; Casting, Barbara Cohen, Mary Gail Artz; an FR Production/Longfellow Pictures Production in association with Simon Fields production, presented in association with Sidney Kimmel Entertainment; Dolby; Deluxe color; Rated R; 104 minutes; Release date: April 27, 2001

Diane Keaton, Goldie Hawn

## CAST

| | |
|---|---|
| Porter Stoddard | Warren Beatty |
| Ellie Stoddard | Diane Keaton |
| Mona | Goldie Hawn |
| Griffin | Garry Shandling |
| Eugenie | Andie MacDowell |
| Alex | Nastassja Kinski |
| Auburn | Jenna Elfman |
| Tom Stoddard | Josh Hartnett |
| Alice Stoddard | Tricia Vessey |
| Mr. Claybourne | Charlton Heston |
| Mrs. Claybourne | Marian Seldes |
| Suttler | Buck Henry |
| Waiter | Vincent Lascoumes |
| Barney | Bill Hootkins |
| Yolanda | Terri Hoyos |
| Omar | Marc Casabani |
| Alejandro | Del Zamora |
| Holly | Katharine Towne |

and Tony Abatemarco (McKlellen), Eve Crawford (Margaret), Faith Geer (Mrs. Hadley), Stephen Fischer (Tour Guide), Ken Kensei (Translator), Masayasu Nakanishi, Akira Takayama (Japanese Guests), Stephen Singer, Lois Robbins, David Lindstedt (Party Guests), Morag Dickson (Griffin's Redhead), Carlos K. McAfee (Golf Caddie), Ian McNeice (Peter Principle), Lisa Ekdahl (Herself), Johnny Brown (Chauffeur), Mark Matheisen (Juke Joint Guy), Harry Boykoff (Henry), Azura Skye (Spider), Chris Tuttle (Quasimodo), Christopher Kubasik (Dinnerware Man), Holland Taylor (Mistress of Ceremonies), Scott Adsit (Cab Driver), Angelo Tiffe (Man at Table), Tom Billett, Michael Bailey Smith (Guards), Bonnie Ellen Miller (Lady on Stairs)

Nastassja Kinski

*Porter Stoddard, a successful and long-married New York architect, finds himself being attracted to several other women, including his friend Mona, whose husband she suspects is having his own affair.*

© New Line Cinema Inc.

Garry Shandling, Jenna Elfman, Warren Beatty

Garry Shandling, Warren Beatty

Til Schweiger, Kip Pardue

Sylvester Stallone, Cristián de la Fuente

Kip Pardue, Gina Gershon, Cristián de la Fuente

Sylvester Stallone, Burt Reynolds

# DRIVEN

**(WARNER BROS.)** Producers, Elie Samaha, Sylvester Stallone, Renny Harlin; Executive Producers, Andrew Stevens, Don Carmody, Kevin King; Director, Renny Harlin; Screenplay, Sylvester Stallone; Story, Jan Skrentny, Neal Tabachnick; Photography, Mauro Fiore; Designer, Charles Wood; Editors, Stuart Levy, Steve Gilson; Co-Executive Producers, Rebecca Spikings, Tracee Stanley; Costumes, Mary McLeod; Line Producer, Mike Drake; Music, BT; Visual Effects Supervisor, Brian M. Jennings; Race Sequences Coordinators, Andy Gill, Steve Kelso; Stunts, Steve Lucescu; Casting, Heidi Levitt, Monika Mikkelsen; a Franchise Pictures presentation; Dolby; Panavision; Deluxe color; Rated PG-13; 117 minutes; Release date: April 27, 2001

## CAST

| | |
|---|---|
| Joe Tanto | Sylvester Stallone |
| Carl Henry | Burt Reynolds |
| Jimmy Bly | Kip Pardue |
| Beau Brandenburg | Til Schweiger |
| Cathy | Gina Gershon |
| Sophia Simone | Estella Warren |
| Memo Heguy | Cristian de la Fuente |
| DeMille Bly | Robert Sean Leonard |
| Lucreatia Jones | Stacy Edwards |
| Crusher | Brent Briscoe |
| Nina | Verona Feldbusch |
| Ingrid | Jasmin Wagner |
| Team Owner | Chip Ganassi |
| Team Manager | John Della Penna |

and Dan Duran, Rob Smith (Commentators), Richard Zeppieri, Tino Monte (Toronto Reporters), Brian Heighton (Toronto Photographer), Renny Harlin (Replacement Driver), Lukas Harlin (Driver's Son), Peter Kosaka (Japanese Tourist), Frank Blanch (Bill), Barry Stillwell (Bob), Brett Heard (Mechanic), Phillip MacKenzie (Dealership Reporter), Liz West (Radio Reporter), Michael Boisvert (Japan Reporter), Jeffrey Knight (Party Reporter), Wayne Best (Target Manager), Jane Moffat (Nurse), Jake Simons (Carl's Assistant), Jean Alesi, Michael Andretti, Kenny Brack, Patrick Carpentier, Cristiano Da Maata, Adrian Fernandez, Christian Fittipaldi, Dario Franchitti, Luiz Garcia, Jr., Mauricio Gugelmin, Michel Jourdain, Jr., Tony Kanaan, Juan Pablo Montoya, Roberto Moreno, Max Papis, Oriol Servia, Alex Tagliani, Paul Tracy, Jimmy Vasser, Jacques Villeneuve (Race Car Drivers)

*Worried that rookie Jimmy Bly is losing focus on the track, car owner Carl Henry asks former race champion Joe Tanto to help train the younger driver.*

© Champs Productions, Inc.

Brendan Fraser, Arnold Vosloo

Brendan Fraser

## THE MUMMY RETURNS

**(UNIVERSAL)** Producers, James Jacks, Sean Daniel; Executive Producers, Bob Ducsay, Don Zepfel; Director/Screenplay, Stephen Sommers; Photography, Adrian Biddle; Designer, Allan Cameron; Editors, Bob Ducsay, Kelly Matsumoto; Music, Alan Silvestri; Costumes, John Bloomfield; Animation Supervisor, Daniel Jeannette; Visual Effects Supervisor, John Berton; Visual Effects Producer, Jennifer Bell; Creature & Makeup Effects, Nick Dudman; Casting, Joanna Colbert, Kate Dowd; Stunts, Steve Dent; an Alphaville production; Dolby; Panavision; Color; Rated PG-13; 129 minutes; Release date: May 4, 2001

### CAST

| | |
|---|---|
| Rick O'Connell | Brendan Fraser |
| Evelyn O'Connell/Nefertiti | Rachel Weisz |
| Jonathan | John Hannah |
| Imhotep | Arnold Vosloo |
| Ardeth Bay | Oded Fehr |
| Meela/Anck-Su-Namun | Patricia Velasquez |
| Alex O'Connell | Freddie Boath |
| Curator | Alun Armstrong |
| The Scorpion King | The Rock |
| Lock-Nah | Adewale Akinnuoye-Agbaje |
| Izzy | Shaun Parkes |
| Red | Bruce Byron |
| Jacques | Joe Dixon |
| Spivey | Tom Fisher |
| The Pharaoh | Aharon Ipalé |
| Shafek | Quill Roberts |

and Donna Air (Show Girl), Trevor Lovell (Mountain of Flesh)

*When mummy Imhotep is once again awoken from his resting place, Rick O'Connell attempts to stop him before the evil spirit can unleash an ancient warrior known as the Scorpion King and absorb his mystical powers. Sequel to the 1999 Universal film* The Mummy, *with Fraser, Weisz, Hannah, Vosloo, Fehr, Ipalé, and Velasquez repeating their roles.*

© Universal Studios

John Hannah, Rachel Weisz, Brendan Fraser, Freddie Boath

45

The Rock

Heath Ledger, Paul Bettany

Heath Ledger

Shannyn Sossamon, Heath Ledger

Mark Addy, Laura Fraser, Alan Tudyk

# A KNIGHT'S TALE

(COLUMBIA) Producers, Brian Helgeland, Tim Van Rellim, Todd Black; Director/Screenplay, Brian Helgeland; Photography, Richard Greatrex; Designer, Tony Burrough; Costumes/Armor Design, Caroline Harris; Editor, Kevin Stitt; Music, Carter Burwell; 2nd Unit/Stunts, Allan Graf; Sword Fight Choreographer, Paul Weston; Casting, Francine Maisler; an Escape Artists/Finestkind production; Dolby; Super 35 Widescreen; Deluxe color; Rated PG-13; 132 minutes; Release date: May 11, 2001

## CAST

William (Sir Ulrich)................................................................Heath Ledger
Count Adhemar ....................................................................Rufus Sewell
Jocelyn ..........................................................................Shannyn Sossamon
Chaucer ...............................................................................Paul Bettany
Kate .....................................................................................Laura Fraser
Roland ..................................................................................Mark Addy
Wat .......................................................................................Alan Tudyk
Christiana.............................................................................Berenice Bejo
Germaine..............................................................................Scott Handy
Colville ...............................................................................James Purefoy
Young William......................................................................Leagh Conwell
John Thatcher ..........................................................Christopher Cazenove
Simon the Summoner.......................................................Steve O'Donnell
Peter the Pardoner ..........................................................Jonathan Slinger
Sir Ector ...............................................................................Nick Brimble
Flanders King of Arms...........................................................Karel Dobry
Rouen King of Arms .....................................................Philip Lenkowsky
Old Bishop............................................................Roger Ashton-Griffiths
and Petr Meissel (Sword Official), Mathew Mills (Colville's Herald), Daniel Rous (Local Earl Lagny), Vladimir Kulhavy (Fence), Miroslav Mokos, Noel Le Bon, Scott Bellefeuille (French Squires), David Schneider (Relic Seller), Rudolf Kubik (Paris Master of Arms), David Fisher (London King of Arms), David Sterne (Retired Knight), Alice Connor (Lone Girl), Alice Vese (Spy), Berwick Kaler (Man in Stocks), Howie Lotker (Lagny Master at Arms), Jan Kuzelka, Vaclav Krejci, Jan Nemejovsky (Smithees)

*The lowborn William unexpectedly fulfills his lifelong dream of becoming a knight when fate allows him to become a jousting champion.*

© Columbia Pictures Industries Inc.

Kaleil Isaza Tuzman

Kaleil Isaza Tuzman

Tom Herman

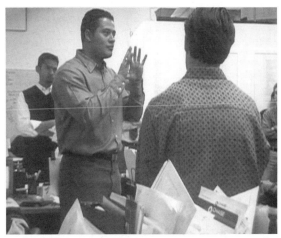

Kaleil Isaza Tuzman (middle)

# STARTUP.COM

**(ARTISAN)** Producer, D. A. Pennebaker; Executive Producers, Frazer Pennebaker, Jehane Noujaim, Chris Hegedus; Directors, Jehane Noujaim, Chris Hegedus; Photography, Jehane Noujaim; Editors, Chris Hegedus, Erez Laufer, Jehane Noujaim; Music Consultants, Sherief El Katsha, Kit Pennebaker; Associate Producers, Rebecca Marshall, Ed Rogoff; a D. A. Pennebaker presentation; Dolby; Color; Rated R; 103 minutes; Release date: May 11, 2001; Documentary on how two friends joined forces to begin an online service.

## FEATURING

Kaleil Isaza Tuzman, Tom Herman, Kenneth Austin, Tricia Burke, Roy Burston, David Camp, Jose Feliciano, Dora Glottman, Julian Herbstein, Christina Ortez, Jonathan Angus, Chieh Cheung, Sean Coar, Ambika Conroy, Patrick Cromer, Jerry Greenberg, Richard Herman, Susan Herman, Tia Herman, Bob Higgins, Maynard Jackson, Brian Locke, Brian Lundy, Spyros Poulios, Marvin Pritchett, Robert Tisch, Ani Tuzman, Kathy Wylde, Kristen Kimball

© Artisan

Office

Princess Fiona, Shrek

Donkey

# SHREK

**(DREAMWORKS)** Producers, Aron Warner, John H. Williams, Jeffrey Katzenberg; Executive Producers, Penney Finkelman Cox, Sandra Rabins; Co-Executive Producer, David Lipman; Directors, Andrew Adamson, Vicky Jenson; Screenplay, Ted Elliott, Terry Rossio, Joe Stillman, Roger S. H. Schulman; Based upon the book by William Steig; Co-Producers, Ted Elliott, Terry Rossio; Music, Harry Gregson-Williams; Editor, Sim Evan-Jones; Designer, James Hegedus; Visual Effects Supervisor, Ken Bielenberg; Supervising Animator, Raman Hui; Associate Producer, Jane Hartwell; Casting, Leslee Feldman; a PDI/Dreamworks production; Dolby; Technicolor; Rated PG; 88 minutes; Release date: May 16, 2001

Shrek

## VOICE CAST

Shrek/Blind Mouse....................................................................Mike Myers
Donkey.................................................................................Eddie Murphy
Princess Fiona....................................................................Cameron Diaz
Lord Farquaad.....................................................................John Lithgow
Monsieur Hood ................................................................Vincent Cassel
Ogre Hunters .....................................................Peter Dennis, Clive Pearse
Captain of Guards............................................................Jim Cummings
Baby Bear ............................................................................Bobby Block
Geppetto/Magic Mirror ........................................................Chris Miller
Pinocchio/Three Pigs............................................................Cody Cameron
Old Woman........................................................................Kathleen Freeman
Peter Pan ...........................................................................Michael Galasso
Blind Mouse/Thelonius .............................................Christopher Knights
Blind Mouse........................................................................Simon J. Smith
Gingerbread Man ..............................................................Conrad Vernon
Wrestling Fan ................................................................Jacquie Barnbrook
Merry Men..................Guillaume Aretos, John Bisom, Matthew Gonder, Calvin Remsberg, Jean-Paul Vignon
Bishop.......................................................................................Val Bettin

*After the evil Lord Farquaad banishes all fairy tale characters from the kingdom, they take up residence in the swamp of an ornery ogre named Shrek. In order to get back his solitude, Shrek cuts a deal with Farquaad to rescue Princess Fiona from a fire-breathing dragon so that she can be the Lord's bride.*

*2001 Academy Award-winner for Best Animated Feature (the first winner in this newly established category). This film received an additional Oscar nomination for adapted screenplay.*

Lord Farquaad, Magic Mirror

© DreamWorks LLC

Donkey, Shrek, Princess Fiona, Lord Farquaad

Shrek

Big Bad Wolf, Shrek

Princess Fiona, Shrek

Princess Fiona, Shrek

Nicole Kidman, Ewan McGregor

Nicole Kidman

Nicole Kidman

Nicole Kidman, Ewan McGregor

Lara Mulcahy, Caroline O'Connor, Natalie Mendoza,
Christine Anu

Ewan McGregor

# MOULIN ROUGE!

(20TH CENTURY FOX) Producers, Martin Brown, Baz Luhrmann, Fred Baron; Director, Baz Luhrmann; Screenplay, Baz Luhrmann, Craig Pearce; Photography, Donald M. McAlpine; Designer, Catherine Martin; Costumes, Catherine Martin, Angus Strathie; Editor, Jill Bilcock; Co-Producer, Catherine Knapman; Choreographer, John O'Connell; Music, Craig Armstrong; Music Director, Marius DeVries; Song: "Come What May" by David Baerwald; Visual Effects Supervisor, Chris Godfrey; Casting, Ronna Kress, Chris King; a Bazmark production; U.S.-Australian; Dolby; Panavision; Deluxe color; Rated PG-13; 126 minutes; Release date: May 18, 2001

## CAST

| | |
|---|---|
| Satine | Nicole Kidman |
| Christian | Ewan McGregor |
| Toulouse Lautrec | John Leguizamo |
| Zidler | Jim Broadbent |
| Duke of Worcester | Richard Roxburgh |
| The Doctor | Garry McDonald |
| The Unconscious Argentinean | Jacek Koman |
| Satie | Matthew Whittet |
| Marie | Kerry Walker |
| Nini Legs in the Air | Caroline O'Connor |
| Audrey | David Wenham |
| Arabia | Christine Anu |
| China Doll | Natalie Mendoza |
| Môme Fromage | Lara Mulcahy |
| Green Fairy | Kylie Minogue |
| Le Chocolat | Deobia Oparei |

and Linal Haft (Warner), Keith Robinson (Le Petomane), Peter Whitford (Stage Manager), Norman Kaye (Doctor), Arthur Dignam (The Father), Carole Skinner (Landlady), Jonathan Hardy (Man in the Moon), Kiruna Stamell (La Petite Princess), Laszlo Lukas (Conductor), Anthony Young (Orchestra Member), Wilson Alcorn, Kerry Casey, Peter Collingwood, Tim Eliott, Nicole Fantl, Judy Howard, Harold Kissin, Paul Maybury, Caroline Nahlous, Scott Peters, David Whitford (Audience Members), Judi Eldred (Patron), Ray Chambers, Darrell Dixon, Otto Luppo, Billy Pat, Adrian Sicari (Fan Bearers), Alexander Houle, Geoffrey Kiem, Peter Muirhead (Stagehands), Pat Evans (Seamstress), Tara Morice (Prostitute), Daniel Scott (Absinthe Drinker/Guitarist), Angus Martin (Pawnbroker), Byron Barriga, Waldo Garrido, Reginald Larner (Musicians), Coralie Eichholtz, Jabe Bromhall (Moulin Rouge Girls), Robert Yearley (Coach), John Pagan (Old Crone), Patrick Hardin-Irmer, Albin Pahernik, Aurel Verne (Waiters), Dee Donavan, Johnny Lockwood, Don Reid (Characer Rakes), Greg Poppleton (Nervous Nellie), Matt Wilson (Slave Trader), Trent Harlow, Troy Harrison, Simon Kriszyk, Chris Pickard, Thern

Ewan McGregor, Nicole Kidman

Reynolds, David Scotchford, Daniel Slater (Dancers), Veronica Beattie, Lisa Callingham, Rosetta Cook, Fleur Denny, Kelly Grauer, Jaclyn Hanson, Michelle Hopper, Fallon King, Wendy McMahon, Tracie Morley, Sue-Ellen Shook, Jenny Wilson, Luke Alleva, Andrew Aroustian, Stephen Colyer, Steven Grace, Mark Hodge, Cameron Mitchell, Deon Nuku, Shaun Parker, Troy Phillips, Rodney Syaranamual, Ashley Wallen, Nathan Wright (Montmartre Dance Team), Susan Black, Nicole Brooks, Danielle Brown, Anastacia Flewin, Fiona Cage, Alex Harrington, Camilla Jakimowicz, Rochelle Jones, Caroline Kaspar, Mandy Liddell, Melanie Mackay, Elise Mann, Charmaine Martin, Michelle Wriggles, Michael Boyd, Lorry D'Ercole, Michael Edge, Glyn Gray, Craig Haines, Stephen Holford, Jamie Jewell, Jason King, Ryan Males, Harlin Martin, Andrew Micallef, Jonathan Schmolzer, Bradley Spargo (Paris Dance Team), Kip Gamblin (Latin Dancer), Dennis Dowlut, Darren Dowlut (Cocoliscious Brothers), Nandy McClean, Maya McClean (Twins), Pina Conti (La Ko Ka Chau), Joseph "Pepe" Ashton, Jordan Ashton, Marcos Falagan, Mitchel Falagan, Chris Mayhew, Hamish Mccann, Adrien Janssen, Shaun Holloway (Tobasco Brothers)

*In the middle of decadent, turn-of-the-century Paris, Christian falls hopelessly in love with Satine, a famous entertainer-courtesan at the city's decadent night-club Moulin Rouge. 2001 Academy Award-winner for Best Costume Design and Art Direction. This film received additional Oscar nominations for picture, actress (Nicole Kidman), cinematography, editing, sound, and makeup.*

© Twentieth Century Fox

Nicole Kidman, Ewan McGregor

Nicole Kidman

Jim Caviezel, Jennifer Lopez

Jim Caviezel

# ANGEL EYES

(**WARNER BROS.**) Producers, Mark Canton, Elie Samaha; Executive Producers, Andrew Stevens, Neil Canton, Don Carmody; Director, Luis Mandoki; Screenplay, Gerald DiPego; Photography, Piotr Sobocinski; Designer, Dean Tavoularis; Co-Producer, Dawn Miller; Costumes, Marie-Sylvie Deveau; Editor, Jerry Greenberg; Music, Marco Beltrami; Music Supervisors, Manish Raval, Tom Wolfe; Casting, Amanda Mackey Johnson, Cathy Sandrich; a Morgan Creek and Franchise Pictures presentation of a Franchise Pictures and Canton Company production; Dolby; Color; Rated R; 103 minutes; Release date: May 18, 2001

## CAST

Sharon Pogue........................................................Jennifer Lopez
Catch .....................................................................Jim Caviezel
Josephine Pogue....................................................Sonia Braga
Robby.....................................................................Terrence Howard
Larry Pogue ...........................................................Jeremy Sisto
Carl Pogue. ............................................................Victor Argo
Kathy Pogue ..........................................................Monet Mazur
Elanora Davis ........................................................Shirley Knight
Larry Jr .................................................................Daniel Magder
Annie .....................................................................Guylaine St. Onge
and Connor McAuley (Max Pogue), Jeremy Ratchford (Ray Micigliano), Peter MacNeill (Lt. Dennis Sanderman), Eldridge Hyndman (Jamal), Karl Matchett (Candace), Michael Cameron (Charlie), Marchello Thadford (Peebo), David Cox (K-Dog), Ron Payne (Priest), Paul A. MacFarlane (Photographer), Daniel Petronijevic (Fighting Kid), Stephen Thomas Kay (Tony Pindella), Grant Nickalls (Joe), Jim Feather, John Shepard (Old Men), Matt Birman (Driver), Eric Coates (Car Man), Chuck Campbell, JJ Authors (Young Men), Stephanie Moore (Officer Vanessa), Ron Johnstone (Bass Player), Nick Ali (Trumpeter), Brian Dickinson (Piano Player), Barry Romberg (Drummer), Neil Brathwaite (Flautist), Kathy Carter (Cop), Darren Marsman (Suspect #2), Brian Jagersky, Chris Lamon (Police Officers), Brenda Adams, Donny Stockford (ND Pedestrians), Matthew Van Hart (Fighting Street Kid #2)

*Chicago policewoman Sharon Pogue is saved by a mysterious man named Catch, with whom she begins an affair, all the while hoping to help him confront his troubled past about which he is so vague.*

© Seraph Productions, Inc.

Jennifer Lopez

Daniel Petronijevic, Jennifer Lopez

Kerry Washington, Anna Simpson, Melissa Martinez

D'Monroe, Melissa Martinez

Melissa Martinez

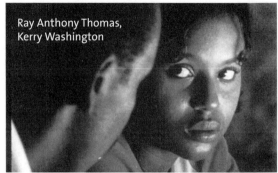

Ray Anthony Thomas,
Kerry Washington

## OUR SONG

(IFC FILMS) Producers, Jim McKay, Paul Mezey, Diana E. Williams; Executive Producers, Caroline Kaplan, Jonathan Sehring, Michael Stipe; Director/Screenplay, Jim McKay; Photography, Jim Denault; Costumes, Tiel Roman; Editor, Alex Hall; Music Supervisor, Julie Panebianco; Co-Producers, Alexa L. Fogel, Joseph Infantolino; Associate Producers, Tyrone Brown, Ashaki "Saki" Fenderson, Susannah Ludwig; a C-Hundred Film Corp. movie, presented in association with Beech Hill Films and Journeyman Pictures; Dolby; Color; Rated R; 96 minutes; Release date: May 23, 2001

### CAST

| | |
|---|---|
| Lanisha Brown | Kerry Washington |
| Joycelyn Clifton | Anna Simpson |
| Maria Hernandez | Melissa Martinez |
| Pilar Brown | Marlene Forte |
| Carl Brown | Ray Anthony Thomas |
| Dawn Clifton | Rosalyn Coleman |
| Rita Hernandez | Carmen Lopez |
| Mr. Miller | Tyrone Brown |
| Kim | Lorraine Berry |
| Keisha | Natasha Frith |
| Benjamin | Chuck Cooper |

and Iris Little Thomas (Clinc Counselor), Kim Howard (Eleanor), Juan Romero, Jr. (Sampson), D'Monroe (Terell), Reginald Washington (Alex), Tommy Axson (Cam), Tyrus Cox (Anthony, The Playa), Taheim Washington (Troy Harper), Starla Benford (Woman with Flowers), Lisa Collins (School Registrar), Greg Haberny (Cute "Guapo" Guy), Eric Byrd (Malik, the Party Kisser), Sidney O'Loughlin (Rasheed), Shannon Phillips (Party DJ), Madeleine T. Gamble (Steppers Booster), Devin Gray (Natasha Up in the Window), Derrick Williams (Rodney), Syron Martin (Ice Cream Scooper), Jan McLaughlin (E.R. Doctor), The Jackie Robinson Steppers Marching Band (Themselves)

*At the end of a hot summer in Crown Heights, Brooklyn, three teenage girl-friends confront the rising tensions in their friendships while rehearsing for marching band.*

© IFC Films

Anna Simpson, Kerry Washington, Melissa Martinez

# PEARL HARBOR

**(TOUCHSTONE)** Producers, Jerry Bruckheimer, Michael Bay; Executive Producers, Mike Stenson, Barry Waldman, Randall Wallace, Chad Oman, Bruce Hendricks; Director, Michael Bay; Screenplay, Randall Wallace; Photography, John Schwartzman; Designer, Nigel Phelps; Editors, Chris Lebenzon, Steven Rosenblum, Mark Goldblatt, Roger Barton; Costumes, Michael Kaplan; Music, Hans Zimmer; Song: "There You'll Be," music and lyrics by Diane Warren/performed by Faith Hill; Visual Effects Supervisor, Eric Brevig; Aerial Coordinator, Alan Purwin; Aerial Unit Director, David B. Nowell; Casting, Bonnie Timmermann; a Jerry Bruckheimer Films presentation; Dolby; Panavision; Technicolor; Rated PG-13; 189 minutes; Release date: May 25, 2001

## CAST

Rafe McCawley ............................................................Ben Affleck
Danny Walker ............................................................Josh Hartnett
Evelyn Johnson ......................................................Kate Beckinsale
Billy ...............................................................William Lee Scott
Anthony R. Fusco ......................................................Greg Zola
Red ..........................................................................Ewen Bremner
Col. James H. Doolittle ..............................................Alec Baldwin
Betty ......................................................................Catherine Kellner
Sandra ....................................................................Jennifer Garner
President Roosevelt ......................................................Jon Voight
Doris "Dorie" Miller ............................................Cuba Gooding, Jr.
Gooz ....................................................................Michael Shannon
Joe ............................................................................Matt Davis
Admiral Yamamoto ........................................................Mako
Nishikura ..................................................................John Fujioka
Genda ..........................................................Cary-Hiroyuki Tagawa
Admiral Kimmel..............................................................Colm Feore
Captain Thurman ........................................................Dan Aykroyd
and Reiley McClendon (Young Danny), Jesse James (Young Rafe), William Fichtner (Danny's Father), Steve Rankin (Rafe's Father), Brian Haley (Training Captain), David Hornsby (Training Captain), Scott Wilson (Gen. Marshall), Graham Beckel (Admiral), Howard Mungo (George), Randy Oglesby (Strategic Analyst), Ping Wu (Japanese Officer), Stan Cahill (Pentagon Lt.), Kevin Wensing (XO U.S.S. West Virginia), Tom Everett (Presidential Aide), Tomas Arana (Vice Admiral), Beth Grant (Motherly Secretary), Sara Rue (Martha), Sung Kang (Listener), Raphael Sbarge (Kimmel's Aide), Marty Belafsky (Louie the Sailor), Yuji Okumoto (Japanese Shy Bomber), Josh Green (Radar Pvt. Ellis), Ian Bohen (Radar Pvt. #2), Michael Milhoan (Army Cmmdr.), Peter Firth (Capt. of West Virginia), Tom Sizemore (Earl), Marco Gould (Pop-Up Sailor), Andrew Bryniarski (Joe the Boxer), Nicholas Downs (Terrified Sailor), Tim Choate (Navy Doctor), John Diehl (Sr. Doctor), Joe Kelly (Medic), Ron Harper (Minister), Ted McGinley (Army Corps Maj.), Madison Mason (Adm. on the Hornet), Kim Coates (Jack Richards), Andrew Baley (Hornet Radio Op), Glenn Morshower (Adm. Halsey), Paul Francis (Doolittle Co-Pilot), Scott Wiper, Eric Christian Olsen (Gunners), Rod Biermann (Navigator), Noriaki Kamata, Garret T. Sato, Eiji Inoue (Japanese Soldiers), Precious Chong (Nursing Supervisor), Jeff Wadlow (Next Guy in Line), Will Gill, Jr. (Train Conductor), Seth Sakai (Japanese Tourist), Curtis Anderson (18-year-old Typist), Blaine Pate (Orderly in Aftermath), John Pyper-Ferguson (Naval Officer in Hospital), Michael Shamus Wiles (Captain of the Hornet), Brett Pedigo (Next Guy in Line #2), Toru M. Tanaka, Jr. (Samoan Bouncer), Sean Gunn (Traction Sailor), Joshua Ackerman, Matt Casper, Fred Koehler (Wounded Sailors), David Kaufman (Young Nervous Doctor), L. L. Ginter (Captain Low), Joshua Aaron Gulledge (Buster), Guy Torry (Teeny Mayfield), Leland Orser (Maj. Jackson), Peter James Smith (Mission Listener), Mark Noon (Medic), Pat Healy (News Reel Guy), Thomas Wilson Brown (Young Flier), Chad Morgan (Pearl Habor Nurse), James Saito, Angel Sing, Tak Kubota (Japanese Aides), Robert Jayne (Sunburnt Sailor), Vic Chao (Japanese Doctor), Michael Gradilone (Screaming Sailor), John Padget

(Hospital Chaplain), Ben Easter, Cory Tucker, Abe Sylvia, Jason Liggett, Mark Panasuk, Bret Roberts (Baja Sailors), John Howry (Lieutenant in Boat), Rufus Dorsey (Dorie's Friend), Patrice Martinez (French Fisherman), Rodney Bursiel (Sailor with Dog), Rob McCabe (Rescue Sailor), Brandon Lozano (Baby Danny), Seiki Moriguchi (Agaki Communication Officer), Brian D. Falk, Christopher Stroop (Helmsmen), Estevan Gonzalo (Bombing Sailor), Sean Faris (Danny's Gunner), Vincent J. Inghilterra (Preacher), Nicholas Farrell (RAF Squadron Leader), Tony Curran (Ian), Viv Weatherall, Benjamin Farry, Daniel Mays (Pilots)

*Two childhood friends, who grow up to become Air Force pilots, both fall in love with the same woman on the eve of the Japanese attack on Pearl Harbor. 2001 Academy Award-winner for Best Sound Effects Editing. This film received additional Oscar nominations for visual effects, sound, and original song ("There You'll Be").*

© Touchstone Pictures and Jerry Bruckheimer, Inc.

(Above) Ben Affleck, Josh Hartnett

(Below) Cuba Gooding, Jr.

Ben Affleck,
Josh Hartnett

(Above) Catherine Kellner, James King, Kate Beckinsale,
Jennifer Garner, Sara Rue. (Below) Dan Aykroyd

(Above) Alec Baldwin
(Below) Jon Voight, Scott Wilson, Ben Affleck

Michael Caton, Rob Schneider

Colleen Haskell, Rob Schneider

# THE ANIMAL

**(COLUMBIA)** Producers, Barry Bernardi, Carr D'Angelo, Todd Garner; Executive Producers, Adam Sandler, Jack Giarraputo; Director, Luke Greenfield; Screenplay, Tom Brady, Rob Schneider; Story, Tom Brady; Photography, Peter Lyons Collister; Designer, Alan Au; Editors, Jeff Gourson, Peck Prior; Costumes, Jim Lapidus; Co-Producers, Tom Brady, John Schneider; Music, Teddy Castellucci; Music Supervision, Michael Dilbeck; Casting, Roger Mussenden, Tracy Kaplan, Elizabeth Boykewich; Stunts, Gregg Smrz; a Revolution Studios presentation of a Happy Madison production; Dolby; Color; Rated PG-13; 83 minutes; Release date: June 1, 2001

## CAST

| | |
|---|---|
| Marvin Mange | Rob Schneider |
| Rianna | Colleen Haskell |
| Sgt. Sisk | John C. McGinley |
| Chief Wilson | Edward Asner |
| Dr. Wilder | Michael Caton |
| Fatty | Louis Lombardi |
| Miles | Guy Torry |
| Bob Harris | Bob Rubin |
| Mrs. De La Rosa | Pilar Schneider |
| Mayor | Scott Wilson |

and Raymond Ma (Mr. Tam), Michael Papajohn (Patrolman Brady), Ron Rogge (Patrolman Jaworski), Holly Maples, Henriette Mantel, Jeremy Kramer, Robb Skyler, Nicko Mariolis (Elkerton Police Officers), Philip Daniel Bolden, Decker Daily, Timmy Deters, Hannah K. Flood, Megan Taylor Harvey, Mitch Holleman, Mollie Rea Patton, Charlie Stewart (Evidence Room Kids), Elizabeth Branson (Heavy-Set Cadet), Sandy Gimpel (Obstacle Course Lady), Paul Short (Burning Man), Arthur Bernard (Elderly Jogger), Tim Herzog (Badger Milk Host), Berglind Olafsdottir (Yolanda), Steven Kravitz (Airport Businessman), Shane Holden, Tom McNulty (Airline Stewards), James Bates (Airport Police), Morisa Taylor Kaplan (Mailbox Girl), Jack Rubens (Old Man Holden), Susan Corwin (TV Anchorwoman), Tom Keische (Bar Patron), Karlee Holden (Waitress), Clare Calvo, Michelle Celestino (Hula Dancers), Luigi Amodeo (Italian Waiter), Wes Takahashi, Fred Stoller (Reporters), Jake Iannarino (Free Press Reporter), John Kirk (Waiter at Party), Brett Smrz (Mayor's Son), Noel Guglielmi (Gang Leader), Adam Sandler (Townie), Norm MacDonald (Mob Member), Brianna Lynn Brown, Amber Collins, John Farley (Other Mob), Pete (Dimples the Dog), Bliss (Nelly the Goat), Kanoozi (Mr. Giggles), Louey (Henry the Orangutan)

*Marvin Mange, a police file clerk, survives a near-fatal car accident only to have an eccentric doctor repair his damaged body using animal organs.*

© Revolution Studios

# WHAT'S THE WORST THAT COULD HAPPEN?

**(MGM)** Producers, Lawrence Turman, David Hoberman, Ashok Armitraj, Wendy Dytman; Executive Producers, John Morrissey, Martin Lawrence, David Nicksay; Director, Sam Weisman; Screenplay, Matthew Chapman; Based upon the novel by Donald E. Westlake; Photography, Anastas Michos; Designer, Howard Cummings; Editors, Garth Craven, Nick Moore; Costumes, Jeffrey Kurland; Music, Tyler Bates, Marc Shaiman; Music Supervisor, Anita Camarata; Co-Producer, Peaches Davis; Casting, John Papsidera; a Turman-Morrissey Company/Hyde Park Entertainment production; Dolby; Deluxe color; Rated PG-13; 95 minutes; Release date: June 1, 2001

## CAST

| | |
|---|---|
| Kevin Caffery | Martin Lawrence |
| Max Fairbanks | Danny DeVito |
| Berger | John Leguizamo |
| Gloria | Glenne Headly |
| Amber Belhaven | Carmen Ejogo |
| Uncle Jack | Bernie Mac |
| Earl Radburn | Larry Miller |
| Lutetia Fairbanks | Nora Dunn |
| Walter Greenbaum | Richard Schiff |
| Det. Alex Tardio | William Fitchner |
| Ann Marie | Ana Gasteyer |
| Tracey Kimberly | Sascha Knopf |
| Edwina | Siobhan Fallon |
| Shelly Nix | GQ |

and Lenny Clarke (Windham), Robin Brown (Auctioneer), Mike Moyer (Large Man at Auction), Darra Herman, Julie Jirousek (Auction Bidders), Kevin H. Chapman (Bartender), Devon Jencks (Officer Keeble), Paul O'Brien (Officer Overkraut), James Baldwin (Older Tennis Player), Jay Carney (Gentleman at Club), Matt Seigel (Banquet Host), Michael Mulheren (Judge Callahan), Michael Jessel, Ryan Hull, Eddie McCabe (Windham Boys), Karen MacDonald (Washington Real Estate Agent), Lonnie Farmer (Washington Condo Doorman), Michelle Youell (Pepper Spray Lady), Tim Gallin, Paul Marini (Washington Cops), Tracy Oliverio (Junior Detective), Cam Neely (Jerry), Elliot Cuker (Senator Richards), George Blumenthal (Senator Engel), Richard McElvain (Senator Schutt), Stephanie Clayman (Sign Language Interpreter), Christy Scott-Cashman (Roxanne), Dan Weisman (Eagle One), Rick Calnan (Cop at Auction), Jimmy Flynn (Fire Captain), Russell Curry, Susie Spear, Richard Saxton (Reporters), Kerry Kilbride (TV Anchor)

*After being captured by the police for breaking into the home of unscrupulous businessman Max Fairbanks, professional thief Kevin Caffrey has his lucky ring taken from him by Fairbanks in retaliation for the intended theft, an act that causes Caffrey to swear revenge.*

© Metro-Goldwyn-Mayer Pictures, Inc.

Danny Devito, Martin Lawrence

John Travolta, Hugh Jackman, Halle Berry

Vinnie Jones, John Travolta

# SWORDFISH

(WARNER BROS.) Producers, Joel Silver, Jonathan D. Krane; Executive Producers, Jim Van Wyck, Bruce Berman; Director, Dominic Sena; Screenplay, Skip Woods; Photography, Paul Cameron; Designer, Jeff Mann; Co-Producers, Dan Cracchiolo, Skip Woods; Music, Christopher Young, Paul Oakenfold; Editor, Stephen Rivkin; Costumes, Ha Nguyen; Visual Effects Supervisor, Boyd Shermis; Stunts, Dan Bradley; Casting, Lora Kennedy; a Silver Pictures/Jonathan D. Krane production, presented in association with Village Roadshow Pictures and NPV Entertainment; Dolby; Panavision; Technicolor; Rated R; 100 minutes; Release date: June 8, 2001

Halle Berry, Hugh Jackman

## CAST

| | |
|---|---|
| Gabriel Shear | John Travolta |
| Stanley Jobson | Hugh Jackman |
| Ginger | Halle Berry |
| Agent Roberts | Don Cheadle |
| Marco | Vinnie Jones |
| Senator Reisman | Sam Shepard |
| Melissa | Drea de Matteo |
| Axl Torvalds | Rudolf Martin |
| A. D. Joy | Zach Grenier |
| Holly | Camryn Grimes |
| Torres | Angelo Pagán |
| SWAT Leader | Chic Daniel |
| Lawyer | Kirk B. B. Woller |
| Agents | Carmen Argenziano, Tim DeKay |
| Helga | Laura Lane |
| Ad Agency Executive | Tait Ruppert |
| Coroner | Craig Braun |

and William Mapother, Ilia Volok, Jonathan Fraser, Shawn Woods, Leo Lee (Gabriel's Crew), Marina Black, Kerry Kletter, Ryan Wulff, Ann Travolta, Margaret Travolta, Dana Hee, Denney Pierce, Jeff Ramsey, Joey Box, Debbie Evans, Samuel S. Travolta, Tim Storms (Hostages), Jason Christopher, Jonathan Pessin (Club Kids), Scott Burkholder, Mark Soper (FBI Geeks), Craig Lally, Rusty McClennon, Mark Riccardi (Customs Agents), Debbie Entin, Natalia Sokolova, Anika Poitier (Helga's Friends), Nick Loren (Dark Suit), Tom Morris, Richard Householder, Michael Arias (Policemen), Brenda Eimers (Holly's Teacher), Timothy Omundson (Agent Thomas), Astrid Veillon (Bank Executive), Dean Rader Duval (Security Guard)

*Convicted computer hacker Stanley Jacobson agrees to assist Gabriel Shear in electronically diverting billions of dollars in laundered funds for his terrorist activities, so that Stanley can get back his daughter whom Gabriel has kidnapped to ensure his participation in the crime.*

© Warner Bros.

John Travolta, Hugh Jackman

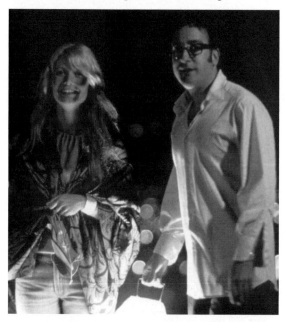

Alan Cumming, Jennifer Jason Leigh

Gwyneth Paltrow, Michael Panes

# THE ANNIVERSARY PARTY

(FINE LINE) Producers, Joanne Sellar, Alan Cumming, Jennifer Jason Leigh; Executive Producer, Andrew Hurwitz; Directors/Screenplay, Jennifer Jason Leigh, Alan Cumming; Photography, John Bailey; Editors, Carol Littleton, Suzanne Spangler; Music, Michael Penn; Co-Producer, Mike Nelson; Associate Producer, Lila Yacoub; Costumes, Christopher Lawrence; Music Supervisor, Robin Urdang; a Joanne Sellar/Pas de Quoi production; Dolby; Color; Rated R; 115 minutes; Release date: June 8, 2001

## CAST

| | |
|---|---|
| Joe Therrian | Alan Cumming |
| Sally Therrian | Jennifer Jason Leigh |
| Clair Forsyth | Jane Adams |
| Monica Rose | Mina Badie |
| Gina Taylor | Jennifer Beals |
| Sophia Gold | Phoebe Cates |
| Jerry Adams | John Benjamin Hickey |
| Cal Gold | Kevin Kline |
| Jeffrey | Matt McGrath |
| Ryan Rose | Denis O'Hare |
| Syke Davidson | Gwyneth Paltrow |
| Levi Panes | Michael Panes |
| Mac Forsyth | John C. Reilly |
| Himself | Otis the Dog |
| Yoga Instructor | Steven Freedman |
| America | Norizzela Monterroso |
| Rosa | Clara Demedrano |
| Jack Gold | Owen Kline |
| Evie Gold | Greta Kline |
| Sanford Jewison | Matt Malloy |
| Mary-Lynn | Mary-Lynn Rajskub |
| Astrid | Blair Tefkin |
| Herself | Anouk the Dog |
| Karen | Karen Kilgariff |

and Molly Bryant, Michael G. Carroll, Craig Chester, Christopher Lawrence, Jessica Queller Jr., W. Reed (Party Guests)

*After a period of estrangement, Joe and Sally Therrian host a sixth-year anniversary party, during which they begin to question their marriage and their relationships to their friends and colleagues. Actors Alan Cumming and Jennifer Jason Leigh make their debuts as motion picture directors.*

© Fine Line Features

Greta Kline, Phoebe Cates, Owen Kline, Kevin Kline

Gwyneth Paltrow, Jennifer Jason Leigh

Jennifer Beals, Alan Cumming, Jennifer Jason Leigh

John Benjamin Hickey, Parker Posey

John C. Reilly, Jane Adams

Mina Badie, Dennis O'Hare

Helga Sinclair, Princess Kida,
Milo Thatch, Commander Rourke

The Ulysses

The Ulysses

Milo Thatch

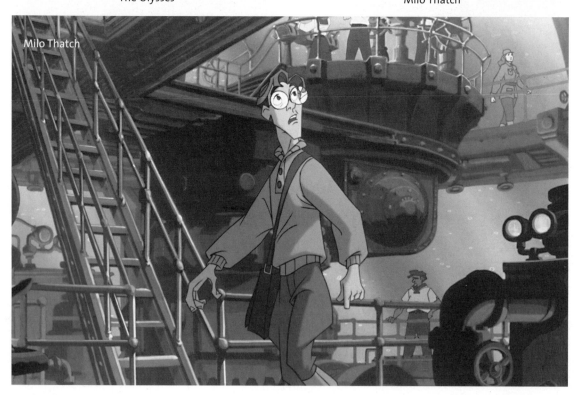

Milo Thatch

# ATLANTIS: THE LOST EMPIRE

(WALT DISNEY PICTURES) Producer, Don Hahn; Directors, Gary Trousdale, Kirk Wise; Screenplay, Tab Murphy; Story, Kirk Wise, Gary Trousdale, Joss Whedon, Bryce Zabel, Jackie Zabel, Tab Murphy; Original Score, James Newton Howard; Song: "Where the Dream Takes You" by Diane Warren (lyrics), Diane Warren, James Newton Howard (music)/Performed by MYA; Associate Producer, Kendra Haaland; Art Director, David Goetz; Artistic Coordinator, Christopher Jenkins; Editor, Ellen Keneshea; Artistic Supervisors: Story, John Sanford; Layout, Ed Ghertner; Background, Lisa Keene; Cleanup, Marshall Toomey; Visual Effects, Marlon West; Computer Graphics Imagery, Kiran Bhakta Joshi; Distributed by Buena Vista Pictures; Dolby; Widescreen; Technicolor; Rated PG; 95 minutes; Release date: June 8, 2001

## VOICE CAST

Milo Thatch ...........................................................Michael J. Fox
Commander Rourke ...........................................................James Garner
Princess Kida ...........................................................Cree Summer
The King of Atlantis ...........................................................Leonard Nimoy
Vinny Santorini ...........................................................Don Novello
Helga ...........................................................Claudia Christian
Audrey ...........................................................Jacqueline Obradors
Preston B. Whitmore ...........................................................John Mahoney
Mole ...........................................................Corey Burton
Fenton Q. Harcourt ...........................................................David Ogden Stiers
Cookie ...........................................................Jim Varney
Mrs. Packard ...........................................................Florence Stanley
Dr. Swee ...........................................................Phil Morris
Young Kida ...........................................................Natalie Strom
and Jim Cummings, Pat Pinney, Steve Barr (Additional Voices)

*Milo Thatch, a linguistics expert and cartographer, is given his grandfather's ancient journal, which may provide the key to finding the lost empire of Atlantis.*

© Disney Enterprises, Inc.

Milo Thatch, Princess Kida

King of Atlantis, Milo Thatch

Cookie, Milo Thatch, Vinny, Audrey, Dr. Sweet

Milo Thatch, Preston B. Whitmore, Commander Rourke

David Duchovny, Orlando Jones

# EVOLUTION

**(DREAMWORKS/COLUMBIA)** Producers, Ivan Reitman, Daniel Goldberg, Joe Medjuck; Executive Producers, Tom Pollock, Jeff Apple, David Rodgers; Director, Ivan Reitman; Screenplay, David Diamond, David Weissman, Don Jakoby; Story, Don Jakoby; Photography, Michael Chapman; Designer, J. Michael Riva; Editors, Sheldon Kahn, Wendy Greene Bricmont; Visual Effects Supervisor, Phil Tippett; Costumes, Aggie Guerard Rodgers; Co-Producer, Paul Deason; Music, John Powell; Casting, Margery Simkin; Stunts, Thomas Robinson Harper; a Montecito Picture Company production; Dolby; Technicolor; Rated PG-13; 103 minutes; Release date: June 8, 2001

David Duchovny, Orlando Jones, Seann William Scott

## CAST

| | |
|---|---|
| Dr. Ira Kane | David Duchovny |
| Allison | Julianne Moore |
| Prof. Harry Block | Orlando Jones |
| Wayne | Seann William Scott |
| Gen. Woodman | Ted Levine |
| Deke | Ethan Suplee |
| Danny | Michael Ray Bower |
| Officer Johnson | Pat Kilbane |
| Flemming | Ty Burrell |
| Governor Lewis | Dan Aykroyd |
| Nadine | Katharine Towne |
| Cartwright | Gregory Itzin |
| Lt. Cryer | Ashley Clark |
| Carla | Michelle Wolff |
| Denise | Sarah Silverman |
| Fire Training Inspector | Richard Moll |
| Fireman | Michael McGrady |
| Judge Guilder | Steven Gilborn |
| Dr. Paulson | Wayne Duvall |
| Sheriff Long | Michael Chapman |
| Officer Drake | Kyle Gass |

David Duchovny, Julianne Moore

and Lucas Dudley (Sgt. Toms), Steven Pierce (Sgt. Larson), Wendy Braun (Nurse Tate), Jennifer Savidge (Claire), Jerry Trainor (Tommy), Stephanie Hodge (Jill Mason), Kristen Meadows (Patty), Winifred Freeman (Debbi), Miriam Flynn (Grace), Mary Pat Gleason (Customer), Tony Mirzoian (Husband), Morgan Nagler (Dressing Room Girl), Andrew Bowen (Road Worker), Steve Kehela, Lee Garlington (Reporters), Joshua Ackerman, Kenny Blank, John Cho, Tressa Pope, Adrienne Smith, Chris Wylde (Students), Marty Belafsky, Lee Weaver (Military Police), Tom Davis, Gary Kent (Governor's Aides), Timothy R. Layton (Guard Gate Soldier), Angelo Vacco (Officer Thompson)

*After a meteor crashes in the Arizona desert, two college professors investigate the matter and discover a rapidly evolving species of alien.*

© DreamWorks LLC and Columbia Pictures

Seann William Scott

# LARA CROFT: TOMB RAIDER

(PARAMOUNT) Producers, Lawrence Gordon, Lloyd Levin, Colin Wilson; Executive Producers, Jeremy Heath-Smith, Stuart Baird; Director/Adaptation, Simon West; Screenplay, Patrick Massett, John Zinman; Story, Sara B. Cooper, Mike Werb, Michael Colleary; Based on the Eidos Interactive game series developed by Core Design; Photography, Peter Menzies; Designer, Kirk M. Petruccelli; Editors, Dallas S. Puett, Glen Scantlebury; Costumes, Lindy Hemming; Co-Producer, Bobby Klein; Music, Graeme Revell; Music Supervsior, Peter Afterman; Special Effects Supervisor, Chris Corbould; 2nd Unit Director/Stunts, Simon Crane; Casting, John Hubbard, Ros Hubbard, Dan Hubbard; a Mutual Film Company presentation of a Lawrence Gordon production in association with Eidos Interactive Limited; Dolby; Panavision; Deluxe color; Rated PG-13; 100 minutes; Release date: June 15, 2001

## CAST

Lara Croft ............................................................Angelina Jolie
Lord Croft ..................................................................Jon Voight
Manfred Powell.............................................................Iain Glen
Bryce ......................................................................Noah Taylor
Alex West .................................................................Daniel Craig
Distinguished Gentleman ...............................Richard Johnson
Hillary.............................................................Christopher Barrie
Mr. Pimms ...........................................Julian Rhind-Tutt
Wilson..................................................................Leslie Phillips
Assault Team Leader ..........................................Robert Phillips
Young Lara .......................................................Rachel Appleton
Boothby's Auctioneer.......................................Henry Wyndham
Head Laborers.....................David Y. Cheung, David K. S. Tse
Little Cambodian Girl ...........................................Ayla Amirali
Young Buddhist Monk ........................................Wai-Keat Lau
Aged Buddhist Monk ................................................Ozzie Yue
Little Inuit Girl...............................................Stephanie Burns
Ancient High Priest...............................................Carl Chase
Imperious Woman ..........................................Richenda Carey
UPS Guy .........................................................Sylvano Clarke
Russian Commander ...........................................Olegar Fedoro
Maid.........................................................Anna Maria Everett

*Adventurer Lara Croft takes on a dangerous secret society in order to locate two halves of an ancient artifact that can grant its possessor great powers.*

© Paramount Pictures Corp.

Angelina Jolie

Jon Voight

Iain Glen

Angelina Jolie, Chris Barrie, Noah Taylor

## SONGCATCHER

**(LIONS GATE)** Producers, Richard Miller, Ellen Rigas-Venetis; Executive Producers, Caroline Kaplan, Jonathan Sehring; Director/Screenplay, Maggie Greenwald; Photography, Enrique Chediak; Designer, Ginger Tougas; Costumes, Kasia Walicka-Maimone; Editor, Keith Reamer; Music, David Mansfield; Casting, Vivian Hasbrouk, Tracy Kilpatrick, Ellen Parks; a Rigas Entertainment in association with the Independent Film Channel Productions presentation of an Ergoarts production; Dolby; Color; Rated PG-13; 105 minutes; Release date: June 22, 2001

### CAST

| | |
|---|---|
| Dr. Lily Penleric | Janet McTeer |
| Tom Bledsoe | Aidan Quinn |
| Viney Butler | Pat Carroll |
| Elna Penleric | Jane Adams |
| Fate Honeycutt | Gregory Cook |
| Rose Gentry | Iris DeMent |
| Alice Kincaid | Stephanie Roth Haberle |
| Earl Giddens | David Patrick Kelly |

and E. Katherine Kerr (Harriet Tolliver), Taj Mahal (Dexter Speaks), Muse Watson (Parley Gentry), Emmy Rossum (Deladis Slocumb), Michael Davis (Dean Arthur Pembroke), Michael Goodwin (Prof. Wallace Aldrich), Bart Hansard (Hilliard), Erin Blake Clanton (Polly), Kristin Hall (Isabel), Mike Harding (Reese Kincaid), Rhoda Griffis (Clementine McFarland), Steve Boles (Ambrose McFarland), Taylor Hayes (Rev. Merriweather), Josh Goforth (Will), Don Pedi (Barn Band, Dulcimer), Sheila Kay Adams (Sheila K. Adams), Bobby McMillon, Hazel Dickens (Singers at Barn Dance), Andrea Powell (Josie Moore), Danny Nelson (Uncle Cratis), David Ducey (Postman Johnson), Steven Sutherland (Cyrus Whittle)

*In the early 1900s, Dr. Lily Penleric, a professor of musicology, arrives in a small Appalachian village to study bluegrass music.*

© Lions Gate Films

Aidan Quinn, Janet McTeer

Janet McTeer

Eddie Murply, Tank the Bear

## DR. DOLITTLE 2

**(20TH CENTURY FOX)** Producer, John Davis; Executive Producers, Neil Machlis, Joe Singer; Director, Steve Carr; Screenplay, Larry Levin; Based on the Doctor Dolittle stories by Hugh Lofting; Photography, Daryn Okada; Designer, William Sandell; Editor, Craig P. Herring; Co-Producers, Michele Imperator Stabile, Heidi Santelli; Visual Effects, Rhythm & Hues, Inc.; Costumes, Ruth Carter; Music, David Newman; Music Supervisor, Spring Aspers; Associate Producer, Aldric La'Auli Porter; Casting, Juel Bestrop, Jeanne McCarthy; a Davis Entertainment Company production; Dolby; Super 35 Widescreen; Deluxe color; Rated PG; 87 minutes; Release date: June 22, 2001

### CAST

| | |
|---|---|
| Dr. John Dolittle | Eddie Murphy |
| Lisa Dolittle | Kristen Wilson |
| Charisse Dolittle | Raven-Symoné |
| Maya Dolittle | Kyla Pratt |
| Eric | Lil'Zane |
| Secretary | Denise Dowse |
| The Crocodile Hunter | Steve Irwin |
| Eldon | James L. Avery |
| Eldon's Wife | Elayn J. Taylor |
| Eugene Wilson | Andy Richter |
| Jack Riley/Voice of Crocodile | Kevin Pollak |
| Judge | Victor Raider-Wexler |
| Joseph Potter | Jeffrey Jones |

and Ken Campbell (Animal Control Officer), Mark Griffin (Logger), Tommy Bush (Farmer), Adam Vernier (Worker), Shaun Robinson (Newscaster), R. Doug Seus (Klondike Brown's Delivery Man), Googy Gress (Bear Announcer), Louise Lennon (Waitress), Lisa Marie Hugueley (Shamu's Trainer), Tank the Bear (Archie); VOICE TALENT: Steve Zahn (Archie), Jacob Vargas (Pepito), Lisa Kudrow (Ava), Mike Epps (Sonny), Jamie Kennedy, Bob Odenkirk, Kenny Campbell, David Cross (Dogs/Animal Groupies), Renee Taylor (Tortoise), Phil Proctor (Drunk Monkey), Michael Rapaport (Joey the Raccoon), Isaac Hayes (Possum), Richard C. Sarafian (God Beaver), Reni Santoni (Rat #20), Andy Dick (Lennie the Weasel), Cedric the Entertainer, John Witherspoon (Zoo Bears), Joey Lauren Adams (Squirrel), Mandy Moore, Frankie Muniz (Bear Cubs), John DiMaggio (Seeing-Eye Dog), Georgia Engel (Giraffe), Clyde Kusatsu, Keone Young (Bees), David L. Lander, Michael McKean (Birds), Tara Mercurio (Deer), David DeLuise, Hal Sparks (School Fish), Norm Macdonald (Lucky), Arnold Schwarzenegger (White Wolf)

*Hoping to help his animal friends save their forest from developers, veterinarian John Dolittle concocts a plan to find an endangered species protected by the law living in the condemned area. Sequel to the 1998 Fox film* Dr. Dolittle, *with Murphy, Wilson, Raven-Symoné, and Pratt repeating their roles.*

© Twentieth Century Fox

# THE FAST AND THE FURIOUS

**(UNIVERSAL)** Producer, Neal H. Moritz; Executive Producers, Doug Claybourne, John Pogue; Director, Rob Cohen; Screenplay, Gary Scott Thompson, Erik Bergquist, David Ayer; Screen Story, Gary Scott Thompson; Photography, Ericson Core; Designer, Waldemar Kalinowski; Editor, Peter Honess; Music, BT; Music Supervisors, Gary Jones, Happy Walters; Costumes, Sanja Milkovic Hays; Stunts/Second Unit Director, Mic Rodgers; Visual Effects Supervisor, Michael J. Wassel; a Neal H. Moritz production, presented in association with Mediastream Film; Dolby; Super 35 Widescreen; Deluxe color; Rated PG-13; 108 minutes; Release date: June 22, 2001

## CAST

| | |
|---|---|
| Brian O'Conner | Paul Walker |
| Dominic Toretto | Vin Diesel |
| Letty | Michelle Rodriguez |
| Mia Toretto | Jordana Brewster |
| Johnny Tran | Rick Yune |
| Jesse | Chad Lindberg |
| Leon | Johnny Strong |
| Vince | Matt Schulze |
| Sgt. Tanner | Ted Levine |
| Edwin | Ja Rule |
| Harry | Vyto Ruginis |
| Agent Bilkins | Thom Barry |
| Muse | Stanton Rutledge |
| Hector | Noel Guglielmi |
| Danny Yamato | RJ De Vera |
| Ted Gassner | Beau Holden |
| Lance Nguyen | Reggie Lee |
| Rasta Racer | David Douglas |
| Samoan Guard | Peter Navy Tuiasosopo |
| Ferrari Driver | Neal H. Moritz |

and Doria Clare Anselmo (Ferrari Passenger), Glenn K. Ota (Johnny's Father), F. Valentino Morales (Dispatcher), Mike White (Night Truck Driver), Delphine Pacific (Racer's Edge Clerk), Monica Tamayo (Monica), Megan Baker (Gimel), Tammy Monica Gegamian (Edwin's Babe)

*High-octane driver Dominic Toretto welcomes Brian O'Conner into the world of L.A. outlaw racing, not realizing that the new guy is, in fact, an undercover cop investigating a series of big-rig hijackings.*

© Universal Studios

Vin Diesel, Paul Walker

(Clockwise from top left) Matt Schulze, Michelle Rodriguez, Vin Diesel, Paul Walker, Jordana Brewster, Rick Yune, Johnny Strong, Chad Lindberg

Paul Walker, Vin Diesel

Ving Rhames, Tyrese Gibson

# BABY BOY

(COLUMBIA) Producer/Director/Screenplay, John Singleton; Executive Producer, Dwight Williams; Photography, Charles E. Mills; Designer, Keith Brian Burns; Editor, Bruce Cannon; Costumes, Ruth Carter; Music, David Arnold; Casting, Kimberly R. Hardin; a New Deal Production; Dolby; Deluxe color; Rated R; 129 minutes; Release date: June 27, 2001

## CAST

| | |
|---|---|
| Jody | Tyrese Gibson |
| Yvette | Taraji P. Henson |
| Sweetpea | Omar Gooding |
| Peanut | Tamara Bass |
| Ms. Herron | Candy Brown Houston |
| Juanita | A. J. Johnson |
| Melvin | Ving Rhames |
| Kim | Angell Conwell |
| Do Dirty | Kareem Grimes |
| Sharika | Tracey Cherelle Jones |
| Joe Joe | Kaylan Bolton |
| Cake Man | Freez Luv |
| Patrice | Mo'Nique Imes-Jackson |
| Rachel | Juanita Jennings |
| Receptionist | Liris Crosse |
| Little Boys | Sylvester Robinson, Maasai Singleton |
| Roger | Mario William Jackson |
| Sneed | Keith Diamond |
| Winston | Frederick Ricks |
| Rodney | Snoop Dogg |
| Ms. Daniels | Selma McPherson |
| Woman | Asondra Hunter |
| Pandora | Tawny Dahl |
| Woman Inside | Alex Wright |
| Sheryl | Serese Teate |
| Chris | Olan Thompson |

and Ephraim Benton, Java Benson (Young Thugs), Dejuan Guy (Looney Toon), Deon Gregory (Tony), Tracey L. Davis, Keiwan Spillman (Knuckleheads), Diamond Dawn Cook, Charlee Miyohshi (Women), Roma Alvarez (Mexican Neighbor), Limary Agosto (Lucy Girl), Amentha Dymally (Elderly Woman), Kym Whitley (Host), Hope Flood, Dannon Green (Guests), Cleopatra Singleton (Lil' Nut), Sheila L. Ward (Mourner), Jamaica Carter (Já Toi), Delores Gilbeaux, Yolanda Jones (Co-Workers), Terrance Holloway, Sir Hondes D. Williams, Sr., Calvin L. Valrie, Jr. (Dice Players), Eddie Clark (Street Vendor)

*Jody, a 20-year-old African-American still living at his mother's house in South Central Los Angeles, realizes he must grow up and face life's responsibilities, including giving attention to the two women by whom he has fathered children.*

© Columbia Pictures Industries Inc.

Snoop Dogg

Tyrese Gibson, Taraji P. Henson

A. J. Johnson, Tyrese Gibson

Jay Hernandez, Kirsten Dunst

Kirsten Dunst, Bruce Davison

Taryn Manning, Kirsten Dunst

Richard Steinmetz, Jay Hernandez

# CRAZY/BEAUTIFUL

(**TOUCHSTONE**) Producers, Mary Jane Ufland, Harry J. Ufland, Rachel Pfeffer; Executive Producer, Guy Riedel; Director, John Stockwell; Screenplay, Phil Hay, Matt Manfredi; Co-Producer, Rick Dallago; Photography, Shane Hurlbut; Designer, Maia Javan; Editor, Melissa Kent; Costumes, Susan Matheson; Music, Paul Haslinger, Music Supervisors, Evyen Klean, P. J. Bloom; Casting, Randi Hiller, Sarah Halley Finn; an Ufland production; Dolby; Technicolor; Rated PG-13; 99 minutes; Release date: June 29, 2001

## CAST

| | |
|---|---|
| Nicole Oakley | Kirsten Dunst |
| Carlos Nuñez | Jay Hernandez |
| Tom Oakley | Bruce Davison |
| Luis | Herman Osorio |
| Eddie | Miguel Castro |
| Victor | Tommy De La Cruz |
| Hector | Rolando Molina |
| Mrs. Nuñez | Soledad St. Hilaire |
| Courtney | Lucinda Jenney |
| Maddy | Taryn Manning |
| Coach Bauer | Richard Steinmetz |
| Rosa | Ana Argueta |
| Jimmy, The Pilot | Neil Looy |
| Morgan | Marion Moseley |
| Dr. Linehan | Mike Jones |
| Mrs. Ellis | Carolyn McKnight |
| Assistant Football Coach Stover | Michael J. Fisher |
| Wilcox | Cory Hardrict |
| Foster | Keram Malicki-Sanchez |
| Lainie | Kimi Reichenberg |
| Davis | Matthew McKane |

and Jim Jackman (Detail Supervisor), Kevin Kane (Mr. Kane), Griselda Diaz (Taco Vendor), Claudia Soundy (Spandexed Latina Girl), Rick Dallago (Photo Teacher), Berenice Ayala (Blanca), Virginia Sanchez (Aunt Eva), Hank Mendoza (Guy on Street), Maria Diaz (Oakley's Receptionist), Louie Liberti (Casey), Bob Sattler, John Marrott (Police Officers), Josh Vaughn (Curtis), Devon Williams, David Benitez (Band Singers), Tracy Claustro (Luz), Jackie Napal (Jackie), Gary Cruz, Magdaleno Robles, Jr. (Dealers), Matt Hobbie (Quarterback), John Pemberton (Football Official)

*Carlos, a straight-A high-school student from East L.A., falls in love with Nicole, the troubled, rebellious daughter of a wealthy congressman.*

© Touchstone Pictures

Jude Law, Haley Joel Osment

Jude Law, Haley Joel Osment

# A.I.: ARTIFICIAL INTELLIGENCE

(WARNER BROS./DREAMWORKS) Producers, Kathleen Kennedy, Steven Spielberg, Bonnie Curtis; Executive Producers, Jan Harlan, Walter F. Parkes; Director/Screenplay, Steven Spielberg; Based on a screenplay story by Ian Watson; Based on the short story *Super Toys Last All Summer* by Brian Aldiss; Photography, Janusz Kaminski; Designer, Rick Carter; Costumes, Bob Ringwood; Editor, Michael Kahn; Music, John Williams; Robot Characters Designed by Stan Winston Studio; Special Visual Effects & Animation, Industrial Light & Magic; Casting, Avy Kaufman; an Amblin/Stanley Kubrick production; Dolby; Technicolor; Rated PG-13; 146 minutes; Release date: June 29, 2001

Haley Joel Osment, Jude Law

## CAST

| | |
|---|---|
| David | Haley Joel Osment |
| Gigolo Joe | Jude Law |
| Monica Swinton | Frances O'Connor |
| Henry Swinton | Sam Robards |
| Martin Swinton | Jake Thomas |
| Lord Johnson-Johnson | Brendan Gleeson |
| Professor Hobby | William Hurt |
| Voice of Teddy | Jack Angel |

### Cybertronics

| | |
|---|---|
| Syatyoo Sama | Ken Leung |
| Colleague | April Grace |
| Executive | Matt Winston |
| Secretary | Sabrina Grdevich |

and Clark Gregg, Kevin Sussman, Tom Gallop, Eugene Osment (Supernerds)

### The Birthday Party

| | |
|---|---|
| Todd | Theo Greenly |

and Jeremy James Kisner, Dillon McEwin, Andy Morrow, Curt Youngberg (Kids)

### Shangri-La Hotel

| | |
|---|---|
| Gigolo Jane | Ashley Scott |
| Mr. Williamson, The Bellman | John Prosky |
| The Murderer | Enrico Colantoni |
| Patricia in the Mirrored Room | Paula Malcomson |

### Flesh Fair

| | |
|---|---|
| Stage Manager | Michael Berresse |
| Amanda | Haley King |
| Teenage Honey | Kathryn Morris |
| Child Singer | Daveigh Chase |
| Backstage Bull | Brian Turk |

and Justina Machado (Assistant), Tim Rigby (Yeoman), Lily Knight (Voice in the Crowd), Vito Carenzo (Big Man), Rena Owen (Ticket Taker), J. Alan Scott (Worker), Adam Alexi-Malle (Crowd Member), Laurence Mason (Tech Director), Brent Sexton (Russell), Ken Palmer, Jason Sutter (Percussionists)

Jude Law (center)

### Rogue City

| | |
|---|---|
| Cop | Michael Shamus Wiles |
| Kate, The Holographic Girl | Kelly McCool |

### Mechas

| | |
|---|---|
| Fern Mecha Nanny | Clara Bellar |
| Roadworker | Keith Campbell |
| Laboratory Technician | Tim Edward Rhoze |
| Chef | Jim Jansen |
| General Circuita | Eliza Coleman |
| Welder | R. David Smith |

and Wayne Wilderson (Comedian), Bobby Harwell (TV Face), Billy Scudder (Mechanic)

### Voices

| | |
|---|---|
| Doctor Know | Robin Williams |
| Specialist/Narrator | Ben Kingsley |
| Blue Mecha | Meryl Streep |
| Comedian | Chris Rock |
| Gardener | Erik Bauersfeld |

and Michael Mantell (Doctor Frasier at Cyrogenic Institute), Miguel Perez, Matt Malloy (Robot Repairmen), Adrian Grenier, Mark Staubach, Michael Fishman (Teens in Van), Jeanine Salla (Sentient Machine Therapist), Laia Salla (Mr. Chan's Assistant), Diane Fletcher (Sentient Machine Security), Kate Nei (Toe Bell Ringing), Red King (Covert Information Retrieval), Al Jourgensen, Paul Barker, Max Brody, Duane Buford, Adam Grossman, Ty Coon (Flesh Fair Band)

*In the distant future, a cybertronic robot boy, David, becomes the surrogate child for a couple whose real son is facing a terminal illness. After David accidentally harms the real child, he is cast out into the world where he finds himself being hunted along with other rejected robots.*

*This film received Oscar nominations for visual effects and original score.*

© Warner Bros. and DreamWorks, LLC

# CATS & DOGS

**(WARNER BROS.)** Producers, Andrew Lazar, Chris Defaria, Warren Zide, Craig Perry; Executive Producers, Bruce Berman, Chris Bender, J. C. Spink; Director, Lawrence Guterman; Screenplay, John Requa, Glenn Ficarra; Photography, Julio Macat; Designer, James Bissell; Editors, Michael Stevenson, Rick W. Finney; Music, John Debney; Costumes, Tish Monaghan; Visual Effects Supervisor/Associate Producer, Ed Jones; Animatronic Effects, David Barclay; Creature Effects, Jim Henson's Creature Shop; Visual Effects, Rhythm & Hues; Casting, Marci Liroff; a Mad Chance/Zide/Perry production, presented in association with Village Roadshow Pictures and NPV Entertainment; Dolby; Technicolor; Rated PG; 87 minutes; Release date: July 4, 2001

## CAST

| | |
|---|---|
| Professor Brody | Jeff Goldblum |
| Carolyn Brody | Elizabeth Perkins |
| Sophie | Miriam Margolyes |
| Scott Brody | Alexander Pollock |

## VOICE CAST

| | |
|---|---|
| Lou | Tobey Maguire |
| Butch | Alec Baldwin |
| Mr. Tinkles | Sean Hayes |
| Ivy | Susan Sarandon |
| Peek | Joe Pantoliano |
| Sam | Michael Clarke Duncan |
| Calico | Jon Lovitz |
| Doberman Drill Sergeant | Victor Wilson |
| Collie at HQ | Salome Jens |
| The Mastiff | Charlton Heston |
| Russian Itty | Glenn Ficarra |
| Ninjas | Danny Mann, Billy West |
| Wolf Blitzer | Paul Pape |

and additional CAST: Myron Natwick (Mr. Mason), Doris Chillcott (Mrs. Calvert), Kirsten Robek (Pie Mom), Frank C. Turner (The Farmer), Mar Andersons (Guard at Gate), Gillian Barber (Factory Receptionist), Carol Ann Susi, Randi Kaplan, Mary Bogue (Sisters), Ivin Sanders, Mark Schooley (Employees), Lou Bollo, Scott Nicholson, Trish Schill (Workers), Babe Dolan (Wife Passenger), Reg Glass, Charles André (Truck Drivers), Peggy Logan (Nurse), Alicia Michelle (Jogger)

*Mr. Tinkles, a Persian cat bent on world domination, plots to alter a vaccine being developed by Professor Brody, so that it will make all humans allergic to dogs.*

© Warner Bros.

Mr. Tinkles

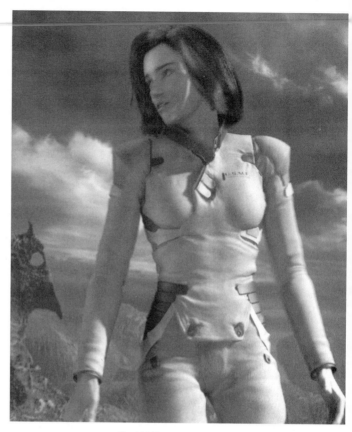

Dr. Aki Ross

# FINAL FANTASY: THE SPIRITS WITHIN

**(COLUMBIA)** Producers, Hironobu Sakaguchi, Jun Aida, Chris Lee; Director/Story, Hironobu Sakaguchi; Co-Director, Moto Sakakibara; Screenplay, Al Reinert, Jeff Vintar; Music, Elliot Goldenthal; Music Supervisor, Richard Rudolph; Associate Producer, Katsuhiko Toyota; Casting/Voice Director, Jack Fletcher; Conceptual Design Artist, Kazunori Nakazawa; Animation Director, Andy Jones; Computer Graphics Supervisor, Gary Mundell; Original Character Designer, Shuko Murase; Editor, Christopher S. Capp; a Square Pictures presentation; U.S.-Japanese; Dolby; Deluxe color; Rated PG-13; 106 minutes; Release date: July 11, 2001

## VOICE CAST

| | |
|---|---|
| Doctor Aki Ross | Ming-Na |
| Captain Gray Edwards | Alec Baldwin |
| Ryan | Ving Rhames |
| Neil | Steve Buscemi |
| Jane | Peri Gilpin |
| Doctor Sid | Donald Sutherland |
| General Hein | James Woods |
| Council Members | Keith David, Jean Simmons |
| Major Elliot | Matt McKenzie |

*In the distant future, when Earth has been taken over by aliens, Aki Ross and her mentor, Dr. Sid, work to develop an antidote to counteract the alien force.*

© Columbia Pictures Industries Inc.

# MADE

**(ARTISAN)** Producers, Vince Vaughn, Jon Favreau; Executive Producer, John Starke; Director/Screenplay, Jon Favreau; Photography, Chris Doyle; Designer, Anne Stuhler; Costumes, Laura Jean Shannon; Co-Producer, Peter Billingsley; Editor, Curtiss Clayton; Music, John O'Brien, Lyle Workman; Music Supervisors, Damon Booth, Pete Giberga, Sean Riciglaino, Tim Riley; Dolby; Color; Rated R; 94 minutes; Release date: July 13, 2001

## CAST

| | |
|---|---|
| Bobby | Jon Favreau |
| Ricky | Vince Vaughn |
| Jessica | Famke Janssen |
| Max | Peter Falk |
| Ruiz | Sean "Puffy" Combs |
| Horrace | Faizon Love |
| Welshman | David O'Hara |
| Jimmy | Vincent Pastore |
| Chloe | Mackenzie Vega |
| Wendy | Jenteal |

and Tom Morello (Best Man), Joe Goossen (Referee), Jonathan Silverman (Bachelor), Kimberley Davies (Bartender), Elizabeth Barondes (Wife), Gary Auerbach (Husband), Bill Capizzi (Arthur), Vernon Vaughn (Coach), Esta-Joy Peters (Salesperson), Jennifer Bransford (Flight Attendant), Jason Delgado (Man on Phone), Leonardo Cimino (Leo), Federico Castelluccio, Matt O'Dwyer, Jason Fabrini (Doormen), Joan Favreau (Zoo Lady), Jamie Harris (Rogue), Tim Gallin (Thug), Dustin Diamond (Himself), Brian Donahue (Westie), Sam Rockwell (Hotel Clerk), Drea de Matteo (Prostitute)

*Bobby and his co-worker Ricky decide that the best way to dig themselves out of their dead-end lives is to take a job with mobster Max, who sends the two men to New York to hook up with money-launderer Ruiz.*

© Artisan

Vince Vaughn, Jon Favreau

Peter Falk

Vince Vaughn, Faizon Love, Sean "Puffy" Combs,
Jon Favreau

Vince Vaughn

Edward Norton, Robert De Niro

Robert De Niro

# THE SCORE

**(PARAMOUNT)** Producers, Gary Foster, Lee Rich; Executive Producers, Bernie Williams, Adam Platnick; Director, Frank Oz; Screenplay, Kario Salem, Lem Dobbs, Scott Marshall Smith; Story, Daniel E. Taylor, Kario Salem; Photography, Rob Hahn; Designer, Jackson De Govia; Music, Howard Shore; Executive Music Producer, Budd Carr; Editor, Richard Pearson; Costumes, Aude Bronson-Howard; Casting, Margery Simkin; a Mandalay Pictures presentation of a Horseshoe Bay/Lee Rich production; Dolby; Panavision; Deluxe color; Rated R; 120 minutes; Release date: July 13, 2001

## CAST

| | |
|---|---|
| Nick Wells | Robert De Niro |
| Jack Teller (Brian) | Edward Norton |
| Max | Marlon Brando |
| Diane | Angela Bassett |
| Burt | Gary Farmer |
| Danny | Paul Soles |
| Steven | Jamie Harrold |
| Laurent | Serge Houde |
| André | Jean Rene Ouellet |
| Jean-Claude | Martin Drainville |
| Albert | Claude Despins |
| Sapperstein | Richard Waugh |
| Sapperstein's Cousin | Mark Camacho |
| Woman in Study | Marie-Josee D'Amours |
| Man in Study | Gavin Svensson |
| Tuan | Thinh Truong Nguyen |
| Cop | Carlo Essagian |
| Drunk | Christian Tessier |
| Storekeeper | Lenie Scoffie |

and Bobby Brown (Tony), Maurice Demers (Philippe), Christian Jacques, Henry Farmer, Dacky Thermidor, Gerard Blouin (Guards), Charles V. Doucet (Old Engineer), Pierre Drolet (Worker), Norman Mikeal Berketa (Bureaucrat Official), Eric Hoziel (Ironclad Tech), John Talbot (Janitor), Richard Zeman, Nick Carasoulis (Thugs), Cassandra Wilson, Mose Allison (Themselves)

*Against his better judgment, master safecracker Nick Wells agrees to team with young thief Jack Teller to steal a valuable item from the Montreal Customs House.*

© Paramount Pictures and MP Film Management TS Productions. GmbH & Co. KG

Robert De Niro, Edward Norton, Marlon Brando

Robert De Niro, Angela Bassett

# BULLY

**(LIONS GATE)** Producers, Chris Hanley, Don Murphy, Fernando Sulichin; Executive Producers, Jordan Gertner, Mark Mower, Manuel Chiche, Arnaud Duteil, Vincent Maraval; Director, Larry Clark; Screenplay, Zachary Long, Roger Pullis; Based on the novel *Bully: A True Story of High School Revenge* by Jim Schutze; Photography, Steve Gainer; Designer, Linda Burton; Costumes, Carleen Ileana Rosado; Editor, Andrew Hafitz; Co-Producers, Guy Stodel, Peter Block, Robert Pfeffer; Associate Producer, Brad Renfro; Casting, Carmen Cuba; a Studio Canal presentation of a Muse/Blacklist Production in association with Gravity Entertainment; Dolby; Color; Rated R; 106 minutes; Release date: July 13, 2001

## CAST

| | |
|---|---|
| Marty Puccio | Brad Renfro |
| Lisa Connelly | Rachel Miner |
| Bobby Kent | Nick Stahl |
| Ali Willis | Bijou Phillips |
| Donny Semenec | Michael Pitt |
| Heather Swallers | Kelli Garner |
| Derek Dzvirko | Daniel Franzese |
| Derek Kaufman, The Hitman | Leo Fitzpatrick |
| Claudia | Nathalie Paulding |
| Blonde | Jessica Sutta |
| Mr. Kent | Edward Amatrudo |
| Mr. Willis | Steven Raulerson |
| Mrs. Willis | Judith Clayton |
| Mr. Puccio | Alan Lilly |
| Mrs. Connelly | Elizabeth Dimon |
| Mr. Kaufman | Larry Clark |

and Jo-Aynne von Born (Claudia's Mother), Marc Pearson (Marty's Brother), Joseph Shrouder (Terry), Scott McHugh (Boy at Beach), John Parker, Phillip Ortiz (Video Game Boys), Lindzee Warren, Alexandra Steele (Girls at Mall), Sam Steele, Anthony Barrineau, Derek Oliveira (Hitman Gang Boy), Rick Amicucci (Hitman's Brother), Rick Seguso (Gay Man), Jesse Dechant (Dildo Man), Det. Frank Ilarraza (Himself), Carlos Hernandez, Danny Norton (Club Dancers on Stage)

*The true story of how a Florida teen's bullying behavior toward his friend led to his murder.*

© Lions Gate Films

Bijou Phillips, Rachel Miner, Brad Renfro

Brad Renfro, Nick Stahl

Bijou Phillips, Kelli Garner, Daniel Franzese

Jennifer Coolidge, Reese Witherspoon

# LEGALLY BLONDE

(MGM) Producers, Marc Platt, Ric Kidney; Director, Robert Luketic; Screenplay, Karen McCullah Lutz, Kirsten Smith; Based on the book by Amanda Brown; Photography, Anthony B. Richmond; Designer, Melissa Stewart; Costumes, Sophie de Rakoff Carbonell; Editors, Anita Brandt Burgoyne, Garth Craven; Music, Rolfe Kent; Music Supervisor, Anita Camarata; Co-Producers, David Nicksay, Christian McLaughlin; Casting, Joseph Middleton; a Marc Platt production; Dolby; Super 35 Widescreen; Color; Rated PG-13; 96 minutes; Release date: July 13, 2001

Selma Blair, Matthew Davis

## CAST

| | |
|---|---|
| Elle Woods | Reese Witherspoon |
| Emmett Richmond | Luke Wilson |
| Vivian Kensington | Selma Blair |
| Warner | Matthew Davis |
| Professor Callahan | Victor Garber |
| Paulette | Jennifer Coolidge |
| Professor Stromwell | Holland Taylor |
| Brooke Taylor Windham | Ali Larter |
| Margot | Jessica Cauffiel |
| Serena | Alanna Ubach |
| Dorky David | Oz Perkins |
| Chutney | Linda Cardellini |
| UPS Guy | Bruce Thomas |
| Enid | Meredith Scott Lynn |
| Mrs. Windham Vandermark | Raquel Welch |
| Claire | Samantha Lemole |

Linda Cardellini, Reese Witherspoon

and Kelly Nyks (Arrogant Aaron), Ted Kairys (Gerard), Michael B. Silver (Bobby), Kimberly McCullough (Amy), Shannon O'Hurley (DA Joyce Rafferty), Greg Serano (Enrique), Francesca P. Roberts (Marina R. Bickford), Lisa Kushell (Boutique Saleswoman), Natalie Barish (Old Lady at Manicurist), Cici Lau (LA Nail Technician), Allyce Beasley (CULA Advisor), Kevin Cooney (Head of Admissions), Ted Rooney, David Moreland, Wayne Federman (Admissions Guys), James Read (Elle's Father), Tane McClure (Elle's Mother), Niklaus Lange (Annoyed 2L), Doug Spinuzza (Intense Ivan Berliner), Lisa K. Wyatt (Jail House Guard), Jason Christopher (Chuck), Corinne Reilly, Victoria Mahoney (Reporters), Lacey Beeman (Nervous 1L Girl), Melissa Young (Blonde Cheerleader), Brody Hutzler (Grant), Chaney Kley (Brandon), John Cantwell (Maurice), Ondrea De Vincentis (Callahan's Assistant), Terrence Michael (Desk Clerk), Nectar Rose (Freshman Girl), Jodi Harris (Another Sister), Patricia Kimes (Blonde Biker), Sasha Barrese (Another Girl), Kelly Driscoll (Blonde Card Carrier), Elizabeth Matthews, Kennedy Stone (Sorority Girls), Moonie (Bruiser), Lily (Rufus)

*Dumped by her politically ambitious boyfriend for not being suitably "serious" enough to further his career, Elle Woods makes it her goal to overcome her "dumb blonde" image by getting into Harvard Law School.*

© Metro-Goldwyn-Mayer Pictures, Inc.

Shannon O'Hurley, Victor Garber,
Luke Wilson, Reese Witherspoon

# JURASSIC PARK III

**(UNIVERSAL)** Producers, Kathleen Kennedy, Larry Franco; Executive Producer, Steven Spielberg; Director, Joe Johnston; Screenplay, Peter Buchman, Alexander Payne, Jim Taylor; Based on characters created by Michael Crichton; Photography, Shelly Johnson; Designer, Ed Verreaux; Editor, Robert Dalva; Music, Don Davis, John Williams; Costumes, Betsy Cox; Animation & Special Visual Effects, Industrial Light & Magic; Visual Effects Supervisor, Jim Mitchell; Visual Effects Producer, Mark S. Miller; Live Action Dinosaurs, Stan Winston; Casting, Nancy Foy; Stunts, Pat Romano; an Amblin Entertainment production; Dolby; Color; Rated PG-13; 91 minutes; Release date: July 18, 2001

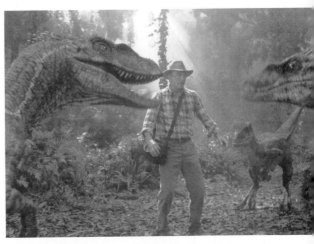

Sam Neill

## CAST

| | |
|---|---|
| Dr. Alan Grant | Sam Neill |
| Paul Kirby | William H. Macy |
| Amanda Kirby | Téa Leoni |
| Billy Brennan | Alessandro Nivola |
| Eric Kirby | Trevor Morgan |
| Udesky | Michael Jeter |
| Cooper | John Diehl |
| Nash | Bruce A. Young |
| Ellie | Laura Dern |
| Mark | Taylor Nichols |
| Ben Hildebrand | Mark Harelik |
| Enrique Cardoso | Julio Oscar Mechoso |
| Charlie | Blake Bryan |
| Cheryl | Sarah Danielle Madison |
| Hannah | Linda Park |
| Symposium Leader | Sonia Jackson |
| Science Reporter | Bruce French |
| Students | Bernard Zilinskas, Rona Benson |
| Man in Suit | Frank Clem |

*Two wealthy adventurers agree to fund Dr. Alan Grant's research project if he will accompany them to Isla Sorna, where genetically engineered prehistoric creatures roam and they hope to locate their missing son. Third in the Universal series following* Jurassic Park *(1993) and* The Lost World: Jurassic Park *(1997); Sam Neill and Laura Dern repeat their roles from the first film.*

© Universal Studios and Amblin Entertainment

Téa Leoni, William H. Macy, Michael Jeter

Michael Jeter, Alessandro Nivola, Téa Leoni, Sam Neill, William H. Macy

John Cameron Mitchell

(Clockwise from center): John Cameron Mitchell, Rob Campbell, Stephen Trask, Miriam Shor, Michael Aronov, Theodore Liscinski

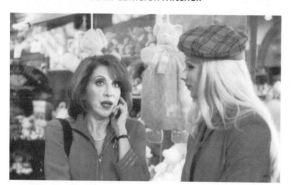

Andrea Martin, John Cameron Mitchell

John Cameron Mitchell

Theodore Liscinski, Stephen Trask, Michael Aronov, John Cameron Mitchell, Miriam Shor, Rob Campbell

John Cameron Mitchell, Michael Pitt

John Cameron Mitchell, Miriam Shor

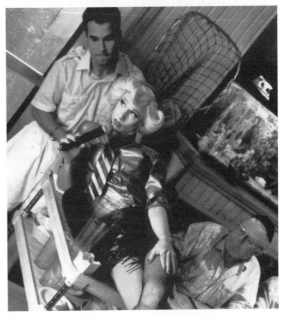

John Cameron Mitchell

# HEDWIG AND THE ANGRY INCH

**(FINE LINE FEATURES)** Producers, Christine Vachon, Katie Roumel, Pamela Koffler; Executive Producers, Michael De Luca, Amy Henkels, Mark Tusk; Director/Screenplay, John Cameron Mitchell; Photography, Frank G. DeMarco; Designer, Thérèse Deprez; Costumes, Arianne Phillips; Music/Lyrics/Original Score, Stephen Trask; Editor, Andrew Marcus; Hedwig's Hair and Makeup, Mike Potter; Animated Sequences and Artwork, Emily Hubley; Executive Music Producer, Alex Steyermark; Line Producer, Colin Brunton; Casting, Susan Shopmaker; a New Line Cinema presentation of a Killer Films production; Dolby; Color; Rated R; 91 minutes; Release date: July 20, 2001

## CAST

| | |
|---|---|
| Hedwig/Hansel Schmidt | John Cameron Mitchell |
| Yitzhak | Miriam Shor |
| Skszp | Stephen Trask |
| Jacek | Theodore Liscinski |
| Krzysztof | Rob Campbell |
| Schlatko | Michael Aronov |
| Phyllis Stein | Andrea Martin |
| Hansel (6 years old) | Ben Mayer-Goodman |
| Hansel's Mom | Alberta Watson |
| Hansel's Dad | Gene Pyrz |
| Tommy Gnosis | Michael Pitt |
| Tommy's Publicist | Karen Hines |
| Goth Menses Boy | Max Toulch |
| Sgt. Luther Robinson | Maurice Dean Wint |
| Fat Man | Ermes Blarasin |
| Kwahg-Yi | Sook-Yin Lee |

and Maggie Moore (Trailer Park Neighbor), Renate Options (Tranny Hooker)

*Having gone through a botched sex-change operation in an effort to get out of East Berlin, Hedwig makes a living as a second-rate singer, trying to capitalize on her celebrity as the supposed ex-lover of noted rock star Tommy Gnosis. John Cameron Mitchell, Miriam Shor, and Stephen Trask repeat their roles from the original 1998 Off-Broadway production.*

© New Line Cinema Inc.

John Cameron Mitchell, Michael Pitt

Scarlett Johansson, Thora Birch

Thora Birch, Steve Buscemi

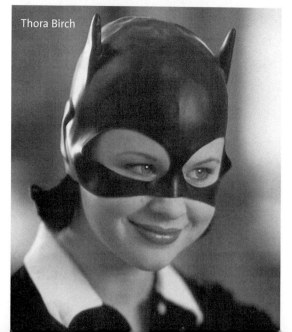

Thora Birch

# GHOST WORLD

**(UNITED ARTISTS)** Producers, Lianne Halfon, John Malkovich, Russell Smith; Executive Producers, Pippa Cross, Janette Day; Director, Terry Zwigoff; Screenplay, Daniel Clowes, Terry Zwigoff; Based on the comic book by Daniel Clowes; Photography, Affonso Beato; Designer, Edward T. McAvoy; Costumes, Mary Zophres; Line Producer, Barbara A. Hall; Editors, Carole Kravetz-Aykanian, Michael R. Miller; Music, David Kitay; Casting, Cassandra Kulukundis; a Granada Film in association with Jersey Shore and Advanced Medien presentation of a Mr. Mudd production; Distributed by MGM Distribution Co.; Dolby; Color; Rated R; 111 minutes; Release date: July 20, 2001

## CAST

Enid.....................................................................Thora Birch
Rebecca ........................................................Scarlett Johansson
Seymour .............................................................Steve Buscemi
Josh...........................................................................Brad Renfro
Roberta .............................................................Illeana Douglas
Enid's Dad.............................................................Bob Balaban
Dana.......................................................................Stacey Travis
Norman ...........................................Charles C. Stevenson, Jr.
Doug .................................................................Dave Sheridan
Joe .....................................................................Tom McGowan
Melorra .................................................................Debra Azar
Sidewinder Boss......................................................Brian George
John Ellis ...................................................................Pat Healy
Graduation Speaker .....................................................Rini Bell
Todd ......................................................................T. J. Thyne
Weird Al .........................................................Ezra Buzzington
Maxine.......................................................................Teri Garr
Vanilla.............................................................Lindsey Girardot
Jade...........................................................................Joy Bisco
Ebony ...................................................Venus DeMilo Thomas
Margaret.............................................................Ashley Peldon
Phillip .............................................................Chachi Pittman
Black Girl .............................................................Janece Jordan
Snotty Girl ............................................................Kaileigh Martin
Hippy Boy ...........................................................Alexander Fors
Angry Guy (Jerome) ...................................................Marc Vann
Asian Guy (Steven) .......................................................James Sie
Fussy Guy (Paul) ..........................................................Paul Keith
Pushy Guy (Gerrold) ....................................................David Cross
Fred Chatman ...............................................J. J. Bad Boy Jones
Red-Haired Girl .....................................................Dylan Jones
MC .........................................................................Martin Grey
Blueshammer..........Steve Pierson, Jake LaBotz, Johnny Irion, Nate Wood and Charles Schneider (Joey McCobb), Edward T. McAvoy (Mr. Satanist), Sid Garza-Hillman, Joshua Wheeler (Zine-O-Phobia Creeps), Patrick Fishler (Masterpiece Video Clerk), Daniel Graves (Masterpiece Video Customer), Matt Doherty (Masterpiece Video Employee), Joel Michaely (Porno Cashier), Debi Derryberry (Rude Coffee Customer), Joe Sikora (Regga Fan), Brett Gilbert (Alien Autopsy Guy), Alex Solowitz (Cineplex Manager), Tony Ketcham (Alcoholic Customer), Mary Bogue (Popcorn Customer), Brian Jacobs (Soda Customer), Patrick Yonally (Garage Sale Hipster), Lauren Bowles (Angry Garage Sale Woman), Lorna Scott (Art Show Curator), Jeff Murray (Roberta's Colleague), Jerry Rector (Dana's Co-Worker), Sheriff John Bunnell (Seymour's Boss), Diane Salinger (Psychiatrist), Anna Berger (Seymour's Mother), Bruce Glover (Feldman, Wheelchair Guy)

*Two teenage girls, Enid and Rebecca, disillusioned with the phony world they live in, play a practical joke on a lonely older man, Seymour, only to have Enid realize that she has found a soul mate in the alienated malcontent.*

*This film received an Oscar nomination for adapted screenplay.*

© United Artists Films, Inc.

Thora Birch, Steve Buscemi

Brad Renfro

Scarlett Johansson, Charles C. Stevenson, Jr., Thora Birch

Bob Balaban, Teri Garr

Illeana Douglas

# AMERICA'S SWEETHEARTS

(COLUMBIA) Producers, Susan Arnold, Donna Arkoff Roth, Billy Crystal; Executive Producers, Charles Newirth, Peter Tolan; Director, Joe Roth; Screenplay, Billy Crystal, Peter Tolan; Photography, Phedon Papamichael; Designer, Garreth Stover; Editor, Stephen A. Rotter; Music, James Newton Howard; Music Supervisor, Kathy Nelson; Costumes, Ellen Mirojnick, Jeffrey Kurland; Casting, Junie Lowry-Johnson, Libby Goldstein; a Roth/Arnold Production, a Face Production; Dolby; Panavision; Deluxe color; Rated PG-13; 102 minutes; Release date: July 20, 2001

John Cusack, Catherine Zeta-Jones

## CAST

| | |
|---|---|
| Kiki Harrison | Julia Roberts |
| Lee Phillips | Billy Crystal |
| Gwen Harrison | Catherine Zeta-Jones |
| Eddie Thomas | John Cusack |
| Hector | Hank Azaria |
| Dave Kingman | Stanley Tucci |
| Hal Weidmann | Christopher Walken |
| Wellness Guide | Alan Arkin |
| Danny Wax | Seth Green |
| Davis | Scot Zeller |
| Themselves | Larry King, Byron Allen |
| Limo Driver | Steve Pink |
| Dave O'Hanlon | Rainn Wilson |
| Security Guards | Eric Balfour, Marty Belafsky |
| Leaf | Keri Lynn Pratt |
| Adinah | Maria Canals |

John Cusack, Julia Roberts

and Charley Steiner (Nevada Anchorman), Shaun Robinson (Nevada Anchorwoman), Jeff Michael (Network Anchor), Sibila Vargas (Reporter), Jane Yamamoto (Reporter on Patio), Wendy Schenker (Maura Klein), Jim Ferguson (Mort Josephson), Lisa Joyner (Laura Messinger), Patrick Stoner (Bob), Sam Rubin (Ken), Susan Katz (Interviewer), Maree Cheatham (Matronly Interviewer), Amber Barretto (Alison), Alex Enberg, Sarah Loew (Larry King Producers), Joseph Feingold (Judge), Sherry Jennings (Bar Hostess), Julie Sorrels (Mother), Austin L. Sorrels (Little Boy), Julie Wagner, Leilani Muenter (Callers), Dimitri Moraitis (Agent), Shawn Driscoll (Sean), Misti See (Misti), Gail Laskowski (Gail)

*In order to save his career, press agent Lee Phillips coaxes estranged movie-star couple Gwen Harrison and Eddie Thomas to appear together at a press junket for their newest film.*

© Revolution Studios

Seth Green                    Alan Arkin

Julia Roberts, Billy Crystal

Stanley Tucci, Billy Crystal

# WET HOT AMERICAN SUMMER

(**USA FILMS**) Producer, Howard Bernstein; Director, David Wain; Screenplay/Co-Producers, Michael Showalter, David Wain; Photography, Ben Weinstein; Designer, Mark White; Costumes, Jill Kliber; Editor, Meg Reticker; Line Producer, Jill Rubin; Music, Theodore Shapiro, Craig Wedren; Casting, Susie Farris; a Eureka Pictures production in association with North Coast Group of a Showalter/Wain Movie; Dolby; DuArt color; Rated R; 97 minutes; Release date: July 27, 2001

## CAST

Beth .....................................................................Janeane Garofalo
Henry .............................................................David Hyde Pierce
Coop/Alan Shemper ........................................Michael Showalter
Katie ...............................................................Marguerite Moreau
Andy ..............................................................................Paul Rudd
J. J. ....................................................................................Zak Orth
Gene...........................................................Christopher Meloni
Gary .......................................................................A. D. Miles
Gail.............................................................Molly Shannon
Aaron ...........................................................Gideon Jacobs
Victor ...........................................................Ken Marino
Neil.............................................................Joe Lo Truglio
McKinley .......................................................Michael Ian Black
Arty ..............................................................Liam Norton
Susie .............................................................Amy Poehler
Ben .............................................................Bradley Cooper
Abby ............................................................Marisa Ryan
Lindsay ........................................................Elizabeth Banks
and Gabriel Millman (Caped Boy), Kevin Sussman (Steve), Kevin Thomas Conroy (Mork Guy), Christopher Cusamano (Medieval Kid), Madeline Blue (Cure Girl), Cassidy Ladden (Mallrat Girl), Nina Hellman (Nancy), Peter Salett (Guitar Dude), Judah Friedlander (Ron), Jacob Shoesmith Fox (Moose), Whitney Vance (Valerie), Benjamin Coppola (Bobby), Jon Benjamin (Can of Vegetables), Jake Fogelnest (Silas), Ian Helfer (Bear Claw Coach), Jordan Maclean (Alexa), Avi Setton (Standup Comic), Kyle Gallner (Bobby's Buddy), Kathleen Pandolfo (Godspell Girl), Zachary Montgomery-Wicks (Gail's Boy Camper), Danny Hopkins, Christopher Connors (Raft Campers), Matt Carmeci (Bunk Boy), Stephen O'Brien, Timothy Gasiewski (Juke Box Kids), Angel Berlane, Christi Berlane (Friends Girls), Bob Walz (Drug Dealer), Joseph Kariuki (Kenyan Runner), Donna Mitchell (Gene's Wife), Joe Bryan, Christine Loebsack, Sandra Kennedy, Keith Oney (Counselors)

*A group of counselors and campers spend a day of wacky high jinks on the final day of summer camp in 1981.*

© USA Films

Bradley Cooper, Janeane Garofalo, Michael Ian Black

Paul Rudd, Marguerite Moreau

Michael Showalter, Christopher Meloni, A.D. Miles

Gideon Jacobs, Molly Shannon

Tim Roth, Mark Wahlberg

Michael Clarke Duncan

Helena Bonham Carter, Erick Avari, Evan Dexter Parke

Paul Giamatti (Left)

# PLANET OF THE APES

(20TH CENTURY FOX) Producer, Richard D. Zanuck; Executive Producer, Ralph Winter; Director, Tim Burton; Screenplay, William Broyles, Jr., Lawrence Konner, Mark Rosenthal; Based on the novel *La Planète des singes (Monkey Planet)* by Pierre Boulle; Photography, Philippe Rousselot; Designer, Rick Heinrichs; Costumes, Colleen Atwood; Editor, Chris Lebenzon; Music, Danny Elfman; Visual Effects Supervisor, Bill George; Special Makeup Effects Designer and Creator, Rick Baker; Casting, Denise Chamian; Stunts, Charles Croughwell; a Zanuck Company production; Dolby; Panavision; Deluxe color; Rated PG-13; 120 minutes; Release date: July 27, 2001

## CAST

| | |
|---|---|
| Captain Leo Davidson | Mark Wahlberg |
| Thade | Tim Roth |
| Ari | Helena Bonham Carter |
| Attar | Michael Clarke Duncan |
| Limbo | Paul Giamatti |
| Daena | Estella Warren |
| Krull | Cary-Hiroyuki Tagawa |
| Sandar | David Warner |
| Karubi | Kris Kristofferson |
| Tival | Erick Avari |
| Birn | Luke Eberl |
| Gunnar | Evan Dexter Parke |
| Senator Nado | Glenn Shadix |
| Bon | Freda Foh Shen |
| Commander Karl Vasich | Chris Ellis |
| Lt. Col. Grace Alexander | Anne Ramsay |
| Major Maria Cooper | Andrea Grano |
| Major Frank Santos | Michael Jace |
| Specialist Hansen | Michael Wiseman |
| Nova | Lisa Marie |
| Leeta | Eileen Weisinger |
| Thade's Father | Charlton Heston |
| Gorilla Kid/Thade's Niece | Deep Roy |
| Red Ape Soldier/Man Hunt Ape | Chad Bannon |
| Limbo's 1st Handler/Ape Commande/2nd Ape Soldier | Kevin Grevioux |
| Limbo's 2nd Handler/1st Ape Soldier | Issac C. Singleton, Jr. |
| Ape Soldier | Quincy Taylor |
| Ape Dinner Guest/Old Man Servant/Old Ape #1 | John Alexander |
| 1st Ape Teenager/2nd Ape Soldier | Jay Caputo |
| 2nd Ape Teenager/Gossiping Male Ape | Philip Tan |
| Little Human Girl | Callie Croughwell |
| Girl Pet | Allie Habberstad |
| Human Kid #1 | Brett Smrz |
| Gorilla | Howard Berger |
| Old Ape #2 | Rick Baker |
| Fruit Vendor | Chet Zar |
| Woman in Cart | Linda Harrison |

and Cameron Croughwell, Joshua Croughwell, Hannah Peitzman, Molly Peitzman, Jesse Tipton, Shane Habberstad (Ape Soccer Kids); Eddie Adams, Todd Babcock, Lorenzo Callender, Shonda Farr, Kam Heskin, Jim Holmes, Todd Kimsey, Candace Kroslak, Joanna Krupa, Elizabeth Lackey, Mark Christopher Lawrence, Melody Perkins, Tate Taylor, Jonna Thompson (Friends at Leo's Party)

*Astronaut Leo Davidson goes through a time warp and crash-lands on a planet where apes rule over humans. Remake of the 1968 20th Century Fox film* Planet of the Apes; *two of the stars of that movie, Charlton Heston and Linda Harrison, make brief appearances here.*

© Twentieth Century Fox

# THE PRINCESS DIARIES

**(WALT DISNEY PICTURES)** Producers, Whitney Houston, Debra Martin Chase, Mario Iscovich; Director, Garry Marshall; Screenplay, Gina Wendkos; Based on the novel by Meg Cabot; Photography, Karl Walter Lindenlaub; Designer, Mayne Berke; Costumes, Gary Jones; Editor, Bruce Green; Music, John Debney; Music Supervisor, Dawn Solér; Co-Producer, Ellen H. Schwartz; Casting, Marcia Ross, Donna Morong, Gail Goldberg; a Brownhouse production; Distributed by Buena Vista Pictures; Dolby; Technicolor; Rated G; 114 minutes; Release date: August 3, 2001

## CAST

| | |
|---|---|
| Queen Clarisse Renaldi | Julie Andrews |
| Mia Thermopolis | Anne Hathaway |
| Joe | Hector Elizondo |
| Lilly Moscovitz | Heather Matarazzo |
| Lana Thomas | Mandy Moore |
| Mia's Mom, Helen | Caroline Goodall |
| Michael Moscovitz | Robert Schwartzman |
| Student Josh Bryant | Erik Von Detten |
| Student Jeremiah Hart | Patrick Flueger |
| Teacher Mr. O'Connell | Sean O'Bryan |
| Vice Principal Gupta | Sandra Oh |
| Charlotte Kutaway | Kathleen Marshall |
| Paolo | Larry Miller |

and Grove High School: Mindy Burbano (Gym Teacher Harbula), Kim Leigh (Music Teacher Wells), Beth Anne Garrison (Cheerleader Anna), Bianca Lopez (Cheerleader Fontana), Tamara Levinson (Cheerleader Lupe), Lenore Thomas (Cable Show Student Melissa), Erik Bragg (Student Bobby Bad), Abigail Green-Dove (Student Linda Green), Meredith Shevory (Student Meredith), Anita Marie Curran (Newspaper Student Anita), Korry Cannon (Newspaper Student Korry), Cassie Rowell (Singing Student Alice), Chrissy Gilman (Beach Student), Todd Lowe (Lana's Date Eric), Joe Unitas (Coach Joe Ewe), Reggie Stanton (Coach Dave Adams) The State Dinner: Joel McCrary (Prime Minister Motaz), Clare Sera (Mrs. Motaz), Juliet Elizondo (Daughter Marissa Motaz), Greg Lewis (Baron Siegfried von Troken), Bonnie Aarons (Baroness Joy von Troken), Darwood Chung (Emperor Sakamoto), Julie Paris (Princess Palisades), Jeff Michalski (Scottish Duke), Erin O'Reilly (Scottish Duchess), Steve Restivo (Count Vitello), Brigitta Lauren (Lady Lindenlaub), Jane Morris (Lady Evergreen), Gary Combs (Lord Fricker), Adam Williams (Dinner Guest Adam), Marvin Braverman, Alan Kent (State Dinner Waiters)

### The Genovian Consulate:

Bob Glaudini (Consulate Valet Adolpho), Bill Ferrell (Consulate Guard Darrell), Joe Ross (Consulate Maitre D'), Steve Totland (Consulate Waiter), Charles Guardino (Limo Driver Mel), Sparrow Heatley, Gwenda Perez (Gretchen & Helga), Barbara Marshall (Lady Jerome), Sam Denoff (Lord Jerome), Tracy Reiner (Press Secretary Spencer), Dale Hikawa (Band Leader Dawn Kawa), Daru Kawalkowski (Countess Puck), Diane Frazen (Ball Guest Diane), Stanley Frazen (Ball Guest Stanley), Barbara J. Nabozny (Ball Guest Barbara), Ira Glick (Ball Guest Dr. Glunk), Sol Rosenthal (Lawyer Ball Guest), Hope Alexander-Willis (Lady Caroline), Joe Allen Price (Father Joseph), Garry Marshall (Ball Guest), Major Willie L. Brown, Jr. (Himself)

### The San Franciscans:

Patrick Richwood (Neighbor Mr. Robutusen), John McGivern (Cable Car Conductor Macintosh), Terry Brown (Policeman Washington), James Brown Orleans (Doctor Motors), Rob Zylowski (Pizza Delivery Man), Karl Makinen (Climbing Manager Schiavone), Sunny Hawks (Climbing Instructor Vivian), Kathy Garver (Cable Tourist), Mary Knoll, Jason Ashland (Trolley Tourists), Erika Young (Umbrella Lady), Ethan Sandler (Tour Bus Driver), Bill Fricker (Autograph Father), Shan Elliot, Harold Carter (Michael's Band Flypaper), Bud Markowitz (Pear Juggler), Michelle Yerger, Wendy Hallin (911 Nuns), Mark Thompson, Brian W. Phelps (DJ's Mark & Brian), Lily Marshall-Fricker, Charlotte Marshall-Fricker (Kid Autograph Seekers)

### Reporters:

Sandra Taylor (Suki Sanchez), Tom Hines (Nelson Davenport), Nicholle Tom (Teen Repoter Cassie), Patrick Noonan (Suki's Cameraman), Ali Gage (Beach Reporter Ali), John Moran (Beach Photographer), Tanya DiFrancesco (Beach Reporter Tanya), Shannon Wilcox, Niloufar Safaie, Tonje Larsgard (Ball Reporters), Flora Chong, Reuben Grundy, Gwen Holloway (Street Reporters), Lori Sigrist, Terri Sigrist (Twin Reporters), Fat Louie (Himself)

*Mia Thermopolis, a drab, unpopular San Francisco high school girl, is stunned to find out that her grandmother is the queen of a small European principality, making Mia the rightful heiress to the throne.*

© Disney Enterprises, Inc.

Julie Andrews, Anne Hathaway

Anne Hathaway, Erik von Detten

Anne Hathaway,
Hector Elizondo

Chris Tucker, Jackie Chan

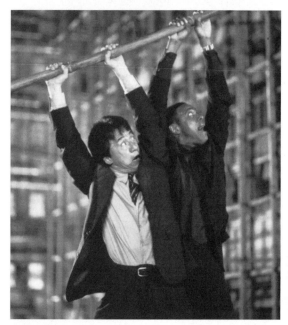

Chris Tucker

# RUSH HOUR 2

**(NEW LINE CINEMA)** Producers, Arthur Sarkissian, Roger Birnbaum, Jay Stern, Jonathan Glickman; Executive Producers, Andrew Z. Davis, Michael De Luca, Toby Emmerich; Director, Brett Ratner; Screenplay, Jeff Nathanson; Based on character created by Ross La Manna; Co-Executive Producer, Leon Dudevoir; Photography, Matthew F. Leonetti; Designer, Terence Marsh; Editor, Mark Helfrich; Costumes, Rita Ryack; Music, Lalo Schifrin; Stunts/2nd Unit Director, Conrad E. Palmisano; Casting, Matthew Barry, Nancy Green-Keyes; an Arthur Sarkissisan and Roger Birnbaum production; Dolby; Panavision; Deluxe color; Rated PG-13; 90 minutes; Release date: August 3, 2001.

## CAST

Chief Inspector Lee .................................................................Jackie Chan
Det. James Carter................................................................Chris Tucker
Ricky Tan ...............................................................................John Lone
Hu Li.....................................................................................Zhang Ziyi
Isabella ..........................................................................Roselyn Sanchez
Agent Sterling.........................................................................Harris Yulin
Steven Reign.............................................................................Alan King
Captain Chin.....................................................................Kenneth Tsang
Receptionist.....................................................................Lisa Lo Cicero
Girls in Car………....…………………….Meiling Melancon, Maggie Q.
Club Hostess..........................................................................Patricia Chan
Karaoke Singer.................................................................Gelbert Coloma
Message Parlor Hostess...............................................................Lucy Lin
Hostess #2 .................................................................................Cindy Lu
Suit Salesman ...................................................................Pang Wing Sang
Chicken Lady .................................................................Mei Ling Wong
Cab Driver........................................................................William Tuen
and Shawn Peretz (Flight Attendant), Audrey Quock (Kenny's Wife), Ernie Reyes, Jr. (Zing), Jeremy Piven (Versace Salesman), Verena Mei (Casino Waitress), Joel McKinnon Miller (Tex), Angela Little, Julia Schultz (Tex's Girlfriends), Saul Rubinek (Box Man), Gianni Russo (Pit Boss), James J. Ghang (Stickman), Michael Chow, Teresa Lin, Tanya Newbould, Matt Barry, James Duke (Gamblers), Don Cheadle (Kenny)

*Detectives Lee and Carter, on vacation in Hong Kong, find themselves investigating the bombing of the American Embassy, their trail of clues leading them to the head of the Fu-Cang-Long Triad, the deadliest gang in China. Sequel to the 1998 New Line Cinema release* Rush Hour *that also starred Jackie Chan and Chris Tucker.*

© New Line Cinema

Zhang Ziyi

Jackie Chan, Chris Tucker

Angelina Jolie, Thomas Jane

Angelina Jolie, Antonio Banderas

# ORIGINAL SIN

(MGM) Producers, Denise Di Novi, Kate Guinzburg, Carol Lees; Executive Producers, Sheldon Abend, Ashok Amritraj, David Hoberman; Director/Screenplay, Michael Cristofer; Based on the novel *Waltz Into Darkness* by Cornell Woolrich; Photography, Rodrigo Prieto; Designer, David J. Bomba; Costumes, Donna Zakowska; Music, Terence Blanchard; Song: "You Can't Walk Away From Me" by Gloria Estefan and Emilo Estefan, Jr./performed by Gloria Estefan; Co-Producer, Edward L. McDonnell; Line Producer, Michael S. Glick; Editor, Eric Sears; Casting, Junie Lowry Johnson, Libby Goldstein; a Via Rosa/Di Novi Pictures production in association with Intermedia/UGC International, presented in association with Hyde Park Entertainment; U.S.-French; Dolby; Panavision; Deluxe color; Rated R; 112 minutes; Release date: August 3, 2001

Angelina Jolie, Antonio Banderas

## CAST

| | |
|---|---|
| Luis Antonio Vargas | Antonio Banderas |
| Julia Russell/Bonny Castle | Angelina Jolie |
| Billy/Walter Downs/Mephisto | Thomas Jane |
| Alan Jordan | Jack Thompson |
| Colonel Worth | Gregory Itzin |
| Augusta Jordan | Allison Mackie |
| Sara | Joan Pringle |
| Emily Russell | Cordelia Richards |
| Faust (Stage) | James Haven |
| Jorge Cortés | Pedro Armendáriz |
| Cuban Priest | Mario Iván Martinez |
| Stage Manager | Harry Porter |
| Wedding Priest | Fernando Torre Lapham |
| Dressmaker Girl | Shaula Vega |
| Margareta (Stage) | Lisa Owen |

and Daniel Martinez (Rafael), Farnesio de Bernal (Bank Clerk), Nitzi Arellano (Prostitute), Roger Cudney (Ship's Captain), Adrián Makala (Ship's Waiter), Francis Laboriel (Ship's Stewardess), Patricio Castillo (French Dining Steward), Derek Rojo (Bell Boy), Abraham Stavans (Mr. Gutiérrez), Roberto Medina, Julian Sedgwick, Alejandro Corp (Card Players), Alejandro Reza (Train Station Man), Guy de Saint Cyr (Chief Jailer), Julio Bracho (Guard), George Belanger, Osami Kawano (Gentlemen in Morocco)

*Luis Vargas marries beautiful Julia Russell only to have her run off with his money, prompting him to look into her past and discover that she is a murderer.*

Angelina Jolie

Antonio Banderas, Angelina Jolie

© Metro-Goldwyn-Mayer Pictures, Inc.

Tilda Swinton

Goran Visnjic, Tilda Swinton

Tilda Swinton

# THE DEEP END

**(FOX SEARCHLIGHT)** Producers/Director/Screenplay, Scott McGehee, David Siegel; Based on the novel *The Blank Wall* by Elisabeth Sanxay Holding; Executive Producer, Robert H. Nathan; Photography, Giles Nuttgens; Editor, Lauren Zuckerman; Designers, Kelly McGehee, Christopher Tandon; Music, Peter Nashel; Associate Producers, Eileen Jones, Mindy Marin; Co-Producer, Laura Greenlee; Casting, Mindy Marin; an I5 Picture; Dolby; Panavision; FotoKem color; Rated R; 99 minutes; Release date: August 8, 2001

## CAST

| | |
|---|---|
| Margaret Hall | Tilda Swinton |
| Alex Spera | Goran Visnjic |
| Beau Hall | Jonathan Tucker |
| Jack Hall | Peter Donat |
| Darby Reese | Josh Lucas |
| Carlie Nagle | Raymond Barry |
| Paige Hall | Tamara Hope |
| Dylan Hall | Jordan Dorrance |
| Sue Lloyd | Heather Mathieson |
| Loan Officer | Holmes Osborne |
| Deputy Sheriff | Richard Gross |
| BVD | Kip Martin |
| Barrish Brother | Franco Delgado |
| Male Nurse | Kip Ellwood |
| Jackie | Margot Krindel |
| Heavy-Set Officer | Michael Pizzuto |

and Tajma Soleil (Nurse), F. W. McGehee (Music Teacher)

*When Margaret Hall discovers the corpse of the man with whom her son has been having an affair, she disposes of the body, only to be blackmailed by a mysterious stranger. Remake of the 1949 Columbia film* The Reckless Moment *that starred Joan Bennett and James Mason.*

© Twentieth Century Fox

Goran Visnjic, Tilda Swinton

## SESSION 9

**(USA FILMS)** Producers, David Collins, Dorothy Aufiero, Michael Williams; Executive Producer, John Sloss; Director/Editor, Brad Anderson; Screenplay, Brad Anderson, Stephen Gevedon; Photography, Uta Briesewitz; Designer, Sophie Carlhian; Costumes, Aimee McCue; Music, Climax Golden Twins; Executive Music Producer, Carson Daly; Casting, Sheila Jaffe, Georgianne Walken; a Scout production; Dolby; HD 24P Widescreen; Color; Rated R; 100 minutes; Release date: August 10, 2001

### CAST

| | |
|---|---|
| Phil. | David Caruso |
| Mike | Stephen Gevedon |
| Bill Griggs | Paul Guilfoyle |
| Hank | Josh Lucas |
| Gordon Fleming | Peter Mullan |
| Jeff | Brendan Sexton III |

and Charles Broderick (Security Guard), Lonnie Farmer (Voice of Doctor), Larry Fessenden (Craig McManus), Jurian Hughes (Voice of Mary Hobbes), Sheila Stasack (Voice of Wendy)

*A group of workmen employed to remove dangerous asbestos from the long-shuttered Danvers State Mental Hospital find themselves becoming unnerved by the mysteries that surround the asylum.*

© USA Films

David Caruso

Brendan Sexton III

Nastassja Kinski, Mae Whitman, Troy Goldwyn

Scarlett Johansson

## AN AMERICAN RHAPSODY

**(PARAMOUNT CLASSICS)** Producers, Colleen Camp, Bonnie Timmermann; Executive Producers, Jay Firestone, Adam Haight, Andrew G. Vajna; Co-Executive Producers, Tony Thatcher, Eric Sandys; Director/Screenplay, Éva Gardos; Co-Producer, Patricia Foulkrod; Associate Producers, Stephanie Poole, Teri Fettis D'Ovidio; Photography, Elemér Rágalyi; Designer, Alex Tavoularis; Costumes, Beatrix Aruna Pasztor, Vanessa Vogel; Editor, Margie Goodspeed; Music, Cliff Eidelman; Casting, Liz Lang Fedrick; a Fireworks Pictures and Peter Hoffman presentation of a Fireworks Entertainment/Seven Arts Pictures production in association with Colleen Camp and Bonnie Timmermann; Dolby; Color; Rated PG-13; 106 minutes; Release date: August 10, 2001

### CAST

| | |
|---|---|
| Margit | Nastassja Kinski |
| Suzanne (15 years old) | Scarlett Johansson |
| Peter | Tony Goldwyn |
| Maria (10 years old) | Mae Whitman |
| Jeno | Balazs Galko |
| Teri | Zsuzsa Czinkoczi |
| Suzanne (6 years old) | Kelly Endresz Banlaki |
| Pattie | Lisa Jane Persky |
| Dottie | Colleen Camp |
| Maria (18 years old) | Larisa Oleynik |

and Raffaella Bánsági (Suzanne, infant), Ági Bánfalvy (Helen), Zoltán Seress (George), Klaudia Szabó (Maria—4 years old), Zsolt Zágoni (Russian Soldier), András Szöke (István), Erzi Pásztor (Ilus), Carlos Laszlo Weiner (Boy on Train), Bori Keresztúri (Suzanne—3 years old), Péter Kállóy Molnár (AVO Officer), Zsuzsa Czinóczi (Teri), Balázs Galkó (Jeno), Kata Dobó (Claire), Éva Soreny (Eva), Don Pugsley (Cafe Supervisor), Vladimir Mashkov (Frank), Imola Gáspár (Stewardess), Tatyana Kanavka (Girl in Airport), Lorna Scott (Neighbor with Poodle), Sandra Staggs (Saleswoman), Jacqueline Steiger (Betty), Robert Lesser (Harold), Lou Beach (Partygoer), Marlee Jackson (Sheila—7 years old), Emmy Rossum (Sheila—15 years old), Timothy Everett Moore (Paul), Joshua Dov (Richard), Kati Bács, Zsuzsa Száger (Women at Market)

*Suzanne, left behind in Budapest while her parents settle in Los Angeles, is raised by an elderly couple. Her mother and father send for her years later, causing her great difficulty in adjusting to her new lifestyle.*

© Paramount Classics

# AMERICAN PIE 2

(UNIVERSAL) Producers, Warren Zide, Craig Perry, Chris Moore; Executive Producers, Adam Herz, Paul Weitz, Chris Weitz; Director, J. B. Rogers; Screenplay, Adam Herz; Story, David H. Steinberg, Adam Herz; Photography, Mark Irwin; Designer, Richard Toyon; Editors, Larry Madaras, Stuart Pappé; Co-Producers, Jane Bartelme, Chris Bender; Associate Producer, Stefan Frank; Music, David Lawrence; Music Supervisors, Gary Jones, Dave Jordan; Costumes, Alexandra Welker; Casting, Joseph Middleton, Michelle Morris Gertz; a Zide/Perry-Liveplanet production; Dolby; Panavision; Deluxe color; Rated R; 105 minutes; Release date: August 10, 2001

## CAST

Jim .................................................................................Jason Biggs
Nadia .......................................................................Shannon Elizabeth
Michelle ....................................................................Alyson Hannigan
Oz..............................................................................Chris Klein
Jessica ......................................................................Natasha Lyonne
Kevin ........................................................................Thomas Ian Nicholas
Vicky ..........................................................................Tara Reid
Stifler.........................................................................Seann William Scott
Heather....................................................................Mena Suvari
Finch ........................................................................Eddie Kaye Thomas
Jim's Dad .................................................................Eugene Levy
Sherman ...................................................................Chris Owen
Jim's Mom...............................................................Molly Cheek
and Denise Faye (Danielle), Lisa Arturo (Amber), John Cho (John), Justin Isfeld (Justin), Eli Marienthal (Stifler's Brother), Casey Affleck (Kevin's Brother), George Wyner (Camp Director), Steven Shenbaum (Counselor), Matthew Peters (Trumpet Kid), Joelle Carter (Natalie), Matthew Frauman (R.A.), Larry Drake (Natalie's Dad), Lee Garlington (Natalie's Mom), Tsianina Joelson (Amy), Bree Turner, Lacey Beeman (Amy's Friends), Lisa Gould (Woman in Bed), Brian Lester (Grand Harbor Sheriff), Nigel Gibbs (Cop), Ernie Lively (Sergeant), Kevin Cooney (Doctor), Marilyn Brett (Bus Driver), Morgan Nagler (Michelle's Friend), Jack Wallace (Enthusiastic Guy), Jesse Heiman (Petey), Joanna Garcia (Christy), Sarah Laine, Nora Zehetner (Girls at Party), David Smigelski, Luke Edwards, Adam Brody (High-School Guys), Amanda Armato (Cowboy Hat Girl), Nancy Stone (Mom), Kevin Kilner (Dad), Cole Petersen (Kid), Paityn James, Joseph D. Reitman (EMTs), Brian Turk (Trucker), Mike Erwin (Cashier), Robert Peters (Grill Guy), Amara Balthrop-Lewis, Jay Rossi (Deputies), Adam Herz (Younger Business Suit), J. B. Rogers (Older Business Suit), Brett Shuttleworth (Abercrombie & Fitch Guy), Amanda Wilmshurst, Devon Jackson (Finch Girls), Daniel Spink (Boy with Monkey), Tamia Richmond (Party Girl), Rachel Blasko (Amy's Friend), Laurie Ellan Reeves (College Party Girl), Derrick Harper (Counselor), Kelley Schneider (Deputy), Jennifer Coolidge

*After spending their first year apart at college, four friends rent a house together and spend a wild summer of partying and looking for the girls of their dreams. Sequel to the 1999 Universal film with most of the cast repeating their roles.*

© Universal Studios

Thomas Ian Nicholas, Jason Biggs,
Seann William Scott, Chris Klein

Alyson Hannigan

Shannon Elizabeth,
Jason Biggs

Joelle Carter, Jason Biggs, Molly Cheek,
Eugene Levy, Larry Drake

# OSMOSIS JONES

**(WARNER BROS.)** Producers, Bradley Thomas, Peter Farrelly, Bobby Farrelly, Zak Penn, Dennis Edwards; Directors, Peter Farrelly, Bobby Farrelly; Animation Directors, Piet Kroon, Tom Sito; Screenplay, Marc Hyman; Photography, Mark Irwin; Designers, Sidney Jackson Bartholomew, Jr.; Costumes, Pamela Ball Withers; Editors, Lois Freeman-Fox, Stephen R. Schaffer, Sam Seig; Music, Randy Edelman; Animation Production Designer, Steve Pilchar; Supervising Animators, Richard Bazley, Dave Brewster, Ricardo Curtis, Tony Fucile, Wendy Perdue, Dean Wellins; Digital and CGI EFX Designer, Allen Foster; 2-D Effects Designer, Caroline Hu; Casting, Rick Montgomery; a Conundrum Entertainment production; Dolby; Clairmont-Scope; Technicolor; Rated PG; 95 minutes; Release date: August 10, 2001

Osmosis Jones

## CAST

Frank ..................................................................Bill Murray
Mrs. Boyd ..........................................................Molly Shannon
Bob......................................................................Chris Elliott
Shane. .................................................................Elena Franklin
and Danny Murphy (Zookeeper Superintendent), Jack McCullough (Zookeeper), Kathy Wege (Volcano Lady), Will Dunn (Oyster Boy), Jackie Flynn (School Janitor), Kelsey Jordan, Anna Byers (Bus Girls), Jesse Peter (Laughing Boy), John Jordan (Pea Soup Manager), Nancy Byers (Pea Soup Supervisor), Kevin Flynn (Docky's Clamshack Waiter), Sean Gildea (Dreamy Photographer), Kathryn Frick, Nikki Tyler-Flynn, Elizabeth Jordan (Nurses), Zen Gesner, Marc Hyman, Zak Penn (Emergency Room Doctors), Nicole Brathwaite, Brianna Cabral, Chandler Vuilleumier, Emily O'Day, Catherine Dunphy (The Volcano Gals), Bill Wade, Bruce McIntyre, Bo Cleary (Pea Soup Staff), Brian Mone, Sean Fitzgerald (Police Officers), Beth Jordan, Mattie Ostiguy, Grace Costa, Maura O'Brien (Emergency Room Nurses)

The Chief, Osmosis Jones

## VOICE CAST

Osmosis Jones........................................................Chris Rock
Thrax......................................................................Laurence Fishburne
Drix ........................................................................David Hyde Pierce
Leah........................................................................Brandy Norwood
The Mayor ..............................................................William Shatner
Tom Colonic ..........................................................Ron Howard
and Robert "Kid Rock" Tichie, Joe C, Uncle Kracker, Kenny Olson, Stefanie Eulenberg, Jason Krause, Jimmie Bones (Kidney Rocks), Jonathan Adams, Carlos Alazraqui, Keith Anthony, Eddie Barth, Sally Ann Brooks, Rodger Bumpass, Michael Carven, Paul Christie, Janis Dardaris, Wendy Dillon, Antonio Fargas, Eddie Frierson, Don Fullilove, Jackie Gonneau, Rif Hutton, Richard Horvitz, Art Kimbro, Joyce Kurtz, Anne Lockhart, Sherry Lynn, Danny Mann, Mickie McGowan, "Stuttering" John Melendez, Hector Mercado, Paul Pape, Marilyn Pasekoff, Chris Phillips, Lynne Redding, Al Rodrigo, Herschel Sparber, Doug Stone, Steve Susskind, Keri Tombazian, Paul Tuerpé, Robert Wisdom (Additional Character Voices)

Elena Franklin, Bill Murray

*A zookeeper in poor health eats a tainted hard-boiled egg prompting the white blood cell police within his body to try to track down the viruses.*

© Warner Bros.

Bill Murray, Chris Elliott

Thrax

Penélope Cruz, Nicholas Cage

Christian Bale

# CAPTAIN CORELLI'S MANDOLIN

**(UNIVERSAL/MIRAMAX)** Producers, Tim Bevan, Eric Fellner, Kevin Loader, Mark Huffam; Director, John Madden; Screenplay, Shawn Slovo; Based on the novel by Louis De Bernieres; Photography, John Toll; Designer, Jim Clay; Costumes, Alexandra Byrne; Editor, Mick Audsley; Music, Stephen Warbeck; Co-Producers, Jane Frazer, Debra Hayward, Liza Chasin; Casting, Mary Selway; a Universal Pictures/Studio Canal/Miramax presentation of a Working Title production; U.S.-British; Dolby; Panavision; Deluxe color; Rated R; 127 minutes; Release date: August 17, 2001

## CAST

| | |
|---|---|
| Captain Antonio Corelli | Nicolas Cage |
| Pelagia | Penélope Cruz |
| Dr. Iannis | John Hurt |
| Mandras | Christian Bale |
| Weber | David Morrissey |
| Drosoula | Irene Papas |
| Carlo | Piero Maggió |
| Stamatis | Gerasimos Skiadaresis |

### The Greeks:

Aspasia Kralli (Mrs. Stamatis), Michalis Giannatos (Kokolios), Dimitris Kamperidis (Father Arsenios), Pedro Sarubbi (Velisarios—The Strongman), Viki Maragaki (Eleni, Pelagia's Friend), Joanna-Daria Adraktas (Lemoni—Younger), Ira Tavlaridis (Lemoni—Older), Katerina Didaskalou (Lemoni's Mother), Emilios Chilakis (Dimitris), Nikos Karathanos (Spiros), Antonis Antoniou (Recruiting Officer), George Kotanidis (Mayor), Tasos Palantzidis (Town Clerk), Kostas Philippoglou (Trembling Man), Froso Korrou (Nun), Maria-Louisa Papadopoulou, Dina Kaferani, Vlassis Zotis, Panagiotis Thanassoulis, Alexia Bouloukou (The Mad People), Babis Artelaris, Gerasimos Iakovatos, Nikos Kalogiratos, Dionysis Karlis, Pavlos Lalis, Angelos Liberatos, Panagis Polichronatos, Christos Rangas, Dimitris Vandoros, Gerasimos Xidias (The Partisans), Dimitris Dimoulas, Pantelis Filipatos, Ilias Theofilatos, Makis Filipatos (Musicians)

### The Italians:

Vincenzo Ricotta (Quartermaster), Roberto Citran (General Ganadin), Federico Fioresi, Sandro Stefanini, Francesco Guzzo, Germano Di Mattia, Simone Spinazzé, Sergio Albelli, Davide Quataro, Paco Reconti, Nuccio Siano, Salvatore Lazzaro, Alessandro Repossi (The Soldiers of La Scal), Massimiliano Pazzaglia (Captain), Tim Hardy (Colonel), Francesco Cabras (Soldier with Cigarette), Nunzio Lombardo (Soldier at Dance), Irini Eleftheriou, Sofia Yannioti, Marina Corelli, Evi Tzortzi, Leticia Moustaki, Angelica Lambri, Maria Philipakopoulou, Irene Christidi (Prostitutes), Giovanni Parricelli, Martin Robertson, Ben Gant, Paul Spong, Eddie Hession, Mike Pickering, Oren Marshall (Waterfront Band)

### The Germans:

Patrick Malahide (Colonel Barge), Martin Glyn Murray, Till Bahlmann, Renny Krupinski (Officers), Peter Stark (Soldier)

*During World War II, Captain Corelli and his troops arrive on the isolated Greek Island of Cephallonia, prompting initial resentment from the inhabitants, including Pelagia, who ultimately finds herself falling for the charming captain.*

© Universal Studios

John Hurt, Penélope Cruz

Wayne Knight,
Rowan Atkinson

# RAT RACE

(PARAMOUNT) Producers, Jerry Zucker, Janet Zucker, Sean Daniel; Executive Producers, James Jacks, Richard Vane; Director, Jerry Zucker; Screenplay, Andy Breckman; Photography, Thomas Ackerman; Designer, Gary Frutkoff; Costumes, Ellen Mirojnick; Editor, Tom Lewis; Music, John Powell; Music Supervisor, Bonnie Greenberg-Goldman; Stunts, Tim Gilbert, John Scott; Casting, Jane Jenkins, Janet Hirshenson; an Alphaville/Zucker production, presented in association with Fireworks Pictures; Dolby; Panavision; Deluxe color; Rated PG-13; 112 minutes; Release date: August 17, 2001

## CAST

| | |
|---|---|
| Enrico Pollini | Rowan Atkinson |
| Donald Sinclair | John Cleese |
| Vera Baker | Whoopi Goldberg |
| Owen Templeton | Cuba Gooding, Jr. |
| Duane Cody | Seth Green |
| Randy Pear | Jon Lovitz |
| Nick Shaffer | Breckin Meyer |
| Beverly Bear | Kathy Najimy |
| Tracy Faucet | Amy Smart |

and Wayne Knight (Zack), Paul Rodriguez (Gus), Vince Vieluf (Blaine Cody), Lanai Chapman (Merrill Jennings), Dean Cain (Shawn), Dave Thomas (Mr. Grisham), Kathy Bates (Squirrel Lady), Jenica Bergere (Hotel Clerk), Carrie Diamond (Casino Bartender), Douglas Haase (Guy at Bar), Chris Myers, Kevin Frazier (Fox Sportscasters), Gloria Allred (Herself), Renee Lee (Witness in Crowd), Corinna Harney Jones, Jane C. Walsh (Cocktail Waitresses), Jillian Marie Hubert (Kimberly Pear), Brody Smith (Jason Pear), Andrew Kavovit (Richie), Mallory Sandler (Guest Services Clerk), Gerard Plunkett, Martin Evans, L. Harvey Gold, David Lereaney, Andy Maton, Manoj Sood, Philip Tsui, Allan Lysell (High Rollers), Marcos Menendez (Other Cabby), Catherine Schreiber (Ticket Agent), Joel Hurt Jones (Charter Pilot), Daryl Sullivan (Man in Line), Kevin Rothery (Air Traffic Controller), Jake Bendel (U Rent It Clerk), Guy Cohen (Rental Car Trainee), Susan Breslau (Rental Car Manager), Steven Tingle, Jared Van Snellenberg (Skinhead Tour Guides), Paul Hayes (Lucy Bus Driver), Anaya Farrell, Peggy Jo Jacobs, Linda Kerns, Christine MacInnis, Christopher Peterson, Deborah Theaker, Roxanne Wong, Charlotte Zucker (Lucys), Kate Zucker (Girl in Lobby), Bob Zucker (Boy in Lobby), Silas Weir Mitchell (Lloyd), Deryl Hayes (Sleeping Trooper), Joanne Resnick (Biker Woman), Gene LeBell (Veteran with Gun), Brandy Ledford (Vicky), John Duerler (Caterer), Rick Cramer (Test Driver), Mike Garibaldi (Press Spokesman), Kathleen Marshall (Reporter), Vic Chao (Engineer), Colleen Camp (Rainbow House Nurse), Junior Ray (Truck Driver), Tristin Leffler (Pierced Girl), Marty Antonini (Monster Truck Driver), Tyler Gauthier, Matthew Gauthier (Baby on Train), Shannon Anderson (Mother), Brian Stollery (Father), Gillian Skupa (Stewardess), Greg Camp, Paul De Lisle, Steve Harwell, Marc Cervantes, Michael Klooster, Michael Urbano (Smash Mouth), Rance Howard (Feed the Earth Spokesman), Lucy Lee Flippin (Feed the Earth Spokeswoman), Jennifer Rugamas (Feed the Earth Girl), Mason Jones (Feed the Earth Boy)

*Las Vegas casino tycoon Donald Sinclair invites six random people to participate in a treasure hunt, giving each of them the key to a locker in Silver City, New Mexico, in which two million dollars in cash is stashed.*

© Paramount Pictures

Christopher Peterson, Cuba Gooding, Jr.

Whoopi Goldberg, John Cleese, Breckin Meyer, Cuba Gooding, Jr., Rowan Atkinson

Jon Lovitz, Seth Green, Amy Smart, Vince Vieluf, Whoopi Goldberg, Rowan Atkinson, Cuba Gooding, Jr., Breckin Meyer, Lanai Chapman

## AMERICAN OUTLAWS

**(WARNER BROS.)** Producer, James G. Robinson; Executive Producer, Jonathan A. Zimbert; Director, Les Mayfield; Screenplay, Roderick Taylor, John Rogers; Story, Roderick Taylor; Photography, Russell Boyd; Designers, Cary White, John Frick; Costumes, Luke Reichle; Editor, Michael Tronick; Music, Trevor Rabin; Music Supervisor, Maureen Crowe; Casting, Pam Dixon Mickelson; a James G. Robinson presentation of a Morgan Creek production; Dolby; FotoKem color; Rated PG-13; 93 minutes; Release date: August 17, 2001

### CAST

| | |
|---|---|
| Jesse James | Colin Farrell |
| Cole Younger | Scott Caan |
| Zee Mimms | Ali Larter |
| Frank James | Gabriel Macht |
| Jim Younger | Gregory Smith |
| Thaddeus Rains | Harris Yulin |
| Ma James | Kathy Bates |
| Allan Pinkerton | Timothy Dalton |
| Bob Younger | Will McCormack |
| Doc Mimms | Ronny Cox |
| Rollin Parker | Terry O'Quinn |

and Nathaniel Arcand (Comanche Tom), Ty O'Neal (Clell Miller), Joe Stevens (Loni Packwood), Barry Tubb (Capt. Malcolm), Jack Watkins (Detective), Tom Schuster (Union Officer), Lee Ritchey (Bank Manager), Robin Christian (Woman), Ed Geldart (Old Man Tucker), Brad Leland (Sheriff), Craig Erickson (Deputy), Mark Walters (Engineer), Michael Costello (Senator), Jack Gould (Head Teller), Morgana Shaw (Lyla), Brady Coleman (Driver), Richard Jones (Pastor), Steven "Dooky" Bland (Man), Jerry Cotton (Teller), Muse Watson (Burly Detective), Lane Thomas Wilson (Boy Soldier), Rony Hayden (Union Lieutenant), Darryl Cox (Jenkins), Riley Flynn (Union Commander), Joe Brown (Pinkerton Commander), Shawn Patrick Nash (Hangman), Jessica Nitsch (Loni's Girl)

*The story of how Jesse James and the Younger brothers formed a gang and became the most notorious outlaws in the Old West. Previous films on the Jesse James saga include* Jesse James *(20th, 1939; with Tyrone Power),* Bad Men of Missouri *(WB, 1941; Alan Baxter),* Kansas Raiders *(Univ, 1950; Audie Murphy),* The Great Missouri Raid *(Par, 1950; Macdonald Carey),* The True Story of Jesse James *(20th, 1956; Robert Wagner),* Young Jesse James *(20th, 1960; Ray Stricklyn), and* The Great Northfield Minnesota Raid *(Univ, 1972; Robert Duvall).*

© Morgan Creek Productions, Inc.

(Top) Colin Farrell, Ali Larter. (Bottom) Will McCormack, Gregory Smith, Colin Farrell, Scott Caan, Gabriel Macht

Laura Kirk, Nat DeWolf, Daniel London

Laura Kirk, Nat DeWolf

## LISA PICARD IS FAMOUS

**(FIRST LOOK)** Producers, Mira Sorvino, Dolly Hall; Executive Producers, Sidney Kimmel, John Penotti, Fisher Stevens, Bradley Yonover, Andrew S. Karsch; Director, Griffin Dunne; Screenplay, Nat DeWolf, Laura Kirk; Photography, William Rexer II; Designer, Mark Ricker; Costumes, Denise Walch; Editor, Nancy Baker; Music, Evan Lurie; Music Supervisor, Barry Cole; Line Producer, Exile Ramirez; Co-Producer, Celeste Peterka; a Stella Maris Films and Dolly Hall production in association with Sidney Kimmel Entertainment/GreeneStreet Films/Longfellow Pictures; Color; Not rated; 87 minutes; Release date: August 22, 2001

### CAST

| | |
|---|---|
| Lisa Picard | Laura Kirk |
| Tate Kelley | Nat DeWolf |
| Boyfriend | Daniel London |
| Andrew | Griffin Dunne |
| Leslie Fitzgerald | Leslie Lyles |
| David Holzman | L. M. Kit Carson |
| Anna Chenier | Sharon Washington |
| Brenda | Joelle Carter |
| Caroline Huff | Karen Kayser |

and Jack Howard (Commercial Stud), Rosanna Scotto (TV Reporter), Neil Butterfield, Robert Rodriguez (Punks), Daniella Rich (Sandy's Assistant), Jeff Whitty (Greg), James Yaegashi (Alex), Sam Catlin (Michael), Tony Rigo (Bartender), Zofia Borucka (Soap Actress), Mark Mortimer (Paul), Sarah Jones (Kirsta), Judie Aronson (Liz), Michael Malone (Jeff), Virginia Louise Smith (Amanda), Quentin Mare (Ken), Gregory Arata (Tate's Boyfriend), Carrie Fisher, Buck Henry, Spike Lee, Charlie Sheen, Mira Sorvino, Fisher Stevens (Themselves)

*Lisa Picard, a struggling, hopelessly self-deluded actress, searches for fame in this mock documentary.*

© First Look Pictures

Woody Allen, David Ogden Stiers, Helen Hunt

Woody Allen

Dan Aykroyd, Helen Hunt

Charlize Theron, Woody Allen

# THE CURSE OF THE JADE SCORPION

**(DREAMWORKS)** Producer, Letty Aronson; Executive Producer, Stephen Tenenbaum; Co-Producer, Helen Robin; Co-Executive Producers, Datty Ruth, Jack Rollins, Charles H. Joffe; Director/Screenplay, Woody Allen; Photography, Zhao Fei; Designer, Santo Loquasto; Costumes, Suzanne McCabe; Editor, Alisa Lepselter; Casting, Juliet Taylor, Laura Rosenthal; a Gravier production, presented in association with VCL Licensing GmbH; Dolby; Technicolor; Rated PG-13; 103 minutes; Release date: August 24, 2001

## CAST

| | |
|---|---|
| CW Briggs | Woody Allen |
| Chris Magruder | Dan Aykroyd |
| Jill | Elizabeth Berkley |
| Betty Ann Fitzgerald | Helen Hunt |
| Al | Brian Markinson |
| George Bond | Wallace Shawn |
| Voltan | David Ogden Stiers |
| Laura Kensington | Charlize Theron |
| Sam | John Tormey |
| Mize | John Schuck |
| Rosie | Kaili Vernoff |
| Office Workers | Maurice Sonnenberg, John Doumanian |
| Ned | Peter Gerety |
| Lunch Delivery Man | Kevin Cahoon |
| Rocky's Waiter | Phil Levy |

and Vince Giordano, Howard Alden, Ted Sommer, Randy Sandke, Peter Ecklund, Joel Helleny, Chuck Wilson, Ray Beckenstein, Lawrence Feldman, Ken Peplowski (Rainbow Room All Stars), Dick Hyman (Band Leader), Carole Bayeux (Voltan's Assistant), Kenneth Edelson, Brian McConnachie, Judy Gold (Voltan's Participants), Herb Lovelle (Night Guard), Carmen (Rose Kensington), Patrick Horgan, Howard Erskine, Ira Wheeler, Tina Sloan (Kensington Guests), Ramsey Faragallah (Fingerprint Detective), Bob Dorian (Mike), Arthur Nascarella (Tom), Trude Klein (Kensington Maid), Professor Irwin Corey (Charlie), Michael Mulheren (Herb Coopersmith), Peter Linari (Joe Coopersmith), Ray Garvey (Police Station Cop), Bruce Brown (Radio Announcer), Dan Moran (Street Contact)

*CW Briggs, a top insurance investigator, is unwittingly hypnotized into committing robberies that he, in his conscious state, tries to solve.*

© DreamWorks LLC

Jason Mewes, Kevin Smith, Ben Affleck

Chris Rock

Will Ferrell, Kevin Smith, Jason Mewes, Jennifer
Schwalbach, Eliza Dushku, Ali Larter

Kevin Smith,
Jason Mewes

# JAY AND SILENT BOB STRIKE BACK

(DIMENSION) Producer, Scott Mosier; Executive Producers, Bob
Weinstein, Harvey Weinstein, Jonathan Gordon; Director/Screenplay,
Kevin Smith; Co-Producer, Laura Greenlee; Photography, Jamie Anderson;
Designer, Robert "Ratface" Holtzman; Editors, Kevin Smith, Scott Mosier;
Music, James L. Venable; Costumes, Isis Mussenden; Visual Effects
Supervisor, Joseph Grossberg; Casting, Christine Sheaks; a View Askew pro-
duction; Distributed by Miramax Films; Dolby; Super 35 Widescreen;
Deluxe color; Rated R; 104 minutes; Release date: August 24, 2001

## CAST

| | |
|---|---|
| Jay | Jason Mewes |
| Silent Bob | Kevin Smith |
| Holden/Chuckie/Himself | Ben Affleck |
| Sissy | Eliza Dushku |
| Justice | Shannon Elizabeth |
| Willenholly | Will Ferrell |
| Chrissy | Ali Larter |
| Brodie/Banky | Jason Lee |
| Chaka | Chris Rock |
| Hitchhiker | George Carlin |
| Cock-Knocker | Mark Hamill |
| Nun | Carrie Fisher |
| Dante | Brian O'Halloran |
| Randal | Jeff Anderson |
| Brent | Seann William Scott |
| Alyssa | Joey Lauren Adams |
| Reg Hartner | Jon Stewart |
| Sheriff | Judd Nelson |
| Dealer | Tracy Morgan |
| Missy | Jennifer Schwalbach |

and Amy Noble (Baby Bob's Mother), Harley Quinn Smith (Baby Silent Bob),
Ever Carradine (Baby Jay's Mother), Brian Andrew Saible (Baby Jay), Gavin
Brooks (Baby Jay Voice), John Willyung (Passerby), Jake Richardson, Nick
Fellinger (Teens), Vincent Pereira (Customer), Ernest O'Donnell (Cop), Marc
Blucas (Guy), Matthew James (Dude), Jane Silvia (Bookish Girl), Carmen
Llywellyn (Beauty), Dan Etheridge (Deputy), Eric Winzenried, Jonathan
Gordon, John Maynard, Robert H. Holtzman, Tom Dorfmeister (Cops), Tango
(Suzanne), Joe Quesada (Pizza Delivery Guy), Michelle Anne Johnson, Merritt
Hicks (Hookers), Steve Kmetko, Jules Asner, Gus Van Sant, Shannen Doherty,
Wes Craven, Jason Biggs, James Van Der Beek, Matt Damon (Themselves),
Diedrich Bader (Security Guard), Scott Mosier (AD "GWH2" William/Guy),
James J. McLauchlin (Clapper/Loader "GWH2"), Scott Winters (Clark), Joseph
D. Reitman (AD "Bluntman & Chronic"), Jamie Kennedy (PA), Paul Dini
(Clapper/Loader "Bluntman & Chronic"), Quentin Wright (William Dusky),
Gregory Owen (Suburban Kid), Ralph Meyer (Receptionist), Bryan Johnson
(Steve-Dave), Walter Flannigan (Walt), Renee Humphrey (Trish), Dwight Ewell
(Hooper), Alanis Morrissette (God), Morris E. Day, Jerome Benton, Stanley
Howard, Gary Johnson, Monte Moir, Torrell Ruffin, Ricky Smith (Morris Day
and the Time)

*New Jersey slackers Jay and Silent Bob head for Hollywood to stop an unau-*
*thorized movie about their alter egos, Bluntman & Chronic.*

© Dimension Films

# TORTILLA SOUP

**(SAMUEL GOLDWYN FILMS)** Producer, John Bard Manulis; Executive Producer, Samuel Goldwyn, Jr.; Director, Maria Ripoll; Screenplay, Ramón Menéndez, Tom Musca, Vera Blasi; Based on the screenplay *Eat Drink Man Woman* by Hui-Ling Wang, Ang Lee, James Schamus; Co-Producer, Lulu Zezza; Associate Producer, Meyer Gottlieb; Photography, Xavier Perez Grobet; Designer, Alicia Maccarone; Costumes, Ileane Meltzer; Music, Bill Conti; Music Supervisor, Julianne Jordan; Editor, Andy Blumenthal; Food and Menus Created and Designed by Mary Sue Milliken, Susan Feniger; Casting, Junie Lowry Johnson, Libby Goldstein, Claudia Becker; a Samuel Goldwyn production, presented in association with Starz/Encore Entertainment; Dolby; Color; Rated PG-13; 110 minutes; Release date: August 24, 2001

## CAST

| | |
|---|---|
| Martin Naranjo | Hector Elizondo |
| Carmen Naranjo | Jacqueline Obradors |
| Leticia Naranjo | Elizabeth Peña |
| Maribel Naranjo | Tamara Mello |
| Andy | Nikolai Kinski |
| Orlando | Paul Rodriguez |
| Hortensia | Raquel Welch |
| Yolanda | Constance Marie |
| Antonio Urgell | Joel Joan |

and Jade Herrera (Eden), Troy Ruptash (Hairdresser), Ken Marino (Jeff), Marisabel Garcia (April), Julio Oscar Mechoso (Gomez), Louis Crugnali (Catering Assistant), Ulysses Cuadra (Snide Student), Mark de la Cruz, Eli Russell Linnetz (April's Classmates), Stoney Westmoreland (Baseball Umpire), Karen Dyer (Jeff's Girlfriend)

*The three Naranjo sisters, who have been devoted to their master-chef father, find their destinies taking them in directions that threaten family tradition.*

© Samuel Goldwyn Films

Jason Statham, Natasha Henstridge, Ice Cube

(Top) Tamara Mello, Jacqueline Obradors, Elizabeth Peña
(Bottom) Hector Elizondo, Raquel Welch

# John Carpenter's GHOSTS OF MARS

**(SCREEN GEMS)** Producer, Sandy King; Director/Music, John Carpenter; Screenplay, Larry Sulkis, John Carpenter; Photography, Gary B. Kibbe; Designer, William Elliott; Costumes, Robin Michel Bush; Special Makeup Effects, Robert Kurtzman, Greg Nicotero, Howard Berger; Editor, Paul Warschilka; Visual Effects Supervisor, Lance Wilhoite; Casting, Reuben Cannon; a Storm King production; Dolby; Panavision; Deluxe color; Rated R; 97 minutes; Release date: August 24, 2001

## CAST

| | |
|---|---|
| James "Desolation" Williams | Ice Cube |
| Lt. Melanie Ballard | Natasha Henstridge |
| Jericho Butler | Jason Statham |
| Helena Braddock | Pam Grier |
| Bashira Kincaid | Clea Duvall |
| Whitlock | Joanna Cassidy |
| Michael Descanso | Liam Waite |
| Akooshay | Wanda DeJesus |
| Uno | Duane Davis |
| Dos | Lobo Sebastian |
| Tres | Rodney A. Grant |
| Rodale | Robert Carradine |
| McSimms | Peter Jason |

and Danielle Burgio (Local Cop), Damon Caro (Shape—Male Intern), Richard Cetrone (Big Daddy Mars), Charlotte Cornwell (Narrator), Rick Edelstein (Zimmerman), Rosemary Forsyth (Inquisitor), Marjean Holden (Young Woman), Michael Krawic (Man in Rover), Rex Linn (Yared), Doug McRath (Benchley), Matt Nolan (Miner), Chad Randall (Big Warrior), Eileen Weisinger (Warrior)

*The Martian Police Force arrives at one of the planet's mining colonies to track down an escaped con, only to find themselves facing former miners who have been infected and driven crazy by a deadly force.*

© Screen Gems, a Sony Pictures Entertainment Company

# HAPPY ACCIDENTS

**(IFC FILMS)** Producer, Susan A. Stover; Executive Producers, Jonathan Sehring, Caroline Kaplan, John Sloss; Director/Screenplay/Editor, Brad Anderson; Photography, Terry Stacey; Designer, Susan Block; Costumes, Victoria Farrell; Line Producer, Derrick Tseng; Music, Evan Lurie; Music Supervisor, Linda Cohen; Executive Music Producer, Alex Steyermark; Casting, Sheila Jaffe, Georgianne Walken; an Accidental production; Color; Rated R; 110 minutes; Release date: August 24, 2001

## CAST

| | |
|---|---|
| Ruby Weaver | Marisa Tomei |
| Sam Deed | Vincent D'Onofrio |
| Gretchen | Nadia Dajani |
| Therapist | Holland Taylor |
| Lillian | Tovah Feldshuh |
| Mark | Sean Gullette |
| Victor | Bronson Dudley |
| Jose | Jose Zuniga |
| Sunil | Jason Chandani |
| Bette | Cara Buono |

and Liana Pai (Claire), Tamara Jenkins (Robin), Richard Portnow (Trip), Saidah Arrika Ekulona (Nurse), Mick Weber (Floor Supervisor), Sam Seder (Ned), Lyn Vaus (Pharmacist), Anthony Michael Hall (Famous Actor), Jon Benjamin, Kathryn Tucker (Revelers), Mike McGlone (Tab), Dan Frazer (Voice of Tom Deed), Michael Buscemi (Pedestrian), Joreen Baquilod (Korean Girl), Elizabeth Gajadharsingh (Sunil's Young Daughter), Steve Gevodan (Frenchman), Larry Fessenden (Junkie), Robert Stanton (Fetishist), Neal Huff (Artist)

*Ruby Weaver, a woman who has pretty much given up on relationships, meets Sam Deed and falls in love with him, only to have him claim that he is a time traveler from the year 2470.*

Jessica Biel, Freddie Prinze, Jr.

Marc Blucas, Matthew Lillard, Freddie Prinze, Jr.

© IFC Films

Vincent D'Onofrio, Marisa Tomei

Holland Taylor

# SUMMER CATCH

**(WARNER BROS.)** Producers, Mike Tollin, Brian Robbins, Sam Weisman; Executive Producer, Herb Gains; Director, Mike Tollin; Screenplay, Kevin Falls, John Gatins; Story, Kevin Falls; Photography, Tim Suhrstedt; Designer, John D. Kretschmer; Costumes, Juliet Polsca; Editor, Harvey Rosenstock; Music, George Fenton; Baseball Coordinator, Mark Ellis; Casting, Marci Liroff; a Tollin/Robbins production; Dolby; Technicolor; Rated PG-13; 104 minutes; Release date: August 24, 2001

## CAST

| | |
|---|---|
| Ryan Dunne | Freddie Prinze, Jr. |
| Tenley Parrish | Jessica Biel |
| Billy Brubaker | Matthew Lillard |
| John Schiffner | Brian Dennehy |
| Sean Dunne | Fred Ward |
| Mike Dunne | Jason Gedrick |
| Dede Mulligan | Brittany Murphy |
| Rand Parrish | Bruce Davison |
| Miles Dalrymple | Marc Blucas |
| Mickey Dominguez | Wilmer Valderrama |

and Corey Pearson (Eric Van Leemer), Christian Kane (Dale Robin), Cedric Pendleton (Calvin Knight), Gabriel Mann (Auggie), Jed Robert Rhein (Pete), Zena Grey (Katie Parrish), Beverly D'Angelo (House Mother), John C. McGinley (Phillies' Scout), Curt Gowdy, Pat Burrell, Dave Collins, Doug Glanville, Ken Griffey, Jr., Jeff Kellogg, Mike Lieberthal, Hank Aaron (Themselves), Dick Allen (Scout in Black Hat), Randi Layne (Vivi Parrish), Traci Dinwiddie (Lauren), Susan Gardner (Marjorie), Jack Baun (Chris Hunt), Tammy Christine Arnold (Vassar Graduate), Tim Lucason (Hyannis Batter), Kenny Gasperson (Statistician), Mark Robert Ellis (Umpire), Herbert W. Gains (Angry Fan), Thaddeus Hill (Coach Sully), Brock Kenne (Chatham Pitcher), Mike Ribaudo, Matt Hobbie (Chatham A's)

*Ryan Dunne, a young man hoping to make it into the major leagues, gets his big chance to impress the talent scouts, but he must overcome his low self-esteem and habit of choking under pressure.*

© Warner Bros.

Mekhi Phifer

Rain Phoenix, Julia Stiles

# O

(LIONS GATE) Producers, Eric Gitter, Anthony Rhulen, Daniel L. Fried; Executive Producers, Michael I. Levy, William Shively; Director, Tim Blake Nelson; Screenplay, Brad Kaaya; Photography, Russell Lee Fine; Designer, Dina Goldman; Costumes, Jill Ohanneson; Co-Executive Producers, Fredrick B. Goodman, Stephen A. Kepniss; Associate Producers, Brad Kaaya, Zack Estrin; Co-Producers, Betsey Danbury, Lisa Gitter; Music, Jeff Danna; Music Supervisor, Barry Cole; Editor, Kate Sanford; Casting, Avy Kaufman; a Chickie the Cop production in association with Filmengine and Daniel Fried productions; Dolby; Deluxe color; Rated R; 95 minutes; Release date: August 31, 2001

## CAST

| | |
|---|---|
| Odin James | Mekhi Phifer |
| Hugo Goulding | Josh Hartnett |
| Desi Brable | Julia Stiles |
| Coach Duke Goulding | Martin Sheen |
| Roger | Elden Henson |
| Michael Casio | Andrew Keegan |
| Emily | Rain Phoenix |
| Dell | Anthony "A. J." Johnson |
| Dean Brable | John Heard |
| Assistant Coach | Chris Freihofer |
| Dutchman Player | Christopher Dong |
| Brandy | Rachel Schumate |
| Radio Announcer | Marshall Gitter |
| Ms. Serney | Lisa Benavides |
| Scout #1 | Ken French |

and Dana Ratliff (TV Announcer), Christopher Jones (Jason), Ronalda Stover (Score Keeper), Kelvin O'Bryant (Ball Boy), Jack "Jay" Munn (Lanny), Mike Flippo (Mr. Bradley), James Middleton (Cop), Julie Fishell (Newscaster), Wally Welch (Mr. Kirby)

*In this contemporary take on Shakespeare's Othello, jealous high-schooler Hugo Goulding sets out to destroy the relationship between popular basketball star Odin James and his girlfriend Desi Brable.*

© Lions Gate Films

Mekhi Phifer, Josh Hartnett

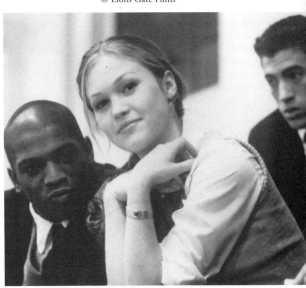

Mekhi Phifer, Julia Stiles, Andrew Keegan

Gina Phillips, Justin Long

Jonathan Breck, Justin Long

Jonathan Breck

# JEEPERS CREEPERS

(UNITED ARTISTS) Producers, Barry Opper, Tom Luse; Executive Producers, Francis Ford Coppola, Linda Reisman, Willi Baer, Mario Ohoven, Eberhard Kayser; Director/Screenplay, Victor Salva; Photography, Don E. FauntLeRoy; Designer, Steven Legler; Costumes, Emae Villalobos; Editor, Ed Marx; Music, Bennet Salvay, Randy Kerber; Co-Producer, J. Todd Harris; Makeup & Creature Effects, Make-up & Monsters Studios; Visual Effects Supervisor, Bob Morgenroth, E+MC2 Digital; Casting, Kimberly Mullen; an American Zoetrope/Cinerenta-Cinebeta production in association with Cinerenta Medienbeteiligungs KG; U.S.-German; Dolby; FotoKem color; Rated R; 89 minutes; Release date: August 31, 2001

## CAST

| | |
|---|---|
| Trish | Gina Phillips |
| Darry | Justin Long |
| The Creeper | Jonathan Breck |
| Jezelle Gay Hartman | Patricia Belcher |
| Sergeant David Tubbs | Brandon Smith |
| The Cat Lady | Eileen Brennan |
| Waitress Beverly | Peggy Sheffield |
| Manager | Jeffrey William Evans |
| Man at Jukebox | Patrick Cherry |
| Trooper Gideon | Jon Beshara |
| Trooper Weston | Avis-Marie Barnes |
| Cellblock Officer | Steven Raulerson |
| Roach | Tom Tarantini |
| Officer with Hole in Chest | Will Hasenzahl |
| Camper Driver | Kim Kahana |
| Dying Boy | Chris Shephardson |

*While driving home for spring break, siblings Darry and Trish chance upon a mysterious cloaked figure that appears to be collecting bodies.*

© United Artists Films Inc.

Justin Long, Eileen Brennan, Gina Phillips

## THE MUSKETEER

(UNIVERSAL/MIRAMAX) Producer, Moshe Diamant; Director/Photography, Peter Hyams; Screenplay, Gene Quintano; based on the novel *The Three Musketeers* by Alexandre Dumas; Executive Producers, Mark Damon, Steven Paul, Rudy Cohen, Frank Hübner, Romain Schroeder; Co-Producer, Jan Fantl; Line Producer, Tom Reeve; Designer, Philip Harrison; Editor, Terry Rawlings; Music, David Arnold; Costumes, Raymond Hughes, Cynthia Dumont; Stunt Choreographer, Xin-Xin Xiong; Casting, Penny Perry, Celestia Fox; a D'Artagnan Productions, Ltd., Apollomedia, Q&Q Media, and Carousel Picture Company production with the support of Film Fund Luxembourg; U.S.-Luxembourg; Dolby; Super 35 Widescreen; Technicolor; Rated PG-13; 105 minutes; Release date: September 7, 2001

### CAST

| | |
|---|---|
| The Queen | Catherine Deneuve |
| Francesca | Mena Suvari |
| Cardinal Richelieu | Stephen Rea |
| Febre | Tim Roth |
| D'Artagnan | Justin Chambers |
| Bonacieux | Bill Treacher |
| King Louis | Daniel Mesguich |
| Rochefort | David Schofield |
| Aramis | Nick Moran |
| Porthos | Steve Speirs |
| Athos | Jan Gregor Kremp |
| Lord Buckingham | Jeremy Clyde |

and Michael Byrne (Treville), Jean-Pierre Castaldi (Planchet), Tsilla Chelton (Madam Lacross), Luc Gentile (D'Artagnan's Father), Catherine Erhardy (D'Artagnan's Mother), Max Dolbey (Young D'Artagnan), Florent Bigot de Nesle (Deleon), Stefan Jürgens (Darcy), Ann Marie Pisani (Buxom Woman), Carrie Mullan (Mathilde), Joachim Paul Assböck (Hessian), Oscar Ortega Sanchez (Marquis de Spota), Sven Walser (Man #1 at Bar), Marco Lorenzini (Inn Keeper), Jean-Francois Wolff (Cardinal's Guard #1), Bertrand Witt (Dumas), Stefan Weinert (Mercenary #2), Patrick Dean (Febre Messenger), Christian Bergmann (Last Febre Man), Sascha Schiffbauer, Frank Ferner (Jail Guards), Sven Nichulski (Guard at Door), Jean-Luc Ristic (Pastry Chef), Roland Stemmer, Dean Gregory, Ciaran Mulhern (Musketeers), Jo Stock (Another Musketeer), Gilles Soeder (Cook), Sigal Diamant (Josephine)

*Swordsman D'Artagnan sets out to join the king's elite guard, the Royal Musketeers, and to find the man who killed his parents when he was a child.*

© Universal Studios

Justin Chambers

Stephen Rea, Tim Roth

Morris Chestnut, Vivica A. Fox

Anthony Anderson, Morris Chestnut

## TWO CAN PLAY THAT GAME

(SCREEN GEMS) Producers, Doug McHenry, Mark Brown, Paddy Cullen; Executive Producers, Larry Kennar, Robert N. Fried, Scott Wynne; Director/Screenplay, Mark Brown; Photography, Alexander Gruszynski; Designer, Amy Ancona; Editor, Earl Watson; Music, Marcus Miller; Music Supervisor, Rashad Liston; Casting, Robi Reed-Humes; a Doug McHenry production in association with C4 Pictures; Dolby; Deluxe color; Rated R; 90 minutes; Release date: September 7, 2001

### CAST

| | |
|---|---|
| Shanté Smith | Vivica A. Fox |
| Keith Fenton | Morris Chestnut |
| Diedre | Mo'Nique |
| Tracye | Tamala Jones |
| Karen | Wendy Raquel Robinson |
| Conny Spalding | Gabrielle Union |
| Michael | Bobby Brown |
| Tony | Anthony Anderson |
| Bill Parker | Ray Wise |
| Dwain | Donré T. Whitfield |
| Jason | David Krumholtz |

and Lee Anthony (Attorney in Elevator), Kristen Herold, Cherise Leana Bangs, Libby Genaro (Miller Girls), Zatella Beatty (Cynthia) Mark Brown, Chris Spencer, Pierre Burgess, Mark Christopher Lawrence (Lying Men), Darrel Heath, Wesley Thompson, Caleb LeConte, Michael Massengale, Mark Taborn, Kelvin Brown (Dinner Guys), Darrell "Silver" Hughes (Patrick), Amy Hunter (Nita), Colby Kane (Calvin), Ian "Blaze" Kelly (Diedre's Man), Jeff Markey (Phil the Attorney), Brian Nakauchi (Delivery Man), A. Doran Reed, Mark Swenson (Help Guys), Jason Singleton (Waiter), Yul L. Spencer (Trent), Alex Thomas (Eddie), La La Vazquez (Bobby the DJ), Natashia Williams (Sexy Young Girl)

*After Shanté discovers that her boyfriend Keith has been cheating on her, she institutes her "Ten Day Plan" to exact revenge and get him to come crawling back to her, only to find out that Keith has a strategy of his own.*

© Screen Gems, a Sony Pictures Entertainment Company

Nick Catanese, Jennifer Aniston, Brian Vander Ark,
Mark Wahlberg, Kara Zediker, Blas Elias

# ROCK STAR

**(WARNER BROS.)** Producers, Robert Lawrence, Toby Jaffe; Executive Producers, Steven Reuther, George Clooney, Mike Ockrent; Director, Stephen Herek; Screenplay, John Stockwell; Photography, Ueli Steiger; Designer, Mayne Berke; Costumes, Auggie Guerard-Rodgers; Music, Trevor Rabin; Co-Producer, Michael Fottrell; Editor, Trudy Ship; Concert Supervisors, Nick Jen, Stephen Nimmer; Casting, Sharon Bialy; a Maysville Pictures/Robert Lawrence production, presented in association with Bel Air Pictures LLC; Dolby; Super 35 Widescreen; Technicolor; Rated R; 106 minutes; Release date: September 7, 2001

Mark Wahlberg

## CAST

| | |
|---|---|
| Chris Cole | Mark Wahlberg |
| Emily Poule | Jennifer Aniston |
| Bobby Beers | Jason Flemyng |
| Rob Malcolm | Timothy Olyphant |
| Mats | Timothy Spall |
| Kirk Cuddy | Dominic West |
| A. C. | Jason Bonham |
| Jorgen | Jeff Pilson |
| Ghode | Zakk Wylde |
| Donny Johnson | Blas Elias |
| Xander Cummins | Nick Catanese |
| Ricki Bell | Brian Vander Ark |
| Tania Asher | Dagmara Dominczyk |
| Joe Jr. | Matthew Glave |
| Mr. Cole | Michael Shamus Wiles |
| Mrs. Cole | Beth Grant |
| Nina | Carey Lessard |
| Samantha | Kristin Willits |

Mark Wahlberg, Jason Flemyng

and Jamie Williams (Mason Bell), Keith Loneker, Eric Weinstein (Roadies), Sami Reed (Amber), Kara Zediker (Marci), Stephen Jenkins (Bradley), Colleen Ann Fitzpatrick, Kirk Enochs (Fans), Kevin Ryder (Cream Reporter), Gene Baxter (Melody Maker Reporter), Gregory Hinton (Bouncer), Sonya Stephens (Nurse), Neil Zlozower (Photographer), Miles Kennedy (Thor), Rachle Hunter (A. C.'s Wife), Heidi Mark (Kirk's Wife), Carrie Stevens (Ghode's Wife), Amy Rolle (Jorgen's Wife), William Martin Brennan (Office Worker), Lorna Scott (Mrs. Andrews), Ralph Saenz (Auditioning Singer), Jennifer Rovero, Natalie Raynes (Topless Cuties), Jamal Weathers (Scalper), Hallie Brennand (2-year-old Girl), Jamie White (MTV Veejay), Jeffrey Wetzel (Metal Head), Frederick E. Kowalo (Guitar Tech), Jennifer Uilani Warren (Girl with P Pass), Chad Azadan, Linda Cevallos, Jennifer Edmond, Brian Friedman, Cynthia Fuhrer, Cati Jean, Edward Jenkins, Kelly Knox, Tabbtah Mays, Udee McGreoy, Ted Napolitano, Tomasian Parrott, Gabriel Ramirez, Ursula Whitaker, Zachary Woodlee (Roxy Dancers)

*Aspiring singer and heavy metal fan Chris Cole is given the chance of a lifetime when he becomes lead singer for his favorite group, Steel Dragon.*

© Warner Bros. Pictures and Bel-Air Pictures, LLC

Mark Wahlberg, Jennifer Aniston, Dagmara Dominczyk

# L.I.E.

**(LOT 47)** Producers, Linda Moran, Rene Bastian, Michael Cuesta; Director, Michael Cuesta; Screenplay, Stephen M. Ryder, Michael Cuesta, Gerald Cuesta; Photography, Romeo Tirone; Designer, Elise Bennett; Costumes, Daniel Glicker; Editors, Eric Carlson, Kane Platt; Music, Pierre Foldes; Co-Producers, Jose Gilberto Molinari-Rosaly, Valerie Romer; Line Producer, Valerie Romer; Associate Producer, Urs Hirschbiegel; Casting, Judy Henderson; an Alter Ego/Belladonna production; Dolby; Color; Rated NC-17; 108 minutes; Release date: September 7, 2001

## CAST

| | |
|---|---|
| Big John Harrigan | Brian Cox |
| Howie Blitzer | Paul Franklin Dano |
| Gary Terrio | Billy Kay |
| Marty Blitzer | Bruce Altman |
| Kevin Cole | James Costa |
| Brian | Tony Donnelly |
| Scott | Walter Masterson |
| Guidance Counselor | Marcia DeBonis |
| Elliot, Marty's Lawyer | Adam LeFevre |
| Newscaster | Michelle Carano |
| Marty's Girlfriend | Tatiana Burgos |
| Anne Harrigan | B. Constance Barry |
| Henry | Brad Silnutzer |
| Clifford | Bob Gerardi |
| Man with Pizza | Frank G. Rivers |
| Tough Kids | Anthony F. Peragine, Jude LoBasso |
| Sylvia Blitzer | Gladys Dano |
| Howie (5 years old) | Emilio Cuesta |
| F.B.I. Woman | Christine Toy Johnson |
| Police Officer | Francis J. Leik |
| Desk Sergeant | Chuck Ardezzone |
| Cop | Risa Ziegler |
| Brian's Father | Ray Garvey |
| Mrs. Cole | Angela Pietropinto |
| Prison Guard | Chance Kelly |

*Howie, a troubled 15-year-old confused about his own sexuality, befriends a middle-aged man whose sexual preferences run towards teenage boys.*

© Lot 47 Films

Billy Kay, Paul Franklin Dano

Brian Cox, Paul Franklin Dano

Tony Donnelly, James Costa, Paul Franklin Dano

Paul Franklin Dano

Leelee Sobieski, Stellan Skarsgård

Leelee Sobieski

Trevor Morgan, Leelee Sobieski

# THE GLASS HOUSE

(COLUMBIA) Producer, Neal H. Moritz; Executive Producer, Michael Rachmil; Director, Daniel Sackheim; Screenplay, Wesley Strick; Photography, Alar Kivilo; Designer, Jon Gary Steele; Editor, Howard E. Smith; Music, Christopher Young; Costumes, Chrisi Karvonides-Dushenko; Casting, Mary Vernieu, Anne McCarthy, Felicia Fasano; an Original Film production; Dolby; Panavision; Deluxe color; Rated PG-13; 106 minutes; Release date: September 14, 2001

## CAST

Ruby Baker .........................................................................Leelee Sobieski
Erin Glass ..............................................................................Diane Lane
Terry Glass ................................................................Stellan Skarsgård
Alvin Begleiter.............................................................................Bruce Dern
Nancy Ryan ...........................................................................Kathy Baker
Rhett Baker.........................................................................Trevor Morgan
Uncle Jack ...............................................................................Chris Noth
Dave Baker .....................................................................Michael O'Keefe
Grace Baker ...............................................................................Rita Wilson
and Gavin O'Connor (Don), Vyto Ruginis (Whitey), Carly Pope (Tasha), China Shavers (E. B.), Agnes Bruckner (Zoe), Michael Paul Chan (Mr. Kim), Rachel Wilson (Hannah), Rutanya Alda (Vice Principal), Erick Avari (Ted Ross), Mia Barrentine (Ruby—5 years old), John Billingsley (Driving Instructor), Richard Anthony Crenna, D. Elliot Woods (Cops), Maya Danziger (Deirdre), Leslie Sackheim (Waitress), Stephanie Ittleson (Officer), Harry Johnson (Minister), January Jones (Girl), Kirk Kinder (Sheriff), Maya McGlaughlin (Receptionist), Wayne Morse (Psycho Killer), Michelle Nordin (Teen Queen), Brent Sexton (Mechanic), Paul Tuerpe (Traffic Cop), Julia Vera (Vicki), Kim Webster (Miss Drake), Alice Hirson (Mrs. Morgan), Drew Snyder (Mr. Morgan)

*Following the death of their parents in an automobile accident, young Ruby Baker and her brother are taken in by friends of their parents, Erin and Terry Glass, a couple Ruby suspects are less benign than they first appear.*

© Columbia Pictures Industries Inc.

# HARDBALL

**(PARAMOUNT)** Producers, Tina Nides, Mike Tollin, Brian Robbins; Executive Producers, Kevin McCormick, Herbert W. Gains, Erwin Stoff; Director, Brian Robbins; Screenplay, John Gatins; Based on the book *Hardball: A Season in the Projects* by Daniel Coyle; Photography, Tom Richmond; Designer, Jaymes Hinkle; Costumes, Francine Jamison-Tanchuck; Editor, Ned Bastille; Music, Mark Isham; Music Supervisor, Michael McQuarn; Casting, Marci Liorr; a Tollins/Robbins production, presented in association with Fireworks Pictures of a Nides/McCormick Production; Dolby; Deluxe color; Rated PG-13; 106 minutes; Release date: September 14, 2001

## CAST

| | |
|---|---|
| Conor O'Neill | Keanu Reeves |
| Elizabeth Wilkes | Diane Lane |
| Ticky Tobin | John Hawkes |
| Matt Hyland | D. B. Sweeney |
| Jimmy Fleming | Mike McGlone |
| Sterling | Sterling Elijah Brim |
| Miles Pennfield II | A. Delon Ellis, Jr. |
| Jefferson Albert Tibbs | Julian Griffith |
| Andre Ray Peetes | Bryan Hearne |
| Jamal | Michael B. Jordan |
| Clarence | Kristopher Lofton |
| Kofi Evans | Michael Perkins |
| Ray-Ray | Brian Reed |
| Alex | Alexander Telles |
| G-Baby | DeWayne Warren |

and Michael B. Chait (Straight-Laced Kid), Carol E. Hall (Pearia Evans), Jacqueline Williams (Lenora Tibbs), Freeman Coffey (Darryl Mackey), Mark Robert Ellis (Waatas Coach), Paul Turner (Bartender), Dawn Lewis (Ellen), Kwame Amoaku, Vince Green (Pizza Guys), Mark Margolis (Fink), Tom Milanovich (Ed), Greg Sandquist (Barber's Son), Stephen Cinabro (Gino), Adam Tomei (Barfly), Father Donald M. Siple (Priest), Sammy Sosa (Himself), Aaron Evans (Aaron), Ronnel Taylor (Gang Member), Alexander Telles (Alex), Andre Morgan, Reginal McKinley (Umpires), Josefus Duanah, Jeffrey Oatlin (Tough Kids), James Currie (Check Cashing Station Cashier)

*In order to pay off his bookies, Conor O'Neill reluctantly agrees to coach a corporate-sponsored little league team consisting of underprivileged kids.*

© Paramount Pictures

Brian Reed, Keanu Reeves, DeWayne Warren

Keanu Reeves, Julian Griffith

Keanu Reeves, DeWayne Warren

Diane Lane, Keanu Reeves

# HEARTS IN ATLANTIS

(**WARNER BROS.**) Producer, Kerry Heysen; Executive Producers, Bruce Berman, Michael Flynn; Director, Scott Hicks; Screenplay, William Goldman; Based on the novel by Stephen King; Photography, Piotr Sobocinski; Designer, Barbara C. Ling; Costumes, Julie Weiss; Editor, Pip Karmel; Music, Mychael Danna; Music Supervisor, John Bissell; a Castle Rock Entertainment presentation in association with Village Roadshow Pictures and NPV Entertainment; Dolby; Panavision; Technicolor; Rated PG-13; 101 minutes; Release date: September 28, 2001

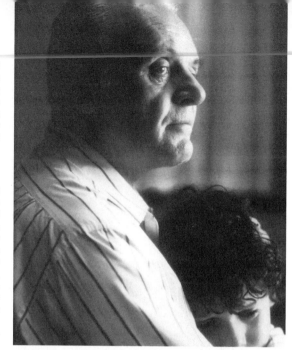

Anthony Hopkins, Anton Yelchin

## CAST

| | |
|---|---|
| Ted Brautigan | Anthony Hopkins |
| Bobby Garfield | Anton Yelchin |
| Liz Garfield | Hope Davis |
| Carol Gerber | Mika Boorem |
| Bobby Garfield (Adult) | David Morse |
| Monte Man | Alan Tudyk |
| Len Files | Tom Bower |
| Alanna Files | Celia Weston |
| Don Biderman | Adam LeFevre |
| Sully-John | Will Rothhaar |
| Harry Doolin | Timmy Reifsnyder |
| Mrs. Gerber | Deirdre O'Connell |
| Mr. Oliver | Terry Beaver |
| Richie O'Rourke | Joe T. Blankenship |
| Willie Shearman | Brett Fleisher |
| Sully's Dad | Joel F. Haberli |
| Sully's Little Brother | Evan Moses |

and Joshua Billings (Cabbie), Valerie Karasek (Sully's Widow), Graham Bardsley (Minister), Keith H. Beyer, Sean Edwards, Robert V. Maine, Mickey Leon McBride (Soldiers at Funeral), Wes Johnson (Sports Announcer)

*Bobby Garfield looks back on the summer of 1960, when a mysterious stranger took a room in his Connecticut home and changed the boy's life.*

© Castle Rock Entertainment

Hope Davis, Anthony Hopkins

Anton Yelchin

Mika Boorem

# DINNER RUSH

(ACCESS MOTION PICTURE GROUP) Producers, Louis DiGiaimo, Patti Greaney; Executive Producers, Phil Suarez, Robert Cheren, Robert Steuer, Michael Baumohl; Director, Bob Giraldi; Screenplay, Rick Shaughnessy, Brian Kalata; Photography, Tim Ives; Designer, Andrew Bernard; Editor, Allyson C. Johnson; Music, Alexander Lasarenko; Music Supervisor, Alex Steyermark; Casting, Stephanie Corsalini; a Giraldi Suarez DiGiaimo Productions presentation of an Entertainment Capital Group Company production; Dolby; Technicolor; Rated R; 100 minutes; Release date: September 28, 2001

Danny Aiello, Kirk Acevedo

## CAST

| | |
|---|---|
| Louis Cropa | Danny Aiello |
| Udo Cropa | Edoardo Ballerini |
| Nicole | Vivian Wu |
| Carmen | Mike McGlone |
| Duncan | Kirk Acevedo |
| Jennifer Freeley | Sandra Bernhard |
| Marti | Summer Phoenix |
| Natalie | Polly Draper |
| Sean | Jamie Harris |
| Fitzgerald | Mark Margolis |
| Ken | John Corbett |
| Paolo | Alex Corrado |

and Frank Bongiorno (Enrico), Sophie Comet (Food Nymph), Tessa Ghylin (Piper), Andre DeLeon (Nino), Walt MacPherson (Det. Drurry), Ajay Naidu (Ademir), Manny Perez (Gabriel), Andre Haynes Richardson (Machine), John Rothman (Gary), Lexie Sperduto (Lucy Clemente), Marita Stavrou (Kisha), Roma Torre, David Diaz (Themselves), Ellen McElduff (Ellen Drury), Zainab Jah (Adrian), Jimmy Shelgin, Nural Raque (Servers), John Patrick Walker (Waiter), Gabriel Jiminez (Pasta Chef), Joe Gatti, Jr. (Harold), Annika Peterson (Bettina), Juan Hernandez (Joseph), Luigi Celentano (Line Chief), Jonathen Chodash (Black-Out Customer), Ted Koch, Doreen Dunlap (Bar Patrons), Julie Zeger (Baby's Mother), David Phillips (Baby's Father), Marcus Schenkenberg, Jennifer Chambers (Customers)

John Corbett, Marita Stavrou

*Gigino's, a fashionable New York restaurant, experiences an especially hectic and crowded evening as various characters converge on the eatery.*

© Access Motion Picture Group

Edoardo Ballerini, Sandra Bernhard

Summer Phoenix, Mike McGlone, Alex Corrado

Michael Douglas, Famke Janssen

Victor Argo, Jennifer Esposito

Brittany Murphy, Michael Douglas

Sean Bean, Shawn Doyle

# DON'T SAY A WORD

**(20TH CENTURY FOX)** Producers, Arnon Milchan, Arnold Kopelson, Anne Kopelson; Director, Gary Fleder; Screenplay, Anthony Peckham, Patrick Smith Kelly; Based on the novel by Andrew Klavan; Executive Procucers, Jeffrey Downer, Bruce Berman; Photography, Amir Mokri; Designer, Nelson Coates; Costumes, Ellen Mirojnick; Editors, William Steinkamp, Armen Minasian; Co-Producers, Andrew Klavan, Nana Greenwald; Music, Mark Isham; Music Supervisor, Peter Afterman; Casting, Avy Kaufman; a Regency Enterprises and Village Roadshow Pictures presentation in association with NPV Entertainment of a Kopelson Entertainment/New Regency/Furthur Films production; Dolby; Panavision; Deluxe color; Rated R; 112 minutes; Release date: September 28, 2001

## CAST

| | |
|---|---|
| Dr. Nathan Conrad | Michael Douglas |
| Patrick B. Koster | Sean Bean |
| Elisabeth Burrows | Brittany Murphy |
| Jessie Conrad | Skye McCole Bartusiak |
| Martin J. Dolen | Guy Torry |
| Detective Sandra Cassidy | Jennifer Esposito |
| Russel Maddox | Shawn Doyle |
| Sydney Simon | Victor Argo |
| Max J. Dunlevy | Conrad Goode |
| Jake | Paul Schulze |
| Arnie Carter | Lance Reddick |
| Aggie Conrad | Famke Janssen |
| Dr. Louis Sachs | Oliver Platt |
| Leon E. Croft | Aidan Devine |
| Jonathan | Alex Campbell |
| Intern | Philip DeWilde |
| Frankie Spaducci | Sam Montesano |

and Arlene Duncan (Aide), Judy Sinclair (Zelda Sinclair), Larry Block (Doorman), David Warshofsky (Ryan), Darren Frost (Janitor), Philip Williams (Large Cop), Louis Vanaria (Cop), Daniel Kash (Detective Garcia), Lucie Laurier (Roommate Vanessa), Isabella Fink (Elisabeth—8 years old), Ray Iannicelli (Man at Marina), Colm Magner (Cop #1), Cyrus Farmer (Officer #1), Martin Roach (Transit Cop), Patricia Mauceri (Sofia)

*In order to retrieve a stolen diamond, a gang of ruthless thieves kidnaps the daughter of Manhattan psychiatrist Nathan Conrad, whose institutionalized patient, Elisabeth Burrows, is the only one who knows the six-digit figure they need to accomplish their task.*

© Regency Entertainment (USA), Inc.

# ZOOLANDER

**(PARAMOUNT)** Producers, Scott Rudin, Ben Stiller, Stuart Cornfeld; Executive Producers, Joel Gallen, Adam Schroeder, Lauren Zalaznick; Director, Ben Stiller; Screenplay, Drake Sather, Ben Stiller, John Hamburg; Story, Drake Sather, Ben Stiller; Photography, Barry Peterson; Designer, Robin Standefer; Costumes, David C. Robinson; Editor, Greg Hayden; Co-Producer, Celia Costas; Music, David Arnold; Music Supervisors, Casting, Juel Bestrop, Jeanne McCarthy, Kathleen Chopin; a Village Roadshow Pictures presentation in association with VH1 and NPV Entertainment; Dolby; Super 35 Widescreen; Deluxe color; Rated PG-13; 89 minutes; Release date: September 28, 2001

## CAST

| | |
|---|---|
| Derek Zoolander | Ben Stiller |
| Hansel | Owen Wilson |
| Matilda Jeffries | Christine Taylor |
| Mugatu | Will Ferrell |
| Katinka | Milla Jovovich |
| Maury Ballstein | Jerry Stiller |
| J. P. Prewitt | David Duchovny |
| Larry Zoolander | Jon Voight |
| Scrappy Zoolander | Judah Friedlander |
| Todd | Nathan Lee Graham |
| Brint | Alexander Manning |
| Rufus | Asio Highsmith |
| Meekus | Alexander Skarsgård |
| Archie | Matt Levin |
| Evil DJ | Justin Theroux |
| Olga the Masseuse | Andy Dick |
| Prime Minister of Malaysia | Woodrow Asai |
| Hansel's Corner Guy | Andrew Wilson |
| Italian Designer | John Vargas |
| American Designer | Jennifer Coolidge |
| French Designer | Tony Kanal |
| German Designer | Endre Hules |
| British Designer | Nora Dunn |
| Mugatu's Dog. | Kiva |
| Coal Mine Tavern Dog | Kahlua |
| Derek's Interview Hairstylist | Ric Pipino |
| VH1 Reporter | Jerry Stahl |
| Mugatu Model | Jennifer McComb |
| Mugatu Bodyguards | Johann Urb, Luc Commeret |
| Tim Magazine Reader | Herb Lieberz |
| Night Club Door Person | Zoya |
| Night Club Security | Colin McNish, Darren Copeland |
| Night Club Bouncer (Biff) | Richard Stanley |
| Night Club Bouncer (Maurice) | Shabazz Richardson |
| Night Club Bouncer | Rohan Quine |
| Billy Zane's Date | Svetlana |
| Rico | Eric Winzenried |
| Abraham Lincoln | Charles Brame |
| John Wilkes Booth | James Marsden |
| JFK Assassins | Rudy Segura, Randall Slavin |
| Monkey Photographer | Patton Oswalt |

and Donald Trump, Christian Slater, Tom Ford, Cuba Gooding, Jr., Steve Kmetko, Tommy Hilfiger, Natalie Portman, Fabio, Lenny Kravitz, Gwen Stefani, Heidi Klum, DJ Mark Ronson, Paris Hilton, David Bowie, Tyson Beckford, Fred Durst, Lance Bass, Li'l Kim, Garry Shandling, Stephen Dorff, Sandra Bernhard, Claudia Schiffer, Veronica Webb, Lukas Haas, Carmen Kass, Frankie Rayder, Little Kingz, Winona Ryder, Laura Salem, Billy Zane (Themselves), Vikram Kashana, Jonah Luber, Michael McAlpin, Eve Salvail, Shavo Odadjian, Eliot Johnson, Richard Gladys, Amy Stiller (Hansel's Posse), Irina Pantaeva (Irina), Stan Chu (Sherpa), Kum Ming Ho (Climber), Theo Kogan (Cool Tattoo Girl), Lam Bor (Dalai Lama Guy), Angel 11:11, Luther Creek, Dechen Thurman, Kenny Max (Funky Loft Guests), Kina (Ennui), David Pressman (Maori Tribesman), Godfrey Danchimah (Janitor Derek), Taj Crown (Janitor Hansel), Richie Rich (Derelicte Doorman), King (Derelicte Bouncer), Frederic Fekkai (Derek's Derelicte Hairstylist), Kevyn Aucoin (Derek's Derelicte Makeup Artist), Boris Kachscovsky (Zoolander Center Student), Mitch Winston (Informercial Director), Mason Webb (Derek, Jr.), Alexa Nikolas (Story Hour Girl), Vince Vaughn (Luke Zoolander), Anne Meara (Protester)

*Looking for meaning in his life after being dethroned as Male Model of the Year, clueless Derek Zoolander gets a comeback assignment from top fashion designer Mugatu, little realizing that he is being used as part of a nefarious assassination plot.*

© Paramount Pictures

Ben Stiller, David Bowie, Owen Wilson

Owen Wilson, Ben Stiller

Ben Stiller, Jerry Stiller

Milla Jovovich, Ben Stiller, Will Ferrell

Denzel Washington, Ethan Hawke

Denzel Washington

# TRAINING DAY

**(WARNER BROS.)** Producers, Jeffrey Silver, Bobby Newmyer; Executive Producers, Bruce Berman, Davis Guggenheim; Director, Antoine Fuqua; Screenplay, David Ayer; Photography, Mauro Fiore; Designer, Naomi Shohan; Costumes, Michele Michel; Editor, Conrad Buff; Music, Mark Mancina; Music Supervisor, John Houlihan; Casting, Mary Vernieu; an Outlaw Production, presented in association with Village Roadshow Pictures and NPV Entertainment; Dolby; Panavision; Technicolor; Rated R; 120 minutes; Release date: October 5, 2001

## CAST

| | |
|---|---|
| Alonzo Harris | Denzel Washington |
| Jake Hoyt | Ethan Hawke |
| Roger | Scott Glenn |
| Stan Gursky | Tom Berenger |
| Doug Rosselli | Harris Yulin |
| Lou Jacobs | Raymond J. Barry |
| Smiley | Cliff Curtis |
| Paul | Dr. Dre |
| Blue | Snoop Dogg |
| Sandman's Wife | Macy Gray |
| Lisa | Charlotte Ayanna |
| Sara | Eva Mendes |
| Tim | Nick Chinlund |
| Mark | Jaime P. Gomez |
| Sniper | Raymond Cruz |
| Moreno | Noel Guglielmi |
| Letty | Samantha Becker |
| Waiter, Dining Car | Richard Browner |
| Gangster | Ronald Ellis |
| Alonzo's Son | Kyjel N. Jolly |
| College Driver | Fran Kranz |
| Waitress, Diner | Janeen Krikorian |
| Wig Store Owner | Princera Lee |
| Veterano | Robert Leon |
| Dreamer | Seidy Lopez |
| College Passengers | Sarah Danielle Madison, Brett Sorenson |
| Pee Wee | Rudy Perez |
| LAPD Pilot | Ben Skorstad |
| Bone | Cle "Shiheed" Sloan |
| Neto | Abel Soto |
| Crackheads | Garland Whitt, Will Foster Stewart |
| Dimitri | Denzel Whitaker |

and Kenneth Allen Madden, Chris Patterson, Darrel Sellers, William English (Dice Players)

*Rookie cop Jake Hoyt goes through a day of training under the wing of veteran narcotics officer Alonzo Harris, whose way of dealing with L.A.'s criminal underworld is no less corrupt than those on the opposite side of the law.*

*2001 Academy Award-winner for Best Actor (Denzel Washington). This film received an additional nomination for supporting actor (Ethan Hawke).*

© Warner Bros.

Denzel Washington, Ethan Hawke

Ethan Hawke, Denzel Washington

Denzel Washington

Macy Gray

Snoop Dogg

Ethan Hawke

Brett Sorenson, Denzel Washington

Kate Beckinsale, John Cusack

# SERENDIPITY

**(MIRAMAX)** Producers, Simon Fields, Peter Abrams, Robert L. Levy; Executive Producers, Bob Osher, Julie Goldstein, Amy Slotnick; Director, Peter Chelsom; Screenplay, Marc Klein; Co-Producers, Amy Kaufman, Andrew Panay; Co-Executive Producer, Robbie Brenner; Photography, John De Borman; Designer, Caroline Hanania; Costumes, Marie-Sylvie Deveau, Mary Claire Hannon; Editor, Christopher Greenbury; Music, Alan Silvestri; Music Supervisor, Laura Ziffren; Casting, Mary Gail Artz, Barbara Cohen, Billy Hopkins, Suzanne Smith, Kerry Barden; a Tapestry Films production in association with Simon Fields Productions; Dolby; Color; Rated PG-13; 91 minutes; Release date: October 5, 2001

Molly Shannon, Kate Beckinsale, Ajay Mehta

## CAST

| | |
|---|---|
| Jonathan Tager | John Cusack |
| Sara Thomas | Kate Beckinsale |
| Dean Kansky | Jeremy Piven |
| Eve | Molly Shannon |
| Halley Buchanan | Bridget Moynahan |
| Lars Hammond | John Corbett |
| Bloomingsdale Salesman | Eugene Levy |
| Caroline Mitchell | Lucy Gordon |
| Courtney | Kate Blumberg |
| Superintendent | Mike Benitez |
| Flight Attendant | Pamela Redfern |
| Hair Stylist | Brenda Logan |
| Hippie Woman | Colleen Williams |
| Host at Serendipity | Stephen Bruce |
| Janitor | Aron Tager |
| Priest | Murray McRae |
| Kenny | Evan Neuman |
| Kip | Kevin Rice |

and Christopher Baker, Neil Claxton (Lars's Band), Leo Fitzpatrick (Leasing Office Temp), Ron Payne (Louis Trager), John Ellison Conlee (Artie), Victor Young (Mr. Buchanan), Eve Crawford (Mrs. Buchanan), Marcia Bennett (Mrs. Trager), Jamie Goodwin (Nick Roberts), Ajay Mehta (Pakistani Driver), Sandra Caldwell (PR Woman), Reggi Wyns (Rastafarian), T. Scott Cunningham (Ryan), Jessica Kelly (Sara Lawson), Simon Jutras (Sebastian), Marquis Bobesich (Street Vendor), Catherine Hernandez (Waitress at Serendipity), Catherine Kuhn (Wedding Coordinator), Clark Middleton (Aiport Cab Driver), David Sparrow (Josh's Dad), Gary Gerbrandt (Josh), Conrad Bergschneider (Check-in Clerk), Lilli Lavine (Bloomingdale's Stock Girl), Buck Henry (Glove Man)

Jeremy Piven, Eugene Levy, John Cusack

*In 1990 Manhattan, two people, Jonathan Trager and Sara Thomas, meet and become smitten with each other only to separate accidentally. Leaving their second meeting up to fate, ten years pass, finding them ready to marry others despite the yearning that still exists within them both.*

© Miramax Films

Kate Beckinsale, John Corbett

# JOY RIDE

**(20TH CENTURY FOX)** formerly *Squelch*; Producers, J. J. Abrams, Chris Moore; Executive Producers, Arnon Milchan, Patrick Markey, Bridget Johnson; Director, John Dahl; Screenplay, Clay Tarver, J. J. Abrams; Photography, Jeffrey Jur; Designer, Rob Pearson; Costumes, Terry Dresbach; Editors, Eric L. Beason, Scott Chestnut, Todd E. Miller, Glen Scantlebury; Music, Marco Beltrami; Casting, Mali Finn, Emily Schweber; Stunts, Terry Leonard; a Regency Enterprises presentation of a New Regency/Bad Robot/Liveplanet production; Dolby; Panavision; Deluxe color; Rated R; 96 minutes; Release date: October 5, 2001

## CAST

Fuller Thomas.............................................................Steve Zahn
Lewis Thomas..............................................................Paul Walker
Venna Wilcox.............................................................Leelee Sobieski
Charlotte Campbell....................................................Jessica Bowman
Danny Rosado (Lewis's Roommate).........................Stuart Stone
Car Salesman.............................................................Basil Wallace
Officer Keeney...........................................................Brian Leckner
Salt Lake City Police Desk Clerk..............................Mary Wickliffe
Asst. Salt Lake City Police Desk Clerk.................McKenzie Satterthwaite
Gas Station Mechanic................................................Dell Yount
Ronald Ellinghouse....................................................Kenneth White
Night Manager...........................................................Luis Cortes
Officer Akins..............................................................Michael McCleery
Sheriff Ritter.............................................................Jim Beaver
Gas Station Manager.................................................Rachel Singer
Ice Truck Man...........................................................Satch Huizenga
Bartender...................................................................Terry Leonard
and James MacDonald (Local in Nebraska Bar), Gwenda Deacon (Truck Stop Waitress), Robert Winley (Truck Stop Manager), Ali Gage (Waitress), Jack Moore (Hotwire Consultant), Hugh Dane (Man at Door), Lee Stepp (Traveling Salesman), Jay Hernandez (Marine), Huey Redwine, John Maynard, Peter Weireter (Policemen), Tim Cooney, Sheryl Giffis, Pamela Senatore (Voice Actors), Matthew Kimbrough (Rusty Nail), Ted Levine (Voice of Rusty Nail)

*During a cross-country drive, irresponsible Fuller Thomas's insistence on playing a hoax on a trucker backfires and he and his brother find themselves being terrorized by the vengeful driver.*

© Monarchy Enterprises S.a.r.l. and Regency Entertainment (USA), Inc.

Paul Walker, Leelee Sobieski, Steve Zahn

Steve Zahn

Paul Walker, Steve Zahn

Leelee Sobieski

Vinessa Shaw, Chris Kattan

Chris Penn, Peter Falk, Peter Berg

## CORKY ROMANO

(**TOUCHSTONE**) Producer, Robert Simonds; Executive Producer, Tracey Trench; Director, Rob Pritts; Screenplay, David Garrett, Jason Ward; Co-Producer, Ira Shuman; Photography, Steven Bernstein; Designer, Peter Politanoff; Costumes, Tom Bronson; Editor, Alan Cody; Music, Randy Edelman; Music Supervisor, Lisa Brown; Casting, Roger Mussenden; a Robert Simonds production; Dolby; Panavision; Technicolor; Rated PG-13; 85 minutes; Release date: October 12, 2001

### CAST

| | |
|---|---|
| Corky Romano | Chris Kattan |
| Agent Kate Russo | Vinessa Shaw |
| Pops | Peter Falk |
| Paulie | Peter Berg |
| Peter | Chris Penn |
| Leo Corrigan | Fred Ward |
| Howard Shuster | Richard Roundtree |
| Agent Brick Davis | Matthew Glave |
| Agent Bob Cox | Roger Fan |
| Agent Terrence Darnell | Dave Sheridan |

and Michael Massee (Angry Gunman), Vincent Pastore (Tony), Fiona Hale (Florence), Al Eben (Dale), Kip King (Dr. Kipper), Adele Craig (Connie), Irene Olga Lopez (Mrs. Hernandez), Sylvester Jenkins (Mr. Langford—Old Man), Jeanette Miller (Phyllis—Old Woman with Cat), Blake Clark (Security Guard), Zach Galifianakis (Dexter—Hacker), April Tran (Vietnamese Man), Eck Stone (Thai Man), Kevin Indio Copeland, Dennis Keiffer, Justin Riemer, Tim Sitarz (Skinheads), Kristina Simonds (Woman in Classroom), Rena Mero (Bouncer), John Farley (Ice Cream Vendor), Howard Weitzman (Attorney), Dilva Henry, Patrick Stinson, James Hill (Reporters), Steven Wilde (Chaz, Bouncer), James Tupper (FBI Agent), Sean Greenhut (Coughing Kid), Flora Burke (Woman with Dog), Grant Silver (Boy with Mouse), Robin Borovic (Secretary), Gary C. Smith (Hank), Ashton Dane, Joseph Dubow (SWAT Team), Gary C. Smith (Precision Driver)

*Corky Romano, a good-natured veterinarian, is ordered by his Mafia-king-pin dad to infiltrate the FBI and steal some important evidence against the old man.*

© Touchstone Pictures

Chris Kattan, Fred Ward

Chris Kattan, Matthew Glave, Richard Roundtree

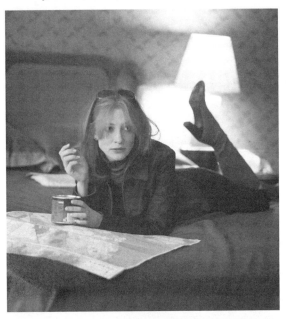

Billy Bob Thornton, Cate Blanchett, Bruce Willis

Cate Blanchett

# BANDITS

(MGM) Producers, Ashok Amritraj, David Hoberman, Arnold Rifkin, Barry Levinson, Paula Weinstein, Michael Birnbaum, Michele Berk; Executive Producers, Patrick McCormick, Harley Peyton, David Willis; Director, Barry Levinson; Screenplay, Harley Peyton; Photography, Dante Spinotti; Designer, Victor Kempster; Editor, Stu Linder; Costumes, Gloria Gresham; Music, Christopher Young; Executive Music Producers, Joel Sill, Allan Mason; Casting, Ellen Chenoweth; an Empire Pictures, Lotus Pictures, Baltimore/Spring Creek Pictures, Cheyenne Enterprises production, presented in association with Hyde Park Entertainment; Dolby; Super 35 Widescreen; Deluxe color; Rated PG-13; 123 minutes; Release date: October 12, 2001

## CAST

| | |
|---|---|
| Joe Blake | Bruce Willis |
| Terry Collins | Billy Bob Thornton |
| Kate Wheeler | Cate Blanchett |
| Harvey Pollard | Troy Garity |
| Darill Miller | Brian F. O'Byrne |
| Cloe Miller | Stacey Travis |
| Darren Head | Bobby Slayton |
| Claire | January Jones |
| Cheri | Azura Skye |
| Mildred Kronenberg | Peggy Miley |
| Charles Wheeler | William Converse-Roberts |
| Lawrence Fife | Richard Riehle |
| Sarah Fife | Micole Mercurio |
| Wildwood Policeman | Scott Burkholder |
| Phil | Anthony Burch |
| Billy Saunders | Sam Levinson |
| Monica Miller | Scout LaRue Willis |
| Erika Miller | Tallulah Belle Willis |

and John Evans (Ralph), John Harrington Bland (Flamingo Clerk), Cindy Goldfield, Heather Matheson, Erin-Kate Whitcomb (Debbie Days), Kim Bogus (Bend Bank Teller), Michael X. Sommers, Rich Sickler (Policemen), Michael Birnbaum (Desk Sergeant), Joe Unitas (Detective), Richard Shuster (LA Chopper Pilot), Jennifer York (LA Reporter), José Guillermo Garcia (Local Youth), Alfred De Contreras (Mexican Priest), Peter Weireter (SWAT Commander), Kerry Kilbride, Jane Velez-Mitchell (Debaters), Mia Lee (Los Angeles Anchor), Louis LeRay, Peter Hutchison, Maya Rossi (Band Members), Joan Palmateer (Bank Teller), Giulio Magnolia (Butler), Rose Aispuro (Bank Hostage), Carrie Casano (Bank Manager), Jaye K. Danford (Alamo Bank Manager), Darryl D. Stewart (Detective), Greg Wilmarth (U.S. Marshal)

*Two escaped cons, making a name for themselves as bank robbers known as "the sleepover bandits," find their lives complicated by a runaway housewife who comes between them.*

© Metro-Goldwyn-Mayer Pictures, Inc.

Troy Garity, January Jones

Cate Blanchett, Troy Garity, Bruce Willis

113

Albert Brooks, Leelee Sobieski

Leelee Sobieski

# MY FIRST MISTER

**(PARAMOUNT CLASSICS)** Producers, Carol Baum, Jane Goldenring, Mitchell Solomon, Sukee Chew, Anne Kurtzman; Executive Producers, Frank Hübner, Gerald Green; Director, Christine Lahti; Screenplay, Jill Franklyn; Co-Executive Producers, Jon F. Vein, Howard Rosenman, Robert Kurtzman; Photography, Jeffrey Jur; Designer, Dan Bishop; Costumes, Kimberly A. Tillman; Music, Steve Porcaro; Music Supervisor, Andy Hill; Editor, Wendy Greene Bricmont; Casting, Amanda Mackey Johnson, Cathy Sandrich; a Total Film Group presentation in association with Film Roman, Inc. of a Firelight/Apollomedia co-production; Dolby; Panavision; Deluxe color; Rated R; 109 minutes; Release date: October 12, 2001

## CAST

Randall ("R")................................................................Albert Brooks
Jennifer ("J")...............................................................Leelee Sobieski
Randy ..........................................................................Desmond Harrington
Bob...............................................................................Michael McKean
Mrs. Benson ................................................................Carol Kane
Patty.............................................................................Mary Kay Place
Benjamin .....................................................................John Goodman
Woman in Apartment...................................................Rutanya Alda
Girl in Vintage .............................................................Natasha Braisewell
Jack Taylor (Salesman) ................................................Henry Brown
Mr. Smithman..............................................................Gary Bullock
Doctor ..........................................................................Kevin Cooney
Blaine (Surfer Boy) ......................................................Nic Costa
Customer.......................................................................William Forward
Woman at R's Store......................................................Shawn Huff
Manager........................................................................Chadwick Palmatier
Bebe..............................................................................Pauley Perrette
Sheila ...........................................................................Lisa Jane Persky
Ashley...........................................................................Katee Sackhoff
and Lorna Scott (Woman in Store), Matthew St. Clair (Kevin), Chris Wylde (Waiter—Coffee House)

*Jennifer, an angry, cynical teenager, gets a job at a clothing store where she forms an unlikely friendship with the manager, Randall, a well-ordered older man who couldn't be less like her.*

© Paramount Classics

Desmond Harrington

Carol Kane

Julie Delpy, Ethan Hawke

# WAKING LIFE

(FOX SEARCHLIGHT) Producers, Palmer West, Jonah Smith, Tommy Pallotta, Anne Walker-McBay; Executive Producers, Jonathan Sehring, Caroline Kaplan, John Sloss; Director/Screenplay, Richard Linklater; Art Director, Bob Sabiston; Editor, Sandra Adair; Music, Glover Gill, Tosca Tango Orchestra; Animators, Jason Archer, Paul Beck, John Bruch, Jean Caffeine, Zoë Charlton, Randy Cole, Kate Dollenmayer, Jennifer Drummond, Rahab El Ewaly, Pat Falconer, Holly Louise Fisher, Dan Gillotte, Nathan Jensen, Matthew Langland, Michael Layne, Travis C. Lindquist, Chris Minley, Katy O'Connor, John Paul, Shannon Pearson, Eric Power, Bob Sabiston, Susan Sabiston, Katie Salen, Divya Srinivasan, Patrick Thornton, Penny Van Horn, Mary Varn, Rosie Q. Weaver, Wiley Wiggins, Constance Wood; Casting, Lizzie Martinez; a Detour Film production, presented by The Independent Film Channel Productions and Thousand Words; Dolby; Color; Rated R; 97 minutes; Release date: October 17, 2001

## CAST

Trevor Jack Brooks, Lorelei Linklater, Wiley Wiggins, Glover Gill, Lara Hicks, Ames Asbell, Leigh Mahoney, Sara Nelson, Jeanine Attaway, Erik Grostic, Bill Wise, Robert C. Solomon, Kim Krizan, Eamonn Healy, J. C. Shakespeare, Ethan Hawke, Julie Delpy, Charles Gunning, David Sosa, Alex Jones, Otto Hofmann, Aklilu Gebrewold, Carol Dawson, Lisa Moore, Steve Fitch, Louis Mackey, Alex Nixon, Violet Nichols, Steven Prince, Ken Webster, Mary McBay, Kregg A. Foote, Jason T. Hodge, Guy Forsyth, John Christensen, Caveh Zahedi, David Jewell, Adam Goldberg, Nicky Katt, E. Jason Liebricht, Brent Green, RC Whittaker, Hymie Samuelson, David Martinez, Ryan Power, Tiana Hux, Speed Levitch, Steve Brudniak, Marta Banda, Steven Soderbergh, Charles Murdock, Mona Lee, Edith Mannix, Bess Cox, Louis Black, Richard Linklater

*In this live-action feature on which the footage was afterward graphically "painted" frame by frame by computer, a young man travels through a surreal series of encounters with various people offering him their philosophies on life.*

© Twentieth Century Fox

Brent Green

Speed Levitch

Marta Banda, Wiley Wiggins

David Jewell, Caveh Zahedi

Meat Loaf Aday

# FOCUS

**(PARAMOUNT CLASSICS)** Producers, Neal Slavin, Michael R. Bloomberg, Robert A. Miller; Executive Producers, Martin Geller, Neil O'Connor, Jamie Rizzo, Anita Slavin; Co-Producers, Thomas D. Adelman, Kip Konwiser; Director, Neal Slavin; Screenplay, Kendrew Lascelles; Based on the novel by Arthur Miller; Line Producer, Thomas D. Adelman; Photography, Juan Ruiz-Anchia; Designer, Vlasta Svoboda; Editor, Tariq Anwar; Music, Mark Adler; Casting, Mary Vernieu, Anne Mcarthy, Felicia Fasano; a Michael R. Bloomberg and Focus Productions presentation of a Robert A. Miller production in association with Carros Pictures; Dolby; Color; Rated PG-13; 104 minutes; Release date: October 19, 2001

## CAST

| | |
|---|---|
| Lawrence Newman | William H. Macy |
| Gertrude Hart | Laura Dern |
| Finkelstein | David Paymer |
| Fred | Meat Loaf Aday |
| Mrs. Newman | Kay Hewtrey |
| Carlson | Michael Copeman |
| Father Crighton | Kenneth Welsh |
| Gargan | Joseph Ziegler |
| Mrs. Dewitt | Arlene Meadows |
| Willy Doyle | Peter Oldring |
| Meeting Hall Man | Robert McCarrol |
| Sullivan | Shaunn Austin-Olsen |
| Cole Stevens | Kevin Jubinville |
| Mel | B. J. McQueen |

and Conrad Bergschneider (Tough's Leader), Brad Austin (1st Tough), David Blacker (Petey), Betariz Pizano (Rape Victim), Rick Braggins (Mr. Lorring), Rodger Barton (Sergeant), Andrew Massingham (Policeman), Bryon Billy (Billy), Anita Burkhart (Speaking Woman on Subway), Olivia Slavin (Mrs. Dewitt's Granddaughter), Wendy Lyon (Elsie), Angela Fusco (2nd Woman on Subway), Barbara Barnes-Hopkins (Maid), Stephan Brogren (Bodyguard), Paulette Sinclair (MP Receptionist), Pat Patterson (Green Grocer), Julia Paton (Waitress), Leo Petrus (Truck Driver), Durward Allen (Photographer), Peter Evans (Man in Theater), Tedde Moore, Anna-Louise Richardson (Women in Theater).

*Mild-mannered Lawrence Newman finds himself unexpectedly facing anti-Semitism when his new pair of glasses leads people to believe that he is Jewish.*

© Paramount Classics

Laura Dern, William H. Macy

David Paymer

William H. Macy, Laura Dern

Mark Ruffalo, Robert Redford

James Gandolfini, Robert Redford

# THE LAST CASTLE

**(DREAMWORKS)** Producer, Robert Lawrence; Executive Producer, Don Zepfel; Director, Rod Lurie; Screenplay, David Scarpa, Graham Yost; Story, David Scarpa; Photography, Shelly Johnson; Designer, Kirk M. Petruccelli; Costumes, Ha Nguyen; Editors, Michael Jablow, Kevin Stitt; Music, Jerry Goldsmith; 2nd Unit Director/Stunts, Mic Rodgers; Casting, Deborah Aquila, Mary Jo Slater; a Robert Lawrence production; Dolby; Panavision; Technicolor; Rated R; 131 minutes; Release date: October 19, 2001

## CAST

| | |
|---|---|
| General Irwin | Robert Redford |
| Colonel Winter | James Gandolfini |
| Yates | Mark Ruffalo |
| Captain Peretz | Steve Burton |
| General Wheeler | Delroy Lindo |
| Dellwo | Paul Calderon |
| Duffy | Samuel Ball |
| Cutbush | Jeremy Childs |
| Aguilar | Clifton Collins, Jr. |
| Thumper | George W. Scott |
| Beaupre | Brian Goodman |
| Enriquez | Michael Irby |
| Doc | Frank Military |
| Rosalie Irwin | Robin Wright Penn |
| Sgt. McLaren | Maurice Bullard |
| Pvt. Niebolt | Nick Kokich |
| Corporal Zamorro | David Alford |

and Dean Hall (Harris), Peg Allen (Secretary, Kelly), Rick Vito (Red Team Leader), Forrest D. Bradford (Simmons), Scott Michael (Gunton), Dean Miller (Carvelli), Kristen Shaw (Clerk, Staff Sgt.), Michael Davis (Honor Guard), Joe Keenan (Trustee, Lester), David Chattam (Wheeler's Aide), Dan Cole (Trustee #2), Hans Mooy (Sgt. Moore), James Jerome Thomas (Rapper), Stephen Sandfort, Jamie Roberto Mantecon, Jeffrey G. Fagan, Lyon Fleming, Darius Willis, Rico Moody, Rocky Abou-Sakher (Inmates), Sean Cameron (Guard), Mary Jean McAdams (Visitor)

Clifton Collins, Jr.

Steve Burton

Frank Military, Robert Redford

*A noted general, court-martialed and stripped of his rank, is sent to a military prison where he clashes with its iron-fisted warden.*

© DreamWorks LLC

# RIDING IN CARS WITH BOYS

(COLUMBIA) Producers, James L. Brooks, Julie Ansell, Richard Sakai, Sara Colleton, Laurence Mark; Executive Producers, Morgan Upton Ward, Bridget Johnson; Director, Penny Marshall; Screenplay, Morgan Upton Ward; Based on the book by Beverly D'Onofrio; Photography, Miroslav Ondricek; Designer, Bill Groom; Costumes, Cynthia Flynt; Editors, Richard Marks, Lawrence Jordan; Music, Hans Zimmer, Heitor Pereira; Co-Producers, Timothy M. Bourne, Amy Lemisch, Beverly Donofrio; Casting, Sheila Jaffe, Georgianne Walken; a Gracie Films production; Dolby; Deluxe color; Rated PG-13; 122 minutes; Release date: October 19, 2001

Steve Zahn, Drew Barrymore

Adam Garcia

## CAST

Beverly Donofrio .................................................................Drew Barrymore
Ray Hasek ................................................................................Steve Zahn
Fay Forrester ....................................................................Brittany Murphy
Jason (20 years old).................................................................Adam Garcia
Mrs. Donofrio ...................................................................Lorraine Bracco
Mr. Donofrio...........................................................................James Woods
Tina ........................................................................................Sara Gilbert
Bobby ...........................................................................Desmond Harrington
Lizard.................................................................................David Moscow
Amelia (20 years old).........................................................Maggie Gyllenhaal
Tommy Butcher .................................................................Peter Facinelli
Janet (19 years old) .................................................................Marisa Ryan
Beverly (11 years old)..............................................................Mika Boorem
Amelia (8 years old)........................................Skye McCole Bartusiak
Jason (8 years old) ...............................................................Logan Lerman
Jason (6 years old) ...................................................................Cody Arens
Jason (3 years old)...................................................................Logan Arens
Shirley .......................................................................................Rosie Perez
Janet (8 years old) .................................................................Celine Marget
Uncle Lou ...........................................................................Vincent Pastore
Aunt Ann.............................................................................Maryann Urbano
Jenny.................................................................................Aleksia Landeau
Cindy ..................................................................................Kristin Proctor
Karen ..................................................................................Temple Brooks
Karen's Friend .........................................................................Lauren Lake
Kevin ....................................................................................Jordan Gelber
Sky Barrister.................................................................Gabriel Carpenter
Mark ......................................................................................Kevin Thoms
Jail Ward .............................................................................Kevin O'Rourke
Mrs. Forrester ......................................................................Susan Forristal
Mr. Forrester ................................................................John Bedford Lloyd
1st Phone Call Flirt........................................................Paz De La Huerta
Janet (12 years old) ....................................................Olivia Morgan Scheck
Wedding Singer Tony...............................................................Dusty Rizzo
Pete .......................................................................................Gene Canfield
Donofrio Cousin ...............................................................Heather Hodder
Zippy .....................................................................................Sean Liotine
Nurse .....................................................................................Tracy Reiner
Jason (newborn)...........................Joseph M. Cannizaro, Noah Hartwick
Jason (baby) .........................................................................Briana Tilden
Jason (1 year old) .....................................................................Skye Arens
and Patrick Salerno, Robert Salerno (Jason—2 years old), Samantha Reale (Amelia—3 years old), Wade Mylius (Al), Jon Korkes (Counselor), Samantha Lucier (Amelia—6 years old), Gaetano Lisi (Sweeny's Owner), Michael Linstroth (Dennis Forrester)

*Beverly Donofrio looks back on how her life was derailed when she got pregnant at age 15 and ended up married to a man with no ambitions and a drug dependency.*

© Columbia Pictures Industries Inc.

Sara Gilbert, David Moscow, Celine Marget, Lorraine Bracco, Drew Barrymore, James Woods, Steve Zahn, Brittany Murphy, Desmond Harrington

# FROM HELL

(20TH CENTURY FOX) Producers, Don Murphy, Jane Hamsher; Executive Producers, Amy Robinson, Thomas M. Hammel, Allen Hughes, Albert Hughes; Director, The Hughes Brothers (Allen Hughes, Albert Hughes); Screenplay, Terry Hayes, Rafael Yglegias; Based on the graphic novel by Alan Moore, Eddie Campbell; Photography, Peter Deming; Designer, Martin Childs; Costumes, Kym Barrett; Editors, Dan Lebental, George Bowers; Music, Trevor Jones; Casting, Joyce Gallie, Sally Osoba; an Underworld Pictures/Don Murphy and Jane Hamsher/Amy Robinson production; Dolby; Panavision; Deluxe color; Rated R; 121 minutes; Release date: October 19, 2001

Johnny Depp

## CAST

| | |
|---|---|
| Fred Abberline | Johnny Depp |
| Mary Kelly | Heather Graham |
| Sir William Gull | Ian Holm |
| Netley | Jason Flemyng |
| Peter Godley | Robbie Coltrane |
| Kate Eddowes | Lesley Sharp |
| Liz Stride | Susan Lynch |
| Ben Kidney | Terence Harvey |
| Dark Annie Chapman | Katrin Cartlidge |
| Ada | Estelle Skornik |
| Dr. Ferral | Paul Rhys |
| Officer Bolt | Nicholas McGaughey |
| Sir Charles Warren | Ian Richardson |
| Polly | Annabelle Apsion |
| Ann Crook | Joanna Page |
| Albert Sickert (Prince Edward) | Mark Dexter |
| Constable Withers | Danny Midwinter |
| Martha Tabram | Samantha Spiro |
| Mcqueen | David Schofield |
| Robert Best | Bryon Fear |
| Lord Hallsham | Peter Eyre |
| Mac (Bartender) | Cliff Parisi |
| Victoria Abberline | Sophia Myles |
| Gordie | Ralph Ineson |
| Gull's Maid | Amy Huck |
| Doss Landlord | Rupert Farley |
| Hospital Director | Donald Douglas |
| Marylebone Governor | John Owens |
| Opium Den Owner | Tony Tang |
| Queen Victoria | Liz Moscrop |
| Sidewalk Preacher | Roger Frost |
| Robert Drudge | Ian McNeice |
| Special Branch Constable | Steve John Shepherd |
| Stonecutter | Al Hunter Ashton |
| Alice Crook | Poppy Rogers |
| Ann Crook's Father | Bruce Byron |
| Ann Crook's Mother | Melanie Hill |

Robbie Coltrane

Heather Graham

and Andy Linden (Carpenter), David Fisher (Carpenter, Letter Writer), Gary Powell, Steve Chaplin, Dominic Cooper (Constables), Vincent Franklin (George Lusk), Louise Atkins (Bold Hooker), Anthony Parker (John Merrick), James Greene (Masonic Governor), Carey Thring (Police Photographer), Vladimir Kulhavy (Rag & Bone Man), Graham Kent (Records Clerk), Ruper Holliday Evans (Sailor), Simon Harrison (Thomas Bond), Paul Moody (Young Doctor), Glen Berry (Young Labourer), Charlie Parish (Labourer #2), Gerry Grennell (Funeral Minister, Ltr. Writer), Pavel Vokoun, John Dent (Horse Masters)

*In 1888 London, Fred Abberline, a brilliant police inspector, is called on by Scotland Yard to help solve the murders of several prostitutes.*

© Twentieth Century Fox

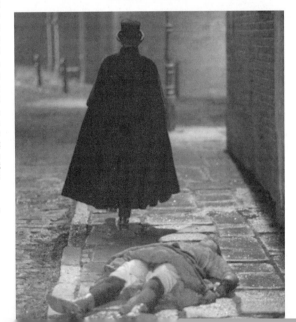

# BONES

**(NEW LINE CINEMA)** Producers, Lloyd Segan, Peter Heller, Rupert Harvey; Executive Producer, Carolyn Manetti; Director, Ernest Dickerson; Screenplay, Adam Simon, Tim Metcalfe; Co-Producer, Leon Dudevoir, Stephen Hollocker; Photography, Flavio Labiano; Designer, Douglas Higgins; Editors, Michael N. Knue, Stephen Lovejoy; Visual Effects Supervisor, Ariel Shaw; Costumes, Dana Campbell; Music, Elia Cmiral; Casting, Susan Taylor Brouse, Anya Colloff, Jennifer Fishman, Amy McIntyre Britt; a Lloyd Segan Company production in association with Heller Highwater Productions; Dolby; Super 35 Widescreen; Deluxe color; Rated R; 96 minutes; Release date: October 24, 2001

Shannon Elizabeth, Tony Shalhoub

## CAST

| | |
|---|---|
| Jimmy Bones | Snoop Dogg |
| Pearl | Pam Grier |
| Lupovich | Michael T. Weiss |
| Jeremiah Peet | Clifton Powell |
| Eddie Mack | Ricky Harris |
| Cynthia | Bianca Lawson |
| Patrick. | Khalil Kain |
| Bill | Merwin Mondesir |
| Maurice | Sean Amsing |

and Katharine Isabelle (Tia), Ronald Selmour (Shotgun), Deezer D (Stank), Garikayi Mutambirwa (Weaze), Erin Wright (Snowflake), Josh Byer (Jason), Kirby Morrow (Palmer), Ellen Ewusie (The Death Lady), Lynda Boyd (Nancy), Boyan Vukelic (Young Cop), Marcus Moldowan (Young Patrick), Mavis D'Andrade (Old Woman, Street), Colin Foo (Elderly Seance Man), Emy Aneke (Clubber), Randy Schooley (Investigator), Tracey Classen (Bones Shadow), Donny Lucas (Crackhead), Shanel Nelson-Murray, Chaynade Knowles, Brittany Moldowan (Skipping Girls), Helena Yea, D. Harland Cutshall, Carlos Joe Costa, Gladys Phillip (Seance People), Jeni Legon (Window Granny), Chaka White (Foxy Lady), Keith Provost, Brantley Bush (Cops), Linda Chow (Jeremiah's 1st Wife), Charles Jones, Jr. (Elderly Man)

*Two men purchase a rundown brownstone in a devastated, drug-ridden area, hoping to turn the place into a nightclub, little realizing that the tormented soul of murdered anti-drug crusader, Jimmy Bones, dwells in the building.*

© New Line Cinema

F. Murray Abraham

(Below) Snoop Dogg, Pam Grier

# THIR13EN GHOSTS

**(WARNER BROS./COLUMBIA)** Producers, Gilbert Adler, Joel Silver, Robert Zemeckis; Executive Producers, Dan Cracchiolo, Steve Richards; Director, Steve Beck; Screenplay, Neal Marshall Stevens, Richard D'Ovidio; Story, Robb White; Co-Producers, Terry Castle, Richard Mirisch; Photography, Gale Tattersall; Designer, Sean Hargreaves; Editors, Derek G. Brechin, Edward A. Warschilka; Visual Effects Supervisor, Dan Glass; Music, John Frizzell; Special Makeup Effects, Howard Berger, Gregory Nicotero, Robert Kurtzman; Casting, Christine Sheaks; a Dark Castle Entertainment production; Dolby; Technicolor; Rated R; 91 minutes; Release date: October 26, 2001

## CAST

| | |
|---|---|
| Arthur Kriticos | Tony Shalhoub |
| Kalina | Embeth Davidtz |
| Rafkin | Matthew Lillard |
| Kathy Kriticos | Shannon Elizabeth |
| Bobby Kriticos | Alec Roberts |
| Ben Moss | JR Bourne |
| Maggie | Rah Diga |
| Cyrus | F. Murray Abraham |
| Damon | Matthew Harrison |

and Jacob Rupp (Cyrus's Assistant), Mike Crestejo, Aubrey Lee Culp, Charles Andre (Team Members), Mikhael Speidel (The First Born Son), Daniel Wesley (The Torso), Laura Mennell (The Bound Woman), Kathryn Anderson (Jean Kriticos), Craig Olejnik (The Torn Prince), Shawna Loyer (The Angry Princess), Xantha Radley (The Pilgrimess), C. Ernst Harth (The Great Child), Laurie Soper (The Dire Mother), Herbert Duncanson (The Hammer), Shayne Wyler (The Jackal), John De Santis (The Juggernaut)

*Widower Arthur Kriticos inherits a magnificent glass home from his estranged Uncle Cyrus, only to find out that it houses twelve spirits in search of a thirteenth ghost. Remake of the 1960 Columbia film* 13 Ghosts *that starred Donald Woods, Charles Herbert, Martin Milner, and Rosemary DeCamp.*

© Warner Bros. and Columbia Pictures

Kevin Spacey, Jeff Bridges

Kevin Spacey

Jeff Bridges, Mary McCormack

## K-PAX

(UNIVERSAL) Producers, Lawrence Gordon, Lloyd Levin, Robert F. Colesberry; Executive Producer, Susan G. Pollock; Director, Iain Softley; Screenplay, Charles Leavitt; Based on the novel by Gene Brewer; Photography, John Mathieson; Designer, John Beard; Costumes, Louise Mingenbach; Editor, Craig McKay; Music, Edward Shearmur; Co-Producer, Michael Levy; Casting, Debra Zane; an Intermedia Films presentation of a Lawrence Gordon production; Dolby; Panavision; Technicolor; Rated PG-13; 120 minutes; Release date: October 26, 2001

### CAST

| | |
|---|---|
| Prot | Kevin Spacey |
| Dr. Mark Powell | Jeff Bridges |
| Rachel Powell | Mary McCormack |
| Claudia Villars | Alfre Woodard |
| Howie | David Patrick Kelly |
| Ernie | Saul Williams |
| Sal | Peter Gerety |
| Mrs. Archer | Celia Weston |
| Dr. Chakraborty | Ajay Naidu |
| Maria | Tracy Vilar |
| Bess | Melanee Murray |
| Russell | John Toles-Bey |
| Joyce Trexler | Kimberly Scott |
| Betty McAllister | Conchata Ferrell |
| Navarro | Vincent Laresca |
| Simms | Mark Christopher Lawrence |
| Steve | Brian Howe |
| Abby | Mary Mara |

and Tess McCarthy (Natalie Powell), Natasha Dorfhuber (Gabby Powell), Brandon Michael DePaul (Josh), Aaron Paul (Michael Powell), William Lucking (Sheriff), Kelly Connell (Walter Fleen), Peter Maloney (Duncan Flynn), Lance Nichols (David Patel), Paul Linke (Stuart Hessler), Christopher Jason Brown (Danny Trexler), Greg Lewis (Dominic McAllister), Clarke Peters (Homeless Veteran), Olga Merediz, Joe Holt (Transit Officers), Lola Pashalinski (Russian Woman), Kateri Walker (Sara Porter), Katya Abelsky (Rebecca Porter), Scott Lincoln (Walker), Clebert Ford (Homeless Man), Norman Alden (Babbling Man), Rawle D. Lewis, Erik Laray Harvey (Security Guards), Zofia Borucka (Woman on Train), Tony Rhune, Vincent Capone (Thugs)

*Psychiatrist Mark Powell tries to find the truth behind Prot, an odd man brought into the mental ward who claims to be a visitor from a distant planet called K-PAX.*

© Universal Studios

Jeff Bridges

# LIFE AS A HOUSE

(NEW LINE CINEMA) Producers, Irwin Winkler, Rob Cowan; Executive Producers, Lynn Harris, Michael DeLuca, Brian Frankish; Director, Irwin Winkler; Screenplay, Mark Andrus; Photography, Vilmos Zsigmond; Designer, Dennis Washington; Costumes, Molly Maginnis; Editor, Julie Monroe; Music, Mark Isham; Casting, Sarah Halley Finn, Randi Hiller; Dolby; Panavision; Deluxe color; Rated R; 124 minutes; Release date: October 26, 2001

## CAST

George Monroe ........................................................................Kevin Kline
Robin Kimball..........................................................Kristin Scott Thomas
Sam .............................................................................Hayden Christensen
Alyssa Beck ....................................................................................Jena Malone
Colleen Beck .........................................................Mary Steenburgen
Adam Kimball ..................................................................Mike Weinberg
Ryan Kimball ............................................................Scotty Leavenworth
Josh....................................................................................Ian Somerhalder
Peter Kimball ...............................................................Jamey Sheridan
Kurt Walker ...........................................................................Scott Bakula
Nurses .........................................................Sandra Nelson, Gwen McGee
David Dokos .............................................................................Sam Robards
Bryan Burke ...........................................................................John Pankow
Bob Larson..........................................................................Kim Delgado
Tom ..............................................................................................Barry Primus
Barbara.......................................................................................Margo Winkler
Marek.......................................................................................Brandon Kessel
Corey ...........................................................................................Jon Foster
Steven Gardner .................................................................Art Chudabula
and Claire Yarlitt (Receptionist), Mike O'Guinne (Dale), Tannis Benedict (Secretary), Anne Betancourt (Officer), Lisa Lovett-Mann (Young Woman), Hillary Tuck (Alyssa's Friend), Steven Artenian (Contractor), J. J. (Guster the Dog)

*Sacked from his job and aware that he is dying, George Monroe insists that his estranged son Sam spend the summer with him, helping rebuild his house.*

© New Line Cinema

Kevin Kline

Kristin Scott Thomas

Mary Steenburgen

Jena Malone, Hayden Christensen

Noah Wyle, Drew Barrymore

Jake Gyllenhaal, Jena Malone, James Duval

Patrick Swayze

Mary McDonnell, Holmes Osborne

# DONNIE DARKO

(NEWMARKET) Producers, Sean McKittrick, Nancy Juvonen, Adam Fields; Executive Producers, Drew Barrymore, Hunt Lowry, Casey La Scala, William Tyrer, Chris J. Ball, Aaron Ryder; Director/Screenplay, Richard Kelly; Photography, Steven Poster; Designer, Alexander Hammond; Costumes, April Ferry; Editors, Sam Bauer, Eric Strand; Line Producer, Tom Hayslip; Music, Michael Andrews; Music Supervisors, Manish Raval, Tom Wolfe; Casting, Joseph Middleton, Michelle Morris Gertz; a Flower Films production presented in association with Pandora; Dolby; Panavision; Color; Rated R; 122 minutes; Release date: October 26, 2001

## CAST

Donnie Darko.................................................................Jake Gyllenhaal
Gretchen Ross................................................................Jena Malone
Ms. Karen Pomeroy ......................................................Drew Barrymore
Frank.............................................................................James Duval
Kittie Farmer ................................................................Beth Grant
Elizabeth Darko ............................................................Maggie Gyllenhaal
Rose Darko ...................................................................Mary McDonnell
Eddie Darko .................................................................Holmes Osborne
Dr. Lilian Thurman ......................................................Katharine Ross
Jim Cunningham ...........................................................Patrick Swayze
Dr. Monnitoff...............................................................Noah Wyle
Seth Devlin...................................................................Alex Greenwald
Sean Smith ...................................................................Gary Lundy
Ricky Danforth .............................................................Seth Rogen
Ronald Fisher................................................................Stuart Stone
and Daveigh Chase (Samantha Darko), Patience Cleveland (Roberta Sparrow/Grandma Death), David Moreland (Principal Cole), Jolene Purdy (Cherita Chen), Arthur Taxier (Dr. Fisher), Mark Hoffman (Police Officer), David St. James (Bob Garland), Tom Tangen (Man in Red Jogging Suit), Jazzie Mahannah (Joanie James), Kristina Malota (Susie Bates), Marina Malota (Emily Bates), Carly Naples (Suzy Bailey), Tiler Peck (Beth Farmer), Lisa K. Wyatt (Linda Connie), Rachel Winfree (Shanda Riesman), Jack Salvatore, Jr. (Larry Riesman), Lee Weaver (Leroy), Phyllis Lyons (Anne Fisher), Ashley Tisdale (Dorky Girl), Alison Jones (Dorky Sister), Jerry Trainor (Lanky Kid), Joan Blair (Mystery Woman), Sarah Hudson (Friend), Fran Kranz (Passenger), Scotty Leavenworth (David)

*When teenager Donnie Darko has a near-death experience, he begins to question his existence, ultimately uncovering a power that could allow him to alter time and destiny.*

© Newmarket Films

Jon Polito, Billy Bob Thornton

Michael Badalucco

Katherine Borowitz

Scarlett Johannson

James Gandolfini

Billy Bob Thornton, James Gandolfini

Jon Polito

# THE MAN WHO WASN'T THERE

(USA FILMS) Producer, Ethan Coen; Executive Producers, Tim Bevan, Eric Fellner; Director, Joel Coen; Screenplay, Joel Coen, Ethan Coen; Co-Producer, John Cameron; Photography, Roger Deakins; Designer, Dennis Gassner; Costumes, Mary Zophres; Music, Carter Burwell; Editors, Roderick Jaynes, Tricia Cooke; Casting, Ellen Chenoweth; a Working Title production; Dolby; Black and white; Rated R; 116 minutes; Release date: October 31, 2001

## CAST

| | |
|---|---|
| Ed Crane | Billy Bob Thornton |
| Doris Crane | Frances McDormand |
| Frank | Michael Badalucco |
| Big Dave Nirdlinger | James Gandolfini |
| Ann Nirdlinger | Katherine Borowitz |
| Creighton Tolliver | Jon Polito |
| Birdy Abundas | Scarlett Johansson |
| Walter Abundas | Richard Jenkins |
| Freddy Riedenschneider | Tony Shalhoub |
| Persky | Christopher Kriesa |
| Krebs | Brian Haley |
| Burns | Jack McGee |
| The New Man | Gregg Binkley |
| Diedrickson | Alan Fudge |
| Medium | Lilyan Chauvin |
| Carcanogues | Adam Alexi-Malle |
| Bingo Caller | Ted Rooney |
| Young Man | Abraham Benrubi |
| Child | Christian Ferratti |
| Costanza | Rhoda Gemignani |
| Customer | E. J. Callahan |
| Sobbing Prisoner | Brooke Smith |
| Banker | Ron Ross |
| Waitress | Hallie Singleton |
| Gatto Eater | Jon Donnelly |
| Bailiff | Dan Martin |
| Tony | Nicholas Lanier |
| Judges | Tom Dahlgren, Booth Colman |
| New Man's Customer | Stanley DeSantis |
| Bartender | Peter Siragusa |
| Macadam Salesman | Christopher McDonald |
| Doctor | John Michael Higgins |
| District Attorney | Rick Scarry |
| Lloyd Garroway | Georges Ives |
| Swimming Boy | Devin Cole Borisoff |
| Prisoner Visitor | Mary Bogue |
| Pie Contest Timer | Don Donati |
| Flophouse Clerk | Arthur Reeves |

Tony Shalhoub, Frances McDormand

Billy Bob Thornton

*In a small northern California town in the late 1940s, Ed Crane, a passive barber, tries to better his lot by investing in a new technique for dry cleaning clothing, a scheme that leads him into blackmail and murder. This film received an Oscar nomination for cinematography.*

© USA Films

Mike Wazowski, Sulley

Sulley, Henry J. Waternoose

Mike Wazowski, Sulley

## MONSTERS, INC.

(WALT DISNEY PICTURES) Producer, Darla K. Anderson; Executive Producers, John Lasseter, Andrew Stanton; Director, Pete Docter; Co-Directors, Lee Unkrich, David Silverman; Associate Producer, Kori Rae; Screenplay, Andrew Stanton, Daniel Gerson; Original Story, Pete Docter, Jill Culton, Jeff Pidgeon, Ralph Eggleston; Music, Randy Newman; Song: "If I Didn't Have You" by Randy Newman/performed by Billy Crystal and John Goodman; Editor, Jim Stewart; Supervising Technical Director, Thomas Porter; Designers, Harley Jessup, Bob Pauley; Art Directors, Tia W. Kratter, Dominique Louis; Supervising Animators, Glenn McQueen, Rich Quade; Layout Supervisor, Ewan Johnson; Modeling Supervisor, Eben Ostby; Simulation & Effects Supervisors, Galyn Susman, Michael Fong; Casting, Ruth Lambert, Mary Hidalgo; a Pixar Animation Studios Film; Dolby; Technicolor; Rated G; 92 minutes; Release date: November 2, 2001

### CAST

James P. "Sulley" Sullivan...................................................John Goodman
Mike Wazowski........................................................................Billy Crystal
Boo.........................................................................................Mary Gibbs
Randall Boggs.....................................................................Steve Buscemi
Henry J. Waternoose ..........................................................James Coburn
Celia......................................................................................Jennifer Tilly
Roz.........................................................................................Bob Peterson
Yeti.................................................................................John Ratzenberger
Fungus........................................................................................Frank Oz
Needleman/Smitty .............................................................Daniel Gerson
Floor Manager ....................................................................Steve Susskind
Flint............................................................................................Bonnie Hunt
Bile...........................................................................................Jeff Pidgeon
George........................................................................................Sam Black

*Sulley and Mike, two employees of Monsters, Inc., a corporation dedicated to scaring children in order to capture their screams for power, find themselves in trouble when a little girl from the human universe accidentally crosses over into their world. 2001 Academy Award-winner for Best Original Song ("If I Didn't Have You"). This film received Oscar nominations for animated feature, sound effects editing, and original score.*

© Disney/Pixar

Mike Wazowski, Sulley

Roz

Mike Wazowski, Celia

Randall Boggs, Mike Wazowski, Sulley

Boo, Sulley

Ethan Hawke

Robert Sean Leonard

Uma Thurman

# TAPE

(LIONS GATE) Producers, Gary Winick, Alexis Alexanian, Anne Walker-McBay, John Sloss; Executive Producers, Jonathan Sehring, Caroline Kaplan; Director, Richard Linklater; Screenplay, Stephen Belber, based on his play; Co-Producers, Robert Cole, David Richenthal; Photography, Maryse Alberti; Designer, Stephen J. Beatrice; Editor, Sandra Adair; Costumes, Catherine Thomas; The Independent Film Channel Productions presentation of an InDigEnt Production in association with Detour Filmproduction; Dolby; Color; Rated R; 86 minutes; Release date: November 2, 2001

## CAST

| | |
|---|---|
| Vince | Ethan Hawke |
| John | Robert Sean Leonard |
| Amy | Uma Thurman |

*John meets up with his one-time high-school friend Vince, whose resentment toward John for dating his ex-girlfriend results in an ugly accusation.*

© Lions Gate Films

# THE ONE

(COLUMBIA) Producers, Glen Morgan, Steven Chasman; Executive Producers, Todd Garner, Charles Newirth, Lata Ryan, Greg Silverman; Director, James Wong; Screenplay, Glen Morgan, James Wong; Photography, Robert McLachlan; Designer, David L. Snyder; Editor, James Coblentz; Music, Trevor Rabin; Music Supervisor, Happy Walters; Costumes, Chrisi Karvonides-Dushenko; Visual Effects Supervisor, Eric Durst; Effects Animation Supervisor, Daniel Roizman; Special Effects Supervisor, Terry Frazee; Martial Arts Choreographer, Cory Yuen; Casting, John Papsidera; Stunts, Gary Hymes; a Revolution Studios presentation of a Hard Eight Pictures production; Dolby; Super 35 Widescreen; Deluxe color; Rated PG-13; 87 minutes; Release date: November 2, 2001

## CAST

| | |
|---|---|
| Gabe/Yulaw/Lawless | Jet Li |
| T. K./Massie Walsh | Carla Gugino |
| Roedecker/Attendant | Delroy Lindo |
| Funsch | Jason Statham |
| Aldrich/"A" World Inmate #1 | James Morrison |
| Yates | Dylan Bruno |
| D'Antoni | Richard Steinmetz |
| MVA Supervisor | Steve Rankin |
| Prison Warden | Tucker Smallwood |
| Nurse Besson | Harriet Sansom Harris |
| MRI Technician | David Keats |
| Sgt. Siegel | Dean Norris |
| Rotten Ronnie | Ron Zimmerman |
| Hugo | Darin Morgan |
| Cesar | Mark Borchardt |
| Dr. Franklin | Joel Stoffer |
| Dr. Hamilton | Kimberly Patton |

and Denney Pierce, Boots Southerland (ER Security Guards), Archie Kao (Woo), Ken Kerman, Kevin Indio Copeland ("A" World Inmates), Marco Verdier, Teddy Lane, Jr. ("C" World Inmates), Narinder Samra (Dr. Hackler), Clement E. Blake, Bill Dunnam (Penal Colony Inmates), Edward James Gage (Factory Worker), B. T. Taylor (Orderly), Thanh T. Tran (Sleeping Boy)

*In the future, when parallel universes exist, a renegade Multiverse agent sets out to destroy his alternate selves, knowing that eradicating each one will give him greater power toward his goal to become the only version of himself.*

© Revolution Studios

(Above) Jet Li. (Below) Jason Statham, Jet Li

Matt O'Leary, John Travolta

John Travolta

Vince Vaughn, Teri Polo

# DOMESTIC DISTURBANCE

(PARAMOUNT) Producers, Donald De Line, Jonathan D. Krane; Director, Harold Becker; Screenplay, Lewis Colick; Story, Lewis Colick, William S. Comanor, Gary Drucker; Photography, Michael Seresin; Designer, Clay A. Griffith; Costumes, Bobbie Read; Editor, Peter Honess; Co-Producer, James R. Dyer; Music, Mark Mancina; Casting, Gretchen Rennell Court; a De Line Pictures and Jonathan D. Krane production; Dolby; J-D-C Scope; Deluxe color; Rated PG-13; 91 minutes; Release date: November 2, 2001

## CAST

| | |
|---|---|
| Frank Morrison | John Travolta |
| Rick Barnes | Vince Vaughn |
| Susan | Teri Polo |
| Danny Morrison | Matt O'Leary |
| Diane | Susan Floyd |
| Ray Coleman | Steve Buscemi |
| Sgt. Edgar Stevens | Ruben Santiago-Hudson |
| Jason | James Lashly |
| Laurie | Rebecca Tilney |
| Theresa | Debra Mooney |
| Coach Mark | Leland L. Jones |
| Don Patterson | William Parry |
| Wedding Coordinator | Suzanne Nystrom |
| Wedding Photographer | George Christy |
| Priest | David Bridgewater |
| Walter Ward | Darryl Warren |
| Patty | Angelica Torn |
| Shady Tree Motel Clerk | Holmes Osborne |
| Detective Warren | Chris Ellis |

and Zach Hanner (Police Technician), Paul Ligotino (Mike), Nick Loren (Cop), Michael Tomlinson (Berman), Terry Loughlin (Judge), Jim Meskimen (Bob Lerner), Steve Roberts (Bartender), Sara Graves (Conroy's Waitress), Dianne Catterton (Waitress), Vipin Patel (Crestview Motel Manger), Patt Noday (TV Reporter), Benton Hill, Jr. (Wedding Band Leader), Vince Beard, Leroy Harper, Brad Lloyd, Brad Merritt, Marc Siegel, Vince Stout, Lee Venters (Wedding Band)

*Young Danny Morrison's dislike of his mother's fiancé, Rick Barnes, proves to be more than justified when he witnesses Barnes murdering a man and disposing of the body.*

John Travolta, Vince Vaughn

© Paramount Pictures

Gene Hackman, Danny DeVito

Gene Hackman, Rebecca Pidgeon

# HEIST

**(WARNER BROS.)** Producers, Art Linson, Elie Samaha, Andrew Stevens; Executive Producers, Don Carmody, Tracee Stanley, James Holt; Director/Screenplay, David Mamet; Photography, Robert Elswit; Designer, David Wasco; Costumes, Renée April; Editor, Barbara Tulliver; Music, Theodore Shapiro; Co-Producers, Cas Donovan, Scott Ferguson; Line Producer, Josette Perrotta; Casting, Avy Kaufman; a Morgan Creek Productions Inc. and Franchise Pictures presentation in association with Indelible Pictures; Dolby; Deluxe color; Rated R; 109 minutes; Release date: November 9, 2001

## CAST

| | |
|---|---|
| Joe Moore | Gene Hackman |
| Mickey Bergman | Danny DeVito |
| Bobby Blane | Delroy Lindo |
| Jimmy Silk | Sam Rockwell |
| Fran | Rebecca Pidgeon |
| Don "Pinky" Pincus | Ricky Jay |
| Betty Croft | Patti LuPone |
| Fast Food Customer | Alan Bilzerian |
| Counterman | Richard L. Friedman |
| Fast Food Cook | Robert Lussier |
| Jewelry Store Guard | Mark Camacho |
| Coffee Cart Man | Mike Tsarouchas |
| D. A. Freccia | Jim Frangione |
| Laszlo | Christopher R. Kaldor |
| Bartender | Danny Blanco Hall |
| Pool Player at Bar | Zodia McLean |
| State Trooper | Andreas Apergis |
| Coffee Man | Tony Calabretta |
| Customs Officer | Ted Whittal |

and Guy Sprung (Pilot), Richard Zeman (Co-Pilot), Don Jordan (Supervisor in Tower), Pierre LeBlanc (Controller in Tower), Richard Robitaille, Gregory Bryant Goossen (Officers), Charles Doucet (Mechanic), Bill Rowat (Official at Cargo Hangar), Benz Antoine (Trooper at Cargo Hangar), Emillie Cassini (Pincus's Niece), Jennifer Moorehouse (Cashier), Marlyne Affleck (Young Woman with Blane)

*Needing money to fund his retirement, thief Joe Moore and his gang agree to one last job to satisfy Joe's fence, Mickey Bergman, who insists his nephew participate in the heist.*

© Heightened Productions, Inc.

Gene Hackman, Sam Rockwell

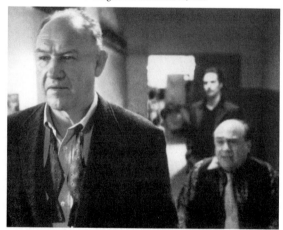

Gene Hackman, Sam Rockwell, Danny DeVito

# SHALLOW HAL

**(20TH CENTURY FOX)** Producers, Bradley Thomas, Charles B. Wessler, Bobby Farrelly, Peter Farrelly; Directors, Bobby Farrelly, Peter Farrelly; Screenplay, Sean Moynihan, Peter Farrelly, Bobby Farrelly; Photography, Russell Carpenter; Designer, Sidney J. Bartholomew, Jr.; Costumes, Pamela Withers; Editor, Christopher Greenbury; Co-Producers, Marc S. Fischer, Mark Charpentier; Music, Ivy; Music Supervisors, Tom Wolfe, Manish Raval; Makeup Effects Designers and Creators, Tony Gardner & Artists' Asylum; Casting, Rick Montgomery; a Condundrum Entertainment production; Dolby; Deluxe color; Rated PG-13; 113 minutes; Release date: November 9, 2001

Gwyneth Paltrow, Jack Black

## CAST

| | |
|---|---|
| Rosemary | Gwyneth Paltrow |
| Hal Larsen | Jack Black |
| Mauricio | Jason Alexander |
| Steve Shanahan | Joe Viterelli |
| Walt | Rene Kirby |
| Reverend Larsen | Bruce McGill |
| Himself | Tony Robbins |
| Jill | Susan Ward |
| Ralph | Zen Gesner |
| Katrina | Brooke Burns |
| Other Hostess | Rob Moran |
| Li'iBoy | Joshua "Li'iBoy" Shintani |

and Kyle Glass (Artie), Laura Kightlinger (Jen), Nan Martin (Nurse Tanya Peeler), Sasha Joseph Neulinger (Young Hal), John E. Jordan (Waiter), Jill Christine Fitzgerald (Mrs. Shanahan), Fawn Irish (Spastic Bella), Erinn Bartlett (Bella), Daniel Greene (Doctor), Danny Murphy (Cabbie), Brian Mone, Bob Mone (Board Members), Don Gavin (David Bouley), Leslie DeAntonio (Maid), Libby Langdon (Waitress), Gigi Moran, Caryl West (Nurses), Brianna Gardner (Sick Kid #1, Cadence), Mariann Neary, Christal Handy (Information Attendants), Jackie Flynn (Manager), Sascha Knopf (Gorgeous Tanya), Mary Wigmore (Cute Hostess), Heather Ann Rosbeck (Doorperson), Steve Tyler (Bocce Club Waiter), Darius Rucker (Maitre D'), Will Coogan, Lyndon Byers (Punks), Sara Stout (Babe on Dance Floor), Allison Anderson, Molly Bergman, Adriana Biega, Keri Bruno, Morgan Clements, Brittney Leigh daCosta, Jessica Nicole Fife, Stacy Fuson, Zoë Graham, Amanda Tascher Harmon, Nichole Hiltz, Katie Holliday, Ashley B. Howard, T Jamison, Mary Lajoinie, Chelsea Marguerite, Danae Miller, Jennifer Pentecost, Jennifer Sky, Christina Della Rose, Amanda Santos, Dana Zimmer (Sorority Girls), Bonnie Aarons, Lisa Brounstein (Spastic Friends), Herb Flynn, Michael Corrente (Homeless Men), Ron Darling (Other Li'iBoy), Anne E. Hodgson, Kelly McRorie (Bar Girls), John Dennis (Guy in Bar), Dean R. Palozej (Bartender), Dede Kinerk (Party Friend), David Kipper (Department Store Clerk), Sayed Badreya (Pediatric Doctor), David Getz (Dr. James Uler), Tom Hohman, James Badstibner (Frat Boys), Jesse Peter, Anna Byers (Sick Kids), Sean P. Gildea (Pool Dad), Robby Johns (Kid in Tree), Tiffany Anne Marie Lucich (Soda Shop Waitress), Hillary Matthews Thomas (Pretty Girl)

*Hal Larsen, a superficial man who judges women strictly on their looks, is put under a spell that forces him to see only a person's inner beauty, thereby allowing him to fall madly in love with a kindly, overweight woman.*

Gwyneth Paltrow

© Twentieth Century Fox

**(Below) Jason Alexander, Jack Black**

Tony Robbins, Jack Black

# HARRY POTTER AND THE SORCERER'S STONE

(WARNER BROS.) a.k.a. *Harry Potter and the Philosopher's Stone*; Producer, David Heyman; Executive Producers, Chris Columbus, Mark Radcliffe, Michael Barnathan, Duncan Henderson; Director, Chris Columbus; Screenplay, Steve Kloves; Based on the novel *Harry Potter and the Philosopher's Stone* by J. K. Rowling; Photography, John Seale; Designer, Stuart Craig; Costumes, Judianna Makovsky; Editor, Richard Francis-Bruce; Music, John Williams; Visual Effects Supervisor, Robert Legato; Creature & Makeup Effects, Nick Dudman; Casting, Susie Figgis; a Heyday Films/1492 Pictures/Duncan Henderson production; Dolby; Panavision; Technicolor; Rated PG; 152 minutes; Release date: November 16, 2001

Daniel Radcliffe

## CAST

| | |
|---|---|
| Harry Potter | Daniel Radcliffe |
| Ron Weasley | Rupert Grint |
| Hermione Granger | Emma Watson |
| Nearly Headless Nick | John Cleese |
| Rubeus Hagrid | Robbie Coltrane |
| Professor Flitwick/Goblin Bank Teller | Warwick Davis |
| Uncle Vernon Dursley | Richard Griffiths |
| Professor Albus Dumbledore | Richard Harris |
| Professor Quirrell | Ian Hart |
| Mr. Ollivander | John Hurt |
| Professor Snape | Alan Rickman |
| Aunt Petunia Dursley | Fiona Shaw |
| Professor Minerva McGonagall | Maggie Smith |
| Mrs. Weasley | Julie Walters |
| Madame Hooch | Zoë Wanamaker |
| Draco Malfoy | Tom Felton |
| Dudley Dursley | Harry Melling |
| Mr. Filch | David Bradley |
| Oliver Wood | Sean Biggerstaff |
| Baby Harry Potter | Saunders Triplets |
| Bartender in Leaky Cauldron | Derek Deadman |
| Diagon Alley Boy | Ben Borowiecki |
| Griphook | Vern Troyer |
| "He Who Must Not Be Named" | Richard Bremmer |
| Lily Potter | Geraldine Somerville |
| Station Guard | Harry Taylor |
| Ginny Weasley | Bonnie Wright |
| Percy Weasley | Chris Rankin |
| Fred Weasely | James Phelps |
| George Weasley | Oliver Phelps |
| Dimpled Woman on Train | Jean Southern |
| Neville Longbottom | Matthew Lewis |
| Crabbe | Jamie Waylett |
| Goyle | Josh Herdman |
| Seamus Finnegan | Devon Murray |
| Dean Thomas | Alfred Enoch |
| The Sorting Hat | Leslie Phillips |
| Susan Bones | Eleanor Columbus |

Maggie Smith

and Terence Bayler (The Bloody Barron), Simon Fisher Becker (Fat Friar), Nina Young (The Grey Lady), Luke Youngblood (Lee Jordan), Elizabeth Spriggs (Fat Lady), Danielle Taylor (Angelina Johnson), Leilah Sutherland (Alicia Spinnet), Emily Dale (Katie Bell), David Holmes (Adrian Pucey), Will Theakston (Marcus Flint), Scott Fern (Terrence Higgs), Adrian Rawlins (James Potter), Ray Fearon (Firenze).

*A young boy, raised by cruel relatives, is startled to discover that he is a wizard and a candidate for Hogwarts School of Witchcraft and Wizardry. This film became the highest-grossing picture to be released in 2001.*

*This film received Oscar nominations for original score, costume design, and art direction.*

© Warner Bros.

(Above) Oliiver Phelps, Daniel Radcliffe, Sean Biggerstaff, James Phelps. (Below) Ian Hart

Daniel Radcliffe, Rupert Grint, Emma Watson

Matthew Lewis, Rupert Grint, Daniel Radcliffe, Emma Watson, Zoë Wanamaker

Richard Harris

Alan Rickman

Richard Griffiths, Daniel Radcliffe, Fiona Shaw, Harry Melling

Robbie Coltrane

Laura Dern

Laura Dern, Steve Martin

# NOVOCAINE

(ARTISAN) Producers, Paul Mones, Daniel M. Rosenberg; Executive Producer, Michele Weisler; Director/Screenplay, David Atkins; Story, Paul Felopulos; Photography, Vilko Filac; Designer, Sharon Seymour; Costumes, Denise Wingate; Editor, Melody London; Music, Steve Bartek; Casting, Mary Colquhoun; a Paul Mones/Daniel M. Rosenberg production; Dolby; Deluxe color; Rated R; 94 minutes; Release date: November 16, 2001

## CAST

Dr. Frank Sangster ...................................................Steve Martin
Susan Ivey...........................................................Helena Bonham Carter
Jean Noble...........................................................Laura Dern
Harlan Sangster ........................................................Elias Koteas
Duane .................................................................Scott Caan
Detective Lunt .......................................................Keith David
Pat .....................................................................Lynne Thigpen
Mike ...................................................................Chelcie Ross
Sally ...................................................................Polly Noonan
Wayne Ponze ..........................................................JoBe Cerny
Sunshine Lounge Bartender.................................Yasen Peyankov
Attractive Complaining Patient .........................Teri Cotruzzola
Mrs. Langston..........................................................Lucina Paquet
Gelding .................................................................Preston Maybank
Chinese Wife ........................................................Sally Kao
Chinese Husband ................................................Quincy Wong
Lance Phelps...........................................................Kevin Bacon
and George Lugg (Liquor Store Owner), Tyler Rostenkowski (Billy), Tom Milanovich (Blue Sands Bartender), Karol Kent (Det. Lily Pons), Eddie Bo Smith (Motel Security Guard), Mary Ann Childers (Anchorwoman), Rich Komenich (Detective), James Chisem (Harris), Joe Kosala (Officer Peter Reilly), Roy Hytower (Skinny Sheriff), Kwame Amoaku (Visiting Room Guard), Christian Stolte (Court Guard), Len Bajenski (Trooper Jarvis), Mindy Bell (Trooper Bunch), Roderick Peeples (Storch)

*A dentist finds himself involved in murder after falling for an unorthodox, mysterious patient who seems to be using him for selfish motives.*

© Artisan

Steve Martin, Helena Bonham Carter

Steve Martin

Robert Redford, Brad Pitt

Catherine McCormack          Stephen Dillane

Robert Redford, Brad Pitt

# SPY GAME

**(UNIVERSAL)** Producers, Douglas Wick, Marc Abraham; Executive Producers, Armyan Bernstein, Iain Smith, Thomas A. Bliss, James W. Skotchdopole; Director, Tony Scott; Screenplay, Michael Frost Beckner, David Arata; Story, Michael Frost Beckner; Photography, Dan Mindel; Designer, Norris Spencer; Costumes, Louise Frogley; Editor, Christian Wagner; Music, Harry Gregson-Williams; Casting, Bonnie Timmermann, Lucinda Syson; a Beacon Pictures presentation of a Douglas Wick production; Dolby; Panavision; Deluxe color; Rated R; 127 minutes; Release date: November 21, 2001

## CAST

| | |
|---|---|
| Nathan Muir | Robert Redford |
| Tom Bishop | Brad Pitt |
| Elizabeth Hadley | Catherine McCormack |
| Charles Harker | Stephen Dillane |
| Troy Folger | Larry Bryggman |
| Gladys Jennip | Marianne Jean-Baptiste |
| Dr. Byars | Matthew Marsh |
| Robert Aiken | Todd Boyce |
| Vincent Vy Ngo | Michael Paul Chan |
| Cy Wilson | Garrick Hagon |
| Andrew Unger | Andrew Grainger |
| Fred Kappler | Bill Buell |
| Henry Pollard | Colin Stinton |
| CIA Administrator | Ted Maynard |
| CIA Lobby Guard | Tom Hodgkins |
| Folger's Secretary | Rufus Wright |
| Billy Hyland | Demetri Goritsas |
| OPS Center Security Officer | Quinn Collins |
| CIA Back Bencher | Yann Johnson |
| Back Bencher | Sam Scudder |
| Cleaner | Pat McGrath |
| Estate Agent | Shane Rimmer |

Hong Kong: David Hemmings (Harry Duncan), James Aubrey (Mitch Alford), In Sook Chappell (Receptionist); Chinese Prison: Benedict Wong (Tran), Ken Leung (Li), Adrian Pang (Jiang), Ho-Yi (Prison Warden), David Y. Cheung (Down's Prisoner), Tony Xu (Interrogator), Mark Sung (Ambulance Driver), David K. S. Tse (Prison Doctor), Logan Wong, Hon Ping Tang (Prison Guards), Daniel Tse (Warden's Lieutenant), Vincent Wang (Outer Gate Guard), Mark Chui (Cell Block Guard); Vietnam: Stuart Milligan (Captain), Joseph Chanet (VC General), Eddie Yeoh (General Hun Chea), Freddie Joe Farnsworth (Radioman); Berlin: Joerg Stadler (Schmidt), Zsolt Zágoni (West German Businessman), Balázs Tardy, Pál Oberfrank (Vopos), Géza Schramek (East German Refugee), Imre Csuja (Bar Owner), Melinda Völgyi (Bar Owner's Wife), Károly Rékasi (East German Border Guard), Kimberly Tufo (Sandy), Iain Smith (Ambassador Cathcart), Gregory Groth (CIA Training Instructor), Peter Linka (CIA Polygraph); Beirut: Omid Djalili (Doumet), Amidou (The Sheik's Doctor), Nabil Massad (Sheik Salameh), Mohamed Picasso (Colonel Ajami), Aziz Ait Essahmi (Checkpoint Guard), Moustapha Moulay (Arab Businessman), Mohamed Quatib (Motorcyclist/Decoy Man), Farid Regragui (Suicide Van Driver); Rescue Sequence: Dale Dye (Commander Wiley), Tim Briggs (Heli Pilot); Reporters: Frank Nall (CNN Reporter), Ian Porter (US-China Reporter), Charlotte Rampling (Anne Cathcart)

*Nathan Muir, a veteran CIA officer on the verge of retirement, discovers that his protégé, Tom Bishop, is detained in a foreign prison and scheduled to die, prompting Muir to plan a rescue.*

© Universal Studios

Robert Redford

# BLACK KNIGHT

**(20TH CENTURY FOX)** Producers, Arnon Milchan, Darryl J. Quarles, Michael Green, Paul Schiff; Executive Producers, Martin Lawrence, Jeffrey Kwatinetz, Peaches Davis, Jack Brodsky; Director, Gil Junger; Screenplay, Darryl J. Quarles, Peter Gaulke, Gerry Swallow; Photography, Ueli Steiger; Designer, Leslie Dilley; Costumes, Marie France; Editor, Michael R. Miller; Co-Producer, Aaron Ray; Music, Randy Edelman; Casting, Sheila Jaffe, Georgianne Walken; a Regency Enterprises presentation of a New Regency/Runteldat Entertainment/The Firm production; Dolby; Panavision; Deluxe color; Rated PG-13; 95 minutes; Release date: November 21, 2001

## CAST

| | |
|---|---|
| Jamal Walker | Martin Lawrence |
| Victoria | Marsha Thomason |
| Knolte | Tom Wilkinson |
| Percival | Vincent Regan |
| Steve | Daryl Mitchell |
| Ernie | Michael Burgess |
| Mrs. Bostick | Isabell Monk |
| Knight #1 | Kevin Stillwell |
| Young Man | Michael Post |
| Puppeteer | Tim Parati |
| Guards | Mark Joy, Joe Inscoe, Zach Hanner |
| Man #2 | Leslie Dilley |
| Vindy | Angel Desai |
| Ling | Elizabeth A. Roberts |
| Phillip | Michael Countryman |
| King Leo | Kevin Conway |
| Princess Regina | Jeannette Weegar |

and Erik Jensen (Derek), Dikran Tulaine (Dennis), Graham F. Smith (Royal Messenger), Mark Jeffrey Miller, Tammy Christine Arnold (Peasants), Helen Carey (The Queen), Richard Fullerton (Will), Jayce Tromsness (Thug), Greg Cooper (Rebel Leader), Mark Pitt (Crowd Member), Miki Shelton (Woman), Jason Chimonides (Soldier #2), Robert Leddy, Jr., Denise S. Bass, Eric Paisley (Rebels), William Boyer (Rebel #2/Guard Captain), Melissa Bolden, Harry D. Campbell, John Cronin, Marty Dew, Traci Dinwiddie, Bonnie Dixon, Mark Evans, Kelly Foxworth, Linda K. Huffman, Krystal Jefferson, Chris Madray, Babs McCullen, Jaime Moffett, Dustin Phillips, Dena Rizzo, Monica Semon, Lara Anne Smith, Veronica Sterling, D'Juan Watts (Dancers)

*Jamal Walker, an employee at Medieval World theme park, finds himself magically transported through time back to the Middle Ages.*

© Twentieth Century Fox and Regency Enterprises

Marsha Thomason, Martin Lawrence

Martin Lawrence, Tom Wilkinson

Martin Lawrence (center)

Martin Lawrence, Kevin Conway

Edward Burns, Heather Graham

# SIDEWALKS OF NEW YORK

(PARAMOUNT CLASSICS) Producers, Margot Bridger, Edward Burns, Cathy Schulman, Rick Yorn; Director/Screenplay, Edward Burns; Photography, Frank Prinzi; Costumes, Catherine Thomas; Editor, David Greenwald; Co-Producers, Richard Patrick, Frank Prinzi; Associate Producers, Brian Burns, Aaron Lubin; Music Consultant, Laura Ziffren; Casting, Laura Rosenthal, Ali Farrell; a Marlboro Road Gang Production in association with Artists Production Group; Dolby; Color; Rated R; 107 minutes; Release date: November 21, 2001

## CAST

| | |
|---|---|
| Tommy | Edward Burns |
| Maria | Rosario Dawson |
| Carpo | Dennis Farina |
| Annie | Heather Graham |
| Ben | David Krumholtz |
| Ashley | Brittany Murphy |
| Griffin | Stanley Tucci |
| Gio/Harry | Michael Leydon Campbell |
| Hilary | Nadia Dajani |
| Sue | Callie Thorne |
| Shari | Aida Turturro |
| Young Hooker | Penny Balfour |
| Katy | Kathleen Doyle |
| Dental Hygenist | Leah Gray |
| Dr. Lance | Tim Jerome |
| Makeup Girl | Libby Langdon |
| Elevator Girl | Alicia Meer |
| Doctor | Ted Neustadt |

*A group of diverse New Yorkers seeks love while attempting to sort out their various romantic problems.*

© Paramount Classics

Edward Burns, Dennis Farina

Heather Graham, Stanley Tucci

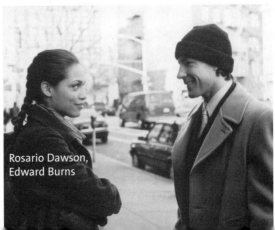

Brittany Murphy, David Krumholtz

Rosario Dawson, Edward Burns

Marisa Tomei, Sissy Spacek, Christopher Adams

Tom Wilkinson, Marisa Tomei

Tom Wilkinson, Sissy Spacek

Sissy Spacek

Marisa Tomei, Nick Stahl

# IN THE BEDROOM

Tom Wilkinson, Sissy Spacek

(MIRAMAX) Producers, Graham Leader, Ross Katz, Todd Field; Executive Producers, Ted Hope, John Penotti; Director, Todd Field; Screenplay, Rob Festinger, Todd Field; Based on the story Killings by Andre Dubus; Co-Producer, Tim Williams; Co-Executive Producers, Stephen Dembitzer, Penn Sicre; Photography, Antonio Calvache; Designer, Shannon Hart; Editor, Frank Reynolds; Music, Thomas Newman; Costumes, Melissa Economy; Casting, Randi Hiller, Belinda Monte; a GreeneStreet Films presentation of a Good Machine production; Dolby; Super 35 Widescreen; Color; Rated R; 138 minutes; Release date: November 23, 2001

## CAST

| | |
|---|---|
| Matt Fowler | Tom Wilkinson |
| Ruth Fowler | Sissy Spacek |
| Frank Fowler | Nick Stahl |
| Natalie Strout | Marisa Tomei |
| Richard Strout | William Mapother |
| Willis Grinnel | William Wise |
| Katie Grinnel | Celia Weston |
| Marla Keyes | Karen Allen |
| Henry | Frank T. Wells |
| Carl | W. Clapham Murray |
| Tim | Justin Ashforth |
| District Attorney | Terry A. Burgess |
| Father McCasslin | Jonathan Walsh |
| Davis's Assistant | Diane E. Hamlin |
| Jason Strout | Camden Munson |
| Duncan Strout | Christopher Adams |
| Young Frank | Henry Field |
| Janelle | Deborah Derecktor |
| Alma Adamson | Harriet Dawkins |
| Elwyn Adamson | Bill Dawkins |
| Tim's Friend | Kevin Chapman |
| Judge | The Honorable Joseph Field |
| Grocery Clerk | Harold Withee |
| Marlboro Man | David Blair |
| Elderly Woman | Elisabeth McClure |
| Young Gymnast | Alida P. Field |
| Waitress | Andrea Walker |
| Reporters | John Campanello, Robert Demkowicz |
| Minister on Television | Veronica Cartwright |
| Red Sox Replay | Daran Norris |
| Bridge Operator | Don Lewis |
| Fork Lift Operator | Doug Rich |

and Sara Armstrong, Elly Barksdale, Erin Barksdale, Adah Holman, Gwendolyn Gilchrist, Shauneen Grou, Jessie Lanoue, Alicia Laplant, Iris Leslie, Erica Towle-Powers, Nichols Wimbiscus, Anna Winsor (Chorus), Lisa Carlton, Rebecca Benner, Francis Mazzeo, Tyler Shane Smith-Campbell, Brian Hagley, Sam Cousins, Jackie Hagley, Comenic Cuccinello III, Ronald Russell, Rachel Freeman, Dale Johnson, Daniel Hendricks, Parker Spear, Sam Johnson, Henry Field, Matthew Maxwell, Shyann Gauthier, Joshua Mills, Bethany Berry, Eric Rahkonen, Hope Berry, Natalie Russell, Chelsea Peasley, Misty Seekins, Daniel Baxter-Leahy, Philip Spearing, Brandon Carleton, Mackenzie Tucker, Owen Thompson, Ben Staples, Ryan Ecker, Jared Mekin (Rockland T-Ball)

Nick Stahl, Sissy Spacek

*Matt and Ruth Fowler's discomfort over their son Frank's relationship with an older single mother is justified when a tragedy results.*

*This film received Oscar nominations for picture, actress (Sissy Spacek), supporting actress (Marisa Tomei), and adapted screenplay.*

© Miramax Films

(Above) Tom Wilkinson. (Below) Nick Stahl, Sissy Spacek, Tom Wilkinson

Gene Hackman

Owen Wilson

Owen Wilson (right)

Owen Wilson

# BEHIND ENEMY LINES

**(20TH CENTURY FOX)** Producer, John Davis; Executive Producers, Stephanie Austin, Wyck Godfrey; Director, John Moore; Screenplay, David Veloz, Zak Penn; Story, James Thomas, John Thomas; Photography, Brendan Galvin; Designer, Nathan Crowley; Editor, Paul Martin Smith; Co-Producer, T. Alex Blum; Music, Don Davis; Visual Effects, Reality Check Studios, Pixel Magic, Riot Pictures, Asylum Visual Effects; Stunts, Steve M. Davison; Casting, Sheila Trezise, Eyde Belasco; a Davis Entertainment Company production; Dolby; Panavision; Deluxe color; Rated PG-13; 106 minutes; Release date: November 30, 2001

## CAST

Lieutenant Chris Burnett .....................................................Owen Wilson
Admiral Reigart ...............................................................Gene Hackman
Stackhouse ......................................................................Gabriel Macht
Rodway .............................................Charles Malik Whitfield
Piquet .............................................................Joaquim de Almeida
O'Malley ...........................................................................David Keith
Lokar .................................................................................Olek Krupa
Tracker ...................................................................Vladimir Mashkov
Bazda ...........................................................................Marko Igonda
Petty Officer Kennedy ...........................................................Eyal Podell
Admiral Donnelly ...............................................................Geoff Pierson
Himself ................................................................Aernout Van Lynden
Serb Soldiers .........................................Igor Hajdarhodzic, Tarik Filipovic
and Sam Jaeger, Shane Mikael Johnson, Don Winston, Elizabeth Perry (Red Crown Operators), Peter Palka (Serb Soldier at Lokar's Mansion), Todd Boyce (Junior Officer), Kamil Kollárik (Babic), Salaudin Bilal (Ejup), Laurence Mason (Brandon), Leon Russom (Ed Burnett), Goran Grgic (Technician), Ivan Urbánek (Father in Minefield), Ismet Bagtasevic (Muslim Passenger), Dragan Marinkovic (Damir), Kamil Mikulcík, Róbert Franko, Lukas Hoffmann (Tigers), Vedrana Seksan (Serb Anchor), Vladimír Oktavec (Petrovic), Dorothy Lucey (Herself), Gregory B. Goossen (CIA Spook), Filip Nola (Serb Solder at Mass Grave), Bumper Robinson (SCIF Technicain), Ann Sorum (Mom Burnett), George Davis (Sky News Cameraman), Tom Mooney (Carrier Commanding Officer), Mark Bocchetti (Navy Rep), Lucia Srncova (Muslim Girl), Daniel Margolius (Muslim Teenager), Jared Chandler (Piquet's Aide)

*After accidentally snapping photographs of a forbidden area while on a routine reconnaissance mission, naval aviator Chris Burnett finds his plane being shot down by the Bosnian military, which is bent on finding the grounded flyer and executing him.*

© Twentieth Century Fox

# THE AFFAIR OF THE NECKLACE

(WARNER BROS.) Producers, Andrew A. Kosove, Broderick Johnson, Charles Shyer, Redmond Morris; Director, Charles Shyer; Screenplay, John Sweet; Co-Producers, Kira Davis, Stacey Attanasio; Photography, Ashley Rowe; Designer, Alex McDowell; Costumes, Milena Canonero; Editor, David Moritz; Music, David Newman; Casting, Gail Stevens, Billy Hopkins, Suzanne Smith, Kerry Barden, Mark Bennett; an Alcon Entertainment presentation; Dolby; Super 35 Widescreen; Technicolor; Rated R; 120 minutes; Release date: November 30, 2001

Hilary Swank, Jonathan Pryce

## CAST

| | |
|---|---|
| Jeanne St. Remy de Valois | Hilary Swank |
| Cardinal Louis de Rohan | Jonathan Pryce |
| Retaux de Vilette | Simon Baker |
| Nicolas De La Motte | Adrien Brody |
| Minister Breteuil | Brian Cox |
| Marie-Antoinette | Joely Richardson |
| Cagliostro | Christopher Walken |
| Young Jeanne | Hayden Panettiere |
| Minister of Titles | Simon Kunz |
| Monsieur Böhmer | Paul Brooke |
| Monsieur Bassenge | Peter Eyre |
| Abel Duphot | Frank McCusker |
| Louis XVI | Simon Shackleton |
| Nicole Leguay d'Oliva | Hermione Gulliford |
| President D'Aligre | Geoffrey Hutchings |
| Maigstrate Titon | James Vaughan |
| Magistrate de Marce | Jonathan Newth |
| Irène de Valois | Kristina Bill |

and James Larkin (Darnell de Valois), Diana Quick (Madame Pomfré), Helen Masters (Madame Campan), Victoria Shalet (Colleen), Christophe Paon (Pierre Charron), Michel D'Oz (Marquis de Favras), Donna Flandrin, Liz Baker (Dowagers in Boat), Dick Brannick (Gamekeeper), Daisy Bevan (The Princess Royal), Thomas Dodgson-Gates (The Dauphin), Caroline Lonco (Madame de Largo), Miranda Pleasence (Rosalie), John Grillo (Dr. Legear), Melodie Berenfeld (Mademoiselle Subur), Ben Miles (Baron Courchamps), Niky Wardley (Madame de Neiss), Bill Thomas (Tailor), Emma Wride (Tailor's Daughter), Stephen Noonan (Camille Desmoulins), Emma Pike (Mademoiselle in Pink), William Chubb (Gendarme), Hallie Meyers-Shyer (Demonstrating Girl), Jocelyn Linder, John Commer (Angry Demonstrators), Angus Wright (Sanson), Christopher Logue (Sir Hargrave), Cate Fowler (Lady Standish)

*A young woman whose family became disenfranchised and fell out of favor with the royal court of France, makes it her life goal to properly regain her place of honor.*

*This film received an Oscar nomination for costume design.*

© Affair Productions, LLC

Joely Richardson

Simon Baker, Hilary Swank, Adrien Brody

Christopher Walken

George Clooney, Brad Pitt, Matt Damon, Elliott Gould, Don Cheadle

Carl Reiner, Brad Pitt

Julia Roberts, George Clooney

Scott Caan, Casey Affleck

Don Cheadle, George Clooney, Shaobo Qin, Casey Affleck

# OCEAN'S ELEVEN

(WARNER BROS.) Producer, Jerry Weintraub; Executive Producers, John Hardy, Susan Ekins, Bruce Berman; Director, Steven Soderbergh; Screenplay, Ted Griffin; Based on a screenplay by Harry Brown and Charles Lederer, and based on a story by George Clayton Johnson and Jack Golden Russell; Photography, Peter Andrews; Designer, Philip Messina; Costumes, Jeffrey Kurland; Editor, Stephen Mirrione; Music, David Holmes; Co-Producer, R. J. Louis; Casting, Debra Zane; a Jerry Weintraub/Section Eight production, presented in association with Village Roadshow Pictures and NPV Entertainment; Dolby; Panavision; CFI color; Rated PG-13; 119 minutes; Release date: December 7, 2001

George Clooney, Brad Pitt

## CAST

| | |
|---|---|
| Danny Ocean | George Clooney |
| Linus Caldwell | Matt Damon |
| Terry Benedict | Andy Garcia |
| Rusty Ryan | Brad Pitt |
| Tess Ocean | Julia Roberts |
| Virgil Malloy | Casey Affleck |
| Turk Malloy | Scott Caan |
| Basher Tarr | Don Cheadle |
| Reuben Tishkoff | Elliott Gould |
| Frank Catton | Bernie Mac |
| Saul Bloom | Carl Reiner |
| Livingston Dell | Eddie Jemison |
| Yen | Shaobo Qin |
| Blackjack Dealer | Lori Galinski |
| Bartender | Mark Gantt |
| Security Guard (Oscar) | Timothy Paul Perez |
| Lockbox Carrier | Frank Patton |
| FBI Men | Jorge R. Hernandez, Tim Snay |
| Explosives Cop | Miguel Perez |
| Technicians | Barry Brandt, William Patrick Johnson |
| Eye-in-the-Sky Technicians | Robert Peters, David Jensen |
| Dancer | Kelly Adkins |
| Sentry | George Stenson |
| Billy Tim Denham | Joe Ladue |
| Hotel Security | John C. Fiore |
| Hotel Bellman | Tommy Kordick |
| Casino Manager (Walsh) | Michael Delano |
| Italian High Roller | Charles La Russa |
| French High Roller | Anthony Allison |
| Japanese High Roller | Ronn Soeda |
| Seller | Robin Sachs |
| Aide-de-Camp | J. P. Manoux |
| High Roller | Jerry Weintraub |
| High Roller Pit Boss (Eddie) | Frankie Jay Allison |
| Baccarat Dealer | James Curatola |
| Bucky Buchanan | Richard Reed |
| Plainclothes Goons | David Sontag, Larry Sontag |
| Guard | William Allison |
| Security Officers | Rusty Meyers, Joe Coyle |
| Bruiser | Scott L. Schwartz |

and John Robotham, Vincent M. Ward (Uzi-Carrying Guards), Scott Clark Beringer (Head Goon), James Alfonso (Police Officer), Cecelia Birt, Paul L. Nolan, Carol Florence (Board Members), Lennox Lewis, Vladimir Klitschko, Topher Grace, Joshua Jackson, Barry Watson, Shane West, Holly Marie Combs, Henry Silva, Eydie Gorme, Angie Dickinson, Steve Lawrence, Wayne Newton, Siegfried Fischbacher, Roy Horn, Jim Lampley, Larry Merchant, Richard Steele (Themselves)

*Fresh out of prison, criminal Danny Ocean gathers together a group of expert thieves to help him pull off an outrageous and seemingly impossible job, robbing three of the top casinos in Las Vegas. Remake of the 1960 Warner Bros. movie that starred Frank Sinatra, Dean Martin, and Sammy Davis, Jr. Angie Dickinson and Henry Silva, who appeared in the earlier film, make cameo appearances here.*

© Warner Bros.

Matt Damon, George Clooney

(Above) Andy Garcia, Carl Reiner. (Below) Andy Garcia, George Clooney, Julia Roberts

Stockard Channing

Julia Stiles

Julia Stiles, Fred Weller, Stockard Channing

Julia Stiles, Stockard Channing

# THE BUSINESS OF STRANGERS

(IFC FILMS) Producers, Susan A. Stover, Robert H. Nathan; Executive Producers, Scott McGehee, David Siegel; Director/Screenplay, Patrick Stettner; Photography, Teodoro Maniaci; Designer, Dina Goldman; Costumes, Kasia Walicka Maimone, Dawn Weisberg; Editor, Keiko Deguchi; Music, Alexander Lasarenko; Line Producer, Derrick Tseng; Associate Producer, Ramsey Fong; Casting, Nicole Arbusto, Joy Dickson; an I5 Picture in association with HeadQuarters; Dolby; Color; Rated R; 84 minutes; Release date: December 7, 2001

## CAST

Julie Styron .................................................... Stockard Channing
Paula Murphy ............................................................ Julia Stiles
Nick Harris .............................................................. Fred Weller
Receptionist ............................................................... Mary Testa
Mr. Fostwick ............................................................ Jack Hallett
Robert .............................................................. Marcus Giamatti
Waiter ............................................................. Buddy Fitzpatrick
Man at Pool .......................................................... Salem Ludwig
Airport Announcer ............................................... Shelagh Ratner

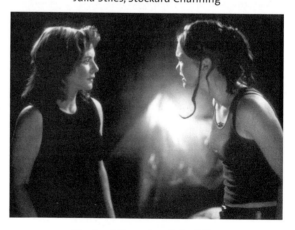

Stockard Channing, Julia Stiles

*Julie Styron, a high-powered business executive, fires her new personal assistant for failing to show up on time to an important presentation, only to find herself forming a strange bond with the young woman at an airport hotel.*

144

© IFC Films

Benjamin Bratt

Talisa Soto, Benjamin Bratt

# PIÑERO

**(MIRAMAX)** Producers, John Penotti, Fisher Stevens, Tim Williams; Co-Executive Producers, John Leguizamo, Kathy Demarco; Director/Screenplay, Leon Ichaso; Co-Producer, Jamie Gordon; Photography, Claudio Chea; Designer, Sharon Lomofsky; Costumes, Sandra Hernandez; Editor, David Tedeschi; Line Producer, Caroline Jaczko; Casting, Ellyn Marshall, Maria Nelson; Produced by GreeneStreet Films and Lower East Side Films; Dolby; Color; Rated R; 103 minutes; Release date: December 13, 2001

## CAST

| | |
|---|---|
| Miguel Piñero | Benjamin Bratt |
| Miguel Algarin | Giancarlo Esposito |
| Sugar | Talisa Soto |
| Tito | Nelson Vasquez |
| Reinaldo Povod | Michael Irby |
| Edgar | Michael Wright |
| Miguel's Mother | Rita Moreno |
| Miguel's Father | Jaime Sanchez |
| Jake | Rome Neal |
| Joseph Papp | Mandy Patinkin |
| Bodega Man | Oscar Colon |
| Bodega Woman | Miriam Cruz |
| Shooting Gallery Man | Lois Caballero |
| Shooting Gallery Woman | Sophia Domoulin |
| Doctor | Robert Klein |
| Miguel (as teen) | Gilbert Callazo |

and Samuel Bruce Campbell (Short Eyes Cop), Loraine Velez (Tutu), Eric Nieves (Nuyorican), Antonia Rey (Señora), Griffin Dunne (Agent), Lisa Rhoden (P.A. Woman), Valentina Quinn (Interviewer), Al D. Rodriguez (Cuqui), Bruno Iannone (Port Authority Cop), Fisher Stevens (Public Theatre Cashier), Jack O'Connell (Chauffeur), Ray Santiago (Willie), Charles Santy (Lincoln), Vanessa Del Sol (Heist Woman), Jamie Tirelli (Marty), O. L. Duke (Paul), Edward Vassallo (Tito Arrest Cop), Amanda KC (Barrio Bar Woman), Bill Boggs (Lennon Anchorman), Tony Vazzo (Auditorium Man 2), Charles Sammarco (Stranger Shower Guy), Lydia Trueheart (Woman with Baby), John Ortiz (Gang Member), Panchito Gomez (Acting Inmate), Amiri Baraka, Pedro Pietri, Jamal Joseph, Miguel Algarin (Themselves), Tara Wilson (Tito's Girlfriend), Joanne Newborn, Francine Berman (Fur Women)

*The true story of explosive playwright/poet Miguel Piñero, who became a temporary sensation on the New York scene before his self-destructive behavior got the best of him.*

© Miramax Films

Giancarlo Esposito, Benjamin Bratt

Benjamin Bratt

Penélope Cruz, Tom Cruise

Tom Cruise, Noah Taylor

# VANILLA SKY

**(PARAMOUNT)** Producers, Tom Cruise, Paula Wagner, Cameron Crowe; Executive Producers, Jonathan Sanger, Danny Bramson; Director/Screenplay, Cameron Crowe; Based on the film *Abre los Ojos (Open Your Eyes)* written by Alejandro Amenábar and Mateo Gil; Photography, John Toll; Designer, Catherine Hardwicke; Costumes, Betsy Heimann; Co-Producer, Donald J. Lee, Jr.; Editors, Joe Hutshing, Mark Livolsi; Music Supervisor, Danny Bramson; Music, Nancy Wilson; Song: "Vanilla Sky," written and performed by Paul McCartney; Associate Producer, Michael Doven; Casting, Gail Levin; a Cruise/Wagner-Vinyl Films production; Dolby; Deluxe color; Rated R; 134 minutes; Release date: December 14, 2001

## CAST

David Aames............................................................Tom Cruise
Sofia Serrano........................................................Penélope Cruz
Julie Gianni ..........................................................Cameron Diaz
McCabe....................................................................Kurt Russell
Brian Shelby ...............................................................Jason Lee
Edmund Ventura .........................................................Noah Taylor
Thomas Tipp ............................................................Timothy Spall
Rebecca Dearborn.....................................................Tilda Swinton
Aaron.................................................................Michael Shannon
David's Assistant ..................................................Delaina Mitchell
Colleen ................................................................Shalom Harlow
Lynette ....................................................................Oona Hart
Emma .................................................................Ivana Milicevic
Peter Brown..........................................................Johnny Galecki
Jamie Berliner..........................................................Jhaemi Willens
and Armand Schultz (Dr. Pomeranz), Cameron Watson (Other Doctor), Robertson Dean (Third Doctor), W. Earl Brown (Barman), Ray Proscia (Doctor from Berlin), Tim Hopper (Man in Blue Coat), Alicia Witt (Libby), Ken Leung (Art Editor), Carolyn Byrne (Beatrice), Mark Pinter (Carlton Keller), Jeff Weiss (Raymond Tooley), Conan O'Brien, Jane Pratt, Patrick McMullen, Steven Colvin, Cindy Crowe, The Great John Sypolt, Steven Spielberg (Themselves), Jim Murtaugh (Benny's Owner), Mark Kozelek (Dude, Fix Your Face Guy), John Fedevich (Silent Ed Vallencourt), Bobby Walsh (Young David), Stacey Sher (Rayna), Fred Shruers (Cryo Man), Jessica Siemens, Julia Carothers Hughes (Sofia's Friends), Holly Raye (Dancer), Marty Collins (Martini Waiter), Mark Bramhall (Sneezy), Jack Hall (Bashful), David Lewison (Sleepy), Jennifer Griffin (Happy), Adam LeGrant (Doc), John Kepley (Dopey), Robin Van Sharner (Grumpy), Laurel Wiley (Dr. Jennifer Ash), Nicole Taylor Hart (Party Videographer), Julia Anne Schuler, Jennifer Marie Kelley, Erin McElmurry (Models), Alice Crowe (Lucid Dreamer), Mel Thompson (Life Extension Man), Jonathan Sanger (Frozen Pediatric Cardiologist), Tommy Lee (Frozen Vintage Car Man), Ana Maria Quintana (Frozen Theologist), Paul Haggar (Frozen Risktaker), Randy Woodside (Frozen Dad), Robert F. Harrison (Laughing Guy), Carly Starr Brullo Niles (Carly), Michael Kehoe (Chef), Danielle R. Wolf (Coat Check Girl), Scotch Ellis Loring (L.E. Building Guard), Brent Sexton, Curt Skaggs (Security Guards), Jennifer Gimenez (Lola), Lori Lezama (Skyscraper Girl), Todd Harrison (Skyscraper Guy), Blossom (Benny the Dog), Laura Fraser (The Future)

*David Aames, a callous and enormously wealthy New York City publisher, falls in love with Sofia Serrano only to have his face hideously damaged in a car accident caused by a jealous girlfriend. Remake of the 1997 Spanish film Abre los Ojos (Open Your Eyes) that was released in the U.S. in 1999 by Artisan Entertainment. Penélope Cruz repeats her role from that film.*

*This film received an Oscar nomination for original song ("Vanilla Sky").*

© Paramount Pictures

Tom Cruise, Jason Lee

Paul Gleason, Cody McMains

# NOT ANOTHER TEEN MOVIE

**(COLUMBIA)** Producer, Neal H. Moritz; Executive Producers, Brad Luff, Michael Rachmil; Director, Joel Gallen; Screenplay, Michael G. Bender, Adam Jay Epstein, Andrew Jacobson, Phil Beauman, Buddy Johnson; Photography, Reynaldo Villalobos; Designer, Joseph T. Garrity; Costumes, Florence-Isabelle Megginson; Editor, Steven Welch; Co-Producers, Phil Beauman, Buddy Johnson, Michael G. Bender; Music, Theodore Shapiro; Casting, Joseph Middleton; a Neal H. Moritz production; Dolby; Deluxe color; Rated R; 89 minutes; Release date: December 14, 2001

## CAST

| | |
|---|---|
| Janey Briggs | Chyler Leigh |
| Jake Wyler | Chris Evans |
| Priscilla | Jaime Pressly |
| Austin | Eric Christian Olsen |
| Catherine | Mia Kirshner |
| Malik | Deon Richmond |
| Ricky | Eric Jungmann |
| Reggie Ray | Ron Lester |
| Mitch Briggs | Cody McMains |
| Ox | Sam Huntington |
| Sandy Sue | Joanna Garcia |
| Amanda Becker | Lacey Chabert |

and Samm Levine (Bruce), Cerina Vincent (Areola), Beverly Polcyn (Sadie), Nectar Rose (Sara Fratelli), Samaire Armstrong (Kara Fratelli), Ed Lauter (The Coach), Paul Gleason (Richard Vernon), Mr. T (Wise Janitor), Molly Ringwald (Flight Attendant), Randy Quaid (Mr. Briggs), Nathan West (Actor), Michelle Holgate (Actress), Jeanette Miller (Grandma Briggs), Michael Ensign (Father O'Flannagan), Benjamin Waldow (Kid), Josh Radnor (Tour Guide), Ross Mulholland, Dean Sheremet, Becca Sweitzer, Hayley Zelniker (Cheerleaders in Front of School), Lukas Behnken, Josh Jacobson (White Guys), Amber Marie Goetz (Window Girl), Joy Bisco (Ashley), Morisa Taylor Kaplan (Heather), Riley Smith (Les), George Wyner (Mr. Cornish), Ned Brower, Peter Simon (Dudes), Joy Gohring (Albino Folk Singer), Tracy Wolfe (Hottie), Jessica Asher (Naked Girl in Locker Room), Sean Smith (Mr. Keller), Heather Brown (Dainty Girl), Ean Mering (Marty), Lyman Ward (Mr. Wyler), Julie Welch (Mrs. Wyler), Daniel Bess (Panicked Student), Jackie Harris (Preston's Mother), James Read (Preston's Father), Robert Patrick Benedict (Preston), Banks McClintock (Keg Guy), Jay Johnston (Roadie), Jennifer Leone (Naked Girl at Party), Daniel Spink (Curious Guy), Oz Perkins (Uninterested Guy), Kyle Cease (Slow Clapper), Jim Wise (Football Announcer), Kimi Bateman, Staci B. Flood, Sarah Christine Smith (Cheerleaders on Football Field), China Shavers (North Compton Cheerleader), Jon Benjamin (Trainer), Paul Goebel (Fat Short-Order Cook), Good Charlotte (Prom Band), Marissa Fedele, Sam Givens, Kimberly Lyon, Zachary Woodlee (Dancers), Alec Murdoch (Man in Line), Cynthena Sanders (Woman in Line), Will Gill, Jr. (Security Guard), Nicholas Z. Cohen (Little Boy)

*The high-school football star makes a bet to turn an outcast girl into the prom queen in this send-up of teen movies.*

© Columbia Pictures Industries Inc.

Chyler Leigh, Eric Jungmann

Dean Richmond, Chris Evans

Beverly Polcyn, Mia Kirshner

Chyler Leigh, Chris Evans

Gwyneth Paltrow, Luke Wilson

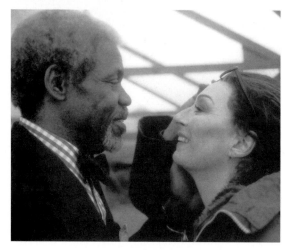

Gene Hackman

# THE ROYAL TENENBAUMS

(TOUCHSTONE) Producers, Wes Anderson, Barry Mendel, Scott Rudin; Executive Producers, Rudd Simmons, Owen Wilson; Director, Wes Anderson; Screenplay, Wes Anderson, Owen Wilson; Photography, Robert Yeoman; Designer, David Wasco; Costumes, Karen Patch; Music, Mark Mothersbaugh; Music Supervisor, Randall Poster; Editor, Dylan Tichenor; Casting, Douglas Aibel; an American Empirical Picture; Dolby; Panavision; Technicolor; Rated R; 108 minutes; Release date: December 14, 2001

## CAST

| | |
|---|---|
| Royal Tenenbaum | Gene Hackman |
| Etheline Tenenbaum | Anjelica Huston |
| Chas Tenenbaum | Ben Stiller |
| Margot Tenenbaum | Gwyneth Paltrow |
| Richie Tenenbaum | Luke Wilson |
| Eli Cash | Owen Wilson |
| Raleigh St. Clair | Bill Murray |
| Henry Sherman | Danny Glover |
| Dusty | Seymour Cassel |
| Pagoda | Kumar Pallana |
| Narrator | Alec Baldwin |
| Ari Tenenbaum | Grant Rosenmeyer |
| Uzi Tenenbaum | Jonah Meyerson |
| Young Chas Tenenbaum | Aram Aslanian-Persico |
| Young Margot Tenenbaum | Irene Gorovaia |
| Young Richie Tenenbaum | Amedeo Turturro |
| Dudley Heinsbergen | Stephen Lea Sheppard |
| Young Eli Cash | James Fitzgerald |
| Peter Bradley | Larry Pine |
| Detective | Don McKinnon |
| Hotel Manager | Frank Wood |
| Walter Sherman | Al Thompson |
| Rachael Tenenbaum | Jennifer Wachtell |
| Hotel Clerk | Donal Ward |
| Farmer Father/Tex Hayward | Andrew Wilson |
| Doctor | Dipak Pallana |
| Sanjay Gandhi | Sanjay Mathew |
| Chas's Secretary | Mary Wigmore |
| Sing-Sang | Sonam Wangmo |
| Neville Smythe-Dorleac | Pawel Wdowczak |
| Yasuo Oshima | Peter Leung |
| Franklin Benedict | William Sturgis |
| Reporter in Blue Cardigan | Liam Craig |
| Eli's Aunt | Sheelagh Tellerday |
| Cote d'Ivoire Attendant | Max Faugno |
| Cote d'Ivoire Radio Operator | Guido Venitucci |
| Frederick (Bellboy) | Ebon Moss-Bacharach |
| Elderly "Baumer" Fans | Brian Smiar, Jan V. E. Austell |
| Cemetery Maintenance Man | Rony Clanton |
| Anwar | Salim Malik |
| Judge | Tom Lacy |
| Royal's Lawyer | Keith Charles |
| Gypsy Cab Driver | Greg Goossen |
| Nurse | Sadiah Arrika Ekulona |
| Sanchez | Vic Mata |

and Michael Conti (Irish Longshoreman), Tatiana Abbey (Parisian Girl), Kalani Queypo (New Guinea Tribesman), Mel Cannon (Punk Rocker), Leo Manuelian, Amir Raissi, Roger Shamas (Eli's Egyptian Friends), Philip Denning (Father Petersen), Gary Evans (Police Officer), Rex Robbins (Mr. Levinson), Nova Landaeus-Skinnar (Elaine Levinson), Sam Hoffman, Brian Tenenbaum, Stephan Dignan (Paramedics), Eric Chase Anderson (Medical Student)

*Royal Tenenbaum shows up after years away from his estranged family, claiming to be terminally ill and in need of a reconciliation with his children, all of whom feel that their early promise was destroyed by their father's behavior. This film received an Oscar nomination for original screenplay.*

© Touchstone Pictures

Danny Glover, Anjelica Huston

Luke Wilson, Gwyneth Paltrow,
Ben Stiller, Gene Hackman

Jonah Mayerson, Gene Hackman

Stephen Lea Sheppard, Bill Murray

Owen Wilson

(Below) Luke Wilson, Gwyneth Paltrow, Gene Hackman, Grant Rosenmeyer, Ben Stiller, Jonah Meyerson, Anjelica Huston, Danny Glover, Kumar Pallana

Cate Blanchett, Elijah Wood

Ian Holm

Christopher Lee

(Above) Dominic Monaghan, Billy Boyd
(Below) Viggo Mortensen

Liv Tyler

Orlando Bloom

# THE LORD OF THE RINGS: THE FELLOWSHIP OF THE RING

(NEW LINE CINEMA) Producers, Barrie M. Osborne, Peter Jackson, Fran Walsh, Tim Sanders; Executive Producers, Mark Ordesky, Bob Weinstein, Harvey Weinstein, Robert Shaye, Michael Lynne; Director, Peter Jackson; Screenplay, Fran Walsh, Philippa Boyens, Peter Jackson; Based on the novel by J. R. R. Tolkien; Co-Producers, Rick Porras, Jamie Selkirk; Photography, Andrew Lesnie; Designer, Grant Major; Costumes, Ngila Dickson, Richard Taylor; Editor, John Gilbert; Music, Howard Shore; Song: "May It Be," music and lyrics by Enya, Nicky Ryan, Roma Ryan/performed by Enya; Special Makeup, Creatures, Armor & Miniatures, Taylor/WETA Workshop Ltd.; Visual Effects Supervisor, Jim Rygiel; Digital Visual Effects, WETA Digital; Stunts, George Marshall Ruge; Casting, John Hubbard, Amy MacLean, Victoria Burrows, Liz Mullane, Ann Robinson; a Wingnut Films production; Dolby; Super 35 Widescreen; Deluxe color; Rated PG-13; 178 minutes; Release date: December 19, 2001.

## CAST

| | |
|---|---|
| Frodo Baggins | Elijah Wood |
| Gandalf | Ian McKellen |
| Arwen Undomiel | Liv Tyler |
| Aragorn (Strider) | Viggo Mortensen |
| Samwise "Sam" Gamgee | Sean Astin |
| Galadriel | Cate Blanchett |
| Gimli | John Rhys-Davies |
| Peregrin "Pippin" Took | Billy Boyd |
| Meriadoc "Merry" Brandybuck | Dominic Monaghan |
| Legolas | Orlando Bloom |
| Saruman | Christopher Lee |
| Elrond | Hugo Weaving |
| Boromir | Sean Bean |
| Bilbo Baggins | Ian Holm |
| Gollum | Andy Serkis |
| Celeborn | Marton Csokas |
| Haldir | Craig Parker |
| Lurtz | Lawrence Makoare |
| Voice of the Ring | Alan Howard |
| Everard Proudfoot | Noel Appleby |
| Sauron | Sala Baker |
| Mrs. Proudfoot | Megan Edwards |
| Gondorian Archivist | Michael Elsworth |
| Gil-Galad | Mark Ferguson |
| Witch King | Brent McIntyre |
| Elendil | Peter Mackenzie |
| Rosie Cotton | Sarah McLeod |
| Bounder | Ian Mune |
| Farmer Maggot | Cameron Rhodes |
| Gate Keeper | Martyn Sanderson |
| Isildur | Harry Sinclair |
| Barliman Butterbur | David Weatherley |
| Cute Hobbit Children | Billy Jackson, Katie Jackson |

and Victoria Beynon-Cole, Les Hartley, Sam La Hood, Chris Streeter, Jonathan Hordan, Semi Kuresa, Clinton Ulyatt, Paul Bryson, Lance Fabian Kemp, Jono Manks, Ben Price, Phillip Grieve (Hero Orcs/Goblins/Uruks/Ringwraiths)

*Hobbit Frodo Baggins and his companions venture forth to return a mystical ring to Mount Doom, in hopes of destroying it and saving civilization from its deadly powers. The first of a three-part trilogy to be followed by* The Lord of the Rings: The Two Towers *(2002) and* The Lord of the Rings: The Return of the King *(2003).*

*2001 Academy Award-winner for Best Cinematography, Visual Effects, Original Score, and Makeup. This film received additional Oscar nominations for picture, director, supporting actor (Ian McKellen), editing, sound, adapted screenplay, costume design, art direction, and original song ("May It Be").*

© New Line Productions, Inc.

Dominic Monaghan

Sean Astin, Elijah Wood

(Above) Hugo Weaving
(Below) Ian McKellen, Elijah Wood

# JIMMY NEUTRON: BOY GENIUS

Jimmy Neutron, Goddard

(PARAMOUNT) Producers, Steve Oedekerk, John A. Davis, Albie Hecht; Executive Producers, Julia Pistor, Keith Alcorn; Director, John A. Davis; Screenplay, John A. Davis, David N. Weiss, J. David Stem, Steve Oedekerk; Story, John A. Davis, Steve Oedekerk; Co-Producer, Paul Marshal, Gina Shay; Music, John Debney; Music Supervisors, Jeff Carson, Frankie Pine; Jimmy Neutron Theme by Brian Causey and Jaret Reddick/performed by Bowling for Soup; Designer, Fred Cline; Editors, Jon Michael Price, Gregory Perler; Animation Production, DNA Productions, Inc.; Art Director/Storyboard Supervisor, James Beihold; Character Designer, Keith Alcorn; Director of Modeling, Sean Jensen; Directors of Animation, Keith Alcorn, John A. Davis; Director of Lighting and Effects, Connon "Corndog" Carey; Casting, Paula Kaplan, Ginny McSwain; a Nickelodeon Movies presentation of an O Entertainment and Nickelodeon production; Dolby; Deluxe color; Rated G; 84 minutes; Release date: December 21, 2001

## VOICE CAST

Jimmy Neutron.................................................................Debi Derryberry
Mom/VOX ...................................................................Megan Cavanagh
Dad/Pilot/Arena Guard ....................................................Mark DeCarlo
Sheen.........................................................................Jeff Garcia
Newscasters......................................................Bob Goen, Mary Hart
Cindy Vortex ............................................................Carolyn Lawrence
Miss Fowl........................................................................Andrea Martin
Nick/Brittany/PJ ...............................................................Candi Milo
Carl/Carl's Mom and Dad/Kid in Classroom/Kid .................Rob Paulsen
Libby .............................................................................Crystal Scales
Ooblar ..........................................................................Martin Short
King Goobot........................................................................Patrick Stewart
Ultra Lord/Mission Control/General................................Jim Cummings
Yokian Guard/Gus ..........................................................David L. Lander
Zachery/Reporter/Angie ................................................Kimberly Brooks
Guard ...........................................................................Paul Greenberg
Hostess ...........................................................................Laraine Newman
and Jeannie Elias (Little Girl/Camera Person), Michael Hagiwara (Chris), John A. Davis (Octapuke Kid/Guard/Bennie), Keith Alcorn (Bobby/Kid/Control Yokian), Richard Allen (Digital Voice), Brian Capshaw, Cheryl Ray (Screamers), Mark Menza (Yokian Incubator Operator), Frank Welker (Orthgot/Worm/Demon/Poultra/Girl-Eating Plant/Oyster), Billy West (Yokian Officer/Jailbreak Cop/Guard/Robobearer /Anchor Boy/Old Man Johnson/Flurp Announcer/Bobby's Twin Brother/Butch), Matthew Russell (Hyperactive Kid/Arena Yokian), Carlos Alazraqui (Sheen's Dad), Dee Bradley Baker (Norad Officer)

Ooblar, King Goobot

*A young scientific whiz kid gets a chance to put his genius to work and save the day when all of the parents from the town of Retroville are abducted by aliens.*

*This film received an Oscar nomination for animated feature.*

© Paramount Pictures and Viacom International Inc.

(Above) Cindy Vortex, Jimmy Neutron, Goddard
(Below) Cindy Vortex, Goddard, Libby, Jimmy Neutron, Sheen, Carl Wheezer

Carl Wheezer, Goddard, Jimmy Neutron

# HOW HIGH

**(UNIVERSAL)** Producers, Danny DeVito, Michael Shamberg, Stacey Sher, Shauna Garr, James Ellis; Executive Producers, Pamela Abdy, Louis G. Friedman, Jonathan Weisgal; Director, Jesse Dylan; Screenplay, Dustin Lee Abraham; Photography, Francis Kenny; Designer, Clark Hunter; Costumes, Cindy Evans; Editor, Larry Bock; Music, Rockwilder; Casting, Matthew Berry, Nancy Green-Keyes; a Jersey Films/Native Pictures production; Dolby; Color; Rated R; 93 minutes; Release date: December 21, 2001

Method Man, Redman

## CAST

| | |
|---|---|
| Silas P. Silas | Method Man |
| Jamal King | Redman |
| Dean Cain | Obba Babatundé |
| Baby Powder | Mike Epps |
| Mrs. King | Anna Maria Horsford |
| Huntley | Fred Willard |
| Vice President | Jeffrey Jones |
| Crew Coach | Hector Elizondo |
| Lauren | Lark Voorhees |

and Al Shearer (I Need Money), Chuck Davis (Ivory), Essence Atkins (Jamie), Chris Elwood (Bart), T. J. Thyne (Gerald), Justin Urich (Jeffrey), Trieu Tran (Tuan), Dennison Samaroo (Amir), Tracey Walter (Prof. Wood), Spalding Gray (Prof. Jackson), Amber Smith (Prof. Garr), Kathy Wagner, Alicia Willis (Intellects), Patrice Fisher (End Table Ass), Sacha Kemp (Hella Back), Scruncho (Baby Wipe), Garrett Morris (PCC Agent), Scott Lincoln (Crackhead), Alem Brhan (Jamaican), Erica Vittina Phillips (Internet Date), Irene Roseen (THC Woman), Dwayne Kennedy, Jimmy Judah (Israelites), Pat Finn (Army Recruiter), Michael Coleman (Priest), James Reese, Rob Nagle (Agents), Judah Friedlander (Student), Joe Ochman (Ben Franklin), Leontine Guilliard, Roz Browne (Mamma's Friends), B-Real, Sen Dog, Bobo (Cypress Hill), Chuck Liddel, Alfonso Alcarez (Tough Guys), Dublin James (Sidekick), Melissa Peterman (Mrs. Cain), David Stebbins (V.P. Aide), Anthony DeSantis (Satanist)

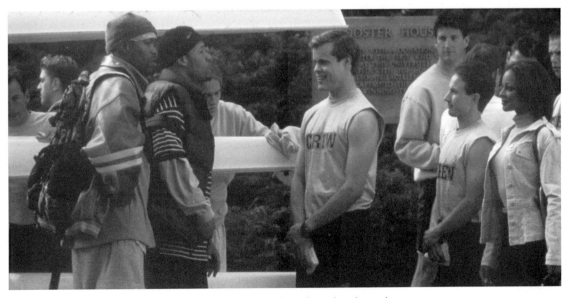

Lark Voorhees, Method Man, Redman

*In an effort to diversify the student body, the Harvard chancellor decides to welcome to the university a pair of stoners who passed the entrance exams with the help of a ghost.*

© Universal Studios

Method Man, Redman, Chris Elwood, Lark Voorhees

Tim Allen, Jim Belushi

# JOE SOMEBODY

**(20TH CENTURY FOX)** Producers, Arnold Kopelson, Anne Kopelson, Matthew Gross, Ken Atchity, Brian Reilly; Executive Producers, Arnon Milchan, Chi-Li Wong, William Wilson III; Director, John Pasquin; Screenplay, John Scott Shepherd; Photography, Daryn Okada; Designer, Jackson De Govia; Costumes, Lou Eyrich, Kathy O'Rear; Editor, David Finfer; Music, George S. Clinton; Music Supervisor, Frankie Pine; Casting, Risa Bramon Garcia; Fight Coordinator, Damon Caro; a Fox 2000 Pictures and Regency Enterprises presentation of a Kopelson Entertainment production; Dolby; Deluxe color; Rated PG; 98 minutes; Release date: December 21, 2001

## CAST

Joe Scheffer...................................................................................Tim Allen
Meg Harper ...................................................................................Julie Bowen
Callie Scheffer................................................................................Kelly Lynch
Natalie Scheffer ...........................................................Hayden Panettiere
Chuck Scarett...............................................................................Jim Belushi
Jeremy.............................................................................................Greg Germann
Pat Chilcutt ...................................................................................Robert Joy
Mark McKinney .............................................................Patrick Warburton
Rick Raglow.....................................................................................Ken Marino
and James Cada (Yoga Exec. Bill), Tawnja Zahradka (Waver "Tawnja"), Tina Lifford (Cassandra Taylor), Anha Brandvik (Neva), Wolfgang Bodison (Cade Raymond), John Riedlinger, Bill McCallum, Gavin Lawrence (In Crowd Guys), Amy Janette McDonald (Reporter), Emil Herrera (Singing Exec.), Cristi L. Conaway (Abby Manheim), Michelle Barnes (Sharone), Michael Haley (Bartender), Peter Eric Syvertsen, Peter Gregory Thomson (Squash Execs), Claudia Wilkens (Deidre), Jim Labriola, Lowell Sanders, Rob Cowin (Guys at Fight), Ross Turner (Basketball Boy), Bob Aden (Old Man), Rod Johnson (Timberwolves Announcer), Shawn Judge (Woman #1), Marquetta Senters (Linda), Jeff Hopkins (First Man), Jane Hajduk (Receptionist), Sean Grande (Play-by-Play Announcer), Jesse Ventura (Himself), Sarah Agnew (Well Wisher), Patrick Coyle (Man in Parking Lot), Cean Okada (Young Woman), William T. Leaf, Frank E. Adams, Kathleen Winter (Fruit Catchers), Kurt David Anderson (Target Employee), William Borea (Muscle Masseur), Brent Seltzer (Starke Commerical Voiceover)

*After being bullied by another employee at his workplace, Joe Scheffer decides to turn his dull existence around and become somebody of value.*

© Twentieth Century Fox and Regency Enterprises

Kelly Lynch, Hayden Panettiere

Greg Germann

Tim Allen, Julie Bowen

Laurie Holden, Jim Carrey

# THE MAJESTIC

**(WARNER BROS.)** Producer/Director, Frank Darabont; Executive Producer, Jim Behnke; Screenplay, Michael Sloane; Photography, David Tattersall; Designer, Gregory Melton; Costumes, Karyn Wagner; Music, Mark Isham; Editor, Jim Page; Associate Producers, Linda Fields Hill, Michael Sloane, Anna Garduño; Casting, Deborah Aquila; a Castle Rock Entertainment presentation in association with Village Roadshow Pictures and NPV Entertainment of a Darkwoods Production; Dolby; Technicolor; Rated PG; 149 minutes; Release date: December 21, 2001

Jim Carrey, Martin Landau, Jeffrey DeMunn

## CAST

| | |
|---|---|
| Peter Appleton (Luke Trimble) | Jim Carrey |
| Harry Trimble | Martin Landau |
| Adele Stanton | Laurie Holden |
| Doc Stanton | David Ogden Stiers |
| Stan Keller | James Whitmore |
| Ernie Cole | Jeffrey DeMunn |
| Kevin Bannerman | Ron Rifkin |
| Congressman Doyle | Hal Holbrook |
| Majority Counsel Elvin Clyde | Bob Balaban |
| Sandra Sinclair | Amanda Detmer |
| Sheriff Cecil Coleman | Brent Briscoe |
| Emmett Smith | Gerry Black |
| Irene Terwilliger | Susan Willis |
| Mabel | Catherine Dent |
| Bob Leffert | Karl Bury |
| Carl Leffert/Voice of Studio Boss | Brian Howe |
| Avery Wyatt | Chelcie Ross |
| Spencer Wyatt | Matt G. Wiens |
| Leo Kubelsky | Allen Garfield |
| Federal Agent Ellerby | Daniel Von Bargen |

and Shawn Doyle (Federal Agent Saunders), Mario Roccuzzo (Jerry the Bartender), Frank Collison (Subpoena Server), Bill Gratton (Daley), Ginger Williams (Louise), Ken Magee (Coastal Engineer), Csilla Horvath (Nurse Muriel), April Ortiz (Vera), Larry Cox (Grauman's Usher), Julie Richardson (Grauman's Bon-Bon Girl), Scotty Leavenworth, Grant Vaught (Boys on Beach), Bob Wells (Reverend), Kevin DeMunn (Western Union Man), Earl Boen (Newsreel Announcer); Sand Pirates of the Sahara: Bruce Campbell (Roland the Intrepid Explorer), Cliff Curtis (The Evil But Handsome Prince Khalid), Michael Sloane (Kindly Old Professor Meredith); Vocal Cameos: Garry Marshall, Paul Mazursky, Sydney Pollack, Carl Reiner, Rob Reiner (Studio Executives), Matt Damon (Luke's Letter)

Jim Carrey

*A Hollywood screenwriter, subpoenaed to appear before the House Un-American Activities Committee, has an accident that causes him to lose his memory. He arrives in a small northern California town where he is mistaken for a presumed-dead war hero.*

© Warner Bros.

Jeffrey DeMunn, Jim Carrey

Mario Van Peebles, Will Smith

# ALI

**(COLUMBIA)** Producers, Jon Peters, James Lassiter, Paul Ardaji, Michael Mann, A. Kitman Ho; Executive Producers, Howard Bingham, Graham King; Director, Michael Mann; Screenplay, Stephen J. Rivele, Christopher Wilkinson, Eric Roth, Michael Mann; Story, Gregory Allen Howard; Photography, Emmanuel Lubezki; Designer, John Myhre; Costumes, Marlene Stewart; Editors, William Goldenberg, Stephen Rivkin, Lynzee Klingman; Music, Lisa Gerrard, Pieter Bourke; Special Makeup Effects, Greg Cannom; Associate Producers, Gusamano Cesaretti, Kathleen M. Shea; Casting, Victoria Thomas; Presented in association with Initial Entertainment Group; a Peters Entertainment/Forward Pass production in association with Lee Caplin/Picture Entertainment Corp. and Overbrook Films; Dolby; Panavision; Deluxe color; Rated R; 158 minutes; Release date: December 25, 2001

## CAST

Cassius Clay/Muhammad Ali .................................................Will Smith
Drew "Bundini" Brown .........................................................Jamie Foxx
Howard Cosell..........................................................................Jon Voight
Malcolm X.............................................................Mario Van Peebles
Angelo Dundee..........................................................................Ron Silver
Howard Bingham...............................................................Jeffrey Wright
Don King.......................................................................Mykelti Williamson
Sonji Roi.................................................................Jada Pinkett Smith
Belinda Boyd........................................................................Nona Gaye
Veronica Porsche.........................................................Michael Michele
Chauncy Eskridge..................................................................Joe Morton
Dr. Ferdie Pacheco.........................................................Paul Rodriguez
Bradley............................................................................Bruce McGill
Herbert Muhammad...............................................Barry Shabaka Henley
Cassius Clay, Sr..............................................................Giancarlo Esposito
Elijah Muhammad..................................................................Albert Hall
Robert Lipsyte.....................................................................David Cubitt
Joe Smiley...............................................................................Ted Levine
Odessa Clay .............................................................Candy Brown Houston
and David Elliott (Sam Cooke), Shari Watson (Singer), Malick Bowens (Joseph Mobutu), Michael Bentt (Sonny Liston), James N. Toney (Joe Frazier), Alfred Cole (Ernie Terrell), Charles Shufford (George Foreman), Rufus Dorsey (Floyd Paterson), Robert Sale (Jerry Quarry), Vincent Cook (Jimmy Ellis), Damien "Bolo" Wills (Ken Norton), David Haines (Rudy Clay/Rahaman Ali), Victoria Dillard (Betty Shabazz), Brad Greenquist (Marlin Thomas), Morgana Van Peebles, Maya Van Peebles (Malcolm X's Daughters), Maestro Harrell (Young Cassius Clay), William Utay (The Doctor), Kim Robillard (Jimmy Cannon), David Purdham (Madison Square Garden Announcer), Gailard Sartain (Gordon Davidson), Wade Andrew Williams (Lt. Jerome Claridge), Guy Van Swearingen (Induction FBI Man), Doug Hale (Judge Ingraham), LaDonna Tittle (Bundini's Landlady), Marc Grapey (Bob Arum), Herb Mitchell (Boxing Commissioner), Eddie Bo Smith, Jr. (Malcolm's Bodyguard), Bob Stuart (Thomas 15x Johnson), Patrick New (Room Service Guy), Ron OJ Parson (Death Newsman), Ellis E. Williams (Family Photo Man), Bokyun Chun (Asian Cosmetologist), John G. Connolly (Assistant Director), Warner

Saunders (Customer), Jack Reiss (Referee Arthur Mercante), Marty Denkin (Frazier Fight 2 Announcer), Tamara Lynch (Flight Attendant), Theron Benymon (Hampton House Announcer), Bill Plaschke (Miami Weigh-In Reporter), Patrick M. Connolly (Referee), Robert Byrd (Willie Reddick), Ronald A. Dinicola (Prosecutor), Moses Hollins (Man on Train), Danaiel E. Gurevitz (Boxing Commission Reporter), Steven Randazzo, Ray Bokhour (Reporters), Leonard Termo, Johnny Ortiz (Madison Square Garden Reporters), Mark Salem, Sheldon Fogel, Jim Gray (New York Reporters), Melvin Brown, Natalie Carter, Reginald Rootman (Harlem Neighbors), Poe Poe (Harlem Reporter), Mel Dick (Louisville Sponsoring Group), Kim Taylor Coleman (Lana Shabazz), Christian Stolte (Miami Cop), Steve Springer (Miami Weigh-In Reporter), Victor Manni (Dressing Weigh-In Guy), Will Gill, Jr. (Dick Sadler), Sylvaine Struck (ORTF Interviewer), Dennis Luposo (Kinshasa Reporter), Sharon Wilkinson (Rose Jennings), Carol Hatchett, Judith Mwale, Keabetowe Notsilanyane (Pointer Sisters), Richard Katanga (Mobutu Aide/Military Aide), Thomas Kariuki (Lt. Nsakala), Larry Hazzard, Sr. (Zack Clayton), Dereck Brown (Larry Holmes), Rommel Hyacinth (The Pilot), Graham Hopkins (London Banker), Daniel Janks (Other CIA Man), Bradford E. Lang, Michael Dorn (Pilots), Dan Robberse, Graham Clarke, Dimitri Caesar, Frank Notaro, Mark Mulder, David Hess (Mozambique Reporters), Henrikennyo Mukenyi Babibingo (Bula), Nathaniel Malekane (Archie Moore), Millard Arnold (Doc Broadus), Edda Collier (Blonde French Reporter), Wei Yi Lu (Chinese Delegate), Lee Cummings (Hunter Thompson), Zaa Nkweta (Foreman Fight Announcer), Themba Gasa (Idi Amin), Andrew P. Jones (Don King's Aide), Marc Kulazite Mboli, Cimanga Kalambay, Jean Bikoi (Additional Aides to Mobutu), James Gilbert (Sparring Partner in Africa)

*The story of boxer Muhammad Ali, from his 1964 defeat of Sonny Liston—which earned him the heavyweight championship title—to his 1974 comeback bout against George Foreman. Previous bio film on Ali was* The Greatest *(Columbia, 1977) in which Ali played himself.*

*This film received Oscar nominations for actor (Will Smith) and supporting actor (Jon Voight).*

© Columbia Pictures

(Above) Jada Pinkett Smith, Will Smith
(Below) Jamie Foxx, Jon Voight, Mykelti Williamson

Will Smith, David Haines, Ron Silver

Will Smith, Michael Michele

Jon Voight, Will Smith

Ron Silver, Paul Rodriguez, Laurence Mason,
Jeffrey Wright, Jamie Foxx

Will Smith, Nona Gaye

Hugh Jackman, Meg Ryan

Bradley Whitford

# KATE & LEOPOLD

**(MIRAMAX)** Producer, Cathy Konrad; Executive Producers, Kerry Orent, Bob Weinstein, Harvey Weinstein, Meryl Poster; Director, James Mangold; Screenplay, James Mangold, Steven Rogers; Story, Steven Rogers; Photography, Stuart Dryburgh; Designer, Mark Friedberg; Costumes, Donna Zakowska; Co-Producer, Christopher Goode; Editor, David Brenner; Music, Rolfe Kent; Song: "Until . . .," written and performed by Sting; Casting, Billy Hopkins, Suzanne Smith, Kerry Barden; a Konrad Pictures production; Dolby; Color; Rated PG-13; 121 minutes; Release date: December 25, 2001

## CAST

| | |
|---|---|
| Kate McKay | Meg Ryan |
| Leopold | Hugh Jackman |
| Stuart Besser | Liev Schreiber |
| Charlie McKay | Breckin Meyer |
| Darci | Natasha Lyonne |
| J. J. Camden | Bradley Whitford |
| Uncle Millard | Paxton Whitehead |
| Dr. Geisler | Spalding Gray |
| Colleague Bob | Josh Stamberg |
| Ad Executive Phil | Matthew Sussman |
| Patrice | Charlotte Ayanna |
| Otis | Philip Bosco |
| Roebling | Andrew Jack |
| Photographer | Stan Tracy |
| Miss Tree | Kristen Schaal |
| Clara | Andrea Barnes |

and James Mangold (Movie Director), William Sanford (Barry), David Aaron Baker (Studio Executive), Arthur Nascarella (Gracy), Robert Manning (Passerby), Roma Torre (TV Newscaster), Viola Davis (Policewoman), Ray Seiden (Sanitation Worker), Jonathan Fried (Faux Wolfgang), Francis Dumaurier (Faux Emeril), Cole Hawkins (Hector), Stephanie Montalvo (CRG Intern), Ebony Jo-Ann (Nurse Ester), George Hahn (Assistant Director), Joe Mosso (Cameraman), Cornelius Byrne (Carriage Driver), Chazz Menendez (Purse Thief), Brandon Parrish (Dennis), Brittney Startzman (Monica), Martha Madison (Office Woman), Stephanie Sanditz (Gretchen), Nai Yuan Hu (Rooftop Violinist), Michael Shelle (Distinguished Actor), Matthew Beisner (Commercial Director), Bill Corsair (Limo Driver), John Rothman, Dennis Rees, Michael Cassady (Executives), Brian Letscher (Ad Executive), Meg Gibson (Executive's Wife), Kevin Daniels (Doorman at Party), Henry Boyle (Cab Driver), Russell Di Perna (Bridge Cop), Frank Arcuri (1876 Doorman)

*Leopold, an English Duke from the 19th century, finds himself transported to modern-day Manhattan where he falls in love with career woman Kate McKay.*

*This film received an Oscar nomination for original song ("Until . . .").*

Meg Ryan, Hugh Jackman

Breckin Meyer, Liev Schreiber

© Miramax Films

Kevin Spacey, Judi Dench

# THE SHIPPING NEWS

**(MIRAMAX)** Producers, Irwin Winkler, Linda Goldstein Knowlton, Leslie Holleran; Executive Producers, Bob Weinstein, Harvey Weinstein, Meryl Poster; Director, Lasse Hallström; Screenplay, Robert Nelson Jacobs; Based on the novel by E. Annie Proulx; Co-Producer, Diana Pokorny; Photography, Oliver Stapleton; Designer, David Gropman; Costumes, Renée Ehrlich Kalfus; Editor, Andrew Mondshein; Music, Christopher Young; Casting, Billy Hopkins, Suzanne Smith, Kerry Barden; an Irwin Winkler production; Dolby; Super 35 Widescreen; Color; Rated R; 111 minutes; Release date: December 25, 2001

## CAST

| | |
|---|---|
| Quoyle | Kevin Spacey |
| Wavey Prowse | Julianne Moore |
| Agnis Hamm | Judi Dench |
| Petal Bear | Cate Blanchett |
| Tert X. Card | Pete Postlethwaite |
| Jack Buggit | Scott Glenn |
| B. Beaufield Nutbeem | Rhys Ifans |
| Billy Pretty | Gordon Pinsett |
| Dennis Buggit | Jason Behr |
| Bayonet Melville | Larry Pine |
| Silver Melville | Jeanetta Arnette |
| EMS Officer | Robert Joy |
| Bunny | Alyssa Gainer, Kaitlyn Gainer, Lauren Gainer |
| Guy Quoyle | John Dunsworth |
| Young Quoyle (7 years old) | Anthony Cipriano |
| Young Quoyle (12 years old) | Kyle Smith |
| Newspaper Boss | Ken James |
| Muscular Man | Roman Podhora |
| Barfly | Luke Fisher |

and Terry Daly (Hunky Guy), Gary Levert (Newspaper Employee), Stephen Morgan (Bartender Dave), Katherine Moennig (Grace Moosup), Daniel Kash (Detective Danzig), Will McAllister (Herry Prowse), Marc Lawrence (Cousin Nolan), Kathryn Fraser (Daycare Mom), Nancy Beatty (Mavis Bangs), R. D. Reid (Alvin York), Deborah Grover (Edna Buggit), Jon Whalen (Big Guy), Nicole Underhay (Betty Buggit), Emma Taylor-Isherwood (Young Agnis), Andrew Fowler (Guy Quoyle—15 years old), John MacEachern (Drunken Guy), Jonathan Creaser (Paramedic)

*Quoyle, a lonely man who has lost his estranged wife in a car accident, moves with his daughter to his ancestors' home in Newfoundland, where he becomes a reporter on the local paper.*

© Miramax Films

Scott Glenn, Kevin Spacey

Cate Blanchett

Michael Gambon, Emily Watson, Richard E. Grant

Ryan Phillippe, Emily Watson

Clive Owen, Kelly Macdonald

# GOSFORD PARK

(USA FILMS) Producers, Robert Altman, Bob Balaban, David Levy; Executive Producers, Jane Barclay, Sharon Harel, Robert Jones, Hannah Leader; Director, Robert Altman; Screenplay, Julian Fellowes; Based on an idea by Robert Altman, Bob Balaban; Photography, Andrew Dunn; Designer, Stephen Altman; Costumes, Jenny Beavan; Editor, Tim Squyres; Music, Patrick Doyle; Co-Producers, Jane Frazer, Joshua Astrachan; Casting, Mary Selway; a Sandcastle 5 production in association with Chicagofilms, presented in association with Capitol Films and the Film Council; U.S.-British; Dolby; Panavision; Technicolor; Rated R; 137 minutes; Release date: December 26, 2001

## CAST

### Above Stairs

Sir William McCordle ....................................................Michael Gambon
Lady Sylvia McCordle ............................................Kristin Scott Thomas
Isobel McCordle.....................................................Camilla Rutherford
Constance, Countess of Trentham ........................................Maggie Smith
Raymond, Lord Stockbridge ................................................Charles Dance
Louisa, Lady Stockbridge ...........................................Geraldine Somerville
Lieutenant Commander Anthony Meredith ....................Tom Hollander
Lady Lavinia Meredith ...............................................Natasha Wightman
The Hon. Freddie Nesbitt ...............................................James Wilby
Mabel Nesbitt ..........................................................Claudie Blakley
Lord Rupert Standish ..................................................Laurence Fox
Jeremy Blond ................................................................Trent Ford
Ivor Novello .........................................................Jeremy Northam
Morris Weissman......................................................Bob Balaban

### Below Stairs

Jennings .................................................................Alan Bates
Mrs. Wilson..............................................................Helen Mirren
Mrs. Croft ...............................................................Eileen Atkins
Probert.................................................................Derek Jacobi
Elsie....................................................................Emily Watson
George ............................................................Richard E. Grant
Arthur ..................................................................Jeremy Swift
Lewis .............................................................Meg Wynn Owen
Dorothy...........................................................Sophie Thompson
Bertha...............................................................Teresa Chucher
Ellen ..................................................................Sarah Flind
Lottie ....................................................................Lucy Cohu
Janet .................................................................Finty Williams
May ...............................................................Emma Buckley
Ethel...............................................................Laura Harling
Maud ...............................................................Tilly Gerrard
Albert..................................................................Will Beer
Fred ...........................................................Greg Henderson Begg
Jim........................................................................Leo Bill
Strutt ..............................................................Ron Puttock
McCordle's Loader.............................................Adrian Preater

### Visiting Servants

Mary Maceachran ....................................................Kelly Macdonald
Robert Parks ..........................................................Clive Owen
Henry Denton .....................................................Ryan Phillippe
Renee....................................................................Joanna Maude
Barnes ...........................................................Adrian Scarborough
Sarah .....................................................................Frances Low
Merriman...............................................................John Atterbury
Burkett...............................................................Frank Thornton

### Outsiders

Inspector Thompson ................................................Stephen Fry
Constable Dexter ....................................................Ron Webster

*A gathering at the posh English estate of Sir William McCordle ends in murder. 2001 Academy Award-winner for Best Original Screenplay. This film received additional Oscar nominations for picture, director, supporting actresses (Helen Mirren, Maggie Smith), costume design, and art direction.*

© USA Films

Kelly Macdonald, Maggie Smith

Ryan Phillippe, Kristin Scott Thomas

Helen Mirren, Stephen Fry

Natasha Wightman, Bob Balaban, Tom Hollander,
Jeremy Northam

Meg Wynn Owen, Richard E. Grant,
Natasha Wightman, Tom Hollander,
Jeremy Swift, Camilla Rutherford,
Maggie Smith, Kristin Scott Thomas

Billy Bob Thornton, Peter Boyle, Heath Ledger

Sean Combs

# MONSTER'S BALL

(LIONS GATE) Producer, Lee Daniels; Executive Producers, Michael Paseornek, Michael Burns, Mark Urman; Director, Marc Foster; Screenplay, Milo Addica, Will Rokos; Photography, Roberto Schaefer; Designer, Monroe Kelly; Costumes, Frank Fleming; Editor, Matt Chesse; Music, Asche and Spencer; Music Supervisor, Joel High; Casting, Billy Hopkins, Suzanne Smith, Kerry Barden, Mark Bennett; a Lee Daniels Entertainment production; Dolby; Panavision; Deluxe color; Rated R; 111 minutes; Release date: December 26, 2001

## CAST

| | |
|---|---|
| Hank Grotowski | Billy Bob Thornton |
| Sonny Grotowski | Heath Ledger |
| Leticia Musgrove | Halle Berry |
| Buck Grotowski | Peter Boyle |
| Lawrence Musgrove | Sean Combs |
| Ryrus Cooper | Mos Def |
| Warden Velasco | Will Rokos |
| Tommy Roulaine | Milo Addica |
| Willie Cooper | Charles Cowan, Jr. |
| Darryl Cooper | Taylor Lagrange |
| Tyrell Musgrove | Coronji Calhoun |
| Lucille | Taylor Simpson |
| Betty | Gabrielle Witcher |
| Vera | Amber Rules |
| Dappa Smith | Anthony Bean |
| Georgia Ann Paynes | Francine Segal |
| Harvey Shoonmaker | John McConnell |
| Phil Higgins | Marcus Lyle Brown |
| Booter | Leah Loftin |
| Correction Officer | Marshall Cain |
| Billy | Anthony Michael Frederick |
| Minister | John Wilmot |
| Clement | Dennis Clement |
| Nurse | Stephanie Claire |
| Hospital Guard | Jamie Haven |
| Detective | Ritchie Montgomery |
| Maggie Cooper | Clara Daniels |
| Mrs. Guillermo | Carol Sutton |
| Deputy Jones | Bernard Johnson |
| Cos | Paul Smith |

*A prison guard, whose personal life is rapidly falling apart, finds himself unexpectedly befriending the lonely widow of a man whose execution he participated in.*

*2001 Academy Award-winner for Best Actress (Halle Berry). This film received an additional Oscar nomination for original screenplay.*

© Lions Gate Films

Halle Berry, Coronji Calhoun

Halle Berry, Billy Bob Thornton

Heath Ledger, Sean Combs, Billy Bob Thornton

Gregory Sporleder, Josh Hartnett

Sam Shepard

(Above) Orlando Bloom, Josh Hartnett

Ewan McGregor

# BLACK HAWK DOWN

(COLUMBIA) Producers, Jerry Bruckheimer, Ridley Scott; Executive Producers, Simon West, Mike Stenson, Chad Oman, Branko Lustig; Director, Ridley Scott; Screenplay, Ken Nolan; Based on the book by Mark Bowden; Photography, Slawomir Idziak; Designer, Arthur Max; Costumes, Sammy Howarth-Sheldon, David Murphy; Editor, Pietro Scalia; Music, Hans Zimmer; Music Supervisors, Kathy Nelson, Bob Badami; Associate Producers, Terry Needham, Harry Humphries, Pat Sandston; Special Effects Supervisor, Neil Corbould; Casting, Bonnie Timmermann; Stunts, Phil Nielson; a Revolution Studios and Jerry Bruckheimer Films presentation of a Jerry Bruckheimer production in association with Scott Free productions; Dolby; Super 35 Widescreen; Technicolor; Rated R; 147 minutes; Release date: December 28, 2001

Thomas Guiry

## CAST

| | |
|---|---|
| Ranger Staff Sgt. Matt Eversmann | Josh Hartnett |
| Ranger Spec. Grimes | Ewan McGregor |
| Ranger Lt. Col. Danny McKnight | Tom Sizemore |
| Delta Sgt. First Class "Hoot" Gibson | Eric Bana |
| Delta Sgt. First Class Jeff Sanderson | William Fichtner |
| Ranger Spec. Shawn Nelson | Ewen Bremner |
| Maj. Gen. William F. Garrison | Sam Shepard |
| Ranger Spec. Mike Kurth | Gabriel Casseus |
| Delta Master Sgt. Chris "Wex" Wexler | Kim Coates |
| Ranger Sgt. First Class Kurt Schmid | Hugh Dancy |
| Chief Warrant Officer Mike Durant | Ron Eldard |
| Ranger Beales | Ioan Gruffudd |
| Ranger Staff Sgt. Ed Yurek | Thomas Guiry |
| Ranger Cpl. Jamie Smith | Charlie Hofheimer |
| Ranger Sgt. Dominick Pilla | Danny Hoch |
| Captain Mike Steele | Jason Isaacs |
| Delta Lt. Col. Gary Harrell | Zeljko Ivanek |
| Lt. Col. Tom Matthews | Glenn Morshower |
| Chief Warrant Officer Cliff Wolcott | Jeremy Piven |
| Ranger Pfc. Richard Kowalewski | Brendan Sexton III |
| Delta Sgt. First Class Randy Shughart | Johnny Strong |
| Delta Staff Sgt. Dan Busch | Richard Tyson |
| Ranger Staff Sgt. Jeff Struecker | Brian Van Holt |
| Delta Master Sgt. Gary Gordon | Nikolaj Coster-Waldau |
| Lt. Col. Joe Cribbs | Steven Ford |
| Ranger Pvt. John Waddell | Ian Virgo |
| Ranger Spec. Lance Twombly | Thomas Hardy |
| Ranger Sgt. Scott Galentine | Gregory Sporleder |
| Ranger Sgt. Mike Goodale | Carmine Giovinazzo |
| Ranger Sgt. James "Casey" Joyce | Chris Beetem |
| Ranger Spec. Brad Thomas | Tac Fitzgerald |
| Ranger Spec. Dale Sizemore | Matthew Marsden |
| Ranger Pvt. First Class Todd Blackburn | Orlando Bloom |
| Ranger Pfc. Clay Othic | Kent Linville |
| Ruiz | Enrique Murciano |
| Ranger Pvt. Maddox | Michael Roof |
| Osman Atto | George Harris |
| Mo'alim | Razaaq Adoti |
| Firimbi | Treva Ettienne |
| Somali Spy | Abdibashir Mohamed Hersi |
| Briley | Pavel Vokoun |
| Fales | Dan Woods |
| Air Force Tech. Sgt. Tim Wilkinson | Ty Burrell |
| Chief Warrant Officer Mike Goffena | Boyd Kestner |
| Chief Warrant Officer Dan Jollata | Jason Hildebrandt |

and Kofi Amankwah, Joshua Quarcoo (Somali Kids), Johann Myers (Somali Father), Lee Geohagen (Somali Son with Gun)

*A group of American soldiers arrives in Mogadishu, Somalia, with the intention of abducting two enemy lieutenants as a peacekeeping strategy, resulting in the biggest military fire fight since Vietnam. 2001 Academy Award-winner for Best Editing and Sound. This film received additional Oscar nominations for director and cinematography.*

© Revolution Studios

Josh Hartnett

Ty Burrell, Jeremy Piven (on stretcher)

Michelle Pfeiffer, Sean Penn

# I AM SAM

**(NEW LINE CINEMA)** Producers, Edward Zwick, Marshall Herskovitz; Executive Producers, Claire Rudnick Polstein, Michael De Luca, David Scott Rubin; Director, Jessie Nelson; Screenplay, Kristine Johnson, Jessie Nelson; Co-Producer, Barbara A. Hall; Photography, Elliot Davis; Designer, Aaron Osborne; Costumes, Susie DeSanto; Editor, Richard Chew; Music, John Powell; Casting, Mary Gail Artz, Barbara Cohen; a Bedford Falls Company/Red Fish, Blue Fish Films production; Dolby; Fotokem color; Rated PG-13; 132 minutes; Release date: December 28, 2001

Sean Penn, Dakota Fanning

## CAST

Sam Dawson .................................................................Sean Penn
Rita Harrison.........................................................Michelle Pfeiffer
Lucy Diamond Dawson ....................................Dakota Fanning
Annie ...................................................................Dianne Wiest
Margaret Calgrove .............................................Loretta Devine
Turner ..................................................................Richard Schiff
Randy Carpenter....................................................Laura Dern
Brad ..........................................................Brad Allan Silverman
Joe.................................................................Joseph Rosenberg
Robert .............................................................Stanley DeSantis
Ifty .....................................................................Doug Hutchison
Lily ....................................................................Rosalind Chao
Judge McNeily..........................................................Ken Jenkins
Miss Wright ........................................................Wendy Phillips
Conner Rhodes..................................................Mason Lucero
Duncan Rhodes ......................................................Scott Paulin
George..................................................................Bobby Cooper
Ms. Davis.............................................................Kit McDonough
Gertie.....................................................................Kimberly Scott
and Michael B. Silver (Dr. Jaslow), Caroline Keenan (Rebecca), Eileen Ryan (Estelle), Mary Steenburgen (Dr. Blake), Marin Hinkle (Patricia), Chase Mackenzie Bebak (Willy), Rafer Weigel (Bruce), Emiko Parise (Nurse), Pamela Dunlap (Grace), Brent Spiner (Shoe Salesman), David Nathan Schwartz (Principal), Kathleen Robertson (Big Boy Waitress), Karen Bankhead (Rita's Colleague), Janet Adderley (Obnoxious Mom), Katie McGloin (Cristina), Steven Maines (Collin), Dennis Fanning (Vice Cop), David Poynter (Cafeteria Worker), R. D. Call (Cop at Park), John Paizis (Starbuck's Father), Russ Fega (Starbuck's Angry Man), Erinn Seaghda Rice Goletz (Starbuck's Barista), Julie Claire (Starbuck's Customer), Marnie Martin (Starbuck's Woman), Tony Abatemarco (Court Clerk), Will Wallace (Bill Carpenter), Scott Weintraub (Scarecrow), Nicholas Mele (Booking Cop), Brian Bialick (Brian), Molly Gordon (Callie), Nora Kroopf (Sara), Allison and Jillian Thormahlen (Lucy, Infant), Ryan Williams (Lucy—6 months old), Felicity Ann and Makindra Sherry Forbes (Lucy—18 months old), Ellie Fanning(Lucy—2 years 10 months old), Amanda Lehaf (Lucy—4 years old)

*A mentally handicapped father enlists a self-absorbed attorney to help him fight a social worker who insists that his young daughter be placed in a foster home.*

*This film received an Oscar nomination for actor (Sean Penn).*

© New Line Cinema

Loretta Devine

Dianne Wiest

Laura Dern, Sean Penn

John C. Holmes in *Wadd: The Life and Times of John C. Holmes* © VCA Pictures

## EXTREME FORCE

(PHAEDRA CINEMA) Executive Producers, Michael Belfonti, Paul Raucci; Director, Michel Qissi; Screenplay, Jonathan Davenport, Michel Qissi; Music, Kays Al-Atrakchi; Editor, Tim Gregoire; Casting, Tracy Frenkel; Stunts, Dale Cannon; from Creative Light Entertainment; Dolby; Color; Rated R; 90 minutes; Release date: January 12, 2001. CAST: Hector Echavarria (Marcos DeSantos), Fitz (Pearl), Tracy Frenkel (Mob Boss), Louis Iocaviello (President Khan), Adam Leadbeater (Vat Kallac), Nikki Lemke (Bianca), Myriam Mesdagh (Sharka), Phi-Long Nguyen (Sniper), Michel Qissi (Kong Li), Youssef Qissi (Cole)

## THE AMATI GIRLS

(PROVIDENCE) Producers, James Alex, Steve C. Johnson, Michael I. Levy, Henry M. Shea, Jr.; Executive Producers, Howard Kazanjian, Craig C. Darian; Director/Screenplay, Anne DeSalvo; Co-Producers, Melanie Backer, Dan Stone; Photography, Frank Byers; Designer, Jane Stewart; Music, Conrad Pope; Costumes, Amy Stofsky; Editor, C. Timothy O'Meara; Casting, Mary Jo Slater; a Fox Family-Providence Entertainment & Tricor Entertainment presentation of a Triple Axel & Heritage Film Group production; Deluxe color; Rated PG; 91 minutes; Release date: January 19, 2001. CAST: Mercedes Ruehl

Lily Knight, Sean Young, Mercedes Ruehl, Dinah Manoff in *The Amati Girls* © Providence Entertainment

Paul Bowles in *NightWaltz* © Owsley Brown

## NIGHT WALTZ:
## THE MUSIC OF PAUL BOWLES

(OWSLEY BROWN PRESENTS) Producers, Owsley Brown III, Robin Burke; Director/Screenplay, Owsley Brown III; Photography, David Golia, Gene Salvitore, Rudy Burckhardt, Nathaniel Dorsky; Editor, Nathaniel Dorsky; Music, Paul Bowles; Produced with support from Telefilm Canada; U.S.-Canadian, 1999; Color/black and white; Not rated; 76 minutes; Release date: January 3, 2001. Documentary on author Paul Bowles's work as a composer, featuring Paul Bowles, Allen Ginsberg, William S. Burroughs.

## WADD: THE LIFE & TIMES OF JOHN C. HOLMES

(VCA PICTURES) Producer/Director, Cass Paley; Executive Producer, Russ Hampshire; Co-Producer/Editor, Christopher Rowland; Photography, Willie Boudevin; Music, Brad Raylius Daniel, Tad Dery; Color; Not rated; 110 minutes; Release date: January 12, 2001. Documentary on porno star John C. Holmes, featuring Linda Adrain, Bill Amerson, Denise Amerson, Sean "Duke" Amerson, P. T. Anderson, Det. Tom Blake, Bunny Blue, Paul Cambria, Bob Chinn, Cicciolina, David Clark, Hon. Ron Coen, "Dawn," Mitchell Egers, Don Fernando, Larry Flint, Al Goldstein, Annette Haven, Bobby Hollander, Jim Holliday, Laurie "Misty Dawn" Holmes, Sharon Holmes, Mike Horner, Ron Jeremy, Det. Tom Lange, Gloria Leonard, John Leslie, Vonda Lia, Jon Martin, Sharon Mitchell, Kitten Natividad, Richard Pachaco, "Aunt Peg," Ann Perry, Ernie Robuck, Candida Royale, Mike Sager, Sheri St. Clair, Det. Bob Souza, "Reb" Sawitz, Joel Sussman, Ken Turan, Bob Vossee

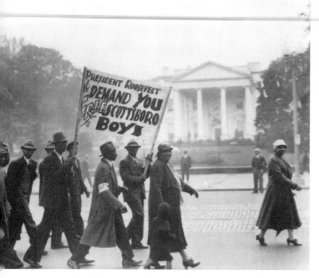

*Scottsboro: An American Tragedy* © Cowboy

## SCOTTSBORO: AN AMERICAN TRAGEDY

(COWBOY BOOKING) Producers/Directors, Daniel Anker, Barak Goodman; Screenplay, Barak Goodman; Photography, Buddy Squires, Tom Hurwitz; Music, Edward Bilous; Editor, Jean Tsien; Narrator, Andre Braugher; a Social Media Prods. production in association with the American Experience; Color; Not rated; 90 minutes; Release date: January 19, 2001. Documentary on how nine black males were accused of the rape of two white women near Scottsboro, AL, in 1931. VOICES: Frances McDormand, Stanley Tucci, Harris Yulin, Jeffrey DeMunn, Daver Morrison.

## A FIGHT TO THE FINISH: STORIES OF POLIO

(KEN MANDEL FILMS) Producers, Ken Mandel, Tony Herring; Executive Producer, J.C. Montgomery Jr.; Director/Photography, Ken Mandel; Screenplay, Ralph Meyers; Editors, Ken Mandel, Ralph Meyers; Music, John Bryant, Frank Hames, Tony Herring; Produced by the Texas Scottish Rite Hospital for Children, Mandel/Herring Productions; Color; Not rated; 90 minutes; Release date: January 19, 2001. A documentary chronicling the fight against polio in the United States.

## TWO NINAS

(CASTLE HILL) Producers, Denise Doyle, Greg Scheinman; Co-Executive Producers, Seth Kanegis, Adam Sender; Director/Screenplay, Neil Turitz; Photography, Joaquin Baca-Asay; Designer, Tony Gasparro; Editor, Jay Chandrasekhar; Music, Joseph Saba; Dolby; Color; Rated R; 89 minutes; Release date: January 26, 2001. CAST: Amanda Peet (Nina Harris), Ron Livingston (Marty Sachs), Cara Buono (Nina Cohen), Bray Poor (Dave Trout), Linda Larkin (Carrie Boxer), John Rothman (Barry Litzer), Jill Hennessy (Mike the Bartender), Leigh Whitney, Denise Doyle, Brooke Leslie, Meredith Lieber, Amy Veltman, Linette Strauss (Blow-off Girls), Mauro Maccione (Nightmare Date Guy), Fred Norris (Eurotrash), Allison Furman (Waitress), Neil Turitz (Guy at Bar), Dave McGuire, Keith Young (Muggers)

(Grace), Paul Sorvino (Joe), Cloris Leachman (Dolly), Sean Young (Christine), Dinah Manoff (Denise), Lily Knight (Dolores), Lee Grant (Aunt Splendora), Mark Harmon (Lawrence), Jamey Sheridan (Paul), Marissa Leigh (Laura), Doug Spinuzza (Armand), Sam McMurray (Brian), Edith Fields (Aunt Loretta), Joe Greco (Uncle Frankie), Cassie Cole (Carla), Kyle Sabihy (Joey), Asher Gold (Peter), Matt Winston (Johnny Barlotta), Garrison Hershberger (Kevin), Anne DeSalvo (Cathy), Sal Viscuso (Father Dedice), Anna Berger (Stella), Don Marino (Sam), Kivi Rogers (Mike), John Capodice (Danny), Robert Picardo (Grace's Doctor), Fred Tucker (Stage Manager), Carol Ann Susi (Ticket Seller), Nikki Harris (Flight Attendant), Maria Cina (Rockie's Girl), Larrisa Joy (Italian Class Student), Jay Acovone (Mr. Moltianni), Michelle Joyner (Moviegoer), Anthony Pontrello (Nick the Bartender)

Ron Livingston, Amanda Peet in *Two Ninas* © Castle Hill Productions

## R2PC: THE ROAD TO PARK CITY

(PHAEDRA CINEMA) Producer, Carolyn Grassl; Director/Screenplay/Photography, Bret Stern; Editor, Peter Vitale; Music, Daniel Gold; Line Producers, Scott Rosenstein, Barbara Steel; Associate Producer, Karl Kempter; a Road to Nowhere Production; Color; Not rated; 83 minutes; Release date: January 26, 2001. CAST: John Viener, Paige Turco, John Mese, Christopher Lawford, Bobby Kennedy Jr., Syd Field, Jed Alpert, Jeannie Macintosh, Allegra Kent, Brody Stevens, Tonia Lynn, Chef Tell (Themselves)

## FORGIVE ME, FATHER

(MYRIAD ENTERTAINMENT) Producer/Director, Ivan Rogers; Screenplay, Blair Latta, Thomas Hartigan Fenton, Marisa Caldero; Executive Producers, Bruce Furr, Paul Baugh, Thomas Balsiger, Jim Payton; Photography, Michael D. Off; Editor, Nate Thompson; Designer, Troy Longest; Music, Gary Koftinoff; CFI color; Rated R; 139 minutes; Release date: January 26, 2001. CAST: Ivan Rogers (Virgil Garrett), Rich Komenich (Izzy Goldman), Charles Napier (Frank Ransom), Chris Elbert (Tony Ransom), Alexander Hill (Clarence Garrett), Jeff Bass (Mike Ransom), Jack Rooney (George Haney), Rebecca O'Gorman (Lt. Lena Sohms), Stephen Jon Cohen (Det. Gil Lansing), John E. Blazier (Father Allston), Brad Griffiths (Det. Jacobs), Derrick Perkins (Nigerian Leader), K.A. Killebrew, Guy Camara, James Penn (Nigerians), Amy Ballard, Rebecca Nelly, Erika Szostak (Topless Dancer), Jon Bond (Neil Marshall), Paul Crump (Lionel Pax), Paul Gillard (Bill Riley), Richard Alan Payne (Tom Paltrow)

## HEAD OVER HEELS

(UNIVERSAL) Producer, Robert Simonds; Executive Producers, Tracey Trench, Julia Dray, Ed Decter, John J. Strauss; Director, Mark Waters; Screenplay, Ron Burch, David Kidd; Story, John J. Strauss, Ed Decter, David Kidd, Ron Burch; Photography, Mark Plummer; Designer, Perry Andelin Blake; Editor, Cara Silverman; Co-Producer, Ira Shuman; Music, Randy Edelman, Steve Porcaro; a Robert Simonds production; Dolby; Panavision; Color; Rated PG-13; 91 minutes; Release date: February 2, 2001. CAST: Monica Potter (Amanda Pierce), Freddie Prinze, Jr. (Jim Winston/Bob), Shalom Harlow (Jade), Ivana Milicevic (Roxana), Sarah O'Hare (Candi), Tomiko Fraser (Holly), China Chow (Lisa), Jay Brazeau (Halloran/Strukov), Stanley DeSantis (Alfredo), Erin-Marie Dykeman (Amanda—10 years old), James Kirk (Tommy), Elysa Hogg (Tommy's Girlfriend), Kristina Lewis (Amanda—17 years old), Ben Silverman (Charlie), Sam MacMillan (Charlie's Date), Betty Linde (Polly), Norma McMillan (Gladys), Bethoe Shirkoff (Noreen), Tom Shorthouse (Mr. Rankin), Timothy Olyphant (Michael), Brenda Schad (Michael's Lover), Theodore Thomas (Doorman), Alex Doduk (Boy with Crutches), Jill Daum (Boy's Mother), Robert Musnicki (Lobby Guy), Russell Porter (Restaurant Guy), Noot Seear (CK Girl), Jonathon Young (Agent Guy), Maria Luisa Cianni, Katie Lee, Katrina Matthews, Jody Thompson (Party Girls), Raoul Ganeev (Harold), Brendan Beiser (Ellis), Alexander Pervakov (Ivan), Gary Jones (Bernie), Tanya Reichert (Megan O'Brien), Joe Pascual (Officer Rodriguez), Colin Lawrence (Officer Jones), J.B. Bivens (Jim's Building Super), Louis Klimam (Newsstand Guy), Andy Whyte, John Bivens (Plumbers), Jan Owen (Hamlet's Owner), John MacDonald (Limo Driver), Jerry Wasserman (FBI Captain Vince), Matthew Moreau (Aquarium Guy)

Charles Napier in *Forgive Me Father*
© Myriad Entertainment

Monica Potter, Freddie Prinze, Jr. in *Head Over Heels*
© Universal Pictures

Henry Thomas, Teri Hatcher in *Fever* © Lions Gate Films

# FEVER

**(LIONS GATE)** Producer, Christian Martin; Executive Producers, Graham Bradstreet, Ali Lou Mitchell, Connie Tavel; Director/Screenplay, Alex Winter; Photography, Joe DeSalvo; Designer, Mark Ricker; Costumes, Azan Kung; Music, Joe Delia; Editor, Thom Zimny; Casting, Todd M. Thaler; from Fever Productions Inc., ICE Media, Sunlight Pictures, Tavel Productions, Unknown Productions; Dolby; Color; Not rated; 93 minutes; Release date: February 2, 2001.CAST: Henry Thomas (Nick Parker), David O'Hara (Will), Teri Hatcher (Charlotte Parker), Bill Duke (Det. Glass), Sándor Técsy (Sidney Miskowitz), Irma St. Paule (Mrs. Miskowitz), Marisol Padilla Sanchez (Soledad), Patricia Dunnock (Sophie Parker), Helen Hanft (Louisa), Remak Ramsey (Richard Parker), Lisby Larson (Eleanor Parker), Jon Tracy (Leonard Wooley), Charles E. Gerber (Bob), Ken Comer (Det. Comer), William Henry Burns (Det. Burns), Alex Kilgore (Adam), Guy Griffis (Jimmy), Nan Wilson (Bea), Yeluda Duenyas (Erle), Tom Rainone (Officer Field), Larry Fishman (Young Nick Parker), Nina Polan (Polish Woman Witness), Tom Stern (Angry Drunk), Jilly Crook (Voice of Louisa), Alex Halpern, Noah Hunter (Art Movers), Donnel Rawlings, Steve Rannell (Cops), Alex Winter (Subway Passenger)

# LEFT BEHIND: THE MOVIE

**(CLOUD TEN PICTURES)** Producers, Peter Lalonde, Paul Lalonde, Joe Goodman, Ralph Winter; Executive Producers, Peter Lalonde, Paul Lalonde, Bobby Neutz, Ron Booth; Director, Vic Sarin; Screenplay, Allan McElroy, Paul Lalonde, Joe Goodman; Co-Producer, Andre van Heerden; Line Producer, Nicholas Tabarrok; Photography, George Jiri Tirl; Designer, Arthur W. Herriot; Editor, Michael Pacek; Music, Jim Covell; Casting, Cathy Henderson, Dori Zukerman; Presented in association with Namesake Entertainment; Color; Not rated; 100 minutes; Release date: February 2, 2001. CAST: Kirk Cameron (Buck Williams), Brad Johnson (Rayford Steele), Janaya Stephens (Chloe Steele), Clarence Gilyard (Bruce Barnes), Colin Fox (Chaim Rosenzweig), Gordon Currie (Nicolae Carpathia), Chelsea Noble (Hattie Durham), Daniel Pilon (Jonathan Stonagal), Tony De Santis (Joshua Cothran), Jack Langedijk (Dirk Burton), Krista Bridges (Ivy Gold), Thomas Hauff (Steve Plank), Neil Crone (Ken Ritz), Sten Eirik (Flattop/Carl), Raven Dauda (Gloria), Marvin Ishmael (Fitzhugh), Philip Akin (Alan Tompkins), Christine MacFadyen (Irene), Jack Manchester (Raymie), Bishop T.D. Jakes (Pastor Billings), Marion Bennett (Young Girl on Plane), David MacNiven (Chris), Thea Andrews (Media Relations Officer), Terry Samuels (General), Robert Levine (Old Man), Alan Rosenthal (Soldier #1), Tufford Kennedy (Husband on Plane), Christine Donato (Wife/Mother), Fran Elliot (Elderly Woman), Lillian Lewis (Old Drunk Lady), David Blacker (Big Man on Plane), Steve Behal (Zombie Man), Stacie Fox (Young Mother on Road), Peter Loung (Washroom Attendant), Chris Gillett (Eric Miller), Richard Hardacre (Tall Man), Katherine Trowell (Woman, Green Blouse), Rufus Crawford, Tony Curtis Bondell (Security Guards), Sherry Hilliard (News Anchor), Regan Moore (Passenger), Rebecca St. James (Buck's Assistant), Bob Carlisle (GNN Reporter), Clay Crosse, Josh Penner, Marty Penner, Toby Penner (U.N. Security Guards), Ava van Heerden (Very Attractive Baby) (This movie had its premiere on video in October of 2000.)

Colin Fox, Kirk Cameron in *Left Behind* © Cloud Ten Pictures

## THE INVISIBLE CIRCUS

(FINE LINE FEATURES) Producers, Julia Chasman, Nick Wechsler; Executive Producer, Tim van Rellim; Director/Screenplay, Adam Brooks; Based on the novel by Jennifer Egan; Photography, Henry Braham; Designer, Robin Standefer; Costumes, Donna Zakowska; Editor, Elizabeth Kling; Music, Nick Laird-Clowes; Casting, Laura Rosenthal; an Industry Entertainment production; Dolby; Color; Rated R; 92 minutes; Release date: February 2, 2001. CAST: Jordana Brewster (Phoebe O'Connor), Christopher Eccleston (Wolf), Cameron Diaz (Faith), Blythe Danner (Gail), Patrick Bergin (Gene), Camilla Belle (Young Phoebe), Isabelle Pasco (Claire), Moritz Bleibtreu (Eric), Ricky Koole (Nikki), Nicola Obermann (Hannah), Philipp Weissert (Safehouse Leader), Robert Getter (American Statesman)

## VALENTINE

(WARNER BROS.) Producer, Dylan Sellers; Executive Producers, Grant Rosenberg, Bruce Berman; Director, Jamie Blanks; Screenplay, Donna Powers, Wayne Powers, Gretchen J. Berg, Aaron Harberts; Based on the novel by Tom Savage; Photography, Rick Bota; Designer, Stephen Geaghan; Editor, Steve Mirkovich; Music, Don Davis; Presented in association with Village Roadshow Pictures and NPV Entertainment; Dolby; Super 35 Widescreen; Technicolor; Rated R; 96 minutes; Release date: February 2, 2001. CAST: David Boreanaz (Adam Carr), Denise Richards (Paige Prescott), Marley Shelton (Kate Davies), Katherine Heigl (Shelley), Jessica Capshaw (Dorothy Wheeler), Jessica Cauffiel (Lily), Hedy Burress (Ruthie), Fulvio Cecere (Det. Vaughn), Daniel Cosgrove (Campbell), Johnny Whitworth (Max Raimi), Woody Jeffreys (Brian), Adam Harrington (Jason), Claude Duhamel (Gary), Wyatt Page (Evan Wheeler), Benita Ha (Kim Wheeler), Paul Magel (Lance), Haig Sutherland (Bookish Guy), Adrian Holmes (Banker), Ty Olsson (Jock), Daniel Boileau (Shy Guy), G. Patrick Currie (Religious Guy), Jo-Ann Fernandes (Maid), Alex Diakun (Pastor), Karina Carreck (Gallery Employee), Aaron Dudley, Dallas Blake, Chris Webb (Video Men), Basia Antos, Carla Boudreau, Vanessa Volker (Video Women), Joel Palmer (Jeremy Melton), Sarah Mjanes (Young Shelley), Brittany Mayers (Young Kate), Kate Logie (Young Dorothy), Chelcie Bugart (Young Paige), Chelsea Florko (Young Lily), Sterling McKay (Joe Tulga), Kendall Saunders (Waitress), Chad Barager (Chad), Noel Fisher, Cody Serpa, Mark Mullan (Tulga Gang Members), Tammy Pentecost (Waitress), Tyler Vradenburg (Med Student)

Jordana Brewster, Christopher Eccleston in *The Invisible Circus* © Fine Line Features

## NEW YORK IN THE FIFTIES

(AVATAR FILMS) Producers, Betsy Blankenbaker, Dorka Keehn; Director, Betsy Blankenbaker; Based on the book by Dan Wakefield; Photography, Bobby Shepard, Dustin Teel, Jeff Watt; Music, Steve Allee; Editor, Steve Marra; Color/black and white; Not rated; 72 minutes; Release date: February 9, 2001. Documentary on the many writers, actors, musicians, artists, and poets who came to Manhattan in the 1950s to flourish in their fields; featuring Dan Wakefield, Gay Talese, Nan Talese, Brock Bower, Ted Steeg, Robert Redford, Mark Van Doren, Joan Didion, John Gregory Dunne, Ed Fancher, Mary Ann DeWees McCoy, Rev. Norm Eddy, Calvin Trillin, Jane Wylie Genth, Nat Hentoff, David Amran, William F. Buckley Jr., James Baldwin, C. Wright Mills, Ned Polsky, Sam Astrachan, Ivan Gold, Ray Grist, Lynn Sharon Schwartz, Knox Burger, J. D. Salinger, Norman Podhoretz, Harvey Shapiro, Bruce Jay Friedman, Art D'Lugoff, Helen Weaver, Ann Brower, Norman Mailer.

Marley Shelton, David Boreanaz in *Valentine*
© Village Roadshow/Warner Bros.

Jesus Chavez in *Split Decision* © First Run Features

## SPLIT DECISION

(FIRST RUN FEATURES) Producer/Director/Editor, Marcy Garriott; Associate Producer, Roman Morales; Photography, Marcy Garriott, Robert Garriott; Color; Not rated; 75 minutes; Release date: February 9, 2001. Documentary on Jesus Gabriel Sandoval Chavez, a boxing hopeful who was deported back to Mexico after serving time in prison for robbery, featuring Jesus Gabriel Sandoval Chavez, Rosario Sandoval, Lidia Sandoval, Jimmy Sandoval, Jesus Sandoval, Hermila Sandoval, Sean Curtin, Marc Kadish, Richard Lord, Lou Duva, Nacho Beristain, Richard Gonzalez, Barbara Hines, Nancy Morawetz.

## RHYTHM 'N' BAYOUS

(COWBOY BOOKING) Producer/Director/Editor, Robert Mugge; Co-Producer, Tim Healey; Executive Producer, Denise Gutnisky; Photography, David Sperling; a Mug-Shot Production in association with Have a Heart Thru Art; Color; Not rated; 107 minutes; Release date: February 16, 2001. Documentary on Louisiana's musical backwater bayous, featuring Frankie Floyd, Kenny Bill Stinson, Felton Pruit, Claude King, Tillman Franks, Dale Hawkins, Ever Ready Gospel Singers, Buddy Flett, Po' Henry & Tookie, Sister Pearlee Tolliver, Rev. Gerald Lewis, Easter Rock Church, Henry Gray & the Hurricanes, Henry Butler, Kermit Ruffins & His Barbecue Swingers, Alida & Moise Viator, La Famille

Alida Viator, Rosie Ledet in *Rhythm 'n' Bayous* © Cowboy

Julie Condra, Pat Hingle in *Road to Redemption* © World Wide Pictures

Viator, Hackberry Ramblers, Jambalaya Cajun Band, Warren Storm, Rod Bernard, Dale & Grace, Lil' Alfred, Nathan & the Zydeco Cha Chas, Rosie Ledet & the Zydeco Playboys, Bill Best, Dr. Michael Luster, Rev. Lionel D. Wilson, Rev. Jimmie Lee Jones, Ben Sandmel, Terry Stewart, Etienne Viator, Deborah-Helen Viator, Floyd Soileau, Shane Bernard, Sid Williams.

## ROAD TO REDEMPTION

(WORLD WIDE PICTURES) Producer, John Shepherd; Co-Producer, John Schmidt; Executive in Charge of Production, Barry Werner; Co-Executive Producers, Dave Ross, Gordon Druvenga; Director/Screenplay, Robert Vernon; Photography, Michael Balog; Editors, John Schmidt, John Pipes; Music, John Campbell, River; Designer, Dave Avanzino; Casting, Beverly Holloway; Presented in association with Dean River Productions; Dolby; Color; Rated PG; 89 minutes; Release date: February 16, 2001. CAST: Pat Hingle (Nathan Tucker), Julie Condra (Amanda Tucker), Leo Rossi (Sully Santoro), Jay Underwood (Alan Fischer), Tony Longo (Vincent), Wes Studi (Frank Lightfoot), Barry Sigismondi (Sheriff), Dennis Agajanian (Biker Leader), Jack Axelrod (Arnold), Gary Bayer (ER Doctor), Noah Poletiek (Paperboy), Leslie David Baker (Tow Truck Driver), Drinda La Lumia (Race Track Teller), Eddie Matthews (Fireman), Peter Moore (Arson Investigator), Susan Fukuda (VA Nurse), Paul Kiernan (Gas Station Attendant), Joan Johnson (Tourist Woman), Joyce Cohen (Marilyn), Christian Stevens (Gas Station Mechanic), Shauna Parsons (TV Reporter), Mathea Lynne Doyle (Cashier), Lauree Melograno (ER Nurse), Brent Smith (Prison Chaplain)

## SOUTHERN COMFORT

**(HBO THEATRICAL)** Producer/Director/Photography/Editor, Kate Davis; Co-Producer, Elizabeth Adams; Music, Joel Harrison; Songs, The DCvers; Supervising Producer for HBO, Nancy Abraham; Executive Producer for HBO, Sheila Nevins; Color; Not rated; 90 minutes; Release date: February 21, 2001. Documentary on Robert Eads, a 52-year-old female-to-male transsexual living in the back hills of Georgia.

## THE FIRST OF MAY

**(CONSTELLATION)** Producers, Gary Rogers, Paul Simons; Supervising Producer, Sandy Watterson; Executive Producers, Reza Badyi, John B. Goodman; Director, Paul Simons; Screenplay, Gary Rogers; Photography, Stephen Campbell; Designer, Orvis Rigsby; Costumes, Beverly Safer; Editor, Oliver Peters; a SHO Entertainment production; Color; Rated G; 11 minutes; Release date: February 23, 2001. CAST: Julie Harris (Carlotta), Charles Nelson Reilly (Dinghy), Robin O'Dell (Michelle), Tom Nowicki (Dan), Joe DiMaggio (Himself), Dan Byrd (Cory), Mickey Rooney (Boss Ed), Gerard Christopher (Zack), Laurie Coleman (Waitress), David E. Conley (Sgt. David Conley), Patricia Clay (Social Worker), Alan Lilly (Bus Driver)

## THE GOSPEL ACCORDING TO PHILIP K. DICK

**(FIRST RUN FEATURES)** Producers, Mark Steensland, Andy Massagli; Director, Mark Steensland; Color; Not rated; 80 minutes; Release date: March 2, 2001. Documentary on science fiction author Philip K. Dick, featuring Ray Nelson, Robert Anton Wilson, Paul Williams, D. Scott Apel.

## CARMAN: THE CHAMPION

**(8XENTERTAINMENT)** Producers, Matthew Crouch, Gary M. Bettman, Lawrence Mortorff; Executive Producer, Paul Crouch; Director, Lee Stanley; Screenplay, Lee Stanley, Carman, Tony Cinciripini, Tadd Callies; Photography, Steve Adcock; Editor, Shane Stanley; Music, Harry Manfredini; Designer, Nanci B. Roberts; Costumes, Jyl Moder; Casting, Jean Scoccimarro; a TBN Films presentation; Dolby; Color; Rated PG-13; 82 minutes; Release date: March 2, 2001. CAST: Carman (Orlando Leone), Michael Nouri (Freddie), Patricia Manterola (Allia), Jeremy Williams (Keshon Banks), Jed Allan (Laracco), Romeo Fabian (Cesar), Betty Carvalho (Geneva), Jay Arlen Jones (Johnny), Bill Boggs, Steve Albert (Themselves), Robert Catrini (Lawrence), Doc Duhame (Doc), Quinn Gonzalez (Party Girl), PaSean Wilson (Teresa), Cory Hodges (Li'l Drac), Jared Huckaby (Bob Jackal), Lori New (Anna)

Lola Cola, Robert Eads in *Southern Comfort* © HBO

## HIT AND RUNWAY

**(LOT 47 FILMS)** Producers, Andrew Charas, Chris D'Annibale, Christopher Livingston; Director, Christopher Livingston; Screenplay, Jaffe Cohen, Christopher Livingston; Photography, David Tumblety; Designer, Mark Helmuth; Editors, Rhonda L. Mitrani, Christopher Livingston; Co-Producer, Jaffe Cohen; Costumes, Jory Adam; Music, Frank Piazza; Casting, Eve Battaglia; Color; Rated R; 105 minutes; Release date: March 9, 2001. CAST: Michael Parducci (Alex Andero), Peter Jacobson (Elliot Springer), Judy Prescott (Gwen Colton), Kerr Smith (Joey Worcieukowski), Hoyt Richards (Jagger Stevens), John Fiore (Frank Andero), J. K. Simmons (Ray Tilman), Teresa De Priest (Lana), Jonathan Hogan (Bob), Bill Cohen (Norman Rizzolli), Rosemary De Angelis (Marie Andero), Marisa Redanty (Barbara), John DiResta (Bruno), Marion Quinn (Eileen), Stephen Singer (Rabbi Pinchas), Nicholas Kepros (Jack Springer), Jaffe Cohen (Comic Actor), David Drake (Michael), Bryan Batt (Carlos), Adoni Anastasse, Arthur Jolly (Villains), Cindy Guyer (Model Hostage), Jo Jo Lowe (Renee), Hillel Meltzer (Woody), Ali Marsh (Geraldine), Mike Arotsky (Harold the Weightlifter), Anderson Gabrych (Gay Bartender), William Severs (Father McWilliams), David Tumblety (Priest), Florence Anglin (Aunt Lois), Bobo Lewis (Cousin Rosalie), Andrew Polk (Gary Shapiro), Alicia Minschew (TV Actress), Julia Novack (Jennifer Andero), Elizabeth Muller (Zoe Springer), David Fillippi (Taxi Driver), David Juskow (Woody's Voice)

Michael Parducci, Peter Jacobson in *Hit and Runaway*
© Lot 47 Films

Joy Bisco, Dante Basco in *The Debut* © 5 Card Productions

## AMERICAN DESI

(EROS) Producers, Piyush Dinker Pandya, Gitesh Pandya, Deep Katdare; Executive Producer, Cyrus Koewing; Director/Screenplay, Piyush Dinker Pandya; Photography, Renato Falcão; Designer, Len Clayton; Music, Wig; Editor, Robert Tate; from American Desi Production, ABCD Productions; Color; Not rated; 100 minutes; Release date: March 16, 2001. CAST: Deep Katdare (Krishns Reddy), Ronobir Lahiri (Jagit Singh), Rizwan Manji (Salim Ali Khan), Kal Penn (Ajay Pandya), Purva Bedi (Nina Shah), Sunita Param (Farah Saaed), Anil Kumar (Rakesh Patel), Aladdin (Gautam Rao), Eric Axen (Eric Berger), Ami Skukla (Priya), Sunil Malhotra (Hemant), Sanjit De Silva (Chandu), Laura Lockwood (Sheila)

## THE DEBUT

(CELESTIAL PICTURES) Producer, Lisa Onodera; Executive Producer/ Director, Gene Cajayon; Screenplay, Gene Cajayon, John Manal Castro; Photography, Hisham Abed; Editor, Kenn Kashima; Music, Wendell Yuponce; Music Supervisor, Kormann Roque; Line Producer, Pia Clemente; Associate Producers, John Manal Castro, Lu Cien Hioe, Patricio Ginelsa, Jr.; a 5 Card Productions presentation in association with National Asian American Telecommunications Association, GMA Network Films, Visual Communications; FotoKem color; Not rated; 90 minutes; Release date: March 16, 2001. CAST: Dante Basco (Ben Mercado), Darion Basco (Augusto), Dion Basco (Rommel), Derek Basco (Edwin Mercado), Eddie Garcia (Lolo Carlos), Tirso Cruz III (Roland Mercado), Gina Alajar (Gina Mercado), Fe de Los Reyes (Alice), Ernie Zarate (Tito Lenny), Bernadette Balagtas (Rose Mercado), Joy Bisco (Annabelle Manalo), Gigi Floresca, Alisha Floresca, Leslye Maninang (Premiere), Conrad Cimarra (Nestor), DJ Icy Ice, DJ E-man, Kayamanan Ng Lahi (Themselves), Jayson Schaal (Doug), Mindy Spence (Jennifer), Nicole Hawkyard (Susie), Gina Honda (Tita Florie), Brian Card (Dave), Rowland Kerr (George), Brandon Martin (Rick), Emelita Moll (Tita Connie), Louie Gonzales (Tito Dante), Rawlins Apilado (Jun Mercado), Robbie Pagatpatan (DJ Robbie Rock), Blas Lorenzo (Car Guy), Arianna Basco (Car Girl), Abe Pagtama (Photographer), Gabe Pagtama (Videographer)

Jaime Gomez, Seidy Lopez in *Gabriela* © Power Point Films

## GABRIELA

(POWER POINT FILMS) Producer/Director/Screenplay, Vincent Jay Miller; Executive Producers, Vincent Francillon, Seth Maxwell, Michael A. Miller, Jeff Silberman; Photography, Adrian Rudomin; Designers, Anne Cartegnie, Kathy Cook; Music, Craig Stuart Garfinkle, Leo Marchildon; Editors, John Hoffhines, Daniel H. Holland, Ray Pond; Casting, Gina Glatis; from Grindstone Pictures; Color; Rated R; 90 minutes; Release date: March 16, 2001. CAST: Jaime Gomez (Mike), Seidy Lopez (Gabriela), Zach Galligan (Pat), Troy Winbush (Douglas), Lupe Ontiveros (Grandma Josie), Stacy Haiduk (Ilona), Evelina Fernandez (Sofia), Frank Medrano (Manny), Sal Lopez, Danny De La Paz (Cops), Liz Torres (Julia), Lamont Bentley (Nick), Patrick Rowe (Gary), Gilbert Garcia (Transvestite), Teddy Lane Jr. (Rex), Jennifer Loto (Staci), Shashani Lombardo (Maria), Colette O'Connell (Ryan), Flora Burke (Ethyl), Patrick M. J. Finerty (Adrian), Anne Cartegnie (French Maid), Steve Valentine (Steven), Joe Rodriguez (Elegant Writer), Yeniffer Behrens (Jesica), Erika Garcia (Tania), Yesica Pineda (Magdalena)

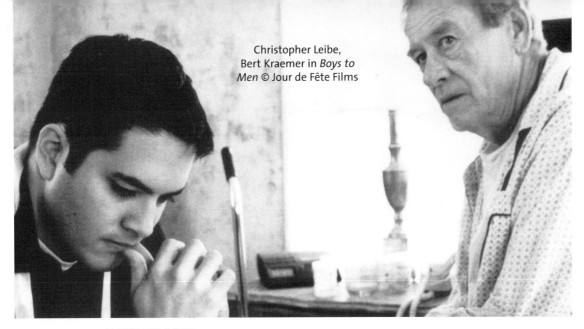

Christopher Leibe,
Bert Kraemer in *Boys to
Men* © Jour de Fête Films

## BOYS TO MEN

**(JOUR DE FÊTE FILMS)** *Crush:* Producer/Director/Screenplay, Phillip Bartell; Photography, Maida Sussman; Editor, Jonathan Knight; Music, Boris Worister; CAST: Ema A. Tuennerman (Tina), Brett Chukerman (Robbie), Weston Mueller (Tim), Rengin Altay (Brenda), Michael Zwiener (Bryan), Margaret Kustermann (Marge), Jack Rogers (Casey), Robert Carson (Lyle), Richard Blake (Jason Hewitt). *The Mountain King:* Producers, Amy Jelenko, Stephen Winter; Director/Screenplay, Duncan Tucker; Photography, Brian Przypek; Editor, Rodney Evans; Casting, Jordan Beswick; CAST: John Sloan, Paul Dawson. . . . *lost:* Producers, Dan Castle, Mike Thomas; Director/Screenplay, Dan Castle; Photography, John Matkowsky; CAST: Wayne Danner, Rick Eichelberger. *The Confession:* Producers, Grace Lee, Jonathan Wald; Director/Screenplay/Editor, Carl Pfirman; Photography, Patti Lee; Music, Barbara Cohen, David Long; CAST: Bert Kraemer (Joseph), Tom Fitzpatrick (Caesar), Christopher Liebe (Father Marcus); Color; Not rated; 75 minutes; Release date: March 16, 2001.

## SAY IT ISN'T SO

**(20TH CENTURY FOX)** Producers, Bobby Farrelly, Bradley Thomas, Peter Farrelly; Director, J. B. Rogers; Screenplay, Peter Gaulke, Gerry Swallow; Photography, Mark Irwin; Designer, Sidney J. Bartholomew, Jr.; Editor, Larry Madaras; Co-Producer, Marc S. Fischer; Music, Mason Daring; Costumes, Lisa Jensen; Casting, Nancy Foy; a Conundrum Entertainment production; Dolby; Color; Rated R; 96 minutes; Release date: March 23, 2001. CAST: Chris Klein (Gilbert Noble), Heather Graham (Josephine Wingfield), Orlando Jones (Dig McCaffey), Sally Field (Valdine Wingfield), Richard Jenkins (Walter Wingfield), John Rothman (Larry Falwell), Jack Plotnick (Leon Pitofsky), Eddie Cibrian (Jack Mitchelson), Mark Pellegrino (Jimmy Mitchelson), Brent Hinkley (Streak), Henry Cho (Freddy), Richard Riehle (Sheriff Merle Hobbs), Brent Briscoe (Det. Vic Bloomfield), Ezra Buzzington (Stewart), Julie White (Ruthie Falwell), David L. Lander (Rev. Stillwater), Judith Maxie (Administrative Nurse), Lin Shaye (Nurse Bautista), Gigi Moran (Gate Agent), Barrow Davis (Angela), Joanne Wolfe (Ticket Agent), Rick Poltaruk (Man in Room), C. Ernst Harth (Mr. Campisi), Joyce Erickson, Alex Green, Mary McDonald (Old Ladies), Connor Widdows (Boy), Courtney Peldon (Cher Falwell), Matthew Peters (Buddy), Andrea Kinsky (Fat Ankles Amy), Annie O'Donnell (Delores), Stacey Goryl (Flight Attendant), Norman Armour, Daniel Boileau, Keith Dallas, E. W. Holden, Rain Draper (Hecklers), Sarah Silverman (Gina), Greg Kean (Front Desk Attendant), Reg Glass (Burly Guy), Alejandro Abellan, Martin Morales (Mexican Men), Dolores Drake (Mrs. Hartunian), Kate Robbins, Gina Stockdale (Elderly Women), Jackie Flynn (Rich Brown), Melanie Wood (Cook), Zahf Hajee (Asian Man), Jordan Weller (Benjy), 'r' Nelson Brown, Marcus Hondro, Pablo Coffey, Shawn Bordoff (Inmates), Mark Olea (Man in Alley), Dan Murphy (Mr. Murphy), Christopher R. Sumpton (Mr. Sumpton), Colin Foo (Mr. Chin), Austin Stark (Animal Shelter Guy), Alícía Calvo (Consuelo), Richard E. Coe (Barber), Michael Gradilone (Paramedic), Charlene Harns (Angry Trailer Park Woman), Floyd Faircrest (Indian Man)

Heather Graham, Chris Klein in *Say It Isn't So*
© Twentieth Century Fox

Jerry O'Connell in *Tomcats* © Revolution Studios

Tobias Schneebaum in *Keep The River on Your Right:
A Modern Cannibal Tale* © IFC Films

## FRIENDLY PERSUASION: IRANIAN CINEMA AFTER THE REVOLUTION

**(COWBOY BOOKING)** Producer/Director/Screenplay, Jamsheed Akrami; Photography, Jamsheed Akrami, Shahram Assadi, Dan Nocera, Albert Xavier; Editors, Jamsheed Akrami, Dah Nankou; Music, Ahmad Pezhman; Narrator, Sara Nodjoums; from Jam-Hi Productions; Color; Not rated; 113 minutes; Release date: March 23, 2001. Documentary featuring Rakshan Bani Etemad, Bahram Bneizai, Ebrahim Hatamikia, Mahmoud Kalari, Niki Karimi, Abbas Kiarostami, Masud Kimiai, Majid Majidi, Mohsen Makhmalbaf, Dariush Mehrjui, Tahmineh Milani, Jafar Panahi, Richard Pena, Kamal Tabizi.

## BUTTERFLY

**(DOUG WOLENS PRODS.)** Producer/Director/Photography, Doug Wolens; Editors, Zack Bennett, Doug Wolens; Associate Producers, Gary Schwartz, Claudia Kussano, Mike Wolens, Lois Wolens; Color; Not rated; 79 minutes; Release date: March 30, 2001. Documentary on Julia Butterly Hill's two-year vigil spent 180 feet high on an ancient redwood tree to prevent it from being cut down. (Note: This film had its premiere on PBS in June 2000.)

## TOMCATS

**(COLUMBIA)** Producers, Alan Riche, Tony Ludwig, Paul Kurta; Executive Producer, Todd Garner; Director/Screenplay, Gregory Poirier; Photography, Charles Minsky; Designer, Robb Wilson King; Costumes, Alix Friedberg; Music, David Kitay; Editor, Harry Keramidas; a Revolution Studios presentation of an Eagle Cover Entertainment production; Dolby; CFI color; Rated R; 95 minutes; Release date: March 30, 2001. CAST: Jerry O'Connell (Michael Delaney), Shannon Elizabeth (Natalie Parker), Jake Busey (Kyle Brenner), Horatio Sanz (Steve), Jaime Pressly (Tricia), Bernie Casey (Officer Hurley), David Ogden Stiers (Dr. Crawford), Travis Fine (Jan), Heather Stephens (Jill), Julia Schultz (Shelby), Scott Beehner (Max), Kam Heskin (Kimberly), J. Kenneth Campbell (Mr. MacDonald), Brandi Andres (Kelly), John Patrick White (Gary), Jason Allen (Otto), Josh Raisin (Dan), David St. James (Priest), Buck Kartalian (Grandfather MacDonald), Alexa Power (Grandmother MacDonald), Anthony Azizi (Sikh Elvis Chaplain), Marisa Parker (Maria), Lauren Moore (Janet), Damon Williams (Tony), Bryan Birge (Vegas Bartender), Amber Smith (Gorgeous Redhead), Philip Jon Schultz (Stick Man), Tommy Canary (Blackjack Dealer), Billy Hufsey (Pit Boss), Christopher Darga, Conrad Goode (Repo Men), Tracy Kay Wolfe (Golfing Girl), Soledad Alberti (Consuela), Nina Kaczorowski (Cheating Wife), Scott Lincoln (Homeless Man), Monica Serene Garnich (Barfing Girl), Amy Hanaiali'i Gilliom (Hawaiian Singer), Florence Stone Fevergeon (Lady in Library), Joan M. Blair (Moustache Lady), Marnie Crossen (Granny), Kinga Phillips (Steve's Nurse), Sandra Taylor (Nurse

Nancy), Katie Lohmann (Centerfold), Lucille M. Oliver (Nurse in Waste Storage), Bill Kohne (Orderly with Sticky Buns), Diana Terranova, Lisa Marie Waishes, Stephanie Chao, Nikita Ager (Girls in Michaael Dream), Doug Carfrae (French Maitre d'), Rachael Sterling (Cherry), Sara Ashlyn, Lisa Lopez, Jovanna Vitiello, Danielle Ciardi, Cinna Bunz-Bowie, Millicent Ally, Candice Beckman, Carrie Carroll, Jenifer Lynn Kinnear (Strippers), Jerry C. Banks (Male Stripper), Shelby Stockton (Mistaken Bride), Eric Gilliom (Mistaken Groom), Dakota Fanning (Little Girl in Park), Barry Sigismondi (Chasing Cop), Robin Kaye Shaw (Animal Rights Activist), Heather Ankeny (Mistaken Natalie), Joseph D. Reitman (Carrot Lover), Christian Whelan, Steve Fitchpatrick (Hollywood Blvd. Cops)

## KEEP THE RIVER ON YOUR RIGHT: A MODERN CANNIBAL TALE

**(IFC FILMS)** Producers/Directors/Screenplay, David Shapiro; Executive Producers, Peter Broderick, Chris Vroom; Associate Producer, Mark Stolaroff; Photography, Jonathan Kovel; Editor, Tula Goenka; Music, Steve Bernstein; a Next Wave Films presentation of a Lifer Film in association with Stolen Car Productions; Dolby; Color; Rated R; 90 minutes; Release date: March 30, 2001. Documentary on Tobias Schneebaum, a seemingly mild-mannered New York art historian whose adventures have taken him into the heart of the Peruvian and Indonesian jungle where he was adopted into a tribe of cannibals.

## ON HOSTILE GROUND

**(COWBOY BOOKING)** Producers, Liz Mermin, Jenny Raskin, Catherine Gund; Directors/Photography/Editors, Liz Mermin, Jenny Raskin; Music, Tom Verlaine, Tom Nishioka; Color; Not rated; 73 minutes; Release date: April 6, 2001. Documentary on the practical, legal, and emotional obstacles faced by three abortion providers, featuring Dr. Richard Stuntz, Susan Cahill, Dr. Morris Wortman.

## BRIGHAM CITY

**(ZION FILMS)** Producer/Director/Screenplay, Richard Dutcher; Photography, Ken Glassing; Line Producer, David Greenlaw Sapp; Designer, Kee L. Miller; Costumes, Camile J. Morris; Editor, Michael Chaskes; Music, Sam Cardon; Casting, Jennifer Buster; Color; Not rated; 119 minutes; Release date: April 6, 2001. CAST: Richard Dutcher (Sheriff Wes Clayton), Matthew A. Brown (Deputy Terry Woodruff), Wilford Brimley (Stu Udall), Carrie Morgan (Peg), Jon Enos (Ed), Tayva Patch (Meredith Cole), Jeff Johnson (Garcia), Wendy Gardiner (April), Richard Clifford (Steve), Sterling Brimley (Glen), Jerry North (Ivan), Jack North (Max), Frank Gerrish (Ralph), Janice Power (Evelyn), Rick Macy (Ernie), Barta Heiner (Clara), Tim Hansen (McKay), Robert Nelson (Parker), Elisabeth Simmons (Jamie), Nick Whitaker (Spencer), Chris Clark (Ben), Christopher E. Kendrick (Mike Sommers), Emily Pearson (Kathleen), Madison Gordon (Sommers Girl #11), Bill Osborn (B. Markham), Kathryn Little (S. Markham), Haley Fife (Jenny Markham), Anne Sward (Carole), Bus Riley (Bob), Jayne Luke (Judy), Jeremy Elliott (Jack), Shannon Engemann (Sherry), Ivan Crosland (John), Shirley Bliss (Mae), Georgia Faux (Georgia), Oscar Rowland (Oscar, Old Man), Ali Seable (Rose), Ryan Shupe (Singer), Kent Richards (Red), Andres Orozco (Bill), Rolland Grubbe (Customer), J. Scott Bronson (Carpenter), Michelle Evans, Becky Christensen (Women), Drew Thueson (Husband), Logan Houston (Son), Teddy Carter, Ethan Dutcher (Boys), Kellen Jones, Ian Ferguson (Priests), Eric Peterson (Scott), Cathleen Mason (Townswoman), Owen Clark (Malachi), Jacque Gray (Caroline Merrill), Sydnie Carter (Red-Headed Girl), Peg Carter (Martha Sorenson)

Susan Cahill in *On Hostile Ground* © Cowboy

Richard Dutcher, Wilford Brimley in *Brigham City* © Zion Films

Carlos Santana in *All Access* © IMAX

## ALL ACCESS

(IMAX) Producers, Jon Shapiro, Peter Shapiro; Executive Producers, Chris J. Ball, William Tyrer, Tisha Fein, Scooter Weintraub; Director, Martyn Atkins; Co-Producers, Kelly Knight, Alex Cornfeld; IMAX Directors of Photography, David Douglas, Reed Smoot, Rodney Taylor; Editor, William Bullen; Music Director, Peter Shapiro; an IMAX Corporation presentation in association with Newmarket of an Ideal Entertainment production, presented by Certs; Dolby; IMAX Panavision; CFI color; Not rated; 64 minutes; Release date: April 6, 2001. Concert documentary, featuring Sting, Cheb Mami, George Clinton & Parliament Funkadelic, Mary J. Blige, Kid Rock, Sheryl Crow, B. B. King, Trey Anastasio and the Roots, Macy Gray, Carlos Santana, Rob Thomas, Al Green, Dave Matthews Band, Moby.

## MAU MAU SEX SEX

(7TH PLANET PICTURES) Producer/Director, Ted Bonnitt; Screenplay, Eddie Muller, Ted Bonnitt; Co-Producer, Eddie Muller; Executive Producer, Keith Robinson; Editors, Ted Bonnitt, Christopher Rowland, Eddie Muller; Color; Not rated; 80 minutes; Release date: April 6, 2001. Documentary on pioneering sexploitation filmmakers Dan Sonney and David Friedman.

Dan Sonney, Dave Friedman in *Mau Mau Sex Sex*
© 7th Planet Productions

## JUST VISITING

(HOLLYWOOD PICTURES) Producers, Patrice Ledoux, Ricardo Mestres; Executive Producer, Richard Hashimoto; Director, Jean-Marie Gaubert; Screenplay, Christian Clavier, Jean-Marie Poire, John Hughes; Based on the film Les Visiteurs written by Jean-Marie Poire, Christian Clavier; Photography, Ueli Steiger; Designer, Doug Kraner; Visual Effects Supervisor, Igor Sekulic; Costumes, Penny Rose; Editor, Michael A. Stevenson; Music, John Powell; Casting, Billy Hopkins, Suzanne Smith, Kerry Barden; a Gaumont presentation; U.S.-French; Dolby; Technicolor; Rated PG-13; 87 minutes; Release date: April 6, 2001. CAST: Jean Reno (Thibault), Christina Applegate (Rosalind/Julia), Christian Clavier (Andre), Matt Ross (Hunter), Tara Reid (Angelique), Bridgette Wilson-Sampras (Amber), John Aylward (Byron), George Plimpton (Dr. Brady), Malcolm McDowell (Wizard), Matt Furlin, Chet Nichols, Martin Aistrope, Ellie Weingardt, Jordan Teplitz, Susan Murray, Michael Skewes, Frederick Husar (Barflies), Karen Vaccaro, Naomi Armstrong, Rebekah Louise Smith, Lisa Dodson, Thomas McElroy, Felipe Camacho, Ike Eichling, Anne Harris (Bystanders), Eric Aviles (Purse Snatcher), Sarah Badel (Queen), Bill Bailey (Thibault's Father), Tab Baker (Cabbie), Doug Barron (Reed Sikes), Clifford Barry (Museum Guard), Janette Bickerton (Screaming Peasant Woman), Kendra Torgan, Lucy Blair (Thibault's Sisters), William Bookston (Peasant), Roy Boutcher (Maitre d'), Richard Bremmer (King Henry), Richard Burton Brown (Irving the Drunk), Daniel Miller, Alexandra Caplan (Kids), Druann Carlson (Elevator Wife), Helen Caro (Screaming Woman), Lorenzo Clemons (Squad Chief), Paul Connell, Alan Kopischke (Crime Scene Cops), Laura Cox (Peasant Woman), William Dambra (Policeman), Oliver Ford Davies (Pit Rivers), Emily Deamer, Sophie Graham (Elevator Girls), Albena Dodeva (Nightclub Waitress), Madeline Fishman (Little Girl—Tammy), Marilyn Dodds Frank (Bag Lady), Jane Galloway Heitz (Dinah the Drunk), Matyelock Gibbs (Rosalind's Nurse), Ross Gibby (Museum Teacher), Chris Gillespie (Daughter at Restaurant), Robert Glenister (Earl of Warwick), Danny Goldring (Bartender), Brian Greene (Old Man with Hearing Aid), Valerie Griffiths (Hag), Molly Price, Amo Gulinello (Teachers), Crispin Harris (Archbishop), Darryl Henriques (Monk), Mike Houlihan (Little Boy's Father), Michelle Hurst (Pawnshop Broker), Rich Komenich (Sid the Drunk), Alexis Loret (Francois), Kevin McClarnon (Police Sgt.), Eric Meyers (Family Man), Larry Neumann, Jr. (Hot Dog Vendor), Steve Owen (Peasant Man), Donna Palmer (Museum Curator), Randall Paul (Bathroom Man), Suzanne Petri (Patsy the Drunk), Beau Sapsford (Little Boy in Elevator), Ric Sarabia (Priest), Adam Shaw (Kitchen Worker), Alan Shaw (Giant Sheriff), Whitney Sneed (Nightclub Woman), Robert Steinman (Cab Driver), Matthew Sussman (Chic Salesman), Kevin Theis (Cop O'Malley), Francesca Vetrano (Nancy the Drunk), Claire Welch (Thibault's Mother), Ruth Winblad (Old Woman), Carl Wright (Station Master), Cedric Young ("Miller"—Museum Guard), Anne Louise Zachry (Young Woman #2)

# THE BODY

**(TRISTAR)** Producer, Rudy Cohen; Executive Producers, Mark Damon, Moshe Diamant; Director/Screenplay, Jonas McCord; Based on the novel by Richard Ben Sapir; Photography, Vilmos Zsigmond; Designer, Allan Starski; Costumes, Caroline Harris; Editor, Alain Jakubowicz; Music, Serge Colbert; Casting, Celestia Fox, Illana Diamant; a Diamant/Cohen production, presented by TriStar Pictures with MDP Worldwide and Helkon Media AG in association with Green Moon Productions; Dolby; Panavision; Color; Rated PG-13; 100 minutes; Release date: April 20, 2001. CAST: Antonio Banderas (Father Matt Gutierrez), Olivia Williams (Sharon Golban), John Shrapnel (Moshe Cohen), Derek Jacobi (Father Lavelle), Jason Flemyng (Father Walter Winstead), John Wood (Cardinal Pesci), Makhram J. Khoury (Nasir Hamid), Vernon Dobtcheff (Monsignor), Ian McNeice (Dr. Sproul), Muhamed Bakri (Abu Yusef), Yoav Dekelbaum (Avi), Sami Samir (Achmel), Jordan Licht (Dorene), Limor Goldstein (Galic), Ariel Horovitz (Reb Mecheal), Roi Horovitz (Zalman), Shai Sharabi (Street Urchin), Lillian Lax (Mrs. Kahn), Arye Elias (Hamied's Father), Sivan Shwartz (Mark), Gilad Bergman (Rani), Halima Abu Aguva (Jasmine)

## HIDDEN WARS OF DESERT STORM

**(FREE WILL PRODS.)** Producers/Directors, Gerard Ungerman, Audrey Brophy; Photography, Gerard Ungerman; Music, Fritz Hede; Narrator, John Hurt; Color; Not rated; 64 minutes; Release date: April 20, 2001. Documentary exploring the unanswered questions about the Gulf War, featuring Gen. Norman Schwarzkopf, Ramsey Clark, Dennis Halliday, Scott Ritter.

## FREDDY GOT FINGERED

**(20TH CENTURY FOX)** Producers, Larry Brezner, Lauren Lloyd, Howard Lapides; Executive Producer, Arnon Milchan; Director, Tom Green; Screenplay, Tom Green, Derek Harvie; Photography, Mark Irwin; Designer, Bob Ziembicki; Editor, Jacqueline Cambas; Co-Producer, Marc S. Fischer; Music, Mike Simpson; Casting, Nancy Mayor; a Regency Enterprises presentation of a New Regency/MBST Production; Dolby; Deluxe color; Rated R; 87 minutes; Release date: April 20, 2001. CAST: Tom Green (Gord Brody), Rip Torn (Jim Brody), Marisa Coughlan (Betty), Eddie Kaye Thomas (Freddy Brody), Harland Williams (Darren), Anthony Michael Hall (Mr. Davidson), Julie Hagerty (Julie Brody),

Jackson Davies (Mr. Malley), Connor Widdows (Andy Malloy), John R. Taylor, Bob Osborne (Farmers), Stephen E. Miller (Ernie), Charles Buettner (Rupert), Cliff Solomon (Big Bear), Fiona Hogan (Pregnant Woman), George Gordon (Doctor), Ronald Selmour (Security Guard, Studio), Drew Barrymore (Davidson's Receptionist), David Neale, Scott Heindl (Men in Restaurant), Wendy Chmelauskas (Woman in Restaurant), 'r' Nelson Brown (Larry, Truck Driver), Jorge Rodriguez, Henry O. Watson (Workers at Pulp Mill), Joe Flaherty (William), Allan Gray (Waiter), Laurie Murdoch (Bank Manager), Lorena Gale (Psychiatrist/Social Worker), Simon Longmore (Cop with Social Worker), Giacomo Baessato (Morose Kid), Mike Bullard (Policeman), Ralph Alderman (Locksmith), Eric Keenleyside (Foreman), Shaquille O'Neal (Shaquille), Darren Moore (Sandwich Customer), Rick Tae (Security Guard), Noel Fisher (Pimply Manager), Irene Karas (Cop at Fancy Restaurant), Ted Friend (Local Field Reporter), Balinder Johal, Kamaljeet Kler (Indian Women)

Olivia Williams, Antonio Banderas in *The Body* © Tin Star

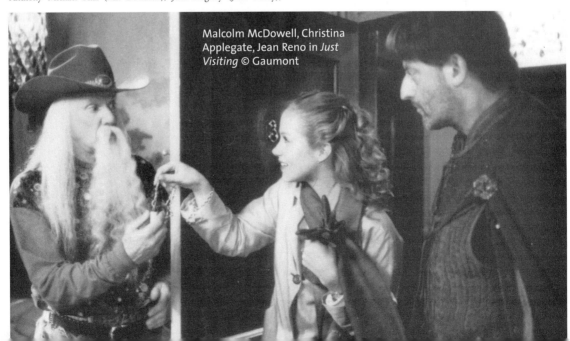

Malcolm McDowell, Christina Applegate, Jean Reno in *Just Visiting* © Gaumont

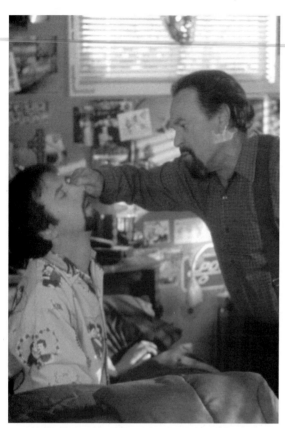

Tom Green, Rip Torn in *Freddie Got Fingered*
© 20th Century Fox

## THE BEST MAN IN GRASS CREEK

(HEARTLAND FILM) Producers, Mark Klitsie, John Newcombe; Director, John Newcombe; Screenplay, John Hines, John Newcombe; Photography, Wes Llewellyn; Music, Deborah Lurie; Editors, Scott Popies, Steve Waller; from Lovestruck Pictures; Color; Not rated; 86 minutes; Release date: April 20, 2001. CAST: Grace Phillips, John Newcombe, John Hines, Oksana Fedunyszyn, Michael Beattie, Tim Farmer, David Jeremiah, Al Leinonen, William Holmes, Mark McCracken, Megan Mullally

## FREAKS, GLAM GODS AND ROCKSTARS

(RYANISLAND FILMS) Director, John T. Ryan; No other credits available; Color; Not rated; 74 minutes; Release date: April 20, 2001. Documentary on Manhattan's underground scene of punks, drag queens, glam rockers, and performance artists, featuring Bernard Scahel, *Bob*, Boob!, Brickbats, Flotilla DeBarge, Jackie Beat, Jayne County, Jimmy James, Justin Bond, Ken Feet, Kevin Aviance, Lee Chappell, Lunachicks, Lilly of the Valley, Mad Juana, Michael T., Miss Understood, Mistress Chaos, Nancy Boy: Donovan Leitch, Jason Nesmith; Patricia Field, Princess Zoraya, Rolando Cevallos, Sister Dimension, Sky Palkowitz, Starr, The "Lady" Bunny, Michael Musto, The Voluptuous Horror of Karen Black, Les Simpson, Toilet Boys, Ultra Nate, Velvet Mafia, Young & Fabulous

## CROCODILE DUNDEE IN LOS ANGELES

(PARAMOUNT) Producers, Lance Hool, Paul Hogan; Executive Producers, Kathy Morgan, Steve Robbins, Jim Reeve; Director, Simon Wincer; Screenplay, Matthew Berry, Eric Abrams; Based on characters created by Paul Hogan; Photography, David Burr; Designer, Leslie Binns; Editor, Terry Blythe; Music, Basil Poledouris; Costumes, Marion Boyce; Casting, Lisa London, Catherine Stroud, Maura Fay, Ann Fay; a Lance Hool/Paul Hogan production in association with Guy Hands; Dolby; Color; Rated PG; 92 minutes; Release date: April 20, 2001. CAST: Paul Hogan (Mick Dundee), Linda Kozlowski (Sue Charleton), Jere Burns (Arnan Rothman), Jonathan Banks (Milos Drubnik), Alec Wilson (Jacko), Gerry Skilton (Nugget O'Cass), Steve Rackman (Donk), Serge Cockburn (Mikey Dundee), Aida Turturro (Jean Ferraro), Paul Rodriguez (Diego), Kaitlin Hopkins (Miss Mathis), David Clendinning (English Tourist), Duke Bannister (American Tourist), Betty Bobbitt (American Lady), Karen Crone (Barmaid Ida), Angela Campbell, Tiriel Mora (Tourist Couple), David Ngoombujarra (Arthur), Patrick Dargan (Troy), Matt Winston (Limo Driver), Morgan O'Neil (Matt), Clare Carey (Skater), Brian Turk, Vladimir McCrary, David Bickford (Drivers), Rhonda Aldrich (Passenger), Kevin Larosa (Chopper Pilot), Daryl Keith Roach, Joe Michael Burke, Jim Davidson (Cops), Hal Fishman, Marta Waller, Mike Tyson, George Hamilton (Themselves), Angelo Perez (Valet), Gerry Del Sol (Barman), Harvey Shain (Ponytail Guy), Keli Daniels (Didi), Lenny Citrano (Actor), Cara Michelle (Model), Matthew Kimbrough (Producer), Grant Piro (Guide), David Baldwin (Grumpy Guy), Gabriella Dilabio (Mrs. Grumpy), Alex Kuzelicki (Lethal Agent), Shanyn Asmar (Claire), John Billingsley (Barry), Jay Acavone (Eric), Gregg Donovan (Concierge), Chad Stephen Taylor (Juggler), Buddy Daniel Friedman (Pickpocket), Mark Kowalewycz, Ty Smith (Trench Coat Men), David Franklin (Assistant Director), Van Markell (Director), Gregory Wheeler (Classmate), Steven Grives (Evil Barron), Alan Zitner (Trainer), Carey Embry (Cowgirl), Mark Adair Rios, Rick Gonzalez (Gang Bangers), Kenneth Ransom (Phil), Nicholas Hammond (Curator), Slim De Grey (Minister), Peter Kent (Carl), Ray Anthony, Darko Tuskan, Ric Anderson, Keir Beck, Ron Vreeken, Nick McKinless, Nick Lawson (Thugs)

Linda Kozlowski, Paul Hogan in *Crocodile Dundee in Los Angeles* © Paramount Pictures

## PIE IN THE SKY: THE BRIGID BERLIN STORY

**(INDEPENDENT/FILM FORUM)** Producers/Directors, Shelly Dunn Fremont, Vincent Fremont; Photography, Vic Losick; Associate Producer, Amy DiPasquale; Editor, Michael Levine; Music, Chris Stein; Color; Not rated; 75 minutes; Release date: April 25, 2001. Documentary on Andy Warhol performer/artist Brigid Berlin, featuring Brigid Berlin, Richard Bernstein, Larry Rivers, John Waters, Bob Colacello, Taylor Mead, Patricia Hearst.

## A SENSIBLE OBSESSION

**(HARVEST ENTERTAINMENT)** Producer/Director/Screenplay/ Photography/Editor/Designer, George Jiha; Executive Producer, Joshua Mashiach; Costumes, Eduardo de la Vega; Music, Juan Salazar; Color; Not rated; 100 minutes; Release date: April 27, 2001. CAST: Mick Shane (Josh), Sylvie Hoffer (Violet), Todd Dylan (Sam), Michelle Russo (Rose), Mike Ellis (Josh's Dad), Patricia Dean (Josh's Mom), Mike Horton (Preacher), Greg Mlacker (Rock Throwing Boy), Virginia Jiha (Singer, Voice)

## THE FORSAKEN

**(SCREEN GEMS)** Producers, Carol Kottenbrook, Scott Einbinder; Director/ Screenplay, J. S. Cardone; Photography, Steven Bernstein; Designer, Martina Buckley; Editor, Norman Buckley; Music, Johnny Lee Schell, Tim Jones; Music Supervisor, Alex Patsavas; Casting, Ferne Cassel; a Sandstorm Films production; Dolby; Color; Rated R; 90 minutes; Release date: April 27, 2001. CAST: Kerr Smith (Sean), Brendan Fehr (Nick), Izabella Miko (Megan), Phina Oruche (Cym), Simon Rex (Pen), Carrie Snodgress (Ina), Johnathon Schaech (Kit), Alexis Thorpe (Teddy), Luis Anaya (Orderly), Ed Anders (Patrolman), Elizabeth Barondes (Oats Diner Waitress), A. J. Buckley (Mike), Jessica R. Butts (Redhead), Sara Downing (Julie), Bert Emmett (Desk Clerk), F. J. Flynn (Hoot), Walter A. Johnson (Mose), Bryan Kirkwood (Merk), Jack Leal (Bus Driver), Jamie Marsh (Mitch), James O'Shea (Racer), Martha Parker (Nurse), Tony Pierce (Mechanic), Matt Reid (Dutton), Julia Schultz (Blonde), Ryan Shuck (Pride), Beth Ann Styne (Garage Woman), Marc Vann (Decker)

## THE END OF THE ROAD

**(JOINT PRODUCTIONS)** Producers, Michael Dong, Douglas Hosdale, Brent Meeske; Director/Editor, Brent Meeske; Photography, Douglas Hosdale, Brent Meeske; Music, Jerry Garcia, Merl Saunders; a Slow Loris Films presentation; Color; Not rated; 97 minutes; Release date: April 27, 2001. Documentary on The Grateful Dead, featuring Mickey Hart, Bill Kreutzman, Phil Lesh, Babatunde Olatunji, Hugh Romney, Merl Saunders, Bob Weir.

Brigid Berlin in *Pie in the Sky*

Kerr Smith, Brendan Fehr in *The Forsaken* © Screen Gems

Steve Railsback in *Ed Gein* © First Look

## ED GEIN

**(FIRST LOOK)** formerly *In the Light of the Moon*; Producers, Michael Muscal, Hamish McAlpine; Executive Producers, Karen Nicholls, Steve Railsback; Director, Chuck Parello; Screenplay, Stephen Johnston; Photography, Vanja Cernjul; Designer, Mark Harper; Music, Robert McNaughton; Costumes, Niklas J. Palm; Makeup, Dan Striepeke; a Tartan Films presentation; Dolby; Color; Rated R; 89 minutes; Release date: May 4, 2001. CAST: Steve Railsback (Ed Gein), Carrie Snodgress (Augusta Gein), Carol Mansell (Collette Marshall), Sally Champlin (Mary Hogan), Steve Blackwood (Brian), Nancy Linehan Charles (Eleanor Adams), Bill Cross (George Gein), Travis McKenna (Ronnie), Jan Hoag (Judy Anderson), Brian Evers (Henry Gein), Pat Skipper (Sheriff Jim Stillwell), Craig Zimmerman (Pete Anderson), Nicholas Stojanovich (Dale), Dylan Kasch (Melvin), Tish Hicks (Leigh Cross), Lee McLaughlin (Phil Anderson), Bill Pirman (Dean Story), Tom Rainone (Butch), Dan Striepeke (Doctor), Heather Gunn (Georgeann), Ryan Thomas Brockington (Ed Gein—16 years old), Austin James Peck (Ed Gein—10 years old), Luke Rowland (Henry Gein—14 years old), Chad Halyard (Roger Johnson), Devin Alexander (Doris Wickstrom), Rick Simpson (Henry Gein—20 years old), Ben Caswell (Officer David Bell), Heather Gettings (Nazi Woman), Melissa Engle (June), Gladell Adelman (Virginia Boyd), Danny Keogh, Jim Kundig, Douglas Hunter (Hunters), Andrew Craig (Harris), Carole Raphaelle Davis (Rosemary)

## ICE FROM THE SUN

**(SUB ROSA STUDIOS)** Producer, Jeremy Wallace; Executive Producer/ Director/Screenplay/Editor, Eric Stanze; Designer, Tommy Biondo; a Wicked Pixel Cinema production; Color; Not rated; 120 minutes; Release date: May 4, 2001. CAST: D. J. Vivona (The Presence), Ramona Midgett (Alison), Angela Zimmerly (Dana), Todd Tevlin (Aaron), Jason Christ (Matt), Tommy Biondo (Keith), Jo Palermo (Buck), Tracey Hein (Pam), Jessica Wyman (The Vision), Charles Heuvelman (Twisted Priest), Alexander Crestwood (Drug Runner), Tony Bridges (Pill Pusher), Leslie A. Unterreiner (Vikki Tonatair), Michael Bradley (Steven), Jeremy Wallace (Hunt 'n' Peck), Rob Cope (Salt Hauler), Jerry Bates (Grave Digger), Dwight Karl Spurgin II (Papa Inbreed), Sandy Garrison (Woods Walker), Jeff Bergeron (Eye Boy), Shana Ko, Robert "Rupe" Daniel (People Pets), George Cousins (Voice of News Broadcaster), Eric Stanze (Voice of TV Program Host), David Berliner, Mark Wallace (Goons), Derek Christian Wallace (Senseless Guard), Mike "Scrub" Champion (Saw Boy), William Clifton (Chess Head), Lisa Morrison (Gun Girl), Paula Morhaus (Doll Mama), Jonny Bitch Esq (Jar Boy), Mandy Cousins (Bic Flicker), Larry O'Neal, Stephanie Strohman, John Fletcher, Nick Normal (Freak Show), Michael Bangert (The Bum), Mark W. Kettler, Jennifer Poirier-Wallace (Inbred Children)

## THE YOUNG GIRL AND THE MONSOON

**(ARTISTIC LICENSE)** Executive Producers, Richard Mehrlich, Beverly Mehrlich; Director/Screenplay, James Ryan; Line Producer, Debi Zelko; Photography, Ben Wolf; Designer, Tina Manfredi; Music, David Carbonara; Editor, John David Allen; Casting, Jeff Block; Color; Not rated; 90 minutes; Release date: May 4, 2001. CAST: Terry Kinney (Hank), Ellen Muth (Constance), Mili Avital (Erin), Diane Venora (Giovanna), Tim Guinee (Jack), Domenick Lombardozzi (Frankie), Christine Mehrlich, Liana Ryan (Teenage Girls), Lee Wong (Waiter), Eugene Leong (Cook), James Ryan (Man on Street), Candyce Mason (Candy), Tina Flaherty (Tina von Gal), Patricia Francy, Connie Meehan, Richard Gibson, Daniela Bar-Illan, Richard Mehrlich, Beverly Mehrlich, Brian Flaherty (Socialites), Slavko Stimac (Milcho), Mark McKennon (Man in Coffin)

Ellen Muth in *The Young Girl and the Monsoon* © Artistic License Films

Jonathan LaPaglia, Vincent Pastore, Michael Rodrick in *Under Hellgate Bridge* © Cavo Pictures

## UNDER HELLGATE BRIDGE

**(CAVO PICTURES)** Producers, Michael Sergio, Isil Bagdadi; Director/Screenplay, Michael Sergio; Executive Producers, Robert G. Dixon, Jr., Frank Marchello; Co-Executive Producers, Vivian Jang, Heinz Kluetmeier, David Anthony; Photography, Leland Krane; Music, Stephan Moccio; Editor, Stan Warnow; Casting, Michele Ortlip; a Fortune Films, Cavo Pictures & D3 Films presentation; Color; Rated R; 90 minutes; Release date: May 11, 2001. CAST: Michael Rodrick (Ryan), Jonathan LaPaglia (Vincent), Dominic Chianese (Father Nichols), Jordan Bayne (Carla), Brian Vincent (Eddie), Vincent Pastore (Mitch), Frank Vincent (Big Sal), Careena Melia (Doreen), Kristen Lee Kelly (Marsha), Frank Bongiorno (Mike), Alex Conlon (Tyler), Marie Barrientos (Teresa), Robert Capelli, Jr. (Ralph), Francesca Buccellato (Big Sal's Girlfriend)

## THE TRUMPET OF THE SWAN

**(TRISTAR)** Producer, Lin Oliver; Executive Producer, Seldon O. Young; Directors, Richard Rich, Terry L. Noss; Screenplay, Judy Rothman Rofé; Based on the book by E. B. White; Co-Producer, Thomas J. Tobin; Music, Marcus Miller; Editor, Joseph L. Campana; a Rich-Crest Animation production of a Lin Oliver production; Dolby; Color; Rated G; 75 minutes; Release date: May 11, 2001. VOICE CAST: Jason Alexander (Father), Mary Steenburgen (Mother), Reese Witherspoon (Serena), Seth Green (Boyd), Carol Burnett (Mrs. Hammerbotham), Joe Mantegna (Monty), Dee Baker (Louie), Sam Gifaldi (Sam), Little Richard (Song Performer), Jeffrey Schoeny (Young Louie), Kath Soucie (Paramedic/Newscaster/Serena), Julie Nathanson (Felicity)

## SORDID LIVES

**(REGENT)** Producers, Sharyn Lane, Victoria Alonso, Max CiVon; Director/Screenplay, Del Shores, based on his play; Photography, Max CiVon; Designer, Steve Cubine; Editor, Ed Marx; Costumes, Jim Echerd; Music, George S. Clinton; Produced in association with Daly/Harris & Davis Classics; Dolby; Color; Not rated; 111 minutes; Release date: May 11, 2001. CAST: Olivia Newton-John (Bitsy Mae Harling), Beau Bridges (G. W. Nethercott), Delta Burke (Noleta Nethercott), Bonnie Bedelia (Latrelle Williamson), Beth Grant (Sissy Hickey), Ann Walker (LaVonda Dupree), Kirk Geiger (Ty Williamson), Leslie Jordan (Brother Boy "Earl" Ingram), Newell Alexander (Wardell "Bubba" Owens), Rosemary Alexander (Dr. Eve Bolinger), Sarah Hunley (Juanita Bartlett), Earl H. Bullock (Odell Owens), Mitch Carter (Bumper), Sharron Alexis (Sara Kaufman), Mary-Margaret Lewis (Ethel), Lorna Scott (Vera Lisso), Dale Dickey (Glyndora), Robert L. Stephenson (Crazy Preacher Man), Carl Balton (Riley), Jane George (Crying Mental Patient), Sharyn Leavitt (Nurse Jackson), Andrew Hawkins (Jason), Beverly Nero (Theater Director), Gloria LeRoy (Peggy Ingram), Luisa Leschin (Leticia Bustamante), Terry Brannon (Tom Ed), Dona Hardy (Mrs. King, Organist), William Edward Phipps (Rev. Barnes)

Ann Walker, Delta Burke in *Sordid Lives*
© Regent Entertainment

Arye Gross, Tim DeKay in *Big Eden* © Jourde Fête

## AUGGIE ROSE

**(ROXIE)** a.k.a. Beyond Suspicion; Producers, Matthew A. Rhodes, Dan Stone; Executive Producers, Mark McGarry, Elie Samaha, Jeremiah Samuels, Andrew Stevens; Director/Screenplay, Matthew Tabak; Photography, Adam Kimmel; Designer, Caroline Hanania; Costumes, Wendy Chuck; Editor, Brian Berdan; Music, Don Harper, Mark Mancina; Casting, Edye Belasco, Richard Pagano; from Franchise Pictures, Persistent Pictures; Dolby; Color; Not rated; 105 minutes; Release date: May 18, 2001. CAST: Jeff Goldblum (John C. Nolan), Anne Heche (Lucy Brown), Nancy Travis (Carol), Timothy Olyphant (Roy Mason), Joe Santos (Emanuel), Richard T. Jones (Officer Decker), Kim Coates (Auggie Rose), Paige Moss (Noreen), Jack Kehler (Oscar Weeks), J. E. Freeman (Pawn Shop Owner), Peter Siragusa (Tony), Nick Chinlund (Car Salesman), Max Perlich (Landlord), Douglas Roberts (Dr. Sachs), Randall Slavin (Robber), Vince Jolivette (Customer in Store), Tony Perez (Det. Cole), Hawthorne James (MacDoogal), Amy Hill (Employment Agency Rep), Tony Genaro (Romeo), Erich Anderson (Paul), Sydney Walsh (Suzanne), Gerald McCullouch (Mr. Lark), Adilah Barnes (Mailperson), Anthony DeSantis (Evidence Attendant), David S. Dunard (Desk Sgt.), Michael Chieffo (Mr. Williams), Tony Abatemarco (Maitre d'), Richard Pagano (Deli Owner #2), Joe Huertas, Tom Miller (Paramedics), Richard Gilbert-Hill (Officer Woods), Tanya Beilke (Waitress), Matthew Tabak (Customer at the End) (Note: This film had its U.S. premiere on cable television on March 18, 2001.)

## EVERYTHING MOVES ALONE

**(HALE MANOR PRODS.)** Producers, Mike Aransky, Philip Guerette, Thomas Edward Seymour; Co-Producer, Jennifer Gray; Director, Mike Aransky; Screenplay, Thomas Edward Seymour; Photography, Mike Aransky, Thomas Edward Seymour; Editors, Mike Aransky, Philip Guerette, Thomas Edward Seymour; Costumes, Jennifer Woymar; Music, Thomas Edward Seymour; Color; Not rated; 100 minutes; Release date: June 1, 2001. CAST: Philip Guerette (Scotch Leary), Thomas Edward Seymour (Anderson), Matt Ford (McDunley), Tina Angelillo (Diane), Mike Aransky (Rob Leary), Kelly Robinson (Mary), Erik Nivison (Josh), Chris Romine, Jennifer Roe (Lawyers), Jen Gorman (Woman in Car), Carmine Capobianco (Used Car Dealer), Jennifer Gray (Barbara J. Frost), James Abucewicz, Abbe Salamon (Deaf Customers), Tim Kulig (Town Drunk), Paul Nelson (Gas Station Attendant), Bruce Seymour (Policeman), Lisa Simlik (New Waitress), Jerry Hemphill (Bus Driver), Vera Hemphill (Bus Passenger), Craig Roel (White Trash Lenny), Matthew Ferelli, Monica Yontef, Mark Woocam, Don Ridgeway (Emma's Customers), Keith Thomassen (Drill Sergeant), Neil Thomassen, Mike Miglietta, Mark Miglietta, Drew Chaplinsky (Soldiers)

## A PACKING SUBURBIA

**(CINEMA ESPERANCA INTL. INC.)** Producers, Steve J. Szklarski, Liz Soldo; Director/Screenplay/Editor, Designer/Costumes, Steve J. Szklarski; Executive Producer, Liz Soldo; Co-Producer/Casting, Donna McKenna; from Suburban Filmworks Inc.; Color; Not rated; 90 minutes; Release date: June 1, 2001. CAST: Thomas Brandise (James Maxwell), Mariana Carreno (Iris), Robert Alexander (Daryl), Aesha Waks (Celeste), Molly Castelloe (Mrs. Maxwell), Ed Kershen (Mr. Musso), Jason Jones (Alando), James Lawrence (Blade), Michael Brown (Bobby), Yvonne Mead (Mrs. Washington), Christine Nagy (News Reporter), Kevin O'Brien (Reggie), Eric Reyes (Jose), Brooke Lewis (Roselle), Carl Low (Nelson), Kenneth Wilson (Harold), Sam Melendez (Sammy), Joseph Minutello (Mr. Maxwell), Henry Marshal (Det. Cooper), Kal Cauthen (Det. Clark), John Fiske (Richard), Judy Prianti (Mrs. Romano), Andrea Frierson (Mrs. King), Johnny Giery (Greg Coleman), Susan Lupo (Gym Teacher), Kelly McKenna, Rick Giannino, Jamie Giannino, Nicole Giannino (Children)

## BIG EDEN

**(JOUR DE FÊTE FILMS)** Producer, Jennifer Chaiken; Director/Screenplay, Thomas Bezucha; Photography, Rob Sweeney; Designer, Stephanie Carroll; Costumes, Sam Hamilton, Rene Holguin; Editor, Andrew London; Music, Joseph Conlan; Casting, David Bloch; a Chaiken Films presentation; Color; Not rated; 118 minutes; Release date: June 1, 2001. CAST: Arye Gross (Henry Hart), Eric Schweig (Pike Dexter), Tim DeKay (Dean Stewart), Louise Fletcher (Grace Cornwell), George Coe (Sam Hart), Nan Martin (Widow Thayer), O'Neal Compton (Jim Soams), Corinne Bohrer (Anna Rudolph), Veanne Cox (Mary Margaret Bishop), Douglas Sebern (John Cornwell), Parker Livingston (Andrew Stewart), Cody Wayne Meixner (Ben Stewart), Josie Adams (Becky Rudolph), Mark Twogood (Lloyd), Christopher Kendra (Bird), Steve Frye (Fulbright), Steven Brian Conard (Leon), Delbert High (Dick), Kenneth R. King (Wheeler), Dori Thompson (Jenny), Mary Cassidy (Carol), Dee Dee Van Zyl (Didi Soams), Tom Cordingley (Rev. Alston), Bekki Vallin, John Lystne (People at Church), Beau Holden (Douglas), Wayne Mansaw (Man at Piano), Christianne Brown, Cori Wolff, Alecia LaRue (Women in Car), Tenika Capouch, Morgan McCarthy, Sarah Dramstad, Amanda Upton

(Schoolgirls), Nicholas Gilhool (Carl at Gallery), Caitlin Carter (Julie Bauer), John Dossett (John Bishop), Justin Fonda (Airline Attendant), Trish Walsh (Airport Security Woman), Brian Grossenbacher (Man in Bar), Amanda Caldwell, Doug Rommereim, Isaac Simpson, Jerry Fletcher (Choir Members), Maxine Rasmussen (Mrs. Stewart), Benny Reynolds (Mr. Stewart), William J. Adamo, Gregory Paul Johnson, James M. Barry, K. Mark Summers, Keith Clark, Brendan Magone (Eligible Men)

## LET IT SNOW

(ARTISTIC LICENSE) Producer/Screenplay, Kipp Marcus; Director, Adam Marcus; Executive Producers, Donny Epstein, Yeeshai Gross; Photography, Ben Weinstein; Designer, Melissa Schrock; Costumes, Bobby Pearce; Editor, Joe Klotz; Line Producer, David Kramer; Casting, Marci Phillips; a Girl and Boy Productions presentation; Dolby; Color; Not rated; 90 minutes; Release date: June 8, 2001. CAST: Kipp Marcus (James Ellis), Alice Dylan (Sarah Milson), Bernadette Peters (Elise Ellis), Henry Simmons (Mitch Jennings), Larry Pine (Wendell Milson), Judith Malina (Grammy), Miriam Shor (Beth), Kristopher Scott Feidel (James—4 years old), Michael Ornstein (Lenny Ellis), Jean-Pierre Lamy (Strange Foreign Man), Wilfredo Medina (Jesus), Anders Hasselblad (Sven), Freeman (Muhammed), Jordan Siwek (James—10 years old), Season Oglesby (Betsy Clotworthy), Jordi Caballero (Jean-Claude), Debra Sullivan (Patricia Milson), Adam Marcus (Facist French Chef), Lou Carbonneau (Aspiring Chef), Sandra Prosper (Jenny), Ann Arvia (Bursar), David Deblinger (Psycho Boss), Kelly Saxon (Bride), Ken Krugman (Groom), Joel Robertson (Kitty-Cat Freak), Christina Ladysh (Crying Woman), Rob Campbell (Small Man), Krista Smith (Regan), Missi Pyle (Ily), Isabel Ruiz de la Prada (Eve), Ned Eisenberg (Carl), Peter Giles (Peter), Bill Migliore (Lonely Guy), Stephen Colbert (Happy Successful Guy), Joanna Bloomer (Sharon), Mary Birdsong (Sneakered Businesswoman), Joseph Siravo (Fredo Andolini), Deborah Langdon (Pat), Susan Lamy (Beverly), Nadya Ginsburg (Store Owner)

## DIRTY COP, NO DONUT

(SUB ROSA STUDIOS) Producer/Director/Screenplay/Photography, Tim Ritter; Editor, Steve McNaughton; Music, R. M. Hoopes & Blue; Special Makeup Effects, Bill Cassinelli; Color; Not rated; 80 minutes; Release date: June 15, 2001. CAST: Joel D. Wynkoop (Officer Friendly), Bill Cassinelli (Tommy), Michael Hoffman, Jr. (Arresting Officer), Andrew Gulbrandsen (Abusive Husband), Lindsay Horgan (Abused Wife), Kathleen Ritter (Drunk Driver), Gertina Willemse (Prostitute)

Joel D. Wynkoop in *Dirty Cop, No Donut*
© Sub Rosa Studios

Kipp Marcus in *Let It Snow* © Artistic License

John Hartford in *Down From the Mountain* © Cowboy

## DOWN FROM THE MOUNTAIN

(COWBOY BOOKING) Producers, Bob Neuwirth, Frazer Pennebaker; Executive Producers, T-Bone Burnett, Ethan Coen, Joel Coen; Directors, Nick Doob, Chris Hegedus, D. A. Pennebaker; Associate Producer, Rebecca Marshall; Filmed and Recorded by Joan Churchill, Jim Desmond, Nick Doob, Chris Hegedus, Bob Neuwirth, Jehane Noujaim, D. A. Pennebaker, John Paul Pennebaker; Editors, Nick Doob, D. A. Pennebaker; Color; Not rated; 98 minutes; Release date: June 15, 2001. Documentary on the American folk music featured in the film O Brother, Where Art Thou?, with The Cox Family, Fairfield Four, John Hartford, Emmylou Harris, Chris Thomas King, Alison Krauss and Union Station, Colin Linden, The Nashville Bluegrass Band, Tim Blake Nelson, The Peasall Sisters, Ralph Stanley, Gillian Welch and David Rawlings, The Whites, House Band, Terry Bulger, T-Bone Burnett, Ethan Coen, Joel Coen, Hairl Hensley, Holly Hunter.

## LIFE & DEBT

(TUFF GONG PICTURES) Producer/Director, Stephanie Black; Photography, Malik Sayeed, Kyle Kibbe, Richard Lannaman, Alex Nepomniaschy; Narration written by Jamaica Kincaid, based on her book A Small Place; Narrator, Belinda Becker; Editor, John Mullen; Color; Not rated; 86 minutes; Release date: June 16, 2001. Documentary on the troubled state of Jamaica's economy.

## W.I.S.O.R.

(COWBOY BOOKING) Producers, Michel Negroponte, Jane Weiner; Director/Photography, Michel Negroponte; Screenplay, Gabriel Morgan; Editor, Tom Cross; Music, Elephant Ears (Beo Morales, Carrie Giunta); Animation/Title Sequence, Lisa Crafts; Presented in association with Independent Television Service and ZDF/Arte; Color/black and white; Not rated; 75 minutes; Release date: June 22, 2001. Documentary on the creation of a Welding and Inspection Steam Operations Robot for use under the streets of New York; featuring the voices of Babi Floyd (Robot), George Bartenieff (Ancestral Voice), Gilbert Giles (Newscaster).

## CHAIN CAMERA

(COWBOY BOOKING) Producers, Dody Dorn, Eddie Schmidt; Supervising Producer, Nancy Abraham; Executive Producers, Kirby Dick, Sheila Nevins; Director, Kirby Dick; Music, Blake Leyh; Editor, Matt Clarke; from Chain Camera Prods., Cinemax Reel Life; Color; Not rated; 90 minutes; Release date: June 22, 2001. Documentary in which ten students at John Marshall High School in Los Angeles filmed their lives; featuring Ethan Adaggio, Silva Arzunyan, Stephanie De La Garza, Leo Diaz, Timothy Docherty, Amy Hattemer, Cinammon Hunter, Mena Mulat, Victor Naranjo, Jesse Ramon, Manuel Ramirez, Lisa Reyes, Fernando Santillana, Suzana Sburlan, Rosemary To, Shannon Whitmore, Winfred Wilson.

## LALEE'S KIN: THE LEGACY OF COTTON

(MAYSLES FILMS) Producers, Susan Fromke, John Hoffman; Executive Producer, Sheila Nevins; Co-Producer, Douglas Graves; Associate Producers, Charles Loxton, Can Parker, Susan Sloan; Directors, Deborah Dickson, Susan Fromke, Albert Maysles; Photography, Albert Maysles; Editor, Deborah Dickson; produced by HBO; Color; 88 minutes; Not rated; Release date: June 22, 2001. Documentary on the legacy of slavery and sharecropping in the Delta, featuring LaLee Wallace, Reggie Barnes.

*W.I.S.O.R.* © Cowboy

## POOTIE TANG

**(PARAMOUNT)** Producers, David Gale, Ali LeRoi, Cotty Chubb, Chris Rock; Executive Producers, Michael Rotenberg, Dave Becky, Van Toffler, Sean Daniel; Director/Screenplay, Louis C. K.; Photography, Willy Kurant; Designer, Amy Silver; Costumes, Amanda Sanders; Editors, Doug Abel, David Lewis Smith; Co-Producers, Blair Breard, Louis C. K.; Music, QD3, Prince Paul; Casting, Brett Goldstein; Presented in association with MTV Films and Chris Rock Productions; an Alphaville/3 Arts Production in association with HBO Downtown Productions; Dolby; Deluxe color; Rated PG-13; 81 minutes; Release date: June 29, 2001. CAST: Lance Crouther (Pootie Tang), J.B. Smoove (Trucky), Jennifer Coolidge (Ireenie), Reg E. Cathey (Dirty Dee), Robert Vaughn (Dick Lecter), Wanda Sykes (Biggie Shorty), Chris Rock (J.B./Radio DJ/Pootie's Father), Mario Joyner (Lacey), Cathy Trien (Stacy), Dave Attell (Frank), Laura Kightlinger (Anchor Woman), Christopher Wynkoop (Sheriff), Rick Shapiro (Shakey), Qiana Drew, Lorria Richards (Singing Ladies), J. D. Williams (Froggy), Tara Jeffers (Solo Girl Singer), Cole Hawkins (Little Pootie), Andy Richter (Record Executive), Kristen Bell (Record Executive's Daughter), Ray Wills, Robert Trumbull (Board Directors), Jim Earl (Eddie), David Cross (Dennis), Chuck Jeffreys (Bad Bitty), Tammy Faye Starlight, Jodi Michelle Pynn (Dirty Dee Girls), Stacy Renae (Sidewalk Girl), Alem Brhan Sapp (Guitar Player), Joseph Dolphin, Todd Barry (Greasies), Keesha Sharp (Party Girl), Gregory Hahn (Prison Guard), John Glaser (Recording Engineer), William Stephenson (Fast Food Cook), Robin Montague (Screaming Woman), Devon Malik Beckford (Sweet Little Boy), Missy Elliott (Diva), Bryan Hearne (Little Trucky), Ebony Jo-Ann (Pootie's Mother), Michelle Robinson (Jilted Woman), Keenan Shimizu (Big Father), Linda Murrell (Burger Joint Reporter), Michael Broughton, Tony Rhune (Bad Bitty Goons), Andy Duppin, David Lomax (Dirty Dee Goons), Bob Colletti (Gorilla), Bob Costas (Himself)

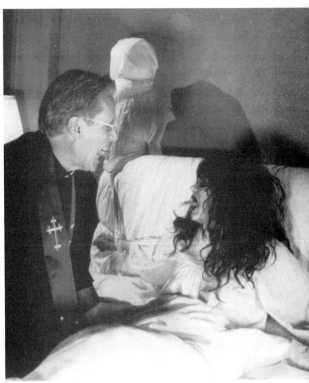

James Woods, Natasha Lyonne in *Scary Movie 2*
© Dimension Films

## SCARY MOVIE 2

**(DIMENSION)** Producer, Eric L. Gold; Executive Producers, Bob Weinstein, Harvey Weinstein, Brad Weston, Peter Schwerin; Director, Keenen Ivory Wayans; Screenplay, Shawn Wayans, Marlon Wayans, Alyson Fouse, Greg Grabianski, Dave Polsky, Michael Anthony Snowden, Craig Wayans; Based on characters created by Shawn Wayans, Marlon Wayans, Buddy Johnson, Phil Beauman, Jason Friedberg, Aaron Seltzer; Co-Executive Producers, Shawn Wayans, Marlon Wayans, Lee R. Mayes, Tony Mark, Lisa Suzanne Blum, Rick Alvarez; Photography, Steven Bernstein; Designer, Cynthia Charette; Editors, Peter Teschner, Richard Pearson; Music Supervisor, Randy Spendlove; Casting, Juel Bestrop, Jeanne McCarthy, Christine Sheaks; a Wayans Bros. Entertainment Production in association with Gold-Miller, Brad Grey Pictures; Dolby; Deluxe color; Rated R; 82 minutes; Release date: July 4, 2001. CAST: Marlon Wayans (Shorty), Shawn Wayans (Ray), Anna Faris (Cindy), Regina Hall (Brenda), Tori Spelling (Alex), Kathleen Robertson (Theo), Andy Richter (Father Harris), Chris Masterson (Buddy), Chris Elliott (Hanson), Tim Curry (The Professor), David Cross (Dwight), Richard Moll (The Ghost), James Woods (Father McFeely), Natasha Lyonne (Megan), Antony Acker, Mark Barrett, Richard Bellos, Suzanne Bianqui, Natale Bosco, Joann Connor, Brad Fisher, Suzanne O'Donnell, Kristi Pearce, Donna Silverberg, Helene Strayer (Exorcist Partygoers), Veronica Cartwright (Mother), Lee R. Mayes (Hip Exorcist Partygoer), Robert Schimmel (Cab Driver), Cordelia Reinhard (Father Harris's Mother), James DeBello (Tommy), Vitamin C (Herself), Matthew Friedman (Bird Voice), Suli McCullough (Clown Voice), Jennifer Curran (Siren), Lester "Beetlejuice" Green (Shorty's Brain)

Chris Rock, J.B. Smoove, Lance Crouther, Mario Joyner in
*Pootie Tang* © Paramount Pictures

Walter Velasquez, Jamal Mackey in *Off the Hook*
© Dendrobium Films

## OFF THE HOOK

**(DENDROBIUM FILMS)** Producers, Adam Watstein, Jennifer Lyne; Director/Screenplay, Adam Watstein; Co-Producers/Story, Walter Velasquez, Anthony Young; Photography, Peter Olsen; Music, Lord Finesse, Dinky Bingham, Pos-Neg; Editor, Ron Kalish; Color; Not rated; 103 minutes; Release date: July 6, 2001. CAST: Walter Velasquez (Himself), Jamal Mackey (Lorenzo), L. Vee Anduze (Lorenzo's Mother), Pamela Johnson (Narine), Kim Anthony (Delene), Anthony Young (Himself), Rene Alberta (Record Executive's Wife), Seanny Cash, Phanatic (Neighbors), Trevor David (Fry), Isaac Davis (Slick Teen), Jasmine Francis (Barbara), Aaron Francis (Lord), Austin Francis (Drug Buyer, Big), William Gee (Record Executive), Barbara J. Gibson (Print Shop Worker), Linwood Holder (Bud), Kash'Shay Jones (Little Girl), Oswald "Oz" Longsworth (Drug Dealer), John Nelson (Music Producer, Street), Mizan Nunes (Walter's Mother), Greg Prather (Sty), George Ratchford (Terry), Patreece Randall, Roslyn Tate (Girls at Office), Roland Sands (Charles), Ronald Smith (Music Producer), Nyrand Thomas (Shooter), Deion Velasquez (Little Boy), Antonio Washington (Shooter, Tall), Mitchell Washington (Terror)

## INBRED REDNECKS

**(SHADOWBOX ENTERPRISES)** Producer/Director/Screenplay/Music, Joshua P. Warren; Color; Not rated; 135 minutes; Release date: July 13, 2001. CAST: Steve Lewis (Monty), Brent Ponder (Billy Bob), Joshua P. Warren (Clovis)

## WAITING

**(MANAYUNK PICTURES)** Producer, John Stefanic; Director/Screenplay/Editor, Patrick Hasson; Co-Producer, Tim Kelly; Photography, Michael Pearlman; Designer, Christopher Jones; Costumes, Chante Brooks; Associate Producer, Will Keenan; Casting, Philadephia Casting; from No Head Films; Color; Not rated; 80 minutes; Release date: July 13, 2001. CAST: Will Keenan (Sean), Kerri Kennedy (Lily), Ron Jeremy (Seedy Father), Kurt Knobelsdorf (Trey), Hannah Dalton (Andrea), Lloyd Kaufman (Mr. Janyszek), Andi Rose (Mrs. Janyszek), Bill Robertson (Garrett), David Hallatt (Shamus), Mickey Goldhaber (Elsie), Casey McGinty (Mary Catherine), Harry Philabosian (Nick Broccoletti), Rocco Rosanio (Enrique "Sticky" Porrini), Rodney Grey (Jerry), Bobbi Martino (Kreg), Frank Ferrara (Michael), Don Allen (John), Aida Davis (Shelby), Eileen Marks (Bobbi), Christopher Thompson (Junior), Samuel Reynolds (Bo), Suzanne Smart (Dolly), Steve Lippe (Baby Poo Poo)

## DOWNTOWN 81

**(ZEITGEIST)** a.k.a. *New York Beat Movie*; Producer, Maripol; Director, Edo Bertoglio; Screenplay/Co-Producer, Glenn O'Brien; Executive Producer, Michael Zilkha; Editor, Pamela French; Produced 1981; Color; Not rated; 73 minutes; Release date: July 13, 2001. Documentary looking at a day in the life of artist Jean Michel Basquiat, featuring Eszter Balint, Jean Michel Basquiat, Victor Bockris, Fab Five Reddie Brathwaite, Clem Burke, Marshall Chess, Diego Cortez, August Darnell, Jimmy Destri, Tav Falco, Fab Five Freddy, Vincent Gallo, Patrick Geoffrois, Giorgio Gomelsky, Debbie Harry, Michael Holman, John Lurie, Compton Maddux, Steve Mass, David McDermott, Daniela Morera, Cookie Mueller, Coati Mundi, Glenn O'Brien, Amos Poe, "Lee" Georges Quinones, Danny Rosen, Lisa Rosen, Anna Schroeder, Walter Sterling, Chris Stein, Betsy Sussler, Marty Thau

## JACKPOT

**(SONY PICTURES CLASSICS)** Producers/Screenplay, Mark Polish, Michael Polish; Director, Michael Polish; Executive Producers, James Egan, Marlise Karlin; Photography, M. David Mullen; Designer, Michele Montague; Costumes, Bic Owen; Music, Stuart Matthewman; Editor, Shawna Callahan; Dolby; HD 24P Widescreen; Color; Rated R; 96 minutes; Release date: July 27, 2001. CAST: Jon Gries (Sunny Holiday), Garrett Morris (Lester Irving), Adam Baldwin (Mel James), Patrick Bauchau (Santa Claus/Voice of Sevon), Crystal Bernard (Cheryl), Mac Davis (Sammy Bones), Anthony Edwards (Tracy), Daryl Hannah (Bobbi), Peggy Lipton (Janice), Rick Overton (Roland), Rosie O'Grady (Sweet Dreams), Larry W. Hunter (Mini-Mart Clerk), Suzanne Krull (Sneezy Waitress), Dig Wayne (Never My Love), Larry Pennell (Truck Driver), Toni Oswald (Truckstop Waitress), Tia Matza (Vicky), Camillia Clouse (Tangerine), Ashley Cohen, Kelly Cohen (Cheerleaders), David Cannizzarro, Allen Fawcett (Karaoke Jockeys), Ricky Trammell (Candy), Gil Gail, Joe Bays (State Troopers), Chip Godwin (Motel Clerk), Mark Polish (Sad Eyes)

## RICHARD THE SECOND

(FARRELL MEDIA) Producer, Joseph Erickson; Executive Producers, Francis P. Rich, Philip Littlehale; Director/Screenplay, John Farrell; Associate Producers, Carol Ann Kando, Ted Arnott; Editor, George Mauro; Music, Liz A. Ficalora, Andrew M. Frazier; Color; Not rated; 93 minutes; Release date: July 27, 2001. CAST: Matte Osian (Richard), Kadina Delejalde (Isabel), Barry Smith (Bolingbroke), Ellen Zachos (Aumerle), Robert F. McCafferty (Northumberland), Daniel Maher (Bushy), Craig Alan Edwards (Green), Frank O'Donnell (Gaunt), David W. Frank (York), Tom Turbiville (Mowbray), Deb Snyder (Queen's Guard), Neil Tadken (Ross), Gary Brenner (Willoughby), Lisa Beth Kovetz (Scroop), Dai Kornberg (Herald), D. J. Kerzner (Gardener), Beth Goldman (Gaunt's Nurse), William Martin (The Keeper)

## ALL OVER THE GUY

(LIONS GATE) Producers, Susan Dietz, Dan Bucatinsky, Donnie Land, Juan Mas; Executive Producers, Susan B. Landau, Don Roos; Director, Julie Davis; Screenplay, Dan Bucatinsky; Photography, Goran Pavicevic; Designer, Fanae Aaron; Costumes, Peter Mitchell; Music, Peter Stuart, Andrew Williams; Editors, Glenn Garland, Mary Morrissey; Casting, Patrick Rush, Sharon Klein; a Susan Dietz/Donnie Land production; Color; Rated R; 92 minutes; Release date: August 10, 2001. CAST: Dan Bucatinsky (Eli), Richard Ruccolo (Tom), Adam Goldberg (Brett), Sasha Alexander (Jackie Samantha Gold), Christina Ricci (Rayna), Lisa Kudrow (Marie), Doris Roberts (Esther), Tony Abatemarco (David), Joanna Kerns (Lydia), Andrea Martin (Ellen), Nicholas Surovy (Jim), Bev Land (Mitch), Michael Harris (Gary), Julie Claire (Lizz), Thea Mann (Donna), Nicole Tocantins (Rachael), Christian Gann (Stripper), Matthew Poage (Bartender), Ben Foreman (Young Eli), Sydney Foreman (Young Rayna), Blaise Garza (Young Tom), Caroline Hope Williams (Waitress)

## THE TURNANDOT PROJECT

(ZEITGEIST) Producer, Margaret Smilov; Executive Producers, Walter Scheuer, Margaret Smilov; Director, Allan Miller; Photography, Tom Hurwitz; Music, Giacomo Puccini; Editors, Donald Klocek, Allan Miller; a co-production of Alternate Currents, EroArts Entertainment and The Four Oaks Foundation; Color; Not rated; 84 minutes; Release date: August 10, 2001. Documentary about the staging of Puccini's opera Turnandot in Beijing's Forbidden City in 1997, featuring Lando Bartolini, Barbara Hendricks, Zubin Mehta, Sharon Sweet, Zhang Yimou.

## HAMLET

(COWBOY BOOKING) Producers, Mary Frances Budig, Jonathan Filley, Campbell Scott; Directors/Adaptation, Campbell Scott, Eric Simonson; Based on the play by William Shakespeare; Co-Producer, Margo Myers; Photography, Dan Gillham; Designer, Chris Shriver; Costumes, Michael Krass; Editor, Andy Keir; Music, Gary DeMichele; Associate Producer,

Adam Baldwin, Garrett Morris, Jon Gries in *Jackpot*
© Sony Pictures Entertainment

Adam Goldberg, Dan Bucatinsky in *All Over the Guy* © Lions Gate Films

Campbell Scott in *Hamlet* © Cowboy

Rebecca Morton; a Hallmark Entertainment presentation of a Spare Room production; Technicolor; Not rated; 178 minutes; Release date: August 17, 2001. CAST: Blair Brown (Gertrude), Roscoe Lee Browne (Polonius), Lisa Gay Hamilton (Ophelia), Campbell Scott (Hamlet), Jamey Sheridan (Claudius), Marcus Giamatti (Guildenstern), John Benjamin Hickey (Horatio), Byron Jennings (Ghost/Player King), Michael Imperioli (Rosencrantz), Denis O'Hare (Osric), Dan Moran (Grave Digger), Sam Robards (Fortinbras), Roger Guenveur Smith (Laertes), Bill Buell (Bernardo), David DeBesse (Francisco), John Campion (Marcellus), Lewis Arlt (Voltemand), Christopher Even Welch (Reynaldo), Leon Addison Brown (Third Player), Lynn Hawley (Player Queen), Matt Malloy (Captain), Robert Simonton (King's Attendant), Elisa Hurt (Queen's Attendant), Eric Simonson (Second Grave Digger), Peter McRobbie (Priest), Ryan Carey (British Ambassador), Clark Carmichael, Jillian Crane, Ramon de Ocampo (Players), Gary DeMichele (Pianist), Peck Allmond, Steve Berger (Musicians)

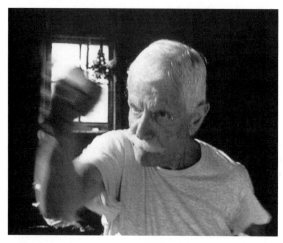

Jan Wiener in *Fighter* © First Run Features

Jake Gyllenhaal, Danny Trejo in *Bubble Boy*
© Touchstone Pictures

# FIGHTER

(FIRST RUN) Producers, Amir Bar-Lev, Jonathan Crosby, Alex Mamlet; Executive Producer, Peter Broderick; Director/Screenplay/Editor, Amir Bar-Lev; Photography, David Collier, Gary Griffin, Jay Danner McDonald, Justin Schein; Music Supervisors, Jeff Daniel, Gillian Melris; a presentation of New Wave Films; Color; Not rated; 91 minutes; Release date: August 24, 2001. Documentary on two European Jews who lived through World War II, featuring Jan Weiner and Arnost Lustig.

# CUPID'S MISTAKE

(PHAEDRA CINEMA) Producers, Young Man Kang, Gregory Hatanaka, Steve Shine; Director/Screenplay, Young Man Kang; Photography, Doo H. Lee; Editor, Bryan Kim; Music, Oliver Lyon; Color; Not rated; 70 minutes; Release date: August 24, 2001. CAST: Susan Petry (Susan), Toya Cho (Toya), Everado Gil (Gil), Ken Yasuda (Ken), Kingston Osagie (Kingston), Young Man Kang (Young)

# BUBBLE BOY

(TOUCHSTONE) Producer, Beau Flynn; Executive Producer, Eric McLeod; Director, Blair Hayes; Screenplay, Cinco Paul, Ken Daurio; Photography, Jerzy Zielinski; Designer, Barry Robison; Costumes, Christopher Lawrence; Editor, Pamela Martin; Music, John Ottman; Music Supervisor, John Houlihan; Special Character Effects Designers and Creators, Alec Gillis, Tom Woodruff, Jr.; Dolby; Casting, John Papsidera; a Bandeira production; Dolby; Panavision; Technicolor; Rated PG-13; 84 minutes; Release date: August 24, 2001. CAST: Jake Gyllenhaal (Jimmy Livingston), Swoosie Kurtz (Mrs. Livingston), Marley Shelton (Chloe), Danny Trejo (Slim), John Carroll Lynch (Mr. Livingston), Verne Troyer (Dr. Phreak), Dave Sheridan (Mark), Brian George (Pushpak), Patrick Cranshaw (Pappy/Pippy), Stephen Spinella (Chicken Man), Ever Carradine (Mark's Sister), Geoffrey Arend (Flipper Boy), Beetlejuice (Li'l Zip), Matthew McGrory (Human Sasquatch), Bonnie Morgan (Rubber Woman), Jason Sklar (Shlomo), Randy Sklar (Dawn), Fabio (Gil), Ping Wu (Emcee), Zach Galifianakis (Bus Stop Man), Boti Ann Bliss (Cashier), Pablo Schreiber, Brian Gattas, Cinco Paul, Ken Daurio, Malik Toure, Leo Fitzpatrick, J. P. Coe, R. J. Durell, Brian Friedman (Todds), Arden Myrin, Merle Kennedy, Shulie Cowen, Alicia Gilley, Mandy Moore (Lorraines), Mitch Holleman (Jimmy— 4 years old), Alex Black (Jimmy—8 years old), Tony Black (Jimmy—10 years old), Robert Bailey, Jr., Oliver A. Kindred, Brandon Depaul (Neighborhood Boys), Steven Van Wormer (Mark's Friend), E. J. Callahan, Charlie Dell, Michael Loprete, Charles Noland, Emily Stewart, Pattie Tierce (Perris Townies), Gary Bullock (Perris Sheriff), Susan Hawk (Perris Waitress), Steven Lawrence (Ice Cream Boy), Raja Fenske (Indian Boy), Cleo King (Minister), Robert Lasardo (Skinny Biker), Jorge Cottini (Big Biker), Madajah McCullum O'Hearn (Red Hot), Stacy Keibler (Working Girl)

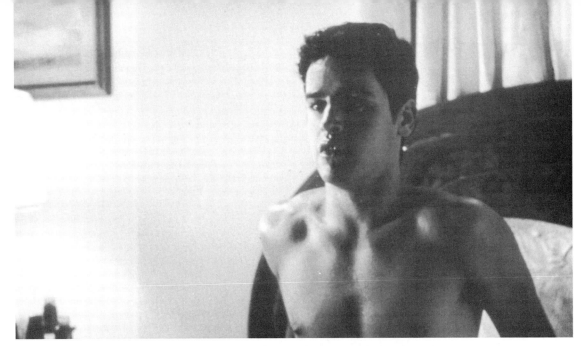

Jesse Bradford in *Speedway Junky* © Regent Entertainment

## SPEEDWAY JUNKY

(REGENT ENTERTAINMENT) Producers, Rodney Omanoff, Randall Emmett, George Furla, Jeff Rice; Executive Producers, Gus Van Sant, Tony Cataldo, Cliff Brune; Director/Screenplay, Nickolas Perry; Photography, Steve Adcock; Designer, Candi Guterres; Music, Stan Ridgway; Editor, Craig A. Colton; Casting, Aaron Griffith; a Miracle Entertainment presentation of a Rodney Omanoff/Randall Emmett production; Dolby; Color; Rated R; 104 minutes; Release date: August 31, 2001. CAST: Jesse Bradford (Johnny), Jordan Brower (Eric), Jonathan Taylor Thomas (Steve), Daryl Hannah (Veronica), Brian Stark (Pez Boy), Justin Urich (Scooby), Erik Alexander Gavica (J. T.), Herbie Ade (Mickey), John Jett (Trish), Patsy Kensit (Donna), Nafisah Tahirah Sayyed (Oreo), Shevonne Durkin (Bridget), Warren G. (Brentley Shaw), Sam Menning (Homeless Man), Susan Gayle Clay (Melanie), Adrienne Frantz (Kelley), Milo Ventimigilia (Travis), Timothy McNeil (Russel), Tiffani-Amber Thiessen (Wilma Price), Faith McDevitt (Vera), Del Monroe (Old Timer), Steve Schirripa (Security Guard), Cynthia Palmer (Teller), Patrick Renna (Bud)

## SOUL SURVIVORS

(ARTISAN) Producers, Neal H. Moritz, Stokley Chaffin; Executive Producers, Michele Weisler, Jonathan Shestack; Director/Screenplay, Steve Carpenter; Photography, Fred Murphy; Designer, Larry Fulton; Costumes, Denise Wingate; Music, Daniel Licht; Editors, Janice Hampton, Todd Ramsay; Special Effects, John Milinac; a Neal H. Moritz production; Dolby; Deluxe color; Rated PG-13; 84 minutes; Release date: September 7, 2001. CAST: Casey Affleck (Sean), Wes Bentley (Matt), Eliza Dushku (Annabel), Angela Featherstone (Raven), Melissa Sagemiller (Cassie), Luke Wilson (Father Jude), Allen Hamilton (Dr. Haverston), Ken Moreno (Hideous Dancer), Carl Paoli (Deathmask), Barbara Robertson (Margaret), Richard Pickren (Ben), Candace Kaye Kroslak (Cool Blonde), Ryan Kitley (Young Cop), Rick Snyder (Father McManus), Danny Goldberg, Scott Benjaminson (Campus Cops), T. J. Jagodowski (ER Doctor), Christine Mary Dunford (ER Nurse), Amy Farrington (ER Doctor, Midtown), Lily Mojekwu (ER Nurse, Midtown), Alex Schlegel, Sam Schlegel (Jump Rope Twins), Michael Sassone (Minister), Lusia Strus (Stern Nurse), Adam Joyce (Student), Kelli Nonnemacher (Coed #1), Jaclyn Barker, Susan Wiltrakis (Halloween Children), Alberto J. Arias, Laurie Canning, Tina Cannon, Shannon Elliot, Nicholas Foote, James Gregg, Devert Hickman, Kelly Tonge Hill, Trisha Lee, Marcellina Marshall, Stephanie Martinez, Elaine McLaurin, Shana Montanez, Eddy Ocampo, Christopher Perricelli, Robyn M. Williams (Dancers)

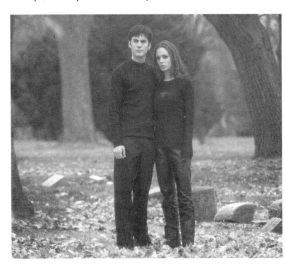

Wes Bentley, Eliza Dushku in *Soul Survivors*
© Artisan Entertainment

Jordan Maldonado in Bounce: *Behind the Velvet Rope*
© Artistic License Films

## BOUNCE: BEHIND THE VELVET ROPE

**(ARTISTIC LICENSE)** Producers, Steven Cantor, Daniel Laikind; Director/Screenplay, Steven Cantor; Music, Samantha Maloney; a Stick Figure production, from HBO; Color; Not rated; 77 minutes; Release date: September 7, 2001. Documentary on nightclub bouncers and doormen, featuring Jordan Maldonado, Alan Crosley, Mike and Frank DeMaio, Homer "Omar" Cook, Lenny "The Guv'nor" McLean, Terence "The Black Prince" Buckley.

## NEW PORT SOUTH

**(TOUCHSTONE)** Producer, Billy Higgins; Executive Producer, John Hughes; Director, Kyle Cooper; Screenplay/Co-Producer, James Hughes; Photography, Juan Ruiz-Anchia; Designer, Maher Ahmad; Editor, Lawrence Jordan; Costumes, Melinda Eshelman; Music, Telefon Tel Aviv, Scott Herren, John Hughes III, Richard Devine; Casting, Billy Hopkins, Suzanne Smith, Kerry Barden; Distributed by Buena Vista; Dolby; Color; Rated PG-13; 95 minutes; Release date: September 7, 2001. CAST: Blake Shields (Maddox), Will Estes (Chris), Kevin Christy (Clip), Melissa George (Amanda), Brad Eric Johnson (Knox), Gabriel Mann (Wilson), Todd Field (Walsh), Nick Sandow (Armstrong), Raymond Barry (Edwards), Lawrence MacGowan (Lawson), Mike Shannon (Stanton), Rebekah Louise Smith (McAmmond), Janelle Snow (Foster), Chad Christ (Morehouse), Dahlia Salem (Kameron), Dennis Williams (Hatchet), Hal Dion (Reporter Garland), Angela Sue Egan (Kassidy #1), Martha Heather Egan (Kassidy #2), Nicholas Downard (Student, Gym), Michael Stahl David (Rossetti), Casey Zeman (Layton), Scott MacFarland (Angry Student), Stephnie Weir (Librarian), Rusty DeWees (School Janitor), Doug James (Anchor Man), Jenniffer Weigel (Anchor Woman), David Engel (Cafeteria Monitor), Jay Kiecolt Wahl (Keith), Marjorie Molitor (School Board Member)

## KILL ME LATER

**(7TH ART)** Producers, Dana Lustig, Ram Bergman, Carole Curb Nemoy, Mike Nemoy; Executive Producer, Federico Pignatelli; Director, Dan Lustig; Screenplay, Annette Goliti Gutierrez; Story, Dana Lustig, Annette Goliti Gutierrez; Photography, David Ferrara; Designer, Tony Devenyi; Editor, Gabriel Wrye; Music, Tal Bergman, Renato Nero; Casting, Mary Margiotta, Karen Margiotta; a Curb Entertainment and Amazon Film Prods. presentation of a Bergman Lustig production; FotoKem color; Not rated; 105 minutes; Release date: September 7, 2001. CAST: Selma Blair (Shawn Holloway), Max Beesley (Charlie Anders), O'Neal Compton (Agent McGinley), Lochlyn Munro (Agent Reed), D. W. Moffett (Matthew Richmond), Brendan Fehr (Billy), Tom Heaton (Jason), David Adams (Ara), Alex Zahara (Officer Larry), Keegan Tracy (Keegan Connor Tracy), Pam Hyatt (Lucy), Stacy Fair (Elizabeth Richmond), Marcel Maillard (Lyle Holloway), Keith Gordey (Elevator Cop), Dana Lustig (Suzan Holloway), Sarah Chalke (Linda), Mecca Menard (Molly), Jillian Fargey, Roger Haskett (Bank Customers), Edward Diaz (Valet), Bethoe Shirkoff (Mrs. Sabatini), Juan Gómez, Octavio Carillo, Mario Valdez (Mariachis), Brett Kelly (Kid), Chris Wild (City Park Policeman), Jeffrey Seymour (Officer in Charge), Robert Marshall (Draftsman)

Blake Shields, Melissa George, Kevin Christy, Will Estes
in *New Port South* © Touchstone Pictures

Rudolf Slansky in *A Trial in Prague* © Cinema Guild

## A TRIAL IN PRAGUE

(CINEMA GUILD) Producers, Zuzana Justman, Jiri Jezek, Zuzana Cervenkova, David Charap; Director/Screenplay, Zuzana Justman; Photography, Miro Gabor, Marek Jicha; Editor, David Charap; Music, Peter Fish; a Pick Production; Color; Not rated; 83 minutes; Release date: September 14, 2001. Documentary on the 1952 trial of fourteen prominent Czechoslovakian communists tried for high treason and espionage.

## HAIKU TUNNEL

(SONY PICTURES CLASSICS) Producers, Brian Benson, Jacob Kornbluth, Josh Kornbluth; Executive Producer, David R. Fuchs; Directors, Jacob Kornbluth, Josh Kornbluth; Screenplay, Josh Kornbluth, Jacob Kornbluth, John Bellucci; Photography, Don Matthew Smith; Designer, Chris Farmer; Editor, Robin Lee; Costumes, Chris Aysta; Music, Marco d'Ambrosio; Casting, Nancy Hayes; a Pandemonium production of a Hello Hooker Productions/Mike's Movies/B9 Films presentation; Dolby; Color; Rated R; 90 minutes; Release date: September 14, 2001. Josh Kornbluth (Himself), Warren Keith (Bob Shelby), Helen Shumaker (Marlina D'Amore), Amy Resnick (Mindy), Brian Thorstenson (Clifford), June Lomena (DaVonne), Harry Shearer (Orientation Leader), Joshua Raoul Brody (System Administrator), Sarah Overman (Julie Faustino), Leah Alperin, Jacob Kornbluth, Stephen Muller, Linda Norton (Temps), Joanna Evangelista (Caryl), Jennifer Laske (Helen the Ex-Girlfriend), Patricia Scanlon (Helen the Ex-Secretary), Joe Bellan (Jimmy the Mail Clerk), Michael X. Sommers (Crack Attorney), Jodean Lawrence (Denise the Receptionist), Adele Proom (Josh's Mom), Tracy O'Neal Heffernan (Lillian), Steve Klinger (Dashiell), Jessica Hird (Ann Dickerson), Margo Hall (Danielle), John Bellucci (Spastic Dancing Nerd), Brian Keith Russell (Security Guard), Baron Bruno (Tim Barnes), David Fine (Oldest Bike Messenger), Todd Hickey (Protester)

Helen Shumaker, Josh Kornbluth in *Haiku Tunnel*
© Sony Pictures Entertainment

## CHILDREN UNDERGROUND

(HBO/CINEMAX) Producer/Director, Edet Belzberg; Executive Producer, Sheilah Kitt McKinnon; Co-Executive Producer, Michel Negroponte; Co-Producers, Jonathan Oppenheim, Alan Oxman; Photography, Wolfgang Held; Editor, Jonathan Oppenheim; HBO Executive Producer, Sheila Nevins; HBO Supervising Producer, Nancy Abraham; Music, Joel Goodman; Presented in association with Red Horse Inc. and Childhope International; Color; Not rated; 108 minutes; Release date: September 19, 2001. Documentary on the street children of Romania, featuring Mihai, Marian, Ana, Cristina, and Macarena.

## IN SEARCH OF PEACE, PART 1, 1948–1967

(7TH ART) Producers, Rabbi Marvin Hier, Richard Trank; Director, Richard Trank; Screenplay, Richard Trank, Martin Gilbert, Rabbi Marvin Hier; Photography, Carl Bartels, Don Lenzer, Jeffrey Victor; Editors, Edgar

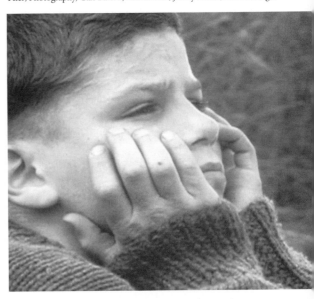

Mihai in *Children Underground* © HBO

Da Brat, Mariah Carey in *Glitter*
© Twentieth Century Fox/Columbia

Burcksen, Lorraine Salk; Music, Lee Holdridge; Color; Not rated; 113 minutes; Release date: September 21, 2001. Documentary on the first two decades of the state of Israel, featuring the voices of Michael Douglas (narrator), Edward Asner, Anne Bancroft, Richard Dreyfuss, Miriam Margolyes, Michael York.

# GLITTER

**(20TH CENTURY FOX/COLUMBIA)** Producer, Laurence Mark; Director, Vondie Curtis Hall; Screenplay, Kate Lanier; Story, Cheryl L. West; Photography, Geoffrey Simpson; Designer, Dan Bishop; Costumes, Joseph G. Aulisi; Editor, Jeff Freeman; Music, Terence Blanchard; Music Supervisor, Robin Urdang; Additional Music, Jimmy Jam, Terry Lewis, Big Jim Wright; Casting, Victoria Thomas; a Maroon Entertainment Production in association with Laurence Mark Productions; Dolby; Super 35 Widescreen; Deluxe color; Rated PG-13; 104 minutes; Release date: September 21, 2001. CAST: Mariah Carey (Billie Frank), Max Beesley (Jonathan Dice), Da Brat (Louise), Tia Texada (Roxanne), Valarie Pettiford (Lillian Frank), Ann Magnuson (Kelly), Terrence Howard (Timothy Walker), Dorian Harewood (Guy Richardson), Grant Nickalls (Jack Bridges), Eric Benét (Rafael), Padma Lakshmi (Sylk), Don Ackerman (Peter), Ed Sahely (Francois), Carmen Wong (Rose), James Allodi (Video Director), Damon D'Olivera (Movie Producer), Mauricio Rodas (Chico), Marcia Bennett (Caseworker), Abdul Shawish (Iranian Cabbie), Chris Tessaro (Stage Manager), Isabel Gomes (Young Billie), Courtnie Beceiro (Young Roxanne), Lindsey Pickering (Young Louise), Kim Roberts (Mrs. Wilson), Bill Sage (Billie's Father), Tim Burd (Engineer), Brian Heighton, Matthew Olver, Colleen Bennett, JC Kenny, Claire Burton (Photographers), Jamia Eaton (Sheba), Emanuel Arruda (Martin), Kyle Thrash (Young Boy), Sonya Hensley (Homeless Woman), Derek Ritschel (Production Assistant), Kevin Keith (B-Boy), Novie Edwards (B-Girl), Dan Chameroy (Gary), Anthony Ashbee (Maitre d'), Tanya Kim (News Reporter), Jeni Anderson (Club Girl), Jose Arias (Manny), Michael Egan (Phone Booth Boy), Judi Mark (Demo Tape Woman), Kate McNeil (Karen Diana), Craig Radioman (Radioman Street Bum), Neisha Folkes (Choreographer), Mark Mclean, Lionel Alston Williams, John T. Davis (Lillian's Band), Rich Brown, Richard Brown (Dice's Band), Dan Sutcliffe, Mike Jackson, Amy Todd, Michelle Carbery (Billie's Dancers), Craig Estrella, Carlos M. Morgan, Pharaoh Lambert, Andrew Craig, Joe Heslip, Simon Craig, Joel Joseph (Billie's Band), David Meinke, Martin Samuel, Rhett George, Louis Paquette (Music Video Dancers), Takeshi Yamamoto, Corrie Daniel, Paul Cantuba, Tony Thompson (Breakdancers)

# GO TIGERS!

**(IFC FILMS)** Producers, Sidney Sherman, Kenneth A. Carlson; Executive Producer, Todd Robinson; Director/Screenplay, Kenneth A. Carlson; Photography, Curt Apduhan; Editor, Jeff Werner; Music, Randy Miller; Original Songs, Katrina Carlson, Ron Alan Cohen; Presented in association with Triple Play; Dolby; Color; Rated R; 102 minutes; Release date: September 21, 2001. Documentary on the dominance of football in the blue-collar town of Massillon, Ohio.

*Go Tigers!*
© IFC Films

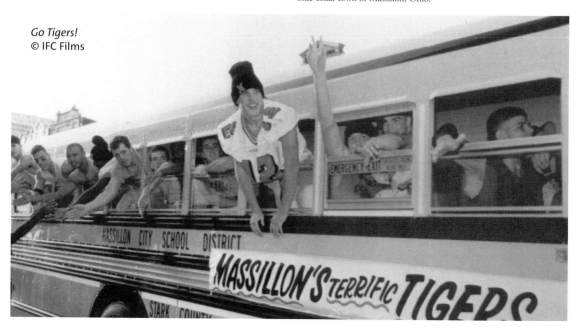

## ROCKY ROAD

**(INTEGRATED PRODS.)** Producer, Laura Caulfield; Co-Producer, Charles Arthur Berg; Director/Screenplay, Patrick Cunningham; Photography, David Trulli; Music, Vincent Callano; Editor, Adam P. Scott; Casting, Akua Campanella, Patrick Cunningham; Release date: September 21, 2001. CAST: Will Wallace (John Johnson), Nicole A. Smith (Talia Jones), Wolf Muser (Bill Johnson), Bob Wisdom (Michael Jones), Natasha Pearce (Tina Jones), Valeri Ross (Yvonne Jones), Bryan Handy (Dwayne Jones), Darryl Dismond (Rodney), James T. Locascio (Paul), Royce Herron (Jane Johnson), Michelle Merserau (Victoria), Reshidatu Foster (Debbie), Nina Womack (Edwina), J. R. Starr (Granddaddy James), Ravell Dameron (Grandma Edith), Sarah Scott Davis (Celia), Bernadette L. Clarke (Rene), Chris Brea, Geoff Cunningham (Paramedics), George Janeck (Byron), Daniel Southworth (James), Yolley DeBold (Cousin Sophie), Darryl Matthews (Gangster), Darrow Igus (Street Man), Alexa Motley (Fundraiser), Elizabeth Wilson (Grandma Louise), Laura A. Caulfield (Secretary), Dee Bryant (Policeman)

## GOD, SEX & APPLE PIE

**(CENTAUR PRODS.)** Producers, Jerome Courshon, Paul Leaf; Executive Producers, Michelle James, Scott Vandiver, Phil Botana; Director, Paul Leaf; Screenplay, Jerome Courshon; Photography, Scott E. Steele; Designer, Colleen Devine; Costumes, Michelle Robinson; Editor, Karen Rasch; Music, John Boegehold; Presented in association with Brimstone Entertainment; Dolby; Color; Rated R; 97 minutes; Release date: September 21, 2001. CAST: Greg Wrangler (Tim), Penelope Crabtree (Bobbie), Mark Porro (Alex), Katy Kurtzman (Maggie), Jerome Courshon (Trent), Andrea Leithe (Debi), Steve Rifkin (Drew), Maria McCann (Tina), Phil Palisoul (Ron), Justina Denney (Cassandra), Lea Hastings (Morgan Tracer), Stephen Polk (Charles Blakely), Teresa Gilmore (Jonelle), Julie Rea (Ellen), Don Ridley (Fisherman)

## SORORITY GIRLS' REVENGE

**(IBEX PRODS.)** Producer/Director/Screenplay, Keith Warn; Photography, Joel Deutsch; Designer, Ernest Hedge; Music, Abnormals; Editors, Chris Gosch, Encar Santos; FotoKem color; Rated R; 90 minutes; Release date: September 21, 2001. CAST: Stacy Oliver, Kevin Wortman, Kelly Kraegel, Tisha Brown, Nicole Holmes, Nikki Trexler, Keith Warn

## MEGIDDO

**(8X ENTERTAINMENT)** Producers, Matthew Crouch, Lawrence Mortorff, Richard J. Cook; Executive Producer, Paul Crouch; Director, Brian Trenchard-Smith; Screenplay, John Fasano, Stephan Blinn; Photography, Bert Dunk; Designer, Charlie Daboub; Costumes, Shawn Holly Cookson; Co-Producers, Gary M. Bettman, Michael York; Music, Peter Bernstein; Editor, John Lafferty; Visual Effects, Rob Bredow; Casting, Jean Scoccimarro; a TBN Films presentation of a Gener8xion Entertainment production; Dolby; FotoKem color; Rated PG-13; 104 minutes; Release date: September 21, 2001. CAST: Michael York (Stone Alexander), Michael Biehn (David Alexander), Diane Venora (Gabriella Francini), R.

Penelope Crabtree, Greg Wrangler in *God, Sex & Apple Pie* © Centaur Productions

Lee Ermey (President Richard Benson), Udo Kier (The Guardian), Franco Nero (Gen. Francini), Jim Metzler (Breckenridge), Noah Huntley (Stone—21 years old), Michael Paul Chan (Chinese Premier), Gil Colon (Col. Rick Howard), David Hedison (Daniel Alexander), Elisa Scialpi (Gabriella—18 years old), Chad Michael Murray (David—16 years old), Eduardo Yanez (Gen. Garcia), Tony Amendola (Father Tirmaco), Forbes Riley (Dana Kincaid), Gavin Fink (Stone—6 years old)

Michael Biehn, Michael York in *Megiddo* © 8x Entertainment

Donnie Wahlberg, Robert Forster in *Diamond Men*
© Panorama Entertainment

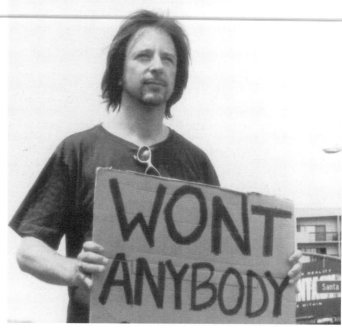

Frank Rogala in *Won't Anybody Listen* © 7th Art

## DIAMOND MEN

(PANORAMA ENTERTAINMENT) Producer/Director/Screenplay, Daniel M. Cohen; Executive Producers, Robert E. Field, Robert Forster; Photography, John Huneck; Designer, Randal P. Earnest; Editor/Co-Producer, Rick Derby; Line Producer, Linda Lester; Music, Garrett Parks; a DMC Films in association with Sidekick Entertainment and Shiprock Productions; Dolby; Color; Not rated; 100 minutes; Release date: September 28, 2001. CAST: Robert Forster (Eddie Miller), Donnie Wahlberg (Bobby Walker), Bess Armstrong (Katie Harnish), Jasmine Guy (Tina), George Coe (Tip Rountree), Jeff Gendelman (Brad), Douglas Allen Johnson (John Lugwig), Kristen Minter (Cherry), Nikki Fritz (Fran), Shannah Laumeister (Amber), Kate Rimmer (Priscilla), Paul Price (Carl), Bruce Smirnoff (Executive), Kate Forster (Customer), Jana Ferner (Emily), Miriam Elizabeth Hyde (Sharon), Irving Simons (Jeweler), Glenn Phillips (Mick), Paul Hewitt (Fess), Leonard Kelly Young (Brennan), James Burns (Detective), Al Vicente (Cab Driver)

## EXTREME DAYS

(PROVIDENCE) Producers, Cindy Bond, Betsy Chasse; Executive Producers, Howard Kazanjian, Craig C. Darian; Director, Eric Hannah; Screenplay, Eric Hannah, Craig Detweiler; Photography, Michael Wojciechowski; Designer, Dan Vivianco; Co-Producer, Alexander H. Gayner; Editor, Andrew Eisen; Music, Klaus Badelt; Line Producer, Scott Altomare; Casting, Heather Johnstone; a Truth Soul Armor presentation of a Norann Entertainment & Tricor Entertainment production; Dolby; Color; Rated PG; minutes; Release date: September 28, 2001. CAST: Dante Basco (Corey), Ryan Browning (Brian), A. J. Buckley (Will), Derek Hamilton (Matt), Cassidy Rae (Jessie), Chao Li Chi (Grandpa G), Virginia Montero (Grandma G), Dylan Bond (Young Brian), Scott Fisher (Young Will), Cameron Clark (Young Matt), Daniel Miranda (Young Corey), Ashlee Bond (Amanda), Jeff Enden (Baboo), John Rosenfeld (Monkey Wrench), Holly McClure (Flight Attendant), Sylva Cox (Waitress), Lee Ann Edwards (Mrs. Davidson), Josh Aver, Jesse Craig, Aaron Tosti, David Tosti (PAX217), Gregory Mark, Scott Hannah, Richard Brown, Scott Brinson (Karate Gang), Scott Lewis, Kory Lewis, Kelsy Lewis (Grandpa G Gang)

## WON'T ANYBODY LISTEN

(7TH ART) Producer/Director, Dov Kelemer; Executive Producers, Frank Rogala, Vince Rogala; Photography, Richard King, Dominic Pereira; Editor, Richard King; a Gestating Pictures production with Integrated Entertainment; Release date: September 28, 2001. Documentary following the attempt of South California rock band NC-17 to make it in the music business, featuring Art Aviles, Robert Aviles, Roxanne Aviles, Lori Graves-Bartolini, Mark Billes, Hugo Burnham, Robin Canada, C. Tucker Cheadle, Keith Dean, Bob Diamond, Bruce Duff, Len Fagen, Lonn Friend, Danny Goodwin, Rich Heaton, Nina Heller, Chuck Hohn, Lance Hubp, Jeff Jampo, Tom Kidd, Chris Martin, Lena Michaels, Ron Perron, Doug Priestap, Frank Rogala, Rose Rogala, Vince Rogala, Billy Rose, Barry Squire, Katherine Turman, Jim Washburn.

A.J. Buckley, Dante Basco, Ryan Browning, Derek Hamilton in *Extreme Days* © Provence Entretainment

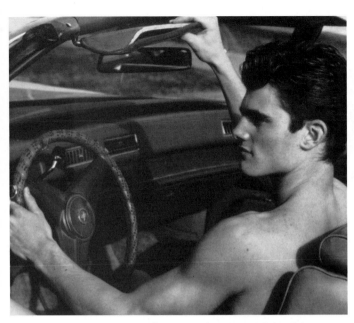

Peter Johnson in *Chop Suey* © Zeitgeist

## CHOP SUEY

(ZEITGEIST) Executive Producer, Nan Bush; Director, Bruce Weber; Screenplay, Bruce Weber, Maribeth Edwards; Photography, Lance Accord, Douglas Cooper, Jim Fealy; Editor, Angelo Corrao; Music, John Leftwich; Associate Producer, Leonard John Bruno; Dolby; Black and white/color; Not rated; 98 minutes; Release date: October 5, 2001. Photographer/filmmaker Bruce Weber's collage of his personal interests, made for model Peter Johnson; featuring Peter Johnson, Frances Faye, the Fletcher Family, the Gracie Family, Robert Mitchum, Teri Shepherd, Sir Wilfred Thesiger, Jan-Michael Vincent, Diana Vreeland, Hoots the Poodle.

## GRATEFUL DAWG

(SONY CLASSICS) Producer/Director, Gillian Grisman; Executive Producers, Craig Miller, David Grisman; Editor, Josh Baron; Associate Producers, John Brittingham, Justin Kreutzmann, Pamela K; Dolby; Color; Rated PG-13; 81 minutes; Release date: October 5, 2001. Filmmaker Gillian Grisman's documentary on the friendship between Grateful Dead guitarist Jerry Garcia and her musician father David Grisman; featuring Jerry Garcia, David Grisman, Joe Craven, Jim Kerwin, Rob Bleetstein, Vassar Clements, Dave Dennison, Bela Fleck, Deborah Koons Garcia, John Goddard, Monroe Grisman, Pamela Grisman, Sam Grisman, Justin Kreutzmann, Dexter Johnson, Richard Loren, Ronnie McCoury, Craig Miller, Steve Parish, Peter Rowan, Eric Thompson, Lawrence Waltman.

Jerry Garcia, David Grisman in *Grateful Dawg* © Sony Pictures Entertainment

## THE LEARNING CURVE

(MOTION PICTURE CORPORATION OF AMERICA) Producers, Oscar Delgado, Carey Westberg, Puntip Limrungroj; Executive Producers, Michael Hofstein, Daarek Szeto, Margaret M. Quitter; Director/Screenplay, Eric Schwab; Photography, Michael Hofstein; Designer, Nya Patrinos; Editor, Adam C. Frank; Music Supervisor, Ted Lowe; Casting, Susan Bluestein; Color; Rated R; 110 minutes; Release date: October 5, 2001. CAST: Carmine Giovinazzo (Paul Cleveland), Monet Mazur (Georgia), Vincent Ventresca (Marshal), Steven Bauer (York), Majandra Delfino (Ashley), Norbert Weisser (Usher), Tim Ransom (Steven), Rod Roesser (Norman), James Eckhouse (Mr. Stevens), Allan Wasserman (Lou), Harry Hutchinson (Barry), Dennis Blake (Hot Dog Server), Phil Nee (Businessman), Kei Rowan-Young (Sandy), Greg Lauren (Todd), Marisa Parker (Receptionist), Noeller Forbes (Secretary), Connie Blankenship (Assistant), Danny Strauss (Quentin), Helen Eigenberg (Cashier), Bayani Ison (Bouncer), Justine E. Boyriven (Hostess), Jarod Carey (Bartender), Stephen Burleigh (Councilman Sherman), Jack Laufer (Councilman Reynolds), Michael Horton (Councilman Nolan), Iheanyi Clemons, Ken Lawson (Beverly Hills Police), Richard Erdman (Ralph), Evan Mackenzie (Walter), Brian Simpson (Stretch), Chris Antonucci (Hip Friend), Mark Newman (Agent Newman), Rita Minor (Agent Minor), Carl Mueller, Marian Green, Phillip Tan (Federal Agents), Milana (Bennett), James McAuley (Policeman)

Carmine Giovinazzo, Vincent Ventresca, Monet Mazur in *The Learning Curve* © MoPic Corp. of America

Zena Grey, Alex D. Linz, Josh Peck in *Max Keeble's Big Move* © Disney Enterprises, Inc.

## MAX KEEBLE'S BIG MOVE

(WALT DISNEY PICTURES) Producer, Mike Karz; Executive Producer, Guy Riedel; Director, Tim Hill; Screenplay, Jonathan Bernstein, Mark Blackwell, James Greer; Story, David Watts, Jonathan Bernstein, Mark Blackwell, James Greer; Co-Producers, Raymond C. Reed, Russell Hollander; Photography, Arthur Albert; Designer, Vincent Jefferds; Editors, Tony Lombardo, Peck Prior; Costumes, Susan Matheson; Music, Michael Wandmacher; Casting, Victoria Burrows, Scot Boland; a Kaz Entertainment production; Dolby; Technicolor; Rated PG; 86 minutes; Release date: October 5, 2001. CAST: Alex D. Linz (Max Keeble), Larry Miller (Jindraike), Jamie Kennedy (Evil Ice Cream Man), Zena Grey (Megan), Josh Peck (Robe), Nora Dunn (Lily Keeble), Robert Carradine (Don Keeble), Clifton Davis (Knebworth), Amy Hill (Mrs. Rangoon), Noel Fisher (Troy McGinty), Orlando Brown (Dobbs), Amber Valletta (Ms. Dingman), Justin Berfield (Caption Writer), Veronica Alicino (Mrs. Talia, Social Studies Teacher), Brooke Anne Smith (Jenna), Greg Lewis (Janitor), Chely Wright (Mrs. Styles, Homeroom Teacher), Jonathan Osser (Worried Kid), Cory Hodges (Yearbook Photographer), Kyle Sullivan (Techie Kid), Jordan Mahome (Marley), Myra (Chelsea), Sarah Rush (Ms. Lane, School Nurse), Chelsea Bond (Mrs. Didion, English Teacher), Shawn Pyfrom (Bus Prankster), Dennis Haskins (Mr. Kohls, Band Teacher), Teddy Lane, Jr. (P.E. Teacher), Martin Spanjers (Runty Band Member), Countess Vaughn (Officer Admin. Asst.), Bryan Matsuura, Andy Morrow (8th Graders), Adam Lamberg (8th Grader on Bike), Nick Albert (8th Grader in Gym), E. J. De La Pena (Pudgy 7th Grader), Marcus Toji (Food Fight Chess Player), Zachary Spound (Julius Klinghoffer), Alexandra Kaplan (Kelly Lloyd), Maximillian Kesmodel (Max—4 years old), Christian Boewe (Troy—6 years old), Jon Ryckman, Steve Provenzano, Joe Unitas (Slavs, Football Players), Lil' Romeo, Tony Hawk (Themselves), Marcus Hopson (Pizza Parlor Kid), Nicholas King (Skater Wannabe)

## THE STRANGE CASE OF SEÑOR COMPUTER

(WORLD ARTISTS) Producer/Director/Screenplay/Editor/Designer, Tom Sawyer; Co-Producers, Adrienne Cox, Darlene Ford, Frenchy O'Brien; Music, Frenchy O'Brien; Photography, Marco Carpetta, Tom Sawyer; from Corrosive Liquid Productions; Black and white; Not rated; 91 minutes; Release date: October 5, 2001. CAST: Rick Ziegler (Charles O'Toole), Tom Sawyer (Voice of Señor Computer), Dr. Spencer Koerner (Lead Detective), Will Lewis, David Damico (Cops), Gladys Hans (Carlotta Sanchez), Lisa Goodman (Linda), Frenchy O'Brien (Delivery Person), Isaiah Jurado (Daniel Kim), Barbara Beneville (Marsha Spillane), Constance Tillotson (Ryan), Precious Chong (Spiritualist)

Cory McAbee in *The American Astronaut*
© Artistic License Films

## STOCKPILE

**(SEVENTH ART)** Producer, Bruce Endie; Executive Producer, Bob Reid; Director/Screenplay, Stephen Trombley; Photography, Stephen McCarthy, Tomasz Mangierski; Editor, Peter Miller; Music, Rob Lane, Simon Whiteside; Narrator, Martin Sheen; a Worldview Pictures production for Discovery Channel in association with Evangelische Omroep (Netherlands) and DRS & TRS (Switzerland); U.S.-Netherlands-Swiss; Color; Not rated; 102 minutes; Release date: October 5, 2001. Documentary on the nuclear arms race between the United States and Russia, featuring Paul White, Vladislav N. Mokhor, Mike Burns, Radi I. Il'Kaev, Siegfried S. Hecker, Harold Agner, John Shaner, Vladimir I. Yuferev, George Vantiem, Hastings Smith, Merri Wood, Steve Younger, Yuri A. Romanov, Yuri A. Truner, Irv Lindemuth, Robert E. Reinovsky, Vladimir K. Chernychev, Ed Grothus.

## THE AMERICAN ASTRONAUT

**(ARTISTIC LICENSE)** Producers, William Perkins, Joshua Taylor, Bobby Lurie; Director/Screenplay, Cory McAbee; Photography, W. Mott Hupfel III; Designer, Geoff Tuttle; Costumes, Dawn Weisberg; Editor, Pete Beaudreau; Co-Producer, Michael Krantz; Music, The Billy Nayer Show; Musical Director, Bobby Lurie; Casting, Ann Goulder; a BNS Production; Black and white; Not rated; 94 minutes; Release date: October 12, 2001. CAST: Cory McAbee (Samuel Curtis), Rocco Sisto (Professor Heiss), Gregory Russell Cook (The Boy), Annie Golden (Cloris), James Ransone (Bodysuit), Joshua Taylor (Blueberry Pirate), Tom Aldredge (Old Man), Peter McRobbie (Lee Vilensky), Bill Buell (Eddie), Mark Manley, Ned Sublette (Henchmen, Hey Boy!). Joseph McKenna (Doorman), Doug McKean (Silver Miner Jake), Melissa Wilder (Lady Venus)

## JAILS, HOSPITALS & HIP-HOP

**(KICKED DOWN PRODS.)** Producers, Mark Benjamin, Garth Belcon; Executive Producers, William O'Neill, Michael Skolnik; Directors, Mark Benjamin, Danny Hoch; Screenplay, Danny Hoch; Photography, Mark Benjamin; Designer, David Ellis; Editor, Brian A. Kates; Co-Producer, Daniel Hank; Associate Producer, Blair Breard; Music, Mix Master Mike; Original Stage Direction & Development, Jo Bonney; Casting, Sue Crystal; Color; Rated R; 90 minutes; Release date: October 12, 2001. CAST: Danny Hoch (Danny/Brooks/Flip/Sam/Gabriel/Victor/Peter/Andy/Emcee Enuff), Lynn Schlansky-Hoch (Herself), Gina Brooke (Maritza), Pablo Herrera (American Tourist), Jeff Peters (Dave), Hector Arias, Jahaira Duarte, Jackie Garcia (Brooklyn Rappers), Doble Filo, Insinto, Obsesion, Primera Base (Cuban Reporters), Susan Blommaert (Dr. Lemmings), Bonz Malone (Sharif)

## THE OPERATOR

**(BLACK WOLF FILMS)** Producer/Director/Screenplay, Jon Dichter; Executive Producer, Jay Barnet; Co-Producers, Douglas Bruce, Betty A. Buckley; Music, Victor Zupanc; Photography, Bert Guthrie; Designers, Bob Butcher, David Sewell McCann, Kara Sutherlin; Costumes, Kari Perkins; Editors, Michael Coleman, Darren Kloomok; Casting, Elizabeth Hayden-Passero, Jeffrey Passero; from Operator Films L.L.C.; Dolby; Color; Rated R: 102 minutes; Release date: October 12, 2001. CAST: Michael Laurence (Gary Wheelan), Jacqueline Kim (The Operator), Brion James (Vernon Woods), Stephen Tobolowsky (Doc), Christa Miller (Janice Wheelan), John Beasley (Rev. James), Frances Bay (Mrs. Sloan), Lori Heuring (Christie), Paul Heckman (Lawyer)

## THINGS BEHIND THE SUN

**(COWBOY BOOKING)** Producers, Daniel Hassid, Doug Mankoff, Robin Alper; Director, Allison Anders; Screenplay, Allison Anders, Kurt Voss; Executive Producers, Gary Barkin, Peter Wetherell, Marla Grossman, Joseph Rice; Co-Producer, Rick Dallago; Photography, Terry Stacey; Designer, Jeffrey Scott Taylor; Costumes, Jody Felz; Editor, Chris Figler; Music, Sonic Youth; Casting, Mark Bennett, Hopkins Smith and Barden; Echo Lake Productions; Color; Rated R; 117 minutes; Release date:

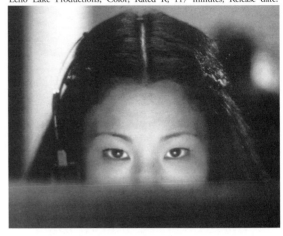

Jacqueline Kim in *The Operator* © Black Wolf Film

Don Cheadle, Kim Dickens in *Things Behind the Sun* © Cowboy

October 12, 2001. CAST: Kim Dickens (Sherry), Gabriel Mann (Owen Richardson), Alison Folland (Lulu), Elizabeth Peña (Carmen), Patsy Kensit (Denise), CCH Pounder (Judge), Shawn Reaves (Tex), Brittany Finamore (Young Sherry), Owen Butler (Young Owen), Justin DePrume (Young Dan), Joshua Leonard (Todd), Jade Gordon (Samantha), Kadu Lennox (Jeremy), Kai Lennox (Colin), Eric Stoltz (Dan), Rosanna Arquette (Pete), Don Cheadle (Chuck), Tom Caffrey (Alex), Alexander Sommer (Randy), Jonathan Osteen (Sonny), Marty Stonerock (AA Speaker), Bill Cordell (AA Secretary), Aria Alpert (Violet), Hal Dion (Public Defender), Talia Osteen (Kathy), Jessica Howell (Jamie), Ruben Anders (Carlos), Jessie Gelaznick (Intern), J. Mascis (Erik), Jeffrey McDonald (Martin), Steve McDonald (Fred), Stephanie Stern (Truck Stop Girl), Rob Sullivan (Bystander) (This film premiered on Showtime cable in August 2001.

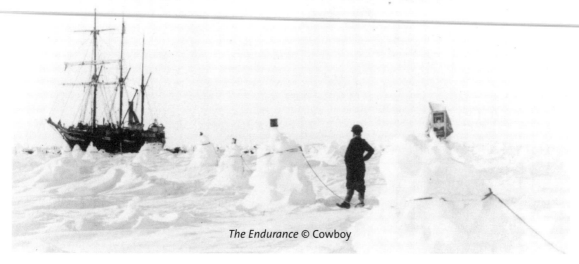

*The Endurance* © Cowboy

## THE ENDURANCE: SHACKLETON'S LEGENDARY ANTARCTIC ADVENTURE

(COWBOY PICTURES) Producer/Director, George Butler; Screenplay, Caroline Alexander, Joseph Dorman; Based on the book by Caroline Alexander; Co-Producer, Louise Rosen; Executive Producer for Nova, Paula Apsell; Executive Producers, Edward R. Pressman, Terrence Malick, L. Dennis Kozlowski, John Mack, Caroline Alexander, Mike Ryan; Photography, Sandi Sissel; Music, Michael Small; Director of Editing and of Still Photo Filming, Joshua Waletzky; Line Producer, Steven Stoke; Narrator, Liam Neeson; a Morgan Stanley presentation of a White Mountain Films/Nova co-production in association with Shackelton Schools, Channel 4, Telepool/Germany, SVT Sweden, Discovery International, the American Museum of Natural History, Zegrahm Expeditions and Outward Bound USA; Color; Rated G; 93 minutes; Release date: October 19, 2001. Documentary on Sir Ernest Shackleton's 1914–16 expedition to Antarctica.

## DOG RUN

(ARROW) Producers, Jeffrey Feldman, Brian Marc, D. Ze'Ev Gilad; Executive Producers, Michael Chambers, Patrick Panzarella; Director, D. Ze'Ev Gilad; Screenplay/Editor, Brian Marc, D. Ze'Ev Gilad; Story/Concept, Brian Marc; Photography, Andrew T. Dunn; Designer, Maria Alindato; Music Supervisors, Jeffrey Twiss, Steve Patch; a C&P Productions presentation of a Zampion Production; Color; Not rated; 100 minutes; Release date: October 19, 2001. CAST: Brian Marc (Eddie), Craig Duplessis (Miles), Lisa Ristorucci (Tara), Elizabeth Horsburgh (Rachel), Gary Cunningham (Lee), Lisa Cork-Twiss (Roberta), Michele Santopietro (Stephanie), Michelle Fierro (Angela), Leon Hartman (Boy on Bus), Ian Reid McCulloch, Jennifer Norton (Rachel's Friends), Jacques Monrose (New Orleans Apt. Guy), Felicia Caplan (New Orleans Apt. Girl), Chris Jones (Roberta's Thug), Ross Giunta (Police Officer), Flip Brown (Mugging Victim), Ayelet Kaznelson (Club Bartender), Al Dilorenzo (Bus Driver), Peter Marquette (Boy's Father), Gary Kittrell (Junkie Mugger), Glenn "Spinner" Jones (Performance Artist), Rajav "Roger" Shillersh (Deli Owner), Duane T. Okubo (Hotel Clerk), Jeffrey Twiss (Club Drug Dealer), Jeffrey Zimberg (Club Doorman), Rachel Plutzer (Club Doorgirl), Jean Daniel Edwards, Lisa Rock, Sarah Huber (Prostitutes), Tracy Feldman (Cute Girl in Bar), Gertrude (Rachel's Cat)

Craig Duplessis, Brian Marc, Lisa Ristorucci in *Dog Run*
© Arrow Releasing Inc.

## ONE WEEK

**(FILM LIFE)** Producers, Amber Washington, Phil James; Executive Producer, Phil James; Director, Carl Seaton; Screenplay, Carl Seaton, Kenny Young; Photography, Jeffery T. Brown; Designer, Danielle Tate; Music, Michael Bearden; from Griot Filmworks; Color; Rated R; 97 minutes; Release date: October 19, 2001. CAST: Kenny Young (Varon Thomas), Saadiqa Mohammad (Kiya Parker), Eric Lane (Tyco), Milauna Jemai (Tasha), Pam Mack (Ms. Watts), Gwen Carter (Big Ma), Cynthia Maddox (Mrs. Parker), Charles Moore (Mr. Parker), Malik Middleton (Hook), J. J. McCormick (Mr. Jones), James T. Alfred (Smitty), P. Francois Battiste (Krew Sports Manager), Rhonda Bedgood (Woman at Ressie's Door), Shayrn Grose (Receptionist), Don Adams (Deandre), Hadrian Hooks, Calvin Richardson (Security Guards), Phil White (Mr. Davis), Tina Jordan (Danielle), Tracy Jones (Danielle's Boyfriend), Eva D (Mrs. Minnie), Makeda Falconer (Stripper), Jesse Sanford (Singer), Phil James (Bartender), Dale Morris, Poncho (Cops), Reggie James, Joe Gibson (Paramedics), Derek Edwards (Detective)

## DANCING AT THE BLUE IGUANA

**(LIONS GATE)** Producers, Etchie Stroh, Ram Bergman, Dana Lustig, Michael Radford, Sheila Kelley, Damian Jones, Graham Broadbent; Director, Michael Radford; Screenplay, Michael Radford, David Linter; Photography, Ericson Core; Designer, Martina Buckley; Costumes, Louise Frogley; Executive Producers, Samuel Hadida, Leslie Jean Porter, Willi Baer; Music, Tal Bergman, Renato Neto; Editor, Roberto Perpignani; Line Producer, Dave Pomier; Casting, Sharon Howard-Field; a Moonstone Entertainment presentation of a Bergman Lustig/Dragon/Gallery production; Dolby; Color; Rated R; 123 minutes; Release date: October 19, 2001. CAST: Charlotte Ayanna (Jessie), Daryl Hannah (Angel), Sheila Kelley (Stormy), Elias Koteas (Sully), Vladimir Mashkov (Sacha), Sandra Oh (Jasmine), Jennifer Tilly (Jo), Robert Wisdom (Eddie), Kristin Bauer (Nico), W. Earl Brown (Bobby), Chris Hogan (Dennis), Rodney Rowland (Charlie), David Amos (Dave), Carolyne Aycaguer (Sophie), R. C. Bates (Jimmy), Jesse Bradford (Jorge), Christina Cabot (Christina), Bill Chott (Angel's Regular), Maurice Compte (Drug Buyer), Jack Conley (Officer Pete Foster), Marta Cunningham (Yolanda), Gino Dentie (Celebrity), Pete Gardner (Jerry), Ruthanna Hopper (Desiree), Stephen Hornyak (Trucker), Kevin Hunt (DJ), Peggy Jo Jacobs (Sarah), Joel Hurt Jones, Isabelle Pasco, Vincent Ricotta (Customers), Jason Kravits (Gordon), Michael Loprete (Stormy's Regular), Ellyn Maybe (Fiona), Tenya Neilsen (Castle), Buckley Norris (Talking Man), Shannon Ransom (Bartender), Harper Roisman (Harry Goldberg), Ted Rooney (Assistant), Lobo Sebastian (Rough Looking Guy), Thomas Shelorke (Jo's Turned On Customer), Iqbal Theba (Clerk), John Thomas (Poetry Man)

## WHITE HOTEL

**(SUB ROSA STUDIOS)** Producers/Directors/Screenplay/Photography, Dianne Griffin, Tobi Solvang; Editors, Tobi Solvang, Dianne Griffin, Pat Barber; Music, Various Artists; a Wake Up! Productions Film; Color; Not rated; 90 minutes; Release date: October 19, 2001. Documentary following an AIDS research team as it travels to Eritrea in East Africa, an area long off-limits to Western visitors.

## A GALAXY FAR, FAR AWAY

**(MORNING STAR PRODS.)** Producers, Terry Tocantins, Biagio Messina, Joke Fincioen; Director/Screenplay/Executive Producer/Narrator, Tariq Jalil; Photography, Jeremy Ides; Music, John Dickson; Color; Not rated; 62 minutes; Release date: October 19, 2001. Documentary on the phenomenal popularity of the Star Wars films, featuring interviews with many fans including appearances by Joe Pesci, Meat Loaf, Christopher Vogler, Roger Corman, Jam Master Jedi.

## HISTORY LESSONS

**(FIRST RUN)** Producer/Director/Photography/Editor, Barbara Hammer; Additional Photography, Carolyn McCartney, Ann T. Rossetti; Music, Eve Beglarian, Lisa Ben, Mikael Karlsson, Gretchen Phillips, Jean Paul Keenon; Archivsts, Ann Maguire, Szu Burgess, Bertrand Grimault, Barbara Hammer, Jenni Olson; Black and white/color; Not rated; 65 minutes; Release date: October 26, 2001. Documentary looking at depictions of lesbianism on film throughout the years; featuring archival footage as well as staged sequences with Carmelita Tropicana, Kaja Aman, Antonio Caputo, Denise Coles, Cambrea Ezell, Mildred Gerestanta, Coco Feliciano, Mo Fisher, Anna Hallberg, Barbara Lempel, Piper Macleod, Kathryn Thomas, Laura Marie Thompson, Sharon Jane Smith, Coco Fusco, Jane Fine, David Del Tredici.

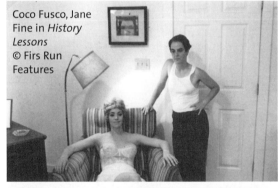

Coco Fusco, Jane Fine in *History Lessons* © Firs Run Features

Charlotte Ayanna in *Dancing at the Blue Iguana* © Lions Gate Films

## ON THE LINE

(MIRAMAX) Producers, Wendy Thorlakson, Rich Hull, Peter Abrams, Robert L. Levy; Executive Producers, Johnny Wright, Lance Bass, Andrew Panay, Bob Osher, Jeremy Kramer, Robbie Brenner; Director, Eric Bross; Screenplay, Eric Aronson, Paul Stanton; Co-Executive Producers, Louise Rosner, Greg Silverman; Co-Producers, Joe Anderson, Far Shariat; Photography, Michael Bernard; Designer, Andrew Jackness; Editor, Eric Sears; Music, Stewart Copeland; Music Supervisors, Randy Spendlove, Jonathan McHugh; Costumes, Margaret Mohr; Casting, Nancy Nayor; a Tapestry Films Production in association with Happy Place; Dolby; Deluxe color; Rated PG; 85 minutes; Release date: October 26, 2001. CAST: Lance Bass (Kevin), Joey Fatone (Rod), Emmanuelle Chriqui (Abbey), GQ (Eric), James Bulliard (Randy), Al Green, Ananda Lewis, Chyna, Brandi Williams, Sammy Sosa, Damon Buford, Eric Young (Themselves), Tamala Jones (Jackie), Richie Sambora (Mick Silver), Amanda Foreman (Julie), Dan Montgomery (Brady), Dave Foley (Higgins), Jerry Stiller (Nathan), David Fraser (Barrett), Jenny Parsons (Margie, Receptionist), Kristin Booth (Sam), Sandra Cladwell (Reebok Client #1), Romona Pringle (Kayla Sanders), Jonathan Watton (Paul), Jeanie Calleja (Tabatha), Tracy Dawson (Goth Girl), Sarah McDonald (Diner Waitress), Kelley Hazen (Woman at Wrigley), Howard E. Brechner (Guy at Wrigley), Alexandra Delory (Girl with Braces), Adrian Churchill (Guy at Bar), Allen Alvarado (Boy), Amanda Brydon (High-School Girl at Party), Steve Clark, Paul Puzzella (Band Members), Dov Tiefenbach (High-School Kid), Sean O'Neil (Puberty-Ravaged Kid), Chip Caray (Cubs TV Announcer)

## PUNKS

(URBANWORLD) Producers, Tracey E. Edmonds, Michael McQuarn, Patrik-Ian Polk; Executive Producers, Kenneth "Babyface" Edmonds, Stacy Spikes; Director/Screenplay, Patrik-Ian Polk; Photography, Rory King; Designer, Liana Reid; Editor, Anne Misawa; Costumes, Linda Stokes; Casting, Doran Reed, Robi Reed-Humes; Tall Skinny Black Boy Productions/e2 Filmworks; Dolby; Color; Rated R; 91 minutes; Release date: November 2, 2001. CAST: Seth Gilliam (Marcus), Dwight Ewell (Hill), Rockmond Dunbar (Darby), Jazzmun (Chris/Crystal), Renoly Santiago (Dante), Loretta Devine (Health Counselor), Vanessa Williams (Jennifer), Devon Odessa (Felicity), Rudolf Martin (Gilbert), Jullian Dulce Vida (Spike), Marc Avalon (Masseur), Kevin Aviance (Miss Smokie), Dustin Blair (Sexy White Guy), Rainbow Borden (Wild Guy #1/Jim), Rodney Chester (Alexis Carrington Colby Dexter), Lamar Damon (Roger), Julio Dolcevita (Spike), Shaun Earl (Monique Jeanville), Nayib Estefan (Wild Guy #2/Mark), Ryan Findlay (Steve, Sexy Guy), Michael Holden (Mr. Geiger, Concierge), Walter E. Hong (Double Rainbow Proprietor), Ron Kochevar (Par), Andre McClain (Chris's Boyfriend), Brian-Paul Mendoza (Bath House Attendant), D-Taylor Murphy (Jo Jo), Jason Olive (Lucas), Phina Oruche, Gregory Keith (Super Model), Rhonda Ray (Bartender), Phillip Rhys (Rodney), Red Savage (Dominique Devereaux), Scott L. Schwartz (Convict), Thea Vidale (Nurse)

Seth Gilliam, Rockmond Dunbar in *Punks*
© Urbanworld Films

GQ, James Buillard, Lance Bass, Joey Fatone in *On the Line* © Miramax Films

## THE ANNIHILATION OF FISH

(REGENT) Producers, Kris Dodge, Paul Heller, William Lawrence Fabrizio, Eric Mitchell, John Remark; Director, Charles Burnett; Screenplay, Anthony C. Winkler; Photography, John Ndiaga Demps, Rick Robinson; Designer, Nina Ruscio; Costumes, Christine Peters; Editor, Nancy Richardson; Music, Laura Karpman; a Paul Heller production in association with American Sterling Productions; Color; Rated R; 108; Release date: November 2, 2001. CAST: Lynn Redgrave (Poinsettia), James Earl Jones (Fish), Margot Kidder (Mrs. Muldroone), Ronald F. Hoiseck (Reno Minister), Tommy Redmond Hicks

## EVERYTHING PUT TOGETHER

(VITAGRAPH FILMS) Producer, Sean Furst; Executive Producer, Adam Forgash; Director, Marc Foster; Screenplay, Catherine Lloyd Burns, Adam Forgash, Marc Forster; Photography, Roberto Schaefer; Designer, Paul Jackson; Editor, Matt Chesse; Music, Thomas Koppel; Dolby; Color; Not rated; 87 minutes; Release date: November 2, 2001. CAST: Radha Mitchell (Angie), Megan Mullally (Barbie), Justin Louis (Russ), Catherine Lloyd Burns (Judith), Alan Ruck (Kessel), Michele Hicks (April), Matt Malloy (Dr. Reiner), Jacqueline Heinze (Jean), Courtney Watkins (H20 Instructor), Mark Boone Junior (Bill), Blake Rossi (Michael), Stephanie Schneider (Party Videographer), Vince Vieluf (Jim), John P. Hunter (Hearse Driver), Kevin Ratliffe (Simon), Arly Jover (Nurse), Pamela Gordon, Octavia L. Spencer (Nurses), Jennie Vaughn (Cashier), Jonathan Slavin (Photo Clerk), Thomas Prisco (Doctor A), Martha Mendoza (Marie), Tom McCleister (Dr. Miller), Garvin Funches (Orderly), Pam Monroe (Loni), Scott Vance (Priest), Henry King, Oliver King (Barbie's Twins), Amy Carlson (Jane), Dakota Leopardi (Justin), Rob Swanson (Man in Park), Roland LaGarde (Mailman), Shelly Desai (Storage Man), Paul Hayes (Dr. Spiegel), Judy Geeson (Angie's Mother)

Lynn Redgrave, James Earl Jones in *The Annihilation of Fish* © Regent Entertainment

## CITIZEN TOXIE: THE TOXIC AVENGER IV

(TROMA) Producers, Lloyd Kaufman, Michael Herz; Executive Producers, Ken Squire, Andrew Learner, James Coleman, Weston Quasha; Director, Lloyd Kaufman; Screenplay, Trent Haaga, Patrick Cassidy, Gabriel Friedman, Lloyd Kaufman; Photography, Brendan Flynt; Designer, Alison Grossman; Editor, Gabriel Friedman; Music, Wes Nagy; Creature Effects, Tim Considine; a Lloyd Kaufman and Michael Herz production; Dolby; Color; Not rated; 108 minutes; Release date: November 2, 2001. CAST: David Mattey, Heidi Sjursen, Clyde Lewis, Debbie Rochon, Ron Jeremy, Paul Krymse, Dan Snow, Trent Haaga, Hank the Angry Dwarf, Joseph Isaac Fleishmaker

Justin Louis, Radha Mitchell in *Everything Put Together* © Vitagraph Films

John Leguizamo in *King of the Jungle*
© Urbanworld Films

## KING OF THE JUNGLE

(URBANWORLD) Producers, Robert S. Potter, Scott Macaulay, Robin O'Hara; Executive Producers, John Leguizamo, Jay Rifkin, Hans Zimmer, Stacy Spikes; Director/Screenplay, Seth Zvi Rosenfeld; Photography, Fortunato Procopio; Designer, Deana Sydney; Costumes, Richard Owings; Music, Harry Gregson-Williams; Editor, Kate Sanford; a Bombo Sports & Entertainment presentation of a Forensic Films/Media Ventures production; DuArt color; Rated R; 86 minutes; Release date: November 9, 2001. CAST: John Leguizamo (Seymour), Rosie Perez (Joanne), Julie Carmen (Mona), Cliff Gorman (Jack), Michael Rapaport (Francis), Marisa Tomei (Det. Costello), Justin Pierce (Lil' Mafsa), Annabella Sciorra (Mermaid), Judy Reyes (Lydia Morreto), Richie Perez (Pucho), Blaze (Dead-Eye), Rafael Nunez, Malcolm Barrett (Basketball Kids), Raymond Vincente (Colon), Yan Ming (Fat Ming), Rosario Dawson (Veronica), Seth Zvi Rosenfeld (Herbie), Raujit Chowdhry (Mr. Sith), William Prael (Officer with Sith), Scott Cohen (Officer Norman Turner), Jason Andrews (Turner's Partner), Jerry Dean (Rober), Eddie Hands (Dum Dum's Friend), Sixto Ramos (Det. Lemons), Carmen Serrano (Woman on Street), Bill Cwikowski (Freddy), Rebecca Cohen Alport (Pregnant Poet)

Laura Linney, Rob Morrow in *Maze* © Andora Pictures

Erin O'Hara, Greg Walloch, Michael Lucas in
*Keeping It Real* © Avatar Films

## I REMEMBER ME

(ZEITGEIST) Producer/Director/Screenplay, Kim A. Snyder; Co-Producer, Sam Counter; Photography, Sam Counter, Lee Daniel, Don Lenzer; Editor, Paula Heredia; Coordinating Producer, Heidi Zecher; Color; Not rated; 74 minutes; Release date: November 9, 2001. Documentary on Chronic Fatigue Syndrome.

## MAZE

(ANDORA PICTURES) Producers, Paul Colichman, Mark R. Harris, Stephen P. Jarchow, Rob Morrow; Executive Producers, Phyllis Carlyle, Joseph Pierson, David Forrest, Beau Rogers; Director, Rob Morrow; Screenplay/Story, Rob Morrow, Bradley White; Photography, Wolfgang Held; Designer, Kalina Ivanov; Costumes, Melissa Toth; Editor, Gary Levy; Music, Bobby Previte; Casting, Sheila Jaffe, Georgianne Walken; a Blockbuster & Starz! Pictures presentation in association with KBK Entertainment & Andora Pictures International of a Regent Entertainment/Bits and Pieces Picture Company/Goldheart Production in association with Cypress Films, Inc. & Carlyle Productions; Dolby; Color; Rated R; 97 minutes; Release date: November 9, 2001. CAST: Rob Morrow (Lyle Maze), Laura Linney (Callie), Craig Sheffer (Mike), Rose Gregorio (Helen), Robert Hogan (Lyle's Father), Gia Carides (Julianne), Betsy Aidem (Lydia), Keenan Shimizu (Korean Market Employee), Matthew Storff (Young Lyle), Sheila Zane (Lenna), Lenny Flaherty (Drunk), Susan Shacter (Photographer), Wally Dunn (Bartender), Billy Strong (Italian Restaurant Patron), Nick Terno (Waiter), Ken Leung (Dr. Mikao), Frank Pugliese (Scott), Brian Greene (Plat Techtonics Man), Merrill Holtzman (Male Nurse), Kathleen Goldpaugh (Birth Nurse), Alla (Fashion Model), Mary Kelsey (Pregnant Woman) (This movie had its premiere on Starz! cable network in 2001.)

## KEEPING IT REAL: THE ADVENTURES OF GREG WALLOCH

**(AVATAR FILMS)** Producers/Screenplay, Eli Kabillio, Greg Walloch; Based on the show White Disabled Talent by Greg Walloch; Executive Producers, TC Rice, Lorna Thomas; Director, Eli Kabillio; Photography, David Sperling, Neil Smith, David Goldsmith; Designer, Niamh Byrne; Music, Melanie Rock, Greg Talenfeld, Martin Trum; Editor, Egon Kirincic; a Mad Dog Films Inc. Production; Color; Not rated; 83 minutes; Release date: November 9, 2001. A part-documentary, -concert film, -comedy based on the life of disabled gay man Greg Walloch; featuring Stephen Baldwin, Paul Borghese, Anne Meara, Michael Musto, Deborah Yates.

## SNIDE AND PREJUDICE

**(VINE INTERNATIONAL)** Line Producer, Rodney Greene; Director/ Producer/Screenplay, Philippe Mora; Photography, J. B. Letchinger; Casting, Felicia Fasano; Bombastic Pictures, Focusfilm Entertainment; Color; Not rated; 90 minutes; Release date: November 9, 2001. CAST: Rene Auberjonois (Dr. Sam Cohen), Joseph Bottoms (Himmler), Sam Bottoms (Schaub), Claudia Christian (Renate Muller), Richard Edson (Hess), Mick Fleetwood (Pablo Picasso), Brion James (Goehring), J. D. Johnson (Sheffield), Angus MacFadyen (Michael Davidson/Adolf Hilter), Brian McDermott (Hindenberg), Richard Moll (Von Ludendorf), Mena Suvari (Geli), Jesse Grey Walken (Christ), T. C. Warner (Tessa Percival/Eva Braun), Michael Zelniker (Goebbels), Mickey Cottrell, Brad Wilson, Jenny Dubasso, Armin Shimerman

## THE WASH

**(LIONS GATE)** Producers, DJ Pooh, Phillip Atwell, Kip Konwiser; Executive Producers, Dr. Dre, Snoop Dogg; Director/Screenplay, DJ Pooh; Co-Producer, Jeremiah Samuels; Photography, Keith Smith; Designer, Albert Cuellar; Costumes, Tracey White; Music, Camara Kambon; Editor, Jack Hofstra; Casting, Monica R. Cooper; a Lithium Entertainment production; Dolby; Color; Rated R; 96 minutes; Release date: November 14, 2001. CAST: Dr. Dre (Sean), Snoop Dogg (Dee Loc), George Wallace

Dr. Dre, George Wallace, Snoop Dogg in *The Wash*
© Lions Gate Films

(Mr. Washington), Angell Conwell (Antoinette), Tommy "Tiny" Lister, Jr. (Bear), Bruce Bruce (DeWayne), Alex Thomas (Jimmy), Shawn Fonteno (Face), Lamont Bentley (C-Money), Shari Watson (Vickey), Arif S. Kinchen (Lil' Dee), Demetrius Navarro (Juan), John Basinger (Mickey), Rashaan Nall (Ronald), Alvin Joiner (Wayne), DJ Pooh (Slim), Frank Chavez (Officer Hoppy), Julio R. Gonzales (Julio G.), Ricardo Brown (Maniac), Jeris Poindexter (Mr. Francis), Marcia Wright (Sharon), Pierre (Mark), Jude S. Walko (Window Man), Derek Thompson (Old Man), Isley (Karen), Tommy Chong (Dee's Connection), Pauly Shore (Man in Trunk), Anthony Albano (Mafia Tony), Shaquille O'Neal (Norman)

## BOMBAY EUNUCH

**(GIDALYA PICTURES)** Producer, Alexandra Shiva; Directors, Alexandra Shiva, Sean MacDonald, Michelle Gucovsky; Photography, Ajay Narohna, Bimal Biswas; Editor, Penelope Falk; Music, John M. Davis; HD Video; Color; Not rated; 71 minutes; Release date: November 16, 2001. Documentary about a group of castrati living in the squalor of Bombay.

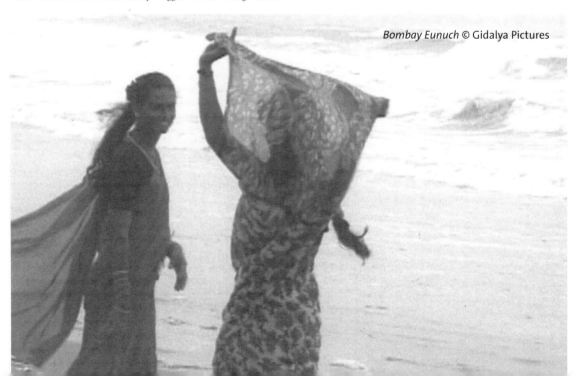

*Bombay Eunuch* © Gidalya Pictures

Michael Cunio in *The Fluffer* © First Run Features/TLA

## THE FLUFFER

**(FIRST RUN FEATURES/TLA RELEASING)** Producers, John Sylla, Victoria Robinson; Executive Producer, Rose Kuo; Directors, Richard Glatzer, Wash West; Screenplay, Wash West; Line Producer, Pat Scanlon; Photography, Mark Putnam; Designer, Devorah Herbert; Costumes, Gitte Meldgaard; Editor, John Binninger; Music, The Bowling Green, John Vaughn; Casting, Elizabeth Jereski; a Fluff and Fold production; Color; Not rated; 94 minutes; Release date: November 16, 2001. CAST: Scott Gurney (Johnny Rebel), Michael Cunio (Sean McGinnis), Roxanne Day (Babylon), Taylor Negron (Tony Brooks), Richard Riehle (Sam Martins), Tim Bagley (Alan Dieser), Adina Porter (Silver), Ruben Madera (Hector), Josh Holland (Brian), Mickey Cottrell (Aunt at Bar, Ralph Shifflett), Guinevere Turner (Video Store Clerk), Robert Walden (Chad Cox), Deborah Harry (Marcella), Heather Shannon Ryan (L.A. Actress), David Pevsner (Casting Man), Gale Van Cott (Casting Woman), Sharon McCormick (Sean's Mama), Andy Zeffer (Rick Daniels), Penn Badgley (Young Sean), Stephen Michael Pace (Jeb Gordon), Zach Richards, Derek Cameron, John Sylla Rex, Chad Donovan, Thomas Lloyd, Chi Chi LaRue, Karen Dior, Bradley Picklesheimer, Louis Re, Jay Lyons, Chris Green, Ron Jeremy, Cole Tucker (Themselves), Squishy (Stacia), Jim Steel (Bartender), Ke (Endowed Go-Go Boy), Lori Alan (Harmony), Christopher Carroll (Businessman at Legg's), Rob Rumsey (Twinkie in a Sling), Johanna Went (Abortion Protester), Judith Benezra (Policewoman), Trev Broudy (TV Reporter), Franklin Hernandez (Mexican Boy)

## THE SIMIAN LINE

**(GABRIEL FILM GROUP)** Producers, Linda Yellen, Robert Renfield; Executive Producers, Montel Williams, Daniel Bennett, Michael Escott; Director, Linda Yellen; Screenplay, Gisela Bernice; Story, Linda Yellen, Michael Leeds; Photography, David Bridges; Designer, Henry Dunn; Costumes, Tim Chappel; Music, Patrick Seymour; Co-Producers, Jordan Walker-Pearlman, Judith Zarin; Editor, Bob Jorissen; an S.L. Production in association with DaWa Movies; Color; Rated R; 106 minutes; Release date: November 16, 2001. CAST: Harry Connick, Jr. (Rick), Cindy Crawford (Sandra), Tyne Daly (Arnita), William Hurt (Edward), Monica Keena (Marta), Samantha Mathis (Mae), Lynn Redgrave (Katharine), Jamey Sheridan (Paul), Eric Stoltz (Sam), Dylan Bruno (Billy), Jeremy Zelig (Jimmy)

## OUT COLD

**(TOUCHSTONE)** Producers, Lee R. Mayes, Michael Aguilar, Jonathan Glickman; Executive Producers, Lauren Shuler Donner, Gary Barber, Roger Birnbaum; Directors, The Malloys (Emmett Malloy, Brendan Malloy); Screenplay, Jon Zack; Photography, Richard Crudo; Designer, Michael Bolton; Costumes, Carla Hetland; Editor, Jeffrey Wolf; Music, Michael Andrews; Casting, Sarah Halley Finn, Randi Hiller; Stunts, J. J. Makaro; a Spyglass Entertainment presentation of a Donnners' Company production, a Barber/Birnbaum production; Dolby; Technicolor; Rated PG-13; 89 minutes; Release date: November 21, 2001. CAST: Jason

Harry Connick, Jr., Lynn Redgrave in *The Simian Line*
© Gabriel Film Group

London (Rick Rambis), Lee Majors (Jack Majors), Willie Garson (Ted Muntz), Zach Galifianakis (Luke), David Koechner (Stumpy), Flex Alexander (Anthony), A. J. Cook (Jenny), David Denman (Lance), Caroline Dhavernas (Anna), Derek Hamilton (Pig Pen), Thomas Lennon (Eric), Victoria Silvstedt (Inga), Lewis Arquette (Papa Muntz), Todd Richards (Barry), Rio Tahara (Tetsuo), Brett Kelly (Kid at Barbeque, Toby), Lee R. Mayes (Whitey), Alexis Glabus, Nicole Amos, Fawnia Mondey, Holly Eglington, Odessa Munroe, Christine Caux, Janette Wu, Kendall Saunders (Solid Gold Dancers), Danny Hagge (Stewart), Adam Harrington (Team Snownook Leader), Rob "Sluggo" Boyce, Scott Heindl (Snownook Guys), Rheta Hutton (Nurse), Jane Sowerby (Powder Room Woman), Peter Kawasaki, Art Irazawa (Japanese Businessmen), Wren Robertz (Snownook Bouncer), Amy Baldwin (Hot Tourist Chick), Lisa Marie Caruk (Other Tourist Chick), Ted Stryker (Tourist Dude in Lineup), Jack Hody Johnson, Adam Topol, Merlo Podlewski (Jack Johnson and Band), Tara Dakides, Devun Walsh, Javas Lehn, Sean Johnson (Themselves), Steve Kahan (Powder Room Bartender)

## TEXAS RANGERS

(DIMENSION) Producers, Alan Greisman, Frank Price; Executive Producers, Bob Weinstein, Harvey Weinstein, Cary Granat, Larry Levinson; Director, Steve Miner; Screenplay, Scott Busby, Martin Copeland; Photography, Daryn Okada; Designer, Herbert Pinter; Music, Trevor Rabin; a Price Entertainment/Greisman Production in association with Larry Levinson Productions, Inc.; Distributed by Miramax Films; Dolby; Panavision; Color; Rated PG-13; 90 minutes; Release date: November 30, 2001. CAST: James Van Der Beek (Lincoln Rogers Dunnison), Dylan McDermott (Leander McNelly), Ashton Kutcher (George Durham), Robert Patrick (Sgt. John Armstrong), Randy Travis (Frank Bones), Usher Raymond (Randolph Douglas Scipio), Alfred Molina (John King Fisher), Jon Abrahams (Berry Smith), Tom Skerritt (Richard Dukes), Rachael Leigh Cook (Caroline Dukes), Leonor Varela (Perdita), Marco Leonardi (Jesus Sandoval), Matt Keeslar (Suh Suh Sam), Vincent Spano (Ed Simms), Bob Bancroft (Auctioneer), Stephen Bridgewater (Older Ranger), Jordan Brower (Jake Dunnison), Anthony Crivello (Ringmaster), Oded Fehr (Pete Marsele), Derek S. Flores (Leary), Breon Gorman (Mrs. Dunnison), Eric Johnson (Rollins), Matthew Kennedy (Ranch Hand Steve), Brad Loree (Outlaw #3), Brian Martell (Jean-Pierre Marsele), Gordon Michaels (Mariachi Guard), David Millbern (Marshal), Billy Morton (Abajo), Kate Newby (Henrietta Dukes), William Prael (Cale Dukes), Joe Renteria (Gen. Cortinas), A. Alexandra Sanford (Fischer's Prostitute), Jim Shield (Baldum), Joe Spano (Mr. Dunnison), Jesse G. Thompson (Purdy Dukes), Gareth Williams (Vigilante Vic)

Jason London, A.J. Cook in *Out Cold*
© Spyglass Entertainment Group

## ABCD

(EROS/LAXMI) Producers, Krutin Patel, Naju Patel; Executive Producer, Madhur Jaffrey; Director/Story, Krutin Patel; Screenplay, Krutin Patel, James McManus; Photography, Milton Kam; Designer, Deborah Schreier; Costumes, Naju Patel; Editor, Ravi Subramanian; Music, Deirdre Broderick; Casting, Glenn Fisher; Color; Not rated; 105 minutes; Release date: November 30, 2001. CAST: Madhur Jaffrey (Anju), Faran Tahir (Raj), Sheetal Sheth (Nina), Aasif Mandvi (Ashok), David Ari (Brian), Jennifer Dorr White (Julia), Adriane Forlana Erdos (Tejal), Rex Young (Sam), Gil Grail (Mark), Bob Bonnet (Cop), Alexander Lasky (Gordon), David Mann (Tony), Janan Raouf (Jennifer), Vince Byrne, Sr. (MacKenzie), Nick Cochrane (Asha), Rashmi Sheth (Shailesh), Susham Bedi (Sona), M. N. Ahmed (Depak), Jessica Lyon (Cindy), Glenn Fisher (Maitre d'), Ismail Bashey (News Vendor), Ralph Amiano (Cashier), Kelly J. Montgomery (Linda), Ami Shukla (Shermila), Nayan Padrai (Prakash), Bipin Bhai (Priest), Naju Patel (Sharmil's Friend), Rahael Elias (Sharmila's Mother), Satish Patel (Sharmila's Father), Clarke Johnson (Minister), Mervin Crook (Samuel), Nancy Johnson (Nancy)

Ashton Kutcher, Usher Raymond, James Van Der Beek in *Texas Rangers* © Dimension Films

Janeane Garofalo, Jerry Stiller in *The Independent*
© Arrow Releasing

# THE INDEPENDENT

(ARROW) Producer, Mike Wilkins; Executive Producer, Jerry Weintraub; Director, Stephen Kessler; Screenplay, Mike Wilkins, Stephen Kessler; Co-Executive Producer, Lesa Lakin Richardson; Co-Producer, Jack Ziga; Photography, Amir Hamed; Designer, Russell Christian; Costumes, Yoona Kwak; Editor, Chris Franklin; Music, Ben Vaughn; Casting, Nicole Arbusto, Joy Dickson; Color; Rated R; 95 minutes; Release date: November 30, 2001. CAST: Jerry Stiller (Morty Fineman), Janeane Garofalo (Paloma Fineman), Max Perlich (Ivan), Ted Demme, Roger Corman, Ron Howard, Karen Black, Peter Bogdanovich, Fred Williamson, Nick Cassavetes (Themselves), Paul Logan (Son), Stacy Fuson (Daughter), Herb Marcus (Old Man/Mr. Witz), Julie Strain (Ms. Kevorkian), Stephen Kessler (Steve), Mike Wilkins (Mike), Ethan Embry (Bert), Kimo Wills (Rob), Phil Proctor (Rob's Dad), Melinda Peterson (Rob's Mom), Louisa Moritz (Sally, Receptionist), Priscilla Taylor (Iris), Greg Behrendt (Redneck), Victoria Silvstedt (Blossom), Devon DeMaria (Violet), Clanton Williams, Joseph Dubow (Businessmen), Danielle Ciardi (Daisy), Lisa McCullough (Leather Girl), Jimmy Briscoe (Morty's Actor Friend), Gary Friedkin (Surfer Guy), Debbie Lee Carrington (Surfer Girl), Susie Rossitto (Morty's Actress Friend), Eric Schaefer (R. F. Fineman), Roy Kerry (Beardo), David Stifel (Hairface), Dennis McCullen (President), S. A. Griffin (Slate), Omer Mohamed (Mr. Singh), Maria Cina (Newscaster), Jennifer Elise Cox (Telluride Booth Girl), Billy Burke (Dwayne), Penelope Pumpkins, Fantasia, Brittany Andrews (Actresses), Amy Stiller (Dr. Rosaria McClesh), Gina Jackson (Foxy Chocolate Robot), John Finnegan (Guard), Larry Hankin (William Henry Ellis), Andy Dick (Maitre d'), Joanne Richter (Tula), Jeff Schoeny (Boy), Ben Stiller (Cop), Ancel Cook (Peter Worth), John Lydon (Baruce), Ginger Lynn Allen (Mayor Kitty Storm), Dr. Michael Robbins (Orthodontist), Ken Michelman (Prosecutor), Dana Gould (Victim), Rob Ingersoll (Christ), Ramon Sison (Mr. Ramos), Jade Herrera (Blue Sky), Anne Meara (Rita), Fred Dryer (Jean-Claude), Richard Paul (Jeffries), Sam Anderson (Ed), Bill Gerber (Dennis), Laura Kightlinger (Dian), Risa Mickenberg (Desk Clerk), Jay Johnson (Soldier), Joseph Griffo (Beach Guy), Bob Odenkirk (Figure), Melissa Daniels (Lover), Owen Bush (VFW Old Man), Aki Aleong (Mr. Ko), Maria Ford (Poster Model)

# PORN STAR: THE LEGEND OF RON JEREMY

(MAELSTROM) Producers, Kirt Eftekhar, Scott J. Gill; Executive Producer, Tim Goldberg; Director/Editor, Scott J. Gill; Photography, Ralph King; Associate Producer, Sean Skelton; Music, Carvin Knowles; Dolby; Color; Not rated; 79 minutes; Release date: November 30, 2001. Documentary on well-endowed porno actor Ron Jeremy.

# FINAL

(COWBOY) Producers, Gary Winick, Alexis Alexanian, Mary Frances Budig, Steve Dunn, Campbell Scott; Executive Producers, Jonathan Sehring, Caroline Kaplan, John Sloss; Director, Campbell Scott; Screenplay, Bruce McIntosh; Photography, Dan Gillham; Designer, Chris Shriver; Costumes, Toni Fusco; Music, Guy Davis; Executive Music Producer, Alex Steyermark; Editor, Andy Keir; Casting, Ellen Lewis, Marcia Debonis; The Independent Film Channel Productions presentation of an InDigEnt production in association with Spare Room Productions; Color; Not rated; 111 minutes; Release date: December 7, 2001. CAST: Denis Leary (Bill), Hope Davis (Ann), J. C. MacKenzie (Todd), Jim Gaffigan (Dayton), Jim Hornyak (Orderly), Maureen Anderman (Supervisor), Marin Hinkle (Sherry), Madison Arnold (Bill's Father), Caroline Kava (Bill's Mother), Mary Diveny (Murse), Janet Hovious (Doctor), Nadine Delallo (Ward Nurse), Bruce McIntosh (Edward), Steve Dunn (Larry), Anthony Pettine (Coloring Patient), Eric Gearity (Puzzle Patient), John Brainard (VCR Patient), Lisa Leguillou (Bookstore Clerk), Danny Drohojowski (Todd's Son), Tina Benko (Blonde in Bar), Guy Davis (Singer), Hélène Cardona (ICU Nurse), Christina Kirk (Mary), Ezra Knight (Lawyer), Seth Barrish, Catherine Brophy (Staff Members), Earl Hindman (Official), Ben Wilson (Attendant), Nancy Wu (Dancing Nurse), Alexis Alexanian (Pushy Nurse), Jody Burke (Coroner)

Ron Jeremy in *Porn Star* © Maelstrom

## KIDS WORLD

**(BLUE STEEL RELEASING)** Producers, Grant Bradley, Tom Taylor; Executive Producers, John Massam, Alex Krem, Devesh Chetty, Walter Josten, Wolfram Tichy; Director, Dale G. Bradley; Screenplay, Michael Lach; Photography, Neil Cervin; Designer, Mark Robbins; Music, Bruce Lynch; Editor, Douglas Braddock; Line Producer, Brian Walden; Associate Producer, Jozsef Fityus; Casting, Roe Baker; a Daybreak Pacific Films and VIF Productions presentation; Color; Rated PG; 93 minutes; Release date: December 7, 2001. CAST: Christopher Lloyd (Leo), Blake Foster (Ryan Mitchell), Michael Purms (Twinkie), Anton Tennet (Stu), Todd Emerson (Detloff), Olivia Tennet (Nicole Mitchell), Anna Wilson (Holly)

## UPRISING

**(BROOKLYN FILMS)** Producers, Jon Avnet, Raffaella De Laurentiis, Jordan Kerner; Executive Producer, Bill Haber; Director, Jon Avnet; Screenplay, Jon Avnet, Paul Brickman; Photography, Denis Lenoir; Designer, Benjamin Fernandez; Costumes, George L. Little; Music, Maurice Jarre; Editor, Sabrina Plisco-Morris; Casting, Debi Manwiller, Rick Pagano, Eva Stefankovicova, Sheila Trezise; Color; Not rated; 163 minutes; Release date: December 7, 2001. CAST: Leelee Sobieski (Tosia Altman), Hank Azaria (Mordechai Anielewicz), David Schwimmer (Yitzak Zuckerman), Jon Voight (Major-General Jurgen Stroop), Donald Sutherland (Adam Czerniakow), Cary Elwes (Dr. Fritz Hippler), Stephen Moyer (Kazik Rodem), Sadie Frost (Zivia Lubetkin), Radha Mitchell (Mira Fruchner), Mili Avital (Devorah Barga), Alexandra Holden (Frania Beatus), John Ales (Marek Edelman), Andy Nyman (Calel Wasser), Eric Lively (Arie Wilner), Nora Brickman (Clara Linder), Jesper Christensen (Gen. Kruger), Melanie Claus (Fergie), Ben Crystal (Julian Wald), Iddo Goldberg (Zygmundt), Luke Moably (Zachariah Artenstein), Nadiv Molcho (Isaac Linder) (Note: This film had its U.S. premiere on television on Nov. 4, 2001.)

## LOST IN THE PERSHING POINT HOTEL

**(NORTHERN ARTS)** Producers, Julia Jay Pierrepont III, Erin Chandler; Executive Producers, Michael Tiberi, Jimmy "Kimo" Ciotti; Director, Julia Jay Pierrepont III; Screenplay, Leslie Jordan; Photography, Sacha Sarchielli; Designer, Cecil Gentry; Costumes, Chantal Thomas; Editor, Ila von Hasperg; Music, Dan Gilboy; Casting, Lisa Pantone, James Pantone; Dolby; Color; Not rated; 107 minutes; Release date: December 7, 2001. CAST: Leslie Jordan (Storyteller), Erin Chandler (Miss Make Do), Mark Pellegrino (Tripper), John Ritter (Christian Therapist), Marilu Henner (Mother), Michelle Phillips (DeeDee Westbrooks), Sheryl Lee Ralph (Nurse Talley-Mae), Kathy Kinney (Redneck Nurse), Carlos Gomez (Nico), Peter Mohawk (Contessa), Luke Eberl (Young Storyteller), Adam Wylie (Duane Striker), Jesse Petrick (Johnny Striker), Sean Moran (Big Tiny), Billy Butler (Irvin), Chad Gordon (Chicken Jimmy), Arthur Hiller (Street Evangelist), Karen Austin (PR Woman), Kris Kamm (Cotton Pine), Bobby McGee (T-Bone), Matt Flanders (Brandon), Ritch Schyder (Storyteller's Father), Badja Djola (Fast Eddie), John Fleck (Weird Guy), Patrick O'Neal (Angry Bartender), Stephanie Blake (Kayla, Stripper), Viveka Davis, Krista Metropolis, Cherise Leana Bangs (Debutantes), Newell Alexander (Preacher), Rosemary Alexander (Church Lady), Jimmy Bangley (Church Man), James Hampton (Pediatrician), Jane Abbott (Jean Jean), Essence (Lucinda), Donna Eskra (Starla), Lisa Smock (Pregnant Prostitute), Edward Ferry (Stairwell John), Vincent Castellanos (Toothpick Jorge), David Higlin (1990s Cabbie), Jeff Key (Wedding Photographer)

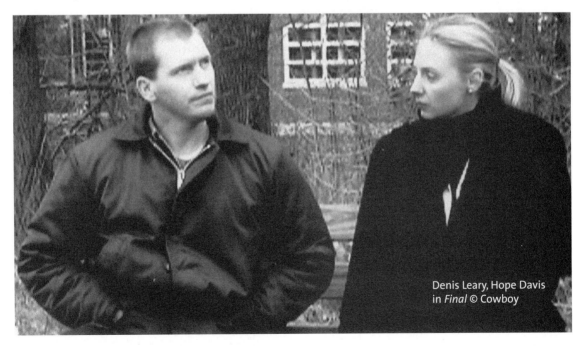

Denis Leary, Hope Davis in *Final* © Cowboy

Giovanni Andrade, Brent Fellows in *Eban & Charley*
© Picture This!

## AS I WAS MOVING AHEAD OCCASIONALLY I SAW BRIEF GLIMPSES OF BEAUTY

**(JONAS MEKAS PRODS.)** Producer/Director/Screenplay/Photography/ Editor, Jonas Mekas; Music, Auguste Varkalis; Color; Not rated; 288 minutes; Release date: December 12, 2001. Filmmaker Jonas Mekas's documentation of glimpses from his life over the past three decades.

## EBAN AND CHARLEY

**(PICTURE THIS!)** Producer, Chris Monlux; Director/Screenplay, James Bolton; Photography, Judy Irola; Editor, Elizabeth Edwards; Music, Stephin Merritt; Color; Not rated; 86 minutes; Release date: December 14, 2001. CAST: Brent Fellows (Eban), Giovanni Andrade (Charley), Ellie Nicholson (Sunshine), Drew Zeller (Kevin), Pam Munter (Eban's Mother), Ron Upton (Eban's Father), Nolan V. Chard (Charley's Father)

## LUSH

**(i5 FILMS)** Producers, Scott McGehee, Patrick Dollard; Executive Producers, Robert H. Nathan, Eileen Jones; Director/Screenplay, Mark Gibson; Photography, Caroline Champetier; Designer, Scott Plauche; Editor, Sarah Flack; Music, Barrett Martin; Co-Producer, Alicia Allain; Casting, Nicole Arbusto, Joy Dickson; Color; Not rated; 93 minutes; Release date: December 28, 2001. CAST: Campbell Scott (Lionel "Ex" Exley), Jared Harris (W. Firmin Carter), Laura Linney (Rachel Van Dyke), Laurel Holloman (Ash Van Dyke), Nick Offerman (Gerry), Kimo Wills (Pats), James R. Hall, Jr. (Buddha), Don Hood (Har), Joe Chrest (Greg), Michael Cahill (Brian), David Sellars (Conner), J. C. Sealy (Miss Billie), Anthony Marble (Brice), Layton Martens (Veteran Cop), Doug Barden (Detective), Marcus Lyle Brown (Rookie Cop), Chris Campbell (Carl), Phil Brady (Fuzzie), Sally Birdsong (Na-Non), Glen Paddie (Bob)

## THE OTHER SIDE OF HEAVEN

**(EXCEL ENTERTAINMENT)** Producers, John Garbett, Gerald R. Molen; Executive Producer, Mitch Davis; Co-Producer, Tim Coddington; Director/Screenplay, Mitch Davis; Based on the book *In the Eye of the Storm* by John H. Groberg; Photography, Brian J. Breheny; Music, Kevin Kiner; Editor, Steven Ramirez; from 3Mark Entertainment, Molen/Garbett Productions; Dolby; Color; Rated PG; 113 minutes; Release date: Dec. 14, 2001. CAST: Christopher Gorham (John Groberg), Anne Hathaway (Jean Sabin), Joe Folau (Feki), Miriama Smith (Lavania), Whetu Fala (Asi), Alvin Fitisemanu (Tomasi), Peter Sa'ena Brown (Kuli), Apii McKinley (Noli), John Sumner (President Stone), Nathaniel Lees, Paki Cherrington, Pua Magasiva, John Paekau, Glynis Paraha

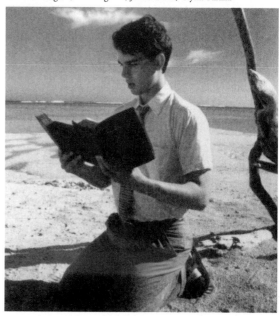

Christopher Gorham in *The Other Side of Heaven*
© Excel Entertainment

# PROMISING NEW ACTORS
## OF 2001

Hayden Christensen
(*Life as a House*)

Aunjanue Ellis
(*The Caveman's Valentine*)

Scarlett Johansson
(*An American Rhapsody, Ghost World,
The Man Who Wasn't There*)

Jay Hernandez
(*Crazy/Beautiful*)

Justin Long
(*Jeepers Creepers*)

Jena Malone
(*Donnie Darko, Life as a House*)

Audrey Tautou
(*Amélie, Happenstance*)

Dominic Monaghan
(*The Lord of the Rings: The Fellowship of the Ring*)

Mos Def
(*Monster's Ball*)

Emma Watson
(*Harry Potter and The Sorcerer's Stone*)

Naomi Watts
(*Mulholland Dr.*)

Daniel Radcliffe
(*Harry Potter and The Sorcerer's Stone,
The Tailor of Panama*)

# ACADEMY AWARD WINNER
## FOR BEST PICTURE OF 2001

Russell Crowe, Ed Harris

Russell Crowe

## A BEAUTIFUL MIND

(UNIVERSAL/DREAMWORKS) Producer, Brian Grazer; Executive Producers, Karen Kehela, Todd Hallowell; Director, Ron Howard; Screenplay, Akiva Goldsman; Based on the book by Sylvia Nasar; Photography, Roger Deakins; Designer, Wynn Thomas; Costumes, Rita Ryack; Editors, Mike Hill, Dan Hanley; Music, James Horner; Co-Producer, Maureen Peyrot; Casting, Jane Jenkins, Janet Hirshenson; an Imagine Entertainment presentation of a Brian Grazer production; Dolby; Deluxe color; Rated PG-13; 134 minutes; Release date: December 21, 2001

### CAST

| | |
|---|---|
| John Forbes Nash, Jr. | Russell Crowe |
| William Parcher | Ed Harris |
| Alicia Larde Nash | Jennifer Connelly |
| Dr. Rosen | Christopher Plummer |
| Charles Herman | Paul Bettany |
| Sol | Adam Goldberg |
| Hansen | Josh Lucas |
| Marcee | Vivien Cardone |
| Bender | Anthony Rapp |
| Ainsley | Jason Gray-Stanford |
| Helinger | Judd Hirsch |
| Thomas King | Austin Pendleton |
| Professor Horner | Victor Steinbach |
| Becky | Tanya Clarke |
| Captain | Thomas F. Walsh |
| General | Jesse Doran |
| Analyst | Kent Cassella |
| MIT Student | Patrick Blindauer |
| Photographer | John Blaylock |
| Governor | Roy Thinnes |
| Young Man | Anthony Easton |
| Harvard Administrator | Cheryl Howard |
| White-Haired Patron | Rance Howard |
| Code-Red Nurse | JJ Chaback |
| Adjunct | Darius Stone |
| Princeton Professor | Josh Pais |
| Toby | Alex Toma |
| Joyce | Valentina Cardinalli |
| Young Professor | Teagle F. Bougere |
| Bar Co-ed | Jill M. Simon |
| Josh Nash, Jr. (13 years old) | David B. Allen |
| Josh Nash, Jr. (20 years old) | Michael Esper |
| Girl at Bar | Catharina Eva Burkley |
| Blonde in Bar | Amy Walz |

Insulin Treatment Nurses .................Kathleen Fellegara, Betsy Klompus and Tracey Toomey, Jennifer Weedon, Yvonne Thomas, Holly Pitrago (Brunettes), Isadore Rosenfeld, Thomas C. Allen, Dave Bayer, Brian Keith Lewis, Tom McNutt, Will Dunham, Glenn Roberts, Ed Jupp (Pen Ceremony Professors), Christopher Stockton, Gregory Dress, Carla Occhiogrosso, Matt Samson, Lyena Nomura (Princeton Students), Stelio Savante, Logan McCall, Bob Broder (Technicians)

*John Nash, an eccentric but brilliant mathematician, is recruited to work as a code breaker during the Cold War, only to find his work hampered when he is diagnosed with paranoid schizophrenia.*

*2001 Academy Award-winner for Best Picture, Director, Supporting Actress (Jennifer Connelly), and Adapted Screenplay. This film received additional Oscar nominations for actor (Russell Crowe), editing, original score, and makeup.*

Russell Crowe, Christopher Plummer, Jennifer Connelly

© Universal Studios

Russell Crowe

Russell Crowe, Paul Bettany

Anthony Rapp, Adam Goldberg, Jennifer Connelly

Russell Crowe, Jennifer Connelly

**DENZEL WASHINGTON**

in *Training Day* © Warner Bros.

## ACADEMY AWARD FOR BEST ACTOR OF 2001

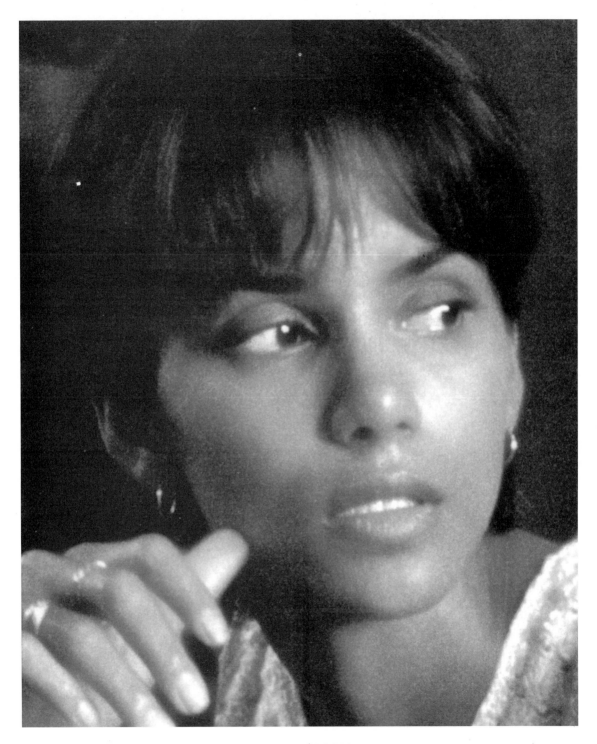

## HALLE BERRY

in *Monster's Ball* © Lions Gate Films

### ACADEMY AWARD FOR BEST ACTRESS OF 2001

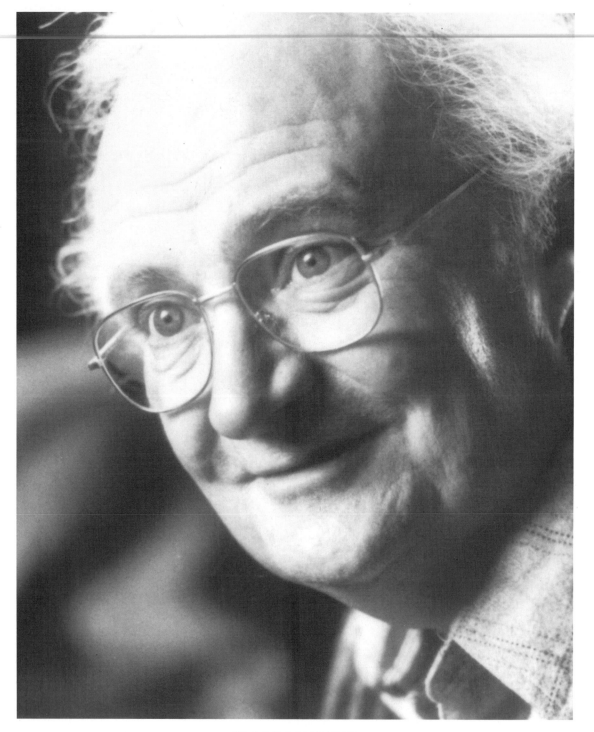

**JIM BROADBENT**

in *Iris* © Miramax Films

ACADEMY AWARD FOR BEST SUPPORTING ACTOR OF 2001

**JENNIFER CONNELLY**

in *A Beautiful Mind* © Universal Studios

## ACADEMY AWARD FOR BEST SUPPORTING ACTRESS OF 2001

# ACADEMY AWARD NOMINEES
## FOR BEST ACTOR

Russell Crowe in *A Beautiful Mind*

Sean Penn in *I Am Sam*

Will Smith in *Ali*

Tom Wilkinson in *In The Bedroom*

# ACADEMY AWARD NOMINEES
## FOR BEST ACTRESS

Judi Dench in *Iris*

Nicole Kidman in *Moulin Rouge!*

Sissy Spacek in *In The Bedroom*

Renée Zellweger in *Bridget Jones's Diary*

# ACADEMY AWARD NOMINEES
## FOR BEST SUPPORTING ACTOR

Ethan Hawke in *Training Day*

Ben Kingsley in *Sexy Beast*

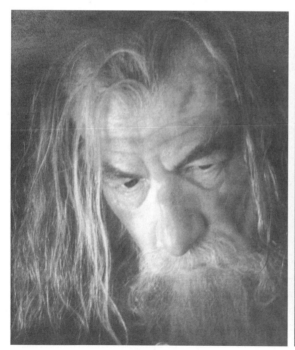

Ian McKellen in *The Lord of the Rings: The Fellowship of the Ring*

Jon Voight in *Ali*

# ACADEMY AWARD NOMINEES
## FOR BEST ACTRESS

Judi Dench in *Iris*

Nicole Kidman in *Moulin Rouge!*

Sissy Spacek in *In The Bedroom*

Renée Zellweger in *Bridget Jones's Diary*

# ACADEMY AWARD NOMINEES
## FOR BEST SUPPORTING ACTOR

Ethan Hawke in *Training Day*

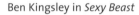

Ben Kingsley in *Sexy Beast*

Ian McKellen in *The Lord of the Rings:
The Fellowship of the Ring*

Jon Voight in *Ali*

# ACADEMY AWARD NOMINEES
## FOR BEST SUPPORTING ACTRESS

Helen Mirren in *Gosford Park*

Maggie Smith in *Gosford Park*

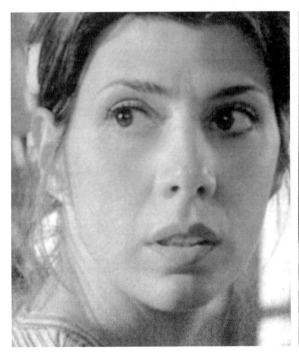

Marisa Tomei in *In The Bedroom*

Kate Winslet in *Iris*

# ACADEMY AWARD WINNER
## FOR BEST FOREIGN LANGUAGE FILM

Rene Bitorajac, Branko Djuric

Rene Bitorajac

## NO MAN'S LAND

(UNITED ARTISTS) Producers, Frédérique Dumas-Zajdela, Marc Baschet, Cedomir Kilar; Co-Producers, Marco Müller, Marion Hänsel, Cat Villiers, Judy Counihan, Dunja Klemenc, Igor Pedicek; Director/Screenplay, Danis Tanovic; Photography, Walther Vanden Ende; Designer, Dusko Milavec; Costumes, Zvonka Makuc; Music, Danis Tanovic; Editor, Francesca Calvelli A.M.C.; a Noé Productions production in co-production with Fabrica Cinema (Italy), Man's Films (Belgium), and with Counihan Villiers Productions (United Kingdom), Studio Maj/Casablanca (Slovenia) in collaboration with the Centre du Cinema et de l'Audiovisuel de la Communauté Française de Belgique and the Télédistributeurs Wallons and Le Fonds Slovène du Cinéma; French-Italian-Belgian-British-Slovenian; Dolby; Color; Rated R; 97 minutes; U.S. release date: December 7, 2001

### CAST

| | |
|---|---|
| Ciki | Branko Djuric |
| Nino | Rene Bitorajac |
| Cera | Filip Sovagovic |
| Marchand | Georges Siatidis |
| Dubois | Serge-Henri Valcke |
| Michel | Sacha Kremer |
| Pierre | Alain Eloy |
| Old Serbian Soldier | Mustafa Nadarevic |
| Serbian Officer | Bogdan Diklic |
| Colonel Soft | Simon Callow |
| Jane Livingstone | Katrin Cartlidge |
| Martha | Tanja Ribic |
| Démineur | Branko Zavrsan |
| Bosnian Guide | Djuro Utjesanovic |
| Bosnian Officer | Mirza Tanovic |

and Boro Stjepanovic, Almir Kurt, Ratko Ristic, Peter Sedmak, Aleksandar Petrovic (Bosnian Soldiers), Boris Cindric (Miralem), Danijel Smon (Serbian Officer 2), Peter Prikratki, Marinko Prga, Darjan Gorela, Srecko Dzumber (Serbian Soldiers), Primoz Ranik (Cameraman), Jure Plesec (Mark), Gordon Wilson (John), Maëlys De Rudder (Olivia), Alan Fairairn (Bill), Michel Obenga, Rok Strehovec (UNPROFOR Soldiers), Zvone Hribar, Ales Valic, Fred M. Liss, Franc Jakob Rac (Journalists), Predrag Brestovac (Rambo), Tadej Troha (Young Bosnian Soldier), Primoz Petrovsek (Serbian Lieutenant, Barricade), Janez Habic (Serbian Soldier, Barricade), Matej Bizjak (Boy Accordionist), Uros Tatomir (Serbian Sergeant), Matej Recer (Bosnian Officer, Barricade), Matija Bulatovic, Uros Furst (Bosnian Soldiers, Barricade)

*A Bosnian and Serbian soldier are stuck in a trench between enemy lines with a wounded soldier, who is lying on a spring-loaded bomb set to explode if he moves.*

Katrin Cartlidge, George Siantidis, Simon Callow

Branko Djuric, Rene Bitorajac

Katrin Cartlidge, Georges Siatidis

Branko Djuric, Rene Bitorajac

Rene Bitorajac, Branko Djuric

Katrin Cartlidge

# TOP BOX OFFICE FILMS
## OF 2001

1. Harry Potter and the Sorcerer's Stone (WB).....................$317,560,000
2. The Lord of the Rings: The Fellowship of the Ring (NL) .......$312,970,000
3. Shrek (DW) ............................................................$267,670,000
4. Monsters, Inc. (BV) ..................................................$255,160,000
5. Rush Hour 2 (NL)......................................................$225,170,000
6. The Mummy Returns (Univ) ........................................$201,900,000
7. Pearl Harbor (BV) .....................................................$198,500,000
8. Ocean's Eleven (WB) .................................................$183,260,000
9. Jurassic Park III (Univ) .............................................$180,190,000
10. Planet of the Apes (20th)...........................................$180,100,000

Milo Thatch in *Atlantis, The Lost Empire*
© Walt Disney Pictures

Daniel Radcliffe in *Harry Potter and The Sorcerer's Stone*
© Warner Bros.

11. A Beautiful Mind (Univ/DW) .......................................$170,710,000
12. Hannibal (MGM/Univ)................................................$165,100,000
13. The Fast and the Furious (Univ) ....................................$144,450,000
14. American Pie 2 (Univ)................................................$144,100,000
15. Lara Croft: Tomb Raider (Par) ......................................$131,170,000
16. Spy Kids (Mir) ........................................................$112,720,000
17. Dr. Dolittle 2 (20th).................................................$111,910,000
18. Black Hawk Down (Col)...............................................$108,270,000
19. The Princess Diaries (BV) ...........................................$108,250,000
20. Vanilla Sky (Par) .....................................................$100,540,000
21. The Others (Mir)......................................................$96,530,000
22. Legally Blonde (MGM) ...............................................$96,450,000
23. America's Sweethearts (Col) ........................................$93,520,000
24. Cats & Dogs (WB).....................................................$93,270,000
25. Save the Last Dance (Par) ...........................................$91,100,000

26. Atlantis: The Lost Empire (BV).......................................$83,920,000
27. Jimmy Neutron: Boy Genius (Par)....................................$80,930,000
28. AI: Artificial Intelligence (WB)........................................$78,580,000
29. Training Day (WB)....................................................$76,190,000
30. Along Came a Spider (Par) ...........................................$74,100,000
31. Bridget Jones's Diary (Mir/Univ).....................................$71,550,000
32. The Score (Par) .......................................................$70,990,000
33. Shallow Hal (20th) ...................................................$70,770,000
34. Scary Movie 2 (Mir) ..................................................$70,310,000
35. Swordfish (WB) .......................................................$69,670,000
36. The Mexican (DW) ....................................................$66,850,000
37. Down to Earth (Par) ..................................................$64,150,000
38. Spy Game (Univ) ......................................................$62,370,000
39. The Wedding Planner (Col) ..........................................$60,410,000
40. Behind Enemy Lines (20th) ..........................................$58,770,000

Renée Zellweger in
*Bridget Jones's Diary*
© Miramax Films

41. Ali (Col) ...............................................................$58,120,000
42. Moulin Rouge! (20th) ................................................$57,230,000
43. Rat Race (Par) .........................................................$56,620,000
44. A Knight's Tale (Col) .................................................$55,790,000
45. The Animal (Col) ......................................................$55,690,000
46. Don't Say a Word (20th) ..............................................$54,940,000
47. The Royal Tenenbaums (BV) ..........................................$52,310,000
48. Blow (NL).............................................................$51,880,000
49. Exit Wounds (WB) ....................................................$51,470,000
50. Enemy at the Gates (Par)..............................................$50,880,000

Nicole Kidman, Ewan
McGregor in *Moulin Rouge!*
© Twentieth Century Fox

51. K-PAX (Univ) .................................................$50,340,000
52. Serendipity (Mir) .............................................$50,300,000
53. Kate & Leopold (Mir) .......................................$47,100,000
54. Zoolander (Par) ...............................................$45,140,000
55. Domestic Disturbance (Par) ..............................$45,100,000
56. The One (Col) .................................................$43,910,000
57. Thirteen Ghosts (WB/Col) .................................$41,770,000
58. Bandits (MGM) ...............................................$41,480,000
59. Gosford Park (USA Films) .................................$41,280,000

Meg Ryan, Hugh Jackman in *Kate & Leopold*
© Miramax Films

60. I Am Sam (NL) ...............................................$40,270,000
61. Hardball (Par) ................................................$40,230,000
62. Heartbreakers (MGM) ......................................$40,150,000
63. Evolution (DW/Col) .........................................$38,350,000
64. Not Another Teen Movie (Col) ...........................$37,890,000
65. Jeepers Creepers (UA) ......................................$37,830,000
66. Kiss of the Dragon (20th) ................................$36,770,000
67. Recess: School's Out (BV) ................................$36,600,000
68. In the Bedroom (Mir) ......................................$35,880,000
69. Black Knight (20th) .........................................$33,370,000
70. See Spot Run (WB) ..........................................$33,240,000
71. Amélie (Mir) ..................................................$33,180,000
72. Driven (WB) ...................................................$32,590,000
73. What's the Worst That Could Happen? (MGM) ............$32,130,000
74. Final Fantasy (Col) ..........................................$32,100,000
75. From Hell (20th) .............................................$31,560,000

Justin Long, Gina Philips in *Jeepers Creepers*
© United Artists Films

76. Monster's Ball (Lions Gate) ..............................$31,260,000
77. How High (Univ) .............................................$31,160,000
78. Jay and Silent Bob Strike Back (Mir) ..................$30,100,000
79. Riding in Cars With Boys (Col) .........................$29,790,000
80. Double Take (BV) .............................................$29,550,000
81. Baby Boy (Col) ...............................................$28,360,000
82. The Majestic (WB) ...........................................$27,800,000
83. The Brothers (Screen Gems) ..............................$27,410,000
84. Someone Like You (20th) ..................................$27,180,000
85. The Musketeer (Univ) ......................................$27,100,000
86. Joe Dirt (Col) .................................................$26,970,000
87. Crocodile Dundee in Los Angeles (Par) ...............$25,540,000
88. Captain Corelli's Mandolin (Univ) .....................$25,500,000
89. Memento (Newmarket) .....................................$25,440,000
90. Sweet November (WB) .....................................$25,180,000

Drew Barrymore, Steve Zahn, Cody Arens in *Riding in Cars With Boys* © Columbia Pictures

91. 15 Minutes (New Line) ....................................$24,410,000
92. Angel Eyes (WB) .............................................$24,100,000
93. Hearts in Atlantis (WB) ...................................$23,950,000
94. Corky Romano (BV) .........................................$23,940,000
95. Heist (WB) .....................................................$23,410,000
96. Kingdom Come (Fox Search) ............................$23,100,000
97. Joe Somebody (20th) .......................................$22,670,000
98. Joy Ride (20th) ...............................................$21,950,000
99. Two Can Play That Game (Screen Gems) ............$21,770,000
100. Valentine (WB) ..............................................$20,360,000

Milla Jovovich, Ben Stiller, Will Ferrell in *Zoolander*
© Paramount Pictures

# FOREIGN FILMS
## RELEASED IN THE US IN 2001

### THE PERSONALS

(FIRST RUN FEATURES) Producer, Hsu Li-kong; Executive Producer, Hsu Li-kong, Chiu Shun-Ching; Director, Chen Kuo-fu; Screenplay, Chen Kuo-fu, Chen Shih-che; Story, Chen Yu-hui; Photography, Ho Nan-hong; Art Director, Wang Yi-bai; Editor, Chang Dar-lung; from Zoom Hunt Int. Productions Co. Ltd., Central Motion Picture Corporation; Taiwan, 2000; Dolby; Color; Not rated; 104 minutes; U.S. release date: January 12, 2001

#### CAST

Du Jiazhen .................................................................Rene Liu
and Chin Shih-chieh, Chen Chao-jung, Wu Bai, Gu Bao-ming, Niu Chen-zer, Shih Yi-nan, Teddy Lo, Sisy Chen, Pu Hsueh-liang

*A successful young eye doctor places a personal ad in the newspaper in order to land a husband and meets up with each of the men who respond.*

© First Run Features

Bibiana Beglau, Alexander Beyer

Bibiana Beglau, Nadja Uhl

Rene Liu (right)

### THE LEGEND OF RITA

(KINO) Producers, Arthur Hofer, Emmo Lempert; Director, Volker Schlöndorff; Screenplay, Wolfgang Kohlhaase, Volker Schlöndorff; Photography, Andreas Höfer, BVK; Art Director, Susanne Hopf; Editor, Peter Przygodda; Costumes, Anne-Gret Oehme; a Babelsberg Film Produktion in association with Mitteldeutsches Filmkontor and MDR; German, 1999; Dolby; Color; Not rated; 101 minutes; U.S. release date: January 24, 2001

#### CAST

Rita ...............................................................................Bibiana Beglau
Erwin Hull ....................................................................Martin Wuttke
Tatjana ..........................................................................Nadja Uhl
Andi ..............................................................................Harald Schrott
Jochen ...........................................................................Alexander Beyer
Friederike ......................................................................Jenny Schily
Klatte.............................................................................Mario Irrek
Gerngross ......................................................................Thomas Arnold
Anna..............................................................................Franca Kastein
The General ...................................................................Dietrich Körner
Milchgesicht ..................................................................Richard Kropf

*Rita, a former West German terrorist, hides out in East Germany, assuming a new identity among the working class until her past catches up with her.*

© Kino International

# FAITHLESS

(GOLDWYN) Producer, Kaj Larsen; Executive Producer, Maria Curman; Director, Liv Ullmann; Screenplay, Ingmar Bergman; Photography, Jörgen Persson FSF; Art Director, Göran Wassberg; Costumes, Inger E Pehrsson; Editor, Sylvia Ingemarsson; an SVT Drama production in collaboration with AB Svensk Filmindustri, NRK, Yle, Classic SRL, RAI and ZDF, with the support of the Swedish Film Institute, Film Commissioner Mats Aréhn and Nordic Film and TV Fund; Presented in association with Fireworks Pictures; Swedish, 2000; Dolby; Color; Rated R; 142 minutes; US release date: January 26, 2001

## CAST

| | |
|---|---|
| Marianne Vogler | Lena Endre |
| Bergman | Erland Josephson |
| David | Krister Henriksson |
| Markus Vogler | Thomas Hanzon |
| Isabelle | Michelle Gylemo |
| Margareta | Juni Dahr |
| Martin Goldman | Philip Zanden |
| Petra Holst | Therese Brunnander |
| Anna Berg | Marie Richardson |
| Eva | Stina Ekblad |
| Johan | Johan Rabaeus |
| Axel | Jan-Olof Strandberg |
| Gustav | Björn Granath |
| Martha | Gertrud Stenung |

*Marianne, an actress married to an orchestra conductor, finds herself involved in an affair with a family friend, a reckless, gloomy film director.*

© Goldwyn/Fireworks

Alana De Roma, Rachel Griffiths

Krister Henriksson, Lena Endre

# AMY

(WORLD WIDE) Producers, Nadia Tass, David Parker; Director, Nadia Tass; Screenplay/Photography, David Parker; Co-Producer, Phil Jones; Designer, Jon Dowding; Editor, Bill Murphy; Costumes, Christiana Plitzco; Music, Phillip Judd; Australian, 1998; Color; Rated PG-13; 103 minutes; US release date: February 2, 2001

## CAST

| | |
|---|---|
| Tanya Rammus | Rachel Griffiths |
| Amy Enker | Alana De Roma |
| Robert Buchanan | Ben Mendelsohn |
| Will Enker | Nick Barker |
| Sarah Trendle | Kerry Armstrong |
| Zac Trendle | Jeremy Trigatti |
| Bill Trendle | William Zappa |
| Luke Lassiter | Torquil Neilson |
| Wayne Lassiter | Sullivan Stapleton |
| Mrs Mullins | Mary Ward |
| Anny Buchanan | Susie Porter |
| Dr Urquhart | Frank Gallacher |
| Susan Hammnett | Jan Friedl |
| Brian Cosgrove | Malcolm Kennard |
| Maurice Reitman | Jeremy Kewley |
| Franco Rammus | Osvaldo Maione |

*A little girl who has retreated into silence following her father's death is encouraged to communicate through music by her mother and by a young musician who lives next door.*

© Beyond Films Ltd.

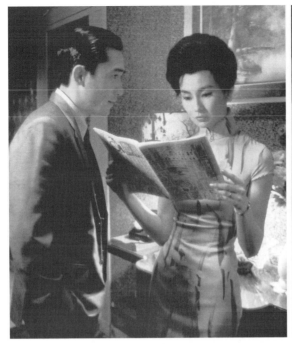

Tony Leung Chiu-wai, Maggie Cheung

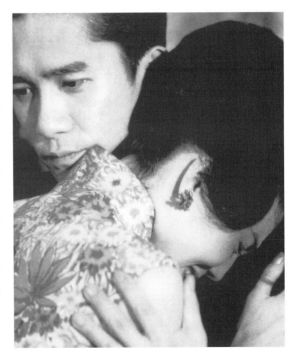

Maggie Cheung, Tony Leung Chiu-wai

# IN THE MOOD FOR LOVE

**(USA FILMS)** Producer/Director/Screenplay, Wong Kar-Wai; Executive Producer, Chan Ye-Cheng; Associate Producer, Jacky Pang Yee-Wah; Photography, Christopher Doyle, Mark Li Ping-Bin; Designer/Costumes, William Chang Suk-Ping; Music, Michael Galasso; a Block 2 Pictures, Inc and Paradis Films presentation of a Jet Tone Films production; Hong Kong-French, 2000; Dolby; Color; Rated PG; 97 minutes; US release date: February 2, 2001

## CAST

Chow Mo-wan .......................................................Tony Leung Chiu-wai
Su Li-zhen .........................................................................Maggie Cheung
Mrs Suen...........................................................................Rebecca Pan
Mr Ho .......................................................................................Lai Chin
Ah Pong ...............................................................................Siu Ping-lam
The Amah ..........................................................................Chin Tsi-ang
and Man-Lei Chan, Kan-wah Koo, Hsien Yu, Po-chun Chow

*In 1962 Hong Kong, a journalist and a secretary, living next door to one another, discover that their spouses are having an affair, leading them to spend a great deal of time together while trying not to act on their growing feelings for one another.*

© USA Films

Tony Leung Chiu-wai, Maggie Cheung

Fernando Ramallo, Jordi Vilches

## NICO AND DANI
### (KRÁMPACK)

**(AVATAR)** Producers, Marta Esteban, Gerardo Herrero; Director, Cesc Gay; Screenplay, Cesc Gay, Tomás Aragay; Based on the play *Krámpack* by Jordi Sánchez; Photography, Andreu Rebês; Music, Riqui Sabatés, Joan Díaz, Jordi Prats; Editor, Frank Gutiérrez; a Messidor Films production; Spanish, 2000; Dolby; Color; Not rated; 90 minutes; US release date: February 2, 2001

### CAST
| | |
|---|---|
| Dani | Fernando Ramallo |
| Nico | Jordi Vilches |
| Elena | Marieta Orozco |
| Berta | Esther Nubiola |
| Julián | Chisco Amado |
| Sonia | Ana Gracia |
| Marianne | Myriam Mézières |
| Dani's Mother | Muntsa Alcañiz |
| Dani's Father | Jesús Garay |
| Mario | Pau Durá |
| Camarero | Eduardo González |
| Chica | Gaelle Poulavec |
| Arturo | Mingo Ràfols |
| Manu | Eloi Yebra |

*During a summer on the Mediterranean coast, 17-year-old Dani's sexual experimentation with his best friend Nico brings him to the realization that he is attracted to men.*

© Avatar Films

Fernando Ramallo, Jordi Vilches

Jordi Vilches, Fernando Ramallo

Bud Cort, Jimmy Smits, Jeremy Davies

# THE MILLION DOLLAR HOTEL

(LIONS GATE) Producers, Deepak Nayar, Bono, Nicholas Klein, Bruce Davey, Wim Wenders; Executive Producer, Ulrich Felsberg; Director, Wim Wenders; Screenplay, Nicholas Klein; Story, Bono, Nicholas Klein; Photography, Phedon Papamichael; Designers, Robert D Freed, Arabella A Serrell; Music, Jon Hassell, Bono, Daniel Lanois, Brian Eno; Costumes, Nancy Steiner; Casting, Heidi Levitt, Monika Mikkelsen; an Icon Entertainment International presentation of a Road Movies production in association with Icon Productions and Kintop Pictures; German-US, 2000; Dolby; Panavision; Color; Rated R; 122 minutes; US release date: February 2, 2001

## CAST

| | |
|---|---|
| Tom Tom | Jeremy Davies |
| Eloise | Milla Jovovich |
| Detective Skinner | Mel Gibson |
| Geronimo | Jimmy Smits |
| Dixie | Peter Stormare |
| Vivien | Amanda Plummer |
| Jessica | Gloria Stuart |
| Hector | Tom Bower |
| Charley Best | Donal Logue |
| Shorty | Bud Cort |
| Terence Scopey | Julian Sands |
| Izzy Goldkiss | Tim Roth |
| Stix | Conrad Roberts |
| Stanley Goldkiss | Harris Yulin |
| Jean Swift | Charlayne Woodard |
| Marlene | Ellen Cleghorne |

and Richard Edson (Joe), Tito Larriva (Jesu), Jon Hassell (Hollow), Justin Lafoe (Marlene's Son), Ezra Buzzington (Reporter), David Stifel (Screamer for Jesus), Winston J. Rochas (Waiter), Frederique Van Der Wal (Diamond Woman), Roger Stoneburner, Erik Rondell (Punks), Bono (Man in Hotel Lobby)

*As childlike Tom Tom jumps from the roof of a shabby LA hotel, he narrates the events that led to this situation, starting when Detective Skinner arrived at the establishment to question its many oddball inhabitants concerning the death of resident Izzy Goldkiss.*

© Lions Gate Films

# THE TASTE OF OTHERS

(OFFLINE) Producers, Christian Bérard, Charles Gassot; Executive Producer, Jacques Hinstin; Director, Agnès Jaoui; Screenplay, Agnès Jaoui, Jean-Pierre Bacri; Photography, Laurent Dailland; Designer, François Emmanuelli; Line Producer, Daniel Chevalier; Editor, Hervé De Luze; Costumes, Jackie Stephens-Budin; Casting, Brigitte Moidon; Presented in association with Miramax Films, Sagittarius Films; French, 2000; Dolby; Super 35 Widescreen; Color; Not rated; 112 minutes; US release date: February 9, 2001

## CAST

| | |
|---|---|
| Clara | Anne Alvaro |
| Castella | Jean-Pierre Bacri |
| Beatrice | Brigitte Catillon |
| Deschamps | Alain Chabat |
| Manie | Agnès Jaoui |
| Moreno | Gerard Lanvin |
| Valerie | Anne Le Ny |
| Angelique | Christiane Millet |
| Antoine | Wladimir Yordanoff |
| Weber | Xavier de Guillebon |
| Benoît | Raphael Dufour |
| Fred | Bob Zarembar |

and Sam Karmann (The Director), Marie-Agnes Brigot (The Secretary), Robert Bacri (Castella's Father), Desir Carre (Passerby), Celine Arnaud (Virginie), Reginald Huguenin (Titus), Jean-Marc Talbot (Antiochus), Jean-François Levistre (Arsace), Didier Mahieu (Hedda's Husband), Stanislas de la Tousche (The Judge)

*Castella, a married man obsessed with Clara, an actress he has seen in a play, is delighted to discover that she is his new English instructor.*

© Artistic License Films

Jean-Pierre Bacri, Anne Alvaro

Regina Casé, Luiz Carlos Vasconcelos

Lima Duarte

## ME YOU THEM

**(SONY PICTURES CLASSICS)** Producers, Andrucha Waddington, Flávio R Tambellini, Pedro B. de Hollanda, Leonardo M. de Barros; Director, Andrucha Waddington; Screenplay, Elena Soárez; Photography, Breno Silveira; Designer, Toni Vanzolini; Costumes, Claudia Kopke; Editor, Vicente Kubrusly; Music, Gilberto Gil; Line Producer, Mariza Figueiredo; Associate Producer, Flora Gil; a Conspiração Filmes, Columbia TriStar Filmes do Brasil presentation; Brazilian-Portuguese, 2000; Dolby; Color; Rated PG-13; 107 minutes; US release date: March 2, 2001

### CAST

| | |
|---|---|
| Darlene | Regina Casé |
| Osias Linares | Lima Duarte |
| Zezinho | Stênio Garcia |
| Ciro | Luís Carlos Vasconcelos |
| Raquel | Nilda Spencer |
| Black Herdsman | Diogo Lopes |
| Darlene's Mother | Helena Araújo |

and Iami Rebouças (Young Woman at Ball), Lucien Paulo (Headman), Borges Cunha (Registry Employee), Plácido Alves Neto (Store Owner), D Dinorah (Osias's Mother), José Pascoal (Young Man at Ball), Zé Brocoió, Clésio Atanásio (Speakers), Fransico Alves Torres (Darlene's Brother), D Maria Isabel Borges, Maria do Roasio, D Luzia Gomes (Mourners), Tarjino Gondim e Banda (Band at São João Festival), Grupo Senhor do Bonfim (Forró Band #1, Darlene's Wedding), Sérgio do Forró e Banda (Forró Band #2), Herbert Medrado (Dimas—1 year old), Joanderson Cruz (Dimas—4 years old), Jocemar Damásio (Dimas—6 years old), Arielson Dos Santos (Baby Edinardo), Pablo Silva (Edinardo—1 year old), Jefferson Souza (Edinardo—4 years old), Vitor Da Conceição (Edinardo—6 years old), Lucas De Castro Silva (Baby Edinaldo), João Lucas De Barros Neto (Edinaldo—1 year old), Jonathan Dantas (Edinaldo—4 years old), Alessandro Dos Santos Ribeiro (Baby Edivaldi)

*Years after Darlene had been abandoned at the altar while pregnant, she moves in with elderly Osias Linhares and becomes lovers with two other men while living in Osias's household.*

© Sony Pictures Entertainment

## LAST RESORT

**(SHOOTING GALLERY)** Producer, Ruth Caleb; Executive Producers, David M Thompson, Alex Holmes; Director/Screenplay, Pavel Pawlikwoski; Photography, Ryszard Lenczewski; Designer, Tom Bowyer; Editor, David Charap; Music, Max de Wardener, Rowan Oliver; Costumes, Julian Day; Casting, Chloe Emerson; from BBC Films; British; Dolby; Soho Images Color; Not rated; 73 minutes; US release date: February 23, 2001

### CAST

| | |
|---|---|
| Tanya | Dina Korzun |
| Alfie | Paddy Considine |
| Artiom | Artiom Strelnikov |
| Les | Lindsey Honey |
| Immigration Officer | Perry Benson |
| Katie | Katie Drinkwater |
| Frank | David Bean |

and Adrian Scarborough, David Auker (Council Officials), Bruce Byron (Police Officer), Jim Trevelyan (Station Guard), Marcus Redwood (Cafe Owner), Zoe Sharpe (Gang Girl), Daniel Mobey (Danny)

*Arriving with her young son in England, where she expects to meet her fiancé, a Russian woman is detained by immigration and taken to a holding area, where she and her child are befriended by an amusement park worker.*

Paddy Considine, Artiom Strelnikov, Dina Korzun

Juliette Binoche

Emir Kusturica

# THE WIDOW OF SAINT-PIERRE

(**LIONS GATE**) Producers, Gilles Legrand, Frédéric Brillion; Director, Patrice Leconte; Screenplay, Claude Faraldo; Adaptation, Patrice Leconte, Michel Duchaussoy, Philippe Magnan, Christian Charmetant, Philippe du Janerand; Photography, Eduardo Sarra; Editor, Joëlle Hache; Designer, Ivan Maussion; Costumes, Christian Gasc; Co-Producers, Denise Robert, Daniel Louis; Music, Pascal Esteve; Directors of Production, Frederic Blum, Paul Laine; an Epithete Films, Cinemaginaire, France 3 Cinema, France 2 Cinema production, with the participation of CNC Canal+, Telefilm Canada Sodec; French-Canadian, 2000; Dolby; Panavision; Color; Rated R; 108 minutes; US release date: March 2, 2001

## CAST

Daniel Auteuil

| | |
|---|---|
| Madame La (Pauline) | Juliette Binoche |
| The Captain (Jean) | Daniel Auteuil |
| Ariel Neel Auguste | Emir Kusturica |
| Judge Venot | Philippe Magnan |
| The Governor | Michel Duchaussoy |
| Supply and Secretariat Officer | Christian Charmetant |
| Customs Officer | Philippe Du Janerand |
| Louis Olivier | Reynald Bouchard |
| M Chevassus | Ghyslain Tremblay |
| Soldier Loic | Marc Béland |
| The Rear-Admiral | Yves Jacques |
| The Governor's Father | Maurice Chevit |
| La Malvilain | Catherine Lascault |
| The Proprietor | Dominique Quesnel |
| The Governor's Wife | Anne-Marie Philipe |
| President Venot's Wife | Isabelle Spade |
| The Governor's Children | Arianne Mallet, Julian Gutierrez |
| Adrienne | Sylvie Moreau |

and Geneviève Cocke, Manon Gauthier (Washhouse Women), Marianne C Miron (Mme Chevassus), Jean-Paul Rouvray (The Priest), Michel Daigle (Father Coupard), Luc Guerin (Captain Dumontier), Niel Kroetsch (Captain of the Marie Galante), Sylvain Eluau (Captain Goelette), Raymond Cloutier (The Adjutant), Patrick Steltzer (The Brigadier), Patrick Caux (Young Soldier), Bernard Tanguay (The Orderly), Serge Christiaenssens (The Drummer), Martin Laroque (Town Crier), Boris Napes (Assessor), Yvon Roy (Granjean), Luc Proulx (Cafe Customer), Kendall Negro (The Child), Stefan Perrault (Oarsman), Sarah McKenna (Emilie)

*On the island of Saint-Pierre, a man awaiting execution for accidentally killing someone during a drunken altercation is placed in custody of the French military commandant and his wife, who begins to question the justice of the death penalty.*

Juliette Binoche, Daniel Auteuil

© Lions Gate Films

# THE GLEANERS AND I

(ZEITGEIST) Director/Narrator, Agnès Varda; Photography, Stéphane Krausz, Didier Rouget, Didier Doussin, Pascal Sautelet, Agnès Varda; Music, Joanna Bruzdowicz; Editors, Agnès Varda, Laurent Pineau; Produced by Ciné Tamaris, with the help of Centre National de la Cinematographie, Procirep and Canal+; French, 2000; Color; Not rated; 82 minutes; US release date: March 7, 2001 A documentary–road-trip throughout France capturing images of gleaners, people who scavenge or pick up items left behind by others

© Zeitgeist Films

Agnès Varda

Rachel Griffiths, Natasha Richardson, Alan Rickman

Josh Hartnett, Rachael Leigh Cook

# BLOW DRY

(MIRAMAX) Producers, Ruth Jackson, William Horberg, David Rubin; Executive Producers, Sydney Pollack, Meryl Poster, Julie Goldstein; Director, Paddy Breathnach; Screenplay, Simon Beaufoy, based on his screenplay *Never Better*; Photography, Cian De Buitléar; Designer, Sophie Becher; Costumes, Rosie Hackett; Co-Producer, Mark Cooper; Associate Producer, David Brown; Music, Patrick Doyle; Make-up and Hair Designer, Jenny Shircore; Casting, Gail Stevens; an Intermedia Films presentation of a Mirage Enterprises/West Eleven Production in association with IMF Productions; British-US; Dolby; Technicolor; Rated R; 90 minutes; US release date: March 7, 2001

## CAST

| | |
|---|---|
| Phil Allen | Alan Rickman |
| Shelly | Natasha Richardson |
| Sandra | Rachel Griffiths |
| Christina Robertson | Rachael Leigh Cook |
| Brian Allen | Josh Harnett |
| Ray Robertson | Bill Nighy |
| Tony | Warren Clarke |
| Daisy | Rosemary Harris |
| Louis | Hugh Bonneville |
| Jasmine | Heidi Klum |
| Vincent | Peter McDonald |
| Robert | Michael McElhatton |
| Noah | David Bradley |
| Saul | Ben Crompton |

and Anne Rye (Margaret, Farmer's Wife), Ray Emmet Brown (TJ), Oliver Ford Davies (Dr Hamilton), Elizabeth Woodcock (Sharon), Mark Benton (George, Journalist #1), Gordon Langford-Rowe (Stanley, Journalist #2), Johnny Leeze (Journalist), Stephen Graham (Photographer), Willie Ross (Louis's Volunteer), Jukka Hiltunen (Biker Volunteer), Paul Copley (Ken), Lorraine Balinska (Ebony), Peter Kay (Cyril the Barman), Janet Henfrey (Aerobics Teacher), Tony Barton, Philip Wright (Workmen), Margaret Blakemore (Receptionist)

*Previous two-time winner of the British Hairdressing Championships, Phil Allen, finds himself facing some stiff competition from reigning champion Ray Robertson, his former rival.*

© Miramax Films

Peter McDonald, Flora Montgomery

# SIMON MAGUS

(FIREWORKS) Producer, Robert Jones; Director/Screenplay, Ben Hopkins; Photography, Nic Knowland; Designer, Angela Davies; Costumes, Michelle Clapton; Line Producer, Anita Overland; Editor, Alan Levy; Music, Deborah Mollison; Casting, Susie Figgis; a FilmFour, Lucky Red, ARP and Hollywood Partners in association with the Arts Council of England presentation of a Jonescompany production; British-German-Italian-French, 1999; Dolby; Super 35 Widescreen; Deluxe color; Not rated; 106 minutes; US release date: March 9, 2001

## CAST

| | |
|---|---|
| Simon Magus | Noah Taylor |
| Dovid | Stuart Townsend |
| Maximilian Hase | Sean McGinley |
| Leah | Embeth Davidtz |
| Sarah | Amanda Ryan |
| Squire | Rutger Hauer |
| Sirius/Boris | Ian Holm |
| Bratislav | Terence Rigby |
| Buchholz | Toby Jones |
| Saul | Jim Dunk |
| Rebecca | Ursula Jones |
| Chaim | Cyril Shaps |

and David De Keyser (Rabbi), Ken Dury (Priest), Tom Fisher (Thomas), Walter Sparrow (Benjamin), Jean Anderson (Roise), Katharine Schlesinger (Askha), Valerie Edmond (Eva), Kathryn Hunter (Grandmother), Maggie Steed (Muttchen), Mimi Potworowska (Angel), Barry Davis (Samuel the Cook), Frank Chersky (Feyder the Forester), Lawrence Werber (Zeidel the Carter), Hayley Carmichael (Rabbit Woman), Phil McKee (Railway Man), Brendan Charleson (Hireling 1), Nitzan Sharron (Joshua—21 years old), Joseph England (Elijah), Joel Freeman (Aaron), Nathan Grower (Anshel), Zoe Buckman (Beyle), Camilla Mars (Shifrah), Sam Davies (Joseph), Joshua Morris (Getsl), Jacob Morris (Simcha), Lexi Rose (Miryem), Elizabeth Margitta Miller (Rachel), Thomas Ingram (Gimpel), James Lewys Cox (Young Joshua), Linden Watts (Matthis), Isla Graham (Railway Man's Daughter)

*In a small 19th-century European village, ruthless businessman Maximilian Hase, eager to bring his town into modern times by the building of a railroad station, enlists the help of outcast Simon Magus to help him plot against his rivals.*

© Fireworks Pictures

# WHEN BRENDAN MET TRUDY

(SHOOTING GALLERY) Producer, Lynda Myles; Executive Producers, David M Thompson, Mike Phillips, Rod Stoneman, Claire Duignan; Director, Kieron J. Walsh; Screenplay/Co-Producer, Roddy Doyle; Photography, Ashley Rowe; Designer, Fiona Daly; Costumes, Consolata Boyle; Editor, Scott Thomas; Music, Richard Hartley; Casting, Leo Davis; a BBC Films, Bord Scannán na hÉireann/The Irish Film Board and Radio Telefís Éireann presentation of a Deadly Films 2 production of a Collins aVenue Film; British-Irish; Dolby; Color; Not rated; 95 minutes; US release date: March 9, 2001

## CAST

| | |
|---|---|
| Brendan | Peter McDonald |
| Trudy | Flora Montgomery |
| Mother | Marie Mullen |
| Nuala | Pauline McLynn |
| Niall | Don Wycherley |
| Edgar | Maynard Eziashi |
| Siobhan | Eileen Walsh |
| Headmaster | Barry Cassin |
| Judge | Niall O'Brien |
| Lynn | Rynagh O'Grady |
| Mary | Ali White |

and Julie Hale, Christ McHallem (Choirsters), Jack Lynch (Conductor), Dr Stewart, Charlie Bird, Gabriel Byrne (Themselves), Robert O'Neill (Dylan), Eoin Manley (Cyril), George McMahon (James), Sean O'Flanagan (Eric), Pat Kinevane, Terry Byrne, Myles Horgan (Teachers), Anne Cassin (Newsreader), Harry Crosbie (Reporter), Luke Boyle (Flach), William O'Sullivan (Oisin), Jonathan White (Wig Man), Philip Judge (Garda Spokesman), Alicia O'Keeffe (Young Woman at Filmhaus), Kieron J Walsh (Young Man at Filmhaus), Berts Folan (School Caretaker), Kevin Sharkey (Celtic Cub), Robbie Doolin (Security Man), Keith McErlean , Martin Murphy, Frank O'Sullivan (Garda), Nuala Kelly, Triona McGarry, Jim Corry (Prison Officers), Ding Dong Denny O'Reilly and the Hairy Bowsies (Pub Band), Conor Evans (Doctor), Patricia Martin (Mrs O'Shaughnessy), Susan Murray, Gail Kainswarren (Wings Women), Amelia Crowley (Bookshop Babe), Robert Mack, James Mack, Coco Kenny, Francis Schurmann, Shauna Nugent (Brendan and Trudy's Children)

*Brendan, a shy high-school teacher, meets Trudy, a free-spirited young woman who turns out to be a cat burglar.*

Noah Taylor

Stuart Townsend, Embeth Davidtz

Sam Neill, Kevin Harrington, Tom Long

# THE DISH

**(WARNER BROS)** Producers, Santo Cilauro, Tom Gleisner, Jane Kennedy, Rob Sitch, Michael Hirsch; Director, Rob Sitch; Screenplay, Santo Cilauro, Tom Gleisner, Jane Kennedy, Rob Sitch; Photography, Graeme Wood; Designer, Carrie Kennedy; Editor, Jill Bilcock; Music, Edmund Choi; Costumes, Kitty Stuckey; Line Producer, Debra Choate; Casting, Jane Kennedy, Yeskel Hicks; a Working Dog presentation in association with Distant Horizon; Australian, 2000; Dolby; Color; Rated PG-13; 102 minutes; US release date: March 14, 2001

## CAST

| | |
|---|---|
| Cliff Buxton | Sam Neill |
| Ross "Mitch" Mitchell | Kevin Harrington |
| Glenn Latham | Tom Long |
| Al Burnett | Patrick Warburton |
| May McIntyre | Genevieve Mooy |
| Rudi Kellerman | Taylor Kane |
| Prime Minister | Bille Brown |
| Mayor Bob McIntyre | Roy Billing |
| Len Purvis | Andrew S. Gilbert |
| Marie McIntyre | Lenka Kripac |
| Keith Morrison | Matthew Moore |
| Janine Kellerman | Eliza Szonert |
| US Ambassador | John McMartin |
| Billy McIntyre | Carl Snell |
| Cameron | Billy Mitchell |
| Miss Nolan | Roz Hammond |
| Damien | Christopher Robin-Street |
| Graeme | Luke Keltie |
| Melanie | Naomi Wright |
| Nicholas | Ben Wright-Smith |

and Beverly Dunn (Secretary Voice-Over), Grant Thompson (Mr. Callen), Bernard Curry (Newspaper Reporter), Kerry Walker (Pearl), Denise Roberts (Bronwyn), Jeff Keogh (Ray), Jason Ritterman (Adrian Hobbs), Alexander Zent (Lead Guitarist), Rowan Macartney (Trumpet), Aidan Macartney (Trombone), Jarrod Factor (Drummer), Oliver McGill (Pianist), Marilyn O'Donnell (Melva), Jane Menelaus (Gwen), John Flaus (Ron), Neil Pigot (Journalist), Darren Davidson (Camera Person), Simon Donaldson (Sound Person), Frank Bennett (Barry Steele), Randall Berger (Ambassador's Aide), Charles "Bud" Tingwell (Reverend Loftus), Mal Walden (ABC Journalist Voice-Over), Rod McNeil (Radio Newsreader Voice-Over), Alister Paterson (ABC-TV Newsreader), Colette Mann (Betty the Bush Poet), Susan Ward (Print Journalist), Roger Crisp (Reporter)

*At Australia's largest satellite dish, Cliff Buxton and his team are chosen to track the progress of Apollo 11 over the southern hemisphere.*

© The Dish Film Productions PYY

Tom Long, Patrick Warburton, Sam Neill, Kevin Harrington

Tom Long

Kevin Harrington, Tom Long, Patrick Warburton, Sam Neill

Rachel Weisz, Jude Law

Joseph Fiennes, Jude Law

Ed Harris

# ENEMY AT THE GATES

**(PARAMOUNT)** Producers, Jean-Jacques Annaud, John D Schofield; Executive Producers, Alain Godard, Alisa Tager; Director, Jean-Jacques Annaud; Screenplay, Alain Godard, Jean-Jacques Annaud; Photography, Robert Fraisse; Designer, Wolf Kroeger; Costumes, Janty Yates; Supervising Sound Editor, Eddy Joseph, MPSE; Visual Effects Supervisor, Peter Chiang; Casting, John and Ros Hubbard, Annette Borgman; a Mandalay Pictures presentation of a Repérage production, co-produced by MP Film Management DOS Productions GmbH & Co KG (Germany), Swanford Films Limited (United Kingdom), and Little Bird Limited (Ireland); German-British-Irish; Dolby; Panavision; Deluxe color; Rated R; 131 minutes; US release date: March 16, 2001

## CAST

| | |
|---|---|
| Danilov | Joseph Fiennes |
| Vassili Zaitsev | Jude Law |
| Tania Chernova | Rachel Weisz |
| Nikita Kruschev | Bob Hoskins |
| Major Konig | Ed Harris |
| Koulikov | Ron Perlman |
| Mother Filipov | Eva Mattes |
| Sacha Filipov | Gabriel Marshall-Thomson |
| General von Paulus | Matthias Habich |
| Ludmilla | Sophie Rois |
| Volody | Ivan Shvetloff |
| Anton | Mario Bandi |
| Red Army General | Hans Martin Stier |
| German Noncom | Clemans Schick |
| Grandfather | Mikhail Matveyev |
| Young Vassili | Alexander Schwan |
| Comrade in Train | Lenn Kudrjawizki |
| Fat Colonel | Hendrik Arnst |
| Aide de Camp | Claudius Freyer |
| Blond Captain | Dietmar Nieder |
| Captain with Lighter | Bernd Lambrecht |
| Stubborn Feldwebel | Jim Dowdall |
| Politruk/Sniper | Maxim Kovalevski |
| Russian Noncom | Gennadi Vengerov |
| Political Officer | Dan van Husen |
| Sweating Officer | Peter Silbereison |
| Stammering Officer | Markus Majowski |
| Spotter | Robert Stadlober |
| Corpse Robber | Gotthard Lange |
| Russian Typist | Anna Böttcher |
| Paulus's Aide de Camp | Holger Handtke |
| Stealing Photographer | Marc Bischoff |
| Russian Captain at Headquarters | Mark Zak |
| Russian Lieutenant | Thomas Petruo |
| Comrade in Shelter | Dimitri Alexandrov |
| Pravda Interviewer | David Pagel |
| Izvestija Interviewer | Galina Dobberstein |
| Krasnaja Zvezda Interviewer | Igor Rozinskij |
| Russian Reporter | Sergwei Tokarev |
| Footsoldier | Tom Wlaschia |
| Woman Plucking Eyebrows | Marischka Schubarth |
| Woman Officer | Natalja Bondar |
| Athletic Sniper | Dana Cebulla |

and Piotr Papierz, Jarek Wozniak, Genia Makarov, Werner Dahn, Birol Ünel, Grigori Kofmann, Alexej Nesterov, Vladimir Vilanov (Politruks), Alexeji Volodin (Junior Politruk), Gennadi Tselbiansky (Senior Politruk), Andrej Kaminski (Russian Trench Officer), Michael Schenk (Russian Officer), Jury Cooper, Manfred Witt (Russian Noncoms), Arslan Kodirov (Tchechen Sniper), Axel Neumann (Gaunt German Prisoner), Morin Smolé, Inna Samian (Snipers), Arslan Kodirov (Sniper/Russian Officer), Keta Burowa (Female Russian Radio Operator)

*During the bloody Battle of Stalingrad, the Russian people find a hero in sniper Vassili Zaitsev, prompting the Nazis to send their best sharpshooter to dispose of him.*

© MP Film Mgmt.

Joseph Fiennes, Jude Law

Joseph Fiennes, Rachel Weisz

Jude Law

Jude Law

Jude Law, Bob Hoskins

Emilio Echevarría

# AMORES PERROS

**(LIONS GATE)** Producer/Director, Alejandro González Iñárritu; Executive Producers, Martha Sosa, Francisco González Compeán; Screenplay, Guillermo Arriaga; Photography, Rodrigo Prieto; Designer, Brigitte Broch; Editors, Alejandro Gonzáles Iñárritu, Luis Carballar, Fernando Perez Unda; Music, Gustavo Santaolalla; Casting, Manuel Teil; an Altavista Films presentation of a Zeta Film and Altavista Films production; Mexican, 2000; Color; Rated R; 153 minutes; US release date: March 30, 2001

## CAST

| | |
|---|---|
| El Chivo | Emilio Echevarría |
| Octavio | Gael García Bernal |
| Valeria | Goya Toledo |
| Daniel | Álvaro Guerrero |
| Susana | Vanessa Bauche |
| Luis | Jorge Salinas |
| Ramiro | Marco Peréz |
| Gustavo | Rodrigo Murray |
| Jorge | Humberto Busto |
| Mauricio | Gerardo Campbell |
| Aunt Luisa | Rosa María Bianchi |
| Susana's Mother | Dunia Saldívar |
| Octavio's Mother | Adriana Barraza |
| Leonardo | José Sefami |
| Maru | Lourdes Echevarría |
| Julieta | Laura Almela |
| Andres Salgado | Ricardo Dalmacci |
| Jarocho | Gustavo Sánchez Parra |
| Alvaro | Dagoberto Gama |
| El Chispas | Gustavo Muñoz |
| Javier | Carlo Bernal |

and Rodrigo Obstab (El Jaibo), Heriberto Castillo (Stranger)

*A car crash in Mexico City brings together three different people: teenager Octavio, model Valeria, and killer-for-hire El Chivo.*

*This film received an Oscar nomination for Foreign Language Film (2000).*

© Lions Gate Films

Gael García Bernal

Goya Toledo

Karma Wangel, Thilen Lhondup

## HIMALAYA

**(KINO)** Producers, Jacques Perrin, Christophe Barratier; Executive Producer, Jean de Trégomain; Director, Eric Valli; Screenplay, Olivier Dazat; Based on a script by Eric Valli, Olivier Dazat, with the assistance of Jean-Claude Guillebaud, Louis Gardel, Nathalie Azoulai, Jacques Perrin; Photography, Eric Guichard AFC, Jean-Paul Meurisse; Art Directors, Jérôme Krowicki, Tenzing Norbu Lama; Editor, Marie-Josèphe Yoyotte; Music, Bruno Coulais; French-Swiss-British-Nepalese; 1999; Color; Not rated; 104 minutes; US release date: March 30, 2001

### CAST

| | |
|---|---|
| Tinle | Thilen Lhondup |
| Karma | Gurgon Kyap |
| Pema | Lhakpa Tsamchoe |
| Passang | Karma Wangel |
| Norbou | Karam Tenzing |
| Labrang | Labrang Tundup |
| Jampa | Jampa Kalsang Tamang |
| Rabkie | Tsering Dorjee |
| Tundup | Rapke Gurung |
| Tensing | Pemba Bika |
| Nene | Karma Chlewang |
| Chopga | Tenzen Charka |

and Karma Chhuldim (Paljor), Karma Tenzing (Urgien), Yangzom (Dawa), Gyalsen Gurung (Chewan), Phuti Bika (Deld), Sangmo Gurung (Angmo), Karma Angbu Gurung (Karma's Father)

*Believing Karma caused the death of his son, Himalayan chieftain Tinle refuses to allow him to lead a caravan, an edict Karma defies.*

© Kino International

## SHADOW MAGIC

**(SONY PICTURES CLASSICS)** Producer/Director, Ann Hu; Executive Producers, Charles Xue, Steve Chang, Chiu Shun-Ching, Han Sanping, Ulrich Felsberg, Eitan Hakami, Katia Milani; Screenplay, Huang Dan, Tang Louyi, Bob McAndrew, Kate Raisz, Ann Hu; Co-Producers, Sandra Schulberg, Zhang Xia, Cheng Zheng, Lee You-Ning; Photography, Nancy Schreiber; Deisgner, Wang Jixian; Editors, Keith Reamer, John Gilroy; Music, Zhang Lida; Costumes, Huang Bao Rong; a C & A Productions in association with Beijing Film Studio, China Film, Taiwan Central Motion Picture Corporation, Post Production Playground, Schulberg, Productions and Road Movies Vierte Produktionen presentation with the supporting of Filmstiftung Nordrhein-Westfalen GmbH; Chinese-German, 2000; Color; Rated PG; 115 minutes; US release date: April 6, 2001

### CAST

| | |
|---|---|
| Raymond Wallace | Jared Harris |
| Liu Jinglun | Xia Yu |
| Ling | Xing Yufei |
| Master Ren | Liu Peiqi |
| Madame Ren | Lu Liping |
| Old Liu | Wang Jingming |
| Lord Tan | Li Yusheng |
| Lao Chang | Zhang Yukui |
| Mi Hu | Chen Chuang |
| Fu Guan | Zheng Zhongwei |
| Jewelry Tower | Mu Qi |
| Widow Jiang | Fang Qingzhuo |
| Empress Ci Xi | Li Bin |

*In 1902 Peking, photographer Liu Jinglun is delighted by the arrival of silent movies, a new invention that visiting opera star Lord Tan believes will steal away his audience.*

© Sony Pictures Entertainment

Xing Yufei, Xia Yu

Eric Bana

## BEAUTIFUL CREATURES

(UNIVERSAL FOCUS) Producers, Alan J Wands, Simon Donald; Director, Bill Eagles; Screenplay, Simon Donald; Photography, James Welland; Designer, Andy Harris; Editor, Jon Gregory ACE; Costumes, Trisha Biggar; Casting, Nina Gold; a DNA Films in association with Universal Pictures International and The Arts Council of England presentation of a Snakeman production; British; Dolby; Technicolor; Rated R; 86 minutes; US release date: April 6, 2001

### CAST

Petula ...................................................................Rachel Weisz
Dorothy ...............................................................Susan Lynch
Tony .........................................................................Iain Glen
Ronnie McMinn .............................................Maurice Roeves
Brian McMinn ..................................................Tom Mannion
Detective Inspector Hepburn ................................Alex Norton
Train Guard ............................................................Jake D'Arcy
Man in Lift ...........................................................Paul Doonan
Man in Kiosk ........................................................Robin Laing
Sheena ................................................................Pauline Lynch
Man on Beach.....................................................John Murtagh
and Shane Cadzow (Small Boy on Beach), Juliet Cadzow (Mother on Beach), Stewart Preston (Duty Sergeant), Ron Donachie (Police Sergeant), Joel Strachan (Sgt Binnie), Stuart Hepburn (Policeman on Bridge), Ellie Haddington (Maureen), Paul Higgins (Aidan), Storm (Pluto)

*Dorothy and Petula, two women who have suffered through bad relationships with men, concoct a plan to convince the police that Petula's boyfriend, Brian, has been kidnapped, when in fact Dorothy has accidentally killed him while defending Petula.*

© Universal Pictures

## CHOPPER

(FIRST LOOK) Producer, Michele Bennett; Executive Producers, Al Clark, Martin Fabinyi; Director/Screenplay, Andrew Dominik; Adapted from the books by Mark Brandon Read; Co-Producer, Michael Gudinski; Photography, Geoffrey Hall, Kevin Hayward; Designer, Paddy Reardon; Editor, Ken Sallows; Music, Mick Harvey; Costumes, Terry Ryan; Casting, Greg Apps; an Image Entertainment presentation in association with The Australian Film Finance Corporation and Mushroom Pictures of a Pariah Films production; Australian, 2000; Dolby; Color; Not rated; 93 minutes; US release date: April 11, 2001

### CAST

Mark Brandon "Chopper" Read .................................Eric Bana
Jimmy Loughan ..................................................Simon Lyndon
Keithy George ........................................................David Field
Bluey.......................................................................Dan Wyllie
Detective Downie ....................................................Bill Young
Neville Bartos.....................................................Vince Colosimo
Keith Read .........................................................Kenny Graham
Tanya ....................................................................Kate Beahan
and Renee Brack (Television Interviewer), Gregory Pitt, Richard Sutherland, Andrew Dunn (Prison Officers), Gary Waddell (Kevin Darcy), Caleb Cluff (Detective Creswell), Hilton Henderson (Detective Wyatt), Fred Barker (Governor Beasley), Alan Close (Medical Officer #1), Mark Stratford (Classification Officer), Carl Price (Brunswick Court Judge), Brian Mannix (Ian James), Johnnie Targan (Paul the Bouncer), Robert Rabiah (Nick), Sam Houli (Robbo), Sarah Jane King (Glamour Queen), Serge Liistro (Sammy the Turk), Pam Western (Tanya's Mother), Peter Hardy (Detective Cooney), Skye Wansey (Mandy), Annalise Emtsis (Shazzy), Marcus Taylor (Jimmy's Mate), Ernie Gray (Crown Prosecutor), David Paterson (Morris Jeffrey), Fletcher Humphrys (Bucky), Terry Willesee (Current Affairs Show Host)

*From his prison cell, Mark "Chopper" Read looks back on his attempts to make a name for himself in the criminal world.*

© First Look Pictures

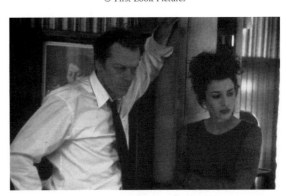

(Above) Iain Glen, Susan Lynch
(Below) Rachel Weisz, Susan Lynch

Nargess Mamizadeh, Maryiam Palvin Almani

# THE CIRCLE

**(WINSTAR)** Producer/Director/Original Idea/Editor, Jafar Panahi; Screenplay, Kambozia Patrovi; Photography, Bahram Badakhshani; Art Director, Iraj Raminfar; Associate Producer, Mohammad Atebbai; Line Producer, Morteza Motevali; a production of Jafar Panahi Film Productions (Iran), Mikado-Lumiere & Co (Italy); Iranian, 2000; Color; Not rated; 91 minutes; US release date: April 16, 2001

## CAST

| | |
|---|---|
| Arezou | Maryiam Palvin Almani |
| Nargess | Nargess Mamizadeh |
| Pari | Fereshteh Sadr Orfani |
| Ticket Seller | Monir Arab |
| Nurse | Elham Saboktakin |
| Mother | Fatemeh Naghavi |
| Prostitute | Mojhan Faramarzi |
| Solmaz | Solmaz Gholami |

*Several Iranian women find themselves on the run to escape the punishment their narrow-minded society enforces on their sex.*

© Winstar Cinema

Maryiam Palvin Almani

Nargess Mamizadeh, Fereshteh Sadr Orfani, Maryiam Parvin Almani

# WITH A FRIEND LIKE HARRY...

(MIRAMAX ZOË) Producer, Michel Saint-Jean; Director, Dominik Moll; Screenplay, Dominik Moll, Gilles Marchand; Photography, Matthieu Poirot-Delpech; Art Director, Michel Barthélémy; Editor, Yannick Kergoat; Music, David Sinclair Whittaker; Casting, Antoinette Boulat; a Michel Saint-Jean presentation of a Diaphana Films, M6 Films Production with the participation of Canal+, M6, Du Centre National De La Cinematographie in association with La Sofica Sofinergie 5 with the support of La Procirep; French, 2000; Dolby; Super 35 Widescreen; Color; Rated R; 117 minutes; US release date: April 20, 2001

## CAST

| | |
|---|---|
| Michel | Laurent Lucas |
| Harry | Sergi Lopez |
| Claire | Mathilde Seigner |
| Plum | Sophie Guillemin |
| Michel's Mother | Liliane Rovere |
| Michel's Father | Dominique Rozan |
| Eric | Michel Fau |
| Jeanne | Victoire De Koster |
| Sarah | Laurie Caminita |
| Iris | Lorena Caminita |

*On the way to a vacation with his wife and kids, Michel meets a former schoolmate he can barely remember, Harry, who insists on joining the family's holiday getaway, becoming an increasingly menacing presence.*

© Miramax Zoë

Sergi Lopez, Sophie Guillemin

Mathilde Seigner, Laurent Lucas

Sergi Lopez, Laurent Lucas

Sophie Guillemin

245

John Turturro, Stuart Wilson, Emily Watson

Emily Watson

Emily Watson, John Turturro

# THE LUZHIN DEFENCE

(SONY CLASSICS) Producers, Caroline Wood, Stephen Evans, Louis Becker, Philippe Guez; Executive Producer, Jody Patton; Director, Marleen Gorris; Screenplay, Peter Berry; Based on the novel by Vladimir Nabokov; Co-Producers, Leo Pescarolo, Eric Robison; Photography, Bernard Lutic; Designer, Tony Burrough; Editor, Michaël Reichwein; Music, Alexandre Desplat; Costumes, Jany Temime; Casting, Celestia Fox; a Renaissance Films in association with Clear Blue Sky Production presentation of a Renaissance and ICE3 production in association with Lantia Cinema, Magic Media, and France 2 Cinéma; British-French, 2000; Dolby; Color; Rated PG-13; 106 minutes; US release date: April 20, 2001

## CAST

| | |
|---|---|
| Alexander Luzhin | John Turturro |
| Natalia | Emily Watson |
| Vera | Geraldine James |
| Valentinov | Stuart Wilson |
| Stassard | Christopher Thompson |
| Turati | Fabio Sartor |
| Ilya | Peter Blythe |
| Anna | Orla Brady |
| Luzhin's Father | Mark Tandy |
| Luzhin's Mother | Kelly Hunter |
| Young Luzhin | Alexander Hunting |
| Officials | Alfredo Pea, Fabio Pasquini |
| Santucci | Luigi Petrucci |
| Hotel Manager | Carlo Greco |
| Tailor | Massimo Sarchielli |
| Fascists | Luca Foggiano, Antonio Carli, David Ambrosi |

*Eccentric, tormented chess master Alexander Luzhin arrives at an Italian lakeside resort to participate in the greatest tournament of his career, and finds himself falling in love with an aristocratic Russian woman whose parents hope to marry her into wealth.*

© Sony Pictures Entertainment

Uma Thurman, Nick Nolte

# THE GOLDEN BOWL

**(LIONS GATE)** Producer, Ismail Merchant; Executive Producers, Paul Bradley, Richard Hawley; Director, James Ivory; Screenplay, Ruth Prawer Jhabvala; Based on the novel by Henry James; Photography, Tony Pierce-Roberts; Designer, Andrew Sanders; Music, Richard Robbins; Editor, John David Allen; Costumes, John Bright; Casting, Celestia Fox; a Merchant Ivory Productions in association with TF1 International presentation; British; Dolby; Panavision; Color; Rated R; 130 minutes; US release date: April 27, 2001

## CAST

| | |
|---|---|
| Maggie Verver | Kate Beckinsale |
| Bob Assingham | James Fox |
| Fanny Assingham | Anjelica Huston |
| Adam Verver | Nick Nolte |
| Prince Amerigo | Jeremy Northam |
| Lady Casteldean | Madeleine Potter |
| Charlotte Stant | Uma Thurman |
| Duke's Older Son | Rossano Rubicondi |
| The Duchess | Marta Paola Richeldi |
| Duke's Younger Son | Francesco Giuffrida |
| The Duke | Mattia Sbragia |
| Shopkeeper | Peter Eyre |
| Lord Castledean | Nicholas Day |
| Principino at Five Years | Daniel Byam Shaw |
| Mr Blint | Robin Hart |
| Lecturer | Nickolas Grace |
| Principino | Billy Monger |

and Pauline Rainer (Nursemaid), Susan Gutfreund (Vivacious Guest), Arturo Venegas (Italian Ambassador), Raymond Green (Photographer), Anthony Bevan (Butler), Neville Phillips (Man Talking to Casteldean), Paul Bradley (Executioner), Lucy Freeman (Lucy Moncrief), Philip Tabor (William Davenport), Catherine Aldrich, Isabel de Pelet, Richard MacRory, Caroline Burnaby-Atkins (Guests at Fawns), Piers Gielgud (The Ballet Pasha), Antonia Franceschi (The Ballet First Queen), Philip Willingham (The Ballet Slave), William Dignon (The Ballet Little Prince), Ray Souza, Leanne Codrington, Amy Bailey, Michaela Burgess, Simon Humphrey, Michaela Burgess, Michela Meazza, Stephen Hughes, Tippi Maravala (Dancers)

*Billionaire Adam Verver and his daughter Maggie both marry only to discover that their spouses are having an affair with one another.*

© Lions Gate Films

Uma Thurman, Jeremy Northam

Nick Nolte, Kate Beckinsale

Uma Thurman, Anjelica Huston, Jeremy Northam

Karen Bach, Raffaëla Anderson

Karen Bach

Karen Bach

Raffaëla Anderson

# BAISE-MOI
## (RAPE ME)

(FILMFIX/REMSTAR) Producer, Philippe Godeau; Executive Producer, Dominique Chiron; Directors/Screenplay, Virginie Despentes, Coralie Trinh Thi; Based on the novel by Virginie Despentes; Photography, Benoît Chamaillard; Art Director, Irène Galitzine; Costumes, Magali Baret, Isabelle Fraysse; Editors, Aïlo Auguste-Judith, Francine Lemaitre; Music, Varou Jan; French, 2000; Color; Not rated; 77 minutes; US release date: April 27, 2001

## CAST

| | |
|---|---|
| Manu | Raffaëla Anderson |
| Nadine | Karen Lancaume/Karen Bach |
| Severine | Delphine MacCarty |
| Karla | Lisa Marshall |
| Alice | Estelle Isaac |
| Martin | H. P. G. (Hervé P. Gustave) |
| Architect | Marc Rioufol |
| Radouan | Ouassini Embarek |

and Adama Niane (Boy with Billiards), Tewfik Saad (Server), Céline Beugnot (Blonde with Billiards), Christophe Claudi (Guy with Counter), Patrick Eudeline (Francis), Hacène Beddrouh (Lakim), Philippe Houillez, Steven Jhonsson, Ian Scott (Rapists), Gil Stuart (Nadine's Client), Karim Sabaddehine (Big Guy), Titof (Little Guy), Alexandre Milor (Receptionist, Hotel Francis), Marc Barrow (Receptionist, Seaside Hotel), Elodie Chérie (Lady Distributor), Rodolphe Antrim (The Local), Jean-Marc Minéo (Arms Seller), Gábor Rassov (Guy with Hood), Patrick Kodjo Topou, Simon Nahoum Karim Chala (Big Thugs), Jean-Louis Costes (Man in Sex Club), Nathalie Dune, Dany, Pascal Saint-James, Sébastien Barriot (BAP), Sylvain Cahen-Delabre, Didier Gardette, Jacques Sans (Dead Bodies)

*Two angry women, one a victim of rape, the other a hardened prostitute, embark on a road trip full of destruction and vengeance aimed at the opposite sex.*

# UNDER THE SAND

(WINSTAR) Producers, Olivier Delbosc, Marc Missonnier; Director, François Ozon; Screenplay, François Ozon, Emmanuèle Bernheim, Marina de Van, Marcia Romano; Photography, Jeanne Lapoirie, Antoine Heberlé; Editor, Laurence Bawedin; Music, Philippe Rombi; Costumes, Pascaline Chavanne; Casting, Antoinette Boulat; a Fidélité Productions presentation in co-production with Euro Space Inc, Haut et Court, Arte France Cinema with the participation of Canal+; French-Japanese, 2000; Dolby; Color; Not rated; 95 minutes; US release date: May 4, 2001

## CAST

| | |
|---|---|
| Marie Drillon | Charlotte Rampling |
| Jean Drillon | Bruno Cremer |
| Vincent | Jacques Nolot |
| Amanda | Alexandra Stewart |
| Gerard | Pierre Vernier |
| Suzanne | Andrée Tainsy |

and Maya Gaugler (German Woman), Damien Abbou (Chief Lifeguard), David Portugais (Young Lifeguard), Pierre Soubestre (Policeman), Agathe Teyssier (In Charge of the Luxury Store), Laurence Martin (Apartment Seller), Jean-François Lapalus (Paris Doctor), Laurence Mercier (Paris Doctor's Secretary), Fabienne Luchetti (Pharmacist), Jo Doumerg (Taxi Driver), Michel Cordes (Superintendent), Maurice Antoni (The Landes Doctor), Patricia Couvillers (Evelyne), Patrick Grieco (José), Axelle Bossard (Student), Charlotte Gerbault (Nurse), Nicole Lartique (Morgue Attendant)

*While on holiday, Marie's husband Jean suddenly disappears, forcing her to go on with her life alone, plunging her into a darker feeling of despair and loss than she is prepared for.*

© Winstar Cinema

Charlotte Rampling, Jacques Nolot

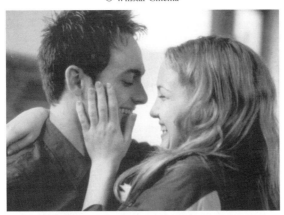

(Above) Stuart Townsend, Kate Hudson
(Below) Stuart Townsend, Frances O'Connor

# ABOUT ADAM

(MIRAMAX) Producers, Anna Devlin, Marina Hughes; Executive Producers, Harvey Weinstein, David M. Thompson, David Aukin, Trea Leventhal, Rod Stoneman; Director/Screenplay, Gerard Stembridge; Photography, Bruno de Keyzer; Designer, Fiona Daly; Editor, Mary Finlay; Music, Adrian Johnston; Costumes, Eimear Ni Mhaoldomhnaigh; Line Producer, Mary Alleguen; Casting, John & Ros Hubbard, Laura Rosenthal; a BBC Films presentation in association with Bord Scannán na hÉireann/The Irish Film Board, a Venus Production; British-Irish-US; Dolby; Color; Rated R; 105 minutes; US release date: May 9, 2001

## CAST

| | |
|---|---|
| Adam | Stuart Townsend |
| Laura Owens | Frances O'Connor |
| Alice Owens | Charlotte Bradley |
| Lucy Owens | Kate Hudson |
| David Owens | Alan Maher |
| Simon | Tommy Tiernan |
| Martin | Brendan Dempsey |
| Karen | Cathleen Bradley |
| Peggy Owens | Rosaleen Linehan |
| Professor McCormick | Roger Gregg |
| Customers | Stewart Roche, Aoife Maloney |
| Andy | Donal Beecher |
| Dympna | Kathy Downes |
| Dracula | Mark Smith |

*Believing she has found the man of her dreams, Lucy Owens brings Adam to meet her family, only to have her sisters fall for the charming young man.*

© Miramax Films

Pilar Padilla, Adrien Brody

George Lopez

# BREAD AND ROSES

(LIONS GATE) Producer, Rebecca O'Brien; Executive Producer, Ulrich Felsberg; Director, Ken Loach; Screenplay, Paul Laverty; Photography, Barry Ackroyd; Designer, Martin Johnson; Costumes, Michele Michel; Music, George Fenton; Editor, Jonathan Morris; Casting, Ronnie Yeskel, Richard Hicks; a Parallax Pictures, Road Movies Filmproduktion and Tornasol/Alta Films production with the participation of British Screeen and BSkyB in association with Bac Films, BIM Distribuzione, Cin-Art and Film Co-Operative, Zurich, and in collaboration with FilmFour, WDR/Arte, La Sept-Arte, ARD/Degeto Film and Filmstiftung Nordrhein-Westfalen; British-German-Spanish-French; Dolby; Color; Rated R; 110 minutes; US release date: May 11, 2001

## CAST

| | |
|---|---|
| Maya | Pilar Padilla |
| Sam | Adrien Brody |
| Rosa | Elpidia Carrillo |
| Perez | George Lopez |
| Bert | Jack McGee |
| Simona | Monica Rivas |
| Luis | Frank Dávila |
| Anna | Lillian Hurst |
| Ben | Mayron Payes |
| Berta | Maria Orellana |
| Cynthia | Melody Garrett |
| Dolores | Gigi Jackman |
| Ella | Beverly Reynolds |
| Juan | Eloy Méndez |
| Maria | Elena Antonenko |
| Olga | Olga Gorelik |
| Oscar | Jesús Pérez |

and Alonso Chávez (Ruben), Estela Maeda (Teresa), José Jiménez (Freddy), Sherman Augustus (Ernest), Julian Orea, Javier Tores (Coyotes), Roscio Saenz (Emma), Blake Clark (Mr Griffin), Pepa Serna (Restaurateur), Tony Rizzoli (Personnel Manager), Tom Gilroy (Director of Campaigns), Neal Baer (Doctor), David Steinberg, Ted Baer (Lawyers), Terry Anzur (Reporter), Greg Montgomery (Supervising Policeman), Clement Blake (Gas Station Attendant), Tom Michael Bailey (Truck Driver), Richard Bravo (IMS Officer), Vanessa Angel, William Atherton, Lara Belmont, Cooper Campbell, Benicio Del Toro, Oded Fehr, Stuart Gordon, Rick Otto, Chris Penn, Ron Perlman, Tim Roth, Robin Tunney, Sam West, Stephanie Zimbalist (Themselves)

*A spirited young Mexican woman, smuggled over the border to Los Angeles where she makes a living cleaning office buildings, is convinced by a union organizer to rally other janitors to fight for their rights.*

© Lions Gate Films

Pilar Padilla

Elpidia Carrillo, Pilar Padilla

Jennifer Jason Leigh

Bruce Davison

Janet McTeer

# THE KING IS ALIVE

(IFC FILMS) Producers, Patricia Krujer, Vibeke Windeløv; Executive Producers, William A Tyrer, Chris J Ball, David Linde, Peter Aalbaek Jensen; Director, Kristian Levring; Screenplay, Kristian Levring, Anders Thomas Jensen; Inspired by *King Lear* by William Shakespeare; Photography, Jens Schlosser; Editor, Nicholas Wayman Harris; Casting, Joyce Nettles, Mali Finn, Moonyeen Lee, Bruno Levi; a Newmarket and Good Machine International presentation of a Zentropa Entertainments production, in co-production with the Danish Broadcasting Corporation in collaboration with SVT Drama and supported by the Danish Film Institute and Nordic Film & TV Fund; Danish-US; Dolby; Color; Rated R; 108 minutes; US release date: May 11, 2001

## CAST

| | |
|---|---|
| Jack | Miles Anderson |
| Catherine | Romane Bohringer |
| Henry | David Bradley |
| Charles | David Calder |
| Ray | Bruce Davison |
| Ashley | Brion James |
| Kanana | Peter Kubheka |
| Moses | Vusi Kunene |
| Gina | Jennifer Jason Leigh |
| Liz | Janet McTeer |
| Paul | Chris Walker |
| Amanda | Lia Williams |

*A group of tourists, stranded in the middle of an African desert, decide to pass the time by staging a production of King Lear, a decision that only forces them to confront their tense situation.*

Jennifer Jason Leigh, Romane Bohringer

© IFC Films

# THE ROAD HOME

(SONY PICTURES CLASSICS) Producer, Zhao Yu; Executive Producer, Zhang Weiping; Director, Zhang Yimou; Screenplay, Bao Shi; Photography, Hou Yong; Designer, Cao Jiuping; Costumes, Dong Huamiao; Editor, Zhai Ru; Music, San Bao; a Columbia Pictures Film Production Asia presentation of a Guangxi Film Studios & Beijing New Picture Distribution Company production; Chinese, 1999; Dolby; Panavision; Color/Black & White; Rated G; 100 minutes; US release date: May 25, 2001

Zhang Ziyi, Zheng Hao

## CAST

| | |
|---|---|
| Zhao Di (Youth) | Zhang Ziyi |
| Luio Yusheng | Sun Honglei |
| Luo Changyu | Zheng Hao |
| Zhao Di (Elderly) | Zhao Yuelin |
| Grandmother | Li Bin |
| Mayor (Elderly) | Chang Guifa |
| Mayor (Youth) | Sung Wencheng |
| Carpenter Xia (Elderly) | Liu Qi |
| Carpenter Xia (Youth) | Ji Bo |
| Crockery Repairman | Zhang Zhongxi |

*Yusheng, returning to his hometown for his father's funeral, recalls the story of how his parents met.*

© Sony Pictures Entertainment

Zhang Ziyi

Zhang Ziyi, Zheng Hao

Johnny Depp

Cate Blanchett, John Turturro

# THE MAN WHO CRIED

(UNIVERSAL FOCUS) Producer, Christopher Sheppard; Executive Producers, Tim Bevan, Eric Fellner; Director/Screenplay, Sally Potter; Co-Producer, Simona Benzakein; Photography, Sacha Vierny ACE; Designer, Carlos Conti; Editor, Hervé Schneid; Costumes, Lindy Hemming; Music, Osvaldo Golijov; Line Producer, Linda Bruce; Casting, Irene Lamb, Mary Colquhoun; a Studio Canal presentation of a Working Title production in association with Adventure Pictures; British-French, 2000; Dolby; Color; Rated R; 97 minutes; US release date: May 25, 2001

## CAST

| | |
|---|---|
| Suzie | Christina Ricci |
| Lola | Cate Blanchett |
| Dante Dominio | John Turturro |
| Cesar | Johnny Depp |
| Felix Perlman | Harry Dean Stanton |
| Father | Oleg Yankovsky |
| Young Suzie | Claudia Lander-Duke |
| Grandmother | Hana Maria Pravda |
| Foster Mother | Diana Hoddinott |
| Foster Father | Richard Albrecht |
| Madame Goldstein | Miriam Karlin |

and Danny Scheinman (Man in Suit), Anna Tzelniker (Mother of Man in Suit), Barry Davis, Thom Osborn, Frank Chersky, Daniel Hart, Peter Majer (Men in Village), Ayala Meir, Abraham Hassan, Lloyd Martin, Uri Meir, Sophie Richman, Theo Wishart (Children), Michael Mount, Harry Flinder (Boys in Cart), Danny Richman (Man in Cart), Victor Sobtchak (Man at Port), Sue Cleaver (Red Cross Woman), Clifford Barry (English Port Official), Paul Clayton (Second Official), Ornella Bryant, Sam Friend, Isabella Melling (Playground Bullies), Alan David (Welsh Teacher), Imogen Claire (Audition Mistress), Consuelo de Haviland (Party Hostess), Katia Labeque, Marielle Labeque (Pianists), George Yiasoumi (Reporter), Pablo Veron (Dancing Romany), Taraf de Haidouks (Romany Band), Odile Roire, Brigitte Boucher, Norah Krief, Helene Hardouin (Opera Chorus), Hugues Dalmagro, Cedric Gary (Romany Brothers), Saifi Ghoul (Romany Boy), Manfred Andrae (German Officer), Richard Sammel (German Officer Pianist), Ahmet Zirek (Father of Boy), Don Fellows (Joe), Joyce Springer (Refugee Worker), Cyril Shaps (Older Man in Sweatshop), Anna Korwin (Woman in Sweatshop), Mark Ivanir, Alfred Hoffman, Bernard Spear (Men in Sweatshop), Damien Puckler (Studio Assistant), David Baxt (Studio Lawyer), Katherine Hogarth (Father's New Wife), Patrick Clarke (Son), Bridget Clarke (Daughter), Chris Gillespie (Nurse)

*Suzie, a Russian Jew, finds herself in Paris where she hopes to make enough money to join her father in America, a goal that becomes even more imperative when the Nazis begin their reign of terror.*

© Universal Studios, Inc.

Christina Ricci

Christina Ricci, Johnny Depp, Cate Blanchett

# BRIDE OF THE WIND

**(PARAMOUNT CLASSICS)** Producer, Lawrence Levy, Evzen Kolar; Executive Producers, Gerald Green, Frank Hübner; Director, Bruce Beresford; Screenplay, Marilyn Levy; Photography, Peter James ACS ASC; Designer, Herbert Pinter; Editor, Timothy Wellburn; Music, Stephen Endelman; Co-Producer, Norbert Blecha; Costumes, Shaun Harwood; Associate Producers, Steven Brown, Kirt Eftekhar; Casting, Joseph Middleton, Ari Raidel; a Total Film Group presentation of an Alma UK Ltd, Apollomedia, Firelight co-production, of a Kolar-Levy production; British-US; Dolby; Deluxe color; Rated R; 99 minutes; US release date: June 8, 2001

## CAST

| | |
|---|---|
| Alma Mahler | Sarah Wynter |
| Gustav Mahler | Jonathan Pryce |
| Oskar Kokoschka | Vincent Perez |
| Walter Gropius | Simon Verhoeven |
| Franz Werfel | Gregor Seberg |
| Anna Moll | Dagmar Schwarz |
| Karl Moll | Wolfgang Hübsch |
| Gustav Klimt | August Schmölzer |
| Bertha Zuckerkandl | Marion Rottenhofer |

and Sophie Schweighofer (Anna Mahler—6 years old), Johannes Silberschneider (Alexander Zemlinsky), Daniele Dadieu (Justine Mahler), Brigitte Antonius (Frau Kokoschka), Johanna Mertinz (Frau Gropius), Erwin Ebenbauer (Dr Alfred Loos), Franziska Becker (Maria Mahler—3 years old), Sonia Madani (Maria Mahler—5 years old), Katrina Sztachovic (Anna Mahler—3 years old), Michaela Illetschko (Anna Mahler—13 years old), Renée Fleming (Frances Alda), Jean-Yves Thibaudet (Alda's Accompanist), Peter Gruber (Dr Blumenthal), Doris Pascher (Sophie Clemenceau), Robert Herzl (Arnold Schonberg), Werner Prinz (Archduke Franz Ferdinand), Patricia Hirschbichler (Duchess Sophie), Bernhard Bauer (Clarinetist), Gordon Catlin (Postman), Michael Rast (Stefan), Helen Zellweger (Helena), Sylvia Haider (Flora), Arthur Denberg (Kurt), Kathy Marothy (Nanny), Marianne Mendt, Angelika Rossaro (Alma's Maids), Heidelinde Theresina (Moll's Maid), Merab Ninidze (Russian Soldier), Josef Schutzhofer (Cavalry Sergeant), Mijou Kovacs, Anita Kolbert (Tobelbad Patients), Monika Mandl (Klimt's Model), Rich Cowan (Mute Waiter), Roby Lakatos, Ernest Bangó (Gypsy Ensemble)

*The story of Alma Mahler, who had love affairs with some of the most influential artists of their day, including composer Gustav Mahler, expressionist painter Oskar Kokoschka, architect Walter Gropius, and novelist Franz Werfel.*

© Paramount Classics

Jonathan Pryce

Sarah Wynter

Vincent Perez

Sarah Wynter, Gregor Seberg

Anna Siskova, Csongor Kassai

Anna Siskova, Boleslav Polivka

Boleslav Polivka

# DIVIDED WE FALL

(SONY PICTURES CLASSICS) Producers, Ondrej Trojan, Pavel Borovan; Executive Producer, Ondrej Trojan; Director, Jan Hrebejk; Screenplay, Petr Jarchovsky, based on his novel; Photography, Jan Malir; Designer, Milan Bycek; Music, Ales Brenzina; Editor, Vladimir Barak; Costumes, Katarina Holla; a Total Helpart (THA) Film Company and Czech Television Production; Czech-German; Dolby; Color; Rated PG-13; 117 minutes; US release date: June 8, 2001

Boleslav Polivka, Richard Tesarik

## CAST

Josef Cizek..........................................................Boleslav Polivka
Marie Cizek............................................................Anna Siskova
Horst Prohaska...................................................Jaroslav Dusek
David Wiener.......................................................Csongor Kassai
Doctor Fischer.................................................................Jiri Kodet
SS Officer..........................................................Vladimir Marek
Captain ...............................................................Richard Tesarik
Frantisek Simacek ......................................................Jiri Pecha
Dr Albrecht Kepk.................................................Martin Huba

*In a small Czech town occupied by the German forces, Josef Cizek shelters a Jewish refugee then hopes to distract attention from this act by taking a job with a Nazi collaborator.*

*This film received an Oscar nomination as foreign-language film for 2000.*

© Sony Pictures Entertainment

Anna Siskova, Jaroslav Dusek

Ben Kingsley, Ray Winstone

Ray Winstone, Alvaro Monje

## SEXY BEAST

**(FOX SEARCHLIGHT)** Producer, Jeremy Thomas; Director, Jonathan Glazer; Screenplay, Louis Mellis, David Scinto; Photography, Ivan Bird; Designer, Jan Houllevigue; Co-Producer, Denise O'Dell; Associate Producers, Hercules Bellville, Peter Watson; Editors, John Scott, Sam Sneade; Music, Roque Baños, UNKLE with South; Costumes, Louise Stjernsward; Casting, Lucy Boulting; a Recorded Picture Company and FilmFour presentation in association with KanZaman SA, of a Jeremy Thomas production developed in association wtih Chronopolis Films; British; Dolby; Super 35 Widescreen; Deluxe color; Rated R; 91 minutes; US release date: June 13, 2001

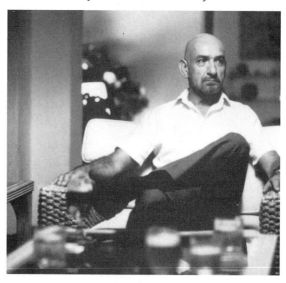

Ben Kingsley

### CAST

| | |
|---|---|
| Gary "Gal" Dove | Ray Winstone |
| Don Logan | Ben Kingsley |
| Teddy Bass | Ian McShane |
| Deedee | Amanda Redman |
| Harry | James Fox |
| Aitch | Cavan Kendall |
| Jackie | Julianne White |
| Enrique | Alvaro Monje |
| Andy | Robert Atiko |
| Air Hostess | Nieves del Amo Oruet |
| Pilot | Enrique Alemán Fabrega |
| Spanish Official | Gerard Barray |
| Felipe's Friends | José Ma Cano Ramos, José López Carrillo |
| Jean | Desirée Erasmus |
| Policias | José Lirola Ramos, Santiago Frías Muñoz, Pedro Zamora Hernández, Juan Manuel Martínez Cobos |
| Ginger Air Steward | José Hernández |
| Maruja (Matronly Woman) | Ana Maldonado Herreria |
| Jimmy | Andy Lucas |

and Antonio Fco Márquez (Steward), Dionisio Mesa (Felipe), Eddie O'Connell (Bruno), Terry Plummer (Mike), Manuel Sánchez Berlanga (Man on Plane), Frank Scinto (Pete), Darkie Smith (Stan), Rocky Taylor (Raymond), Chris Webb (Nicky)

*Don Logan, a volatile and dangerous gangster, shows up at the Spanish villa of retired mobster Gal Dove to force Gal to participate in one final bank job.*

*This film received an Oscar nomination for supporting actor (Ben Kingsley).*

© Twentieth Century Fox

Ray Winstone, Ben Kingsley

Benno Fürmann, Franka Potente

Franka Potente

# THE PRINCESS AND THE WARRIOR

(SONY PICTURES CLASSICS) Producers, Stefan Arndt, Maria Köpf; Director/Screenplay, Tom Tykwer; Photography, Frank Griebe; Designer, Ulli Hanisch; Costumes, Monika Jacobs; Editor, Mathilde Bonnefoy; Music, Tom Tykwer, Johnny Kilmek, Reinhold Heil; Casting, Filmcast; an X Filme, Creative Pool production; German, 2000; Dolby; Panavision; Color; Rated R; 130 minutes; US release date: June 22, 2001

## CAST

| | |
|---|---|
| Sissi (Simone) | Franka Potente |
| Bodo | Benno Fürmann |
| Walter | Joachim Kròl |
| Sissi's Mother | Marita Breuer |
| Schmatt | Jürgen Tarrach |
| Steini | Lars Rudolph |
| Otto | Melchior Beslon |
| Werner Dürr | Ludger Pistor |
| Bruno Kramer | Steffen Schult |
| Dieter Strack | Rolf Dannemann |
| Paul Rummenhöller | Gottfried Breitfuss |
| Ali Gören | Susanne Bredehöft |
| Sigrun Mölke | Christa Fast |
| Maria | Sybille Jacqueline Schedwill |

and Sebastian Schipper, Armin Krug (Security Types), Jörg Reimers (Watchman), Natja Brunckhorst (Meike), Ali Nejat-uei (Ali Gören), Friederike Frerichs (Corinna), Stefanie Mühlhahn (Andrea), Irma Schmitt (Sandra), Max Urlacher (Holger), Thomas Gimbel (Markus), Alexander Wipprecht (Martin), Jan André Zinnschlag (Stefan), Sabina Riedel (Marita), Karl-Heinz Dickmann (Bank Clerk), Jana Schröder (Bank Trainee), Georg-Martin Bode (Bank Branch Manager), Georg Zurhelle (Postman), Peter Götz Korn (Birkenhof Porter), Marcel Segmüller (Rotzbalg), Michael Hanemann (Hartwich), Heiner Voigt (Priest), Eva Wolfertz (Meike's Mother), Ralf Knebel, Piet Paes (Filling Station Man), Jürgen Blumenthal (Lorry Driver), Ercan Sagnak, Winfried Walgenbach (Casualty Team), Manfred Götting, Tom Spiess (Schmatt Shop Customers), Axel Siefer (Casualty Doctor), Eva Pilego (Casualty Nurse), Frank Dubowski (Casualty Male Nurse), Frank Plasberg (Aktuelle Stunde Newsreader), Ina Kiesewetter (Lokalzeit Newsreader), Dirk Brand (Pump Attendant), Thomas Wüpper (Policeman at Birkenhof), Frauke Jacob (Nurse at Birkenhof)

*Following a horrific car accident, a shy nurse is rescued by a mysterious savior who turns out to be a crook on the run from the law.*

© Sony Pictures Entertainment

Franka Potente, Joachim Kròl

Benno Fürmann

Jérémie Elkaïm, Stéphane Rideau

Jérémie Elkaïm, Stéphane Rideau

# COME UNDONE
## (PRESQUE RIEN)

(PICTURE THIS! ENTERTAINMENT) aka Almost Nothing; Producers, Jean-Christophe Colson, Cecile Amillat, Christian Tison; Director, Sébastien Lifshitz; Screenplay, Stéphane Bouquet, Sébastien Lifshitz; Photography, Pascal Poucet; Designer, Roseanna Sacco; Costumes, Elisabeth Mehu; Music, Perry Blake; Associate Producers, Marion Hansel, Arlette Zylberberg; Editor, Yann Dedet; a Lancelot Films & Man's Films presentation in association with Arte France Cinema, RTBF (Television Belge), with the participation of Centre National de la Cinematographie, La Procirep, Canal+, Centre du Cinema et de L'Audiovisuel, and La Coummunaute Francaise de Belgique; French, 2000; Dolby; Color; Not rated; 94 minutes; US release date: June 27, 2001

Jérémie Elkaïm

## CAST

| | |
|---|---|
| Mathieu | Jérémie Elkaïm |
| Cédric | Stéphane Rideau |
| Annick | Marie Matheron |
| Mother | Dominique Reymond |
| Sarah | Laetitia Legrix |
| Pierre | Nils Ohlund |
| Psychiatrist | Réjane Kerdaffrec |
| Cédric Father | Guy Houssier |
| Pierre's Mother | Violeta Ferrer |
| Cafe Owner | Robert Darmel |
| Nurses | Marie-Claire Durand, Charline Levaque |
| Waffle Seller | Sarah Reviasse |
| Annick's Friend | Eric Savin |
| Club Bouncer | Gildas Chotard |
| Boy on the Beach | Maxence Rabrit |

*Mathieu, an 18-year-old boy on summer holiday with his family, finds himself falling in love with another boy.*

Jérémie Elkaïm, Stéphane Rideau

Daniel Auteuil, Michèle Laroque

Gérard Depardieu, Daniel Auteuil

© Picture This! Entertainment

# THE CLOSET
## (LE PLACARD)

**(MIRAMAX ZOË)** Producer, Alain Poiré; Director/Screenplay, Francis Veber; Directors of Production, Philippe Desmoulins, Henri Brichetti; Photography, Luciano Tovoli; Editor, Georges Klotz; Art Director, Hugues Tissander; Music, Vladimir Cosma; Costumes, Jacqueline Bouchard; Casting, François Menidrey; Presented in association with Gaumont and Efve Films; a co-production of Gaumont/Efve Films/TF1 Films production; Dolby; Technovision; Color; Rated R; 87 minutes; US release date: June 27, 2001

Michel Aumont, Daniel Auteuil

## CAST

| | |
|---|---|
| Francois Pignon | Daniel Auteuil |
| Félix Santini | Gérard Depardieu |
| Guillaume | Thierry Lhermitte |
| Mlle Bertrand | Michèle Laroque |
| Belone | Michel Aumont |
| Kopel, Company Director | Jean Rochefort |
| Christine | Alexandra Vandernoot |
| Franck | Stanislas Crevillén |
| Mathieu | Edgar Givry |
| Victor | Thierry Ashanti |
| Ariane | Michèle Garcia |
| Alba | Laurent Gamelon |
| Ponce | Vincent Moscato |
| Martine | Irina Ninova |
| Suzanne | Marianne Groves |
| The Cop | Philippe Vieux |
| Moreau | Luq Hamet |
| Maitre D'Hotel | Eric Vanzetta |
| Wine Waiter | Michel Caccia |
| Photographer | Joel Demarty |
| Removal Man | Dominique Thomas |

and Akihiro Nishida, Hiro Uchiyama, Yongsou Cho, Onochi Seietsu (Japanese Clients)

*Francois Pignon, a dull employee at a condom factory, pretends to be gay in order to keep himself from being fired.*

Daniel Auteuil

Thierry Lhermitte, Gérard Depardieu

© Miramax Zoë

Samantha Morton, Emily Woof, John Hannah, Linus Roache

# PANDAEMONIUM

**(USA FILMS)** Producer, Nick O'Hagan; Executive Producers, David M Thompson, Mike Phillips, Tracey Scoffield; Co-Producer, Michael Kustow; Director, Julien Temple; Screenplay, Frank Cottrell Boyce; Photography, John Lynch; Designer, Laurence Dorman; Editor, Niven Howie; Costumes, Annie Symons; Line Producer, Jane Robertson; Hair & Makeup Designer, Liz Daxauer; Music, Dario Marianelli; Casting, Liora Reich; a BBC Films presentation of a Mariner Films production in association with The Arts Council of England and Moonstone Entertainment; Dolby; Color; Rated PG-13; 125 minutes; US release date: June 27, 2001

## CAST

| | |
|---|---|
| Samuel Coleridge | Linus Roache |
| William Wordsworth | John Hannah |
| Sara Coleridge | Samantha Morton |
| Dorothy Wordsworth | Emily Woof |
| Mary Wordsworth | Emma Fielding |
| John Thelwall | Andy Serkis |
| Robert Southey | Samuel West |
| Walsh | Michael N. Harbour |
| Tom Poole | William Scott-Masson |
| Dr. Gillman | Clive Merrison |
| Humphry Davy | Dexter Fletcher |

and Guy Lankester (Lord Byron), Andrea Lowe (Edith Southey), Jacqueline Defferary (Miss Holland), Andy de la Tour (Andre Crosse), John Kane (Jones), Colin McCredie (Messenger), Glyn Owen (Fisherman), Peter Harkness (Journalist), Niall Vincent (Hartley Coleridge—4 years old), Jason & Miles Quick (Hartley Coleridge—18 months old), Eleanor Russell (Hartley Coleridge—2 months old), Juno Temple (Emma Southey), Leo Temple (Herbert Southey), Rowena Gaukroger (Edith Mae Southey)

*A drama about the friendship, and ultimate betrayal, of two of the most celebrated poets at the turn of the 19th century, William Wordsworth and Samuel Taylor Coleridge.*

© USA Films

# EVERYBODY'S FAMOUS!

**(MIRAMAX)** Producers, Loret Meus, Dominique Deruddere; Director/Screenplay, Dominique Deruddere; Photography, Willy Stassen; Sets, Hubert Pouille; Music, Raymond van het Groenewoud; Editor, Ludo Troch; Costumes, Loret Meus; Co-Producers, Volkert Struycken, Errol Nayci, Pascal Judelewicz, Anne-Dominique Toussaint; Line Producer, Gérard Vercruysse; an Otomatic, Get Reel Productions, Les Films des Tournelles presentation; Belgian-French-Dutch, 2000; Dolby; Color; Rated R; 99 minutes; US release date: July 3, 2001

## CAST

| | |
|---|---|
| Jean Vereecken | Josse De Pauw |
| Willy van Outreve | Werner De Smedt |
| Marva Vereecken | Eva Van Der Gucht |
| Debbie | Thekla Reuten |
| Michael Jansen | Victor Löw |
| Chantal Vereecken | Gert Portael |
| Gaby | Ianka Fleerackers |
| Lies | Alice Reys |
| Julio Iglesia Imitation | Steve Ryckier |
| Freddy Mercury Imitation | Olivier Ythier |
| Otis Redding Imitation | Hein Sienkiewicz |
| State Police Warrant Officer | Jef Van Der Kuylen |
| Jim Poppe | Matthias Sercu |
| Rik de Visser | Wim Opbroeck |
| Georges | Marc Van Eeghem |
| Greet | Sylke Aerts |

and Heidi Verheyden, Viko Cockx, Frank Iwens, Mario Despiegeleer, Jan Van Der Kuylen, Christophe Vercouillie, Gunter Van Den Bergh, Wouter Talon, Michel Van Herck (State Police Officers), Caroline Rottier (Hair Stylist), Lut Hannes (Friend), George Arrendell (Dave), Hilt Devos (Woman on Talk Show), Sylvia Claes (Announcer), Christian Nolens, Miriam Thys, Bert Vannieuwenhuyse (Newscasters), Filip Peeters (State Police Officer), Tanja Cloeck (Singer in Restroom), Carl Ridders (Producer), Sien Eggers (Neighbor), Siegred Vincke (Teacher), Francois Beukelaers (NTO Director), Damiaan Deschrijver (State Police Spokesperson), Dominiek Vansteertegem (DJ), Hugo Van Den Bremt (Yup Host), Marc Didden (Talk Show Director), Jan Roos ("Song Organ" Director), Ivo Kuyl (Pharmacist), Christophe Stienlet (VJ), Alain Van Goethem ("Green Room" Singers), Annick Vandercruyssen ("Lonesome Zorra" Sound Mixer), Silvia Anglade (Spanish Newscaster), Mieke Verdin (Psychiatrist), Guy Dermul, Max Thijsen (Hosts)

*A blue-collar worker, intent on seeing his far-from-talented daughter make it as a singer, kidnaps a popular vocalist in hopes of attaining his goal.*

© Miramax Films

Eva Van Der Gucht

Jet Li

Jet Li, Bridget Fonda

## KISS OF THE DRAGON

**(20TH CENTURY FOX)** Producers, Luc Besson, Jet Li, Steven Chasman, Happy Walters; Director, Chris Nahon; Screenplay, Luc Besson, Robert Mark Kamen; Story, Jet Li; Photography, Thierry Arbogast AFC; Designer, Jacques Bufnoir; Editor, Marco Cave; Action Director, Cory Yuen; Music, Craig Armstrong; Co-Producer, Bernard Grenet; Stunts, Philippe Guegan, Pascal Guegan; a Europa Corp production in association with Quality Growth International Ltd; French-US; Dolby; Technovision; Color; Rated R; 97 minutes; US release date: July 6, 2001

Bridget Fonda

### CAST

| | |
|---|---|
| Liu Jian | Jet Li |
| Jessica | Bridget Fonda |
| Richard | Tchéky Karyo |
| Aja | Laurence Ashley |
| Uncle Tai | Burt Kwouk |
| Twins | Cyril Raffaelli, Didier Azoulay |
| Max | John Forgeham |
| Lupo | Max Ryan |
| Lupo's Assistant | Colin Prince |
| Pluto | Vincent Glo |
| Mister Big | Ric Young |
| Minister Tang | Vincent Wong |
| Chen | Kentaro |
| Aides | Stefano Sao Nelet, Peter Lee |
| Isabel | Isabelle Duhauvelle |

*A top government agent comes to Paris to assist a police official only to find himself betrayed by the man, accused of a murder he didn't commit and on the run from the law.*

© Twentieth Century Fox

Tchéky Karyo

Mischa Barton, Piper Perabo, Jessica Paré

## LOST AND DELIRIOUS

**(LIONS GATE)** Producers, Lorraine Richard, Louis-Philippe Rochon, Greg Dummett; Director, Léa Pool; Screenplay, Judith Thompson; Based on the novel *The Wives of Bath* by Susan Swan; Photography, Pierre Gill; Designer, Serge Bureau; Costumes, Aline Gilmore; Editor, Gaëtan Huot; Music, Yves Chamberland; Casting, Gail Carr, Lucie Robitaille, Lina Todd; a Cité-Amérique/Dummett Films production; Canadian; Dolby; Color; Not rated; 103 minutes; US release date: July 6, 2001

### CAST

| | |
|---|---|
| Pauline Oster | Piper Perabo |
| Victoria Moller | Jessica Paré |
| Mary "Mouse" Bradford | Mischa Barton |
| Faye Vaughn | Jackie Burroughs |
| Joseph Menzies | Graham Greene |
| Eleanor Bannet | Mimi Kuzyk |
| Jake | Luke Kirby |
| Kara | Caroline Dhavernas |
| Cordelia | Amy Stewart |
| Morley Bradford | Noel Burton |

and Emily Van Camp (Allison), Alan Fawcett (Bruce), Peter Oldring (Phil), Grace Lynn Kung (Lauren), Stephen Mwinga (John), Lydia Zadel (Monica), Felicia Schulman (Sal Bedford), Gabrielle Boni, Sheena Bernett, Meaghan Rath, Melissa Pirrera (Allison's Friends), David Dean (Boy of RAB), Jonathan Eliot (Tim), Phong Doan Huy (Fencing Teacher), Catherine Florent (Pauline's Fencing Opponent), Sophie Barsanti, Genevieve LaVallee, Myrtho Ouellette (Flutists)

*Mouse Bradford becomes close friends with her two senior roommates at college until those girls are caught in a compromising position, tearing their relationship apart.*

© Lions Gate Entertainment

## JUMP TOMORROW

**(IFC)** Producer, Nicola Usborne; Executive Producers, Tim Perell, Paul Webster; Director/Screenplay, Joel Hopkins; Co-Producer, Jake Myers; Photography, Patrick Cady; Designer, John Paino; Costumes, Sarah J Holden; Associate Producers, Howard Gertler, Gill Holland; Editor, Susan Littenberg; Music, John Kimbrough; Casting, Ali Farrell; a Eureka Pictures/Jorge Productions, Inc production for FilmFour; British-US; Dolby; Technicolor; Rated PG; 96 minutes; US release date: July 6, 2001

### CAST

| | |
|---|---|
| George | Tunde Adebimpe |
| Gerard | Hippolyte Girardot |
| Alicia | Natalia Verbeke |
| Consuelo | Patricia Mauceri |
| George's Uncle | Isiah Whitlock, Jr |
| Heather Leather | Kaili Vernoff |
| Old Man | Gene Ruffini |
| Sophie | Abiola Wendy Abrams |
| Other Student in Class | Amy Sedaris |
| Priest | Deen Badarou |
| Nathan | James Wilby |

and Murielle Arden (Claudette), Cherie Jimenez (Maria), Raul A Reyes (Co-Worker), Alan Gryfe (Teacher), Arthur Anderson (Jeweler), Leisa Heintzelman (Airport Official), William Barry (Compere), Carole Bayeux (PVC Girl), Anthony Genco (Boy at Falls), Charles Temo (Border Guard)

*George, a shy man scheduled to marry a Nigerian woman his family has select-ed for him, finds himself questioning his destiny when he meets Alicia, a beau-tiful Spanish girl who is also heading for an uncertain marriage.*

© IFC Films

Hippolyte Girardot, Tunde Adebimpe

263

Beat Takeshi, Joy Nakagawa

Claude Maki, Beat Takeshi, Omar Epps

Beat Takeshi

Wanda-Lee Evans, Omar Epps, Tatyana M. Ali

# BROTHER

(SONY PICTURES CLASSICS) Producers, Masayuki Mori, Jeremy Thomas; Director/Screenplay/Editor, Takeshi Kitano; Line Producer, Shinji Komiya; Associate Producer, Peter Watson; Co-Producers, Takio Yoshida, Ann Carli; Photography, Katsumi Yanagijima; Designer, Norihiro Isoda; Costumes, Yohji Yamamoto; Music, Joe Hisaishi; Casting, Takefumi Yoshikawa, Robi Reed; a Recorded Picture Company and Office Kitano presentation in association with FilmFour and Bac Films; Japanese-British-French-U.S., 2000; Dolby; Color; Rated R; 107 minutes; US release date: July 20, 2001

## CAST

Yamamoto............................................................Beat Takeshi
Denny ...................................................................Omar Epps
Ken.......................................................................Claude Maki
Shirase .................................................................Masaya Kato
Kato......................................................................Susumu Terajima
Jay ........................................................................Royale Watkins
Mo ........................................................................Lombardo Boyar
Harada..................................................................Ren Ohsugi
Ishihara ................................................................Ryo Ishibashi
Sugimoto..............................................................James Shigeta
Latifa....................................................................Tatyana M. Ali
Chief of Police .....................................................Makolo Ohtake
Hanaoka...............................................................Koen Okumura
Hisamatsu.............................................................Naomasa Musaka
and Rino Katase (Night Club Madame), Tetsuya Watari (Jinseikai Boss), Ren Murakami (Minamino), Joy Nakagawa (Marina), Wanda-Lee Evans (Denny's Mother), Tony Colitti (Roberto), Koyo Into (Nishida), Alan Garcia (Bellboy), Antwon Tanner (Colin), Joseph Ragno (Mafia Ross Rossi), Nynno Ali (Oscar), Paul Feddersen (Limo Driver), Dan Gunther (Killer Waiter), Robert Covarrubias, Anthony Vatsula (Mexican Mafia Officers), Al Vicente, Luis Angel (Victor's Henchmen), Brad "The Animal" Lesley (Moose), Lobo Sebastian (Yamamoto Bodyguard), Tomas Chavez (Victor's Driver), Don Sato (Sushi Bar Owner), Hideo Kimura (Sushi Bar Part-Timer), Yayoi Otani (Sushi Bar Waitress), Tuesday Night (Prostitute), Yuji Hasegawa (Whorehouse Customer), Chuma Hunter-Gault (Sly), Kool Mo Dee (Jack), Peter Spellos (Taxi Driver), Amaury Nolasco (Victor), Jack Ong, Mike Wu (Chinese Bosses), Tad Horino (Coffee Shop Owner), Alvin Ing (Doctor), Herschel Sparber (Geppetti's Bodyguard), John Aprea (Mafia Boss Geppetti), Christopher Dergregorian, Manny Perez (Mexican Mafia Hitmen), Eddie Garcia (Mexican Mafia Henchman), Rainbow Borden, Manny Gavino, Hiroshi Otaguro, Darryl M Bell (Yamamoto's Henchmen), Eiji Inoue (Shirase's Henchman), Akira Kaneda (Mafia Hitman), Geoff Meed (Rossi's Bodyguard), Shoken Kunimoto (Ohyama), Shuhei Saga (Matsumoto)

*A Japanese yakuza, forced to leave Tokyo, ends up in Los Angeles where he finds himself reverting to his violent ways, forming a gang, and taking over a major drug operation.*

© Sony Pictures Entertainment

Bruno Ganz

# BREAD AND TULIPS

**(FIRST LOOK PICTURES)** Producer, Daniele Maggioini; Director, Silvio Soldini; Screenplay/Story, Doriana Leondeff, Silvio Soldini; Photography, Luca Bigazzi; Art Director, Paola Bizzarri; Costumes, Silvia Nebiolo; Editor, Carlotta Cristiani; Music, Giovanni Venosta; Casting, Jorgelina Depetris; a co-production of Amka Films, Instituto Luce, Monogatari, Rai Cinemafiction, Televisione Svizzera Italian (TSI); Italian-Swiss, 2000; Dolby; Cinecitta color; Rated PG-13; 114 minutes; US release date: July 27, 2001

## CAST

| | |
|---|---|
| Rosalba Barletta | Licia Maglietta |
| Fernando Girasoli | Bruno Ganz |
| Constantino | Giuseppe Battiston |
| Grazia | Marina Massironi |
| Mimmo Barletta | Antonio Catania |
| Fermo | Felice Andreasi |
| Ketty | Vitalba Andrea |
| Adele | Tatiana Lepore |
| Eliseo | Ludovico Paladin |
| Nic | Tiziano Cucchiarelli |
| Salvo | Matteo Febo |
| Constantino's Mother | Silvana Bosi |
| Man at the Station | Manrico Gammarota |
| Goran | Massimiliano Speziani |
| Man in Car | Fausto Russo Alesi |
| Ballad Singer | Don Backy |
| Tour Guide | Nunzio Daniele |

and Pierantio Micciarelli (Salesman), Daniela Piperno (Woman in Car), Lina Bernardi (Nancy), Antonia Miccoli (Sami), Mauro Marino (Lello), Paola Brolati (Florist Customer), Giselda Volodi (Pensione Housekeeper)

*An unhappy housewife, accidentally left behind while on holiday, makes her way to Venice where she decides to stay on and take a job in a florist shop, finding all the joys that had been absent from her routine life.*

© First Look Pictures

Licia Maglietta

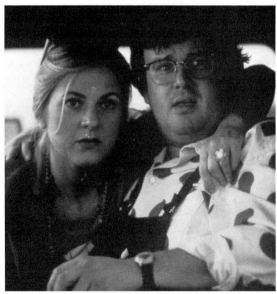

Licia Maglietta, Bruno Ganz

Marina Massironi, Antonio Catania

Natasha Little, Clive Owen

# GREENFINGERS

**(SAMUEL GOLDWYN)** Producers, Travis Swords, Daniel J Victor, Trudie Styler; Executive Producer, Daniel J Victor; Director/Screenplay, Joel Hershman; Photography, John Daly BSC; Designer, Tim Hutchinson; Costumes, Frances Tempest; Music, Guy Dagul; Editor, Justin Krish; Casting, Michelle Guish; a Fireworks Pictures and Samuel Goldwyn Films and Boneyard Entertainment presentation in association with Xingu Films and Travis Swords Productions; British; Dolby; Color; Rated R; 91 minutes; US release date: July 27, 2001

## CAST

| | |
|---|---|
| Colin Briggs | Clive Owen |
| Georgina Woodhouse | Helen Mirren |
| Fergus Wilk | David Kelly |
| Governor Hodge | Warren Clarke |
| Tony | Danny Dyer |
| Raw | Adam Fogerty |
| Jimmy | Paterson Joseph |
| Primrose Woodhouse | Natasha Little |
| Dudley | Peter Guinness |
| Holly | Lucy Punch |
| Susan Hodge | Sally Edwards |
| Nigel | Donald Douglas |
| Laurence | Kevin McMonagle |
| Sarah | Julie Saunders |
| John | Jordan Maxwell |

and David Lyon (Home Secretary), Jan Chappell (Peggy Tortworth), Timothy Carlton (Hampton Court Official), Sudha Bhuchar, Ian East, Paul Ridley (Prison Board Officials), Brenda Cowling (Book Shop Customer), Charles De'Ath (Julian), Trevor Bowen (Royal Horticultural Society President), Lindsay Swan (Royal Horticultural Society Publicist), Cate Fowler (Nurse), Chris Barnes (Reporter), Emily Stott (Interviewer), Elwyn A David (Bodybuilder), James Wooley (Parole Judge)

*Two inmates find meaning in their lives when the flowers they have planted impress the governor so much that he allows them to cultivate the prison's first official garden.*

© Fireworks/Goldwyn

David Kelly, Clive Owen

Helen Mirren

Clive Owen

Helena Bergström

# UNDER THE SUN

**(SHADOW DISTRIBUTION)** Producer/Director, Colin Nutley; Screenplay, Colin Nutley, Johanna Hald, David Neal; Based on the short story *The Little Farm* by H E Bates; Photography, Jens Fischer; Music, Paddy Maloney; Editor, Perry Schaffer; Costumes, Camilla Thulin; Produced by Sweetwater in cooperation with Svensk Filmindustri, SVT Goteborg/Drama, Film I Vast and Nordisk Film and TV-Fond; Swedish, 1998; Dolby; CinemaScope; Color; Not rated; 118 minutes; US release date: August 3, 2001

## CAST

| | |
|---|---|
| Olof | Rolf Lassgård |
| Ellen | Helena Bergström |
| Erik | Johan Widerberg |
| Newspaper Receptionist | Gunilla Röör |
| Preacher | Jonas Falk |
| Lena | Linda Ulvaeus |

and Bergljót Arnadóttir (Shop Assistant), Per Sandberg (Undertaker)

*In rural 1956 Sweden, an illiterate, isolated farmer advertises for a housekeeper and gets a response from the beautiful, worldly Ellen.*

© Shadow Distribution

Helena Bergström, Rolf Lassgård

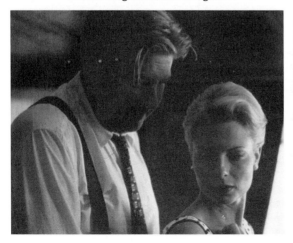

Rolf Lassgård, Helena Bergström

Johan Widerberg, Helena Bergström

Lena Headey

## AUDITION

**(VITAGRAPH)** Producers, Akemi Suyama, Satoshi Hukushima; Executive Producer, Toyoyuki Yokohama; Director, Takashi Miike; Screenplay, Daisuke Tengan; Story, Ryû Murakami; Photography, Hideo Yamamoto; Designer, Tatsuo Ozeki; Editor, Yasushi Shimamura; Music, Kôji Endô; Japanese, 1999; Color; Not rated; 115 minutes; US release date: August 8, 2001

### CAST

Shigeharu Aoyama.................................................Ryô Ishibashi
Asami Yamazaki .......................................................Eihi Shiina
Shigehiko Aoyama .................................................Tetsu Sawaki
Yasuhisa Yoshikawa...............................................Jun Kunimura
Old Man in Wheelchair.......................................Renji Ishibashi
Ryôko Aoyama.....................................................Miyuki Matsuda
and Toshie Negishi (Rie), Ren Osugi (Shibata), Shigeru Saiki (Toastmaster), Ken Mitsuishi (Director), Yuriko Hirooka (Michiyo Yanagida), Fumiyo Kohinata (TV Station Presenter), Misato Nakamura (Misuzu Takagi), Yuuto Arima (Shigeharu as a Child), Ayaka Izumi (Asami as a Child)

*Widower Aoyama holds auditions for a non-existent movie in hopes of finding a bride. After choosing the seemingly demure Asami, he is shocked when their relationship takes an unexpected turn.*

© Vitagraph

## ABERDEEN

**(FIRST RUN FEATURES)** Producer, Petter J Borgli; Executive Producer, Tom Remlov; Director, Hans Petter Moland; Screenplay, Kristin Amundsen, Hans Petter Moland; Story, Lars Bill Lundholm; Photography, Philip Øgaard; Designer, Janusz Sosnowski; Costumes, Anne Pedersen; Music, Zbigniew Preisner; Editor, Sophie Hesselberg; Co-Producers, Kastro Khatib, John McGrath; Casting, Jeremy Zimmerman; from Filmfabriken Baltic Sea AB (Sweden), Freeway Films (UK), and Norsk Film A/S (Norway); British-Norwegian-Swedish, 2000; Dolby; Color; Not rated; 106 minutes; American release date: August 10, 2001

### CAST

Tomas...............................................................Stellan Skarsgård
Kaisa .......................................................................Lena Headey
Clive..........................................................................Ian Hart
Helen ................................................................Charlotte Rampling
Nurse.....................................................................Louise Goodall
Perkins ............................................................Jason Hetherington

*Helen convinces her daughter to journey to Norway under the pretense of bringing her estranged alcoholic father to Scotland for rehab.*

© First Run Features

Ryô Ishibashi, Jun Kunimura

Eihi Shiina

Alakina Mann, Nicole Kidman, James Bentley

Nicole Kidman (Above and Below)

# THE OTHERS

**(MIRAMAX)** Producers, Fernando Bovaira, José Luis Cuerda, Sunmin Park; Executive Producers, Tom Cruise, Paula Wagner, Bob Weinstein, Harvey Weinstein, Rick Schwartz; Director/Screenplay/Music, Alejandro Amenábar; Photography, Javier Aguirresarobe AEC; Designer, Benjamín Fernández; Costumes, Sonia Grande; Casting, Jina Jay; a Cruise-Wagner Productions/Sogecine/Las Producciones Del Escorpión production; Spanish-US; Dolby; Deluxe color; Rated PG-13; 101 minutes; US release date: August 10, 2001

## CAST

| | |
|---|---|
| Grace Stewart | Nicole Kidman |
| Mrs. Mills | Fionnula Flanagan |
| Charles Stewart | Christopher Eccleston |
| Anne Stewart | Alakina Mann |
| Nicholas | James Bentley |
| Mr Tuttle | Eric Sykes |
| Lydia | Elaine Cassidy |
| Old Lady | Renée Asherson |
| Assistants | Gordon Reid, Ricardo López |
| Mr Marlish | Keith Allen |
| Mrs Marlish | Michelle Fairley |
| Victor | Alexander Vince |
| Gardene | Aldo Grilo |

*During the final days of World War II, Grace, who protects her two young children from extreme exposure to the light by shutting them up in her Victorian mansion, begins to sense the eerie presence of intruders in the house.*

© Dimension Films

Julia Blake, Charles Tingwell

Kristine Van Pellicom, Kenny Aernouts
© Fireworks Pictures

# INNOCENCE

(FIREWORKS/CINEVAULT) Producers, Paul Cox, Mark Patterson; Executive Producer, William T Marshall; Director/Screenplay, Paul Cox; Photography, Tony Clark ASC; Designer, Tony Cronin; Music, Paul Grabowsky; Associate Producer, Willem Thijssen; Editor, Simon Whitington; a Strand/New Oz Productions/Showtime Australia in association with the South Australian Film Corporation, Film Victoria, a division of Cinemedia, with HET Fonds Film in Vlaanderen and the International Film Festival Ghent and Illumination Films in association with Cinété presentation; Australian; Dolby; Color; Not rated; 95 minutes; US release date: August 17, 2001

## CAST

| | |
|---|---|
| Claire | Julia Blake |
| Andreas | Charles Tingwell |
| John | Terry Norris |
| David | Robert Menzies |
| Monique | Marta Dusseldorp |
| Young Claire | Kristine Van Pellicom |
| Young Andreas | Kenny Aernouts |
| Minister | Chris Haywood |
| Gerald | Norman Kaye |
| Sally | Joey Kennedy |
| Maudie | Liz Windsor |

*Fifty years after their brief but passionate love affair in post-war Belgium, music teacher Andreas Borg discovers that Claire still lives in the same town as he does, prompting him to contact her.*

# MAYBE BABY

(USA FILMS) Producer, Phil McIntyre; Executive Producers, Ernst Goldschmidt, David M Thompson; Director/Screenplay, Ben Elton; Associate Producer, Lucy Ansbro; Line Producer, Mary Richards; Photography, Roger Lanser ACS; Designer, Jim Clay; Editor, Peter Hollywood; Costumes, Anna Sheppard; Music, Colin Towns; Song: Maybe Baby by Charles Hardin, Norman Petty/performed by Paul McCartney; Casting, Mary Selway; a Pandora and BBC Films presentation of a Phil McIntyre production; British; Dolby; Deluxe color; Rated R; 93 minutes; US release date: August 24, 2001

## CAST

| | |
|---|---|
| Sam Bell | Hugh Laurie |
| Lucy Bell | Joely Richardson |
| George | Adrian Lester |
| Carl Phipps | James Purefoy |
| Ewan Proclaimer | Tom Hollander |
| Sheila | Joanna Lumley |
| Joanna | Rachael Stirling |
| Nigel | Matthew Macfadyen |
| Mr James | Rowan Atkinson |
| Charlene | Dawn French |
| Druscilla | Emma Thompson |

and Yasmin Bannerman (Melinda), Dave Thompson (Dave the Comedian/Mrs Furblob), Stephen Simms (Trevor), John Brenner (Kit), Jaz Wilson (Baby Cuthbert), Guy Barrett, Delia Bhujoo, Abbey Careford, Marina Fiorato (Nigel's Posse), Richard Leaf (Justin Cocker), Lidija Zovkic (Petra), Connor Pearce (Boy on Bike in Park), Henrietta Garden (Mother in Park), Richard Sandells (Man Wrestling for Cab), Emma Cooke, Shelley Conn (Nurses), Stephanie Bartczak, Chris Belgrave, Catriona Pearson, Judith Shekoni (Ewan's Posse), Paul Ready (Student Doctor), Paul Tripp (Mr Furblob), Gemma Aston (Roz), Lisa Palfrey (Jan), Serena Evans (Dr Cooper), Katisha Kenyon, Anneli Harrison, Caroline Hayes (Commerical Girls), Elizabeth Woodcock (Tilda), John Lightbody (Hospital Administrator), Mina Anwar (Yasmin), Junix Nocian (Chinese Practitioner), John Fortune (Acupuncturist), Sally Reeve (Masseuse), Kelly Reilly (Nimh), Emma Buckley (IVF Surgeon), Karen Bryson (Actor Playing Doctor), Bill & Ben (William the Dog)

*A successful married couple tries every method imaginable to have a baby.*

© USA Films

Joely Richardson, Hugh Laurie

Michael Nyqvist, Lisa Lindgren

Ola Norell

Jessica Liedberg, Lisa Lindgren

# TOGETHER

(IFC FILMS) Producer, Lars Jönsson; Director/Screenplay, Lukas Moodysson; Photography, Ulf Brantås; Art Director, Carl Johan de Geer; Costumes, Mette Möller; Editors, Michal Leszczylowski SFK, Fredrik Abrahamsen; Casting, Imor Hermann; Produced by Memfis Film in co-production with Zentropa Entertainments, Film i Väst, SVT Drama Göteborg, Keyfilms Roma, Nordisk Film & TV-Fond; Swedish-Danish, 2000; Dolby; Color; Not rated; 107 minutes; US release date: August 24, 2001

## CAST

| | |
|---|---|
| Elisabeth | Lisa Lindgren |
| Rolf | Michael Nyqvist |
| Eva | Emma Samuelsson |
| Stefan | Sam Kessel |
| Goran | Gustaf Hammarsten |
| Lena | Anja Lundqvist |
| Anna | Jessica Liedberg |
| Lasse | Ola Norell |
| Tet | Axel Zuber |
| Klas | Shanti Roney |
| Erik | Olle Sarri |
| Signe | Cecilia Frode |
| Sigvard | Lars Frode |
| Mane | Emil Moodysson |
| Fredrik | Henrik Lundstrom |
| Margit | Therese Brunnander |
| Ragnar | Claes Hartelius |
| Birger | Sten Ljunggren |

*Elisabeth, a housewife tired of her husband's abusive behavior, takes her two young children and moves into a commune.*

© IFC Films

Ola Norell, Shanti Roney

Michael Nyqvist, Lisa Lindgren

Tillsammans' Members

Giorgio Maiocchi

# THE IRON LADIES

(STRAND) Producer, Visute Poolvoralaks; Co-Producers, Chatchavarian Klainak, Prasert Wiwatananonpong, Chanajai Tonsaithong; Director, Yongyoot Thongkongtoon; Screenplay, Visuthichai Boonyakarinjana, Jira Maligool, Yongyoot Thongkongtoon; Photography, Jira Maligool; Art Director, Narucha Vijitvarit; Costumes, Ekkawsit Meeprasertkul; Music, Wild at Heart; Editor, Sunit Assavinikul; a Tai Entertainment presentation; Thai, 2000; Dolby; Color; Not rated; 105 minutes; US release date: September 7, 2001

## CAST

| | |
|---|---|
| Jung | Chaichan Nimpoonsawas |
| Mon | Sahaparp Virakamin |
| Nong | Giorgio Maiocchi |
| Pia | Gokgorn Benjathikul |
| Chai | Jessdaporn Pholdee |
| Wit | Ekachai Buranapanit |
| Coach Bee | Siridhana Hongsophon |
| April | Phromsit Sittichumroenkhun |
| May | Suttipong Sittichumroenkhun |
| June | Anucha Chatkaew |
| Man | Suraphan Chaupaknam |
| Muk | Sujira Arunpipat |
| Chat | Pakorn Vipatawat |

and Pairote Jaisinga (Jung's Father), Wiyada Umarin (Jung's Mother), Saneh Srisuwan (Sheriff), Umnuay Sirichan (Coach Bee's Father), Siriwan Suridej (Seller), Prawin Pattanaphong (Coach Chatree), Patcharapon Hitanant (Street Vendor), Sudjai Sunthornwipat (Grandma on Train), Damrong Puttarn, Sanya Kunakorn (TV Hosts), Weeraprawat Wonguapan (Wit's Father), Piatip Kumwong (Witt's Mother), Sukanya Raiwint (Juli), Komsan Meesombat (Referee), Suraphon Chonwilai (Wedding Photographer), Anupon Puwapoonphon (Northern Dialect MC), Samruay Saengtubtim (Nan Province Coach), Kritt Uttaseri, Wasan Utamayothin (TV Hosts), Kroi Samkao, Boonyod Sukthinthai (Referees), Theerachai Preukpiman (Coach), Kittipat Chainuwat (Kitti)

*The true story of how a male volleyball team, consisting mostly of homosexuals, transvestites, and transsexuals, won the 1996 National Championships.*

© Strand Releasing

# A MATTER OF TASTE

(ATTITUDE FILMS/TLA RELEASING) Producers, Catherine Dussart, Chantal Perrin; Director, Bernard Rapp; Screenplay, Gilles Taurand, Bernard Rapp; Based on the novel *Affairs de Gout* by Philippe Balland; Photography, Gérard de Battista; Designer, François Comtet; Costumes, Martine Rapin; Music, Jean-Philippe Goude; Editor, Juliette Welfling; Casting, Gérard Moulévrier; French, 2000; Dolby; Color; Not rated; 90 minutes; US release date: September 7, 2001

## CAST

| | |
|---|---|
| Frédéric Delamont | Bernard Giraudeau |
| Nicolas Rivière | Jean-Pierre Lorit |
| Béatrice | Florence Thomassin |
| René Rousset | Charles Berling |
| Magistrate | Jean-Pierre Léaud |
| Flavert | Artus de Penguern |
| Doctor Rossignon | Laurent Spielvogel |
| Caroline | Elisabeth Macocco |
| Doctor Ferrières | Anne-Marie Philipe |
| Nathalie | Delphine Zingg |
| Marco | David D'ingeo |
| Fèlix | Frédéric de Goldfiem |

*Frédéric Delamont, a wealthy, eccentric businessman, hires handsome waiter Nicolas to be his food taster, resulting in an increasingly unsettling relationship between the two, as Delamont becomes more demanding and obsessive.*

© Attitude Films/TLA

Florence Thomassin, Jean-Pierre Lorit

Bernard Giraudeau, Jean-Pierre Lorit

# OUR LADY OF THE ASSASSINS

**(PARAMOUNT CLASSICS)** Producers, Margaret Menegoz, Barbet Schroeder; Director, Barbet Schroeder; Screenplay, Fernando Vallejo, based on his novel *La Virgen de los Sicarios*; Photography, Rodrigo Lalinde; Designer/Costumes, Monica Marulanda; Editor, Elsa Vasquez; Music, Jorge Arriagada; Casting, Marlin Franco, Margarita Florez, Ana Isabel Velasquez; a co-production of Les Films du Losange/Le Studio Canal+; French; Dolby; Color; Rated R; 100 minutes; US release date: September 7, 2001

## CAST

Fernando ...................................................................Germàn Jaramillo
Alexis...............................................................Anderson Ballesteros
Wilmar...................................................................Juan David Restrepo
Alfonso ...........................................................................Manuel Busquets
Child Sniffing Glue.........................................................Wilmar Agudelo
4X4 Thief .........................................................................Juan Carlos Alvarez
Taxi Driver—Santo Domingo....................................................Jairo Alzate
Waitress ................................................................................Zulma Arango
Alexis's Mother ....................................................................Cenobia Cano
and José Luis Bedoya (Taxi Sabaneta #1), Eduardo Carvajal (Taxi Driver Clinic), Olga Lucía Collazos (Pregnant Woman), Jorge A Correa (Dead Man), Phanor Delgado (Taxi Driver with Machette), Albeiro Lopera (Punk), Wilson Lòpez (Taxi Driver Sabaneta #2), Alexander Molina, Juan Tejada (Alexis's Brothers), Anibal Moncada (Don Anibal), Jaime Osorio (Forensic Pathologist), Carlos Ordòñez (Old Fool), Teyler Pérez (4X4 Youth), Edwin Porras, Ohn Mario Restrepo (Bad Guys), Gustavo Restrepo (Wounded Man), Carlos A Danita (Wounded Man's Friend), Nicolàs Franco, Juan Fdo Leòn (Hired Assassins), Hector Galàn (Tango Singer), Rubi Henao (Beggar), John Jaramillo (Child Beggar), Carlos Zapata (Motel Receptionist), Serafin Zapata (Clown), Martha Libia Zuluaga (Dead Punk Waitress)

*Fernando, a wearied and cynical Colombian writer, returns to his home town of Medellín where he witnesses the devastation and crime that has become the norm to the population, including his younger lover, Alexis, who believes it is his duty to dispose of the underbelly of society.*

© Paramount Classics

Germàn Jaramillo

Anderson Ballesteros

Anderson Ballesteros, Germàn Jaramillo

Claire Hackett, Anthony Borrows, Ian Hart

# LIAM

(LIONS GATE) Producers, Colin McKeown, Martin Tempia; Executive Producers, David M Thompson, Tessa Ross, Sally Hibbin; Co-Producer, Ulrich Felsberg; Director, Stephen Frears; Screenplay, Jimmy McGovern; Photography, Andrew Dunn; Designer, Stephen Fineren; Costumes, Alex Caulfield; Editor, Kristina Hetherington; Music, John Murphy; Casting, Pippa Hall, Leo Davis; a BBC Films presentation of a Liam Films production in co-production with Road Movies and in association with MIDA, Diaphana, BIM, WDR/Arte, ARD/Degeto Film; British-German-Italian; Dolby; Color; Rated R; 90 minutes; US release date: September 21, 2001

Anthony Borrows

## CAST

| | |
|---|---|
| Dad Tom Sullivan | Ian Hart |
| Mum Sullivan | Claire Hackett |
| Mrs. Abernathy | Anne Reid |
| Liam Sullivan | Anthony Borrows |
| Con Sullivan | David Hart |
| Teresa Sullivan | Megan Burns |
| Father Ryan | Russell Dixon |
| Auntie Aggie | Julia Deakin |
| Uncle Tom | Andrew Schofield |
| Lizzie | Bernadette Shortt |
| Lizzie's Husband | David Carey |
| Mr. Samuels | David Knopov |
| Mrs. Samuels | Jane Gurnett |
| Jane Samuels | Gema Loveday |
| David | Martin Hancock |
| Nunny | Sylvie Gatrill |
| Nunny's Husband | Chris Darwin |
| Lofty | James Foy |
| Pawnbroker | Arnold Brown |

and Billy Moocho (Clubman), Stephen Walters (Black Shirt), Bryan Reagan (Gaffer), Sean Styles (Big Micky), Sean McKee (Little Micky), George Maudsley (Man at Political Rally)

*A young boy, growing up in poverty in 1930 Liverpool, sees his desperate father join a group of fascists after he has convinced himself that the Jews are responsible for him losing his job at the shipyard.*

© Lions Gate Films

Anthony Borrows, Megan Burns

(Above) Hélène De Fougerolles, Sergio Castellitto
(Below) Jeanne Balibar

## BORN ROMANTIC

(UNITED ARTISTS) Producer, Michele Camarda; Executive Producers, David M Thompson, Alistair MacLean-Clark, Melvyn Singer; Director/Screenplay, David Kane; Photography, Robert Alazraki AFC; Designer, Sarah Greenwood; Costumes, Jill Taylor; Editor, Michael Parker; Music, Simon Boswell; Choreographers, Jose Ordonez Fernandes De Souza, Rodolpho Fournier; Casting, Jina Jay; a BBC Films and Harvest Pictures presentation of a Kismet Film Company production; British; Dolby; Deluxe color; Rated R; 96 minutes; US release date: September 28, 2001

### CAST

Frankie..................................................................Craig Ferguson
Second Cab Driver ...........................................................Ian Hart
Mo ...................................................................Jane Horrocks
Jimmy...............................................................Adrian Lester
Jocelyn ...................................................Catherine McCormack
Eddie ...................................................................Jimi Mistry
Fergus ...........................................................David Morrissey
Eleanor..............................................................Olivia Williams
and Paddy Considine (Ray), Kenneth Cranham (Barney), Louise Delamere (Maria), Jose Ordonez Fernandes De Souza (Souza), Tony Maudsley (Turnkey), Hermione Norris (Carolanne), Sally Phillips (Suzy), Mel Raido (Brian), Martin Savage (Wayne), Jessica Stevenson (Libby), John Thomson (1st Driver), Ashley Walters (Lee), Victoria Willing (Frankie's Barmaid), Vanessa Samson, Alison Allen, Philip Langlais Garcia, Maria Legaspi, Sarah Davis, Rodolfo Fournier, Delena Dunster, Ernesto Estryou, Roisin Ahearne, Leonel Gamboa, Yamile Berral, Bill Williams, Homero Gonzalez, Stacey Dore, Cherryl Hancock, Ashwin Musiban, Gordon Haynes (Salsa Club Dancers), Simon Boswell, Jeff Clyne, Harry Dixon, Jimmy Hastings, Lew Hooper, George Patterson, Peter Strange, Eddie Taylor (Frankie's Band)

*Three single London men searching for love find themselves pursuing seemingly unsuitable women.*

© United Artists Films, Inc.

## VA SAVOIR
## (WHO KNOWS?)

(SONY PICTURES CLASSICS) Producer, Martine Marignac; Director, Jacques Rivette; Screenplay, Pascal Bonitzer, Christine Laurent, Jacques Rivette; Dialogue, Pascal Bonitzer, Christine Laurent, Jacques Rivette; Photography, William Lubtchansky; Designer, Manu de Chauvigny; Editor, Nicole Lubtchansky; Associate Producer, Maurice Tinchant; Costumes, Laurence Struz, Christine Laurent; a Pierre Grise Productions presentation; a co-production of Pierre Grise Productions, France 2 Cinema VM Productions (France), Mikado (Italy), Kinowelt (Germany), with the participation of Canal+, Cofimage 12, Gimages 4, Centre National de la Cinematographie with the support of Eurimages and La Procirep; French-Italian-German; Dolby; Color; Rated PG-13; 150 minutes; US release date: September 29, 2001

### CAST

Camille Renard ....................................................Jeanne Balibar
Ugo Bassani .................................................Sergio Castellitto
Sonia ............................................................Marianne Basler
Pierre Mauduit ............................................Jacques Bonnaffé
Dominique "Do" Desprez.....................Hélène de Fougerolles
Arthur Delamarche .......................................Bruno Todeschini
Madame Desprez, Do's Mother.......................Catherine Rouvel
Autograph Librarian ...............................................Claude Berri

## CAST OF
## As You Desire Me
## (Come tu mi vuoi)

Salter .................................................................Attilio Cucari
Greta (Mop) ......................................................Bettina Kee
Bruno ...........................................Arturo Armone Caruso
Lena ...........................................................Luciana Castellucci
Salesio .......................................................Emanuele Vacca
Ines.............................................................Valeria Cavalli
Silvio ....................................................Fausto Maria Sciarappa
The Madwoman ..............................................Paola Andrea
and Enrico Marassi, Cesare Panzera Capitani, Roberto Manieri, Constantino Raimondi (Four Young Men), Christiana Visentin (Pamina), Fosco Perinti (Administrator), Walter Zoon (Doctor)

*French actress Camille Renard returns to Paris after a three-year absence to participate in an Italian company's production of* As You Desire Me, *directed by her lover, Ugo, who becomes obsessed with finding the lost manuscript of a play by Italian playwright Goldoni.*

© Sony Pictures Entertainment

David Morrissey, Jimi Mistry, Craig Ferguson

Naomi Watts, Laura Elena Harring

Justin Theroux

Ann Miller, Naomi Watts

© Universal Studios, Inc.

# MULHOLLAND DR.

(UNIVERSAL) Producers, Mary Sweeney, Alain Sarde, Neal Edelstein, Michael Polaire, Tony Krantz; Executive Producer, Pierre Edelman; Director/Screenplay, David Lynch; Photography, Peter Fleming; Designer, Jack Fisk; Editor, Mary Sweeney; Costumes, Amy Stofsky; Music, Angelo Badalamenti; a co-production of Les Films Alain Sarde, Studio Canal, Picture Factory; French-US; Dolby; Color; Rated R; 146 minutes; US release date: October 8, 2001

## CAST

| | |
|---|---|
| Adam Kesher | Justin Theroux |
| Betty Elms/Diane Selwyn | Naomi Watts |
| Rita/Camilla Rhodes | Laura Elena Harring |
| Coco Lenoix | Ann Miller |
| Vincenzo Castigliane | Dan Hedaya |
| Joe | Mark Pellegrino |
| Detective Domgaard | Brent Briscoe |
| Detective Harry McKnight | Robert Forster |
| Cynthia | Katharine Towne |
| Louise Bonner | Lee Grant |
| Limo Driver | Scott Wulff |
| Gene | Billy Ray Cyrus |
| Jimmy Katz | Chad Everett |
| Linney James | Rita Taggart |
| Wally Brown | James Karen |
| Lorraine | Lori Heuring |
| Luigi Castigliane | Angelo Badalamenti |
| Billy | Michael Des Barres |
| Mr Darby | Marcus Graham |
| Waitress at Winkies | Melissa Crider |
| Ray Hott | Robert Katims |
| Irene | Jeanne Bates |
| Irene's Companion | Dan Birnbaum |
| Aunt Ruth | Maya Bond |
| Dan | Patrick Fischler |
| Herb | Michael Cooke |
| Bum | Bonnie Aarons |
| Mr Roque | Michael J. Anderson |
| Roque's Manservant | Joseph Kearney |
| Back of Head Man | Enrique Buelna |
| Hairy-Armed Man | Richard Mead |
| Cab Driver at LAX | Sean E. Markland |
| Valet Attendant | Daniel Rey |
| Robert Smith | David Schroeder |
| Espresso Man | Tom Morris |
| Camilla Rhodes | Melissa George |
| Castigliane Limo Driver | Matt Gallini |
| Ed | Vincent Castellanos |

and Diane Nelson (Heavy-Set Woman), Charlie Croughwell (Vacuum Man), Rena Riffel (Laney), Tad Horino (Taka), Tony Longo (Kenny), Geno Silva (Cookie), Lafayette Montgomery (Cowboy), Kate Forster (Martha Johnson), Wayne Grace (Bob Booker), Michele Hicks (Nicki), Lisa Ferguson (Julia Chadwick/Dancer), William Ostrander (1st Assistant Director), Elizabeth Lackey (Carol), Brian Beacock, Blake Lindsley, Adrien Curry, Tyrah M Lindsey (Backup Singers), Michael Weatherred (Hank, Assistant Director), Michael Fairman (Jason), Johanna Stein (Woman in #12), Richard Green (The Magician), Conte Candoli (Trumpet Player), Cori Glazer (Blue-Haired Lady), Rebekah Del Rio (Herself), Lyssie Powell (Blonde in Bed), Scott Coffey (Wilkins), Kimberly Clever, Joshua Collazo, David Frutos, Peter Loggins, Theresa Salazar, Thea Samuels, Christian Thompson (Dancers)

*A naive aspiring actress arrives in Hollywood where she meets up with an amnesiac who has just escaped death, leading the two of them into a hellish and puzzling adventure.*

*This film received an Oscar nomination for director.*

Anaïs Reboux, Roxane Mesquida

Anaïs Reboux, Roxane Mesquida

Anaïs Reboux

Libero De Rienzo, Roxane Mesquida

# FAT GIRL

(COWBOY PICTURES) Director/Screenplay, Catherine Breillat; Photography, Yorgos Arvanitis AFC; Art Directors, Francois Renaud Labarthe, Yann Richard, Cecilia Blom, Fabienne David, Christophe Graziani, Fabrice Heraud, Gerald Lemaire, Jean-Luc Molle; Costumes, Catherine Meillan; Editors, Pascale Chavance, Gwenola Heaulme, Frederic Barbe; Casting, Michael Weill; a Jean-François Lepetit presentation of a Flach Film-CB Films Production, Immagine & Cinema-Urbania Pictures, with the participation of Canal+ and the Centre National de la Cinématographie; French-Italian; Color; Not rated; 83 minutes; US release date: October 10, 2001

## CAST

Anaïs ............................................................................Anaïs Reboux
Elena ..........................................................................Roxane Mesquida
Fernando ......................................................................Libero De Rienzo
Mother ..........................................................................Arsinée Khanjian
Father............................................................................Romain Goupil
Fernando's Mother ................................................................Laura Betti
The Killer ......................................................................Albert Goldberg
and Odette Barriere, Ann Matthijsse, Pierre Renverseau, Jean-Marc Boulanger (Friends at Residence), Frederick Bodin (Waiter), Michel Guillemin (Janitor), Josette Cathalan (Saleswoman), Claude Sese (Police Officer), Marc Samuel (Inspector)

*While on vacation with her family, Anaïs, an introverted overweight girl, finds herself jealous of her gorgeous sister's sexual dalliance with a young Italian.*

© Cowboy Booking

Libero De Rienzo, Roxane Mesquida

Yu Rong Guang

## INTIMACY

**(EMPIRE)** Producers, Jacques Hinstin, Patrick Cassavetti; Executive Producer, Charles Gassot; Director, Patrice Chereau; Screenplay, Patrice Chereau, Anne-Louise Trividic; Based on the stories *Intimacy* and *Night Light* by Hanif Kureishi; Photography, Eric Gautier; Designer, Hayden Griffin; Costumes, Caroline De Vivaise; Line Producer, Lesley Stewart; Music, Eric Neveux; Editor, Francois Gedigier; Casting, Karen Lindsay-Stewart; Studio Canal; French; Dolby; CinemaScope; Color; Not rated; 119 minutes; US release date: October 17, 2001

### CAST

Jay .................................................................................Mark Rylance
Claire ......................................................................................Kerry Fox
Andy ..............................................................................Timothy Spall
Victor.......................................................................Alastair Galbraith
Ian ...........................................................................Philippe Calvario
Betty.......................................................................Marianne Faithfull
Susan ......................................................................Susannah Harker
Pam...........................................................................Rebecca Palmer
Dave .............................................................................Fraser Ayres
and Michael Fitzgerald, Robert Addie (Bar Owners), Deborah McLaren (Theatre Course Student), Greg Sheffield, Vinnie Hunter (Jay's Children), Joe Prospero (Claire's Son), Siân Reeves (Claire's Neighbor at Audition), Paola Dionisotti (Amanda in *The Glass Menagerie*), Marcello Walton (Tom in *The Glass Menagerie*), Christian Malcolm (Jim in *The Glass Menagerie*), Katie Campbell, Roderic Culver, Jonathan Emmett, Gideon Gent, Alison Lintott, Xavier Loira, Kate Orr, Clare Wayland

*A man and woman meet every week to have sex, trying not to become emotionally attached, a vow they find hard to keep.*

© Empire Pictures

## IRON MONKEY

**(MIRAMAX)** Producer, Tsui Hark; Executive Producers, Raymond Chow, Wang Ying Hsiang; Director, Yuen Wo Ping; Screenplay, Tsui Hark, Elsa Tang, Lau Tai Mok; Co-Producer, Raymond Lee; Photography, Arthur Wong, Tam Chi Wai; Designer, Ringo Cheung; Costumes, Bo Bo Ng; Music, James L Venable; Editors, Angie Lam, Chan Chi Wai; Martial Arts Choreographers, Yuen Cheung Yan, Yuen Shun Yi, Ku Huen Chiu; a Media Asia, Golden Harvest and Quentin Tarantino presentation of an LS Pictures Ltd Film Work Shop Production; Hong Kong, 1993; Dolby; Color; Rated PG-13; 85 minutes; US release date: October 12, 2001

### CAST

Dr Yang (Iron Monkey)......................................Yu Rong Guang
Wong Kei-Ying...........................................................Donnie Yen
Miss Orchid..................................................................Jean Wang
Wong Fei Hong......................................................Tsang Sze Man
Chief Fox ...............................................................Yuen Shun Yi
Governor...................................................................James Wong
Royal Minister....................................................Yen Yee Kwan
Virgin Assassin .................................................................Lee Fai
Scarred Assassin ...............................................Hau Yin Chung
Governor's Favorite Wife ..............................Cheung Fung Nay
and Chun Kwai Bo, Chan Siu Wah, Yip Choi Nam, Ko Man Dick (Monks)

*In 19th-century eastern China, an evil governor attempts to increase food prices during a famine, prompting a mysterious fighter known as the Iron Monkey to try to save his village from this oppression.*

© Miramax Films

(Above) Kerry Fox, Mark Rylance
(Below) Mark Rylance, Kerry Fox

Mark (right)

## BURNT MONEY
### (PLATA QUEMADA)

(STRAND) Producer, Oscar Kramer; Director, Marcelo Piñeyro; Screenplay, Marcelo Figueras; Photography, Alfredo Mayo; Designers, Jorge Ferrari, Juan Mario Roust; Editor, Juan Carlos Macias; Music, Osvaldo Montes; a Cabezas, Mandarin, Taxi Films SA production; Argentine, 2000; Dolby; Color; Not rated; 125 minutes; US release date: October 19, 2001

### CAST

| | |
|---|---|
| Angel | Eduardo Noriega |
| Nene | Leonardo Sbaraglia |
| Cuervo | Pablo Echarri |
| Giselle | Leticia Brédice |
| Fontana | Ricardo Bartis |
| Vivi | Dolores Fonzi |
| Nando | Carlos Roffé |
| Tabaré | Daniel Valenzuela |
| Losardo | Héctor Alterio |
| Realtor | Claudio Rissi |
| Florian Reyes | Luis Zembosky |
| Carlos Tulian | Harry Havilio |
| Parisi | Roberto Vallejo |
| Cantante Cabaret | Adriana Varela |

*A pair of gay lovers, dubbed "The Twins" by the police, become noted criminals of the Buenos Aires underworld until a botched heist forces them to escape to Uruguay.*

© Strand Releasing

## TREMBLING BEFORE G-D

(NEW YORKER) Producers, Sandi Simcha DuBowski, Marc Smolowitz; Co-Producers, James Velaise, Philippa Kowarsky; Director, Sandi Simcha DuBowski; Creative Collaboration, Susan Korda; Editors, Susan Korda, Johanna Prenner; Music, John Zorn; Photography, Various; Music Supervisors, Carole Sue Baker, Jon L Fine; Pretty Pictures (Paris), Cinephil Ltd (Tel Aviv); Israeli-French; Color; Not rated; 84 minutes; US release date: October 24, 2001 Documentary on gay Hasidic and Orthodox Jews who practice Judaism despite their religion's condemnation of homosexuality.

© New Yorker Films

Eduardo Noriega

Leonardo Sbaraglia, Eduardo Noriega

Ariane Ascaride, Gérard Meylan

Ariane Ascaride

Julie-Marie Parmentier, Ariane Ascaride

# THE TOWN IS QUIET

(NEW YORKER) Director, Robert Guédiguian; Screenplay, Jean-Louis Milesi, Robert Guédiguian; Photography, Bernard Cavalié; Designer, Michel Vandestien; Editor, Bernard Sasia; Costumes, Catherine Keller; Director of Production, Malek Hamzaoui; a co-production of Agat & CIE/Diaphana with the participation of Canal+; French; Dolby; Color; Not rated; 132 minutes; US release date: October 26, 2001

## CAST

| | |
|---|---|
| Michèle | Ariane Ascaride |
| Fiona | Julie-Marie Parmentier |
| Claude | Pierre Banderet |
| Gérard | Gérard Meylan |
| Paul | Jean-Pierre Darroussin |
| Paul's Father | Jacques Boudet |
| Paul's Mother | Pascale Roberts |
| Viviane Froment | Christine Brücher |
| Yves Froment | Jacques Pieiller |
| Abderamane | Alexandre Ogou |
| Momo, Abderamane's Brother | Amar Toulé |
| Farid | Farid Ziane |
| Ameline | Véronique Balme |
| SarkisJulien | Sevan Papazian |

and Danielle Stefan (The Prostitute), Patrick Bonnel (The Post Office Worker), Yann Trégouët (The Young Woman Who Provokes Gérard), Frédérique Bonnal (The Woman From the "National Preference"), Jacques Germain (Mr "National Preference"), Alain Lenglet (The Piano Mover), Emilie Angélini, Margaux Tartour, Noé Tellier (The Three Babies)

*The lives of several Marseilles inhabitants overlap and influence one another, including a fishmonger and her heroin-addicted daughter, a dockworker-turned-cabbie, a bartender who deals drugs, and a young North African ex-con.*

© New Yorker Films

Alexandre Ogou, Christine Brücher

Audrey Tautou

Frédéric Bouraly, Franck Bussi

Faudel

Eric Savin, Lysiane Meis

© Lot 47 Films

# HAPPENSTANCE

(LOT 47) Producers, Anne-Dominique Toussaint, Pascal Judelewicz; Director/Screenplay, Laurent Firode; Executive Producer, Franck Landron; Photography, Jean-Rene Duveau; Music, Peter Chase; Costumes, Najat Kas; Editor, Didier Ranz; Casting, Stephane Gaillard; a co-production of Les Films des Tournelles and Les Films en Hiver; French; Dolby; Color; Not rated; 90 minutes; US release date: November 2, 2001

## CAST

| | |
|---|---|
| Younes | Faudel |
| Irene | Audrey Tautou |
| Richard | Eric Slavin |
| Luc | Eric Feldman |
| Stephanie | Irene Ismailoff |
| Elsa | Lysiane Meis |
| Marie | Nathalie Besancon |
| Bobby | Frederique Bouraly |

and Franck Bussi (The Boy from the Filosophic Cafe), Marina Tome (Julie), Antoine Coesens (The Clochard), Said Serrari (The Pickpocket), Lily Boulogne (Luc's Mother), Gilbert Robin (The Destiny Man), Manu Layotte (Cailluox's Lanceurs), Husky Kihal (The Magazine Owner), Nor-eddin Abboud (The SAV Salesman), Louison Roblin (Irene's Neighbor), Felicite Wouassi (The Vigilant), Manuela Gourary (Elsa's Mother), Mathieu Ducrez (Franck), Abdessamada Chahidi (The Clandestine Moroccan), Sylvie Herbert (The Nurse), Michel Baladi (The Waiter From the Coffee Shop), Louise Vincent (The Gitane), Charlotte Maury-Sentier (The Horoscope Woman), Edith Le Merdy (The Subway Passenger), Oleg Imbert, Ludmila Imbert (The Russian Tourists), Francois Chattot (Marc), Pierre Bellemare (Taxi Driver)

*A group of seemingly unconnected individuals becomes instrumental in reuniting two people who have interacted on the Metro and accidentally separated.*

Audrey Tautou in *Amélie*

Audrey Tautou in *Amélie*

Audrey Tautou in *Amélie*

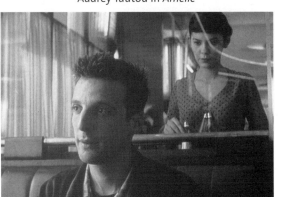

Mathieu Kassovitz, Audrey Tautou in *Amélie*

Audrey Tautou in *Amélie*

# AMÉLIE

(MIRAMAX ZOË) Producer, Claudie Ossard; Director, Jean Pierre Jeunet; Screenplay, Guillaume Laurant, Jean Pierre Jeunet; Dialogue, Guillaume Laurant; Photography, Bruno Delbonnel; Sets, Aline Bonetto; Costumes, Madeline Fontaine; Music, Yann Tiersen; Editor, Herve Schneid ACE; Visual Effects, Alain Carsoux, Duboi; Casting, Pierre Jacques Benichou; Presented in association with Claudie Ossard and UGC; a Victoires Productions, Tapioca Films, France 3 Cinema, MMC Independent Gmbh co-production in collaboration with the Sofica Sofinergie 5 and the support of the Filmstiftung with the participation of Canal+; French; Dolby; Technovision; Color; Rated R; 120 minutes; US release date: November 2, 2001

## CAST

| | |
|---|---|
| Amélie Poulain | Audrey Tautou |
| Nino Quicampoix | Mathieu Kassovitz |
| Raphael Poulain (Amélie's Father) | Rufus |
| Madeleine Wallace (Concierge) | Yolande Moreau |
| Hipolito (The Writer) | Artus de Penguern |
| Collignon (The Grocer) | Urbain Cancellier |
| Joseph | Dominique Pinon |
| Bretodeau (The Box Man) | Maurice Benichou |
| Eva (The Strip Teaser) | Claude Perron |
| Old Man Collignon | Michel Robin |
| Georgette | Isabelle Nanty |
| Suzanne | Claire Maurier |
| Gina | Clotilde Mollet |
| Dufayel | Serge Merlin |
| Lucien | Jamel Debbouze |
| Amandine Poulain | Lorella Cravotta |
| Philomene | Armelle |
| Amélie, 8 years old | Flora Guiet |
| Nino as a Child | Amaury Babault |
| The Blind Man | Jean Darie |
| The Photo Booth Man | Ticky Holgado |
| The Stranger | Marc Amyot |
| The Screaming Neighbor | Dominique Bettenfeld |
| Eugene Koler | Eugène Berthier |

and Andrée Damant (Mrs. Collignon), Franckie Pain (The Newsstand Woman), Marion Pressburger (Credits Helper), Charles-Roger Bour (The Urinal Man), Luc Palun (Amandine's Grocer), Fabienne Chaudat (Woman in Coma), Jacques Viala (The Customer Who Humiliates His Friend), Fabien Behar (The Humiliated Customer), Jonathan Joss (The Humiliated Customer's Son), Jean-Pierre Becker (The Bum), Theirry Gibault (The Endive Client), François Bercovici (His Buddy), Guillaume Viry (The Vagrant), Valérie Zarrouk (Dominique Bredoteau Woman), Kevin Fernandes (Bretodeau as a Child), Marie-Laure Descouraux (The Dead Man's Concierge), Sophie Tellier (Aunt Josette), Gérald Weingand (The Teacher), François Viaur (The Bar Owner), Paule Dare (His Employee), Myriam Labbe (The Tobacco Buyer), Robert Gendreu (Cafe Patron), Julianne Kovacs (Grocer's Client), Philippe Paimblanc (Train Ticket Taker), Mady and Monette Malroux (The Twins), Valériane de Villeneuve (The Laughing Woman), Isis Peyrade (Samantha) Raymonde Heudeline (Phantom Train Cashier), Christiane Bopp (Woman by the Merry-Go-Round), Thierry Arfeuilleres (Statue Man), Jerry Lucas (The Sacré-Couer Boy), Patrick Paroux (The Street Prompter), Francois Aubineau (The Concierge's Postman), Philippe Beautier (Poulain's Postman), Règis Iacono (Felix L'Herbier); Off-Screen Voices: Frank-Oliver Bonnet (Palace Video), Alain Floret (The Concierge's Husband), Jean-Pol Brissart (The Postman), Jacques Thebault (Voice-Over), André Dussollier (Voice)

*A waitress decides to transform the lives of her neighbors by doing anonymous deeds for them, while forsaking her own chance at happiness.*

*This film received Oscar nominations for foreign-language film, cinematography, original screenplay, and art direction.*

Audrey Tautou

Audrey Tautou

Mathieu Kassovitz

© Miramax Zoë

Iñigo Garcés

Irene Visedo

Marisa Paredes, Eduardo Noriega

# THE DEVIL'S BACKBONE

(SONY CLASSICS) Executive Producers, Augstín Almodóvar, Berta Navarro; Director, Guillermo Del Toro; Screenplay, Guillermo Del Toro, Antonio Trashorras, David Muñoz; Co-Producer, Rosa Bosch; Photography, Guillermo Navarro; Director of Production, Esther García; Art Director, Cesar Macarrón; Costumes, José Vico; Editor, Luis De La Madrid; Music, Javier Navarrete; Associate Producer, Michel Ruben; Digital Special Effects, Telson; Special Effects Makeup, DDT—David Martín; a Pedro and Augustín Almodóvar presentation, an El Deseo, SA, Tequila Gang and Anhelo Producciones co-production; Spanish; Dolby; Color; Rated R; 108 minutes; US release date: November 21, 2001

## CAST

Jacinto ...........................................................................Eduardo Noriega
Carmen ...........................................................................Marisa Paredes
Cásares ...........................................................................Federico Luppi
Jaime...............................................................................Iñigo Garcés
Carlos..............................................................................Fernando Tielve
and Irene Visedo (Conchita), Berta Ojea (Alma), Paco Maestre (El Puerco), José Manuel Lorenzo (Marcelo), Junio Valverde (Santi), Victor Barroso, Javier Gonzalez, Daniel Esparza, Adrián Lamana (Boys)

*At an isolated school during the last days of the Spanish Civil War, ten-year old Carlos becomes aware of the ghost of a former student who was brutally murdered.*

© Sony Pictures Entertainment

Victor Barroso, Javier Gonzalez, Daniel Esparza, Iñigo Garcés, Fernando Tielve, Adrián Lamana

# THE WAY WE LAUGHED

**(NEW YORKER)** Producers, Vittorio and Rita Cecchi Gori (Tiger CinCa srl); Executive Producer, Mario Conte (Pacific Pictures); Director/Screenplay, Gianni Amelio; Photography, Luca Bigazzi; Designer, Giancarlo Basili; Costumes, Gianna Gissi; Editor, Simona Paggi; Music, Franco Piersanti; Casting, Nicola Conticello, Lorella Chiapatti; a Tiger CinCa srl and Pacific Pictures production; Italian, 1998; Dolby; Color; Not rated; 124 minutes; US release date: November 21, 2001

## CAST
### Arrivals

| | |
|---|---|
| Pietro | Francesco Guiffrida |
| Giovanni | Enrico Lo Verso |
| The Father of the Family from Foggia | Guiliano Spadaro |
| His Wife | Patrizia Marino |
| His Son | Giuseppe Sangari |
| His Daughter | Francesca Monchiero |

and Calogero Caruana, Roberto Marzo, Davide Negro, Giorgio Pittau, Pasqualino Vona, Giuseppe Zarbano (Giovanni's Friends), Salvatore Refano (The Old Sicilian), Giorgia Scuderi (Assuntina), Maria Terranova (Giovanni's Aunt), Antonio Trigilla (Giovanni's Uncle), Michele Trigilla (Giovanni's Cousin), Alessandro Bretti (The Young Cousin)

### Deceptions

| | |
|---|---|
| Rosario | Claudio Contartese |
| Girl at the Bar | Barbara Braga |
| Sardinian Lance Corporal | Giovanni Leoni |
| Corporal's Assistant | Luigi Mauro |
| Neapolitan Janitor | Edoardo Ciciriello |

and Aldo Rendina (The Dance Teacher), Sabrina Rubino (The Dancer/The Maid), Rosaria Danze (Lucia)

### Money

| | |
|---|---|
| Giovanni's Assistant | Vittorio Rondella |
| The Boy from Lecce | Antonio Madaro |
| Alessandra, the Student | Erika Doria |
| Mrs Verusio | Iolanda Donnini |
| Carmelo, the Mason | Massimo Greco |
| The Train Thief | Emanuele Aquilino |

and Aldo Boarino (The Thief), Rosina Borgi (The Thief's Wife), Paolo Sansalone (The Boy in Public Baths), Bruno Casetta (The Restaurant's Waiter)

### Letters

| | |
|---|---|
| Female Student | Irene Vistarini |
| Male Student | Fabrizio Nicastro |
| The Janitor from Turin | Renato Liprandi |

and Domenico Ragusa (Simone, the Guard), Francesco Guzzo (Man in the Bar)

Enrico Lo Verso, Francesco Giuffrida

Enrico Lo Verso

Francesco Giuffrida, Enrico Lo Verso

### Blood

| | |
|---|---|
| The Exam Professors | Antonio Prestipino, Corrado Borsa, Pierfranco Ghisleni |
| Rosini, the Teacher | Paolo Sena |
| Director of the Cooperative | Domenico Mungo |
| The Unemployed Calabrian | Valerio Contartese |

and Marco Testa (The Singer at the Feast), Davide Pecetto (The Accordion Player), Mirella Ferrera (The Engaged Woman), Giuseppe D'Angelo (Giovanni's Assistant), Giannicola Resta (Young Thug)

### Families

| | |
|---|---|
| Ada | Simonetta Benozzo |
| Pelaia, the Educator | Fabrizio Gifuni |
| Battista, the Father | Pietro Paglietti |
| The Mother | Rosanna Rovere |
| Brother-in-Law | Nanni Tormen |
| Sister-in-Law | Ileana Spalla |
| The Grandson | Gianluigi Marcone |

and Luisella Tamietto, Tiziana Catalano (The Aunt), Clara Droetto (The Aunt)

*In a story that takes place on six different days during a six-year span, illiterate Sicilian immigrant Giovanni encourages his younger brother to get a diploma and become a teacher so that he may have the rewards of knowledge.*

© New Yorker Films

Javier Bardem, Jordi Mollá

## SECOND SKIN (SEGUNDA PIEL)

**(MENEMSHA)** Producer, Andrés Vicente Gómez; Director, Gerardo Vera; Screenplay, Andrés González Sinde; Photography, Júlio Madurga; Art Director, Ana Alvargonzález; Costumes, Macarena Soto; Music, Roque Baños; Editor, Nicholas Wentworth; Associate Producer, Marco Gómez; Produced by Antena 3 Television, Lolafilms S.A., Via Digital; Spanish, 1999; Color; Not rated; 110 minutes; American release date: November 30, 2001

### CAST

| | |
|---|---|
| Diego | Javier Bardem |
| Alberto Garcia | Jordi Mollà |
| Elena | Ariadna Gil |
| Eva | Cecilia Roth |
| Rafael | Gil Albala |
| Adrian | Adrian Sac |
| Maria Elena | Mercedes Sampietro |
| Ana Mari | Cristina Espinosa |
| Neus | Pilar Castro |
| Oriol | Ramiro Alonso |
| Engineer | Silvia Espigado |
| Nurse | Carmen Grey |
| Tomasa | Ángela Rosal |
| Aitor | Luis B. Santiago |
| Luis | Christian Queipo |
| Ivan | Ivan Mateo |

*Diego, a doctor, falls in love with Alberto Garcia, a married man with a child, leading to an affair that has profound repercussions for all parties involved including Alberto's wife.*

## CODE UNKNOWN

**(LEISURE TIME FEATURES/KIMSTIM)** Producers, Alain Sarde, Marin Karmitz; Executive Producer, Yvon Crenn; Director/Screenplay, Michael Haneke; Photography, Jürgen Jürges; Designer, Manu de Chauvigny; Costumes, Francoise Clavel; Editors, Karin Hartusch, Andreas Prochaska; Casting, Kris Portier Debellair; French-German-Romanian, 2000; Dolby; Color; Not rated; 117 minutes; US release date: November 30, 2001

### CAST

| | |
|---|---|
| Anne | Juliette Binoche |
| Georges | Thierry Neuvic |
| Le Paysan | Sepp Bierbichler |
| Jean | Alexandre Hamidi |
| Amadou | Ona Lu Yenke |
| Maria | Luminata Gheorghiu |
| Aminate | Maimouna Hélène Diarra |
| The Father | Djibril Kouyaté |
| Irina | Crenguta Hariton Stoica |

and Bob Nicolaescu (Dragos), Bruno Todeschini (Pierre), Paulus Manker (Perrin), Didier Flamand (The Director), Walid Afkir (The Young Arab), Maurice Bénichou (The Old Arab), Carlo Brandt (Henry), Philippe Demarle (Paul), Marc Duret (The Policeman), Arsinée Khanjian (Francine), Florence Loiret (Amadou's Friend), Nathalie Richard (Mathilde), Andrée Tainsy (Mrs Becker), Jean-Yves Chatelais (Shop Owner), Laurent Suire (Policeman), Malick Bowens (Witch Doctor), Ioan Marian Boris (Nicu), Monica Popa (Nuta), Ada Navrot (Florica), Dominique Douret (David), Tsuyu Bridwell (David's Friend), Antoine Mathieu (Restaurant Waiter), Constantin Barbulescu (Mihai Popa), Domeke Meite (Demba)

*Several Parisians, including an aspiring actress, a music teacher for deaf-mute children, and a beggar, find themselves linked in unexpected ways.*

© Leisure Time Features

Juliette Binoche

Michael Caine, Bob Hoskins, Tom Courtenay,
David Hemmings

Helen Mirren, Bob Hoskins

# LAST ORDERS

(SONY CLASSICS) Producers, Fred Schepisi, Elisabeth Robinson; Executive Producers, Nik Powell, Rainer Mockert, Gary Smith, Chris Craib; Director/Screenplay, Fred Schepisi; Based upon the novel by Graham Swift; Photography, Brian Tufano BSC; Designer, Tim Harvey; Costumes, Jill Taylor; Music, Paul Grabowsky; Editor, Kate Williams; Casting, Patsy Pollock, Shaheen Baig; from MBP, Scala Productions, Winchester Films; British-German; Dolby; Digitalscope; Color; Rated R; 109 minutes; US release date: December 7, 2001

## CAST

| | |
|---|---|
| Jack | Michael Caine |
| Vic | Tom Courtenay |
| Lenny | David Hemmings |
| Ray | Bob Hoskins |
| Amy | Helen Mirren |
| Vince | Ray Winstone |
| Young Jack | J.J. Feild |
| Young Vic | Cameron Fitch |
| Young Lenny | Nolan Hemmings |
| Young Ray | Anatol Yusef |
| Young Amy | Kelly Reilly |
| Young Vince | Stephen McCole |
| Bernie | Georges Innes |
| June | Laura Morelli |
| Mandy | Sally Hurst |
| Carol | Denise Black |

and Sue James (Pam), Meg Wynn Owen (Joan), Kitty Leigh (Young Carol), Alex Reid (Young Pam), Tracey Murphy (Young Joan), Claire Harman (Young Sally), John Baker (11-year-old Vince), Emma Deigman (10-year-old Sally), Tom Baker (7-year-old Vince), Laura Deigman (5-year-old Sally), Simon Oats (Andy), Patricia Valentine (Sue), Lois Winstone (Kath), Brian Osborne (Tally Man), Joanna Bacon (Woman Picker), Teresa Lloyd (Ray's Prostitute), Alan Taylor (Sideshow Man), Charlotte Atkinson (Rochester Barmaid), Dani Foreman (Woman in Bar), Bea Sewell (Fairfax Home Receptionist), Aislinn Sands (Nurse Kelly)

David Hemmings

Tom Courtenay, Bob Hoskins

*A group of friends, gathering to spread the ashes of one of them who has passed away, reminisce on their lives.*

© Sony Pictures Entertainment

Denis Lavant, Chulpan Hamatova

Phillippe Clay

## TUVALU

(INDICAN) Producer/Director, Veit Helmer; Screenplay, Michaela Beck, Veit Helmer; Executive Producers, Vladimir Andreev, George Balkanski; Photography, Emil Christov; Art Director, Alexander Manasse; Costumes, Boriana Mintcheva; Editor, Araksi Mouhibian; Music, Jürgen Knieper; a Veit Helmer-Filmproduktion from Borough Film, Bavarai Film International; German, 1999; Dolby; Cinemascope; Color; Rated R; 100 minutes; US release date: December 7, 2001

### CAST

Anton ....................................................................................Denis Lavant
Eva ..................................................................Chulpan Hamatova
Karl ........................................................................Philippe Clay
Gregor ...............................................................Terrence Gillespie
Inspector ..............................................................E. J. Callahan
Gustav............................................................................Djoko Rosic
Martha ..........................................................Catalina Murgea
Policeman ...........................................................Todor Georgiev

*Anton, a shy attendant in a crumbling bathhouse, falls in love with Eva, whose father has been killed by falling debris at the pool.*

© Indican

## IN JULY

(FILM PHILOS) Producers, Stephan Schubert, Ralph Schwingel; Director/Screenplay, Fatih Akin; Photography, Pierre Aim; Designer, Jurgen Schnell; Costumes, Helen Achtermann; Music, Ulrich Kodjo Wendt; Editor, Andrew Bird; Casting, Ingeborg Molitoris; Produced by Argos Filmcilik Turizm, Quality Pictures, Wuste Filmproduktion; German, 2000; Dolby; Color; Not rated; 99 minutes; US release date: December 7, 2001

### CAST

Daniel Bannier ...................................................................Moritz Bleibtreu
Juli ..............................................................................Christiane Paul
Isa ...........................................................................Mehmet Kurtulus
Melek ...............................................................................Idil Ünel
Leo.......................................................................Jochen Nickel
Luna...............................................................................Branka Katic
Club Doyen ...........................................................Birol Ünel
Marion............................................................Sandra Borgmann
and Cem Akin (Turkish Border Guard), Fatih Akin (Romanian Border Guard), Dylan Gray (Hungarian Border Guard)

© Film Philos

Christiane Paul

Christiane Paul, Moritz Bleibtreu

Nelofer Pazira

Afghan Women

## KANDAHAR

**(AVATAR)** Producer/Director/Screenplay/Editor, Mohsen Makhmalbaf; Photography, Ebrahim Ghafori; Set Designer, Akbar Meshkini; Music, Mohamad Reza Darvishi; a Makhmalbaf Film House presentation produced by Makhmalbaf Film House (Iran) and Bac Films (France); Iranian-French; Color; Not rated; 85 minutes; US release date: December 14, 2001

### CAST

| | |
|---|---|
| Nafas | Nelofer Pazira |
| Tabib Sahid | Hassan Tantaï |
| Khak | Sadou Teymouri |
| Hayat | Hoyatala Hakimi |

*Nafas, an exiled Afghan journalist, attempts to cross over the border back into her homeland to find her sister who is suffering under Taliban rule.*

© Avatar Films

Zahra Bahrami

## BARAN
### (RAIN)

**(MIRAMAX)** Producers, Majid Majidi, Fouad Nahas; Director/Screenplay, Majid Majidi; Photography, Mohammad Davudi; Designer, Behzad Kazzazi; Costumes, Behzad Kazzazi, Malek Jahan Khazai; Editor, Hassan Hassandust; Music, Ahmad Pejman; a Majid Majidi & Fouad Nahas production; Iranian; Dolby; Color; Rated PG; 94 minutes; US release date: December 7, 2001

### CAST

| | |
|---|---|
| Lateef | Hossein Abedini |
| Memar | Mohammad Reza Naji |
| Rahmat & Baran | Zahra Bahrami |
| Soltan | Hossein Rahimi |
| Najaf | Gholam Ali Bakhshi |

*Lateef, a conniving, lazy Iranian teen who works as a caretaker at construction site manned by Afghan refugees, becomes resentful when his job is given over to a new employee, Rahmat, less capable of handling the more taxing labor.*

© Miramax Films

Hossein Abedini

Judi Dench, Jim Broadbent

Judi Dench

# IRIS

**(MIRAMAX)** Producers, Robert Fox, Scott Rudin; Executive Producers, Guy East, David M Thompson, Tom Hedley, Harvey Weinstein, Anthony Minghella, Sydney Pollack; Director, Richard Eyre; Screenplay, Richard Eyre, Charles Wood; Based on John Bayley's books *Iris: A Memoir* and *Elegy for Iris*; Line Producer, Michael Dreyer; Photography, Roger Pratt BSC; Designer, Gemma Jackson; Editor, Martin Walsh; Music, James Horner; Solo Violin, Joshua Bell; Costumes, Ruth Myers; Hair and Makeup Designer, Lisa Westcott; Casting, Celestia Fox; a BBC Films, Intermedia Films presentation of a Mirage Enterprises/Robert Fox/Scott Rudin Production; British-US; Dolby; Color; Rated R; 91 minutes; US release date: December 14, 2001

## CAST

Iris Murdoch .............................................................Judi Dench
John Bayley ...........................................................Jim Broadbent
Young Iris Murdoch ..............................................Kate Winslet
Young John Bayley .........................................Hugh Bonneville
Janet Stone ........................................................Penelope Wilton
Young Maurice ........................................................Samuel West
Old Maurice ...........................................................Timothy West
Principal, Somerville College..................................Eleanor Bron
Hostess...................................................................Angela Morant
Check-out Girl........................................................Siobhan Hayes
Young Janet Stone..................................................Juliet Aubrey
BBC Presenter ........................................................Joan Bakewell
BBC PA ..................................................................Nancy Carroll
Dr. Gudgeon ...........................................................Kris Marshall
Neurologist..............................................................Tom Mannion
Postman ...........................................................Derek Hutchinson
Phillida Stone............................................................Saira Todd
Emma Stone ..........................................................Juliet Howland
and Charlotte Arkwright (Young Phillida Stone), Harriet Arkwright (Young Emma Stone), Matilda Allsopp (Little Stone), Steve Edis (Pianist), Emma Handy (Policewoman), Stephen Marcus (Taxi Driver), Pauline McGlynn (Maureen), Gabrielle Reidy (Tricia)

*The courtship of independent writer Iris Murdoch and John Bayley is contrasted with Iris's last years, when Alzheimer's disease began to destroy her mind*

*2001 Academy Award-winner for Best Supporting Actor (Jim Broadbent) This film received an additional Oscar nomination for actress (Judi Dench).*

© Miramax Films

Kate Winslet

Hugh Bonneville, Kate Winslet

Jim Broadbent, Judi Dench

Judi Dench

Jim Broadbent

Hugh Bonneville, John Bayley, Kate Winslet

Kate Winslet

Geoffrey Rush

Barbara Hershey

Anthony LaPaglia, Kerry Armstrong

Rachael Blake

# LANTANA

**(LIONS GATE)** Producer, Jan Chapman; Executive Producer, Rainer Mockert, Mikael Borglund; Director, Ray Lawrence; Screenplay, Andrew Bovell, based on his play Speaking in Tongues; Photography, Mandy Walker; Designer, Kim Buddee; Costumes, Margot Wilson; Music, Paul Kelly; Editor, Karl Sodersten; Line Producer, Catherine Jarman; Casting, Susie Maizels, Sarah Beardsall; an MBP, Australian Film Finance Corporation, Jan Chapman Films presentation; Australian; Dolby; Panavision; Color; Rated R; 121 minutes; US release date: December 14, 2001

## CAST

| | |
|---|---|
| Leon Zat | Anthony LaPaglia |
| John Knox | Geoffrey Rush |
| Dr Valerie Somers | Barbara Hershey |
| Sonja Zat | Kerry Armstrong |
| Jane O'May | Rachael Blake |
| Nik Daniels | Vince Colosimo |
| Michael | Russell Dykstra |
| Paula Daniels | Daniela Farinacci |
| Patrick Phelan | Peter Phelps |
| Claudia | Leah Purcell |
| Pete O'May | Glenn Robbins |
| Steve | Jon Bennett |
| Lisa | Melissa Marinez |
| Old Man in Pajamas | Owen McKenna |
| Sam Zat | Nicholas Cooper |
| Dylan Zat | Marc Dwyer |

and Puven Panther (Drug Dealer), Lionel Tozer, Glen Suter (Police Officers), Natasha Guthrie (Young Girl), James Cullington (Man at Book Launch), Ashley Fitzgerald (Eleanor), Keira Wingate (Hannah Daniels), Angus Cripps, William Cripps (Harry), Kay Armstrong (Dance Partner), Jacomb Borra (Jacob), Ben Mortley (Jose), Gabriella Maselli (Sarah), Richard Morecroft (News Reader), Lani Tupu (Patrick's Lover), Lesley Hancock (Lover's Wife), Angus McGulgan (Lover's Child)

*Police detective Leon Zat's investigation into the mysterious death of a woman reveals unexpected connections between a disparate group of people in Sydney, Australia.*

Anthony LaPaglia

© Lions Gate Films

Veronika Zilková, Little Otik

© Zeitgeist Films

# LITTLE OTIK
## (OTESÁNEK)

(ZEITGEIST) Producer, Jaromir Kallista; Director/Screenplay/Story, Jan Svankmajer; Artistic Directors, Eva Svankmajerová, Jan Svankmajer; Photography, Juraj Galvanek; Editor, Marie Zemanová; Animators, Bedrich Glaser, Martin Kublák; Produced with financial contributions from the State Fund of the Czech Republic for the Support and Promotion of Czech Cinematography, Czech Literary Fund Foundation, REN Corporation Ltd, Ceskyk Ltd (Tokyo); Czech Republic, 2000; Dolby; Color; Not rated; 127 minutes; US release date: December 19, 2001

## CAST

| | |
|---|---|
| Bozena Horakova | Veronika Zilková |
| Karel Horak | Jan Hartl |
| Mrs Stadlerova | Jaroslava Kretschmerová |
| Franisek Stadler | Pavel Novy |
| Alzbetka | Kristina Adamcová |
| The Caretaker | Dagmar Stribrna |
| Mr Zlabek | Zdenek Kozak |
| Social Worker Bulankova | Jitka Smutna |
| The Policeman at the Station | Jiri Labus |

*A couple, who have longed to have a baby without success, find a tree stump resembling a small child and decide to raise the inanimate object as their offspring.*

# BEHIND THE SUN

(MIRAMAX) Producer, Arthur Cohn; Executive Producers, Lillian Birnbaum, Mauricio A Ramos; Director, Walter Salles; Screenplay, Walter Salles, Sérgio Machado, Karim Aïnouz; Inspired by the novel *Broken April* by Ismail Kadaré; Photography, Walter Carvalho; Designer, Cassio Amarante; Costumes, Cao Albuquerque; Editor, Isabelle Rathery; Music, Antonio Pinto, Ed Cortes, Beto Villares; Associate Producers, Jean Labadie, Carole Scotta; Line Producer, Marcelo Torres; an Arthur Cohn production, a Videofilms-Haut and Court-Bac Films-Dan Valley AG co-production; Brazilian-French-Swiss; Dolby; Super 35 Widescreen; Color; Rated PG-13; 105 minutes; US release date: December 21, 2001

## CAST

| | |
|---|---|
| Father | José Dumont |
| Tonho | Rodrigo Santoro |
| Mother | Rita Assemany |
| Salustiano | Luís Carlos Vasconcelos |
| Pacu | Ravi Ramos Lacerda |
| Clara | Flavia Marco Antonio |
| Old Blind Man | Everaldo de Souza Pontes |
| Mr Lourenço | Othon Bastos |
| Inácio | Caio Junqueira |
| Widow | Mariana Loureiro |
| Isaias | Servilio de Holanda |
| Matheus | Wagner Moura |
| Reginaldo | Gero Camilo |

and Vinicius de Oliveira, Sôia Lira, Maria do Socorro Nobre (Ferreira Family)

*A long-standing land dispute between two Brazilian families forces the middle son of the Breves clan to avenge his brother's death.*

© Miramax FIlms

Rodrigo Santoro, Ravi Ramos Lacerda

Cate Blanchett

Michael Gambon, Billy Crudup

# CHARLOTTE GRAY

(WARNER BROS) Producers, Sarah Curtis, Douglas Rae; Executive Producers, Paul Webster, Robert Bernstein, Hanno Huth; Co-Producers, Elinor Day, Catherine Kerr; Director, Gillian Armstrong; Screenplay, Jeremy Brock; Based on the novel by Sebastian Faulks; Photography, Dion Beebe; Designer, Joseph Bennett; Costumes, Janty Yates; Music, Stephen Warbeck; Editor, Nicholas Beauman; an Ecosse Films production and a Pod Film production, presented in association with FilmFour and Senator Film; British; Dolby; Technicolor; Rated PG-13; 121 minutes; US release date: December 28, 2001

## CAST

Charlotte Gray (Dominique) ............................................Cate Blanchett
Julien Levade ......................................................................Billy Crudup
Levade....................................................................................Michael Gambon
Peter Gregory ..................................................................Rupert Penry Jones
Renech ..................................................................................Anton Lesser
Mirabel...................................................................................Ron Cook
Richard Cannerly..............................................................James Fleet
Daisy ....................................................................................Abigail Cruttenden
Sally .......................................................................Charlotte McDougall
Borowski ..........................................................................Robert Hands
Psychiatrist .......................................................................Hugh Ross
Assault Course Instructor..............................................Martin Oldfield
Mr Jackson.........................................................................Nicholas Farrell
Morse Code Instructor......................................................Mike Burnside
Gun Instructor ..........................................................Damian Myerscough
Instructor ..............................................................................Miranda Bell
Agent ....................................................................................Angus Wright
Andre.....................................................................................Lewis Crutch
Jacob ...................................................................................Matthew Plato
Auguste ...............................................................................Charlie Condou
and Tom Goodman-Hill, Michael Fitzgerald (Businessmen at Party), Victoria Scarborough (Claire Monceau), David Birkin (Jean-Paul), John Pierce Jones (Monsieur Monceau), Louise Vincent (Madame Cariteau), Gillian Barge (Madame Galliot), Michael Mellinger (Old Man Roudil), Carole Barbier, Francoise Heraut, Severine Bouche (Housewives), Rosanna Lavelle (Sophie the Telephonist), John Hug (Bartender), Helen McCrory (Francoise), John Benfield (Loque), Robert Shannon (Bernard), John Bennett (Gerard), Mathias Jung (German Sergeant), Jean-Pierre Roane (Mayor), Jack Shepherd (Pichon), Erich Redman (German Corporal), Wolf Kahler (Oberlieutenant Lindermann), Maurice Yeoman (German Soldier), Robin Pearce (Gendarme Claude), Amy Marston (Pregnant Mother)

*During World War II, Charlotte Gray agrees to become a secret agent for Britain in hopes of finding her lover whose plane has been shot down over France.*

© FilmFour Ltd.

Cate Blanchett

Lewis Crutch, Matthew Plato, Billy Crudup

# DARK BLUE WORLD

(SONY CLASSICS) Producers, Eric Abraham, Jan Sverak; Co-Producers, Werner Koenig, Domenico Proccaci; Director, Jan Sverak; Screenplay, Zdenek Sverak; Photography, Vladimir Smutny; Designer, Jan Vlasak; Costumes, Vera Mirova; Editor, Alois Fisarek; Music, Ondrej Soukup; Visual Effects Designer, Milos Kohout; Casting, Sona Tichackova, Doreen Jones; a Portobello Pictures, Biograf, Jan Sverak Film in co-production with Helkon Media, Phoenix Film Investments, Fandango and Czech Television with the support of Eurimages and the Czech Film Fund; Czech-British; Dolby; Widescreen; Color; Rated R; 119 minutes; US release date: December 28, 2001

Kryštof Hàdek, Ondřej Vetchy

## CAST

Frantisek Slama .......................................................Ondrej Vetchy
Karel Vojtisek ........................................................Krystof Hadek
Susan ...........................................................................Tara Fitzgerald
Wing-Commander Bentley...............................Charles Dance
Machaty.......................................................................Oldrich Kaiser
Mrtvy............................................................................David Novotny
Hanicka ......................................................................Linda Rybova
Kanka ..........................................................................Jaromir Dulava
Tom Tom ....................................................................Lukas Kantor
Sysel .............................................................................Radim Fiala
Gregora .......................................................................Juraj Bernath
Houf ..............................................................................Miroslav Taborsky
Doctor Blaschke.........................................Hans-Jorg Assmann
German Officer Hesse ....................................Thure Riefenstein
English Teacher.......................................................Anna Massey
Major Skokan ..........................................................Viktor Preiss
and John Warnaby (RAF Instructor), Caroline Holdaway (Mrs Brett), Timothy Otis, William McEnchroe, Jeff Tyler (Radio Operators), Cestmir Randa (Pavlata—Armorer), Sophie Wilcox (WAAF Jane), Charlotte Fairman (WAAF Sally), Rhian Heppleston, Lucy Fillery, Amy Huck (WAAFs), Jeremy Swift (Private Pierce), William S Masson (Susan's Husband), Ashley Clish (Beth—4 years old), Lexie Peel (David—7 years old), Gemma Scrimgeour (Girl—10 years old), Blaise Colangelo (Twin—Ann), Sienna Colangelo (Twin—Mary), Noel Le Bon (Telephone Operator), Jan Dvorak (Bustik—Prison Guard), Petr Burian (Vrba Vlastik), Joseph John Comer (English Mechanic), John Norton (Rear Gunner Captain), Jiri Labus (Pub Landlord), Daniela Kolarova (Pecharova), Anna Vesela (Jeannette), Frantisek Vyskocil, Martin Dostal (German Motorcyclists), David Fisher (Telephonist)

Tara Fitzgerald, Ondřej Vetchy

*Escaping to England after the Nazis invade Czechoslovakia, a fighter pilot and his young protégé become flyers for their adopted country, only to find themselves falling in love with the same woman.*

© Sony Pictures Entertainment

Kryštof Hàdek

Ondřej Vetchy, Charles Dance

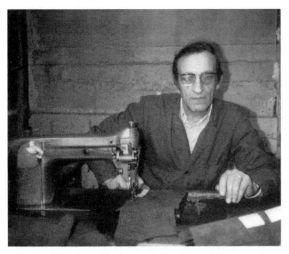

Raymond Kojitski in *Terrorists in Retirement* © Zek Prods.

## TERRORISTS IN RETIREMENT

(ZEK PRODS.) Director, Mosco Boucault; Photography, Jean Orjollet; Editor, Christiane Leherissey; Music, Jean Schwarz; Narrators, Simone Signoret, Gerard Desarthe; French, 1984; Color; Not rated; 84 minutes; U.S. release date: January 10, 2001. Documentary about the French Resistance in Nazi-occupied Paris.

## A MONKEY'S TALE

(PROVIDENCE) Producers, Gerd Hecker, Patrick Moine, Steve Walsh; Director, Jean-François Laguionie; Screenplay, Norman Hudis, Jean-François Laguionie; Artistic Director, Zoltan Szilagyi Varga; Music, Alexandre Desplat; Editor, Soazic Veillon; Animation Directors, Ginger Gibbons, Henri Heidsieck; French, 1999; Color; Not rated; 76 minutes; U.S. release date: January 26, 2001. VOICE CAST: Matt Hill (Kom), John Hurt (Sebastian), Michael York (The King), Rik Mayall (Gerard the Gormless), Sally Ann Marsh (Gina), Michael Gambon (Master Martin), Shirley Ann Field (The Governess), French Tickner (Korkonak), Diana Quick (Princess Ida), William Vanderpuye (Lionel), Paul Dobson (Gavin), Janyse Jaud (Kom's Mother), Peter Elliott (Monkey Cries)

Lou Doillon, Maud Forget in *Bad Company*
© Menemsha

Jonny Lee Miller in *Love, Honour & Obey*
© Keystone Releasing

## FALLEN ANGELS PARADISE

(ARTMATTAN PRODS.) Producer, Al Batrik; Director, Ossama Fawzi; Screenplay, Moustafa Zekri; Based on a novel by George Amado; Photography, Tarek Telmessani; Editor, Khaled Merhi; Music, Fathi Salama; Set Designer, Nehad Bahgat; an Art Production; Egyptian, 2000; Dolby; Color; Not rated; 100 minutes; U.S. release date: February 1, 2001. CAST: Mahmoud Hemida (Tabl), Lebleba (Hobba), Caroline Khalil (Salwa), Safwa (Shawkia), Amr Waked (Nonna), Serri Al Nagar (Adel), Salah Fahmi (Boussy), Saeed Al Saleh (George), Menha Al Batrawi (The Wife), Menha Zeytoun (The Aunt), Maged Kedwani (Atef), Kamal Soleiman (Abou Rasha), Raafat Ragi (Halim), Geena (The Girl Driver), Mohammad Dardiry (The Doctor), Tamer Habib (The Dentist)

## BAD COMPANY

(FLACH PYRAMIDE/MENEMSHA) Producers, Philippe Godeau, Alain Sarde; Director, Jean-Pierre Ameris; Screenplay, Alain Layrac; Photography, Yves Vandermeeren; Editor, Martine Giordano; French, 1999; Color; Not rated; 98 minutes; U.S. release date: February 7, 2001. CAST: Maud Forget (Delphine), Lou Doillon (Olivia), Robinson Stevenin (Laurent), Maxime Mansion (Alain), Delphine Rich (Claire), François Berleand (Rene), Micheline Presle (Mamie)

## LOVE, HONOUR & OBEY

(KEYSTONE) Producers/Directors/Screenplay, Dominic Anciano, Ray Burdis; Executive Producers, David M. Thompson, Jane Tranter, Jim Beach; Photography, John Ward; Designer, Nick Burnell; Costumes, Ali Brown; Line Producer, Mark Hudson; Editor, Rachel Meyrick; Song: Force of Nature written and performed by Noel Gallagher; Casting, Geraldine Geraghty; a BBC Films presentation of a Fugitive production; British, 2000; Dolby; Color; Rated R; 95 minutes; U.S. release date:

February 9, 2001. CAST: Sadie Frost (Sadie), Jonny Lee Miller (Jonny), Jude Law (Jude), Sean Pertwee (Sean), Kathy Burke (Kathy), Denise Van Outen (Maureen), Rhys Ifans (Matthew), Dominic Anciano (Dominic), Ray Burdis (Ray), John Beckett (John), Trevor H. Laird (Trevor), William Scully (Bill), Perry Benson (Perry "Fat Alan"), Mark Burdis (Mark), Laila Morse (Laila), Sam Smart, Rory Muir, Dane Keenan, Ryan Moore, Calum Callaghan, Eddie Cooper, Ricky Grover, Hugh Sachs, Mario Renzullo, Damien Anciano, Tom Shirley, Nancy-Jane Maun, Nula Conwell, Sky Burdis, Andy Denyer, David Gillespie, Derek Avery, Enoch Frost, Alan Fordham, John Davis, Phytos Neophytou, Eamonn Tully, Culver Greenidge, Mo Kahn, Jerry Mulcahy, Rick English, Cliff Tarr, Danny Sullivan, Louise Strachan, Megan Strachan, John Brooks, Ayiko, Lisa Moorish, Lucy Bowen, Dr. David Lomas

## JOURNEY TO THE SUN

(CINEMA VILLAGE FEATURES) Producer, Behrooz Hashemian; Executive Producer, Ezel Akay; Director/Screenplay, Yesim Ustaoglu; Photography, Jacek Petrycki; Art Director, Natali Yeres; Editor, Nicolas Gaster; Music, Vlatko Stefanovski; an IFR Production, in collaboration with the Film Company Amsterdam, Media Res, Berlin, Fabrica & ZDF/Arte; Turkish-German-Dutch; Dolby; Color; Not rated; 104 minutes; U.S. release date: February 9, 2001. CAST: Newroz Baz (Mehmet), Nazmi Quirix (Berzan), Mizgin Kapazan (Arzu), Nigar Aktar (Laundromat Owner), Iskender Bagcilar (Police Interrogator), Ara Guler (Mehmet's Boss)

## SIGNS & WONDERS

(STRAND) Producer, Marin Karmitz; Executive Producers, Nick Wechsler, Jed Alpert; Director, Jonathan Nossiter; Screenplay, James Lasdun, Jonathan Nossiter; Story, James Lasdun; Photography, Yorgos Arvanitis; Costumes, Kathryn Nixon; Music, Adrian Utley; Line Producer, Yvon Crenn; Editor, Madeleine Gavin; an MK2 production, presented in association with Idefixe Productions, Industry Entertainment, Sunshine Amalgamedia & GoatWorks Films; French, 2000; Dolby; Color; Not rated; 108 minutes; U.S. release date: February 9, 2001. CAST: Stellan Skarsgård (Alec Fenton), Charlotte Rampling (Marjorie Fenton), Deborah Kara Unger (Katherine), Dimitris Katalifos (Andreas), Ashley Remy (Siri), Michael Cook (Marcus), Dave Simonds (Kent), Arto Apartian (Police Interpreter), Alexandros Mylonas (Police Captain), Dimitris Kamberidis (Sotiris), Steven Goldstein (American Businessman)

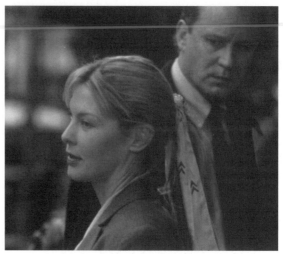

Deborah Kara Unger, Stellan Skarsgård in
*Signs & Wonders* © Strand Releasing

## THE PRICE OF MILK

(LOT 47) Producer, Fiona Copland; Executive Producer, Tim Sanders; Director/Screenplay, Harry Sinclair; Photography, Leon Narbey; Designer/Costumes, Kristy Cameron; Editor, Cushla Dillon; a John Swimmer presentation in association with The New Zealand Film Commission; New Zealand; Dolby; Widescreen; Color; Rated PG-13; 87 minutes; U.S. release date: February 14, 2001. CAST: Danielle Cormack (Lucinda), Karl Urban (Rob), Willa O'Neill (Drosophilia), Michael Lawrence (Bernie), Rangi Motu (Auntie)

Karl Urban, Danielle Cormack in *The Price of Milk*
© Lot 47 Films

Houari Djerir, Akhenhaton in *The Magnet* © Two Boots

## YOM YOM

(KINO) Producers, Eyal Shiray, Laurent Truchot; Executive Producer, Ilan Moscovitch; Director, Amos Gitai; Screenplay, Jacky Cukier, Amos Gitai; Photography, Renato Berta; Editors, Nili Richter, Ruben Kornfeld; Art Director, Thierry François; Music, Philippe Eidel; an Agav Films and Cinema Factory production, in association with Canal+, Intereurop, Mikadoo, M.P. Productions, Telad, Arte, and Rai Due; Israeli-French-Italian, 1998; Dolby; Color; Not rated; 105 minutes; U.S. release date: February 16, 2001. CAST: Moshe Ivgi (Moshe), Hanna Maron (Hanna), Juliano Mer (Jules), Dalit Kahan (Didi), Yussef Abu Warda (Yussef), Nataly Atiya (Grisha), Anne Petit-Lagrange (The Doctor), Shmuel Calderon (Shmul), Gassan Abass (Nadim), Keren Mor (Mimi)

## IN CHINA THEY EAT DOGS

(ENTERTECH) Producer, Steen Herdel; Executive Producer, Michael Brask; Director/Editor, Lasse Spang Olsen; Screenplay, Anders Thomas Jensen; Photography, Morten Søborg; Music, George Keller; from ScanBox, TiMe Filmverleih; Danish-German, 1999; Color; Not rated; 91 minutes; U.S. release date: February 16, 2001. CAST: Kim Bodnia (Harald), Dejan Cukic (Arvid), Nikolaj Lie Kaas (Martin), Tomas Villurn

Shi Yu in *So Close to Paradise* © Cinema Village Features

Jensen (Peter), Peter Gantzler (Franz), Trine Dyrholm (Hanne), Line Kruse (Astrid), Brian Patterson (Vuk), Søren Sætter-Lassen (Jenning), Lester Wiese (Richard), Jesper Christensen (Bartender), Lasse Lunderskov (Jørgen), Preben Harris (Erling), Slavko Labovic (Ratko), Anne Britt Mathiaseen (Gunna), Martin Spang Olsen (Preben), Niels Brinch (Interviewer)

## THE KITE

(PHAEDRA) Director, Gil Portes; Screenplay, Butch Dalisay, Gil Portes; No other credits available; Philippine, 1999; Color; Not rated; 85 minutes; U.S. release date: February 22, 2001. CAST: Ricky Davao (Homer), Lester Llannsong (Rex), Jennifer Sevilla (Anita)

## THE MAGNET

(INDEPENDENT/TWO BOOTS) Producer, Richard Grandpierre; Executive Producer, Why Not Productions; Directors/Screenplay, Kamel Saleh, Akhenaton; Photography, Denis Rouden; Music, Bruno Coulais, Akhenaton; Editor, Fabrice Sallinié; a co-production of Le Studio Canal+, La Société 361, with the participation of the Centre National de la Cinematographie; French, 2000; Color; Not rated; 100 minutes; U.S. release date: March 9, 2001. CAST: Kamel Saleh (Cahuete), Houari Djerir (Houari), Brahim Aimad (Bra-Bra), Sofiane Madjid Mammeri (Christian), Kamel Ferrat (Fouad), Titoff (Santino), Akhenaton (Sauveur), Malek Brahimi (Kakou), Georges Neri, Bernard Fischetti, Raymond La Science, Loule Bilione, José Tygat, Elie du Mas (The Mafiosi), Khalil Mohamed (Kader), Virginie Gallo (Nathalie), Nadège Mignien (Beatrice), Bérangère Topart (Sylvie), Ahamed Abdou (Jackson), Jerome-Jérôme Esposito (The Informer), Diana Hamidovich (Diana), Samira Berriche (Linda), Hanane Mohim (Soraya), Nadéra Mouthoub (Sandra), Farida Bessa, Linda Tortoza (Flirt Girls), Samir Mohamed, Dadou (Little Boys)

## SO CLOSE TO PARADISE

(CINEMA VILLAGE FEATURES) Producer, Han Sanping; Director, Wang Xiaoshuai; Executive Producers, Zhang Gonggu, Li Xiaogeng; Creators, Tian Zhuangzhuang, Li Buo; Screenplay, Wang Xiaoshuai, Pang Ming; Photography, Yang Tao; Editors, Liu Fang, Yang Hong Yu; Art

Venus Seye, Sosie Pathé in *Faat-Kine* © New Yorker FIlms

Director, Cheng Guangming; Music, Liu Lin; a co-production of the Beijing Film Studio and Beijing Goldenplate Film TV & Art Production Co. in association with Beijing Pegase Cultural Communication Centre; Chinese, 1998; Dolby; Color; Not rated; 90 minutes; U.S. release date: March 9, 2001. CAST: Wang Tong (Ruan Hong), Shi Yu (Dong Zi), Guo Tao (Gao Ping), Wu Tao (Su Wu)

## FAAT-KINE

(NEW YORKER) Producer, Wongue Mbengue; Director/Screenplay, Ousmane Sembene; Photography, Dominique Gentil; Editor, Kahena Attia Riveill; Music, Yandé Codou Sène; Senegalese, 2000; Color; Not rated; 118 minutes; U.S. release date: March 28, 2001. CAST: Venus Seye (Faat-Kine), Mame Ndoumbé Diop (Maamy, Her Mother), Tabara Ndiaye (Amy Kasse), Awa Sène Sarr (Mada), Ndiagne Dia (Djip, Her Son), Mariama Balde (Aby, Her Daughter), Sosie Pathé

## SMELL OF CAMPHOR, FRAGRANCE OF JASMINE

(NEW YORKER) Producer, Morteza Shayesteh; Executive Producer, Fazlollah Yousefpour; Director/Screenplay, Bahman Farmanara; Photography, Mahmoud Kalari; Art Director, Zilla Mehrjouii; Music, Ahmad Pejman; Iranian; Color; Not rated; 93 minutes; U.S. release date: April 6, 2001. CAST: Bahman Farmanara (Bahman Farjami), Roya Nonahali (Woman Hitchhiker), Reza Kianian (Dr. Arasteh, The Attorney), Valiyollah Shirandami (Homayouni, The Actor), Hossein Kasbian (Abdollah, The Servant), Firouz Behjat Mohammadi (Memorial Sign Rental), Parivash Nazarieh (Farzaneh), Mantaj Nojoomi (Bahman's Sister)

## POKÉMON THE MOVIE 3

(WARNER BROS.) Producers, Norman J. Grossfeld, Choji Yoshikawa, Yukako Matsusako, Takemoto Mori; Executive Producers, Masakazu Kubo, Takashi Kawaguchi, Alfred R. Kahn; Directors, Kunihiko Yuyama, Michael Haigney; Screenplay, Takeshi Shudo, Hideki Sonoda; American Adaptation, Michael Haigney, Norman J. Grossfeld; Based on characters created by Satoshi Tajiri; Photography, Hisao Shirai; Art Director, Katsuyoshi Kanemura; Editors, Jay Film, Toshio Henmi, Yutaka Ito;

Music, Ralph Schuckett; Animation Supervisor, Yoichi Kotabe; a 4Kids Entertainment production; Japanese; Dolby; Color; U.S. release date: April 6, 2001. VOICE CAST: Veronica Taylor (Ash Ketchum/Mrs. Delia Ketchum), Eric Stuart (Brock/James), Rachael Lillis (Misty/Jessie), Maddie Blaustein (Meowth), Ikoue Ôtani (Pikachu), Stan Hart (Professor Oak), Ken Gates, Dan Green, Amy Birnbaum, Lisa Ortiz, Kathy Pilon, Peter R. Bird, Kayzie Rogers, Ed Paul, Tara Jayne, Lee Quick, Roger Kay (Additional Voices)

(Above) Bahman Farmanara in *Smell of Camphor, Fragrance of Jasmine* © New Yorker Films
(Below) Ash, Pikachu, Misty in *Pokémon The Movie 3* © Pikachu Projects

Agathe de La Boulaye, Claire Keim in *The Girl*
© Artistic License Films

Aidan Gillen in *The Low Down* © Shooting Gallery

## THE DAY I BECAME A WOMAN

(SHOOTING GALLERY) Producer, Mohsen Makhmalbaf; Director, Marzieh Meshkini; Screenplay, Mohsen Makhmalbaf, Marzieh Meshkini; Photography, Mohamad Ahmadi, Ebrahim Ghafori; Art Director, Akbar Meshkini; Editors, Mezsaam Makhmalbaf, Shahrzad Pouya; Music, Ahmad Reza Darvish; a Makhmalbaf Production; Iranian, 2000; Color; Not rated; 78 minutes; U.S. release date: April 6, 2001. CAST: Fatemeh Cherag Akhar (Hava), Hassan Nebhan (Hassan), Shahr Banou Sisizadeh (Mother), Ameneh Passand (Grandmother), Shabhnam Toloui (Ahoo), Sirous Kahvarinegad (Husband), Mahram Zeinal Zadeh (Osmann), Norieh Mahigiran (Rival Cyclist), Azizeh Segidhi (Hoora), Badr Iravani (Young Boy)

## THE GIRL

(ARTISTIC LICENSE) Producer, Dolly Hall; Executive Producers, Sue Delisle, Gil Donaldson; Director, Sande Zeig; Screenplay, Sande Zeig, Monique Wittig; Story, Monique Wittig; Co-Producer/Casting, Claude Martin; Photography, George Lechaptois; Designer, Phillipe Renucci; Editors, Geraldine Peroni; Music, Richard Robbins; a Dolly Hall production in association with Method Films; French, 1999; Color; Not rated; 84 minutes; U.S. release date: April 20, 2001. CAST: Claire Keim (The Girl), Agathe de la Boulaye (The Narrator), Cyril Lecomte (The Man), Sandra N'Kake (Bu Savé), Ronald Guttman (Bartender), Cyrille Hertel (Bodyguard), Pascal Cervo (Hotel Clerk), Franck Prevost (Piano Player)

## THE CHARCOAL PEOPLE

(CINEMA GUILD) Producer/Screenplay, José Padilha; Director, Nigel Noble; Co-Producers, Marcos Prado, Jozine Resende; Photography, Flávio Zangrandi; Editor, Ann Collins; from Les Zazen Producoes; Brazilian; Color; Not rated; 72 minutes; U.S. release date: April 20, 2001. Documentary on Brazilian migrant workers.

## THE LOW DOWN

(SHOOTING GALLERY) Producers, Sally Llewellyn, John Stewart; Director/Screenplay, Jamie Thraves; Photography, Igor Jadue-Lillo; Designer, Lucy Reeves; Costumes, Julie Jones; Music, Nick Currie, Fred Thomas; Editor, Lucia Zucchetti; Casting, Amanda Tabak; a production of Bozie, British Screen, Channel Four Films, Oil Factory, and Sleeper Films; British; Color; Not rated; 96 minutes; U.S. release date: April 20, 2001. CAST: Aiden Gillen (Frank), Kate Ashfield (Ruby), Dean Lennox Kelly (Mike), Tobias Menzies (John), Rupert Procter (Terry), Samantha Power (Lisa), Deanna Smiles (Susan), Maggie Lloyd Williams (Jean), Agnieszka Liggett (Anna), Adam Buxton (Adam), Joe Cornish (Joe), Paula Hamilton (Cashpoint Woman), Alicya Eyo (Paul Girl), Dorian Lough (Squash Player), Clint Dyer (Nathan), Rachel Issac (Nicola), Elliot Levey (Peter), Martin Freeman (Solomon), Liz Liew (Vera), Michael Hodgson, Michael McKell, Alex Palmer (Pubman), Vass Anderson (Landlord), Anthony Warren, Paul Dungworth, Barry Dobbin (Street Corner Men)

*The Charcoal People* © Cimena Guild

# RAT

**(UNIVERSAL FOCUS)** Producers, Steve Barron, Alison Owen; Director, Steve Barron; Screenplay, Wesley Burrowes; Photography, Brendan Galvin; Designer, Mark Geraghty; Costumes, Siobhan Barron; Music, Pete Briquette, Bob Geldof; Editor, David Yardley; Casting, Nina Gold; from United International Pictures; British-Irish, 2000; Dolby; Color; Rated PG; 88 minutes; U.S. release date: April 27, 2001. CAST: Imelda Staunton (Conchita Flynn), Pete Postlethwaite (Hubert Flynn), Frank Kelly (Uncle Matt), David Wilmot (Phelim Spratt), Andrew Lovern (Pius Flynn), Kerry Condon (Marietta Flynn), Hubert (Hubert the Rat), Veronica Duffy (Daisy), Ed Byrne (Randolph), Niall Toibin (Father Geraldo), Alfie (Mickey the Dog), Peter Caffrey (Mick the Barman), Rita Hamill (Estate Woman), Roxanna Williams (Hopscotch Child), Geoffrey Palmer (The Doctor), Stanley Townsend (Newsreader), Simon Delaney (Bookies Manager), Niall O'Brien, John O'Toole (Men in Bookies), Jer O'Leary, Mick Nolan (Men in Pub), Gavin Dowdall, Jamie McCormack, Keith O'Brien, Sian Napper, Aaron Joseph-Galvin (Kids), Pat Kinevane (Mr. Reilly), Mark Doherty (Barrister), Arthur Riordan (Sergeant), Michael Hayes (Young Garda), Billie Traynor, Mary Moynihan, Margaret Twomey (Women Shopping), Keith Moran, Aaron Moran, John Farrell, Shane Moran (Buskers)

# NORA

**(ANDORA PICTURES)** Producers, Bradley Adams, Damon Bryant, Tracey Seaward, Tiernan MacBride; Executive Producers, Guy Collins, Rod Stoneman, Tony Miller; Director, Pat Murphy; Screenplay, Pat Murphy, Gerard Stembridge; Based on the biography by Brenda Maddox; Photography, Jean François Robin; Designer, Alan MacDonald; Editor, Pia Di Ciaula; Music, Stanislas Syrewicz; Costumes, Consolata Boyle; Casting, Nuala Moiselle, Frank Moiselle, Shaila Rubin; a Natural Nylon Entertainment in association with IAC Holdings/Volta Films/Road Movies Vierte Produktionen/Gam Film/Metropolitan Films production; British-Irish-German-Italian, 1999; Dolby; Deluxe color; Not rated; 107 minutes; U.S. release date: May 4, 2001. CAST: Ewan McGregor (James Joyce), Susan Lynch (Nora Barnacle), Peter McDonald (Stanislas Joyce), Roberto Citran (Roberto Prezioso), Andrew Scott (Michael Bodkin),

Susan Lynch, Ewan McGregor in *Nora* © Andora Pictures

Vincent McCabe (Uncle Tommy), Veronica Duffy (Annie Barnacle), Aedin Moloney (Eva Joyce), Pauline McLynn (Miss Kennedy), Neili Conroy, Sile Nugent (Maids), Daragh Kelly (Cosgrave), Alan Devine (Gogarty), Paul Hickey (Curran), Kate O'Toole (Miss Delahunty), Martin Murphy (George Russell), Karl Scully (John McCormack), Frances Burke (Old Woman), Monica Scattini (Amalia Globonik), Adrian McCourt (Eyers), Ignazio Oliva (Alessandro Francini Bruni), Stefania Montorsi (Clothilde Francini Bruni), Franco Trevisi (Tullio Sylvestri), Eamonn Hunt (George Roberts), Manuel Bragato (Baby Giorgio), Liam McCourt, Odin O'Sullivan (Giorgio, 2 years old), Dylan Mooney (Giorgio, 4 years old), Ben Harding (Giorgio, 6 years old), Robin Mooney (Lucia, 2 years old), Lauren Mulhall (Lucia, 4 years old)

Imelda Staunton in *Rat* © Universal Pictures International

Koji Yakusho, Masaru Miyazaki, Aoi Miyazaki in *Eureka*
© Shooting Gallery

## EUREKA

(SHOOTING GALLERY) Producer, Takenori Sento; Director/Screenplay/Editor, Shinji Aoyama; Co-Producer, Philippe Avril; Photography, Masaki Tamura; Designer, Takeshi Shimizu; Music, Shinji Aoyama, Isao Yamada; a co-production of Dentsu, Imagica Corp., J Works, Les Films de L'Observatoire, Suncent Cinema Works, Tokyo Theaters Co.; Japanese, 2000; Black and white; Not rated; 217 minutes; U.S. release date: May 4, 2001. CAST: Koji Yakusho (Makoto Sawai), Aoi Miyazaki (Kozue Tamura), Masaru Miyazaki (Naoki Tamura), Yoichiro Saito (Akihiko), Sayuri Kokusho (Yumiko), Ken Mitsuishi (Shigeo), Gô Rijû (Busjack Man), Yutaka Matsushige (Matsuoka), Sansei Shiomi (Yoshiyuki Sawai), Kimie Shingyoji (Mother), Machiko Ono (Mikiko)

## TIME AND TIDE

(TRISTAR) Producer/Executive Producer/Director, Tsui Hark; Screenplay, Koan Hui, Tsui Hark; Photography, Ko Chiu Lam, Herman Yau; Editor, Marco Mak; Music, Tommy Wai; Line Producer, Ng Kam Chiu; a Columbia Pictures Film Production Asia presentation of a Film Workshop Company Limited production; Hong Kong; Dolby; Color; Rated R; 113 minutes; U.S. release date: May 4, 2001. CAST: Nicholas Tse (Tyler), Wu Bai (Jack), Anthony Wong (Uncle Ji), Joventino Couto Remotigue (Miguel), Candy Lo (Ah Hui), Cathy Chui (Ah Jo)

## PAVILION OF WOMEN

(UNIVERSAL FOCUS) Producer, Luo Yan; Executive Producer, Hugo Shong; Co-Producer, Simon Edery; Director, Yim Ho; Screenplay, Luo Yan, Paul R. Collins; Based on the novel by Pearl S. Buck; Photography, Poon Hang Sang; Designer, James Leung; Editors, Duncan Burns, Claudia Finkle; Music, Conrad Pope; a Luo Yan production, a co-production with Beijing Film Studio in association with the China Film Co-Production Corporation; Chinese; Dolby; Color; Rated R; 119 minutes; U.S. release date: May 4, 2001. CAST: Willem Dafoe (Father Andre), Luo Yan (Madame Wu), Shek Sau (Mr. Wu), John Cho (Fengmo), Yi Ding (Chiuming), Koh Chieng Mun (Ying), Anita Loo (Old Lady), Amy Hill (Madame Kang), Kate McGregor-Stewart (Sister Shirley), Liu Jia Dong (Mr. Lang), Chen Shu (Head Servant), Poon Hang Sang (Fat Cook), Wang Li (Kang Lin Yi), Xu You Jin (Matchmaker), Gu Ding Yuan (Mayor), Zhao Pei Ying (Midwife), Mao Xiao Dong (Liangmo), Huang Lan (Meng), Sun Yang, Yu En Ti, Yan Huai Bo (Fengmo's Friends), Zhang Kang (Boldman), Jin Ge (Loud Mouth), Yang Rong (Kang's Maid), John Dunn (Kang's Doorman), Miu Yan Lei, Sun Li, Gun Xin-Qi, Guao Xuan Ming (Wu's Relatives), Yang Ge (Head of Police), Song Min Qi (Orphanage Woman), Zhang Lei, Gu Ying, Irene Zhen (Kang's Wives), Jin Ying Chun (Bride Carrier), Zauang Zhi Fang (Masseur), Pu Hong Kui (Land Steward), Hong Zi Yuan (Wu's Doorman), Zhu Shou Gen (Accountant), Linq Yim (Policeman), Zhuang Cun (KMT General), Chen Yin, Liu Hui Dong (Japanese Generals), Chen Yu Feng (Japanese Soldiers), Cao Xu Bai, Gu En Hao (Kang's Children), Cai Yue (Duck Kid), Mo Chen Hao, Qi Lin Hui, Dong Xu Chao, Yang Xi, Zhang Zhao, Ye De Jie, Jiang Yi Fei, Xu Ding, Xue Tian Yun, Huang Yin Yuan, Zhang Jian Wen, Liu Meng Shi, Zeng Ling Yuan (Orphans)

Cathy Chui,
Nicholas Tse in
*Time and Tide*
© Tri Star
Pictures

Princess Margaret, Lord Glenconner in *The Man Who Bought Mustique* © First Run Features

## THE MAN WHO BOUGHT MUSTIQUE

**(FIRST RUN FEATURES)** Producer, Vikram Jayanti; Executive Producer, Andre Singer; Director, Joseph Bullman; Editor, Sally Hilton; Photography, Ian Liggett, Peter Cannon, David Smith; Music, Dario Marianelli; British, 2000; Color; Not rated; 78 minutes; U.S. release date: May 9, 2001. Documentary follows Colin Tennant as he returns to Mustique, the Caribbean island he once owned.

## FAST FOOD, FAST WOMEN

**(LOT 47)** Producers, Avram Ludwig, Hengameh Panahi; Director/ Screenplay, Amos Kollek; Photography, Jean-Marc Fabre; Designer, Stacey Tanner; Music, David Carbonara; Editor, Sheri Bylander; Costumes, Pascal Gosset; Casting, Caroline Sinclair; a Lumen Films presentation of a BIM Distribuzione, Lumen Films, Pandora Film, Paradis Films and Dryly Films production; French-Italian-U.S., 2000; Dolby; Color; Not rated; 96 minutes; U.S. release date: May 18, 2001. CAST: Anna Thomson (Bella), Jamie Harris (Bruno), Louise Lasser (Emily), Lonette McKee (Sherry-Lynn), Robert Modica (Paul), Victor Argo (Seymour), Angelica Torn (Vitka), Austin Pendleton (George), Valerie Geffner (Wanda), Mark Margolis (Graham), Judith Roberts (Bella's Mother), Salem Ludwig (Leo), Loulou Katz (Betsy), Irma St. Paul (Mugging Victim), Joe Davieau (Jasper), Lynn Cohen (Jesse), Ellee Panahi (Shawn)

## STRANGE FITS OF PASSION

**(LEISURE TIME FEATURES)** Producer, Lucy Maclaren; Executive Producers, Tim White, Carole Sklan, Bryce Menzies, Ian Fairweather, Roslyn Walker; Director/Screenplay, Elisa McCredie; Photography, James Grant; Designer, Macgregor Knox; Editors, Chris Branagan, Ken Sallows; Music, Cezary Skubiszewski; Costumes, Kerri Mazzocco; Casting, Alison Telford; from Meridian Films, presented by ABC-TV Arena Film, Victoria; Australian, 2000; Color; Not rated; 83 minutes; U.S. release date: May 18, 2001. CAST: Michela Noonan (She), Mitchell Butel (Jimmy), Samuel Johnson (Josh), Steve Adams (Pablo), Anni Finsterer (Judy), Boyana Novakovic (Jaya), Rob Carlton (Blackson), Jack Finsterer (Francis), Nathan Page (Simon), Barry Dickins (Mr. Selditt), Jodie J. Hill (Penny), Luke Anderson (Lachlan), James Liotta (James), Howard Stanley (Jimmy's Father), Judith Roberts (Jimmy's Mother), Donni Frizzell (Boy at Bar), Sim Gray (Girl at Bar), Glenn Burns (Barman), Tommy Dysart (Taxi Driver), Tom Healey, James Wardlaw (Supermarket Men), Elizabeth Welch (Store Detective), Bradley Hulme (Slick Businessman), Genevieve Mooris (Church Woman), Maud Davey (Woman in Gay Bookshop), David Lih (Christian Boy), Paul Bongiovanni, Libby Stone (Nurses), Andrea Swifte (Doctor), Johanna Hanley, Michael Isaacs (Hot Dog Customers), David Schofield (Jaya's New Man), Jeremy Engelman (Simon's Other Man), Nick Barker (Boy in Hot Dog Shop), Natasha Lyne (Beautiful Young Girl), Eric Kowalewski (Mason, Soap Opera), Constance Lansberg (Charity, Soap Opera), Davage Thomas, Dave Morris, Justin "Juddy" Dwyer (Live Pussies)

Angelica Torn, Robert Modica in *Fast Food, Fast Women*
© Lot 47 Films

Michela Noonan in *Strange Fits of Passion*
© Leisure Time Features

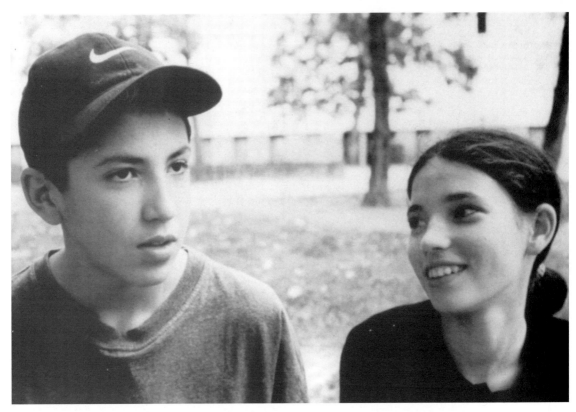

Iliès Sefraoui, Stéphanie Touly in *Petits Freres* © First Run Features

## PETITS FRERES ("LITTLE FELLAS")

**(FIRST RUN FEATURES)** Producer, Marin Karmitz; Director/ Screenplay, Jacques Doillon; Photography, Manuel Teran; Music, Oxmo Puccino; Editor, Camille Cotte; Casting, Lola Doillon, Emmanuelle Gaborit, Stéphane Foenkinos; a co-production of MK2 Productions-France 3 Cinema; French, 1999; Dolby; Color; Not rated; 92 minutes; U.S. release date: May 18, 2001. CAST: Stéphanie Touly (Talia), Iliès Sefraoui (Iliès), Mustapha Goumane (Mous), Nassim Izem (Nassim), Rachid Mansouri (Rachid), Dembo Goumane (Dembo), Sabrina Mansar (Sabrina), Gérald Dantsoff (Talia's Stepfather), Simone Zouari Sayada (Talia's Mother), Myriam Goumane (Myriam), Goundo Goumane (Goundo), Halimatou Goumane (Halimatou), Fedora Saidi (Talia's Kid Sister), Ludmilla Saidi (Ludmilla), Mohamed Fekiri (Momo), Karim Ferdjallah (Karim), Anthony Schmit (Anthony), David Estevez (David), Max Saint Jean (Lieutenant Leroy), Philippe Guyral (Police Inspector)

## NO ONE SLEEPS

**(GALERIA ALASKA PRODS.)** Producer/Director/Screenplay, Jochen Hick; Photography, Tom Harting, Michael Maley; Designers, Craig T. Copher, Bernard Homann; Editor, Bernard Homann; Music, James Hardway; Costumes, Maria Rivera; German, 2000; Dolby; Color; Rated R; 108 minutes; U.S. release date: May 25, 2001. CAST: Kenn Lyon (Jon), Irit Levi (Louise Tolliver), Robert A. Bustamante (Fast Food Guy), Kalene Parker (Maureen Finley), Randy Wendelin (Sgt. Flinter), David Rice (Presidio Victim), Michael Lovaglia (Sascha), Earl Kingston (Prof. Witkins), Patricia Miller (Student), Lisa Kang (Dr. Givens), Jim Thalman (Jeffrey Russo), Richard Conti (Dr. Richard Burroughs), Karl Fischer (Nurse from AIDS Project), Brian Yates (Volunteer at AIDS Project), Lino Antonio Lezama-Aguilar (Boy with Cross), Brian A. Vouglas (Doorman at Sacrifice), Aaron Place (Clown Boy), Cody Bayne (Cowboy), Jon Gale (Man in Harness), Ron Athey (Performer at Club), Paradox Pollack (Victim #2), Jason Mannino (Ron), John M. Stevens (Doorman at Safe Sex Club), Curtiss Craig (Man in Safe Sex Club), Ed Burke (Stefan's Father), Paul C. Moffett (Mail Box Clerk), Steve Casavant (Verona Maid), Peter Hadres (Agent Morgan), Joe Wilson (Carlos), James Marks (Boy from Porn Arcade), William Brogan (Headquarters Boy), Charles Shaw Robinson (Tom), Jeffrey J. Davis (Beggar), Dolores Moloney (Hospital Receptionist), Gene Thompson (Doctor), Verona Paul Arthur (Hotel Clerk), Joseph Blosk (Police Officer at Headquarters), Gary Wayne Farris (Headquarters Victim), Michael Gaffrey (Confessing Sexaholic), Heather Plakke (Burroughs's Receptionist), Scott Walker (TV Cameraman), Robert K. Hedrick, Jr. (Senator Michael Atwood), Sherry Al-Mufti (Atwood's Wife), Benjamin McGee (Receptionist at Sir Francis Drake Hotel), Alberto Rosas (Bellboy), John Swenson (Opera Singer), Glorinda Marie (Mexican Woman), Jimbei Suzuki (Officer Brown), Michal Gizinski (Officer Burton), Antonio Ferrelli (Stefan's New Boyfriend)

## ENLIGHTENMENT GUARANTEED

**(CAPITOL ENTERTAINMENT)** Producer, Franz X. Gernstl; Executive Producer, Louis Saul; Director, Doris Dörrie; Screenplay, Doris Dörrie, Ruth Stadler; Photography, Hans Karl Hu; Art Director, Ruth Stadler; Editors, Inez Regnier, Anne Sinwell; from Megaherz TV Fernsehproduktion GmbH; German, 2000; Dolby; Color; Not rated; 109

minutes; U.S. release date: June 1, 2001. CAST: Uwe Ochsenknecht (Uwe), Gustav-Peter Wohler (Gustav), Petra Zieser (Petra), Ulrike Kriener (Ulrike), Anica Dobra (Anica), Heiner Lauterbach (Heiner), Franz X. Gernstl, Gisela Gernstl (Ehepaar), Jimmy Ochsenknecht (Jimmy), Wilson Ochsenknecht (Wilson), Leopold Zieser (Leopold), Emilia Zieser (Emilia), Pierre Sanoussi-Bliss (Ulrikes Liebhaber), Imaseki (Sumo-Ringer)

## A REAL YOUNG GIRL

(CINEMA VILLAGE FEATURES) Producer, André Génovès; Director/ Screenplay/Designer, Catherine Breillat; Based on the novel by Andé Génovès; Photography, Pierre Fattori; Music, Mort Shuman; Editor, Annie Charrier; from Artédis, C.B. Films S.A., and Centre National de La Cinematographie; French, 1976; Color; Not rated; 94 minutes; U.S. release date: June 1, 2001. CAST: Charlotte Alexandria (Alice), Hiram Keller (Jim), Rita Maiden (Mother), Bruno Balp (Father), Georges Guéret (Martial), Shirley Stoler (Shopkeeper)

## A LOVE DIVIDED

(CINEMA GUILD) Producers, Alan Moloney, Tim Palmer, Gerry Gregg; Executive Producers, David Blake Knox, Barbara McKissack, Rod Stoneman; Director, Sydney Macartney; Screenplay, Stuart Hepburn; Photography, Cedric Culliton; Designer, Alan Farquharson; Costumes, Allison Byrne; Editor, Ray Roantree; Music, Fiachra Trench; Casting, Nuala Moiselle; a Parallel Films production; Irish-British; Dolby; Color; Not rated; 98 minutes; U.S. release date: June 1, 2001. CAST: Liam Cunningham (Sean Cloney), Orla Brady (Sheila Kelly Cloney), Tony Doyle (Father Stafford), Peter Caffrey (Andy Bailey), John Kavanagh (Bishop Staunton), Brian McGrath (Fred Kelly), Jim Norton (Rev. Fischer), Ali White (Dorothy Kelly), Garrett Keogh (Jimmy Kennedy), Ian McElhinney (Rev. Hamilton), Rynagh O'Grady (Minnie Kennedy), Ger Ryan (Anna Walsh), Sarah Bolger (Eileen Cloney), Nicole Bohan (Mary Cloney), Joe Gallagher (Alec Auld), Doreen Keogh (Lucy Knipe), Peter Gowen (Patrick Pelly), Helen Norton (Katie Anderson), Melissa Bolger (Rebecca Auld), Grace Bolger (Rebecca's Sister), Emma Walsh (Molly Kennedy), Alvin Reid (William Auld), Eleanor Methven (Georgia Simpson), Brendan Conroy (The Drunk), Brian de Salvo (The Judge), Alan Barry (Ambrose), David Wilmot (Ted Nealan), Martin O'Malley (Reporter), Eileen Pollock (Helen Pottinger), Mark Mulholland (Mr. Pottinger), Peter Vollebregt (Callum), Gemma Hayes (Scottish Singer), Oliver O'Donohue (Papal)

## FAREWELL, HOME SWEET HOME

(INDEPENDENT) Producer, Martine Marignac; Director/Screenplay, Otar Ioseliani; Photography, William Lubtchansky; Designer, Emmanuel de Chauvigny; Music, Nicholas Zourabichvili; Editors, Otar Ioseliani, Eva Lenkiewicz; French-Swiss-Italian, 1999; Color; Not rated; 118 minutes; U.S. release date: June 1, 2001. CAST: Nico Tarielashvili (Son), Lily Lavina (Mother), Philippe Bas (Moto Driver), Stephanie Hainque (Girl at Bar), Mirabelle Kirkland (Maid), Amiran Amiranashvili (Hobo), Joachim Salinger (Beggar), Emmanuel de Chauvigny (Lover), Otar Ioseliani (Father), Narda Blanchet (Old Lady)

Orla Brady, Liam Cunningham in *A Love Divided*
© Cinema Guild

## THE WIDE BLUE ROAD

(MILESTONE) Producer, Maleno Malenotti; Director, Gillo Pontecorvo; Screenplay, Franco Solinas, Ennio De Concini, Gillo Pontecorvo; Based on the novella Squarciò by Franco Solinas; Photography, Mario Montuori; Music, Carlo Franci; Editor, Eraldo Da Roma; Costumes, Lucia Mirisola; from G.E.S.I. Cinematografica (Roma), Play-Art (Paris), Eichberg Film (Monaco), Triglav Film (Lubiana); Italian, 1957; Superscope; Ferraniacolor; Not rated; 90 minutes; U.S. release date: June 6, 2001. CAST: Yves Montand (Squarciò), Alida Valli (Rosetta), Francisco Rabal (Salvatore), Umberto Spadaro (Gaspare, 1st Coast Guard Officer), Peter Carsten (Riva, 2nd Coast Guard Officer), Federica Ranchi (Diana), Mario Girotti (Renato), Ronaldino Bonacchi (Bore), Giancarlo Soblone (Tonino)

Alida Valli, Yves Montand in *The Wide Blue Road*
© Milestone Film

Sho Aikawa in
*Dead or Alive*
© Viz Films

## DEAD OR ALIVE

**(VIZ FILMS)** Producers, Katsumi Ono, Makoto Okada; Executive Producers, Mitsuru Kurosawa, Tsutomu Tsuchikawa; Director, Takashi Miike; Screenplay, Ichiro Ryu; Photography, Hideo Yamamoto; Art Director, Akira Ishige; Music, Kouri Endou; Editor, Taiji Shimamura; a Daiei Co./Toei Video Co. production; Japanese, 2000; Color; Not rated; 104 minutes; U.S. release date: June 8, 2001. CAST: Riki Takeuchi (Ryuichi), Sho Aikawa (Detective Jojima), Renji Ishibashi (Aoki), Hitoshi Ozawa (Satake), Shingo Tsurumi (Tsin), Kaoru Sugita (Mrs. Jojima)

## WHATEVER HAPPENED TO HAROLD SMITH?

**(USA FILMS)** Producers, David Brown, Ruth Jackson; Executive Producers, Guy East, Nigel Sinclair; Director, Peter Hewitt; Screenplay, Ben Steiner; Photography, David Tattersall; Designer, Gemma Jackson; Costumes, Marie France; Music, Harry Gregson-Williams; Editor, Martin Walsh; Casting, Nina Gold; a co-production of the Arts Council of England, Intermedia Films, October Films, and West Eleven Films; British, 2000; Dolby; Color; Rated R; 95 minutes; U.S. release date: June 8, 2001. CAST: Tom Courtenay (Harold Smith), Michael Legge (Vince Smith), Laura Fraser (Joanna Robinson), Stephen Fry (Dr. Peter Robinson), Charlotte Roberts (Lucy Robinson), Amanda Root (Margaret Robinson), Lulu (Irene Smith), David Thewlis (Nesbit), Charlie Hunnam (Daz), Matthew Rhys (Ray Smith), James Corden (Walter), Rosemary Leach (Harold's Mother), Charles Simon (Oobie), Mark Williams (Roland Thornton), John Higgins (The Reverend Anthony Cooper), Keith Chegwin (Hugh Pimm), Jeremy Child (Dr. Bannister), Patrick Monckton (Peter Pringle), Andy Rashleigh (Sgt. Higgins), Iain Rogerson (North Now Presenter), Rebecca Hill, Janita Appa (Disco Girls), Dave Cooke (Boyfriend), Richenda Carey (Mary Blackcottage), Janus Stark (The Clique), Gizz Butt (Clique Lead Singer), Andrew Pincham (Clique Drummer), Swapan Nandi (Clique Bass Player), Matt Biffa (Clique Manager), Angela Rippon, John Craven, Alan Wicker, Jan Leeming (Themselves), David Law, Charlie Wathen, Sharon Holland (Harold Smith Followers), Jim Barclay, Simon Holmes, Peter Speedwell, Simon Scott (Journalists), Robert Curbishley, Jonah Russell, Ian Kirkby (Policemen), Anna Keaveney (Woman in Street), Dick Ward (Man in Street), John Harrison (Bus Driver)

## THE ADVENTURES OF FELIX

**(WINSTAR)** Producer, Philippe Martin; Directors/Screenplay, Olivier Ducastel, Jacques Martineau; Photography, Matthieu Poirot-Delpech; Designer, Louis Soubrier; Costumes, Juliette Chanaud; Editor, Sabine Mamou; Songs performed by Blossom Dearie; a co-production of ARTE France Cinema and Pyramide Productions, in association with Gimages 2, with the participation of Canal+ and the Centre National de la Cinematographie; French, 2000; Dolby; Widescreen; Color; Not rated; 95 minutes; U.S. release date: June 15, 2001. CAST: Sami Bouajila (Felix), Patachou (Mathilde), Ariane Ascaride (Isabelle), Pierre-Loup Rajot (Daniel), Charly Sergue (Jules), Maurice Bénichou (Fisherman), Philippe Garziano (Railroader), Didier Mahieu (Friend/Unionist), Aliette Langloff-Colas (Unemployment Secretary), Christiane Millet (Woman on Bitherapy), Arno Feffer (Man on Pentatherapy), Clément Dupré (Teenager with Kite), Clément Révérend (Laurent, the Assailant), Daniel Lesur (Bar Owner), Antoine Marneur (Salesman), Lisa Guez (Little Girl), Jean-Stéphan Havert (Dancer at Zizy Folies), Jean-Michel Colon (Zizy

Tom Courtenay in
*Whatever Happened to Harold Smith?* © USA Films

Sami Bouajila, Charly Sergue in *The Adventures of Felix* © Winstar Cinema

Folies Owner), Virginie Blanc (Louise), Florian Rollez (Nicolas), Adrien Auzias (Antoine), Gilles Barba (Driver in Car Accident), Pascal Billon (Antoine's Father)

## RUSSIAN DOLL

**(LOT 47)** Producers, Allanah Zitserman, Hugo Weaving; Executive Producer, Bruno Charlesworth; Director, Stavros Kazantzidis; Screenplay, Stavros Kazantzidis, Allanah Zitserman; Photography, Justin Brickle; Editor, Andrew MacNeil; Designer, Elizabeth Mary Moore; Casting, Sandra Wolfson; a co-production of Beyond Films, Screen Artists, and the Australian Film Finance Corp.; Australian; Dolby; Color; Rated R; 90 minutes; U.S. release date: June 15, 2001. CAST: Hugo Weaving (Harvey), Natalia Novikova (Katia), David Wenham (Ethan), Rebecca Frith (Miriam), Sacha Horler (Liza), Helen Dallimore (Alison)

## SAUDADE DO FUTURO

**(LATERIT PRODS.)** Producers, Marie-Clémence Blanc-Paes, César Paes; Director, César Paes; Screenplay, Marie-Clémence Blanc-Paes, César Paes; Photography, Michel Berck, César Paes; Music, Fabio Freire, Thomas Rohrer; Editor, Agnès Contensou; Brazilian-French-Belgian, 2000; Color; Not rated; 92 minutes; U.S. release date: June 20, 2001. Documentary, featuring Luiza Erundina, Fabio Freire, Ezequias Lira, Thomas Rohrer.

## JIN-ROH: THE WOLF BRIGADE

**(VIZ/TIDEPOINT)** Producers, Satoshi Kanuma, Toshifumi Yoshida; Director, Hiroyuki Okiura; Screenplay/Creator, Mamoru Oshii; Music, Hajime Mizoguchi; Key Animation Supervisor, Tetsuya Nishio; English Adaptation Producers, Bandai Entertainment and Viz Communications; English Script, Kevin McKeown, Robert Chomiack; Voice Director, Karl Willems; Casting, InterPacific Productions and Randi Riediger; Japanese, 1999, Color, Not rated, 102 minutes, U.S. release date: June 22, 2001. VOICE CAST: Michael Dobson (Kazuki Fuse), Moneca Stori (Kei Amemiya), Doug Abrahams (Hachiroh Tohbe), Colin Murdock (Atsushi Henmi), Dale Wilson (Bunmei Muroto), Michael Kopsa (Hajime Handa), Ron Halder (Shiroh Tatsumi), French Tickner (Isao Aniya), Maggie Blue O'Hara (Nanmi Agawa)

Natalia Novikova, Hugo Weaving in *Russian Doll* © Lot 47 FIlms

*Saudade Do Futuro* © Laterit Prods.

Ian Hart in *Strictly Sinatra* © Universal Studios

## STRICTLY SINATRA

(UNIVERSAL FOCUS) a.k.a. *Cocozza's Way*; Producer, Ruth Kenley-Letts; Executive Producers, Duncan Kenworthy, Andrew Macdonald; Director/Screenplay, Peter Capaldi; Photography, Stephen Blackman; Designer, Martyn John; Costumes, Kate Carin; Music, Stanislas Syrewicz; a co-production of the Arts Council of England, DNA Films, and Saracen Street; British; Dolby; Technicolor; Rated R; 97 minutes; U.S. release date: June 22, 2001. CAST: Ian Hart (Toni Cocozza), Kelly Macdonald (Irene), Alun Armstrong (Bill), Brian Cox (Chisholm), Tommy Flanagan (Michelangelo), Iain Cuthbertson (Connolly), Una McLean (Dainty), Jimmy Chisholm (Kenny), Jimmy Yuill (Rod Edmunds), Richard E. Grant, Jimmy Tarbuck (Themselves), Stewart Ennis (Doorman), Paul Dennan (Nicol), Anne Lacey (Coat Check Girl), Alex Howden (Kojak), Douglas Badie (Hard Man), Jamie Murphy (Drowned Rat), Brian McDermott (Youth in Supermarket), Alex McAvoy (Aldo), Pauline Lockhart ("Big T" Assistant), Billy McColl (John the Watchman), Iain Fraser (Joe the Bartender), Callum Beaton (Boy on Stairs)

## LUMUMBA

(ZEITGEIST) Executive Producer, Jacques Bidou; Director, Raoul Peck; Screenplay, Raoul Peck, Pascal Bonitzer; Photography, Bernard Lutic; Art Director, Andrew Fosny; Costumes, Charlotte David; Editor, Jacques Comets; Music, Jean-Claude Petit; Casting, Sylvie Brocheré; a JBA Productions (France), Entre Chine et Loup (Belgium), Essential Filmproduktion (Germany), Velvet S.A. (Haiti), Arte France Cinema, RTBF (Belgian Television), ARTE ZDF, Liberator Productions, FMB Films, SFP Cinema and Canal+, VRT, Cofimage 10; French-Belgian-Haitian-German, 2000; Dolby; Color; Not rated; 115 minutes; U.S. release date: June 27, 2001. CAST: Eriq Ebouaney (Patrice Lumumba), Alex Descas (Joseph Mobutu), Maka Kotto (Joseph Kasa Vubu), Théophile Moussa Sowié (Maurice Mpolo), Dieudonné Kabongo Bashila (Godefroid Munungo), Pascal Nzonzi (Moise Tshombe), André Debaar (Walter J. Ganshof Van der Meersch), Cheik Doukouré (Joseph Okito), Oumar Diop Makena (Thomas Kanza), Mariam Kaba (Pauline Lumumba), Rudi Delhem (General Emile Janssens)

## THE CRIMSON RIVERS

(TRISTAR) Producer, Alain Goldman; Director, Mathieu Kassovitz; Screenplay, Jean-Christophe Grangé, Mathieu Kassovitz; Based on the novel *Red Blood Rivers* by Jean-Christophe Grangé; Photography, Thierry Arbogast; Designer, Thierry Flamand; Editor, Maryline Monthieux; Music, Bruno Coulais; a production Gaumont-Legende Enterprises-TF1 Films Production with the participation of Canal+; French, 2000; Dolby; Panavision; Color; Rated R; 106 minutes; U.S. release date: June 27, 2001. CAST: Jean Reno (Pierre Niemans), Vincent Cassel (Max Kerkerian), Nadia Farès (Fanny Ferreira), Jean-Pierre Cassel (Dr. Bernard Chernezé), Karim Belkhadra (Capt. Dahmane), Didier Flamand (The Rector), Laurent Avare (Rémy Caillois), Francine Berge (The Headmistress), Dominique Bettenfeld (The Idea Policeman), Tonio Descanvelle, Olivier Rousset (Policemen, Sarzac), Robert Gendreu (The Cemetery Warden), Alain Guerillot (Skinhead Cafe Owner), Nicolas Koretzky (Computer Cop), Laurent Lafitte (The Rector's Son), Francois Levantal (The Lawyer), Francoise Loreau (Sister at the Convent), Olivier Morel (Philippe Sertys), Philippe Nahon (Man at Motorway Services), Christophe Bernard, Nicky Naude (Skinheads), Alexis Robin (Child), Christophe Rossignon (The Bridge Break Policeman), Dominique Sanda (Sister Andrée), Vincent Schimenti (Policeman), Sami Zitouni, Slim Zitouni (Youths at Sarzac Estate)

Nadia Ferès, Jean Reno in *The Crimson Rivers* © Tristar Pictures

## UNDER THE FLUTTERING MILITARY FLAG

**(INDEPENDENT/SCREENING ROOM)** Producers, Seishi Matsumaru, Eigasha Shinsei, Shohei Tokizane; Director, Kinji Fukasaku; Screenplay, Kinji Fukasaku, Norio Osada, Kaneto Shindô; Based on the novel by Shoji Yuki; Photography, Hiroshi Segawa; Music, Hiroshi Hayashi; Editor, Keiichi Uraoka; Japanese, 1972; Color; Not rated; 96 minutes; U.S. release date: July 6, 2001. CAST: Sachiko Hidari, Tetsuro Tamba, Noboru Mitani, Sanae Nakahara, Kanemon Nakamura

## THE VERTICAL RAY OF THE SUN

**(SONY PICTURES CLASSICS)** Producer, Christophe Rossignon; Executive Producer, Benoit Jaubert; Director/Screenplay, Tran Anh Hung; Photography, Mark Lee Ping-Bin; Art Director, Benoît Barouh; Costumes, Susan Lu; Editor, Mario Battistel; Music, Ton That Tiet; Produced by Lazennec in association with Studio Canal+, Arte France Cinema; French-Vietnamese; Dolby; Color; Rated PG-13; 112 minutes; U.S. release date: July 6, 2001. CAST: Tran Nu Yên-Khé (Liên), Nguyen Nhu Quynh (Suong), Lê Khanh (Khanh), Ngô Quang Hai (Hai), Tran Manh Cuong (Kiên), Chu Ngoc Hung (Quôc), Le Tuan Anh (Tuân), Lê Van Lôc (Lôc)

## ADANGGAMAN

**(NEW YORKER)** Producer, Tiziana Soudani; Director, Roger Gnoan M'Bala; Screenplay, Roger Gnoan M'Bala, Jean-Marie Adlaffi, Bertin Akaffou; Photography, Mohammed Soudani; Art Director, Jean-Baptiste Lerro; Costumes, Aïssatou Traoré; Editor, Monica Goux; Music, Lokua Kanza; a co-production of Abyssa Film, Amka Films, Canal+ Horizon, Direction de la Cinematographie Nationale, Fabrica, IMTM Films, Renardes Productions, Televisione Svizzera Italiana (TSI); French-Italian-Swiss-Ivory Coast-Burkina Faso; Dolby; Color; Not rated; 90 minutes; U.S. release date: July 11, 2001. CAST: Rasmane Ouedraogo (Adanggman), Albertine N'Guessan (Mo Akassi), Ziablé Honoré Goore (Ossei), Mylene-Perside Boti Kouame (Naka), Bintou Bakayoko (Ehua), Nicole Suzis Menyeng (Adjo), Mireille André Boti (Mawa), Tie Dijian Patrick (Kanga), Lou Nadege Blagone (Safo Aboua), Anastasie Tode Bohi (The Castanet Girl), Didier Grandidier (Bangalajan), Mylène-Perside Boti Kouame (Naka), Étienne Goheti Bi Gore (Poro), Zie Soro (Sory)

*101 Reykjavik* © Menemsha Entertainment

## 101 REYKJAVIK

**(MENEMSHA ENTERTAINMENT)** Producers, Ingvar Thordarson, Baltasar Kormakur; Director/Screenplay, Baltasar Kormakur; Based on the novel by Hallgrimur Helgason; Photography, Peter Steuger; Designer, Arni Pall Johannsson; Costumes, Thorunn Sveinsdottir, Sigridur Gudjonsdottir; from Zentropa Prods., Filmhuset, Liberator, Troik Entertainment; Icelandic-Danish-Norweigan-French-German, 2000; Dolby; Color; Not rated; 93 minutes; U.S. release date: July 25, 2001. CAST: Victoria Abril (Lola Milagros), Hilmir Snaer Gudnason (Hlynur), Hanna Maria Karlsdottir (Berglind), Thrudur Vihjalmsdottir (Hofi), Baltasar Kormakur (Throstur), Olafur Darri Olafsson (Marri), Throstur Leo Gunnarsson (Brusi), Eyvindur Erlendsson (Hafsteinn), Halldora Bjornsdottir (Elsa), Hilmar Jonsson (Maggi), Johann Sigurdarson (Pall), Edda Heidrun Backman (Pall's Wife), Gudmundur Ingi Thorvaldsson (Ellert)

Tran Nu Yën-Khé, Ngö Quang Hai in *The Vertical Ray of The Sun* © Sony Pictures Entertainment

Susie Porter, Kelly McGillis in *The Monkey's Mask*
© Strand Releasing

Dennis Hopper, Matthew Modine in *The Blackout*
© Trimark

## THE MONKEY'S MASK

**(STRAND)** Producers, Robert Connolly, John Maynard; Director, Samantha Lang; Screenplay, Annie Kennedy; Based on the novel in poetry by Dorothy Porter; Co-Producer, Domenico Procacci; Photography, Garry Philips; Designer, Michael Philips; Costumes, Emily Seresin; Editor, Dany Cooper; Casting, Ann Robinson, Leo Davis; an Arenafilm Pty Ltd./Australian Film Finance Corporation/New South Wales Film and Television Office; Australian; Dolby; Color; Not rated; 91 minutes; U.S. release date: July 27, 2001. CAST: Susie Porter (Jill Fitzpatrick), Kelly McGillis (Diana), Marton Csokas (Nick), Deborah Mailman (Lou), Abbie Cornish (Mickey), Jean-Pierre Mignon (Tony Brach), Caroline Gillmer (Barbara Brach), Brendan Cowell (Hayden), Bojana Novakovic (Tianna), John Noble (Mr. Norris), Linden Wilkinson (Mrs. Norris), Jim Holt (Bill McDonald), Annie Jones (Evelyn McDonald), Chris Haywood (Dad Fitzgerald), John Batchelor (Steve), William Zappa (Det. Sgt. Wesley), Charlotte Rose Regan (Cerebral Girl), Johnny Lee (Tai Chi Instructor), Sara Nunn (Comforting Policewoman), Brian Wood (Brian the Poet), Amanda Herbert, Cassandra McGann (Strippers), Robert Choy, Sky Tse (Asian Fishermen), Billy Mitchell (Stan), Kathryn Hartman (Policewoman)

## CURE

**(COWBOY BOOKING)** Producers, Tetsuya Ikeda, Satoshi Kanno, Tsutomu Tsuchikawa, Atsuyuki Shimoda; Director/Screenplay, Kiyoshi Kurosawa; Executive Producer, Hiroyuki Kato; Photography, Takusho Kikumura; Designer, Tomoyuki Maruo; Music, Gary Shiya; Editor, Kan Suzuki; a Code Red and Daiei Co. Ltd. presentation; Japanese, 1997; Color; Not rated; 111 minutes; U.S. release date: July 27, 2001. CAST: Koji Yakusho (Ken-ichi Takabe), Tsuyoshi Ujiki (Makoto Sakuma), Anna Nakagawa (Fumie Takabe), Masato Hagiwara (Kunio Mamiya), Yoriko Douguchi (Dr. Miyajima), Yukijiro Hotaru (Inchiro Kuwano), Denden (Oida), Ren Osugi (Fujiwara)

## THE BLACKOUT

**(TRIMARK)** Producers, Edward R. Pressman, Clayton Townsend; Executive Producers, Alessandro Camon, Mark Damon; Director, Abel Ferrara; Screenplay, Abel Ferrara, Marla Hanson, Christ Zois; Photography, Ken Kelsch; Designer, Richard Hoover; Costumes, Melinda Eshelman; Editor, Anthony Redman; Casting, Lori Eastside; a co-production of CIPA, Les Films Number One, MDP Worldwide; French-U.S., 1997; Dolby; Color; Not rated; 98 minutes; U.S. release date: August 3, 2001. CAST: Matthew Modine (Matty), Claudia Schiffer (Susan), Dennis Hopper (Mickey Wayne), Beatrice Dalle (Annie 1), Sarah Lassez (Annie 2), Steven Bauer, Laura Bailey, Nancy Ferrara, Andy Fiscella, Vincent Lamberti (Mickey's Studio Actors), Victoria Duffy (Script Girl), Nicholas De Cegli (Miami Dealer), Daphne Duplaix, Mercy Lopez (Fly Girls), Lori Eastside (That Girl), Shareef Malnik (Gold Carder), Peter Cannold (Movie Investor) (Note: This film had its U.S. premiere on cable television in 2000.)

Koji Yakusho (right) in *Cure* © Cowboy Booking

Aylin Yay in *Thomas in Love* © IFC Films

## THOMAS IN LOVE

(IFC FILMS) Producer, Diana Elbaum; Co-Producers, Jacques Bidou, Arlette Zylberberg; Director, Pierre Paul Renders; Screenplay, Philippe Blasband; Photography, Virginie Saint Martin; Art Director, Pierre Gerbaux; Costumes, Anne Fournier; Editor, Ewin Ryckaert; Music, Igor Sterpin; a co-production of JBA Productions, RTBF (Belgian Television); French-Belgian; Dolby; Color; Not rated; 97 minutes; U.S. release date: August 3, 2001. CAST: Benoît Verhaert (Thomas), Aylin Yay (Eva), Magali Pinglault (Melodie), Micheline Hardy (Nathalie, the Mother), Alexandre von Sivers (Insurance Agent), Frédéric Topart (Psychologist), Serge Larivière (Receptionist), Eric Kasongo (Ken)

## BROOKLYN BABYLON

(ARTISAN) Producers, Henri M. Kessler, Ezra Swerdlow; Executive Producers, Alex Gibney, David Peipers, John Sloss; Associate Producers, Bonz Malone, Lisa West; Director, Marc Levin; Screenplay, Marc Levin, Bonz Malone, Pam Widener; Photography, Mark Benjamin; Designer, Andrea Stanley; Editor, Emir Lewis; Casting, Brett Goldstein; a co-production of Bac Films, Le Studio Canal+, Off Line Entertainment Group; French-U.S., 2000; Dolby; Color; Rated R; 89 minutes; U.S. release date: August 17, 2001. CAST: Tariq Trotter (Solomon), Karen Goberman (Sara), Bonz Malone (Scratch), David Vadim (Judah), Rahzel (Narrator), Earl Contasti (Ras Don), Carol Woods (Cislyn), Slick Rick (Buddah), Mad Cobra (Key Bouncer), Camille Cruse (Cindy), Ahmir Thompson, James "Mala" Gray, Leonard "Hub" Hubbard, Kyle "Scratch" Jones (Members of the Lions), Mina Bern (Nann), Joanne Baron (Aunt Rose), Daniel Serafini-Sauli (Abe), Steve "Simcha" Gottlieb (Sara's Father), Spragga Benz, Yossi Piamenta (Themselves)

Jalil Nazari (center), Mahmoud Behraznia in *Djomeh*
© New Yorker Films

## DJOMEH

(NEW YORKER) Producer, Ahmad Moussazadeh; Director/Screenplay/Editor, Hassan Yektapanah; Co-Producer, Mehran Haguigui; Photography, Ali Loghmani; Iranian; Color; Not rated; 94 minutes; U.S. release date: September 5, 2001. CAST: Jalil Nazari (Djomeh), Mahmoud Behraznia (Agha Mohmoud), Rashid Akbari (Habib), Mahbobeh Khalili (Setareh)

## VENGO

(COWBOY BOOKING) Director/Screenplay, Tony Gatlif; Adaptation and Dialogues, Tony Gatlif, David Trueba; Photography, Thierry Pouget; Editor, Pauline Dairou; Casting, Hélèna Odier, Carmen Sanz, Matilde Rubio; a Code Red and Princes Films presentation; French-Spanish, 2000; Color; Not rated; 90 minutes; U.S. release date: September 7, 2001. CAST: Antonio Canales (Caco), Orestes Villasan Rodriguez (Diego), Antonio Perez Dechent (Primo Alejandro), Bobote (Primo Antonio), Juan Luis Corrientes (Primo Tres), Fernando Guerrero Rebollo (Fernando Caravaca), Francisco Chavero Rios (Francisco Caravaca), Jose Ramirez El Cheli, Juan-Luis Barrios Llorente, Jesus Maria Ventura (Primos Caravaca), El Moror (Pepe Sardina), Manuel Vega Salazar (Anselmo), Maria Faraco (La Catalana), Natasha Mayghine (Alma), Maria Altea Maya (La Coneja)

*Vengo* © Cowboy Booking

Han Suk-kyu, Shim Eun-ha in *Tell Me Something*
© Kino International

## TELL ME SOMETHING

(KINO) Producers, Koo Bon-han, Chang Youn-hyun; Executive Producer, Choi Gwi-duk; Director, Chang Youn-Hyun; Screenplay, Chang Youn-Hyun, Kong Su-chang, In Eun-Ah, Shim Hae-weon, Kim Eun-jung; Story, Koo Bon-han; Photography, Kim Sung-bok; Editor, Kim Sang-bum; Art Director, Chung Ku-ho; Music, Cho Young-ook, Bang Joon-suk; a Koo & C Film production in association with Cinema Service & Kookmin Venture Capital; South Korean, 2000; Dolby; Color; Not rated; 116 minutes; U.S. release date: September 14, 2001. CAST: Han Suk-kyu (Detective Cho), Shim Eun-ha (Su-Yeon Chae), Chang Hang-sun (Detective Oh), Yum Jung-ah (Sung-min)

D in *Vampire Hunter D: Bloodlust* © Urban Vision

Mouna Noureddine, Sabah Bouzouita in
*The Season of Men* © Cowboy Booking

## VAMPIRE HUNTER D: BLOODLUST

(URBAN VISION) Producers, Mataichiro Yamamoto, Masao Maruyama, Takayuki Nagasawa; Director/Screenplay, Yoshiaki Kawajiri; Based on a novel by Hideyuki Kikuchi; Based on character illustrations by Yoshitaka Amano; Conceptual Designer, Yasushi Nirasawa; Mechanical Designer, Ken Koike; Art Director, Yuji Ikehata; from Madhouse Animation Studios; a Mata Yamamoto production from Filmlink International; Japanese, 2000; Dolby; Color; Rated R; 105 minutes; U.S. release date: September 21, 2001. VOICE CAST: Andrew Philpot (D), Pamela Segall (Leila), John Rafter Lee (Meier Link), Wendee Lee (Charlotte), Mike McShane (Left Hand), Julia Fletcher (Carmila), Matt McKenzie (Borgoff), John DiMaggio (Nolt/Sheriff/Mashira/John Elbourne), Alex Fernandez (Kyle), Jack Fletcher (Grove), John Hostetter (Polk), Dwight Schultz (Benge/Old Man of Barbarois), John Demita (Alan Elbourne/Priest), Mary Elizabeth McGlynn (Caroline), Debi Derryberry (Young Girl)

## THE SEASON OF MEN

(COWBOY BOOKING) Producers, Margaret Menegoz, Mohamed Tlatli; Director/Screenplay, Moufida Tlatli; Adaptation & Dialogue, Nouri Bouzid; Photography, Chedli Chaouachi; Costumes, Nadia Anane, Naama Mejri; Editor, Isabelle Devinck; Music, Anouar Brahem; a co-production of Les Films Du Losange, Maghrebfilms Carthage and Arte France Cinema; Tunisian-French; Dolby; Color; Not rated; 124 minutes; U.S. release date: September 28, 2001. CAST: Rabiaa Ben Abdallah (Aïcha), Sabah Bouzouita (Zeineb), Ghania Ben Ali (Meriem), Hend Sabri (Emna), Ezzedine Gannoun (Saïd), Mouna Noureddine (Ommi), Azza Baaziz (Meriem's Child), Lilia Falkat (Emna's Child), Adel Hergal (Aziz), Houyem Rassaa (Zohra), Kaouther Bel Haj Ali (Fatma)

## LA CIÉNAGA

**(COWBOY BOOKING)** Producer, Lita Stantic; Director/Screenplay, Lucrecia Martel; Co-Producers, Diego Guebel, Ana Aizenberg, Mario Pergolini; Photography, Hugo Colace; Art Director, Graciela Oderigo; Editor, Santiago Ricci; an Orfeo Films International presentation of a 4K Films Production; Argentine, 2000; Color; Not rated; 103 minutes; U.S. release date: October 3, 2001. CAST: Martín Adjemian (Gregorio), Diego Baenas (Joaquín), Leonora Balcarce (Verónica), Silvia Bayle (Mercedes), Sofia Bertolotto (Momi), Juan Cruz Bordeu (José), Graciela Borges (Mecha), Noelia Bravo Herrera (Agustina), Maria Micol Ellero (Mariana), Andrea Lopez (Isabel), Sebastián Montagna (Luciano), Mercedes Moran (Tali), Daniel Valenzuela (Rafael), Franco Veneranda (Martín), Fabio Villafañe (Perro)

## THE HIDDEN HALF

**(ARTA FILM)** Producers, Tahmineh Milani, Mohammad Nikbin; Director/Screenplay, Tahmineh Milani; Photography, Mahmoud Kalari; Designer, Iraj Raminfar; Music, Amir Moini; Editor, Bahram Dehghani; Produced by the Iranian Film Society; Iranian; Color; Not rated; 103 minutes; U.S. release date: October 5, 2001. CAST: Niki Marimi (Fereshteh), Mohammad Nikbin (Khosro), Atila Pesiani (Husband), Soghra Abissi, Akbar Moazezi, Afarin Obeisi

*Werckmeister Harmonies* © Menemsha Entertainment

## WERCKMEISTER HARMONIES

**(MENEMSHA ENTERTAINMENT)** Producers, Franz Goëss, Paul Saadoun, Miklós Szita, Joachim von Vietinghoff; Director, Béla Tarr; Screenplay, László Krasznahorkai, Béla Tarr; Additional Dialogue, Péter Dobai, Gyuri Dósa Kiss, György Fehér; Based on the novel The Melancholy of Resistance by László Krasznahorkai; Photography, Miklós Gurbán, Erwin Lanzensberger, Gábor Medvigy, Emil Novak, Rob Tregenza, Patrick de Ranter; Costumes, János Breckl; Music, Mihály Vig; Editor, Ágnes Hranitzky; German-French-Hungarian, 2000; Stereo; Black and white; 145 minutes; U.S. release date: October 10, 2001. CAST: Lars Rudolph (János Valuska), Peter Fitz (György Eszter), Hanna Schygulla (Tünde Eszter), Éva Almássy Albert (Aunt Piri), Irén Szajki (Mrs. Harrer), Alfréd Járai (Lajos Harrer), György Barkó (Mr. Nadabán), Lajos Dobák (Mr. Volent), András Fekete (Mr. Árgyelán), János Derzsi (Man in the Broad-Cloth Coat), Djoko Rosic (Man in Western Boots), Tamás Wichmann (Man in the Sailor Cap), Matuas Drafi (Man in the Fur Cap), Ferenc Kállai (Director), Mihály Kormos (Factotum), Putyi Horváth (Porter), Péter Dobai (Chief Constable), Kati Lázár (Sorter), László Fe-Lugossy (Housepainter), Gyula Pauer (Mr. Hagelmayer), Barna Mihók (Coachman), Viktor Lois (Loader), Béla Máriáss (Mr. Mádai), Sandor Bese (The Prince)

Silvia Bayle, Juan Cruz Bordeu in *La Ciénaga*
© Cowboy Booking

Yehuda Lerner in *Sobibor: October 14, 1943, 4 P.M.*
© New Yorker Films

## SOBIBOR: OCTOBER 14, 1943, 4 P.M.

**(NEW YORKER)** Director, Claude Lanzmann; Photography, Caroline Champetier, Dominique Chapuis; Editors, Chantal Hymans, Sabine Marnou; a co-production of Why Not Productions-Les Films Aleph-France 2 Cinema, with the participation of Canal+ and France Television Images; French; DTS Stereo; Color; Not rated; 95 minutes; U.S. release date: October 12, 2001. Documentary on the only successful uprising ever staged by Jewish prisoners at an extermination camp against the Nazis, featuring Yehuda Lerner.

## YANA'S FRIENDS

**(FRIENDS OF FILM)** Producers, Marek Rozenbaum, Moshe Levinson, Uri Sabag, Einat Bikel; Director, Arik Kaplun; Screenplay, Arik Kaplun, Simeon Vinokur; Photography, Valentin Belonogov; Art Director, Ariel Roshko; Music, Avi Binyamin; Israeli; Color; Not rated; 90 minutes; U.S. release date: October 12, 2001. CAST: Evelyne Kaplun (Yana), Nir Levi (Eli), Shmil Ben-Ari (Yuri), Moscu Alcalay (Yitzhak), Dalia Friedland (Rosa), Vladimir Friedman (Alik), Israel Demidov (Fima), Lena Sachanova (Mila), Jenya Fleischer (Edik), Eviatar Lazar (Daniel), Lucy Dubinchik (Yuri's Daughter)

Nir Levi, Evelyne Kaplun in *Yana's Friends* © Friends of Film

*Berlin Babylon* © S.U.M.O. Film

## SPRIGGAN

**(ADV FILMS)** Director, Hirotsuge Kawasaki; Screenplay, Yasutaka Itô; General Supervisor, Katsuhiro Ôtomo; Character Designer/Animation Director, Hisashi Eguchi; CGI Director, Akiko Saito; Japanese, 1998; Dolby; Color; Rated R; 90 minutes; U.S. release date: October 12, 2001. VOICE CAST: Chris Patton (Yu Ominae), Kevin Corn (Gen. MacDougall), Ted Pfister (Dr. Meisel), Andy McAvin (Jean-Jacques Mondo), Kelly Manison (Margaret), Mike Kleinhenz (Fattman), Spike Spencer (Little Boy), John Paul Shepard (Yamamoto), John Swasey (Mr. Smith), Brett Weaver (Classmate A), Jason Douglas, Tiffany Grant, Adam Taylor (Additional Voices)

## BERLIN BABYLON

**(S.U.M.O. FILM)** Producers, Hubertus Siegert, E.N. Wilsdorf, Boris Wilsdorf; Director/Screenplay, Hubertus Siegert; Photography, Ralf K. Dobrick, Thomas Plenert; Music, Einstürzende Neubauten; a co-production of S.U.M.O. Film Hubertus Siegert and Philip Gröning Filmproduktion; German; 2000; Dolby; Color; Not rated; 88 minutes; U.S. release date: October 17, 2001. Documentary about the building campaign of various international companies eager to establish themselves in Berlin following the fall of the Berlin Wall in 1989.

## COOL & CRAZY

**(FIRST RUN FEATURES)** Producer, Tom Remlov; Director, Knut Erik Jensen; Line Producer, Jan-Erik Gammleng; Photography, Svein Krøvel, Aslaug Holm; Editor, Aslaug Holm; a Norsk Film AS co-production with Barentsfilm AS and Giraff Film AB; Norweigan; Color; Not rated; U.S. release date: October 19, 2001. Documentary on the Berlevåg Male Choir, featuring Odd Marino Frantzen (Conductor), Einar F. L. Strand, Arne Wensel, Kåre Wensel, Arne Blomsø, Leif Roger Ananiassen, Eirik Daldorff, Odd-Arne Olsen, Eirik Nilsen, Nils Grønberg (1st Tenor), Reidar Strand, Ragnar Rotnes, Randulf Antonsen, Ole Jonny Larsen, Einar Kristian Straumsne (2nd Tenor), Alf Håkon Pedersen, Harald Wensel, Kolbjørn Svendsen, Karl Ananiassen, Bjarne Mathisen, Tommy Bergersen, Oddvar Hansen, Einar Sætervoll, Terje Håkon Blickfeldt (1st Bass), Arne Nygård, Ken-Hugo Jensen, Trygg Lund, Kai Olav Jakobsen, Hilmar Wensel, Brynjar Langås (2nd Bass).

Berlevåg Male Choir in *Cool & Crazy* © First Run Features

## BETTER THAN SEX

**(GOLDWYN/FIREWORKS)** Producers, Bruna Papandera, Frank Cox; Executive Producer, Marc Bonduel; Director/Screenplay, Jonathan Teplitzky; Photography, Garry Phillips; Designer, Tara Kamath; Costumes, Kelly May; Music, David Hirschfelder; Editor, Shawn Seet; Casting, Nicki Barrett; The New South Wales Film & Television Office, France Television Distribution, Meercat & NewVision Films presentation of a Better Than production; Australian-French, 2000; Dolby; Color; Not rated; 84 minutes; U.S. release date: October 24, 2001. CAST: David Wenham (Josh), Susie Porter (Cin), Catherine McClements (Sam), Kris McQuade (Taxi Driver), Simon Bossell (Tim), Imelda Corcoran (Carole), Dina Gillespie (Girl "B"), Emily Saunders (Girl "C"), Laura Keneally (Girl "D"), Leah Vandenberg (Girl "E"), Tammy MacIntosh (Girl "F"), Mark Priestley (Guy "A"), Tamblyn Lord (Guy "B"), Jason Clarke (Guy "C"), Jason Chong (Guy "D"), Tim Richards (Guy "E"), Harry Bragg (Old Man), Pauline Anderson (Old Woman)

## MY VOYAGE TO ITALY
### (Il Mio Viaggio in Italia)

**(MIRAMAX)** Producers, Barbara De Fina, Giuliana Del Punta, Bruno Restuccia; Executive Producers, Giorgio Armani, Riccardo Tozzi; Director, Martin Scorsese; Screenplay, Suso Cecchi D'Amico, Raffaele Donato, Kent Jones, Martin Scorsese; Editor, Thelma Schoonmaker; Associate Producer, Caterina D'Amico; Co-Executive Producer, Raffaele Donato; a Mediatrade presentation in association with Cappa Productions; a Mediatrade production in conjunction with Paso Doble Film; Italian-U.S.; Dolby; Color; Rated PG-13; 243 minutes; U.S. release date: October 24, 2001. Documentary hosted by director Martin Scorsese as he explores Italian movie history.

(Above) Susie Porter, David Wenham in *Better Than Sex*
© Goldman-Fireworks
(Below) Martin Scorsese in *My Voyage to Italy*
© Miramax Films

Pisek Intrakanchit in *Bangkok Dangerous*
© First Look Features

## BANGKOK DANGEROUS

(FIRST LOOK FEATURES) Producer, Nonzee Nimibutr; Executive Producers, Pracha Maleenont, Brian L. Marcar, Adirek Wattaleela; Directors/Screenplay/Editors, Oxide Pang, Danny Pang; Photography, Decha Srimantra; Designer, Wut Chaoslip; Music, Orange Music; Thailand, 1999; Dolby; Color; Not rated; 105 minutes; American release date: October 19, 2001. CAST: Pawalit Mongkolpisit (Kong), Premsinee Ratanasopha (Fon), Patharawarin Timkul (Aom), Pisek Intrakanchit (Jo)

## GINGER SNAPS

(TVA INTERNATIONAL) Producers, Steve Hoban, Karen Lee Hall; Executive Producers, Noah Segal, Alicia Reilly-Larson, Daniel Lyon; Director, John Fawcett; Screenplay, Karen Walton; Story, Karen Walton, John Fawcett; Photography, Thom Best; Designer, Todd Cherniawsky; Editor, Brett Sullivan; Costumes, Lea Carlson; Special Make-up and Creature Effects, Paul Jones; Music, Michael Shields; Casting, Robin D. Cook, Linda Philips-Palo, Robert McGee; a Copper Heat Entertainment/Water Pictures in association with Lions Gate Films and Unapix Entertainment presentation; Canadian; Dolby; Color; Not rated; 108 minutes; American release date: October 26, 2001. CAST: Emily Perkins (Brigitte Fitzgerald), Katharine Isabelle (Ginger Fitzgerald), Kris Lemche (Sam), Mimi Rogers (Pamela Fitzgerald), Jesse Moss (Jason), Danielle Hampton (Trina Sinclair), John Bourgeois (Henry Fitzgerald), Peter Keleghan (Mr. Wayne), Christopher Redman (Ben), Jimmy MacInnis (Tim), Lindsey Leese (Nurse Ferry), Nick Nolan (Creature & Gingerwolf), Wendii Fulford (Ms. Sykes), Ann Baggley (Mother), Graeme Robertson, Maxwell Robertson (Toddlers), Pak-Kong Ho (Janitor), Bryon Bully (Hockey Kid), Steven Taylor (Puppy Kid), Lucy Lawless (Announcer on School's PA System)

## OUCH!

(NEW YORKER) Producers, Martine Marignac, Maurice Tinchant; Director/Screenplay, Sophie Fillieres; Photography, Christophe Pollock; Designer, Antoine Platteau; Editor, Valerie Loiseleux; Music, Michel Portal; Pierre Grise Productions; French, 2000; Dolby; Color; Not rated; 106 minutes; U.S. release date: October 26, 2001. CAST: André Dussollier (Robert), Hélène Fillieres (Aie), Emmanuelle Devos (Claire), Anne Le Ny (Marie), Gisèle Casadesus (Robert's Mother), Lucien Pascal (Robert's Father), Lucienne Hamon (Aie's Mother), Alain Rimoux (Aie's Father), Jean-Baptiste Malartre (David), Olivier Cruveiller (Francois)

## HIGH HEELS AND LOW LIFES

(TOUCHSTONE) Producers, Uri Fruchtmann, Barnaby Thompson; Director, Mel Smith; Screenplay/Associate Producer, Kim Fuller; Story, Kim Fuller, Georgia Pritchett; Co-Producer, Nicky Kentish Barnes; Photography, Steven Chivers; Designer, Michael Pickwood; Costumes, Jany Temime; Editor, Christopher Blunden; Music, Charlie Mole; Casting, Kate Rhodes James, Deborah Aquila; a Fragile Films production, Distributed by Buena Vista; Dolby; Color; Rated R; 86 minutes; U.S.

Emily Perkins (right) in *Ginger Snaps* © TVA International

release date: October 26, 2001. CAST: Minnie Driver (Shannon), Mary McCormack (Frances), Kevin McNally (Mason), Michael Gambon (Kerrigan), Danny Dyer (Danny), Mark Williams (Tremaine), Kevin Eldon (McGill), Len Collin (Barry Tarson), Julian Wadham (Chief Inspector Rogers), Darren Boyd (Ray), Simon Scardifield (Tony), Jane Partridge (Receptionist), Jason Griffiths, Ben Lemel, Sophie Millet (Paramedics), Ranjit Krishnamma (Doctor), Mark Meadows (Romantic Actor), Ben Walden (Bloodied Actor), Mike Attwell (Duty Sergeant), Danny Babington (Suspect), John Sessions (Director), Paul Bown (Barman), James Cameron (Reporter), James Garbutt (Mr. Winters), Eve Slickie (Patient), Patrick Baladi (Car Driver), Barry Ewart (Busybody), Tom Ellis (Uniformed Officer), Ben Farrow (Julian), Junior Simpson (Mickey), Darren Tighe (Clubber), Kier Charles (Young Guy), Stewart Wright (Officer), Hugh Bonneville (Farmer), James Taylor (Ticket Collector), Liam Noble (Delivery Man)

## MYSTERIOUS OBJECT AT NOON

**(INDEPENDENT/ANTHOLOGY FILM ARCHIVES)** Producers, Gridthiya Gaweewong, Mingmongkol Sonakul; Director, Apichatpong Weerasethakul; Photography, Prasong Klinborrom, Apichatpong Weerasethakul; Editors Tony Morias, Peter Jones; Story, Villagers of Thailand; Thailand, 2000; Black and white; Not rated; 85 minutes; U.S. release date: November 1, 2001. Part-fiction, part-documentary depiction of the lives of several inhabitants of Bangkok, Thailand, featuring Somsri Pinyopol, Duangjai Hiransri, To Hanudomlapr, Kannikar Narong, Kongkiert Komsiri, Mee Madmoon, Chakree Duangklao, Jaruwan Techasatiern, Somsri Pinyopol, Jarunee Jandang, Deaw, Jack of Ayuddhaya.

Minnie Driver, Mary McCormack in
*High Heels and Low Lifes* © Touchstone Pictures

## ASOKA

**(ARCLIGHTZ)** Executive Producer, Sanjiv Chawla; Director/Photography, Santosh Sivan; Screenplay, Saket Chaudhary, Santosh Sivan; Editor, Shreekar Prasad; Art Director, Sabu Cyril; Music, Sandeep Chowta; Indian; Color; Not rated; 169 minutes; U.S. release date: November 2, 2001. CAST: Shah Rukh Khan (Asoka), Kareena Kapoor (Kaurwaki), Danny Denzongpa (Virat), Ajit (Susima), Rahul Dev (Bheema), Hrishita Bhatt (Devi), Umesh Mehra (Chandragupta), Gerson Da Cuhna (Bindusara), Subhashini (Dharma), Suraj Balaje (Arya), Johnny Lever, Raghuvir Yadav, Suresh Menon (Magadha Soldiers), Rani Rajlaxmi (Bar Girl), Gayatri Jayaraman (Dancer), Shilpa R. Mehta (Queen), Shweta Menon (Nandaneshwari), Shabir Massani (Giri), Vinit Sharma (Sugatra), Vivek Sharma (Sugidha), Usha Jerajani (Nanny), N. Shyam Sunder (Radhagupta), C. L. Gurnani (Pandit), Mithilesh Chaturvedi (Kalinga Minister), P. Mantu Mohaputra (Kalinga Minister's Goon), Madhu (Vitasoka), Karan Dewani (Young Asoka), Jitendra Shriamali (Milkman), Shampa (Milkman's Wife), Rajendra Mehra (Village Head), Anu Ansari (Headman's Daughter), Master Hardik (Headman's Grandsom), Anjan Ghosh (Magadha General), Vijay Kumar, Bahadur (Buddhist Monks), Arvind Ayer (Assassin in the River), Ashok Mapara (Assassin in the Monastery), Samir Sarkar (Messenger), S. Krishna, Milind Vereker (Thugs), Balakrishna (Arya's Father), Sanghamitra Jena (Arya's Mother), Bomie E. Dotiwala (Devi's Father), Bunty (Groom), Col. Suresh Rege (Groom's Father), Chetan Motiwala (Announcer), Mangilal (Arya's Caretaker), Monika Kale (Flower Girl)

Shah Rukh Khan in *Asoka* © Overseas Film Group

Isaach de Bankolé in *Otomo* © ArtMattan

Béatrice Dalle, Alex Descas in *Trouble Every Day*
© Lot 47 Films

## OTOMO

(ARTMATTAN) Producers, Thomas Lechner, Claudia Tronnier, Irene von Alberti; Director, Frieder Schlaich; Screenplay, Frieder Schlaich, Klaus Pohl; Photography, Volker Tittel; Designer, Anne Schlaich; Editor, Magdolna Rokob; Costumes, Henrike Luz; Produced by Filmgalerie 451, Zweites Deutsches Fernsehen; German, 1999; Color; Not rated; 85 minutes; U.S. release date: November 2, 2001. CAST: Isaach de Bankolé (Frederic Omoto), Hanno Friedrich (Heinz), Barnaby Metschurat (Rolf), Lara Kugler (Simone), Eva Mattes (Gisela), Siegrid Burkholder, Gottfried Breitfuss, Traute Hoess, Stefan Moos, Katja Schmidt-Ohen, Hansjuergen Gerth

*Jung (War) in the Land of the Mujaheddin*
© Karousel Films

## THE PRINCE OF LIGHT: THE LEGEND OF RAMAYANA

(SHOWCASE ENTERTAINMENT) Producers, Krishna Shah, Yugo Sata; Executive Producer, Atsushi Matsuo; Director, Yugo Sako; Screenplay, Krishna Shah, Yugo Sako; Based on The Ramayana by Valmiki; Animation Director, Kazuyuki Koyabayashi, for WRS Motion Picture and Video Lab; Art Director, Hajime Matsuoka; Editors, Makato Arai, Wayne Schmidt; Music, Vanraj Bhatia, Alan Howarth; a Showcase Entertainment and Krishna Shah presentation of a Nippon Ramayana & MRI Inc. production; Japanese-Indian-U.S.; Dolby; Color; Rated PG; 96 minutes; U.S. release date: November 9, 2001. VOICE CAST: Bryan Cranston, Edie Mirman, Tom Wyner, Richard Cansino, Michael Sorich, Mike L. Reynolds, Tony Pope, Mari Devon, Simon Prescott, Barbera Goodson, Kirk Thornton, Steve Bulen, Eddie Friarson, Jeff Winkless, Catherine Battisone, Michael McConnohie

## JUNG (WAR) IN THE LAND OF THE MUJAHEDDIN

(KAROUSEL FILMS) Directors, Fabrizio Lazzaretti, Alberto Vendemmiati; Line Producer/Editor, Giuseppe Petitto; Photography, Fabrizio Lazzaretti; Music, Mario Crispi; a Human Rights Watch International Film Festival presentation; Italian, 2000; Color; Not rated; 114 minutes; U.S. release date: November 23, 2001. Documentary on Dr. Gino Strada and his efforts to build a hospital near the front lines in northern Afghanistan.

## TROUBLE EVERY DAY

(LOT 47) Producers, Georges Benayoun, Jean-Michel Rey, Philippe Liégeois; Director, Claire Denis; Screenplay, Jean-Pol Fargeau, Claire Denis; Photography, Agnes Godard; Designer, Arnaud de Moléron; Editor, Nelly Quettier; Music, Tindersticks; Casting, Nicolas Lublin, James Calleri; a Messaouda Films, Rezo Prods., Arte France Cinema, Dacia Films Kinetique Inc. production with the participation of Canal+, Arte/ZDF, Rezo Films; French; Dolby; Color; Not rated; 102 minutes; U.S. release date: November 30, 2001. CAST: Vincent Gallo (Shane

Brown), Tricia Vessey (June Brown), Béatrice Dalle (Core), Alex Descas (Leo Semeneau), Florence Loiret-Caille (Christelle), Nicolas Duvauchelle (Erwan), Jose Garcia (Choart), Hélène Lapiower (Malecot), Marilu Marini (Friessen), Aurore Clément (Jeanne), Raphaël Neal (Ludo), Bakary Sangare (Night Watchman), Lionel Goldstein (Receptionist), Céline Samie (Woman in Brasserie), Arnaud Churin (Truck Driver), Slimane Brahimi (Christelle's Friend), Alice Houri (Young Girl in Metro), Véra Chidyvar (Woman in Metro), Nelly Zargarian, Rosa Nikolic, Csilla Lukacs-Molnar (Chambermaids), Lacrita Massix (Air Hostess), Myriam Theodoresco, Alexandre Uzureau de Martynoff (Couple), Laure Guerard (Woman in High Heels), Albert Szpiro (Community Clinic Boss)

## B-52

(BITOMSKY) Producers, Albert Schwinges, Hartmut Bitomsky; Director/Screenplay, Hartmut Bitomsky, from an idea by Ben Nicholson; Photography, Volker Langhoff, Hugo Kroiss; Editor, Theo Bromin; German-U.S.-Swiss; Not rated; 122 minutes; U.S. release date: December 5, 2001. Documentary on the history of the powerful warplane, the B-52.

## PRINCESA

(STRAND) Producer, Rebecca O'Brien; Director, Henrique Goldman; Screenplay, Henrique Goldman, Ellis Freeman; Based on the book by Fernanda Farias de Albuquerque; Photography, Guillermo Escalon; Costumes, Nivea Sibulka; Editor, Kerry Kohler; Music, Giovanni Venosta; a co-production of Bac Films, British Screen, Filmstiftung Nordrhein-Westfalen, Manga Films SL, Parallax Pictures Ltd., Road Movies Filmproduktion, Telepiu, Westdeutscher Rundfunk; French-Italian-German-British-Brazilian; Dolby; Color; Not rated; 96 minutes; U.S. release date: December 7, 2001. CAST: Ingrid de Souza (Fernanda), Cesare Bocci (Gianni), Lulu Pecorari (Karin), Biba Lerhue (Charlo), Sonia Morgan (Fofao), Mauro Pirovano (Fabrizio), Alessandra Acciai (Lidia)

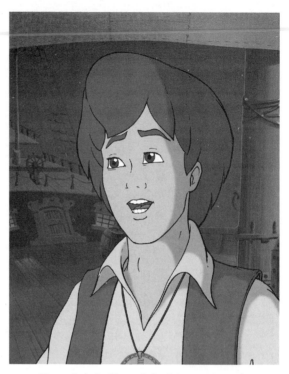

Marco Polo in *Marco Polo: Return to Xanadu*
© Tooniversal Company

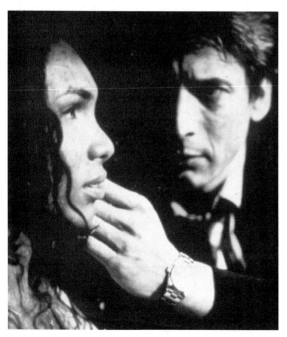

Ingrid de Souza, Cesare Bocci in *Princesa*
© Strand Releasing

## MARCO POLO: RETURN TO XANADU

(THE TOONIVERSAL COMPANY) Producers, Igor Meglic, Chris Holter, Ron Merk; Director, Ron Merk; Screenplay, Chris Holter, Ron Merk, Sheldon Moldoff; Associate Producer, Yan Luo; Production Designers/Animation Directors, Jaroslav Baran, Arne Wong; an Afanti International Animation Corporation, Interline s.r.o., Druzba Film Associates Ltd. presentation; Chinese-Slovakian-Korean-Canadaian-U.S.; Dolby; Eastmancolor; Rated G; 82 minutes; U.S. release date: December 21, 2001. VOICE CAST: Nicholas Gonzalez (Young Marco), John Matthew (Delicate Dinosaur/Marco Polo), Elea Bartling (Princess Ming-Yu), Tony Pope (Foo-Ling/Reginald the Seagull/Babu), Michael Kostroff (Kubla Khan/Lo Fat), John C. Hyke (Malgor), Robert Kramer (Grandpa/The Helmsman), Paul Ainsley (Wong Wei), Alan Altshuld (Pangu), Terry Wood, Joe Pizzulo, Steve Lively (Singers)

F. Murray Abraham

Adam Arkin

Anne Bancroft

Antonio Banderas

# BIOGRAPHICAL DATA

**AAMES, WILLIE** (William Upton): Los Angeles, July 15, 1960.

**AARON, CAROLINE:** Richmond, VA, Aug. 7, 1954. Catholic U.

**ABBOTT, DIAHNNE:** NYC, 1945.

**ABBOTT, JOHN:** London, England, June 5, 1905.

**ABRAHAM, F. MURRAY:** Pittsburgh, PA, Oct. 24, 1939. U TX.

**ACKLAND, JOSS:** London, Feb. 29, 1928.

**ADAMS, BROOKE:** NYC, Feb. 8, 1949. Dalton.

**ADAMS, CATLIN:** Los Angeles, Oct. 11, 1950.

**ADAMS, DON:** NYC, Apr. 13, 1926.

**ADAMS, EDIE** (Elizabeth Edith Enke): Kingston, PA, Apr. 16, 1927. Juilliard, Columbia.

**ADAMS, JOEY LAUREN:** Little Rock, AR, Jan. 6, 1971.

**ADAMS, JULIE** (Betty May): Waterloo, IA, Oct. 17, 1926. Little Rock, Jr. College.

**ADAMS, MASON:** NYC, Feb. 26, 1919. U WI.

**ADAMS, MAUD** (Maud Wikstrom): Lulea, Sweden, Feb. 12, 1945.

**ADJANI, ISABELLE:** Germany, June 27, 1955.

**AFFLECK, BEN:** Berkeley, CA, Aug. 15, 1972.

**AFFLECK, CASEY:** Falmouth, MA, Aug. 12, 1975.

**AGAR, JOHN:** Chicago, IL, Jan. 31, 1921.

**AGUTTER, JENNY:** Taunton, England, Dec. 20, 1952.

**AIELLO, DANNY:** NYC, June 20, 1933.

**AIMEE, ANOUK** (Dreyfus): Paris, France, Apr. 27, 1934. Bauer-Therond.

**AKERS, KAREN:** NYC, Oct. 13, 1945, Hunter College.

**ALBERGHETTI, ANNA MARIA:** Pesaro, Italy, May 15, 1936.

**ALBERT, EDDIE** (Eddie Albert Heimberger): Rock Island, IL, Apr. 22, 1908. U MN.

**ALBERT, EDWARD:** Los Angeles, Feb. 20, 1951. UCLA.

**ALBRIGHT, LOLA:** Akron, OH, July 20, 1925.

**ALDA, ALAN:** NYC, Jan. 28, 1936. Fordham.

**ALEANDRO, NORMA:** Buenos Aires, Argentina, Dec. 6, 1936.

**ALEJANDRO, MIGUEL:** NYC, Feb. 21, 1958.

**ALEXANDER, JANE** (Quigley): Boston, MA, Oct. 28, 1939. Sarah Lawrence.

**ALEXANDER, JASON** (Jay Greenspan): Newark, NJ, Sept. 23, 1959. Boston U.

**ALICE, MARY:** Indianola, MS, Dec. 3, 1941.

**ALLEN, DEBBIE** (Deborah): Houston, TX, Jan. 16, 1950. Howard U.

**ALLEN, JOAN:** Rochelle, IL, Aug. 20, 1956. E IL U.

**ALLEN, KAREN:** Carrollton, IL, Oct. 5, 1951. U MD.

**ALLEN, NANCY:** NYC, June 24, 1950.

**ALLEN, TIM:** Denver, CO, June 13, 1953. W. MI. U.

**ALLEN, WOODY** (Allan Stewart Konigsberg): Brooklyn, NY, Dec. 1, 1935.

**ALLEY, KIRSTIE:** Wichita, KS, Jan. 12, 1955.

**ALLYSON, JUNE** (Ella Geisman): Westchester, NY, Oct. 7, 1917.

**ALONSO, MARIA CONCHITA:** Cuba, June 29, 1957.

**ALT, CAROL:** Queens, NY, Dec. 1, 1960. Hofstra.

**ALVARADO, TRINI:** NYC, Jan. 10, 1967.

**AMIS, SUZY:** Oklahoma City, OK, Jan. 5, 1958. Actors Studio.

**AMOS, JOHN:** Newark, NJ, Dec. 27, 1940. CO U.

**ANDERSON, GILLIAN:** Chicago, IL, Aug. 9, 1968. DePaul.

**ANDERSON, KEVIN:** Waukeegan, IL, Jan. 13, 1960.

**ANDERSON, LONI:** St. Paul, MN, Aug. 5, 1946.

**ANDERSON, MELISSA SUE:** Berkeley, CA, Sept. 26, 1962.

**ANDERSON, MELODY:** Edmonton, Canada, 1955. Carlton.

**ANDERSON, MICHAEL, JR.:** London, England, Aug. 6, 1943.

**ANDERSON, RICHARD DEAN:** Minneapolis, MN, Jan. 23, 1950.

**ANDERSSON, BIBI:** Stockholm, Sweden, Nov. 11, 1935. Royal Dramatic Sch.

**ANDES, KEITH:** Ocean City, NJ, July 12, 1920. Temple, Oxford.

**ANDRESS, URSULA:** Bern, Switzerland, Mar. 19, 1936.

**ANDREWS, ANTHONY:** London, England, Dec. 1, 1948.

**ANDREWS, JULIE** (Julia Elizabeth Wells): Surrey, England, Oct. 1, 1935.

**ANGLIM, PHILIP:** San Francisco, CA, Feb. 11, 1953.

**ANISTON, JENNIFER:** Sherman Oaks, CA, Feb. 11, 1969.

**ANN-MARGRET** (Olsson): Valsjobyn, Sweden, Apr. 28, 1941. Northwestern.

**ANSARA, MICHAEL:** Lowell, MA, Apr. 15, 1922. Pasadena Playhouse.

**ANSPACH, SUSAN:** NYC, Nov. 23, 1945.

**ANTHONY, LYSETTE:** London, England, 1963.

**ANTHONY, TONY:** Clarksburg, WV, Oct. 16, 1937. Carnegie Tech.

**ANTON, SUSAN:** Yucaipa, CA, Oct. 12, 1950. Bernardino College.

**ANTONELLI, LAURA:** Pola, Italy, Nov. 28, 1941.

**ANWAR, GABRIELLE:** Laleham, England, Feb. 4, 1970

**APPLEGATE, CHRISTINA:** Hollywood, CA, Nov. 25, 1972.

**ARCHER, ANNE:** Los Angeles, Aug. 25, 1947.

**ARCHER, JOHN** (Ralph Bowman)**:** Osceola, NB, May 8, 1915. USC.

**ARDANT, FANNY:** Monte Carlo. Mar 22, 1949

**ARKIN, ADAM:** Brooklyn, NY, Aug. 19, 1956.

**ARKIN, ALAN:** NYC, Mar. 26, 1934. LACC.

**ARMSTRONG, BESS:** Baltimore, MD, Dec. 11, 1953.

**ARNAZ, DESI, JR.:** Los Angeles, Jan. 19, 1953.

**ARNAZ, LUCIE:** Hollywood, CA, July 17, 1951.

**ARNESS, JAMES** (Aurness)**:** Minneapolis, MN, May 26, 1923. Beloit College.

**ARQUETTE, DAVID:** Winchester, VA, Sept. 8, 1971.

**ARQUETTE, PATRICIA:** NYC, Apr. 8, 1968.

**ARQUETTE, ROSANNA:** NYC, Aug. 10, 1959.

**ARTHUR, BEATRICE** (Frankel)**:** NYC, May 13, 1924. New School.

**ASHER, JANE:** London, England, Apr. 5, 1946.

**ASHLEY, ELIZABETH** (Elizabeth Ann Cole)**:** Ocala, FL, Aug. 30, 1939.

**ASHTON, JOHN:** Springfield, MA, Feb. 22, 1948. USC.

**ASNER, EDWARD:** Kansas City, KS, Nov. 15, 1929.

**ASSANTE, ARMAND:** NYC, Oct. 4, 1949. AADA.

**ASTIN, JOHN:** Baltimore, MD, Mar. 30, 1930. U MN.

**ASTIN, MacKENZIE:** Los Angeles, May 12, 1973.

**ASTIN, SEAN:** Santa Monica, CA, Feb. 25, 1971.

**ATHERTON, WILLIAM:** Orange, CT, July 30, 1947. Carnegie Tech.

**ATKINS, CHRISTOPHER:** Rye, NY, Feb. 21, 1961.

**ATKINS, EILEEN:** London, England, June 16, 1934.

**ATKINSON, ROWAN:** England, Jan. 6, 1955. Oxford.

**ATTENBOROUGH, RICHARD:** Cambridge, England, Aug. 29, 1923. RADA.

**AUBERJONOIS, RENE:** NYC, June 1, 1940. Carnegie Tech.

**AUDRAN, STEPHANE:** Versailles, France, Nov. 8, 1932.

**AUGER, CLAUDINE:** Paris, France, Apr. 26, 1942. Dramatic Cons.

**AULIN, EWA:** Stockholm, Sweden, Feb. 14, 1950.

**AUTEUIL, DANIEL:** Alger, Algeria, Jan. 24, 1950.

**AVALON, FRANKIE** (Francis Thomas Avallone)**:** Philadelphia, PA, Sept. 18, 1939.

**AYKROYD, DAN:** Ottawa, Canada, July 1, 1952.

**AZARIA, HANK:** Forest Hills, NY, Apr. 25, 1964. AADA, Tufts.

**AZNAVOUR, CHARLES** (Varenagh Aznourian)**:** Paris, France, May 22, 1924.

**AZZARA, CANDICE:** Brooklyn, NY, May 18, 1947.

**BACH, CATHERINE:** Warren, OH, Mar. 1, 1954.

**BACALL, LAUREN** (Betty Perske)**:** NYC, Sept. 16, 1924. AADA.

**BACH, BARBARA:** Queens, NY, Aug. 27, 1946.

**BACKER, BRIAN:** NYC, Dec. 5, 1956. Neighborhood Playhouse.

**BACON, KEVIN:** Philadelphia, PA, July 8, 1958.

**BAIN, BARBARA:** Chicago, IL, Sept. 13, 1934. U IL.

**BAIO, SCOTT:** Brooklyn, NY, Sept. 22, 1961.

**BAKER, BLANCHE:** NYC, Dec. 20, 1956.

**BAKER, CARROLL:** Johnstown, PA, May 28, 1931. St. Petersburg, Jr. College.

**BAKER, DIANE:** Hollywood, CA, Feb. 25, 1938. USC.

**BAKER, JOE DON:** Groesbeck, TX, Feb.12, 1936.

**BAKER, KATHY:** Midland, TX, June 8, 1950. UC Berkley.

**BAKULA, SCOTT:** St. Louis, MO, Oct. 9, 1955. Kansas U.

**BALABAN, BOB:** Chicago, IL, Aug. 16, 1945. Colgate.

**BALDWIN, ADAM:** Chicago, IL, Feb. 27, 1962.

**BALDWIN, ALEC:** Massapequa, NY, Apr. 3, 1958. NYU.

**BALDWIN, DANIEL:** Massapequa, NY, Oct. 5, 1960.

**BALDWIN, STEPHEN:** Massapequa, NY, 1966.

**BALDWIN, WILLIAM:** Massapequa, NY, Feb. 21, 1963.

**BALE, CHRISTIAN:** Pembrokeshire, West Wales, Jan. 30, 1974.

**BALK, FAIRUZA:** Point Reyes, CA, May 21, 1974.

**BALLARD, KAYE:** Cleveland, OH, Nov. 20, 1926.

**BANCROFT, ANNE** (Anna Maria Italiano)**:** Bronx, NY, Sept. 17, 1931. AADA.

**BANDERAS, ANTONIO:** Malaga, Spain, Aug. 10, 1960.

**BANERJEE, VICTOR:** Calcutta, India, Oct. 15, 1946.

**BANES, LISA:** Chagrin Falls, OH, July 9, 1955. Juilliard.

**BARANSKI, CHRISTINE:** Buffalo, NY, May 2, 1952. Juilliard.

**BARBEAU, ADRIENNE:** Sacramento, CA, June 11, 1945. Foothill College.

**BARDEM, JAVIER:** Gran Canaria, Spain, May 1, 1969.

**BARDOT, BRIGITTE:** Paris, France, Sept. 28, 1934.

**BARKIN, ELLEN:** Bronx, NY, Apr. 16, 1954. Hunter College.

**BARNES, CHRISTOPHER DANIEL:** Portland, ME, Nov. 7, 1972.

**BARR, JEAN-MARC:** San Diego, CA, Sept. 1960.

**BARRAULT, JEAN-LOUIS:** Vesinet, France, Sept. 8, 1910.

**BARRAULT, MARIE-CHRISTINE:** Paris, France, Mar. 21, 1944.

**BARREN, KEITH:** Mexborough, England, Aug. 8, 1936. Sheffield Playhouse.

**BARRETT, MAJEL** (Hudec)**:** Columbus, OH, Feb. 23, 1939. Western Reserve.

**BARRIE, BARBARA:** Chicago, IL, May 23, 1931.

**BARRY, GENE** (Eugene Klass)**:** NYC, June 14, 1919.

**BARRY, NEILL:** NYC, Nov. 29, 1965.

**BARRYMORE, DREW:** Los Angeles, Feb. 22, 1975.

**BARRYMORE, JOHN DREW:** Beverly Hills, CA, June 4, 1932. St. John's Military Academy.

**BARYSHNIKOV, MIKHAIL:** Riga, Latvia, Jan. 27, 1948.

**BASINGER, KIM:** Athens, GA, Dec. 8, 1953. Neighborhood Playhouse.

**BASSETT, ANGELA:** NYC, Aug. 16, 1958.

**BATEMAN, JASON:** Rye, NY, Jan. 14, 1969.

**BATEMAN, JUSTINE:** Rye, NY, Feb. 19, 1966.

**BATES, ALAN:** Allestree, Derbyshire, England, Feb. 17, 1934. RADA.

**BATES, JEANNE:** San Francisco, CA, May 21, 1918. RADA.

**BATES, KATHY:** Memphis, TN, June 28, 1948. S. Methodist U.

**BAUER, STEVEN** (Steven Rocky Echevarria)**:** Havana, Cuba, Dec. 2, 1956. U Miami.

**BAXTER, KEITH:** South Wales, England, Apr. 29, 1933. RADA.

**BAXTER, MEREDITH:** Los Angeles, June 21, 1947. Interlochen Academy.

**BAYE, NATHALIE:** Maineville, France, July 6, 1948.

**BEACH, ADAM:** Winnipeg, Manitoba, Canada, Nov. 11, 1972.

**BEACHAM, STEPHANIE:** Casablanca, Morocco, Feb. 28, 1947.

**BEALS, JENNIFER:** Chicago, IL, Dec. 19, 1963.

**BEAN, ORSON** (Dallas Burrows): Burlington, VT, July 22, 1928.

**BEAN, SEAN:** Sheffield, Yorkshire, England, Apr. 17, 1958.

**BEART, EMMANUELLE:** Gassin, France, Aug. 14, 1965.

**BEATTY, NED:** Louisville, KY, July 6, 1937.

**BEATTY, WARREN:** Richmond, VA, Mar. 30, 1937.

**BECK, JOHN:** Chicago, IL, Jan. 28, 1943.

**BECK, MICHAEL:** Memphis, TN, Feb. 4, 1949. Millsap College.

**BECKINSALE, KATE:** England, July 26, 1974.

**BEDELIA, BONNIE:** NYC, Mar. 25, 1946. Hunter College.

**BEGLEY, ED, JR.:** NYC, Sept. 16, 1949.

**BELAFONTE, HARRY:** NYC, Mar. 1, 1927.

**BEL GEDDES, BARBARA:** NYC, Oct. 31, 1922.

**BELL, TOM:** Liverpool, England, 1932.

**BELLER, KATHLEEN:** NYC, Feb. 10, 1957.

**BELLWOOD, PAMELA** (King): Scarsdale, NY, June 26, 1951.

**BELMONDO, JEAN PAUL:** Paris, France, Apr. 9, 1933.

**BELUSHI, JAMES:** Chicago, IL, June 15, 1954.

**BELZER, RICHARD:** Bridgeport, CT, Aug. 4, 1944.

**BENEDICT, DIRK** (Niewoehner): White Sulphur Springs, MT, March 1, 1945. Whitman College.

**BENEDICT, PAUL:** Silver City, NM, Sept. 17, 1938.

**BENIGNI, ROBERTO:** Tuscany, Italy, Oct. 27, 1952.

**BENING, ANNETTE:** Topeka, KS, May 29, 1958. SF St. U.

**BENJAMIN, RICHARD:** NYC, May 22, 1938. Northwestern.

**BENNENT, DAVID:** Lausanne, Switzerland, Sept. 9, 1966.

**BENNETT, ALAN:** Leeds, England, May 9, 1934. Oxford.

**BENNETT, BRUCE** (Herman Brix): Tacoma, WA, May 19, 1909. U WA.

**BENNETT, HYWEL:** Garnant, So. Wales, Apr. 8, 1944.

**BENSON, ROBBY:** Dallas, TX, Jan. 21, 1957.

**BENTLEY, WES:** Jonesboro, AR, Sept. 4, 1978.

**BERENGER, TOM**: Chicago, IL, May 31, 1950. U MO.

**BERENSON, MARISA:** NYC, Feb. 15, 1947.

**BERG, PETER:** NYC, March 11, 1964. Malcalester College.

**BERGEN, CANDICE:** Los Angeles, May 9, 1946. U PA.

**BERGEN, POLLY:** Knoxville, TN, July 14, 1930. Compton, Jr. College.

**BERGER, HELMUT:** Salzburg, Austria, May 29, 1942.

**BERGER, SENTA:** Vienna, Austria, May 13, 1941. Vienna Sch. of Acting.

**BERGER, WILLIAM:** Austria, Jan. 20, 1928. Columbia.

**BERGERAC, JACQUES:** Biarritz, France, May 26, 1927. Paris U.

**BERGIN, PATRICK:** Dublin, Ireland, Feb. 4, 1951.

**BERKLEY, ELIZABETH:** Detroit, MI, July 28, 1972.

**BERKOFF, STEVEN:** London, England, Aug. 3, 1937.

**BERLE, MILTON** (Berlinger): NYC, July 12, 1908.

**BERLIN, JEANNIE:** Los Angeles, Nov. 1, 1949.

**BERLINGER, WARREN:** Brooklyn, NY, Aug. 31, 1937. Columbia.

**BERNHARD, SANDRA:** Flint, MI, June 6, 1955.

**BERNSEN, CORBIN:** Los Angeles, Sept. 7, 1954. UCLA.

**BERRI, CLAUDE** (Langmann): Paris, France, July 1, 1934.

**BERRIDGE, ELIZABETH:** Westchester, NY, May 2, 1962. Strasberg Inst.

**BERRY, HALLE:** Cleveland, OH, Aug. 14, 1968.

**BERRY, KEN:** Moline, IL, Nov. 3, 1933.

**BERTINELLI, VALERIE:** Wilmington, DE, Apr. 23, 1960.

**BEST, JAMES:** Corydon, IN, July 26, 1926.

**BETTGER, LYLE:** Philadelphia, PA, Feb. 13, 1915. AADA.

**BEY, TURHAN:** Vienna, Austria, Mar. 30, 1921.

**BEYMER, RICHARD:** Avoca, IA, Feb. 21, 1939.

**BIALIK, MAYIM:** San Diego, CA, Dec. 12, 1975.

**BIEHN, MICHAEL:** Anniston, AL, July 31, 1956.

**BIGGERSTAFF, SEAN:** Glasgow, Scotland, Mar. 15, 1983.

**BIGGS, JASON:** Pompton Plains, NJ, May 12, 1978.

**BIKEL, THEODORE:** Vienna, Austria, May 2, 1924. RADA.

**BILLINGSLEY, PETER:** NYC, Apr. 16, 1972.

**BINOCHE, JULIETTE:** Paris, France, Mar. 9, 1964.

**BIRCH, THORA:** Los Angeles, Mar. 11, 1982.

**BIRKIN, JANE:** London, England, Dec. 14, 1947

**BIRNEY, DAVID:** Washington, DC, Apr. 23, 1939. Dartmouth, UCLA.

**BIRNEY, REED:** Alexandria, VA, Sept. 11, 1954. Boston U.

**BISHOP, JOEY** (Joseph Abraham Gotllieb): Bronx, NY, Feb. 3, 1918.

**BISHOP, JULIE** (Jacqueline Wells): Denver, CO, Aug. 30, 1917. Westlake School.

**BISSET, JACQUELINE:** Waybridge, England, Sept. 13, 1944.

**BLACK, KAREN** (Ziegler): Park Ridge, IL, July 1, 1942. Northwestern.

**BLACK, JACK:** Edmonton, Alberta, Canada, Apr. 7, 1969.

**BLACK, LUCAS:** Danville, AL, Nov. 29, 1982.

**BLACKMAN, HONOR:** London, England, Aug. 22, 1926.

**BLADES, RUBEN:** Panama City, Panama, July 16, 1948. Harvard.

**BLAIR, BETSY** (Betsy Boger): NYC, Dec. 11, 1923.

**BLAIR, JANET** (Martha Jane Lafferty): Blair, PA, Apr. 23, 1921.

**BLAIR, LINDA:** Westport, CT, Jan. 22, 1959.

**BLAIR, SELMA:** Southfield, MI, June 23, 1972.

**BLAKE, ROBERT** (Michael Gubitosi): Nutley, NJ, Sept. 18, 1933.

**BLAKELY, SUSAN:** Frankfurt, Germany, Sept. 7, 1950. U TX.

**BLAKLEY, RONEE:** Stanley, ID, 1946. Stanford U.

**BLANCHETT, CATE:** Melbourne, Australia, May 14, 1969.

**BLETHYN, BRENDA:** Ramsgate, Kent, England, Feb. 20, 1946.

**BLOOM, CLAIRE:** London, England, Feb. 15, 1931. Badminton School.

**BLOOM, VERNA:** Lynn, MA, Aug. 7, 1939. Boston U.

**BLOUNT, LISA:** Fayettville, AK, July 1, 1957. U AK.

**BLUM, MARK:** Newark, NJ, May 14, 1950. U MN.

**BLYTH, ANN:** Mt. Kisco, NY, Aug. 16, 1928. New Waybum Dramatic School.

**BOCHNER, HART:** Toronto, Canada, Oct. 3, 1956. U San Diego.

**BOCHNER, LLOYD:** Toronto, Canada, July 29, 1924.

**BOGOSIAN, ERIC:** Woburn, MA, Apr. 24, 1953. Oberlin College.

**BOHRINGER, RICHARD:** Paris, France, Jan. 16, 1941.

**BOLKAN, FLORINDA** (Florinda Soares Bulcao): Ceara, Brazil, Feb. 15, 1941.

**BOLOGNA, JOSEPH:** Brooklyn, NY, Dec. 30, 1938. Brown.

**BOND, DEREK:** Glasgow, Scotland, Jan. 26, 1920. Askes School.

**BONET, LISA:** San Francisco, CA, Nov. 16, 1967.

**BONHAM-CARTER, HELENA:** London, England, May 26, 1966.

**BOONE, PAT:** Jacksonville, FL, June 1, 1934. Columbia.

**BOOTHE, JAMES:** Croydon, England, Dec. 19, 1930.

**BOOTHE, POWERS:** Snyder, TX, June 1, 1949. S. Methodist U.

**BORGNINE, ERNEST** (Borgnino): Hamden, CT, Jan. 24, 1917. Randall School.

**BOSCO, PHILIP:** Jersey City, NJ, Sept. 26, 1930. Catholic U.

**BOSLEY, TOM:** Chicago, IL, Oct. 1, 1927. DePaul U.

**BOSTWICK, BARRY:** San Mateo, CA, Feb. 24, 1945. NYU.

**BOTTOMS, JOSEPH:** Santa Barbara, CA, Aug. 30, 1954.

**BOTTOMS, SAM:** Santa Barbara, CA, Oct. 17, 1955.

Ned Beatty    David Bowie    Josh Brolin    Eleanor Bron

**BOTTOMS, TIMOTHY:** Santa Barbara, CA, Aug. 30, 1951.

**BOULTING, INGRID:** Transvaal, South Africa, 1947.

**BOUTSIKARIS, DENNIS:** Newark, NJ, Dec. 21, 1952. Catholic U.

**BOWIE, DAVID** (David Robert Jones)**:** Brixton, South London, England, Jan. 8, 1947.

**BOWKER, JUDI:** Shawford, England, Apr. 6, 1954.

**BOXLEITNER, BRUCE:** Elgin, IL, May 12, 1950.

**BOYLE, LARA FLYNN:** Davenport, IA, Mar. 24, 1970.

**BOYLE, PETER:** Philadelphia, PA, Oct. 18, 1933. LaSalle College.

**BRACCO, LORRAINE:** Brooklyn, NY, 1955.

**BRACKEN, EDDIE:** NYC, Feb. 7, 1920. Professional Children's School.

**BRAEDEN, ERIC** (Hans Gudegast)**:** Kiel, Germany, Apr. 3, 1942.

**BRAGA, SONIA:** Maringa, Brazil, June 8, 1950.

**BRANAGH, KENNETH:** Belfast, Northern Ireland, Dec. 10, 1960.

**BRANDAUER, KLAUS MARIA:** Altaussee, Austria, June 22, 1944.

**BRANDIS, JONATHAN:** CT, Apr. 13, 1976.

**BRANDO, JOCELYN:** San Francisco, Nov. 18, 1919. Lake Forest College, AADA.

**BRANDO, MARLON:** Omaha, NB, Apr. 3, 1924. New School.

**BRANDON, CLARK:** NYC, Dec. 13, 1958.

**BRANDON, MICHAEL** (Feldman)**:** Brooklyn, NY, Apr. 20, 1945.

**BRANTLEY, BETSY:** Rutherfordton, NC, Sept. 20, 1955. London Central Sch. of Drama.

**BRATT, BENJAMIN:** San Francisco, CA, Dec. 16, 1963.

**BRENNAN, EILEEN:** Los Angeles, Sept. 3, 1935. AADA.

**BRENNEMAN, AMY:** Glastonbury, CT, June 22, 1964.

**BRIALY, JEAN-CLAUDE:** Aumale, Algeria, 1933. Strasbourg Cons.

**BRIDGES, BEAU:** Los Angeles, Dec. 9, 1941. UCLA.

**BRIDGES, JEFF:** Los Angeles, Dec. 4, 1949.

**BRIMLEY, WILFORD:** Salt Lake City, UT, Sept. 27, 1934.

**BRINKLEY, CHRISTIE:** Malibu, CA, Feb. 2, 1954.

**BRITT, MAY** (Maybritt Wilkins)**:** Sweden, Mar. 22, 1936.

**BRITTANY, MORGAN** (Suzanne Cupito)**:** Los Angeles, Dec. 5, 1950.

**BRITTON, TONY:** Birmingham, England, June 9, 1924.

**BROADBENT, JIM:** Lincoln, England, May 24, 1959.

**BRODERICK, MATTHEW:** NYC, Mar. 21, 1962.

**BRODY, ADRIEN:** NYC, Dec. 23, 1976.

**BROLIN, JAMES:** Los Angeles, July 18, 1940. UCLA.

**BROLIN, JOSH:** Los Angeles, Feb. 12, 1968.

**BROMFIELD, JOHN** (Farron Bromfield)**:** South Bend, IN, June 11, 1922. St. Mary's College.

**BRON, ELEANOR:** Stanmore, England, Mar. 14, 1934.

**BRONSON, CHARLES** (Buchinsky)**:** Ehrenfield, PA, Nov. 3, 1920.

**BROOKES, JACQUELINE:** Montclair, NJ, July 24, 1930. RADA.

**BROOKS, ALBERT** (Einstein)**:** Los Angeles, July 22, 1947.

**BROOKS, MEL** (Melvyn Kaminski)**:** Brooklyn, NY, June 28, 1926.

**BROSNAN, PIERCE:** County Meath, Ireland, May 16, 1952.

**BROWN, BLAIR:** Washington, DC, Apr. 23, 1947. Pine Manor.

**BROWN, BRYAN:** Panania, Australia, June 23, 1947.

**BROWN, GARY** (Christian Brando)**:** Hollywood, CA, 1958.

**BROWN, GEORGE STANFORD:** Havana, Cuba, June 24, 1943. AMDA.

**BROWN, JAMES:** Desdemona, TX, Mar. 22, 1920. Baylor U.

**BROWN, JIM:** St. Simons Island, NY, Feb. 17, 1935. Syracuse U.

**BROWNE, LESLIE:** NYC, 1958.

**BROWNE, ROSCOE LEE:** Woodbury, NJ, May 2, 1925.

**BUCHHOLZ, HORST:** Berlin, Germany, Dec. 4, 1933. Ludwig Dramatic School.

**BUCKLEY, BETTY:** Big Spring, TX, July 3, 1947. TX CU.

**BUJOLD, GENEVIEVE:** Montreal, Canada, July 1, 1942.

**BULLOCK, SANDRA:** Arlington, VA, July 26, 1964.

**BURGHOFF, GARY:** Bristol, CT, May 24, 1943.

**BURGI, RICHARD:** Montclair, NJ, July 30, 1958.

**BURKE, PAUL:** New Orleans, LA, July 21, 1926. Pasadena Playhouse.

**BURNETT, CAROL:** San Antonio, TX, Apr. 26, 1933. UCLA.

**BURNS, CATHERINE:** NYC, Sept. 25, 1945. AADA.

**BURNS, EDWARD:** Valley Stream, NY, Jan. 28, 1969.

**BURROWS, DARREN E.:** Winfield, KS, Sept. 12, 1966.

**BURROWS, SAFFRON:** London, England, 1973.

**BURSTYN, ELLEN** (Edna Rae Gillhooly)**:** Detroit, MI, Dec. 7, 1932.

**BURTON, LeVAR:** Los Angeles, Feb. 16, 1958. UCLA.

**BUSCEMI, STEVE:** Brooklyn, NY, Dec. 13, 1957.

**BUSEY, GARY:** Goose Creek, TX, June 29, 1944.

**BUSFIELD, TIMOTHY:** Lansing, MI, June 12, 1957. E. Tenn. St. U.

**BUTTONS, RED** (Aaron Chwatt)**:** NYC, Feb. 5, 1919.

**BUZZI, RUTH:** Westerly, RI, July 24, 1936. Pasadena Playhouse.

**BYGRAVES, MAX:** London, England, Oct. 16, 1922. St. Joseph's School.

**BYRNE, DAVID:** Dumbarton, Scotland, May 14, 1952.

**BYRNE, GABRIEL:** Dublin, Ireland, May 12, 1950.

**BYRNES, EDD:** NYC, July 30, 1933.

Dean Cain

Michael Caine

Neve Campbell

Jim Carrey

**CAAN, JAMES:** Bronx, NY, Mar. 26,1939.

**CAESAR, SID:** Yonkers, NY, Sept. 8, 1922.

**CAGE, NICOLAS** (Coppola): Long Beach, CA, Jan.7, 1964.

**CAIN, DEAN** (Dean Tanaka): Mt. Clemens, MI, July 31, 1966.

**CAINE, MICHAEL** (Maurice Micklewhite): London, England, Mar. 14, 1933.

**CAINE, SHAKIRA** (Baksh): Guyana, Feb. 23, 1947. Indian Trust College.

**CALLAN, MICHAEL** (Martin Calinieff): Philadelphia, PA, Nov. 22, 1935.

**CALLOW, SIMON:** London, England, June 15, 1949. Queens U.

**CALVERT, PHYLLIS:** London, England, Feb. 18, 1917. Margaret Morris School.

**CAMERON, KIRK:** Panorama City, CA, Oct. 12, 1970.

**CAMP, COLLEEN:** San Francisco, CA, 1953.

**CAMPBELL, BILL:** Chicago, IL, July 7, 1959.

**CAMPBELL, GLEN:** Delight, AR, Apr. 22, 1935.

**CAMPBELL, NEVE:** Guelph, Ontario, Canada, Oct. 3, 1973.

**CAMPBELL, TISHA:** Oklahoma City, OK, Oct. 13, 1968.

**CANALE, GIANNA MARIA:** Reggio Calabria, Italy, Sept. 12, 1927.

**CANNON, DYAN** (Samille Diane Friesen): Tacoma, WA, Jan. 4, 1937.

**CAPERS, VIRGINIA:** Sumter, SC, Sept. 25, 1925. Juilliard.

**CAPSHAW, KATE:** Ft. Worth, TX, Nov. 3, 1953. U MO.

**CARA, IRENE:** NYC, Mar. 18, 1958.

**CARDINALE, CLAUDIA:** Tunis, N. Africa. Apr. 15, 1939. College Paul Cambon.

**CAREY, HARRY, JR.:** Saugus, CA, May 16, 1921. Black Fox Military Academy.

**CAREY, PHILIP:** Hackensack, NJ, July 15, 1925. U Miami.

**CARIOU, LEN:** Winnipeg, Manitoba, Canada, Sept. 30, 1939.

**CARLIN, GEORGE:** NYC, May 12, 1938.

**CARLYLE, ROBERT:** Glasgow, Scotland, Apr. 14, 1961.

**CARMEN, JULIE:** Mt. Vernon, NY, Apr. 4, 1954.

**CARMICHAEL, IAN:** Hull, England, June 18, 1920. Scarborough College.

**CARNE, JUDY** (Joyce Botterill): Northampton, England, 1939. Bush-Davis Theatre School.

**CARNEY, ART:** Mt. Vernon, NY, Nov. 4, 1918.

**CARON, LESLIE:** Paris, France, July 1, 1931. National Conservatory, Paris.

**CARPENTER, CARLETON:** Bennington, VT, July 10, 1926. Northwestern.

**CARRADINE, DAVID:** Hollywood, CA, Dec. 8, 1936. SF St. U.

**CARRADINE, KEITH:** San Mateo, CA, Aug. 8, 1950. CO St. U.

**CARRADINE, ROBERT:** San Mateo, CA, Mar. 24, 1954.

**CARREL, DANY:** Tourane, Indochina, Sept. 20, 1936. Marseilles Cons.

**CARRERA, BARBARA:** Managua, Nicaragua, Dec. 31, 1945.

**CARRERE, TIA** (Althea Janairo): Honolulu, HI, Jan. 2, 1965.

**CARREY, JIM:** Jacksons Point, Ontario, Canada, Jan. 17, 1962.

**CARRIERE, MATHIEU:** Hannover, West Germany, Aug. 2, 1950.

**CARROLL, DIAHANN** (Johnson): NYC, July 17, 1935. NYU.

**CARROLL, PAT:** Shreveport, LA, May 5, 1927. Catholic U.

**CARSON, JOHN DAVID:** California, Mar. 6, 1952. Valley College.

**CARSON, JOHNNY:** Corning, IA, Oct. 23, 1925. U NE.

**CARSTEN, PETER** (Ransenthaler): Weissenberg, Bavaria, Apr. 30, 1929. Munich Akademie.

**CARTER, NELL:** Birmingham, AL, Sept. 13, 1948.

**CARTLIDGE, KATRIN:** London, England, 1961.

**CARTWRIGHT, VERONICA:** Bristol, England, Apr 20, 1949.

**CARUSO, DAVID:** Forest Hills, NY, Jan. 7, 1956.

**CARVEY, DANA:** Missoula, MT, Apr. 2, 1955. SF St. College.

**CASELLA, MAX:** Washington D.C., June 6, 1967.

**CASEY, BERNIE:** Wyco, WV, June 8, 1939.

**CASSAVETES, NICK:** NYC, 1959, Syracuse U, AADA.

**CASSEL, JEAN-PIERRE:** Paris, France, Oct. 27, 1932.

**CASSEL, SEYMOUR:** Detroit, MI, Jan. 22, 1935.

**CASSIDY, DAVID:** NYC, Apr. 12, 1950.

**CASSIDY, JOANNA:** Camden, NJ, Aug. 2, 1944. Syracuse U.

**CASSIDY, PATRICK:** Los Angeles, Jan. 4, 1961.

**CATES, PHOEBE:** NYC, July 16, 1962.

**CATTRALL, KIM:** Liverpool, England, Aug. 21, 1956. AADA.

**CAULFIELD, MAXWELL:** Glasgow, Scotland, Nov. 23, 1959.

**CAVANI, LILIANA:** Bologna, Italy, Jan. 12, 1937. U Bologna.

**CAVETT, DICK:** Gibbon, NE, Nov. 19, 1936.

**CAVIEZEL, JIM:** Mt. Vernon, WA, Sept. 26, 1968.

**CHAKIRIS, GEORGE:** Norwood, OH, Sept. 16, 1933.

**CHAMBERLAIN, RICHARD:** Beverly Hills, CA, March 31, 1935. Pomona.

**CHAMPION, MARGE** (Marjorie Belcher): Los Angeles, Sept. 2, 1923.

**CHAN, JACKIE:** Hong Kong, China, Apr. 7, 1954

**CHANNING, CAROL:** Seattle, WA, Jan. 31, 1921. Bennington.

**CHANNING, STOCKARD** (Susan Stockard): NYC, Feb. 13, 1944. Radcliffe.

**CHAPIN, MILES:** NYC, Dec. 6, 1954. HB Studio.

**CHAPLIN, BEN:** London, England, July 31, 1970.

**CHAPLIN, GERALDINE:** Santa Monica, CA, July 31, 1944. Royal Ballet.

**CHAPLIN, SYDNEY:** Los Angeles, Mar. 31, 1926. Lawrenceville.

**CHARISSE, CYD** (Tula Ellice Finklea): Amarillo, TX, Mar. 3, 1922. Hollywood Professional School.

**CHARLES, JOSH:** Baltimore, MD, Sept. 15, 1971.

**CHARLES, WALTER:** East Strousburg, PA, Apr. 4, 1945. Boston U.

**CHASE, CHEVY** (Cornelius Crane Chase): NYC, Oct. 8, 1943.

**CHAVES, RICHARD:** Jacksonville, FL, Oct. 9, 1951. Occidental College.

**CHAYKIN, MAURY:** Canada, July 27, 1954.

**CHEADLE, DON:** Kansas City, MO, Nov. 29, 1964.

**CHEN, JOAN** (Chen Chung): Shanghai, China, Apr. 26, 1961. Cal. St. U.

**CHER** (Cherilyn Sarkisian): El Centro, CA, May 20, 1946.

**CHILES, LOIS:** Alice, TX, Apr. 15, 1947.

**CHONG, RAE DAWN:** Vancouver, Canada, Feb. 28, 1962.

**CHONG, THOMAS:** Edmonton, Alberta, Canada, May 24, 1938.

**CHRISTIAN, LINDA** (Blanca Rosa Welter): Tampico, Mexico, Nov. 13, 1923.

**CHRISTIE, JULIE:** Chukua, Assam, India, Apr. 14, 1941.

**CHRISTOPHER, DENNIS** (Carrelli): Philadelphia, PA, Dec. 2, 1955. Temple U.

**CHRISTOPHER, JORDAN:** Youngstown, OH, Oct. 23, 1940. Kent State.

**CILENTO, DIANE:** Queensland, Australia, Oct. 5, 1933. AADA.

**CLAPTON, ERIC:** London, England, Mar. 30, 1945.

**CLARK, CANDY:** Norman, OK, June 20, 1947.

**CLARK, DICK:** Mt. Vernon, NY, Nov. 30, 1929. Syracuse U.

**CLARK, MATT:** Washington, DC, Nov. 25, 1936.

**CLARK, PETULA:** Epsom, England, Nov. 15, 1932.

**CLARK, SUSAN:** Sarnid, Ont., Canada, Mar. 8, 1943. RADA.

**CLAY, ANDREW DICE** (Andrew Silverstein): Brooklyn, NY, Sept. 29, 1957. Kingsborough College.

**CLAYBURGH, JILL:** NYC, Apr. 30, 1944. Sarah Lawrence.

**CLEESE, JOHN:** Weston-Super-Mare, England, Oct. 27, 1939. Cambridge.

**CLOONEY, ROSEMARY:** Maysville, KY, May 23, 1928.

**CLOSE, GLENN:** Greenwich, CT, Mar. 19, 1947. William & Mary College.

**COBURN, JAMES:** Laurel, NB, Aug. 31, 1928. LACC.

**CODY, KATHLEEN:** Bronx, NY, Oct. 30, 1953.

**COFFEY, SCOTT:** HI, May 1, 1967.

**COLE, GEORGE:** London, England, Apr. 22, 1925.

**COLEMAN, GARY:** Zion, IL, Feb. 8, 1968.

**COLEMAN, DABNEY:** Austin, TX, Jan. 3, 1932.

**COLEMAN, JACK:** Easton, PA, Feb. 21, 1958. Duke U.

**COLIN, MARGARET:** NYC, May 26, 1957.

**COLLET, CHRISTOPHER:** NYC, Mar. 13, 1968. Strasberg Inst.

**COLLETTE, TONI:** Sydney, Australia, Nov. 1, 1972.

**COLLINS, JOAN:** London, May 21, 1933. Francis Holland School.

**COLLINS, PAULINE:** Devon, England, Sept. 3, 1940.

**COLLINS, STEPHEN:** Des Moines, IA, Oct. 1, 1947. Amherst.

Jim Caviezel     Billy Connolly

**COLON, MIRIAM:** Ponce, PR., 1945. U PR.

**COLTRANE, ROBBIE:** Rutherglen, Scotland, Mar. 30, 1950.

**COMBS, SEAN "Puffy," "P. Diddy":** NYC, Nov. 4, 1969.

**COMER, ANJANETTE:** Dawson, TX, Aug. 7, 1942. Baylor, Tex. U.

**CONANT, OLIVER:** NYC, Nov. 15, 1955. Dalton.

**CONAWAY, JEFF:** NYC, Oct. 5, 1950. NYU.

**CONNELLY, JENNIFER:** NYC, Dec. 12, 1970

**CONNERY, SEAN:** Edinburgh, Scotland, Aug. 25, 1930.

**CONNERY, JASON:** London, England, Jan. 11, 1963.

**CONNICK, HARRY, JR.:** New Orleans, LA, Sept. 11, 1967.

**CONNOLLY, BILLY:** Glasgow, Scotland, Nov. 24, 1942.

**CONNORS, MIKE** (Krekor Ohanian): Fresno, CA, Aug. 15, 1925. UCLA.

**CONRAD, ROBERT** (Conrad Robert Falk): Chicago, IL, Mar. 1, 1935. Northwestern.

**CONSTANTINE, MICHAEL:** Reading, PA, May 22, 1927.

**CONTI, TOM:** Paisley, Scotland, Nov. 22, 1941.

**CONVERSE, FRANK:** St. Louis, MO, May 22, 1938. Carnegie Tech.

**CONWAY, GARY:** Boston, MA, Feb. 4, 1936.

**CONWAY, KEVIN:** NYC, May 29, 1942.

**CONWAY, TIM** (Thomas Daniel): Willoughby, OH, Dec. 15, 1933. Bowling Green St.

**COOGAN, KEITH** (Keith Mitchell Franklin): Palm Springs, CA, Jan. 13, 1970.

**COOK, RACHAEL LEIGH:** Minneapolis, MN, Oct. 4, 1979.

**COOPER, BEN:** Hartford, CT, Sept. 30, 1930. Columbia.

**COOPER, CHRIS:** Kansas City, MO, July 9, 1951. U MO.

**COOPER, JACKIE:** Los Angeles, Sept. 15, 1921.

**COPELAND, JOAN:** NYC, June 1, 1922. Brooklyn College, RADA.

**CORBETT, GRETCHEN:** Portland, OR, Aug. 13, 1947. Carnegie Tech.

**CORBIN, BARRY:** Dawson County, TX, Oct. 16, 1940. Texas Tech. U.

**CORCORAN, DONNA:** Quincy, MA, Sept. 29, 1942.

**CORD, ALEX** (Viespi): Floral Park, NY, Aug. 3, 1931. NYU, Actors Studio.

**CORDAY, MARA** (Marilyn Watts): Santa Monica, CA, Jan. 3, 1932.

**COREY, JEFF:** NYC, Aug. 10, 1914. Fagin School.

**CORNTHWAITE, ROBERT:** St. Helens, OR, Apr. 28, 1917. USC.

**CORRI, ADRIENNE:** Glasgow, Scotland, Nov. 13, 1933. RADA.

**CORT, BUD** (Walter Edward Cox): New Rochelle, NY, Mar. 29, 1950. NYU.

Billy Crystal    John Cusack    Joan Cusack    Hope Davis

**CORTESA, VALENTINA:** Milan, Italy, Jan. 1, 1924.

**COSBY, BILL:** Philadelphia, PA, July 12, 1937. Temple U.

**COSTER, NICOLAS:** London, England, Dec. 3, 1934. Neighborhood Playhouse.

**COSTNER, KEVIN:** Lynwood, CA, Jan. 18, 1955. Cal St. U.

**COURTENAY, TOM:** Hull, England, Feb. 25, 1937. RADA.

**COURTLAND, JEROME:** Knoxville, TN, Dec. 27, 1926.

**COX, BRIAN:** Dundee, Scotland, June 1, 1946. LAMDA.

**COX, COURTENEY:** Birmingham, AL, June 15, 1964.

**COX, RONNY:** Cloudcroft, NM, Aug. 23, 1938.

**COYOTE, PETER** (Cohon): NYC, Oct. 10, 1941.

**CRAIG, MICHAEL:** Poona, India, Jan. 27, 1929.

**CRAIN, JEANNE:** Barstow, CA, May 25, 1925.

**CRAVEN, GEMMA:** Dublin, Ireland, June 1, 1950.

**CRAWFORD, MICHAEL** (Dumbel-Smith): Salisbury, England, Jan. 19, 1942.

**CREMER, BRUNO:** Paris, France, 1929.

**CRENNA, RICHARD:** Los Angeles, Nov. 30, 1926. USC.

**CRISTAL, LINDA** (Victoria Moya): Buenos Aires, Argentina, Feb. 25, 1934.

**CROMWELL, JAMES:** Los Angeles, CA, Jan. 27, 1940.

**CRONYN, HUME** (Blake): Ontario, Canada, July 18, 1911.

**CROSBY, DENISE:** Hollywood, CA, Nov. 24, 1957.

**CROSBY, HARRY:** Los Angeles, Aug. 8, 1958.

**CROSBY, MARY FRANCES:** Los Angeles, Sept. 14, 1959.

**CROSS, BEN:** London, England, Dec. 16, 1947. RADA.

**CROSS, MURPHY** (Mary Jane): Laurelton, MD, June 22, 1950.

**CROUSE, LINDSAY:** NYC, May 12, 1948. Radcliffe.

**CROWE, RUSSELL:** New Zealand, Apr. 7, 1964.

**CROWLEY, PAT:** Olyphant, PA, Sept. 17, 1932.

**CRUDUP, BILLY:** Manhasset, NY, July 8, 1968. UNC/Chapel Hill.

**CRUISE, TOM** (T. C. Mapother, IV): July 3, 1962, Syracuse, NY.

**CRUZ, PENELOPE** (P.C. Sanchez): Madrid, Spain, Apr. 28, 1974.

**CRYER, JON:** NYC, Apr. 16, 1965, RADA.

**CRYSTAL, BILLY:** Long Beach, NY, Mar. 14, 1947. Marshall U.

**CULKIN, KIERAN:** NYC, Sept. 30, 1982.

**CULKIN, MACAULAY:** NYC, Aug. 26, 1980.

**CULLUM, JOHN:** Knoxville, TN, Mar. 2, 1930. U TN.

**CULLUM, JOHN DAVID:** NYC, Mar. 1, 1966.

**CULP, ROBERT:** Oakland, CA, Aug. 16, 1930. U WA.

**CUMMING, ALAN:** Perthshire, Scotland, Jan. 27, 1965.

**CUMMINGS, CONSTANCE:** Seattle, WA, May 15, 1910.

**CUMMINGS, QUINN:** Hollywood, CA, Aug. 13, 1967.

**CUMMINS, PEGGY:** Prestatyn, North Wales, Dec. 18, 1926. Alexandra School.

**CURRY, TIM:** Cheshire, England, Apr. 19, 1946. Birmingham U.

**CURTIN, JANE:** Cambridge, MA, Sept. 6, 1947.

**CURTIS, JAMIE LEE:** Los Angeles, CA, Nov. 22, 1958.

**CURTIS, KEENE:** Salt Lake City, UT, Feb. 15, 1925. U UT.

**CURTIS, TONY** (Bernard Schwartz): NYC, June 3, 1924.

**CUSACK, JOAN:** Evanston, IL, Oct. 11, 1962.

**CUSACK, JOHN:** Chicago, IL, June 28, 1966.

**CUSACK, SINEAD:** Dalkey, Ireland, Feb. 18, 1948.

**DAFOE, WILLEM:** Appleton, WI, July 22, 1955.

**DAHL, ARLENE:** Minneapolis, Aug. 11, 1928. U MN.

**DALE, JIM:** Rothwell, England, Aug. 15, 1935.

**DALLESANDRO, JOE:** Pensacola, FL, Dec. 31, 1948.

**DALTON, TIMOTHY:** Colwyn Bay, Wales, Mar. 21, 1946. RADA.

**DALTREY, ROGER:** London, England, Mar. 1, 1944.

**DALY, TIM:** NYC, Mar. 1, 1956. Bennington College.

**DALY, TYNE:** Madison, WI, Feb. 21, 1947. AMDA.

**DAMON, MATT:** Cambridge, MA, Oct. 8, 1970.

**DAMONE, VIC** (Vito Farinola): Brooklyn, NY, June 12, 1928.

**DANCE, CHARLES:** Plymouth, England, Oct. 10, 1946.

**DANES, CLAIRE:** NYC, Apr. 12, 1979.

**D'ANGELO, BEVERLY:** Columbus, OH, Nov. 15, 1953.

**DANGERFIELD, RODNEY** (Jacob Cohen): Babylon, NY, Nov. 22, 1921.

**DANIELS, JEFF:** Athens, GA, Feb. 19, 1955. E MI St.

**DANIELS, WILLIAM:** Brooklyn, NY, Mar. 31, 1927. Northwestern.

**DANNER, BLYTHE:** Philadelphia, PA, Feb. 3, 1944. Bard College.

**DANNING, SYBIL** (Sybille Johanna Danninger): Vienna, Austria, May 4, 1949.

**DANSON, TED:** San Diego, CA, Dec. 29, 1947. Stanford, Carnegie Tech.

**DANTE, MICHAEL** (Ralph Vitti): Stamford, CT, 1935. U Miami.

**DANZA, TONY:** Brooklyn, NY, Apr. 21, 1951. U Dubuque.

**D'ARBANVILLE-QUINN, PATTI:** NYC, 1951.

**DARBY, KIM** (Deborah Zerby): North Hollywood, CA, July 8, 1948.

**DARCEL, DENISE** (Denise Billecard): Paris, France, Sept. 8, 1925. U Dijon.

**DARREN, JAMES:** Philadelphia, PA, June 8, 1936. Stella Adler School.

Catherine Deneuve

Gérard Depardieu

Johnny Depp

Angie Dickinson

**DARRIEUX, DANIELLE:** Bordeaux, France, May 1, 1917. Lycee LaTour.
**DAVENPORT, NIGEL:** Cambridge, England, May 23, 1928. Trinity College.
**DAVID, KEITH:** NYC, June 4, 1954. Juilliard.
**DAVIDOVICH, LOLITA:** Toronto, Ontario, Canada, July 15, 1961.
**DAVIDSON, JAYE:** Riverside, CA, 1968.
**DAVIDSON, JOHN:** Pittsburgh, PA, Dec. 13, 1941. Denison U.
**DAVIES, JEREMY** (Boring): Rockford, IA, Oct. 28, 1969.
**DAVIS, CLIFTON:** Chicago, IL, Oct. 4, 1945. Oakwood College.
**DAVIS, GEENA:** Wareham, MA, Jan. 21, 1957.
**DAVIS, HOPE:** Tenafly, NJ, 1967.
**DAVIS, JUDY:** Perth, Australia, Apr. 23, 1955.
**DAVIS, MAC:** Lubbock, TX, Jan. 21,1942.
**DAVIS, NANCY** (Anne Frances Robbins): NYC, July 6, 1921. Smith College.
**DAVIS, OSSIE:** Cogdell, GA, Dec. 18, 1917. Howard U.
**DAVIS, SAMMI:** Kidderminster, Worcestershire, England, June 21, 1964.
**DAVISON, BRUCE:** Philadelphia, PA, June 28, 1946.
**DAWBER, PAM:** Detroit, MI, Oct. 18, 1954.
**DAY, DORIS** (Doris Kappelhoff): Cincinnati, Apr. 3, 1924.
**DAY, LARAINE** (Johnson): Roosevelt, UT, Oct. 13, 1917.
**DAY LEWIS, DANIEL:** London, England, Apr. 29, 1957. Bristol Old Vic.
**DAYAN, ASSI:** Israel, Nov. 23, 1945. U Jerusalem.
**DEAKINS, LUCY:** NYC, 1971.
**DEAN, JIMMY:** Plainview, TX, Aug. 10, 1928.
**DEAN, LOREN:** Las Vegas, NV, July 31, 1969.
**DeCARLO, YVONNE** (Peggy Yvonne Middleton): Vancouver, BC, Canada, Sept. 1, 1922. Vancouver School of Drama.
**DEE, FRANCES:** Los Angeles, Nov. 26, 1907. Chicago U.
**DEE, JOEY** (Joseph Di Nicola): Passaic, NJ, June 11, 1940. Patterson State College.
**DEE, RUBY:** Cleveland, OH, Oct. 27, 1924. Hunter College.
**DEE, SANDRA** (Alexandra Zuck): Bayonne, NJ, Apr. 23, 1942.
**DeGENERES, ELLEN:** New Orleans, LA, Jan. 26, 1958.
**DeHAVEN, GLORIA:** Los Angeles, July 23, 1923.
**DeHAVILLAND, OLIVIA:** Tokyo, Japan, July 1, 1916. Notre Dame Convent School.
**DELAIR, SUZY** (Suzanne Delaire): Paris, France, Dec. 31, 1916.
**DELANY, DANA:** NYC, March 13, 1956. Wesleyan U.

**DELPY, JULIE:** Paris, France, Dec, 21, 1969.
**DELON, ALAIN:** Sceaux, France, Nov. 8, 1935.
**DELORME, DANIELE:** Paris, France, Oct. 9, 1926. Sorbonne.
**DEL TORO, BENICIO:** Santurce, Puerto Rico, Feb. 19, 1967.
**DeLUISE, DOM:** Brooklyn, NY, Aug. 1, 1933. Tufts College.
**DeLUISE, PETER:** NYC, Nov. 6, 1966.
**DEMONGEOT, MYLENE:** Nice, France, Sept. 29, 1938.
**DeMORNAY, REBECCA:** Los Angeles, Aug. 29, 1962. Strasberg Inst.
**DEMPSEY, PATRICK:** Lewiston, ME, Jan. 13, 1966.
**DeMUNN, JEFFREY:** Buffalo, NY, Apr. 25, 1947. Union College.
**DENCH, JUDI:** York, England, Dec. 9, 1934.
**DENEUVE, CATHERINE:** Paris, France, Oct. 22, 1943.
**De NIRO, ROBERT:** NYC, Aug. 17, 1943. Stella Adler.
**DENNEHY, BRIAN:** Bridgeport, CT, Jul. 9, 1938. Columbia.
**DENVER, BOB:** New Rochelle, NY, Jan. 9, 1935.
**DEPARDIEU, GERARD:** Chateauroux, France, Dec. 27, 1948.
**DEPP, JOHNNY:** Owensboro, KY, June 9, 1963.
**DEREK, BO** (Mary Cathleen Collins): Long Beach, CA, Nov. 20, 1956.
**DERN, BRUCE:** Chicago, IL, June 4, 1936. UPA.
**DERN, LAURA:** Los Angeles, Feb. 10, 1967.
**DeSALVO, ANNE:** Philadelphia, PA, Apr. 3, 1949.
**DEVANE, WILLIAM:** Albany, NY, Sept. 5, 1939.
**DeVITO, DANNY:** Asbury Park, NJ, Nov. 17, 1944.
**DEY, SUSAN:** Pekin, IL, Dec. 10, 1953.
**DeYOUNG, CLIFF:** Los Angeles, Feb. 12, 1945. Cal. St. U.
**DIAMOND, NEIL:** NYC, Jan. 24, 1941. NYU.
**DIAZ, CAMERON:** Long Beach, CA, Aug. 30, 1972.
**DiCAPRIO, LEONARDO:** Hollywood, CA, Nov.11, 1974.
**DICKINSON, ANGIE** (Angeline Brown): Kulm, ND, Sept. 30, 1932. Glendale College.
**DIESEL, VIN:** NYC, July 18, 1967.
**DIGGS, TAYE** (Scott Diggs): Rochester, NY, 1972.
**DILLER, PHYLLIS** (Driver): Lima, OH, July 17, 1917. Bluffton College.
**DILLMAN, BRADFORD:** San Francisco, CA, Apr. 14, 1930. Yale.
**DILLON, KEVIN:** Mamaroneck, NY, Aug. 19, 1965.
**DILLON, MATT:** Larchmont, NY, Feb. 18, 1964. AADA.
**DILLON, MELINDA:** Hope, AR, Oct. 13, 1939. Goodman Theatre School.

**DIXON, DONNA:** Alexandria, VA, July 20, 1957.

**DOBSON, KEVIN:** NYC, Mar. 18, 1944.

**DOBSON, TAMARA:** Baltimore, MD, May 14, 1947. MD Inst. of Art.

**DOHERTY, SHANNEN:** Memphis, TN, Apr. 12, 1971.

**DOLAN, MICHAEL:** Oklahoma City, OK, June 21, 1965.

**DONAT, PETER:** Nova Scotia, Canada, Jan. 20, 1928. Yale.

**DONNELLY, DONAL:** Bradford, England, July 6, 1931.

**D'ONOFRIO, VINCENT:** Brooklyn, NY, June 30, 1959.

**DONOHOE, AMANDA:** London, England, June 29 1962.

**DONOVAN, MARTIN:** Reseda, CA, Aug. 19, 1957.

**DONOVAN, TATE:** NYC, Sept. 25, 1963.

**DOOHAN, JAMES:** Vancouver, BC, Mar. 3, 1920. Neighborhood Playhouse.

**DOOLEY, PAUL:** Parkersburg, WV, Feb. 22, 1928. U WV.

**DORFF, STEPHEN:** CA, July 29, 1973.

**DOUG, DOUG E.** (Douglas Bourne): Brooklyn, NY, Jan. 7, 1970.

**DOUGLAS, DONNA** (Dorothy Bourgeois): Baywood, LA, Sept. 26, 1935.

**DOUGLAS, ILLEANA:** MA, July 25, 1965.

**DOUGLAS, KIRK** (Issur Danielovitch): Amsterdam, NY, Dec. 9, 1916. St. Lawrence U.

**DOUGLAS, MICHAEL:** New Brunswick, NJ, Sept. 25, 1944. U CA.

**DOUGLASS, ROBYN:** Sendai, Japan, June 21, 1953. UC Davis.

**DOURIF, BRAD:** Huntington, WV, Mar. 18, 1950. Marshall U.

**DOWN, LESLEY-ANN:** London, England, Mar. 17, 1954.

**DOWNEY, ROBERT, JR.:** NYC, Apr. 4, 1965.

**DRAKE, BETSY:** Paris, France, Sept. 11, 1923.

**DRESCHER, FRAN:** Queens, NY, Sept. 30, 1957.

**DREW, ELLEN** (formerly Terry Ray): Kansas City, MO, Nov. 23, 1915.

**DREYFUSS, RICHARD:** Brooklyn, NY, Oct. 19, 1947.

**DRILLINGER, BRIAN:** Brooklyn, NY, June 27, 1960. SUNY/Purchase.

**DRIVER, MINNIE** (Amelia Driver): London, England, Jan. 31, 1971.

**DUCHOVNY, DAVID:** NYC, Aug. 7, 1960. Yale.

**DUDIKOFF, MICHAEL:** Torrance, CA, Oct. 8, 1954.

**DUGAN, DENNIS:** Wheaton, IL, Sept. 5, 1946.

**DUKAKIS, OLYMPIA:** Lowell, MA, June 20, 1931.

**DUKE, BILL:** Poughkeepsie, NY, Feb. 26, 1943. NYU.

**DUKE, PATTY** (Anna Marie): NYC, Dec. 14, 1946.

**DULLEA, KEIR:** Cleveland, NJ, May 30, 1936. SF St. College.

**DUNAWAY, FAYE:** Bascom, FL, Jan. 14, 1941, Fla. U.

**DUNCAN, SANDY:** Henderson, TX, Feb. 20, 1946. Len Morris College.

**DUNNE, GRIFFIN:** NYC, June 8, 1955. Neighborhood Playhouse.

**DUNST, KIRSTEN:** Point Pleasant, NJ, Apr. 30, 1982.

**DUPEREY, ANNY:** Paris, France, 1947.

**DURBIN, DEANNA** (Edna): Winnipeg, Manitoba, Canada, Dec. 4, 1921.

**DURNING, CHARLES:** Highland Falls, NY, Feb. 28, 1923. NYU.

**DUSHKU, ELIZA:** Boston, MA, Dec. 30, 1980.

**DUSSOLLIER, ANDRE:** Annecy, France, Feb. 17, 1946.

**DUTTON, CHARLES:** Baltimore, MD, Jan. 30, 1951. Yale.

**DUVALL, ROBERT:** San Diego, CA, Jan. 5, 1931. Principia College.

**DUVALL, SHELLEY:** Houston, TX, July 7, 1949.

**DYSART, RICHARD:** Brighton, ME, Mar. 30, 1929.

**DZUNDZA, GEORGE:** Rosenheim, Germany, July 19, 1945.

**EASTON, ROBERT:** Milwaukee, WI, Nov. 23, 1930. U TX.

**EASTWOOD, CLINT:** San Francisco, CA, May 31, 1930. LACC.

**EATON, SHIRLEY:** London, England, 1937. Aida Foster School.

**EBSEN, BUDDY** (Christian, Jr.)**:** Belleville, IL, Apr. 2, 1910. U FL.

**ECKEMYR, AGNETA:** Karlsborg, Sweden, July 2. Actors Studio.

**EDELMAN, GREGG:** Chicago, IL, Sept. 12, 1958. Northwestern.

**EDEN, BARBARA** (Huffman): Tucson, AZ, Aug. 23, 1934.

**EDWARDS, ANTHONY:** Santa Barbara, CA, July 19, 1962. RADA.

**EDWARDS, LUKE:** Nevada City, CA, Mar. 24, 1980.

**EGGAR, SAMANTHA:** London, England, Mar. 5, 1939.

**EICHHORN, LISA:** Reading, PA, Feb. 4, 1952. Queens Ont. U, RADA.

**EIKENBERRY, JILL:** New Haven, CT, Jan. 21, 1947.

**EILBER, JANET:** Detroit, MI, July 27, 1951. Juilliard.

**EKBERG, ANITA:** Malmo, Sweden, Sept. 29, 1931.

**EKLAND, BRITT:** Stockholm, Sweden, Oct. 6, 1942.

**ELDARD, RON:** Long Island, NY, Feb. 20, 1965.

**ELFMAN, JENNA** (Jennifer Mary Batula): Los Angeles, Sept. 30, 1971.

**ELIZONDO, HECTOR:** NYC, Dec. 22, 1936.

**ELLIOTT, ALISON:** San Francisco, CA, 1969.

**ELLIOTT, CHRIS:** NYC, May 31, 1960.

**ELLIOTT, PATRICIA:** Gunnison, CO, July 21, 1942. U CO.

**ELLIOTT, SAM:** Sacramento, CA, Aug. 9, 1944. U OR.

**ELWES, CARY:** London, England, Oct. 26, 1962.

**ELY, RON** (Ronald Pierce): Hereford, TX, June 21, 1938.

**EMBRY, ETHAN** (Ethan Randall): Huntington Beach, CA, June 13, 1978.

**ENGLUND, ROBERT:** Glendale, CA, June 6, 1949.

**ERBE, KATHRYN:** Newton, MA, July 2, 1966.

**ERDMAN, RICHARD:** Enid, OK, June 1, 1925.

**ERICSON, JOHN:** Dusseldorf, Germany, Sept. 25, 1926. AADA.

**ERMEY, R. LEE** (Ronald): Emporia, KS, Mar. 24, 1944

**ESMOND, CARL** (Willy Eichberger): Vienna, Austria, June 14, 1906. U Vienna.

**ESPOSITO, GIANCARLO:** Copenhagen, Denmark, Apr. 26, 1958.

**ESTEVEZ, EMILIO:** NYC, May 12, 1962.

**ESTRADA, ERIK:** NYC, Mar. 16, 1949.

**EVANS, JOSH:** NYC, Jan. 16, 1971.

**EVANS, LINDA** (Evanstad): Hartford, CT, Nov. 18, 1942.

**EVERETT, CHAD** (Ray Cramton): South Bend, IN, June 11, 1936.

**EVERETT, RUPERT:** Norfolk, England, 1959.

**EVIGAN, GREG:** South Amboy, NJ, Oct. 14, 1953.

**FABARES, SHELLEY:** Los Angeles, Jan. 19, 1944.

**FABIAN** (Fabian Forte): Philadelphia, Feb. 6, 1943. ·

**FABRAY, NANETTE** (Ruby Nanette Fabares): San Diego, Oct. 27, 1920.

**FAHEY, JEFF:** Olean, NY, Nov. 29, 1956.

**FAIRCHILD, MORGAN** (Patsy McClenny): Dallas, TX, Feb. 3, 1950. UCLA.

**FALK, PETER:** NYC, Sept. 16, 1927. New School.

**FARENTINO, JAMES:** Brooklyn, NY, Feb. 24, 1938. AADA.

**FARGAS, ANTONIO:** Bronx, NY, Aug. 14, 1946.

**FARINA, DENNIS:** Chicago, IL, Feb. 29, 1944.

**FARINA, SANDY** (Sandra Feldman): Newark, NJ, 1955.

**FARR, FELICIA:** Westchester, NY, Oct. 4. 1932. Penn St. College.

**FARRELL, COLIN:** Castleknock, Ireland, Mar. 31, 1976.

**FARROW, MIA** (Maria): Los Angeles, Feb. 9, 1945.

**FAULKNER, GRAHAM:** London, England, Sept. 26, 1947. Webber-Douglas.

Rupert Everett     Colin Farrell     Jon Favreau     Harrison Ford

**FAVREAU, JON:** Queens, NY, Oct. 16, 1966.

**FAWCETT, FARRAH:** Corpus Christie, TX, Feb. 2, 1947. TX U.

**FEINSTEIN, ALAN:** NYC, Sept. 8, 1941.

**FELDMAN, COREY:** Encino, CA, July 16, 1971.

**FELDON, BARBARA** (Hall): Pittsburgh, Mar. 12, 1941. Carnegie Tech.

**FELDSHUH, TOVAH:** NYC, Dec. 27, 1953, Sarah Lawrence College.

**FELLOWS, EDITH:** Boston, MA, May 20, 1923.

**FENN, SHERILYN:** Detroit, MI, Feb. 1, 1965.

**FERRELL, CONCHATA:** Charleston, WV, Mar. 28, 1943. Marshall U.

**FERRELL, WILL:** Irvine, CA, July 16, 1968.

**FERRER, MEL:** Elbeton, NJ, Aug. 25, 1912. Princeton.

**FERRER, MIGUEL:** Santa Monica, CA, Feb. 7, 1954.

**FERRIS, BARBARA:** London, England, 1943.

**FIEDLER, JOHN:** Plateville, WI, Feb. 3, 1925.

**FIELD, SALLY:** Pasadena, CA, Nov. 6, 1946.

**FIELD, SHIRLEY ANNE:** London, England, June 27, 1938.

**FIELD, TODD** (William Todd Field): Pomona, CA, Feb. 24, 1964.

**FIENNES, JOSEPH:** Salisbury, Wiltshire, England, May 27, 1970.

**FIENNES, RALPH:** Suffolk, England, Dec. 22, 1962. RADA.

**FIERSTEIN, HARVEY:** Brooklyn, NY, June 6, 1954. Pratt Inst.

**FINCH, JON:** Caterham, England, Mar. 2, 1941.

**FINLAY, FRANK:** Farnworth, England, Aug. 6, 1926.

**FINNEY, ALBERT:** Salford, Lancashire, England, May 9, 1936. RADA.

**FIORENTINO, LINDA:** Philadelphia, PA, Mar. 9, 1960.

**FIRTH, COLIN:** Grayshott, Hampshire, England, Sept. 10, 1960.

**FIRTH, PETER:** Bradford, England, Oct. 27, 1953.

**FISHBURNE, LAURENCE:** Augusta, GA, July 30, 1961.

**FISHER, CARRIE:** Los Angeles, CA, Oct. 21, 1956. London Central School of Drama.

**FISHER, EDDIE:** Philadelphia, PA, Aug. 10, 1928.

**FISHER, FRANCES:** Orange, TX, 1952.

**FITZGERALD, TARA:** London, England, Sept. 17, 1968.

**FITZGERALD, GERALDINE:** Dublin, Ireland, Nov. 24, 1914. Dublin Art School.

**FLAGG, FANNIE:** Birmingham, AL, Sept. 21, 1944. U AL.

**FLANAGAN, FIONNULA:** Dublin, Ireland, Dec. 10, 1941.

**FLANNERY, SUSAN:** Jersey City, NJ, July 31, 1943.

**FLEMING, RHONDA** (Marilyn Louis): Los Angeles, Aug. 10, 1922.

**FLEMYNG, ROBERT:** Liverpool, England, Jan. 3, 1912. Haileybury College.

**FLETCHER, LOUISE:** Birmingham, AL, July 22 1934.

**FLOCKHART, CALISTA:** Stockton, IL, Nov. 11, Rutgers.

**FOCH, NINA:** Leyden, Holland, Apr. 20, 1924.

**FOLEY, DAVE:** Toronto, Canada, Jan. 4, 1963.

**FOLLOWS, MEGAN:** Toronto, Canada, Mar. 14, 1968.

**FONDA, BRIDGET:** Los Angeles, Jan. 27, 1964.

**FONDA, JANE:** NYC, Dec. 21, 1937. Vassar.

**FONDA, PETER:** NYC, Feb. 23, 1939. U Omaha.

**FONTAINE, JOAN:** Tokyo, Japan, Oct. 22, 1917.

**FOOTE, HALLIE:** NYC, 1953. UNH.

**FORD, GLENN** (Gwyllyn Samuel Newton Ford): Quebec, Canada, May 1, 1916.

**FORD, HARRISON:** Chicago, IL, July 13, 1942. Ripon College.

**FOREST, MARK** (Lou Degni): Brooklyn, NY, Jan. 1933.

**FORLANI, CLAIRE:** London, England, July 1, 1972.

**FORREST, FREDERIC:** Waxahachie, TX, Dec. 23, 1936.

**FORREST, STEVE:** Huntsville, TX, Sept. 29, 1924. UCLA.

**FORSLUND, CONNIE:** San Diego, CA, June 19, 1950. NYU.

**FORSTER, ROBERT** (Foster, Jr.): Rochester, NY, July 13, 1941. Rochester U.

**FORSYTHE, JOHN** (Freund): Penn's Grove, NJ, Jan. 29, 1918.

**FORSYTHE, WILLIAM:** Brooklyn, NY, June 7, 1955

**FOSSEY, BRIGITTE:** Tourcoing, France, Mar. 11, 1947.

**FOSTER, JODIE** (Ariane Munker): Bronx, NY, Nov. 19, 1962. Yale.

**FOSTER, BEN:** Boston, MA, Oct. 29, 1980.

**FOSTER, MEG:** Reading, PA, May 14, 1948.

**FOX, EDWARD:** London, England, Apr. 13, 1937. RADA.

**FOX, JAMES:** London, England, May 19, 1939.

**FOX, MICHAEL J.:** Vancouver, BC, Canada, June 9, 1961.

**FOX, VIVICA A.:** Indianapolis, IN, July 30, 1964.

**FOXWORTH, ROBERT:** Houston, TX, Nov. 1, 1941. Carnegie Tech.

Brendan Fraser          Cuba Gooding, Jr.          Heather Graham          Bruce Greenwood

**FRAIN, JAMES:** Leeds, England, 1969.

**FRAKES, JONATHAN:** Bethlehem, PA, Aug. 19, 1952. Harvard.

**FRANCIOSA, ANTHONY** (Papaleo): NYC, Oct. 25, 1928.

**FRANCIS, ANNE:** Ossining, NY, Sept. 16, 1932.

**FRANCIS, ARLENE** (Arlene Kazanjian): Boston, MA, Oct. 20, 1908. Finch School.

**FRANCIS, CONNIE** (Constance Franconero): Newark, NJ, Dec. 12, 1938.

**FRANCKS, DON:** Vancouver, BC, Canada, Feb. 28, 1932.

**FRANKLIN, PAMELA:** Tokyo, Japan, Feb. 4, 1950.

**FRANZ, ARTHUR:** Perth Amboy, NJ, Feb. 29, 1920. Blue Ridge College.

**FRANZ, DENNIS:** Chicago, IL, Oct. 28, 1944.

**FRASER, BRENDAN:** Indianapolis, IN, Dec. 3, 1968.

**FRAZIER, SHEILA:** NYC, Nov. 13, 1948.

**FRECHETTE, PETER:** Warwick, RI, Oct. 1956. URI.

**FREEMAN, AL, JR.:** San Antonio, TX, Mar. 21, 1934. CCLA.

**FREEMAN, MONA:** Baltimore, MD, June 9, 1926.

**FREEMAN, MORGAN:** Memphis, TN, June 1, 1937. LACC.

**FREWER, MATT:** Washington, DC, Jan. 4, 1958, Old Vic.

**FRICKER, BRENDA:** Dublin, Ireland, Feb. 17, 1945.

**FRIELS, COLIN:** Glasgow, Scotland, Sept. 25, 1952.

**FRY, STEPHEN:** Hampstead, London, Eng., Aug. 24, 1957.

**FULLER, PENNY:** Durham, NC, 1940. Northwestern.

**FUNICELLO, ANNETTE:** Utica, NY, Oct. 22, 1942.

**FURLONG, EDWARD:** Glendale, CA, Aug. 2, 1977.

**FURNEAUX, YVONNE:** Lille, France, 1928. Oxford U.

**GABLE, JOHN CLARK:** Los Angeles, Mar. 20, 1961. Santa Monica College.

**GABOR, ZSA ZSA** (Sari Gabor): Budapest, Hungary, Feb. 6, 1918.

**GAIL, MAX:** Derfoil, MI, Apr. 5, 1943.

**GAINES, BOYD:** Atlanta, GA, May 11, 1953. Juilliard.

**GALECKI, JOHNNY:** Bree, Belgium, Apr. 30, 1975.

**GALLAGHER, PETER:** NYC, Aug. 19, 1955. Tufts.

**GALLIGAN, ZACH:** NYC, Feb. 14, 1963. Columbia.

**GALLO, VINCENT:** Buffalo, NY, Apr. 11, 1961.

**GAM, RITA:** Pittsburgh, PA, Apr. 2, 1928.

**GAMBLE, MASON:** Chicago, IL, Jan. 16, 1986.

**GAMBON, MICHAEL:** Dublin, Ireland, Oct. 19, 1940.

**GANDOLFINI, JAMES:** Westwood, NJ, Sept. 18, 1961.

**GANZ, BRUNO:** Zurich, Switzerland, Mar. 22, 1941.

**GARBER, VICTOR:** Montreal, Canada, Mar. 16, 1949.

**GARCIA, ADAM:** Wahroonga, New So. Wales, Australia, June 1, 1973.

**GARCIA, ANDY:** Havana, Cuba, Apr. 12, 1956. FL Inst.

**GARFIELD, ALLEN** (Allen Goorwitz): Newark, NJ, Nov. 22, 1939. Actors Studio.

**GARFUNKEL, ART:** NYC, Nov. 5, 1941.

**GARLAND, BEVERLY:** Santa Cruz, CA, Oct. 17, 1926. Glendale College.

**GARNER, JAMES** (James Baumgarner): Norman, OK, Apr. 7, 1928. OK U.

**GAROFALO, JANEANE:** Newton, NJ, Sept. 28, 1964.

**GARR, TERI:** Lakewood, OH, Dec. 11, 1949.

**GARRETT, BETTY:** St. Joseph, MO, May 23, 1919. Annie Wright Seminary.

**GARRISON, SEAN:** NYC, Oct. 19, 1937.

**GARY, LORRAINE:** NYC, Aug. 16, 1937.

**GAVIN, JOHN:** Los Angeles, Apr. 8, 1935. Stanford.

**GAYLORD, MITCH:** Van Nuys, CA, Mar. 10, 1961. UCLA.

**GAYNOR, MITZI** (Francesca Marlene Von Gerber): Chicago, IL, Sept. 4, 1930.

**GAZZARA, BEN:** NYC, Aug. 28, 1930. Actors Studio.

**GEARY, ANTHONY:** Coalsville, UT, May 29, 1947. U UT.

**GEDRICK, JASON:** Chicago, IL, Feb. 7, 1965. Drake.

**GEESON, JUDY:** Arundel, England, Sept. 10, 1948. Corona.

**GELLAR, SARAH MICHELLE:** NYC, Apr. 14, 1977.

**GEOFFREYS, STEPHEN** (Miller): Cincinnati, OH, Nov. 22, 1959. NYU.

**GEORGE, SUSAN:** West London, England, July 26, 1950.

**GERARD, GIL:** Little Rock, AR, Jan. 23, 1940.

**GERE, RICHARD:** Philadelphia, PA, Aug. 29, 1949. U MA.

**GERROLL, DANIEL:** London, England, Oct. 16, 1951. Central.

**GERSHON, GINA:** Los Angeles, June 10, 1962.

**GERTZ, JAMI:** Chicago, IL, Oct. 28, 1965.

**GETTY, BALTHAZAR:** Los Angeles, Jan. 22, 1975.

**GETTY, ESTELLE:** NYC, July 25, 1923. New School.

**GHOLSON, JULIE:** Birmingham, AL, June 4, 1958.

**GHOSTLEY, ALICE:** Eve, MO, Aug. 14, 1926. OK U.

**GIANNINI, GIANCARLO:** Spezia, Italy, Aug. 1, 1942. Rome Academy of Drama.

**GIBB, CYNTHIA:** Bennington, VT, Dec. 14, 1963.
**GIBSON, HENRY:** Germantown, PA, Sept. 21, 1935.
**GIBSON, MEL:** Peekskill, NY, Jan. 3, 1956. NIDA.
**GIBSON, THOMAS:** Charleston, SC, July 3, 1962.
**GIFT, ROLAND:** Birmingham, England, May 28 1962.
**GILBERT, MELISSA:** Los Angeles, May 8, 1964.
**GILES, NANCY:** NYC, July 17, 1960, Oberlin College.
**GILLETTE, ANITA:** Baltimore, MD, Aug. 16, 1938.
**GILLIAM, TERRY:** Minneapolis, MN, Nov. 22, 1940.
**GILLIS, ANN** (Alma O'Connor): Little Rock, AR, Feb. 12, 1927.
**GINTY, ROBERT:** NYC, Nov. 14, 1948. Yale.
**GIRARDOT, ANNIE:** Paris, France, Oct. 25, 1931.
**GISH, ANNABETH:** Albuquerque, NM, Mar. 13, 1971. Duke.
**GIVENS, ROBIN:** NYC, Nov. 27, 1964.
**GLASER, PAUL MICHAEL:** Boston, MA, Mar. 25, 1943. Boston U.
**GLASS, RON:** Evansville, IN, July 10, 1945.
**GLEASON, JOANNA:** Winnipeg, Manitoba, Canada, June 2, 1950. UCLA.
**GLEASON, PAUL:** Jersey City, NJ, May 4, 1944.
**GLENN, SCOTT:** Pittsburgh, PA, Jan. 26, 1942. William and Mary College.
**GLOVER, CRISPIN:** NYC, Sept 20, 1964.
**GLOVER, DANNY:** San Francisco, CA, July 22, 1947. SF St. College.
**GLOVER, JOHN:** Kingston, NY, Aug. 7, 1944.
**GLYNN, CARLIN:** Cleveland, Oh, Feb. 19, 1940. Actors Studio.
**GOLDBERG, WHOOPI** (Caryn Johnson): NYC, Nov. 13, 1949.
**GOLDBLUM, JEFF:** Pittsburgh, PA, Oct. 22, 1952. Neighborhood Playhouse.
**GOLDEN, ANNIE:** Brooklyn, NY, Oct. 19, 1951.
**GOLDSTEIN, JENETTE:** Beverly Hills, CA, 1960.
**GOLDTHWAIT, BOB:** Syracuse, NY, May 1, 1962.
**GOLDWYN, TONY:** Los Angeles, May 20, 1960. LAMDA.
**GOLINO, VALERIA:** Naples, Italy, Oct. 22, 1966.
**GONZALEZ, CORDELIA:** San Juan, PR, Aug. 11, 1958. U PR.
**GONZALES-GONZALEZ, PEDRO:** Aguilares, TX, Dec. 21, 1926.
**GOODALL, CAROLINE:** London, England, Nov. 13, 1959. Bristol U.
**GOODING, CUBA, JR.:** Bronx, N.Y., Jan. 2, 1968.
**GOODMAN, DODY:** Columbus, OH, Oct. 28, 1915.
**GOODMAN, JOHN:** St. Louis, MO, June 20, 1952.
**GORDON, KEITH:** NYC, Feb. 3, 1961.
**GORDON-LEVITT, JOSEPH:** Los Angeles, Feb. 17, 1981.
**GORMAN, CLIFF:** Jamaica, NY, Oct. 13, 1936. NYU.
**GORSHIN, FRANK:** Pittsburgh, PA, Apr. 5, 1933.
**GORTNER, MARJOE:** Long Beach, CA, Jan. 14, 1944.
**GOSSETT, LOUIS, JR.:** Brooklyn, NY, May 27, 1936. NYU.
**GOULD, ELLIOTT** (Goldstein): Brooklyn, NY, Aug. 29, 1938. Columbia.
**GOULD, HAROLD:** Schenectady, NY, Dec. 10, 1923. Cornell.
**GOULD, JASON:** NYC, Dec. 29, 1966.
**GOULET, ROBERT:** Lawrence, MA, Nov. 26, 1933. Edmonton.
**GRAF, DAVID:** Lancaster, OH, Apr. 16, 1950. OH St. U.
**GRAFF, TODD:** NYC, Oct. 22, 1959. SUNY/ Purchase.
**GRAHAM, HEATHER:** Milwaukee, WI, Jan. 29, 1970.
**GRANGER, FARLEY:** San Jose, CA, July 1, 1925.
**GRANT, DAVID MARSHALL:** Westport, CT, June 21, 1955. Yale.
**GRANT, HUGH:** London, England, Sept. 9, 1960. Oxford.
**GRANT, KATHRYN** (Olive Grandstaff): Houston, TX, Nov. 25, 1933. UCLA.

Rachel Griffiths      Ioan Gruffudd

**GRANT, LEE:** NYC, Oct. 31, 1927. Juilliard.
**GRANT, RICHARD E:** Mbabane, Swaziland, May 5, 1957. Cape Town U.
**GRAVES, PETER** (Aurness): Minneapolis, Mar. 18, 1926. U MN.
**GRAVES, RUPERT:** Weston-Super-Mare, England, June 30, 1963.
**GRAY, COLEEN** (Doris Jensen): Staplehurst, NB, Oct. 23, 1922. Hamline.
**GRAY, LINDA:** Santa Monica, CA, Sept. 12, 1940.
**GRAY, SPALDING:** Barrington, RI, June 5, 1941.
**GRAYSON, KATHRYN** (Zelma Hedrick): Winston-Salem, NC, Feb. 9, 1922.
**GREEN, KERRI:** Fort Lee, NJ, Jan. 14, 1967. Vassar.
**GREEN, SETH:** Philadelphia, PA, Feb. 8, 1974.
**GREENE, ELLEN:** NYC, Feb. 22, 1950. Ryder College.
**GREENE, GRAHAM:** Six Nations Reserve, Ontario, Canada, June 22, 1952
**GREENWOOD, BRUCE:** Quebec, Canada, Aug. 12, 1956.
**GREER, MICHAEL:** Galesburg, IL, Apr. 20, 1943.
**GREIST, KIM:** Stamford, CT, May 12, 1958.
**GREY, JENNIFER:** NYC, Mar. 26, 1960.
**GREY, JOEL** (Katz): Cleveland, OH, Apr. 11, 1932.
**GREY, VIRGINIA:** Los Angeles, Mar. 22, 1917.
**GRIECO, RICHARD:** Watertown, NY, Mar. 23, 1965.
**GRIEM, HELMUT:** Hamburg, Germany, Apr. 6, 1932. Hamburg U.
**GRIER, DAVID ALAN:** Detroit, MI, June 30, 1955. Yale.
**GRIER, PAM:** Winston-Salem, NC, May 26, 1949.
**GRIFFITH, ANDY:** Mt. Airy, NC, June 1, 1926. UNC.
**GRIFFITH, MELANIE:** NYC, Aug. 9, 1957. Pierce Col.
**GRIFFITH, THOMAS IAN:** Hartford, CT, Mar. 18, 1962.
**GRIFFITHS, RACHEL:** Melbourne, Australia, 1968.
**GRIFFITHS, RICHARD:** Tornaby-on-Tees, England, July 31, 1947.
**GRIMES, GARY:** San Francisco, CA, June 2, 1955.
**GRIMES, SCOTT:** Lowell, MA, July 9, 1971.
**GRIMES, TAMMY:** Lynn, MA, Jan. 30, 1934. Stephens College.
**GRIZZARD, GEORGE:** Roanoke Rapids, NC, Apr. 1, 1928. U NC.
**GRODIN, CHARLES:** Pittsburgh, PA, Apr. 21, 1935.
**GROH, DAVID:** NYC, May 21, 1939. Brown U, LAMDA.
**GROSS, MARY:** Chicago, IL, Mar. 25, 1953.
**GROSS, MICHAEL:** Chicago, IL, June 21, 1947.
**GRUFFUDD, IOAN:** Cardiff, Wales, Oct. 6, 1973.
**GUEST, CHRISTOPHER:** NYC, Feb. 5, 1948.

**GUEST, LANCE:** Saratoga, CA, July 21, 1960. UCLA.

**GUILLAUME, ROBERT** (Williams): St. Louis, MO, Nov. 30, 1937.

**GULAGER, CLU:** Holdenville, OK, Nov. 16 1928.

**GUTTENBERG, STEVE:** Massapequa, NY, Aug. 24, 1958. UCLA.

**GUY, JASMINE:** Boston, MA, Mar. 10, 1964.

**HAAS, LUKAS:** West Hollywood, CA, Apr. 16, 1976.

**HACK, SHELLEY:** Greenwich, CT, July 6, 1952.

**HACKETT, BUDDY** (Leonard Hacker): Brooklyn, NY, Aug. 31, 1924.

**HACKMAN, GENE:** San Bernardino, CA, Jan. 30, 1930.

**HAGERTY, JULIE:** Cincinnati, OH, June 15, 1955. Juilliard.

**HAGMAN, LARRY** (Hageman): Weatherford, TX, Sept. 21, 1931. Bard.

**HAID, CHARLES:** San Francisco, CA, June 2, 1943. Carnegie Tech.

**HAIM, COREY:** Toronto, Canada, Dec. 23, 1972.

**HALE, BARBARA:** DeKalb, IL, Apr. 18, 1922. Chicago Academy of Fine Arts.

**HALEY, JACKIE EARLE:** Northridge, CA, July 14, 1961.

**HALL, ALBERT:** Boothton, AL, Nov. 10, 1937. Columbia.

**HALL, ANTHONY MICHAEL:** Boston, MA, Apr. 14, 1968.

**HALL, ARSENIO:** Cleveland, OH, Feb. 12, 1959.

**HAMEL, VERONICA:** Philadelphia, PA, Nov. 20, 1943.

**HAMILL, MARK:** Oakland, CA, Sept. 25, 1952. LACC.

**HAMILTON, CARRIE:** NYC, Dec. 5, 1963.

**HAMILTON, GEORGE:** Memphis, TN, Aug. 12, 1939. Hackley.

**HAMILTON, LINDA:** Salisbury, MD, Sept. 26, 1956.

**HAMLIN, HARRY:** Pasadena, CA, Oct. 30, 1951.

**HAMPSHIRE, SUSAN:** London, England, May 12, 1941.

**HAMPTON, JAMES:** Oklahoma City, OK, July 9, 1936. N TX St. U.

**HAN, MAGGIE:** Providence, RI, 1959.

**HANDLER, EVAN:** NYC, Jan. 10, 1961. Juilliard.

**HANKS, TOM:** Concord, CA, Jul. 9, 1956. Cal. St. U.

**HANNAH, DARYL:** Chicago, IL, Dec. 3, 1960. UCLA.

**HANNAH, PAGE:** Chicago, IL, Apr. 13, 1964.

**HARDEN, MARCIA GAY:** LaJolla, CA, Aug. 14, 1959.

**HARDIN, TY** (Orison Whipple Hungerford, II): NYC, June 1, 1930.

**HAREWOOD, DORIAN:** Dayton, OH, Aug. 6, 1950. U Cincinnati

**HARMON, MARK:** Los Angeles, Sept. 2, 1951. UCLA.

**HARPER, JESSICA:** Chicago, IL, Oct. 10, 1949.

**HARPER, TESS:** Mammoth Spring, AK, 1952. SW MO St.

**HARPER, VALERIE:** Suffern, NY, Aug. 22, 1940.

**HARRELSON, WOODY:** Midland, TX, July 23, 1961. Hanover College.

**HARRINGTON, PAT:** NYC, Aug. 13, 1929. Fordham.

**HARRIS, BARBARA** (Sandra Markowitz): Evanston, IL, July 25, 1935.

**HARRIS, ED:** Tenafly, NJ, Nov. 28, 1950. Columbia.

**HARRIS, JULIE:** Grosse Point, MI, Dec. 2, 1925. Yale Drama School.

**HARRIS, MEL** (Mary Ellen): Bethlehem, PA, 1957. Columbia.

**HARRIS, RICHARD:** Limerick, Ireland, Oct. 1, 1930. London Academy.

**HARRIS, ROSEMARY:** Ashby, England, Sept. 19, 1930. RADA.

**HARRISON, GREGORY:** Catalina Island, CA, May 31, 1950. Actors Studio.

**HARRISON, NOEL:** London, England, Jan. 29, 1936.

**HARROLD, KATHRYN:** Tazewell, VA, Aug. 2, 1950. Mills College.

**HARRY, DEBORAH:** Miami, IL, July 1, 1945.

**HART, ROXANNE:** Trenton, NJ, 1952, Princeton.

**HART, IAN:** Liverpool, England, 1964.

**HARTLEY, MARIETTE:** NYC, June 21, 1941.

**HARTMAN, DAVID:** Pawtucket, RI, May 19, 1935. Duke.

**HASSETT, MARILYN:** Los Angeles, Dec. 17, 1947.

**HATCHER, TERI:** Sunnyvale, CA, Dec. 8, 1964.

**HATOSY, SHAWN:** Fredrick, MD, Dec. 29, 1975.

**HAUER, RUTGER:** Amsterdam, Holland, Jan. 23, 1944.

**HAVER, JUNE:** Rock Island, IL, June 10, 1926.

**HAUSER, COLE:** Santa Barbara, CA, Mar. 22, 1975.

**HASUER, WINGS** (Gerald Dwight Hauser): Hollywood, CA, Dec. 12, 1947.

**HAVOC, JUNE** (Hovick): Seattle, WA, Nov. 8, 1916.

**HAWKE, ETHAN:** Austin, TX, Nov. 6, 1970.

**HAWN, GOLDIE:** Washington, DC, Nov. 21, 1945.

**HAYEK, SALMA:** Coatzacoalcos, Veracruz, Mexico, Sept. 2, 1968.

**HAYES, ISAAC:** Covington, TN, Aug. 20, 1942.

**HAYS, ROBERT:** Bethesda, MD, July 24, 1947, SD St. College.

**HEADLY, GLENNE:** New London, CT, Mar. 13, 1955. Amherst.

**HEALD, ANTHONY:** New Rochelle, NY, Aug. 25, 1944. MI St. U.

**HEARD, JOHN:** Washington, DC, Mar. 7, 1946. Clark.

**HEATHERTON, JOEY:** NYC, Sept. 14, 1944.

**HECHE, ANNE:** Aurora, OH, May 25, 1969.

**HEDAYA, DAN:** Brooklyn, NY, July 24, 1940.

**HEDISON, DAVID:** Providence, RI, May 20, 1929. Brown.

**HEDREN, TIPPI** (Natalie): Lafayette, MN, Jan. 19, 1931.

**HEGYES, ROBERT:** Metuchen, NJ, May 7, 1951.

**HELMOND, KATHERINE:** Galveston, TX, July 5, 1934.

**HEMINGWAY, MARIEL:** Ketchum, ID, Nov. 22, 1961.

**HEMMINGS, DAVID:** Guilford, England, Nov. 18, 1941.

**HEMSLEY, SHERMAN:** Philadelphia, PA, Feb. 1, 1938.

**HENDERSON, FLORENCE:** Dale, IN, Feb. 14, 1934.

**HENDRY, GLORIA:** Jacksonville, FL, 1949.

**HENNER, MARILU:** Chicago, IL, Apr. 6, 1952.

**HENRIKSEN, LANCE:** NYC, May 5, 1940.

**HENRY, BUCK** (Henry Zuckerman): NYC, Dec. 9, 1930. Dartmouth.

**HENRY, JUSTIN:** Rye, NY, May 25, 1971.

**HENSTRIDGE, NATASHA:** Springdale, Newfoundland, Canada, Aug. 15, 1974.

**HEPBURN, KATHARINE:** Hartford, CT, May 12, 1907. Bryn Mawr.

**HERRMANN, EDWARD:** Washington, DC, July 21, 1943. Bucknell, LAMDA.

**HERSHEY, BARBARA** (Herzstein): Hollywood, CA, Feb. 5, 1948.

**HESSEMAN. HOWARD:** Lebanon, OR, Feb. 27, 1940.

**HESTON, CHARLTON:** Evanston, IL, Oct. 4, 1922. Northwestern.

**HEWITT, JENNIFER LOVE:** Waco, TX, Feb. 21, 1979.

**HEWITT, MARTIN:** Claremont, CA, Feb. 19, 1958. AADA.

**HEYWOOD, ANNE** (Violet Pretty): Birmingham, England, Dec. 11, 1932.

**HICKMAN, DARRYL:** Hollywood, CA, July 28, 1933. Loyola.

**HICKMAN, DWAYNE:** Los Angeles, May 18, 1934. Loyola.

**HICKS, CATHERINE:** NYC, Aug. 6, 1951. Notre Dame.

**HIGGINS, ANTHONY** (Corlan): Cork City, Ireland, May 9, 1947. Birmingham Sch. of Dramatic Arts.

**HIGGINS, MICHAEL:** Brooklyn, NY, Jan. 20, 1926. Am. Th. Wing.

Marcia Gay Harden

Ed Harris

Shawn Hatosy

Dan Hedaya

**HILL, ARTHUR:** Saskatchewan, Canada, Aug. 1, 1922. U Brit. College.

**HILL, BERNARD:** Manchester, England, Dec. 17, 1944.

**HILL, STEVEN:** Seattle, WA, Feb. 24, 1922. U WA.

**HILL, TERRENCE** (Mario Girotti): Venice, Italy, Mar. 29, 1941. U Rome.

**HILLER, WENDY:** Bramhall, Cheshire, England, Aug. 15, 1912. Winceby House School.

**HILLERMAN, JOHN:** Denison, TX, Dec. 20, 1932.

**HINES, GREGORY:** NYC, Feb.14, 1946.

**HINGLE, PAT:** Denver, CO, July 19, 1923. TX U.

**HIRSCH, JUDD:** NYC, Mar. 15, 1935. AADA.

**HOBEL, MARA:** NYC, June 18, 1971.

**HODGE, PATRICIA:** Lincolnshire, England, Sept. 29, 1946. LAMDA.

**HOFFMAN, DUSTIN:** Los Angeles, Aug. 8, 1937. Pasadena Playhouse.

**HOFFMAN, PHILIP SEYMOUR:** Fairport, NY, July 23, 1967.

**HOGAN, JONATHAN:** Chicago, IL, June 13, 1951.

**HOGAN, PAUL:** Lightning Ridge, Australia, Oct. 8, 1939.

**HOLBROOK, HAL** (Harold): Cleveland, OH, Feb. 17, 1925. Denison.

**HOLLIMAN, EARL:** Tennessa Swamp, Delhi, LA, Sept. 11, 1928. UCLA.

**HOLM, CELESTE:** NYC, Apr. 29, 1919.

**HOLM, IAN:** Ilford, Essex, England, Sept. 12, 1931. RADA.

**HOLMES, KATIE:** Toledo, OH, Dec. 18, 1978.

**HOMEIER, SKIP** (George Vincent Homeier): Chicago, IL, Oct. 5, 1930. UCLA.

**HOOKS, ROBERT:** Washington, DC, Apr. 18, 1937. Temple.

**HOPE, BOB** (Leslie Townes Hope): London, England, May 26, 1903.

**HOPKINS, ANTHONY:** Port Talbot, So. Wales, Dec. 31, 1937. RADA.

**HOPPER, DENNIS:** Dodge City, KS, May 17, 1936.

**HORNE, LENA:** Brooklyn, NY, June 30, 1917.

**HORROCKS, JANE:** Rossendale Valley, England, Jan. 18, 1964.

**HORSLEY, LEE:** Muleshoe, TX, May 15, 1955.

**HORTON, ROBERT:** Los Angeles, July 29, 1924. UCLA.

**HOSKINS, BOB:** Bury St. Edmunds, England, Oct. 26, 1942.

**HOUGHTON, KATHARINE:** Hartford, CT, Mar. 10, 1945. Sarah Lawrence.

**HOUSER, JERRY:** Los Angeles, July 14, 1952. Valley Jr. College.

**HOWARD, ARLISS:** Independence, MO, 1955. Columbia College.

**HOWARD, KEN:** El Centro, CA, Mar. 28, 1944. Yale.

**HOWARD, RON:** Duncan, OK, Mar. 1, 1954. USC.

**HOWARD, RONALD:** Norwood, England, Apr. 7, 1918. Jesus College.

**HOWELL, C. THOMAS:** Los Angeles, Dec. 7, 1966.

**HOWELLS, URSULA:** London, England, Sept. 17, 1922.

**HOWES, SALLY ANN:** London, England, July 20, 1930.

**HOWLAND, BETH:** Boston, MA, May 28, 1941.

**HUBLEY, SEASON:** NYC, May 14, 1951.

**HUDDLESTON, DAVID:** Vinton, VA, Sept. 17, 1930.

**HUDSON, ERNIE:** Benton Harbor, MI, Dec. 17, 1945.

**HUDSON, KATE:** Los Angeles, Apr. 19, 1979.

**HUGHES, BARNARD:** Bedford Hills, NY, July 16, 1915. Manhattan College.

**HUGHES, KATHLEEN** (Betty von Gerkan): Hollywood, CA, Nov. 14, 1928. UCLA.

**HULCE, TOM:** Plymouth, MI, Dec. 6, 1953. NC Sch. of Arts.

**HUNNICUT, GAYLE:** Ft. Worth, TX, Feb. 6, 1943. UCLA.

**HUNT, HELEN:** Los Angeles, June 15, 1963.

**HUNT, LINDA:** Morristown, NJ, Apr. 1945. Goodman Theatre.

**HUNT, MARSHA:** Chicago, IL, Oct. 17, 1917.

**HUNTER, HOLLY:** Atlanta, GA, Mar. 20, 1958. Carnegie-Mellon.

**HUNTER, KIM** (Janet Cole): Detroit, Nov. 12, 1922.

**HUNTER, TAB** (Arthur Gelien): NYC, July 11, 1931.

**HUPPERT, ISABELLE:** Paris, France, Mar. 16, 1955.

**HURLEY, ELIZABETH:** Hampshire, England, June 10, 1965.

**HURT, JOHN:** Lincolnshire, England, Jan. 22, 1940.

**HURT, MARY BETH** (Supinger): Marshalltown, IA, Sept. 26, 1948. NYU.

**HURT, WILLIAM:** Washington, DC, Mar. 20, 1950. Tufts, Juilliard.

**HUSSEY, RUTH:** Providence, RI, Oct. 30, 1917. U MI.

**HUSTON, ANJELICA:** Santa Monica, CA, July 9, 1951.

**HUTTON, BETTY** (Betty Thornberg): Battle Creek, MI, Feb. 26, 1921.

**HUTTON, LAUREN** (Mary): Charleston, SC, Nov. 17, 1943. Newcomb College.

**HUTTON, TIMOTHY:** Malibu, CA, Aug. 16, 1960.

**HYER, MARTHA:** Fort Worth, TX, Aug. 10, 1924. Northwestern.

Janet Jackson

Samuel L. Jackson

Lainie Kazan

Nastassja Kinski

**ICE CUBE** (O'Shea Jackson): Los Angeles, June 15, 1969.
**IDLE, ERIC:** South Shields, Durham, England, Mar. 29, 1943. Cambridge.
**INGELS, MARTY:** Brooklyn, NY, Mar. 9, 1936.
**IRELAND, KATHY:** Santa Barbara, CA, Mar. 8, 1963.
**IRONS, JEREMY:** Cowes, England, Sept. 19, 1948. Old Vic.
**IRONSIDE, MICHAEL:** Toronto, Canada, Feb. 12, 1950.
**IRVING, AMY:** Palo Alto, CA, Sept. 10, 1953. LADA.
**IRWIN, BILL:** Santa Monica, CA, Apr. 11, 1950.
**ISAAK, CHRIS:** Stockton, CA, June 26, 1956. U Pacific.
**IVANEK, ZELJKO:** Lujubljana, Yugoslavia, Aug. 15, 1957. Yale, LAMDA.
**IVEY, JUDITH:** El Paso, TX, Sept. 4, 1951.
**IZZARD, EDDIE:** Aden, Yemen, Feb. 7, 1962.
**JACKSON, ANNE:** Alleghany, PA, Sept. 3, 1926. Neighborhood Playhouse.
**JACKSON, GLENDA:** Hoylake, Cheshire, England, May 9, 1936. RADA.
**JACKSON, JANET:** Gary, IN, May 16, 1966.
**JACKSON, KATE:** Birmingham, AL, Oct. 29, 1948. AADA.
**JACKSON, MICHAEL:** Gary, IN, Aug. 29, 1958.
**JACKSON, SAMUEL L.:** Atlanta, GA, Dec. 21, 1948.
**JACKSON, VICTORIA:** Miami, FL, Aug. 2, 1958.
**JACOBI, DEREK:** Leytonstone, London, England, Oct. 22, 1938. Cambridge.
**JACOBI, LOU:** Toronto, Canada, Dec. 28, 1913.
**JACOBS, LAWRENCE-HILTON:** Virgin Islands, Sept. 14, 1953.
**JACOBY, SCOTT:** Chicago, IL, Nov. 19, 1956.
**JAGGER, MICK:** Dartford, Kent, England, July 26, 1943.
**JAMES, CLIFTON:** NYC, May 29, 1921. OR U.
**JANNEY, ALLISON:** Dayton, OH, Nov. 20, 1960. RADA.
**JARMAN, CLAUDE, JR.:** Nashville, TN, Sept. 27, 1934.
**JASON, RICK:** NYC, May 21, 1926. AADA.
**JEAN, GLORIA** (Gloria Jean Schoonover): Buffalo, NY, Apr. 14, 1927.
**JEFFREYS, ANNE** (Carmichael): Goldsboro, NC, Jan. 26, 1923. Anderson College.
**JEFFRIES, LIONEL:** London, June 10, 1926. RADA.
**JERGENS, ADELE:** Brooklyn, NY, Nov. 26, 1922.
**JETER, MICHAEL:** Lawrenceburg, TN, Aug. 26, 1952. Memphis St. U.

**JILLIAN, ANN** (Nauseda): Cambridge, MA, Jan. 29, 1951.
**JOHANSEN, DAVID:** Staten Island, NY, Jan. 9, 1950.
**JOHN, ELTON** (Reginald Dwight): Middlesex, England, Mar. 25, 1947. RAM.
**JOHNS, GLYNIS:** Durban, S. Africa, Oct. 5, 1923.
**JOHNSON, DON:** Galena, MO, Dec. 15, 1950. U KS.
**JOHNSON, PAGE:** Welch, WV, Aug. 25, 1930. Ithaca.
**JOHNSON, RAFER:** Hillsboro, TX, Aug. 18, 1935. UCLA.
**JOHNSON, RICHARD:** Essex, England, July 30, 1927. RADA.
**JOHNSON, ROBIN:** Brooklyn, NY, May 29, 1964.
**JOHNSON, VAN:** Newport, RI, Aug. 28, 1916.
**JOLIE, ANGELINA** (Angelina Jolie Voight): Los Angeles, June 4, 1975.
**JONES, CHRISTOPHER:** Jackson, TN, Aug. 18, 1941. Actors Studio.
**JONES, DEAN:** Decatur, AL, Jan. 25, 1931. Actors Studio.
**JONES, GRACE:** Spanishtown, Jamaica, May 19, 1952.
**JONES, JACK:** Bel-Air, CA, Jan. 14, 1938.
**JONES, JAMES EARL:** Arkabutla, MS, Jan. 17, 1931. U Mich.
**JONES, JEFFREY:** Buffalo, NY, Sept. 28, 1947. LAMDA.
**JONES, JENNIFER** (Phyllis Isley): Tulsa, OK, Mar. 2, 1919. AADA.
**JONES, L.Q.** (Justice Ellis McQueen): Aug 19, 1927.
**JONES, ORLANDO:** Mobile, AL, Apr. 10, 1968.
**JONES, SAM J.:** Chicago, IL, Aug. 12, 1954.
**JONES, SHIRLEY:** Smithton, PA, March 31, 1934.
**JONES, TERRY:** Colwyn Bay, Wales, Feb. 1, 1942.
**JONES, TOMMY LEE:** San Saba, TX, Sept. 15, 1946. Harvard.
**JOURDAN, LOUIS:** Marseilles, France, June 19, 1920.
**JOVOVICH, MILLA:** Kiev, Ukraine, Dec. 17, 1975.
**JOY, ROBERT:** Montreal, Canada, Aug. 17, 1951. Oxford.
**JUDD, ASHLEY:** Los Angeles, Apr. 19, 1968.
**JURADO, KATY** (Maria Christina Jurado Garcia): Guadalajara, Mex., Jan. 16, 1927.
**KACZMAREK, JANE:** Milwaukee, WI, Dec. 21, 1955.
**KANE, CAROL:** Cleveland, OH, June 18, 1952.
**KAPLAN, MARVIN:** Brooklyn, NY, Jan. 24, 1924.
**KAPOOR, SHASHI:** Calcutta, India, Mar. 18, 1938.
**KAPRISKY, VALERIE** (Cheres): Paris, France, Aug. 19, 1962.
**KARRAS, ALEX:** Gary, IN, July 15, 1935.
**KARTHEISER, VINCENT:** Minneapolis, MN, May 5, 1979.
**KASSOVITZ, MATHIEU:** Paris, France, Aug. 3, 1967.

**KATT, WILLIAM:** Los Angeles, Feb. 16, 1955.

**KATTAN, CHRIS:** Mt. Baldy, CA, Oct. 19, 1970.

**KAUFMANN, CHRISTINE:** Lansdorf, Graz, Austria, Jan. 11, 1945.

**KAVNER, JULIE:** Burbank, CA, Sept. 7, 1951. UCLA.

**KAZAN, LAINIE** (Levine): Brooklyn, NY, May 15, 1942.

**KAZURINSKY, TIM:** Johnstown, PA, March 3, 1950.

**KEACH, STACY:** Savannah, GA, June 2, 1941. U CA, Yale.

**KEATON, DIANE** (Hall): Los Angeles, Jan. 5, 1946. Neighborhood Playhouse.

**KEATON, MICHAEL:** Coraopolis, PA, Sept. 9, 1951. Kent State.

**KEEGAN, ANDREW:** Los Angeles, Jan. 29, 1979.

**KEEL, HOWARD** (Harold Leek): Gillespie, IL, Apr. 13, 1919.

**KEENER, CATHERINE:** Miami, FL, 1960.

**KEESLAR, MATT:** Grand Rapids, MI, 1972.

**KEITEL, HARVEY:** Brooklyn, NY, May 13, 1939.

**KEITH, DAVID:** Knoxville, TN, May 8, 1954. U TN.

**KELLER, MARTHE:** Basel, Switzerland, 1945. Munich Stanislavsky Sch.

**KELLERMAN, SALLY:** Long Beach, CA, June 2, 1936. Actors Studio West.

**KELLY, MOIRA:** Queens, NY, Mar. 6, 1968.

**KEMP, JEREMY** (Wacker): Chesterfield, England, Feb. 3, 1935. Central Sch.

**KENNEDY, GEORGE:** NYC, Feb. 18, 1925.

**KENNEDY, LEON ISAAC:** Cleveland, OH, 1949.

**KENSIT, PATSY:** London, England, Mar. 4, 1968.

**KERR, DEBORAH:** Helensburg, Scotland, Sept. 30, 1921. Smale Ballet Sch.

**KERR, JOHN:** NYC, Nov. 15, 1931. Harvard, Columbia.

**KERWIN, BRIAN:** Chicago, IL, Oct. 25, 1949.

**KEYES, EVELYN:** Port Arthur, TX, Nov. 20, 1919.

**KIDDER, MARGOT:** Yellow Knife, Canada, Oct. 17, 1948. U BC.

**KIDMAN, NICOLE:** Hawaii, June 20, 1967.

**KIEL, RICHARD:** Detroit, MI, Sept. 13, 1939.

**KIER, UDO:** Koeln, Germany, Oct. 14, 1944.

**KILMER, VAL:** Los Angeles, Dec. 31, 1959. Juilliard.

**KINCAID, ARON** (Norman Neale Williams, III): Los Angeles, June 15, 1943. UCLA.

**KING, ALAN** (Irwin Kniberg): Brooklyn, NY, Dec. 26, 1927.

**KING, PERRY:** Alliance, OH, Apr. 30, 1948. Yale.

**KINGSLEY, BEN** (Krishna Bhanji): Snaiton, Yorkshire, England, Dec. 31, 1943.

**KINNEAR, GREG:** Logansport, IN, June 17, 1963.

**KINSKI, NASTASSJA:** Berlin, Germany, Jan. 24, 1960.

**KIRBY, BRUNO:** NYC, Apr. 28, 1949.

**KIRK, TOMMY:** Louisville, KY, Dec.10 1941.

**KIRKLAND, SALLY:** NYC, Oct. 31, 1944. Actors Studio.

**KITT, EARTHA:** North, SC, Jan. 26, 1928.

**KLEIN, CHRIS:** Hinsdale, IL, March 14, 1979.

**KLEIN, ROBERT:** NYC, Feb. 8, 1942. Alfred U.

**KLINE, KEVIN:** St. Louis, MO, Oct. 24, 1947. Juilliard.

**KLUGMAN, JACK:** Philadelphia, PA, Apr. 27, 1922. Carnegie Tech.

**KNIGHT, MICHAEL E.:** Princeton, NJ, May 7, 1959.

**KNIGHT, SHIRLEY:** Goessel, KS, July 5, 1937. Wichita U.

**KNOX, ELYSE:** Hartford, CT, Dec. 14, 1917. Traphagen School.

**KOENIG, WALTER:** Chicago, IL, Sept. 14, 1936. UCLA.

**KOHNER, SUSAN:** Los Angeles, Nov. 11, 1936. U CA.

**KORMAN, HARVEY:** Chicago, IL, Feb. 15, 1927. Goodman.

**KORSMO, CHARLIE:** Minneapolis, MN, July, 1978.

Lisa Kudrow          Anthony LaPaglia

**KOTEAS, ELIAS:** Montreal, Quebec, Canada, 1961. AADA.

**KOTTO, YAPHET:** NYC, Nov. 15, 1937.

**KOZAK, HARLEY JANE:** Wilkes-Barre, PA, Jan. 28, 1957. NYU.

**KRABBE, JEROEN:** Amsterdam, The Netherlands, Dec. 5, 1944.

**KREUGER, KURT:** St. Moritz, Switzerland, July 23, 1917. U London.

**KRIGE, ALICE:** Upington, South Africa, June 28, 1955.

**KRISTEL, SYLVIA:** Amsterdam, The Netherlands, Sept. 28, 1952.

**KRISTOFFERSON, KRIS:** Brownsville, TX, June 22, 1936. Pomona College.

**KRUGER, HARDY:** Berlin, Germany, April 12, 1928.

**KRUMHOLTZ, DAVID:** NYC, May 15, 1978.

**KUDROW, LISA:** Encino, CA, July 30, 1963.

**KURTZ, SWOOSIE:** Omaha, NE, Sept. 6, 1944.

**KUTCHER, ASHTON** (Christopher A. K.): Cedar Rapids, IA, Feb. 7, 1978.

**KWAN, NANCY:** Hong Kong, May 19, 1939. Royal Ballet.

**LaBELLE, PATTI:** Philadelphia, PA, May 24, 1944.

**LACY, JERRY:** Sioux City, IA, Mar. 27, 1936. LACC.

**LADD, CHERYL** (Stoppelmoor): Huron, SD. July 12, 1951.

**LADD, DIANE** (Ladner): Meridian, MS, Nov. 29, 1932. Tulane.

**LAHTI, CHRISTINE:** Detroit, MI, Apr. 4, 1950. U MI.

**LAKE, RICKI:** NYC, Sept. 21, 1968.

**LAMAS, LORENZO:** Los Angeles, Jan. 28, 1958.

**LAMBERT, CHRISTOPHER:** NYC, Mar. 29, 1958.

**LANDAU, MARTIN:** Brooklyn, NY, June 20, 1931. Actors Studio.

**LANDRUM, TERI:** Enid, OK, 1960.

**LANE, ABBE:** Brooklyn, NY, Dec. 14, 1935.

**LANE, DIANE:** NYC, Jan. 22, 1963.

**LANE, NATHAN:** Jersey City, NJ, Feb. 3, 1956.

**LANG, STEPHEN:** NYC, July 11, 1952. Swarthmore College.

**LANGE, HOPE:** Redding Ridge, CT, Nov. 28, 1931. Reed College.

**LANGE, JESSICA:** Cloquet, MN, Apr. 20, 1949. U MN.

**LANGELLA, FRANK:** Bayonne, NJ, Jan. 1, 1940. Syracuse U.

**LANSBURY, ANGELA:** London, Oct. 16, 1925. London Academy of Music.

**LaPAGLIA, ANTHONY:** Adelaide, Australia. Jan 31, 1959.

**LARROQUETTE, JOHN:** New Orleans, LA, Nov. 25, 1947.

**LASSER, LOUISE:** NYC, Apr. 11, 1939. Brandeis.

**LATIFAH, QUEEN** (Dana Owens): East Orange, NJ, 1970.

**LAUGHLIN, JOHN:** Memphis, TN, Apr. 3.

Cyndi Lauper · Jude Law · Robert Sean Leonard · Patti LuPone

**LAUGHLIN, TOM:** Minneapolis, MN, 1938.
**LAUPER, CYNDI:** Queens, NY, June 20, 1953.
**LAURE, CAROLE:** Montreal, Canada, Aug. 5, 1951.
**LAURIE, HUGH:** Oxford, England, June 11, 1959.
**LAURIE, PIPER** (Rosetta Jacobs): Detroit, MI, Jan. 22, 1932.
**LAUTER, ED:** Long Beach, NY, Oct. 30, 1940.
**LAVIN, LINDA:** Portland, ME, Oct. 15 1939.
**LAW, JOHN PHILLIP:** Hollywood, CA, Sept. 7, 1937. Neighborhood Playhouse, U HI.
**LAW, JUDE:** Lewisham, England, Dec. 29, 1972.
**LAWRENCE, BARBARA:** Carnegie, OK, Feb. 24, 1930. UCLA.
**LAWRENCE, CAROL** (Laraia): Melrose Park, IL, Sept. 5, 1935.
**LAWRENCE, MARTIN:** Frankfurt, Germany, Apr. 16, 1965.
**LAWRENCE, VICKI:** Inglewood, CA, Mar. 26, 1949.
**LAWSON, LEIGH:** Atherston, England, July 21, 1945. RADA.
**LEACHMAN, CLORIS:** Des Moines, IA, Apr. 30, 1930. Northwestern.
**LEARY, DENIS:** Boston, MA, Aug. 18, 1957.
**LEAUD, JEAN-PIERRE:** Paris, France, May 5, 1944.
**LeBLANC, MATT:** Newton, MA, July 25, 1967.
**LEDGER, HEATH:** Perth, Australia, Apr. 4, 1979.
**LEE, CHRISTOPHER:** London, England, May 27, 1922. Wellington College.
**LEE, JASON:** CA, Apr. 25, 1970.
**LEE, MARK:** Sydney, Australia, 1958.
**LEE, MICHELE** (Dusiak): Los Angeles, June 24, 1942. LACC.
**LEE, PEGGY** (Norma Delores Egstrom): Jamestown, ND, May 26, 1920.
**LEE, SHERYL:** Augsburg, Germany, Apr. 22, 1967.
**LEE, SPIKE** (Shelton Lee): Atlanta, GA, Mar. 20, 1957.
**LEGROS, JAMES:** Minneapolis, MN, Apr. 27, 1962.
**LEGUIZAMO, JOHN:** Colombia. July 22, 1965. NYU.
**LEIBMAN, RON:** NYC, Oct. 1l, 1937. Ohio Wesleyan.
**LEIGH, JANET** (Jeanette Helen Morrison): Merced, CA, July 6, 1926. College of Pacific.
**LEIGH, JENNIFER JASON:** Los Angeles, Feb. 5, 1962.
**LeMAT, PAUL:** Rahway, NJ, Sept. 22, 1945.
**LEMMON, CHRIS:** Los Angeles, Jan. 22, 1954.
**LENO, JAY:** New Rochelle, NY, Apr. 28, 1950. Emerson College.
**LENZ, KAY:** Los Angeles, Mar. 4, 1953.
**LENZ, RICK:** Springfield, IL, Nov. 21, 1939. U MI.

**LEONARD, ROBERT SEAN:** Westwood, NJ, Feb. 28, 1969.
**LEONI, TÉA** (Elizabeth Tea Pantaleoni): NYC, Feb. 25, 1966.
**LERNER, MICHAEL:** Brooklyn, NY, June 22, 1941.
**LESLIE, JOAN** (Joan Brodell): Detroit, Jan. 26, 1925. St. Benedict's.
**LESTER, MARK:** Oxford, England, July 11, 1958.
**LETO, JARED:** Bossier City, LA, Dec. 26, 1971.
**LEVELS, CALVIN:** Cleveland, OH, Sept. 30, 1954. CCC.
**LEVIN, RACHEL:** NYC, 1954. Goddard College.
**LEVINE, JERRY:** New Brunswick, NJ, Mar. 12, 1957, Boston U.
**LEVY, EUGENE:** Hamilton, Canada, Dec. 17, 1946. McMaster.
**LEWIS, CHARLOTTE:** London, Aug.7, 1967.
**LEWIS, GEOFFREY:** San Diego, CA, Jan. 1, 1935.
**LEWIS, JERRY** (Joseph Levitch): Newark, NJ, Mar. 16, 1926.
**LEWIS, JULIETTE:** Los Angeles, June 21, 1973.
**LI, JET:** Beijing, China, Apr. 26, 1963.
**LIGON, TOM:** New Orleans, LA, Sept. 10, 1945.
**LILLARD, MATTHEW:** Lansing, MI, Jan. 24, 1970.
**LINCOLN, ABBEY** (Anna Marie Woolridge): Chicago, IL, Aug. 6, 1930.
**LINDEN, HAL:** Bronx, NY, Mar. 20, 1931. CCNY.
**LINDO, DELROY:** London, England, Nov. 18, 1952.
**LINDSAY, ROBERT:** Ilketson, Derbyshire, England, Dec. 13, 1951, RADA.
**LINN-BAKER, MARK:** St. Louis, MO, June 17, 1954. Yale.
**LINNEY, LAURA:** NYC, Feb. 5, 1964.
**LIOTTA, RAY:** Newark, NJ, Dec. 18, 1955. U Miami.
**LISI, VIRNA:** Rome, Italy, Nov. 8, 1937.
**LITHGOW, JOHN:** Rochester, NY, Oct. 19, 1945. Harvard.
**LIU, LUCY:** Queens, NY, Dec. 2, 1967.
**LL COOL J** (James Todd Smith): Queens, NY, Jan. 14, 1968.
**LLOYD, CHRISTOPHER:** Stamford, CT, Oct. 22, 1938.
**LLOYD, EMILY:** London, England, Sept. 29, 1970.
**LOCKE, SONDRA:** Shelbyville, TN, May, 28, 1947.
**LOCKHART, JUNE:** NYC, June 25, 1925. Westlake School.
**LOCKWOOD, GARY:** Van Nuys, CA, Feb. 21, 1937.
**LOGGIA, ROBERT:** Staten Island, NY, Jan. 3, 1930. U MO.
**LOLLOBRIGIDA, GINA:** Subiaco, Italy, July 4, 1927. Rome Academy of Fine Arts.
**LOM, HERBERT:** Prague, Czechoslovakia, Jan. 9, 1917. Prague U.
**LOMEZ, CELINE:** Montreal, Canada, May 11, 1953.
**LONE, JOHN:** Hong Kong, China, Oct 13, 1952. AADA.

LONG, NIA: Brooklyn, NY, Oct. 30, 1970.

LONG, SHELLEY: Ft. Wayne, IN, Aug. 23, 1949. Northwestern.

LOPEZ, JENNIFER: Bronx, NY, July 24, 1970.

LOPEZ, PERRY: NYC, July 22, 1931. NYU.

LORDS, TRACY (Nora Louise Kuzma): Steubenville, OH, May 7, 1968.

LOREN, SOPHIA (Sophia Scicolone): Rome, Italy, Sept. 20, 1934.

LOUIS-DREYFUS, JULIA: NYC, Jan. 13, 1961.

LOUISE, TINA (Blacker): NYC, Feb. 11, 1934, Miami U.

LOVE, COURTNEY (Love Michelle Harrison): San Francisco, CA, July 9, 1965.

LOVETT, LYLE: Klein, TX, Nov. 1, 1957.

LOVITZ, JON: Tarzana, CA, July 21, 1957.

LOWE, CHAD: Dayton, OH, Jan. 15, 1968.

LOWE, ROB: Charlottesville, VA, Mar. 17, 1964.

LOWITSCH, KLAUS: Berlin, Germany, Apr. 8, 1936, Vienna Academy.

LUCAS, LISA: Arizona, 1961.

LUCKINBILL, LAURENCE: Fort Smith, AK, Nov. 21, 1934.

LUFT, LORNA: Los Angeles, Nov. 21, 1952.

LULU (Marie Lawrie): Glasgow, Scotland, Nov. 3, 1948.

LUNA, BARBARA: NYC, Mar. 2, 1939.

LUNDGREN, DOLPH: Stockolm, Sweden, Nov. 3, 1959. Royal Inst.

LuPONE, PATTI: Northport, NY, Apr. 21, 1949, Juilliard.

LYDON, JAMES: Harrington Park, NJ, May 30, 1923.

LYNCH, KELLY: Minneapolis, MN, Jan. 31, 1959.

LYNLEY, CAROL (Jones): NYC, Feb. 13, 1942.

LYON, SUE: Davenport, IA, July 10, 1946.

LYONNE, NATASHA (Braunstein): NYC, Apr. 4, 1979.

MacARTHUR, JAMES: Los Angeles, Dec. 8, 1937. Harvard.

MACCHIO, RALPH: Huntington, NY, Nov. 4, 1961.

MacCORKINDALE, SIMON: Cambridge, England, Feb. 12, 1953.

MACDONALD, KELLY: Glasgow, Scotland, Feb. 23, 1976.

MacDOWELL, ANDIE (Rose Anderson MacDowell): Gaffney, SC, Apr. 21, 1958.

MacFADYEN, ANGUS: Scotland, Oct. 21, 1963.

MacGINNIS, NIALL: Dublin, Ireland, Mar. 29, 1913. Dublin U.

MacGRAW, ALI: NYC, Apr. 1, 1938. Wellesley.

MacLACHLAN, KYLE: Yakima, WA, Feb. 22, 1959. U WA.

MacLAINE, SHIRLEY (Beaty): Richmond, VA, Apr. 24, 1934.

MacLEOD, GAVIN: Mt. Kisco, NY, Feb. 28, 1931.

MacNAUGHTON, ROBERT: NYC, Dec. 19, 1966.

MACNEE, PATRICK: London, England, Feb. 1922.

MacNICOL, PETER: Dallas, TX, Apr. 10, 1954. U MN.

MacPHERSON, ELLE: Sydney, Australia, 1965.

MacVITTIE, BRUCE: Providence, RI, Oct. 14, 1956. Boston U.

MACY, WILLIAM H. (W. H.): Miami, FL, Mar. 13, 1950. Goddard College.

MADIGAN, AMY: Chicago, IL, Sept. 11, 1950. Marquette.

MADONNA (Madonna Louise Veronica Cicone): Bay City, MI, Aug. 16, 1958. U MI.

MADSEN, MICHAEL: Chicago, IL, Sept. 25, 1958.

MADSEN, VIRGINIA: Winnetka, IL, Sept. 11, 1963.

MAGNUSON, ANN: Charleston, WV, Jan. 4, 1956.

MAGUIRE, TOBEY: Santa Monica, CA, June 27, 1975.

MAHARIS, GEORGE: Queens, NY, Sept. 1, 1928. Actors Studio.

MAHONEY, JOHN: Manchester, England, June 20, 1940, WU Ill.

MAILER, STEPHEN: NYC, Mar. 10, 1966. NYU.

MAJORS, LEE: Wyandotte, MI, Apr. 23, 1940. E KY St. College.

Natasha Lyonne

William H. Macy

MAKEPEACE, CHRIS: Toronto, Canada, Apr. 22, 1964.

MAKO (Mako Iwamatsu): Kobe, Japan, Dec. 10, 1933. Pratt Inst.

MALDEN, KARL (Malden Sekulovich): Gary, IN, Mar. 22, 1914.

MALKOVICH, JOHN: Christopher, IL, Dec. 9, 1953, IL St. U.

MALONE, DOROTHY: Chicago, IL, Jan. 30, 1925.

MANN, TERRENCE: KY, 1945. NC Sch. Arts.

MANOFF, DINAH: NYC, Jan. 25, 1958. Cal. Arts.

MANTEGNA, JOE: Chicago, IL, Nov. 13, 1947. Goodman Theatre.

MANZ, LINDA: NYC, 1961.

MARAIS, JEAN: Cherbourg, France, Dec. 11, 1913. St. Germain.

MARCEAU, SOPHIE (Maupu): Paris, France, Nov. 17, 1966.

MARCOVICCI, ANDREA: NYC, Nov. 18, 1948.

MARGULIES, JULIANNA: Spring Valley, NY, June 8, 1966.

MARIN, CHEECH (Richard): Los Angeles, July 13, 1946.

MARIN, JACQUES: Paris, France, Sept. 9, 1919. Conservatoire National.

MARINARO, ED: NYC, Mar. 31, 1950. Cornell.

MARS, KENNETH: Chicago, IL, 1936.

MARSDEN, JAMES: Stillwater, OK, Sept. 18, 1973.

MARSH, JEAN: London, England, July 1, 1934.

MARSHALL, KEN: NYC, 1953. Juilliard.

MARSHALL, PENNY: Bronx, NY, Oct. 15, 1942. U NM.

MARSHALL, WILLIAM: Gary, IN, Aug. 19, 1924. NYU.

MARTIN, ANDREA: Portland, ME, Jan. 15, 1947.

MARTIN, DICK: Battle Creek, MI Jan. 30, 1923.

MARTIN, GEORGE N.: NYC, Aug. 15, 1929.

MARTIN, MILLICENT: Romford, England, June 8, 1934.

MARTIN, PAMELA SUE: Westport, CT, Jan. 15, 1953.

MARTIN, STEVE: Waco, TX, Aug. 14, 1945. UCLA.

MARTIN, TONY (Alfred Norris): Oakland, CA, Dec. 25, 1913. St. Mary's College.

MASON, MARSHA: St. Louis, MO, Apr. 3, 1942. Webster College.

MASSEN, OSA: Copenhagen, Denmark, Jan. 13, 1916.

MASTERS, BEN: Corvallis, OR, May 6, 1947. U OR.

MASTERSON, MARY STUART: Los Angeles, June 28, 1966, NYU.

MASTERSON, PETER: Angleton, TX, June 1, 1934. Rice.

MASTRANTONIO, MARY ELIZABETH: Chicago, IL, Nov. 17, 1958. U IL.

MASUR, RICHARD: NYC, Nov. 20, 1948.

MATHESON, TIM: Glendale, CA, Dec. 31, 1947. Cal. St.

MATHIS, SAMANTHA: NYC, May 12, 1970.

MATLIN, MARLEE: Morton Grove, IL, Aug. 24, 1965.

MATTHEWS, BRIAN: Philadelphia, Jan. 24. 1953. St. Olaf.

MAY, ELAINE (Berlin): Philadelphia, PA, Apr. 21, 1932.

MAYO, VIRGINIA (Virginia Clara Jones): St. Louis, MO, Nov. 30, 1920.

MAYRON, MELANIE: Philadelphia, PA, Oct. 20, 1952. AADA.

MAZURSKY, PAUL: Brooklyn, NY, Apr. 25, 1930. Bklyn College.

MAZZELLO, JOSEPH: Rhinebeck, NJ, Sept. 21, 1983.

McCALLUM, DAVID: Scotland, Sept. 19, 1933. Chapman College.

McCAMBRIDGE, MERCEDES: Jolliet, IL, Mar. 17, 1918. Mundelein College.

McCARTHY, ANDREW: NYC, Nov. 29, 1962, NYU.

McCARTHY, KEVIN: Seattle, WA, Feb. 15, 1914. MN U.

McCARTNEY, PAUL: Liverpool, England, June 18, 1942.

McCLANAHAN, RUE: Healdton, OK, Feb. 21, 1934.

McCLORY, SEAN: Dublin, Ireland, Mar. 8, 1924. U Galway.

McCLURE, MARC: San Mateo, CA, Mar. 31, 1957.

McCLURG, EDIE: Kansas City, MO, July 23, 1950.

McCORMACK, CATHERINE: Alton, Hampshire, Eng., Jan. 1, 1972.

McCOWEN, ALEC: Tunbridge Wells, England, May 26, 1925. RADA.

McCRANE, PAUL: Philadelphia, PA, Jan. 19. 1961.

McCRARY, DARIUS: Walnut, CA, May 1, 1976.

McDERMOTT, DYLAN: Waterbury, CT, Oct. 26, 1962. Neighborhood Playhouse.

McDONALD, CHRISTOPHER: NYC, 1955.

McDONNELL, MARY: Wilkes Barre, PA, Apr. 28, 1952.

McDORMAND, FRANCES: Illinois, June 23, 1957.

McDOWELL, MALCOLM (Taylor): Leeds, England, June 19, 1943. LAMDA.

McELHONE, NATASCHA (Natasha Taylor): London, England, Mar. 23, 1971.

McENERY, PETER: Walsall, England, Feb. 21, 1940.

McENTIRE, REBA: McAlester, OK, Mar. 28, 1955. Southeastern St. U.

McGAVIN, DARREN: Spokane, WA, May 7, 1922. College of Pacific.

McGILL, EVERETT: Miami Beach, FL, Oct. 21, 1945.

McGILLIS, KELLY: Newport Beach, CA, July 9, 1957. Juilliard.

McGINLEY, JOHN C.: NYC, Aug. 3, 1959. NYU.

McGOOHAN, PATRICK: NYC, Mar. 19, 1928.

McGOVERN, ELIZABETH: Evanston, IL. July 18, 1961. Juilliard.

McGOVERN, MAUREEN: Youngstown, OH, July 27, 1949.

McGREGOR, EWAN: Perth, Scotland, March 31, 1971

McGUIRE, BIFF: New Haven, CT, Oct. 25. 1926. MA St. Col.

McHATTIE, STEPHEN: Antigonish, NS, Feb. 3. Acadia U, AADA.

McKAY, GARDNER: NYC, June 10, 1932. Comell.

McKEAN, MICHAEL: NYC, Oct. 17, 1947.

McKEE, LONETTE: Detroit, MI, July 22, 1955.

McKELLEN, IAN: Burnley, England, May 25, 1939.

McKENNA, VIRGINIA: London, England, June 7, 1931.

McKEON, DOUG: Pompton Plains, NJ, June 10, 1966.

McKERN, LEO: Sydney, Australia, Mar. 16, 1920.

McKUEN, ROD: Oakland, CA, Apr. 29, 1933.

McLERIE, ALLYN ANN: Grand Mere, Canada, Dec. 1, 1926.

McMAHON, ED: Detroit, MI, Mar. 6, 1923.

McNAIR, BARBARA: Chicago, IL, Mar. 4, 1939. UCLA.

McNAMARA, WILLIAM: Dallas, TX, Mar. 31, 1965.

McNICHOL, KRISTY: Los Angeles, Sept. 11, 1962.

McQUEEN, ARMELIA: NC, Jan. 6, 1952. Bklyn Consv.

McQUEEN, CHAD: Los Angeles, Dec. 28, 1960. Actors Studio.

McRANEY, GERALD: Collins, MS, Aug. 19, 1948.

McSHANE, IAN: Blackburn, England, Sept. 29, 1942. RADA.

McTEER, JANET: York, England, 1961.

MEADOWS, JAYNE (Jayne Cotter): Wuchang, China, Sept. 27, 1924. St. Margaret's.

MEANEY, COLM: Dublin, Ireland, May 30, 1953.

MEARA, ANNE: Brooklyn, NY, Sept. 20, 1929.

MEAT LOAF (Marvin Lee Aday): Dallas, TX, Sept. 27, 1947.

MEDWIN, MICHAEL: London, England, 1925. Inst. Fischer.

MEKKA, EDDIE: Worcester, MA, June 14, 1952. Boston Cons.

MELATO, MARIANGELA: Milan, Italy, 1941. Milan Theatre Acad.

MEREDITH, LEE (Judi Lee Sauls): Oct. 22, 1947. AADA.

MERKERSON, S. EPATHA: Saganaw, MI, Nov. 28, 1952. Wayne St. U.

MERRILL, DINA (Nedinia Hutton): NYC, Dec. 29, 1925. AADA.

MESSING, DEBRA: Brooklyn, NY, Aug. 15, 1968.

METCALF, LAURIE: Edwardsville, IL, June 16, 1955. IL St. U.

METZLER, JIM: Oneonta, NY, June 23, 1955. Dartmouth.

MEYER, BRECKIN: Minneapolis, MN, May 7, 1974.

MICHELL, KEITH: Adelaide, Australia, Dec. 1, 1926.

MIDLER, BETTE: Honolulu, HI, Dec. 1, 1945.

MILANO, ALYSSA: Brooklyn, NY, Dec. 19, 1972.

MILES, JOANNA: Nice, France, Mar. 6, 1940.

MILES, SARAH: Ingatestone, England, Dec. 31, 1941. RADA.

MILES, SYLVIA: NYC, Sept. 9, 1934. Actors Studio.

MILES, VERA (Ralston): Boise City, OK, Aug. 23, 1929. UCLA.

MILLER, ANN (Lucille Ann Collier): Chireno, TX, Apr. 12, 1919. Lawler Professional School.

MILLER, BARRY: Los Angeles, Feb. 6, 1958.

MILLER, DICK: NYC, Dec. 25, 1928.

MILLER, JONNY LEE: Surrey, England, Nov. 15, 1972.

MILLER, LINDA: NYC, Sept. 16, 1942. Catholic U.

MILLER, PENELOPE ANN: Santa Monica, CA, Jan. 13, 1964.

MILLER, REBECCA: Roxbury, CT, 1962. Yale.

MILLS, DONNA: Chicago, IL, Dec. 11, 1945. U IL.

MILLS, HAYLEY: London, England, Apr. 18, 1946. Elmhurst School.

MILLS, JOHN: Suffolk, England, Feb. 22, 1908.

MILLS, JULIET: London, England, Nov. 21, 1941.

MILNER, MARTIN: Detroit, MI, Dec. 28, 1931.

MIMIEUX, YVETTE: Los Angeles, Jan. 8, 1941. Hollywood High.

MINNELLI, LIZA: Los Angeles, Mar. 19, l946.

MIOU-MIOU (Sylvette Henry): Paris, France, Feb. 22, 1950.

MIRREN, HELEN (Ilynea Mironoff): London, July 26, 1946.

MITCHELL, JAMES: Sacramento, CA, Feb. 29, 1920. LACC.

MITCHELL, JOHN CAMERON: El Paso, TX, Apr. 21, 1963. Northwestern.

MITCHUM, JAMES: Los Angeles, CA, May 8, 1941.

MODINE, MATTHEW: Loma Linda, CA, Mar. 22, 1959.

MOFFAT, DONALD: Plymouth, England, Dec. 26, 1930. RADA.

MOFFETT, D. W.: Highland Park, IL, Oct. 26, 1954. Stanford.

MOHR, JAY: NJ, Aug. 23, 1971.

MOKAE, ZAKES: Johannesburg, South Africa, Aug. 5, 1935. RADA.

Frances McDormand

Breckin Meyer

Demi Moore

Viggo Mortensen

**MOLINA, ALFRED:** London, England, May 24, 1953. Guildhall.

**MOLL, RICHARD:** Pasadena, CA, Jan. 13, 1943.

**MONAGHAN, DOMINIC:** Berlin, Germany, Dec. 8, 1976.

**MONK, DEBRA:** Middletown, OH, Feb. 27, 1949.

**MONTALBAN, RICARDO:** Mexico City, Mexico, Nov. 25, 1920.

**MONTENEGRO, FERNADA** (Arlete Pinheiro): Rio de Janiero, Brazil, 1929.

**MONTGOMERY, BELINDA:** Winnipeg, Manitoba, Canada, July 23, 1950.

**MOODY, RON:** London, England, Jan. 8, 1924. London U.

**MOOR, BILL:** Toledo, OH, July 13, 1931. Northwestern.

**MOORE, CONSTANCE:** Sioux City, IA, Jan. 18, 1919.

**MOORE, DEMI** (Guines): Roswell, NM, Nov. 11, 1962.

**MOORE, DICK:** Los Angeles, Sept. 12, 1925.

**MOORE, DUDLEY:** Dagenham, Essex, England, Apr. 19, 1935.

**MOORE, JULIANNE** (Julie Anne Smith): Fayetteville, NC, Dec. 30, 1960.

**MOORE, KIERON:** County Cork, Ireland, 1925. St. Mary's College.

**MOORE, MARY TYLER:** Brooklyn, NY, Dec. 29, 1936.

**MOORE, ROGER:** London, England, Oct. 14, 1927. RADA.

**MOORE, TERRY** (Helen Koford): Los Angeles, Jan. 7, 1929.

**MORALES, ESAI:** Brooklyn, NY, Oct. 1, 1962.

**MORANIS, RICK:** Toronto, Canada, Apr. 18, 1954.

**MOREAU, JEANNE:** Paris, France, Jan. 23, 1928.

**MORENO, RITA** (Rosita Alverio): Humacao, PR, Dec. 11, 1931.

**MORGAN, HARRY (HENRY)** (Harry Bratsburg): Detroit, MI, Apr. 10, 1915. U Chicago.

**MORGAN, MICHELE** (Simone Roussel): Paris, France, Feb. 29, 1920. Paris Dramatic School.

**MORIARTY, CATHY:** Bronx, NY, Nov. 29, 1960.

**MORIARTY, MICHAEL:** Detroit, MI, Apr. 5, 1941. Dartmouth.

**MORISON, PATRICIA:** NYC, Mar. 19, 1915.

**MORITA, NORIYUKI "PAT":** Isleton, CA, June 28, 1932.

**MORRIS, GARRETT:** New Orleans, LA, Feb. 1, 1937.

**MORRIS, HOWARD:** NYC, Sept. 4, 1919. NYU.

**MORROW, ROB:** New Rochelle, NY, Sept. 21, 1962.

**MORSE, DAVID:** Hamilton, MA, Oct. 11, 1953.

**MORSE, ROBERT:** Newton, MA, May 18, 1931.

**MORTENSEN, VIGGO:** NYC, Oct. 20, 1958.

**MORTON, JOE:** NYC, Oct. 18, 1947. Hofstra.

**MORTON, SAMANTHA:** Nottingham, England, 1977.

**MOSES, WILLIAM:** Los Angeles, Nov. 17, 1959.

**MOSS, CARRIE-ANNE:** Vancouver, BC, Canada, Aug. 21, 1967.

**MOSTEL, JOSH:** NYC, Dec. 21, 1946. Brandeis U.

**MOUCHET, CATHERINE:** Paris, France, 1959. Ntl. Consv.

**MUELLER-STAHL, ARMIN:** Tilsit, East Prussia, Dec. 17, 1930.

**MULDAUR, DIANA:** NYC, Aug. 19, 1938. Sweet Briar College.

**MULGREW, KATE:** Dubuque, IA, Apr. 29, 1955. NYU.

**MULHERN, MATT:** Philadelphia, PA, July 21, 1960. Rutgers.

**MULL, MARTIN:** N. Ridgefield, OH, Aug. 18, 1941. RI Sch. of Design.

**MULRONEY, DERMOT:** Alexandria, VA, Oct. 31, 1963. Northwestern.

**MUMY, BILL** (Charles William Mumy, Jr.): San Gabriel, CA, Feb. 1, 1954.

**MURPHY, BRITTANY:** Atlanta, GA, Nov. 10, 1977.

**MURPHY, DONNA:** Queens, NY, March 7, 1958.

**MURPHY, EDDIE:** Brooklyn, NY, Apr. 3, 1961.

**MURPHY, MICHAEL:** Los Angeles, May 5, 1938. U AZ.

**MURRAY, BILL:** Wilmette, IL, Sept. 21, 1950. Regis College.

**MURRAY, DON:** Hollywood, CA, July 31, 1929.

**MUSANTE, TONY:** Bridgeport, CT, June 30, 1936. Oberlin College.

**MYERS, MIKE:** Scarborough, Canada, May 25, 1963.

**NABORS, JIM:** Sylacauga, GA, June 12, 1932.

**NADER, GEORGE:** Pasadena, CA, Oct. 19, 1921. Occidental College.

**NADER, MICHAEL:** Los Angeles, 1945.

**NAMATH, JOE:** Beaver Falls, PA, May 31, 1943. U AL.

**NAUGHTON, DAVID:** Hartford, CT, Feb. 13, 1951.

**NAUGHTON, JAMES:** Middletown, CT, Dec. 6, 1945.

**NEAL, PATRICIA:** Packard, KY, Jan. 20, 1926. Northwestern.

**NEESON, LIAM:** Ballymena, Northern Ireland, June 7, 1952.

**NEFF, HILDEGARDE** (Hildegard Knef): Ulm, Germany, Dec. 28, 1925. Berlin Art Acad.

**NEILL, SAM:** Northern Ireland, Sept. 14, 1947. U Canterbury.

**NELL, NATHALIE:** Paris, France, Oct. 1950.

**NELLIGAN, KATE:** London, Ontario, Canada, Mar. 16, 1951. U Toronto.

**NELSON, BARRY** (Robert Nielsen): Oakland, CA, Apr. 16, 1920.

**NELSON, CRAIG T.:** Spokane, WA, Apr. 4, 1946.

Paul Newman          Clive Owen          Amanda Peet          Joaquin Phoenix

**NELSON, DAVID:** NYC, Oct. 24, 1936. USC.

**NELSON, JUDD:** Portland, ME, Nov. 28, 1959, Haverford College.

**NELSON, LORI** (Dixie Kay Nelson): Santa Fe, NM, Aug. 15, 1933.

**NELSON, TRACY:** Santa Monica, CA, Oct. 25, 1963.

**NELSON, WILLIE:** Abbott, TX, Apr. 30, 1933.

**NEMEC, CORIN:** Little Rock, AK, Nov. 5, 1971.

**NERO, FRANCO** (Francisco Spartanero): Parma, Italy, Nov. 23, 1941.

**NESMITH, MICHAEL:** Houston, TX, Dec. 30, 1942.

**NETTLETON, LOIS:** Oak Park, IL, 1931. Actors Studio.

**NEUWIRTH, BEBE:** Princeton, NJ, Dec. 31, 1958.

**NEWHART, BOB:** Chicago, IL, Sept. 5, 1929. Loyola.

**NEWMAN, BARRY:** Boston, MA, Nov. 7, 1938. Brandeis.

**NEWMAN, LARAINE:** Los Angeles, Mar. 2, 1952.

**NEWMAN, NANETTE:** Northampton, England, 1934.

**NEWMAN, PAUL:** Cleveland, OH, Jan. 26, 1925. Yale.

**NEWMAR, JULIE** (Newmeyer): Los Angeles, Aug. 16, 1933.

**NEWTON, THANDIE:** Zambia, 1972.

**NEWTON-JOHN, OLIVIA:** Cambridge, England, Sept. 26, 1948.

**NGUYEN, DUSTIN:** Saigon, Vietnam, Sept. 17, 1962.

**NICHOLAS, DENISE:** Detroit, MI, July 12, 1945.

**NICHOLAS, PAUL:** London, England, 1945.

**NICHOLS, NICHELLE:** Robbins, IL, Dec. 28, 1933.

**NICHOLSON, JACK:** Neptune, NJ, Apr. 22, 1937.

**NICKERSON, DENISE:** NYC, 1959.

**NICOL, ALEX:** Ossining, NY, Jan. 20, 1919. Actors Studio.

**NIELSEN, BRIGITTE:** Denmark, July 15, 1963.

**NIELSEN, LESLIE:** Regina, Saskatchewan. Canada, Feb. 11, 1926. Neighborhood Playhouse.

**NIMOY, LEONARD:** Boston, MA, Mar. 26, 1931. Boston College, Antioch College.

**NIXON, CYNTHIA:** NYC, Apr. 9, 1966. Columbia.

**NOBLE, JAMES:** Dallas, TX, Mar. 5, 1922, SMU.

**NOIRET, PHILIPPE:** Lille, France, Oct. 1, 1930.

**NOLAN, KATHLEEN:** St. Louis, MO, Sept. 27, 1933. Neighborhood Playhouse.

**NOLTE, NICK:** Omaha, NE, Feb. 8, 1940. Pasadena City College.

**NORRIS, BRUCE:** Houston, TX, May 16, 1960. Northwestern.

**NORRIS, CHRISTOPHER:** NYC, Oct. 7, 1943. Lincoln Square Academy

**NORRIS, CHUCK** (Carlos Ray): Ryan, OK, Mar. 10, 1940.

**NORTH, HEATHER:** Pasadena, CA, Dec. 13, 1950. Actors Workshop.

**NORTH, SHEREE** (Dawn Bethel): Los Angeles. Jan. 17, 1933. Hollywood High.

**NORTHAM, JEREMY:** Cambridge, England, Dec. 1, 1961.

**NORTON, EDWARD:** Boston, MA, Aug. 18, 1969.

**NORTON, KEN:** Jacksonville, IL, Aug. 9, 1945.

**NOSEWORTHY, JACK:** Lynn, MA, Dec. 21, 1969.

**NOURI, MICHAEL:** Washington, DC, Dec. 9, 1945.

**NOVAK, KIM** (Marilyn Novak): Chicago, IL, Feb. 13, 1933. LACC.

**NOVELLO, DON:** Ashtabula, OH, Jan. 1, 1943. U Dayton.

**NUYEN, FRANCE** (Vannga): Marseilles, France, July 31, 1939. Beaux Arts School.

**O'BRIAN, HUGH** (Hugh J. Krampe): Rochester, N,. Apr. 19, 1928. Cincinnati U.

**O'BRIEN, CLAY:** Ray, AZ, May 6, 1961.

**O'BRIEN, MARGARET** (Angela Maxine O'Brien): Los Angeles, Jan. 15, 1937.

**O'CONNELL, JERRY** (Jeremiah O'Connell): NYC, Feb. 17, 1974.

**O'CONNOR, CARROLL:** Bronx, NY, Aug. 2, 1924. Dublin National U.

**O'CONNOR, DONALD:** Chicago, IL, Aug. 28, 1925.

**O'CONNOR, GLYNNIS:** NYC, Nov. 19, 1955. NYSU.

**O'DONNELL, CHRIS:** Winetka, IL, June 27, 1970.

**O'DONNELL, ROSIE:** Commack, NY, March 21, 1961.

**O'HARA, CATHERINE:** Toronto, Canada, Mar. 4, 1954.

**O'HARA, MAUREEN** (Maureen Fitz-Simons): Dublin, Ireland, Aug. 17, 1920.

**O'HERLIHY, DAN:** Wexford, Ireland, May 1, 1919. National U.

**O'KEEFE, MICHAEL:** Larchmont, NY, Apr. 24, 1955. NYU, AADA.

**OLDMAN, GARY:** New Cross, South London, England, Mar. 21, 1958.

**OLIN, KEN:** Chicago, IL, July 30, 1954. U PA.

**OLIN, LENA:** Stockholm, Sweden, Mar. 22, 1955.

**OLMOS, EDWARD JAMES:** Los Angeles, Feb. 24, 1947. CSLA.

**O'LOUGHLIN, GERALD S.:** NYC, Dec. 23, 1921. U Rochester.

**OLSON, JAMES:** Evanston, IL, Oct. 8, 1930.

**OLSON, NANCY:** Milwaukee, WI, July 14, 1928. UCLA.

OLYPHANT, TIMOTHY: HI, May 20, 1968.

O'NEAL, GRIFFIN: Los Angeles, 1965.

O'NEAL, RON: Utica, NY, Sept. 1, 1937. OH St.

O'NEAL, RYAN: Los Angeles, Apr. 20, 1941.

O'NEAL, TATUM: Los Angeles, Nov. 5, 1963.

O'NEIL, TRICIA: Shreveport, LA, Mar. 11, 1945. Baylor.

O'NEILL, ED: Youngstown, OH, Apr. 12, 1946.

O'NEILL, JENNIFER: Rio de Janeiro, Brazil, Feb. 20, 1949. Neighborhood Playhouse.

ONTKEAN, MICHAEL: Vancouver, BC, Canada, Jan. 24, 1946.

O'QUINN, TERRY: Newbury, MI, July 15, 1952.

ORBACH, JERRY: Bronx, NY, Oct. 20, 1935.

ORMOND, JULIA: Epsom, England, Jan. 4, 1965.

O'SHEA, MILO: Dublin, Ireland, June 2, 1926.

OSMENT, HALEY JOEL: Los Angeles, Apr. 10, 1988.

O'TOOLE, ANNETTE (Toole): Houston, TX, Apr. 1, 1953. UCLA.

O'TOOLE, PETER: Connemara, Ireland, Aug. 2, 1932. RADA.

OVERALL, PARK: Nashville, TN, Mar. 15, 1957. Tusculum College.

OWEN, CLIVE: Coventry, England, 1965.

OZ, FRANK (Oznowicz): Hereford, England, May 25, 1944.

PACINO, AL: NYC, Apr. 25, 1940.

PACULA, JOANNA: Tamaszow Lubelski, Poland, Jan. 2, 1957. Polish Natl. Theatre Sch.

PAGET, DEBRA (Debralee Griffin): Denver, CO, Aug. 19, 1933.

PAIGE, JANIS (Donna Mae Jaden): Tacoma, WA, Sept. 16, 1922.

PALANCE, JACK (Walter Palanuik): Lattimer, PA, Feb. 18, 1920. U NC.

PALIN, MICHAEL: Sheffield, Yorkshire, England, May 5, 1943, Oxford.

PALMER, BETSY: East Chicago, IN, Nov. 1, 1926. DePaul.

PALMER, GREGG (Palmer Lee): San Francisco, Jan. 25, 1927. U UT.

PALMINTERI, CHAZZ (Calogero Lorenzo Palminteri): NYC, May 15, 1952.

PALTROW, GWYNETH: Los Angeles, Sept. 28, 1973.

PAMPANINI, SILVANA: Rome, Italy, Sept. 25, 1925.

PANEBIANCO, RICHARD: NYC, 1971.

PANKIN, STUART: Philadelphia, PA, Apr. 8, 1946.

PANTOLIANO, JOE: Jersey City, NJ, Sept. 12, 1954.

PAPAS, IRENE: Chiliomodion, Greece, Mar. 9, 1929.

PAQUIN, ANNA: Winnipeg, Manitoba, Canada, July, 24, 1982.

PARE, MICHAEL: Brooklyn, NY, Oct. 9, 1959.

PARKER, COREY: NYC, July 8, 1965. NYU.

PARKER, ELEANOR: Cedarville, OH, June 26, 1922. Pasadena Playhouse.

PARKER, FESS: Fort Worth, TX, Aug. 16, 1925. USC.

PARKER, JAMESON: Baltimore, MD, Nov. l8, 1947. Beloit College.

PARKER, JEAN (Mae Green): Deer Lodge, MT, Aug. 11, 1912.

PARKER, MARY-LOUISE: Ft. Jackson, SC, Aug. 2, 1964. Bard College.

PARKER, NATHANIEL: London, England, 1963.

PARKER, SARAH JESSICA: Nelsonville, OH, Mar. 25, 1965.

PARKER, SUZY (Cecelia Parker): San Antonio, TX, Oct. 28, 1933.

PARKER, TREY: Auburn, AL, May 30, 1972.

PARKINS, BARBARA: Vancouver, BC, Canada, May 22, 1943.

PARKS, MICHAEL: Corona, CA, Apr. 4, 1938.

PARSONS, ESTELLE: Lynn, MA, Nov. 20, 1927. Boston U.

PARTON, DOLLY: Sevierville, TN, Jan. 19, 1946.

PATINKIN, MANDY: Chicago, IL, Nov. 30, 1952. Juilliard.

PATRIC, JASON: NYC, June 17, 1966.

PATRICK, DENNIS: Philadelphia, PA, Mar. 14, 1918.

PATTERSON, LEE: Vancouver, BC, Canada, Mar. 31, 1929. Ontario College.

PATTON, WILL: Charleston, SC, June 14, 1954.

PAULIK, JOHAN: Prague, Czechoslovakia, 1975.

PAVAN, MARISA (Marisa Pierangeli): Cagliari, Sardinia, June 19, 1932. Torquado Tasso College.

PAXTON, BILL: Fort Worth, TX, May 17, 1955.

PAYMER, DAVID: Long Island, NY, Aug. 30, 1954.

PAYS, AMANDA: Berkshire, England, June 6, 1959.

PEACH, MARY: Durban, South Africa, 1934.

PEARCE, GUY: Ely, England, Oct. 5, 1967.

PEARSON, BEATRICE: Dennison, TX, July 27, 1920.

PECK, GREGORY: La Jolla, CA, Apr. 5, 1916. U CA.

PEET, AMANDA: NYC, Jan. 11, 1972.

PEÑA, ELIZABETH: Cuba, Sept. 23, 1961.

PENDLETON, AUSTIN: Warren, OH, Mar. 27, 1940. Yale.

PENHALL, BRUCE: Balboa, CA, Aug. 17, 1960.

PENN, SEAN: Burbank, CA, Aug. 17, 1960.

PEREZ, JOSE: NYC, 1940.

PEREZ, ROSIE: Brooklyn, NY, Sept. 6, 1964.

PERKINS, ELIZABETH: Queens, NY, Nov. 18, 1960. Goodman School.

PERKINS, MILLIE: Passaic, NJ, May 12, 1938.

PERLMAN, RHEA: Brooklyn, NY, Mar. 31, 1948.

PERLMAN, RON: NYC, Apr. 13, 1950. U MN.

PERREAU, GIGI (Ghislaine): Los Angeles, Feb. 6, 1941.

PERRINE, VALERIE: Galveston, TX, Sept. 3, 1943. U AZ.

PERRY, LUKE (Coy Luther Perry, III): Fredricktown, OH, Oct. 11, 1966.

PESCI, JOE: Newark, NJ. Feb. 9, 1943.

PESCOW, DONNA: Brooklyn, NY, Mar. 24, 1954.

PETERS, BERNADETTE (Lazzara): Jamaica, NY, Feb. 28, 1948.

PETERS, BROCK: NYC, July 2, 1927. CCNY.

PETERSEN, PAUL: Glendale, CA, Sept. 23, 1945. Valley College.

PETERSEN, WILLIAM: Chicago, IL, Feb. 21, 1953.

PETERSON, CASSANDRA: Colorado Springs, CO, Sept. 17, 1951.

PETTET, JOANNA: London, England, Nov. 16, 1944. Neighborhood Playhouse.

PETTY, LORI: Chattanooga, TN, 1964.

PFEIFFER, MICHELLE: Santa Ana, CA, Apr. 29, 1958.

PHIFER, MEKHI: NYC, Dec. 12, 1975.

PHILLIPPE, RYAN (Matthew Phillippe): New Castle, DE, Sept. 10, 1975.

PHILLIPS, LOU DIAMOND: Phillipines, Feb. 17, 1962, U TX.

PHILLIPS, MacKENZIE: Alexandria, VA, Nov. 10, 1959.

PHILLIPS, MICHELLE (Holly Gilliam): Long Beach, CA, June 4, 1944.

PHILLIPS, SIAN: Bettws, Wales, May 14, 1934. U Wales.

PHOENIX, JOAQUIN: PR, Oct. 28, 1974.

PICARDO, ROBERT: Philadelphia, PA, Oct. 27, 1953. Yale.

PICERNI, PAUL: NYC, Dec. 1, 1922. Loyola.

PIDGEON, REBECCA: Cambridge, MA, 1963.

PIERCE, DAVID HYDE: Saratoga Springs, NY, Apr. 3, 1959.

PIGOTT-SMITH, TIM: Rugby, England, May 13, 1946.

PINCHOT, BRONSON: NYC, May 20, 1959. Yale.

PINE, PHILLIP: Hanford, CA, July 16, 1920. Actors' Lab.

PISCOPO, JOE: Passaic, NJ, June 17, 1951.

PISIER, MARIE-FRANCE: Vietnam, May 10, 1944. U Paris.

PITILLO, MARIA: Mahwah, NJ, 1965.

PITT, BRAD (William Bradley Pitt): Shawnee, OK, Dec. 18, 1963.

PIVEN, JEREMY: NYC, July 26, 1965.

PLACE, MARY KAY: Tulsa OK, Sept. 23, 1947. U Tulsa.

PLATT, OLIVER: Oct. 10, 1960.

PLAYTEN, ALICE: NYC, Aug. 28, 1947. NYU.

PLESHETTE, SUZANNE: NYC, Jan. 31, 1937. Syracuse U.

PLIMPTON, MARTHA: NYC, Nov. 16, 1970.

PLOWRIGHT, JOAN: Scunthorpe, Brigg, Lincolnshire, England, Oct. 28, 1929. Old Vic.

PLUMB, EVE: Burbank, CA, Apr. 29, 1958.

PLUMMER, AMANDA: NYC, Mar. 23, 1957. Middlebury College.

PLUMMER, CHRISTOPHER: Toronto, Canada, Dec. 13, 1927.

PODESTA, ROSSANA: Tripoli, Libya, June 20, 1934.

POITIER, SIDNEY: Miami, FL, Feb. 27, 1927.

POLANSKI, ROMAN: Paris, France, Aug. 18, 1933.

POLITO, JON: Philadelphia, PA, Dec. 29, 1950. Villanova.

POLITO, LINA: Naples, Italy, Aug. 11, 1954.

POLLACK, SYDNEY: South Bend, IN, July 1, 1934.

POLLAK, KEVIN: San Francisco, CA, Oct. 30, 1958.

POLLAN, TRACY: NYC, June 22, 1960.

POLLARD, MICHAEL J.: Passaic, NJ, May 30, 1939.

POLLEY, SARAH: Jan. 8, 1979.

PORTMAN, NATALIE; Jerusalem, Israel, June 9, 1981.

POSEY, PARKER: Baltimore, MD, Nov. 8, 1968.

POSTLETHWAITE, PETE: London, England, Feb. 7, 1945.

POTTER, MONICA: Cleveland, OH, June 30, 1971.

POTTS, ANNIE: Nashville, TN, Oct. 28, 1952. Stephens College.

POWELL, JANE (Suzanne Burce): Portland, OR, Apr. 1, 1928.

POWELL, ROBERT: Salford, England, June 1, 1944. Manchester U.

POWER, TARYN: Los Angeles, Sept. 13, 1953.

POWER, TYRONE, IV: Los Angeles, Jan. 22, 1959.

POWERS, MALA (Mary Ellen): San Francisco, CA, Dec. 29, 1921. UCLA.

POWERS, STEFANIE (Federkiewicz): Hollywood, CA, Oct. 12, 1942.

PRENTISS, PAULA (Paula Ragusa): San Antonio, TX, Mar. 4, 1939. Northwestern.

PRESLE, MICHELINE (Micheline Chassagne): Paris, France, Aug. 22, 1922. Rouleau Drama School.

PRESLEY, PRISCILLA: Brooklyn, NY, May 24, 1945.

PRESNELL, HARVE: Modesto, CA, Sept. 14, 1933. USC.

PRESTON, KELLY: Honolulu, HI, Oct. 13, 1962. USC.

PRESTON, WILLIAM: Columbia, PA, Aug. 26, 1921. PA St. U.

PRICE, LONNY: NYC, Mar. 9, 1959. Juilliard.

PRIESTLEY, JASON: Vancouver, BC, Canada, Aug, 28, 1969.

PRIMUS, BARRY: NYC, Feb. 16, 1938. CCNY.

PRINCE (P. Rogers Nelson): Minneapolis, MN, June 7, 1958.

PRINCIPAL, VICTORIA: Fukuoka, Japan, Jan. 3, 1945. Dade Jr. College.

PRINZE, FREDDIE, JR.: Los Angeles, March 8, 1976.

PROCHNOW, JURGEN: Berlin, Germany, June 10, 1941.

PROSKY, ROBERT: Philadelphia, PA, Dec. 13, 1930.

PROVAL, DAVID: Brooklyn, NY, May 20, 1942.

PROVINE, DOROTHY: Deadwood, SD, Jan. 20, 1937. U WA.

PRYCE, JONATHAN: Wales, UK, June 1, 1947, RADA.

PRYOR, RICHARD: Peoria, IL, Dec. 1, 1940.

PULLMAN, BILL: Delphi, NY, Dec. 17, 1954. SUNY/Oneonta, U MA.

PURCELL, LEE: Cherry Point, NC, June 15, 1947. Stephens.

PURDOM, EDMUND: Welwyn Garden City, England, Dec. 19, 1924. St. Ignatius College.

QUAID, DENNIS: Houston, TX, Apr. 9, 1954.

QUAID, RANDY: Houston, TX, Oct. 1, 1950. U Houston.

QUINLAN, KATHLEEN: Mill Valley, CA, Nov. 19, 1954.

QUINN, AIDAN: Chicago, IL, Mar. 8, 1959.

RADCLIFFE, DANIEL: London, England, July 23, 1989.

RAFFERTY, FRANCES: Sioux City, IA, June 16, 1922. UCLA.

RAFFIN, DEBORAH: Los Angeles, Mar. 13, 1953. Valley College.

RAGSDALE, WILLIAM: El Dorado, AK, Jan. 19, 1961. Hendrix College.

RAILSBACK, STEVE: Dallas, TX, 1948.

RAINER, LUISE: Vienna, Austria, Jan. 12, 1910.

RALSTON, VERA (Vera Helena Hruba): Prague, Czechoslovakia, July 12, 1919.

RAMIS, HAROLD: Chicago, IL, Nov. 21, 1944. Washington U.

RAMPLING, CHARLOTTE: Surmer, England, Feb. 5, 1946. U Madrid.

RAMSEY, LOGAN: Long Beach, CA, Mar. 21, 1921. St. Joseph.

RANDALL, TONY (Leonard Rosenberg): Tulsa, OK, Feb. 26, 1920. Northwestern.

RANDELL, RON: Sydney, Australia, Oct. 8, 1920. St. Mary's College.

RAPAPORT, MICHAEL: March 20, 1970.

RAPP, ANTHONY: Chicago, IL, Oct. 26, 1971.

RASCHE, DAVID: St. Louis, MO, Aug. 7, 1944.

REA, STEPHEN: Belfast, Northern Ireland, Oct. 31, 1949.

REAGAN, RONALD: Tampico, IL, Feb. 6, 1911. Eureka College.

REASON, REX: Berlin, Germany, Nov. 30, 1928. Pasadena Playhouse.

REDDY, HELEN: Melbourne, Australia, Oct. 25, 1942.

REDFORD, ROBERT: Santa Monica, CA, Aug. 18, 1937. AADA.

REDGRAVE, CORIN: London, England, July 16, 1939.

REDGRAVE, LYNN: London, England, Mar. 8, 1943.

REDGRAVE, VANESSA: London, England, Jan. 30, 1937.

REDMAN, JOYCE: County Mayo, Ireland, 1919. RADA.

REED, PAMELA: Tacoma, WA, Apr. 2, 1949.

REEMS, HARRY (Herbert Streicher): Bronx, NY, 1947. U Pittsburgh.

REES, ROGER: Aberystwyth, Wales, May 5, 1944.

REESE, DELLA: Detroit, MI, July 6, 1932.

REEVE, CHRISTOPHER: NYC, Sept. 25, 1952. Cornell, Juilliard.

REEVES, KEANU: Beiruit, Lebanon, Sept. 2, 1964.

REGEHR, DUNCAN: Lethbridge, Canada, Oct. 5, 1952.

REID, ELLIOTT: NYC, Jan. 16, 1920.

REID, TIM: Norfolk, VA, Dec, 19, 1944.

REILLY, CHARLES NELSON: NYC, Jan. 13, 1931. U CT.

REILLY, JOHN C.: Chicago, IL, May 24, 1965.

REINER, CARL: NYC, Mar. 20, 1922. Georgetown.

REINER, ROB: NYC, Mar. 6, 1947. UCLA.

Burt Reynolds

Christina Ricci

Cliff Robertson

Mimi Rogers

**REINHOLD, JUDGE** (Edward Ernest, Jr.): Wilmington, DE, May 21, 1957. NC Sch. of Arts.

**REINKING, ANN:** Seattle, WA, Nov. 10, 1949.

**REISER, PAUL:** NYC, Mar. 30, 1957.

**REMAR, JAMES:** Boston, MA, Dec. 31, 1953. Neighborhood Playhouse.

**RENFRO, BRAD:** Knoxville, TN, July 25, 1982.

**RENO, JEAN** (Juan Moreno): Casablanca, Morocco, July 30, 1948.

**REUBENS, PAUL** (Paul Reubenfeld): Peekskill, NY, Aug. 27, 1952.

**REVILL, CLIVE:** Wellington, New Zealand, Apr. 18, 1930.

**REY, ANTONIA:** Havana, Cuba, Oct. 12, 1927.

**REYNOLDS, BURT:** Waycross, GA, Feb. 11, 1935. FL. St. U.

**REYNOLDS, DEBBIE** (Mary Frances Reynolds): El Paso, TX, Apr. 1, 1932.

**RHOADES, BARBARA:** Poughkeepsie, NY, Mar. 23, 1947.

**RHODES, CYNTHIA:** Nashville, TN, Nov. 21, 1956.

**RHYS-DAVIES, JOHN:** Salisbury, England, May 5, 1944.

**RHYS-MEYERS, JONATHAN:** Cork, Ireland, July 27, 1977.

**RIBISI, GIOVANNI:** Los Angeles, Dec. 17, 1974.

**RICCI, CHRISTINA:** Santa Monica, CA, Feb. 12, 1980.

**RICHARD, CLIFF** (Harry Webb): India, Oct. 14, 1940.

**RICHARDS, DENISE:** Downers Grove, IL, Feb. 17, 1972.

**RICHARDS, MICHAEL:** Culver City, CA, July 14, 1949.

**RICHARDSON, JOELY:** London, England, Jan. 9, 1965.

**RICHARDSON, MIRANDA:** Southport, England, Mar. 3, 1958.

**RICHARDSON, NATASHA:** London, England, May 11, 1963.

**RICKLES, DON:** NYC, May 8, 1926. AADA.

**RICKMAN, ALAN:** Hammersmith, England, Feb. 21, 1946.

**RIEGERT, PETER:** NYC, Apr. 11, 1947. U Buffalo.

**RIFKIN, RON:** NYC, Oct. 31, 1939.

**RIGG, DIANA:** Doncaster, England, July 20, 1938. RADA.

**RILEY, JOHN C.:** Chicago, IL, May 24, 1965.

**RINGWALD, MOLLY:** Rosewood, CA, Feb. 16, 1968.

**RITTER, JOHN:** Burbank, CA, Sept. 17, 1948. USC.

**RIVERS, JOAN** (Molinsky): Brooklyn, NY, June 8, 1933.

**ROACHE, LINUS:** Manchester, England, 1964.

**ROBARDS, SAM:** NYC, Dec. 16, 1963.

**ROBBINS, TIM:** NYC, Oct. 16, 1958. UCLA.

**ROBERTS, ERIC:** Biloxi, MS, Apr. 18, 1956. RADA.

**ROBERTS, JULIA:** Atlanta, GA, Oct. 28, 1967.

**ROBERTS, RALPH:** Salisbury, NC, Aug. 17, 1922. UNC.

**ROBERTS, TANYA** (Leigh): Bronx, NY, Oct. 15, 1954.

**ROBERTS, TONY:** NYC, Oct. 22, 1939. Northwestern.

**ROBERTSON, CLIFF:** La Jolla, CA, Sept. 9, 1925. Antioch College.

**ROBERTSON, DALE:** Oklahoma City, OK, July 14, 1923.

**ROBINSON, CHRIS:** West Palm Beach, FL, Nov. 5, 1938. LACC.

**ROBINSON, JAY:** NYC, Apr. 14, 1930.

**ROBINSON, ROGER:** Seattle, WA, May 2, 1940. USC.

**ROCHEFORT, JEAN:** Paris, France, 1930.

**ROCK, CHRIS:** Brooklyn, NY, Feb. 7, 1966.

**ROCKWELL, SAM:** Daly City, CA, Nov. 5, 1968.

**ROGERS, MIMI:** Coral Gables, FL, Jan. 27, 1956.

**ROGERS, WAYNE:** Birmingham, AL, Apr. 7, 1933. Princeton.

**RONSTADT, LINDA:** Tucson, AZ, July 15, 1946.

**ROOKER, MICHAEL:** Jasper, AL, Apr. 6, 1955.

**ROONEY, MICKEY** (Joe Yule, Jr.): Brooklyn, NY, Sept. 23, 1920.

**ROSE, REVA:** Chicago, IL, July 30, 1940. Goodman.

**ROSEANNE** (Barr): Salt Lake City, UT, Nov. 3, 1952.

**ROSS, DIANA:** Detroit, MI, Mar. 26, 1944.

**ROSS, JUSTIN:** Brooklyn, NY, Dec. 15, 1954.

**ROSS, KATHARINE:** Hollywood, Jan. 29, 1943. Santa Rosa College.

**ROSSELLINI, ISABELLA:** Rome, Italy, June 18, 1952.

**ROSSOVICH, RICK:** Palo Alto, CA, Aug. 28, 1957.

**ROTH, TIM:** London, England, May 14, 1961.

**ROUNDTREE, RICHARD:** New Rochelle, NY, Sept. 7, 1942. Southern IL.

**ROURKE, MICKEY** (Philip Andre Rourke, Jr.): Schenectady, NY, Sept. 16, 1956.

**ROWE, NICHOLAS:** London, England, Nov. 22, 1966, Eton.

**ROWLANDS, GENA:** Cambria, WI, June 19, 1934.

**RUBIN, ANDREW:** New Bedford, MA, June 22, 1946. AADA.

**RUBINEK, SAUL:** Fohrenwold, Germany, July 2, 1948.

**RUBINSTEIN, JOHN:** Los Angeles, Dec. 8, 1946. UCLA.

**RUCK, ALAN:** Cleveland, OH, July 1, 1960.

**RUCKER, BO:** Tampa, FL, Aug. 17, 1948.

**RUDD, PAUL S.:** Boston, MA, May 15, 1940.

**RUDD, PAUL:** Passaic, NJ, Apr. 6, 1969.

Susan Sarandon    Diana Scarwid    Stellan Skarsgård    Christian Slater

**RUDNER, RITA:** Miami, FL, Sept. 17, 1955.
**RUEHL, MERCEDES:** Queens, NY, Feb. 28, 1948.
**RULE, JANICE:** Cincinnati, OH, Aug. 15, 1931.
**RUPERT, MICHAEL:** Denver, CO, Oct. 23, 1951. Pasadena Playhouse.
**RUSH, BARBARA:** Denver, CO, Jan. 4, 1927. U Calif.
**RUSH, GEOFFREY:** Toowoomba, Queensland, Australia, July 6, 1951. U Queensland.
**RUSSELL, JANE:** Bemidji, MI, June 21, 1921. Max Reinhardt Sch.
**RUSSELL, KURT:** Springfield, MA, Mar. 17, 1951.
**RUSSELL, THERESA** (Paup): San Diego, CA, Mar. 20, 1957.
**RUSSO, JAMES:** NYC, Apr. 23, 1953.
**RUSSO, RENE:** Burbank, CA, Feb. 17, 1954.
**RUTHERFORD, ANN:** Toronto, Canada, Nov. 2, 1920.
**RYAN, JOHN P.:** NYC, July 30, 1936. CCNY.
**RYAN, MEG:** Fairfield, CT, Nov. 19, 1961. NYU.
**RYAN, TIM** (Meineslschmidt): Staten Island, NY, 1958. Rutgers.
**RYDER, WINONA** (Horowitz): Winona, MN, Oct. 29, 1971.
**SACCHI, ROBERT:** Bronx, NY, 1941. NYU.
**SÄGEBRECHT, MARIANNE:** Starnberg, Bavaria, Aug. 27, 1945.
**SAINT, EVA MARIE:** Newark, NJ, July 4, 1924. Bowling Green St. U.
**SAINT JAMES, SUSAN** (Suzie Jane Miller): Los Angeles, Aug. 14, 1946. CT College.
**ST. JOHN, BETTA:** Hawthorne, CA, Nov. 26, 1929.
**ST. JOHN, JILL** (Jill Oppenheim): Los Angeles, Aug. 19, 1940.
**SALA, JOHN:** Los Angeles, Oct. 5, 1962.
**SALDANA, THERESA:** Brooklyn, NY, Aug. 20, 1954.
**SALINGER, MATT:** Windsor, VT, Feb. 13, 1960. Princeton, Columbia.
**SALT, JENNIFER:** Los Angeles, Sept. 4, 1944. Sarah Lawrence College.
**SAMMS, EMMA:** London, England, Aug. 28, 1960.
**SAN GIACOMO, LAURA:** Orange, NJ, Nov. 14, 1961.
**SANDERS, JAY O.:** Austin, TX, Apr. 16, 1953.
**SANDLER, ADAM:** Bronx, NY, Sept. 9, 1966. NYU.
**SANDS, JULIAN:** Yorkshire, England, Jan 15, 1958.
**SANDS, TOMMY:** Chicago, IL, Aug. 27, 1937.
**SAN JUAN, OLGA:** NYC, Mar. 16, 1927.
**SARA, MIA** (Sarapocciello): Brooklyn, NY, June 19, 1967.

**SARANDON, CHRIS:** Beckley, WV, July 24, 1942. U WV, Catholic U.
**SARANDON, SUSAN** (Tomalin): NYC, Oct. 4, 1946. Catholic U.
**SARRAZIN, MICHAEL:** Quebec City, Quebec, Canada, May 22, 1940.
**SAVAGE, FRED:** Highland Park, IL, July 9, 1976.
**SAVAGE, JOHN** (Youngs): Long Island, NY, Aug. 25, 1949. AADA.
**SAVIOLA, CAMILLE:** Bronx, NY, July 16, 1950.
**SAVOY, TERESA ANN:** London, England, July 18, 1955.
**SAXON, JOHN** (Carmen Orrico): Brooklyn, NY, Aug. 5, 1935.
**SBARGE, RAPHAEL:** NYC, Feb. 12, 1964.
**SCACCHI, GRETA:** Milan, Italy, Feb. 18, 1960.
**SCALIA, JACK:** Brooklyn, NY, Nov. 10, 1951.
**SCARWID, DIANA:** Savannah, GA, Aug. 27, 1955, AADA. Pace U.
**SCHEIDER, ROY:** Orange, NJ, Nov. 10, 1932. Franklin-Marshall.
**SCHEINE, RAYNOR:** Emporia, VA, Nov. 10. VA Commonwealth U.
**SCHELL, MARIA:** Vienna, Austria, Jan. 15, 1926.
**SCHELL, MAXIMILIAN:** Vienna, Austria, Dec. 8, 1930.
**SCHLATTER, CHARLIE:** Englewood, NJ, May 1, 1966. Ithaca College.
**SCHNEIDER, JOHN:** Mt. Kisco, NY, Apr. 8, 1960.
**SCHNEIDER, MARIA:** Paris, France, Mar. 27, 1952.
**SCHREIBER, LIEV:** San Francisco, CA, Oct. 4, 1967.
**SCHRODER, RICK:** Staten Island, NY, Apr. 13, 1970.
**SCHUCK, JOHN:** Boston, MA, Feb. 4, 1940.
**SCHULTZ, DWIGHT:** Milwaukee, WI, Nov. 10, 1938. Marquette.
**SCHWARZENEGGER, ARNOLD:** Austria, July 30, 1947.
**SCHWARTZMAN, JASON:** Los Angeles, June 26, 1980.
**SCHWIMMER, DAVID:** Queens, NY, Nov. 12, 1966.
**SCHYGULLA, HANNA:** Katlowitz, Germany, Dec. 25, 1943.
**SCIORRA, ANNABELLA:** NYC, Mar. 24, 1964.
**SCOFIELD, PAUL:** Hurstpierpoint, England, Jan. 21, 1922. London Mask Theatre Sch.
**SCOGGINS, TRACY:** Galveston, TX, Nov. 13, 1959.
**SCOLARI, PETER:** Scarsdale, NY, Sept. 12, 1956. NYCC.
**SCOTT, CAMPBELL:** South Salem, NY, July 19, 1962. Lawrence.
**SCOTT, DEBRALEE:** Elizabeth, NJ, Apr. 2, 1953
**SCOTT, GORDON** (Gordon M. Werschkul): Portland, OR, Aug. 3, 1927. Oregon U.
**SCOTT, LIZABETH** (Emma Matso): Scranton, PA, Sept. 29, 1922.

**SCOTT, MARTHA:** Jamesport, MO, Sept. 22, 1914. U MI.

**SCOTT THOMAS, KRISTIN:** Redruth, Cornwall, England, May 24, 1960.

**SEAGAL, STEVEN:** Detroit, MI, Apr. 10, 1951.

**SEARS, HEATHER:** London, England, Sept. 28, 1935.

**SEDGWICK, KYRA:** NYC, Aug. 19, 1965. USC.

**SEGAL, GEORGE:** NYC, Feb. 13, 1934. Columbia.

**SELBY, DAVID:** Morganstown, WV, Feb. 5, 1941. UWV.

**SELLARS, ELIZABETH:** Glasgow, Scotland, May 6, 1923.

**SELLECK, TOM:** Detroit, MI, Jan. 29, 1945. USC.

**SERBEDZIJA, RADE:** Bunic, Yugoslavia, July 27, 1946.

**SERNAS, JACQUES:** Lithuania, July 30, 1925.

**SERRAULT, MICHEL:** Brunoy, France. Jan. 24, 1928. Paris Cons.

**SETH, ROSHAN:** New Delhi, India. 1942.

**SEWELL, RUFUS:** Twickenham, England, Oct. 29, 1967.

**SEYMOUR, JANE** (Joyce Frankenberg): Hillingdon, England, Feb. 15, 1952.

**SHALHOUB, TONY:** Oct. 7, 1953.

**SHARIF, OMAR** (Michel Shalhoub): Alexandria, Egypt, Apr. 10, 1932. Victoria College.

**SHANDLING, GARRY:** Chicago, IL, Nov. 29, 1949.

**SHATNER, WILLIAM:** Montreal, Canada, Mar. 22, 1931. McGill.

**SHAVER, HELEN:** St. Thomas, Ontario, Canada, Feb. 24, 1951.

**SHAW, FIONA:** Cork, Ireland, July 10, 1955. RADA.

**SHAW, STAN:** Chicago, IL, 1952.

**SHAWN, WALLACE:** NYC, Nov. 12, 1943. Harvard.

**SHEA, JOHN:** North Conway, NH, Apr. 14, 1949. Bates, Yale.

**SHEARER, HARRY:** Los Angeles, Dec. 23, 1943. UCLA.

**SHEARER, MOIRA:** Dunfermline, Scotland, Jan. 17, 1926. London Theatre School.

**SHEEDY, ALLY:** NYC, June 13, 1962. USC.

**SHEEN, CHARLIE** (Carlos Irwin Estevez): Santa Monica, CA, Sept. 3, 1965.

**SHEEN, MARTIN** (Ramon Estevez): Dayton, OH, Aug. 3, 1940.

**SHEFFER, CRAIG:** York, PA, Apr. 23, 1960. E Stroudsberg U.

**SHEFFIELD, JOHN:** Pasadena, CA, Apr. 11, 1931. UCLA.

**SHELLEY, CAROL:** London, England, Aug. 16, 1939.

**SHEPARD, SAM** (Rogers): Ft. Sheridan, IL, Nov. 5, 1943.

**SHEPHERD, CYBILL:** Memphis, TN, Feb. 18, 1950. Hunter College, NYU.

**SHER, ANTONY:** England, June 14, 1949.

**SHERIDAN, JAMEY:** Pasadena, CA, July 12, 1951.

**SHIELDS, BROOKE:** NYC, May 31, 1965.

**SHIRE, TALIA:** Lake Success, NY, Apr. 25, 1946. Yale.

**SHORT, MARTIN:** Toronto, Canada, Mar. 26, 1950. McMaster.

**SHUE, ELISABETH:** S. Orange, NJ, Oct. 6, 1963. Harvard.

**SIEMASZKO, CASEY:** Chicago, IL, March 17, 1961.

**SIKKING, JAMES B.:** Los Angeles, Mar. 5, 1934.

**SILVA, HENRY:** Brooklyn, NY, 1928.

**SILVER, RON:** NYC, July 2, 1946. SUNY.

**SILVERMAN, JONATHAN:** Los Angeles, Aug. 5, 1966. USC.

**SILVERSTONE, ALICIA:** San Francisco, CA, Oct. 4, 1976.

**SILVERSTONE, BEN:** London, England, Apr. 9, 1979.

**SIMMONS, JEAN:** London, England, Jan. 31, 1929. Aida Foster School.

**SIMON, PAUL:** Newark. NJ, Nov. 5, 1942.

**SIMON, SIMONE:** Bethune, France, Apr. 23, 1910.

**SIMPSON, O. J.** (Orenthal James): San Francisco, CA, July 9, 1947. UCLA.

**SINBAD** (David Adkins): Benton Harbor, MI, Nov. 10, 1956.

**SINCLAIR, JOHN** (Gianluigi Loffredo): Rome, Italy, 1946.

Kerr Smith

Paul Sorvino

**SINDEN, DONALD:** Plymouth, England, Oct. 9, 1923. Webber-Douglas.

**SINGER, LORI:** Corpus Christi, TX, May 6, 1962. Juilliard.

**SINISE, GARY:** Chicago, IL, Mar. 17. 1955.

**SIZEMORE, TOM:** Detroit, MI, Sept. 29, 1964.

**SKARSGÅRD, STELLAN:** Gothenburg, Vastergotland, Sweden, June 13, 1951.

**SKERRITT, TOM:** Detroit, MI, Aug. 25, 1933. Wayne St. U.

**SKYE, IONE** (Leitch): London, England, Sept. 4, 1971.

**SLATER, CHRISTIAN:** NYC, Aug. 18, 1969.

**SLATER, HELEN:** NYC, Dec. 15, 1965.

**SMITH, CHARLES MARTIN:** Los Angeles, Oct. 30, 1953. Cal. St. U.

**SMITH, JACLYN:** Houston, TX, Oct. 26, 1947.

**SMITH, JADA PINKETT:** Baltimore, MD, Sept. 18, 1971.

**SMITH, KERR:** Exton, PA, Mar. 9, 1972.

**SMITH, KEVIN:** Red Bank, NJ, Aug. 2, 1970.

**SMITH, KURTWOOD:** New Lisbon, WI, July 3, 1942.

**SMITH, LANE:** Memphis, TN, Apr. 29, 1936.

**SMITH, LEWIS:** Chattanooga, TN, 1958. Actors Studio.

**SMITH, LOIS:** Topeka, KS, Nov. 3, 1930. U WA.

**SMITH, MAGGIE:** Ilford, England, Dec. 28, 1934.

**SMITH, ROGER:** South Gate, CA, Dec. 18, 1932. U AZ.

**SMITH, WILL:** Philadelphia, PA, Sept. 25, 1968.

**SMITHERS, WILLIAM:** Richmond, VA, July 10, 1927. Catholic U.

**SMITS, JIMMY:** Brooklyn, NY, July 9, 1955. Cornell.

**SNIPES, WESLEY:** NYC, July 31, 1963. SUNY/Purchase.

**SNODGRESS, CARRIE:** Chicago, IL, Oct. 27, 1946. UNI.

**SOBIESKSI, LEELEE** (Liliane Sobieski): NYC, June 10, 1982.

**SOLOMON, BRUCE:** NYC, 1944. U Miami, Wayne St. U.

**SOMERS, SUZANNE** (Mahoney): San Bruno, CA, Oct. 16, 1946. Lone Mt. College.

**SOMMER, ELKE** (Schletz): Berlin, Germany, Nov. 5, 1940.

**SOMMER, JOSEF:** Greifswald, Germany, June 26, 1934.

**SORDI, ALBERTO:** Rome, Italy, June 15, 1920.

**SORVINO, MIRA:** Tenafly, NJ, Sept. 28, 1967.

**SORVINO, PAUL:** NYC, Apr. 13, 1939. AMDA.

**SOTO, TALISA** (Miriam Soto): Brooklyn, NY, Mar. 27, 1967.

SOUL, DAVID: Chicago, IL, Aug. 28, 1943.

SPACEK, SISSY: Quitman, TX, Dec. 25, 1949. Actors Studio.

SPACEY, KEVIN: So. Orange, NJ, July 26, 1959. Juilliard.

SPADE, DAVID: Birmingham, MS, July 22, 1964.

SPADER, JAMES: Buzzards Bay, MA, Feb. 7, 1960.

SPANO, VINCENT: Brooklyn, NY, Oct. 18, 1962.

SPENSER, JEREMY: Ceylon, 1937.

SPINELLA, STEPHEN: Naples, Italy, Oct. 11, 1956. NYU.

SPRINGFIELD, RICK (Richard Spring Thorpe): Sydney, Australia, Aug. 23, 1949.

STACK, ROBERT: Los Angeles, Jan. 13, 1919. USC.

STADLEN, LEWIS J.: Brooklyn, NY, Mar. 7, 1947. Neighborhood Playhouse.

STAHL, NICK: Dallas, TX, Dec. 5, 1979.

STALLONE, FRANK: NYC, July 30, 1950.

STALLONE, SYLVESTER: NYC, July 6, 1946. U Miami.

STAMP, TERENCE: London, England, July 23, 1939.

STANG, ARNOLD: Chelsea, MA, Sept. 28, 1925.

STANTON, HARRY DEAN: Lexington, KY, July 14, 1926.

STAPLETON, JEAN: NYC, Jan. 19, 1923.

STAPLETON, MAUREEN: Troy, NY, June 21, 1925.

STARR, RINGO (Richard Starkey): Liverpool, England, July 7, 1940.

STEELE, BARBARA: England, Dec. 29, 1937.

STEELE, TOMMY: London, England, Dec. 17, 1936.

STEENBURGEN, MARY: Newport, AR, 1953. Neighborhood Playhouse.

STEIGER, ROD: Westhampton, NY, Apr. 14, 1925.

STERLING, JAN (Jane Sterling Adriance): NYC, Apr. 3, 1923. Fay Compton Sch.

STERLING, ROBERT (William Sterling Hart): Newcastle, PA, Nov. 13, 1917. U Pittsburgh.

STERN, DANIEL: Bethesda, MD, Aug. 28, 1957.

STERNHAGEN, FRANCES: Washington, DC, Jan. 13, 1932.

STEVENS, ANDREW: Memphis, TN, June 10, 1955.

STEVENS, CONNIE (Concetta Ann Ingolia): Brooklyn, NY, Aug. 8, 1938. Hollywood Professional School.

STEVENS, FISHER: Chicago, IL, Nov. 27, 1963. NYU.

STEVENS, STELLA (Estelle Eggleston): Hot Coffee, MS, Oct. 1, 1936.

STEVENSON, PARKER: Philadelphia, PA, June 4, 1953. Princeton.

STEWART, ALEXANDRA: Montreal, Quebec, Canada, June 10, 1939. Louvre.

STEWART, ELAINE (Elsy Steinberg): Montclair, NJ, May 31, 1929.

STEWART, FRENCH (Milton French Stewart): Albuquerque, NM, Feb. 20, 1964.

STEWART, JON (Jonathan Stewart Liebowitz): Trenton, NJ, Nov. 28, 1962.

STEWART, MARTHA (Martha Haworth): Bardwell, KY, Oct. 7, 1922.

STEWART, PATRICK: Mirfield, England, July 13, 1940.

STIERS, DAVID OGDEN: Peoria, IL, Oct. 31, 1942.

STILES, JULIA: NYC, Mar. 28, 1981.

STILLER, BEN: NYC, Nov. 30, 1965.

STILLER, JERRY: NYC, June 8, 1931.

STING (Gordon Matthew Sumner): Wallsend, England, Oct. 2, 1951.

STOCKWELL, DEAN: Hollywood, CA, Mar. 5, 1935.

STOCKWELL, JOHN (John Samuels, IV): Galveston, TX, Mar. 25, 1961. Harvard.

STOLTZ, ERIC: Whittier, CA, Sept. 30, 1961. USC.

STONE, DEE WALLACE (Deanna Bowers): Kansas City, MO, Dec. 14, 1948. U KS.

STORM, GALE (Josephine Cottle): Bloomington, TX, Apr. 5, 1922.

STOWE, MADELEINE: Eagle Rock, CA, Aug. 18, 1958.

STRASSMAN, MARCIA: NJ, Apr. 28, 1948.

STRATHAIRN, DAVID: San Francisco, CA, Jan. 26, 1949.

STRAUSS, PETER: NYC, Feb. 20, 1947.

STREEP, MERYL (Mary Louise): Summit, NJ, June 22, 1949. Vassar, Yale.

STREISAND, BARBRA: Brooklyn, NY, Apr. 24, 1942.

STRITCH, ELAINE: Detroit, MI, Feb. 2, 1925. Drama Workshop.

STROUD, DON: Honolulu, HI, Sept. 1, 1937.

STRUTHERS, SALLY: Portland, OR, July 28, 1948. Pasadena Playhouse.

STUDI, WES (Wesley Studie): Nofire Hollow, OK, Dec. 17, 1947.

SUMMER, DONNA (LaDonna Gaines): Boston, MA, Dec. 31, 1948.

SUTHERLAND, DONALD: St. John, New Brunswick, Canada, July 17, 1935. U Toronto.

SUTHERLAND, KIEFER: Los Angeles, Dec. 18, 1966.

SUVARI, MENA: Newport, RI, Feb. 9, 1979.

SVENSON, BO: Goreborg, Sweden, Feb. 13, 1941. UCLA.

SWANK, HILARY: Bellingham, WA, July 30, 1974.

SWAYZE, PATRICK: Houston, TX, Aug. 18, 1952.

SWEENEY, D. B. (Daniel Bernard Sweeney): Shoreham, NY, Nov. 14, 1961.

SWINTON, TILDA: London, England, Nov. 5, 1960.

SWIT, LORETTA: Passaic, NJ, Nov. 4, 1937, AADA.

SYLVESTER, WILLIAM: Oakland, CA, Jan. 31, 1922. RADA.

SYMONDS, ROBERT: Bistow, AK, Dec. 1, 1926. TX U.

SYMS, SYLVIA: London, England, June 1, 1934. Convent School.

SZARABAJKA, KEITH: Oak Park, IL, Dec. 2, 1952. U Chicago.

T, MR. (Lawrence Tero): Chicago, IL, May 21, 1952.

TABORI, KRISTOFFER (Siegel): Los Angeles, Aug. 4, 1952.

TAKEI, GEORGE: Los Angeles, Apr. 20, 1939. UCLA.

TALBOT, NITA: NYC, Aug. 8, 1930. Irvine Studio School.

TAMBLYN, RUSS: Los Angeles, Dec. 30, 1934.

TARANTINO, QUENTIN: Knoxville, TN, Mar. 27, 1963.

TATE, LARENZ: Chicago, IL, Sept. 8, 1975.

TAUTOU, AUDREY: Beaumont, France, Aug. 9, 1978.

TAYLOR, ELIZABETH: London, England, Feb. 27, 1932. Byron House School.

TAYLOR, LILI: Glencoe, IL, Feb. 20, 1967.

TAYLOR, NOAH: London, England, Sept. 4, 1969.

TAYLOR, RENEE: NYC, Mar. 19, 1935.

TAYLOR, ROD (Robert): Sydney, Australia, Jan. 11, 1929.

TAYLOR-YOUNG, LEIGH: Washington, DC, Jan. 25, 1945. Northwestern.

TEEFY, MAUREEN: Minneapolis, MN, 1954, Juilliard.

TEMPLE, SHIRLEY: Santa Monica, CA, Apr. 23, 1927.

TENNANT, VICTORIA: London, England, Sept. 30, 1950.

TERZIEFF, LAURENT: Paris, France, June 25, 1935.

TEWES, LAUREN: Braddock, PA, Oct. 26, 1954.

THACKER, RUSS: Washington, DC, June 23, 1946. Montgomery College.

THAXTER, PHYLLIS: Portland, ME, Nov. 20, 1921. St. Genevieve.

James Spader

Hilary Swank

Jennifer Tilly

Marisa Tomei

**THELEN, JODI:** St. Cloud, MN, 1963.

**THERON, CHARLIZE:** Benoni, South Africa, Aug. 7, 1975.

**THEWLIS, DAVID:** Blackpool, England, 1963.

**THOMAS, HENRY:** San Antonio, TX, Sept. 8, 1971.

**THOMAS, JAY:** New Orleans, LA, July 12, 1948.

**THOMAS, JONATHAN TAYLOR (Weiss):** Bethlehem, PA, Sept. 8, 1981.

**THOMAS, MARLO (Margaret):** Detroit, Nov. 21, 1938. USC.

**THOMAS, PHILIP MICHAEL:** Columbus, OH, May 26, 1949. Oakwood College.

**THOMAS, RICHARD:** NYC, June 13, 1951. Columbia.

**THOMPSON, EMMA:** London, England, Apr.15, 1959. Cambridge.

**THOMPSON, FRED DALTON:** Sheffield, AL, Aug. 19, 1942

**THOMPSON, JACK (John Payne):** Sydney, Australia, Aug. 31, 1940.

**THOMPSON, LEA:** Rochester, MN, May 31, 1961.

**THOMPSON, REX:** NYC, Dec. 14, 1942.

**THOMPSON, SADA:** Des Moines, IA, Sept. 27, 1929. Carnegie Tech.

**THORNTON, BILLY BOB:** Hot Spring, AR, Aug. 4, 1955.

**THORSON, LINDA:** Toronto, Canada, June 18, 1947. RADA.

**THULIN, INGRID:** Solleftea, Sweden, Jan. 27, 1929. Royal Drama Theatre.

**THURMAN, UMA:** Boston, MA, Apr. 29, 1970.

**TICOTIN, RACHEL:** Bronx, NY, Nov. 1, 1958.

**TIERNEY, LAWRENCE:** Brooklyn, NY, Mar. 15, 1919. Manhattan College.

**TIFFIN, PAMELA (Wonso):** Oklahoma City, OK, Oct. 13, 1942.

**TIGHE, KEVIN:** Los Angeles, Aug. 13, 1944.

**TILLY, JENNIFER:** Los Angeles, Sept. 16, 1958.

**TILLY, MEG:** Texada, Canada, Feb. 14, 1960.

**TOBOLOWSKY, STEPHEN:** Dallas, TX, May 30, 1951. So. Methodist U.

**TODD, BEVERLY:** Chicago, IL, July 1, 1946.

**TODD, RICHARD:** Dublin, Ireland, June 11, 1919. Shrewsbury School.

**TOLKAN, JAMES:** Calumet, MI, June 20, 1931.

**TOMEI, MARISA:** Brooklyn, NY, Dec. 4, 1964. NYU.

**TOMLIN, LILY:** Detroit, MI, Sept. 1, 1939. Wayne St. U.

**TOPOL (Chaim Topol):** Tel Aviv, Israel, Sept. 9, 1935.

**TORN, RIP:** Temple, TX, Feb. 6, 1931. U TX.

**TORRES, LIZ:** NYC, Sept. 27, 1947. NYU.

**TOTTER, AUDREY:** Joliet, IL, Dec. 20, 1918.

**TOWSEND, ROBERT:** Chicago, IL, Feb. 6, 1957.

**TRAVANTI, DANIEL J.:** Kenosha, WI, Mar. 7, 1940.

**TRAVIS, NANCY:** Queens, NY, Sept. 21, 1961.

**TRAVOLTA, JOEY:** Englewood, NJ, 1952.

**TRAVOLTA, JOHN:** Englewood, NJ, Feb. 18, 1954.

**TREMAYNE, LES:** London, England, Apr. 16, 1913. Northwestern, Columbia, UCLA.

**TRINTIGNANT, JEAN-LOUIS:** Pont-St. Esprit, France, Dec. 11, 1930. Dullin Balachova Drama School.

**TRIPPLEHORN, JEANNE:** Tulsa, OK, 1963.

**TSOPEI, CORINNA:** Athens, Greece, June 21, 1944.

**TUBB, BARRY:** Snyder, TX, 1963. Am. Cons. Th.

**TUCCI, STANLEY:** Katonah, NY, Jan. 11, 1960.

**TUCKER, CHRIS:** Decatur, GA, Aug. 31, 1972.

**TUCKER, JONATHAN:** Boston, MA, May 31, 1982.

**TUCKER, MICHAEL:** Baltimore, MD, Feb. 6, 1944.

**TUNE, TOMMY:** Wichita Falls, TX, Feb. 28, 1939.

**TURNER, JANINE (Gauntt):** Lincoln, NE, Dec. 6, 1963.

**TURNER, KATHLEEN:** Springfield, MO, June 19, 1954. U MD.

**TURNER, TINA (Anna Mae Bullock):** Nutbush, TN, Nov. 26, 1938.

**TURTURRO, JOHN:** Brooklyn, NY, Feb. 28, 1957. Yale.

**TUSHINGHAM, RITA:** Liverpool, England, Mar. 14, 1940.

**TWIGGY (Lesley Hornby):** London, England, Sept. 19, 1949.

**TWOMEY, ANNE:** Boston, MA, June 7, 1951. Temple U.

**TYLER, BEVERLY (Beverly Jean Saul):** Scranton, PA, July 5, 1928.

**TYLER, LIV:** Portland, ME, July 1, 1977.

**TYRRELL, SUSAN:** San Francisco, CA, 1946.

**TYSON, CATHY:** Liverpool, England, June 12, 1965. Royal Shake. Co.

**TYSON, CICELY:** NYC, Dec. 19, 1933. NYU.

**UGGAMS, LESLIE:** NYC, May 25, 1943. Juilliard.

**ULLMAN, TRACEY:** Slough, England, Dec. 30, 1959.

**ULLMANN, LIV:** Tokyo, Japan, Dec. 10, 1938. Webber-Douglas Academy.

**ULRICH, SKEET (Bryan Ray Ulrich):** NC, Jan. 20, 1969.

**UMEKI, MIYOSHI:** Otaru, Hokaido, Japan, Apr. 3, 1929.

**UNDERWOOD, BLAIR:** Tacoma, WA, Aug. 25, 1964. Carnegie-Mellon.

**UNGER, DEBORAH KARA:** Victoria, BC, Canada, 1966.

**URICH, ROBERT:** Toronto, Canada, Dec. 19, 1946.

**USTINOV, PETER:** London, England, Apr. 16, 1921. Westminster School.

**VACCARO, BRENDA:** Brooklyn, NY, Nov. 18, 1939. Neighborhood Playhouse.

**VALANDREY, CHARLOTTE** (Anne Charlone Pascal)**:** Paris, France, 1968.

**VALLI, ALIDA:** Pola, Italy, May 31, 1921. Academy of Drama.

**VALLONE, RAF:** Riogio, Italy, Feb. 17, 1916. Turin U.

**VAN ARK, JOAN:** NYC, June 16, 1943. Yale.

**VAN DAMME, JEAN-CLAUDE** (J-C Vorenberg)**:** Brussels, Belgium, Apr. 1, 1960.

**VAN DE VEN, MONIQUE:** The Netherlands, 1952.

**VAN DER BEEK, JAMES:** Cheshire, CT, March 8, 1977.

**VAN DEVERE, TRISH** (Patricia Dressel)**:** Englewood Cliffs, NJ, Mar. 9, 1945. Ohio Wesleyan.

**VAN DIEN, CASPER:** Ridgefield, NJ, Dec. 18, 1968.

**VAN DOREN, MAMIE** (Joan Lucile Olander)**:** Rowena SD, Feb. 6, 1933.

**VAN DYKE, DICK:** West Plains, MO, Dec. 13, 1925.

**VANITY** (Denise Katrina Smith)**:** Niagara, Ontario, Canada, Jan. 4, 1959.

**VAN PALLANDT, NINA:** Copenhagen, Denmark, July 15, 1932.

**VAN PATTEN, DICK:** NYC, Dec. 9, 1928.

**VAN PATTEN, JOYCE:** NYC, Mar. 9, 1934.

**VAN PEEBLES, MARIO:** NYC, Jan. 15, 1958. Columbia.

**VAN PEEBLES, MELVIN:** Chicago, IL, Aug. 21, 1932.

**VANCE, COURTNEY B.:** Detroit, MI, Mar. 12, 1960.

**VAUGHN, ROBERT:** NYC, Nov. 22, 1932. USC.

**VAUGHN, VINCE:** Minneapolis, MN, Mar. 28, 1970.

**VEGA, ISELA:** Mexico, 1940.

**VELJOHNSON, REGINALD:** NYC, Aug. 16, 1952.

**VENNERA, CHICK:** Herkimer, NY, Mar. 27, 1952. Pasadena Playhouse.

**VENORA, DIANE:** Hartford, CT, 1952. Juilliard.

**VERNON, JOHN:** Montreal, Quebec, Canada, Feb. 24, 1932.

**VEREEN, BEN:** Miami, FL, Oct. 10, 1946.

**VICTOR, JAMES** (Lincoln Rafael Peralta Diaz)**:** Santiago, Dominican Republic, July 27, 1939. Haaren HS/NYC.

**VINCENT, JAN-MICHAEL:** Denver, CO, July 15, 1944. Ventura.

**ULTRA VIOLET** (Isabelle Collin-Dufresne)**:** Grenoble, France, 1935.

**VITALE, MILLY:** Rome, Italy, July 16, 1928. Lycee Chateaubriand.

**VOHS, JOAN:** St. Albans, NY, July 30, 1931.

**VOIGHT, JON:** Yonkers, NY, Dec. 29, 1938. Catholic U.

**VON BARGEN, DANIEL:** Cincinnati, OH, June 5, 1950. Purdue.

**VON DOHLEN, LENNY:** Augusta, GA, Dec. 22, 1958. U TX.

**VON SYDOW, MAX:** Lund, Sweden, July 10, 1929. Royal Drama Theatre.

**WAGNER, LINDSAY:** Los Angeles, June 22. 1949.

**WAGNER, NATASHA GREGSON:** Los Angeles, Sept. 29, 1970.

**WAGNER, ROBERT:** Detroit, MI, Feb. 10, 1930.

**WAHL, KEN:** Chicago, IL, Feb. 14, 1953.

**WAITE, GENEVIEVE:** South Africa, 1949.

**WAITE, RALPH:** White Plains, NY, June 22, 1929. Yale.

**WAITS, TOM:** Pomona, CA, Dec. 7, 1949.

**WALKEN, CHRISTOPHER:** Astoria, NY, Mar. 31, 1943. Hofstra.

**WALKER, CLINT:** Hartfold, IL, May 30, 1927. USC.

**WALKER, PAUL:** Glendale, CA, Sept. 12, 1973.

**WALLACH, ELI:** Brooklyn, NY, Dec. 7, 1915. CCNY, U TX.

**WALLACH, ROBERTA:** NYC, Aug. 2, 1955.

**WALLIS, SHANI:** London, England, Apr. 5, 1941.

**WALSH, M. EMMET:** Ogdensburg, NY, Mar. 22, 1935. Clarkson College, AADA.

**WALTER, JESSICA:** Brooklyn, NY, Jan. 31, 1944. Neighborhood Playhouse.

**WALTER, TRACEY:** Jersey City, NJ, Nov. 25, 1942.

**WALTERS, JULIE:** London, England, Feb. 22, 1950.

**WALTON, EMMA:** London, England, Nov. 1962. Brown.

**WANAMAKER, ZOË:** NYC, May 13, 1949.

**WARD, BURT** (Gervis)**:** Los Angeles, July 6, 1945.

**WARD, FRED:** San Diego, CA, Dec. 30, 1942.

**WARD, RACHEL:** London, England, Sept. 12, 1957.

**WARD, SELA:** Meridian, MS, July 11, 1956.

**WARD, SIMON:** London, England, Oct. 19, 1941.

**WARDEN, JACK** (Lebzelter)**:** Newark, NJ, Sept. 18, 1920.

**WARNER, DAVID:** Manchester, England, July 29, 1941. RADA.

**WARNER, MALCOLM-JAMAL:** Jersey City, NJ, Aug. 18, 1970.

**WARREN, JENNIFER:** NYC, Aug. 12, 1941. U WI.

**WARREN, LESLEY ANN:** NYC, Aug. 16, 1946.

**WARREN, MICHAEL:** South Bend, IN, Mar. 5, 1946. UCLA.

**WARRICK, RUTH:** St. Joseph, MO, June 29, 1915. U MO.

**WASHINGTON, DENZEL:** Mt. Vernon, NY, Dec. 28, 1954. Fordham.

**WASSON, CRAIG:** Ontario, OR, Mar. 15, 1954. U OR.

**WATERSTON, SAM:** Cambridge, MA, Nov. 15, 1940. Yale.

**WATLING, JACK:** London, England, Jan. 13, 1923. Italia Conti School.

**WATSON, EMILY:** London, England, Jan. 14, 1967.

**WATSON, EMMA:** Oxford, England, Apr. 15, 1990.

**WAYANS, DAMON:** NYC, Sept. 4, 1960.

**WAYANS, KEENEN, IVORY:** NYC, June 8, 1958. Tuskegee Inst.

**WAYNE, PATRICK:** Los Angeles, July 15, 1939. Loyola.

**WEATHERS, CARL:** New Orleans, LA, Jan. 14, 1948. Long Beach CC.

**WEAVER, DENNIS:** Joplin, MO, June 4, 1924. U OK.

**WEAVER, FRITZ:** Pittsburgh, PA, Jan. 19, 1926.

**WEAVER, SIGOURNEY** (Susan)**:** NYC, Oct. 8, 1949. Stanford, Yale.

**WEAVING, HUGO:** Nigeria, Apr. 4, 1960. NIDA.

**WEBER, STEVEN:** Queens, NY, March 4, 1961.

**WEDGEWORTH, ANN:** Abilene, TX, Jan. 21, 1935. U TX.

**WEISZ, RACHEL:** London, England, Mar. 7, 1971.

**WELCH, RAQUEL** (Tejada)**:** Chicago, IL, Sept. 5, 1940.

**WELD, TUESDAY** (Susan)**:** NYC, Aug. 27, 1943. Hollywood Professional School.

**WELDON, JOAN:** San Francisco, CA, Aug. 5, 1933. SF Cons.

**WELLER, PETER:** Stevens Point, WI, June 24, 1947. Am. Th. Wing.

**WENDT, GEORGE:** Chicago, IL, Oct. 17, 1948.

**WEST, ADAM** (William Anderson)**:** Walla Walla, WA, Sept. 19, 1929.

**WEST, SHANE:** Baton Rouge, LA, June 10, 1978.

**WETTIG, PATRICIA:** Cincinatti, OH, Dec. 4, 1951. Temple.

**WHALEY, FRANK:** Syracuse, NY, July 20, 1963. SUNY/Albany.

**WHALLEY-KILMER, JOANNE:** Manchester, England, Aug. 25, 1964.

**WHEATON, WIL:** Burbank, CA, July 29, 1972.

**WHITAKER, FOREST:** Longview, TX, July 15, 1961.

**WHITAKER, JOHNNY:** Van Nuys, CA, Dec. 13, 1959.

WHITE, BETTY: Oak Park, IL, Jan. 17, 1922.
WHITE, CHARLES: Perth Amboy, NJ, Aug. 29, 1920. Rutgers.
WHITELAW, BILLIE: Coventry, England, June 6, 1932.
WHITMAN, STUART: San Francisco, CA, Feb. 1, 1929. CCLA.
WHITMORE, JAMES: White Plains, NY, Oct. 1, 1921. Yale.
WHITNEY, GRACE LEE: Detroit, MI, Apr. 1, 1930.
WHITTON, MARGARET: Philadelphia, PA, Nov, 30, 1950.
WIDDOES, KATHLEEN: Wilmington, DE, Mar. 21, 1939.
WIDMARK, RICHARD: Sunrise, MN, Dec. 26, 1914. Lake Forest.
WIEST, DIANNE: Kansas City, MO, Mar. 28, 1948. U MD.
WILBY, JAMES: Burma, Feb. 20, 1958.
WILCOX, COLIN: Highlands, NC, Feb. 4, 1937. U TN.
WILDER, GENE (Jerome Silberman): Milwaukee, WI, June 11, 1935. U IA.
WILKINSON, TOM: Leeds, England, 1948. U Kent.
WILLIAMS, BILLY DEE: NYC, Apr. 6, 1937.
WILLIAMS, CARA (Bernice Kamiat): Brooklyn, NY, June 29, 1925.
WILLIAMS, CINDY: Van Nuys, CA, Aug. 22, 1947. KACC.
WILLIAMS, CLARENCE, III: NYC, Aug. 21, 1939.
WILLIAMS, ESTHER: Los Angeles, Aug. 8, 1921.
WILLIAMS, JOBETH: Houston, TX, Dec 6, 1948. Brown.
WILLIAMS, MICHELLE: Kalispell, MT, Sept. 9, 1980.
WILLIAMS, PAUL: Omaha, NE, Sept. 19, 1940.
WILLIAMS, ROBIN: Chicago, IL, July 21, 1951. Juilliard.
WILLIAMS, TREAT (Richard): Rowayton, CT, Dec. 1, 1951.
WILLIAMSON, FRED: Gary, IN, Mar. 5, 1938. Northwestern.
WILLIAMSON, NICOL: Hamilton, Scotland, Sept. 14, 1938.
WILLIS, BRUCE: Penns Grove, NJ, Mar. 19, 1955.
WILLISON, WALTER: Monterey Park, CA, June 24, 1947.
WILSON, DEMOND: NYC, Oct. 13, 1946. Hunter College.
WILSON, ELIZABETH: Grand Rapids, MI, Apr. 4, 1925.
WILSON, LAMBERT: Paris, France, 1959.
WILSON, LUKE: Dallas, TX, Sept. 21, 1971.
WILSON, OWEN: Dallas, TX, Nov. 18, 1968.
WILSON, SCOTT: Atlanta, GA, 1942.
WINCOTT, JEFF: Toronto, Canada, May 8, 1957.
WINCOTT, MICHAEL: Toronto, Canada, Jan. 6, 1959. Juilliard.
WINDE, BEATRICE: Chicago, IL, Jan. 6.
WINDOM, WILLIAM: NYC, Sept. 28, 1923. Williams College.
WINFIELD, PAUL: Los Angeles, May 22, 1940. UCLA.
WINFREY, OPRAH: Kosciusko, MS, Jan. 29, 1954. TN St. U.
WINGER, DEBRA: Cleveland, OH, May 17, 1955. Cal. St.
WINKLER, HENRY: NYC, Oct. 30, 1945. Yale.
WINN, KITTY: Washington, DC, Feb, 21, 1944. Boston U.
WINNINGHAM, MARE: Phoenix, AZ, May 6, 1959.
WINSLET, KATE: Reading, England, Oct. 5, 1975.
WINSLOW, MICHAEL: Spokane, WA, Sept. 6, 1960.
WINTER, ALEX: London, England, July 17, 1965. NYU.
WINTERS, JONATHAN: Dayton, OH, Nov. 11, 1925. Kenyon College.
WINTERS, SHELLEY (Shirley Schrift): St. Louis, Aug. 18, 1922. Wayne St. U.
WITHERS, GOOGIE: Karachi, India, Mar. 12, 1917. Italia Conti.
WITHERS, JANE: Atlanta, GA, Apr. 12, 1926.
WITHERSPOON, REESE (Laura Jean Reese Witherspoon): Nashville, TN, Mar. 22, 1976.
WOLF, SCOTT: Newton, MA, June 4, 1968.
WONG, B.D.: San Francisco, CA, Oct. 24,1962.
WONG, RUSSELL: Troy, NY, Mar. 1, 1963. Santa Monica College.
WOOD, ELIJAH: Cedar Rapids, IA, Jan 28, 1981.

Diane Venora | Billy Dee Williams

WOODARD, ALFRE: Tulsa, OK, Nov. 2, 1953. Boston U.
WOODLAWN, HOLLY (Harold Ajzenberg): Juana Diaz, PR, 1947.
WOODS, JAMES: Vernal, UT, Apr. 18, 1947. MIT.
WOODWARD, EDWARD: Croyden, Surrey, England, June 1, 1930.
WOODWARD, JOANNE: Thomasville, GA, Feb. 27, 1930. Neighborhood Playhouse.
WORONOV, MARY: Brooklyn, NY, Dec. 8, 1946. Cornell.
WORTH, IRENE (Hattie Abrams): Nebraska, June 23, 1916. UCLA.
WRAY, FAY: Alberta, Canada, Sept. 15, 1907.
WRIGHT, AMY: Chicago, IL, Apr. 15, 1950.
WRIGHT, MAX: Detroit, MI, Aug. 2, 1943. Wayne St. U.
WRIGHT, ROBIN: Dallas, TX, Apr. 8, 1966.
WRIGHT, TERESA: NYC, Oct. 27, 1918.
WUHL, ROBERT: Union City, NJ, Oct. 9, 1951. U Houston.
WYATT, JANE: NYC, Aug. 10, 1910. Barnard College.
WYLE, NOAH: Los Angeles, June 2, 1971.
WYMAN, JANE (Sarah Jane Fulks): St. Joseph, MO, Jan. 4, 1914.
WYMORE, PATRICE: Miltonvale, KS, Dec. 17, 1926.
WYNN, MAY (Donna Lee Hickey): NYC, Jan. 8, 1930.
WYNTER, DANA (Dagmar): London, June 8. 1927. Rhodes U.
YORK, MICHAEL: Fulmer, England, Mar. 27, 1942. Oxford.
YORK, SUSANNAH: London, England, Jan. 9, 1941. RADA.
YOUNG, ALAN (Angus): North Shield, England, Nov. 19, 1919.
YOUNG, BURT: Queens, NY, Apr. 30, 1940.
YOUNG, CHRIS: Chambersburg, PA, Apr. 28, 1971.
YOUNG, SEAN: Louisville, KY, Nov. 20, 1959. Interlochen.
YULIN, HARRIS: Los Angeles, Nov. 5, 1937.
CHOW YUN-FAT: Lamma Island, Hong Kong, China, May 18, 1955.
ZACHARIAS, ANN: Stockholm, Sweden, 1956.
ZADORA, PIA: Hoboken, NJ, May 4, 1954.
ZELLWEGER, RENEE: Katy, TX, Apr. 25, 1969.
ZERBE, ANTHONY: Long Beach, CA, May 20, 1939.
ZETA-JONES, CATHERINE: Swansea, Wales, Sept. 25, 1969.
ZIMBALIST, EFREM, JR.: NYC, Nov.30, 1918. Yale.
ZUNIGA, DAPHNE: Berkeley, CA, Oct.28,1963. UCLA.

# OBITUARIES
## FOR 2001

**LARRY ADLER, 87,** Baltimore-born harmonica player-composer, died on Aug. 7, 2001 in London. In addition to his stage appearances he was seen performing in movies such as *The Singing Marine, The Big Broadcast of 1937, St. Martin's Lane (Sidewalks of London)*, and *Music for Millions*. Survived by his son, three daughters, two granddaughters, and two great-grandchildren.

**SAMUEL Z. ARKOFF, 83,** Iowa-born motion picture executive and producer who, together with his late partner James H. Nicholson, established American International Pictures, died on Sept. 16, 2001 in Burbank, CA. His studio output of "B" exploitation pictures that became a staple in drive-in theaters from the mid-1950s throughout the 1970s included titles such as *I Was a Teenage Werewolf, Invasion of the Saucer Men, I Was a Teenage Frankenstein, Attack of the Puppet People, Bucket of Blood, The Pit and the Pendulum, Beach Party, What's Up Tiger Lily?, The Wild Angels, Wild in the Streets, Bloody Mama, The Abominable Dr. Phibes, Black Caesar*, and *Blacula*. He is survived by his son, Louis Arkoff, and a daughter, Donna Roth, both of whom are producers; five grandchildren; and a great-grandson.

Pat Ast

Jean-Pierre Aumont

**LEWIS ARQUETTE, 65,** Chicago-born film and television character player, died of congestive heart failure on Feb. 10, 2001 in Los Angeles. The son of comedian Cliff Arquette (Charley Weaver), he appeared in movies such as *The China Syndrome, Big Business, Tango & Cash, The Linguini Incident, Sleep With Me, Twilight, Best in Show*, and *Little Nicky*. He is survived by his brother, a sister, and five children, Rosanna, Richmond, Patricia, Alexis, and David Arquette, all of whom are actors.

**PAT AST, 59,** Brooklyn-born actress, died of natural causes at her home in West Hollywood, CA, on Oct. 2, 2001. She could be seen in movies such as *Heat* (1972), *The Duchess and the Dirtwater Fox, The World's Greatest Lover, Foul Play, The Incredible Shrinking Woman, The Pursuit of D. B. Cooper*, and *Reform School Girls*. No reported survivors.

Sandy Baron

Budd Boetticher

**JEAN-PIERRE AUMONT (J-P Salomons), 90,** Paris-born star of French and American films, died on Jan. 30, 2001 at his home in Saint-Tropez. His films include *Hotel du Nord, Flight Into Darkness, Assignment in Brittany, The Cross of Lorraine, Heartbeat, Song of Scheherazade, Sirens of Atlantis, The First Gentleman, Lili, Royal Affairs in Versailles, Charge of the Lancers, Hilda Crane, John Paul Jones, The Devil at 4 O'Clock, Five Miles to Midnight, Castle Keep, Day for Night, Mahogany, Cat and Mouse, Becoming Colette, Jefferson in Paris*, and *The Proprietor*. He is survived by his second wife, actress Marisa Pavan, their two sons, and his daughter from his marriage to actress Maria Montez.

**SANDY BARON (Sanford Beresofsky), 64,** Brooklyn-born comedian-actor died on Jan. 21, 2001 in Van Nuys, CA, after suffering for years from emphysema. Among the films he appeared in were *Targets, Sweet November* (1968), *If It's Tuesday This Must Be Belgium, The Out of Towners* (1970), *Straight*

*Time, Broadway Danny Rose, Birdy, Vamp, The Grifters,* and *The Hi-Lo Country.* He is survived by his sister.

**JAMES BERNARD, 75,** British composer-writer, who won the Academy Award for collaborating with Paul Dehn on the screenplay for *Seven Days to Noon,* died of unspecified causes on July 12, 2001 in London. As a composer at Hammer Studios he scored movies such as *The Quatermass Experiment* (*The Creeping Unknown*), *The Curse of Frankenstein, Dracula* (*Horror of Dracula*), *The Hound of the Baskervilles* (1959), *The Terror of the Tongs, These Are the Damned, She* (1965), *The Devil Rides Out,* and *Dracula Has Risen From the Grave.* Survived by a sister.

**BUDD BOETTICHER (Oscar Boetticher, Jr.), 85,** Chicago-born motion picture director, best known for low-budget westerns such as *Seminole* and *The Tall T,* died on Nov. 29, 2001 at his home in Ramona, CA. His other films include *Bullfighter and the Lady, The Cimarron Kid, Bronco Buster, Red Ball Express, Horizons West, City Beneath the Sea, The Man From the Alamo, East of Sumatra, The Magnificent Matador, Seven Men From Now, Decision at Sundown, Buchanan Rides Alone, Ride Lonesome, Comanche Station,* and *The Rise and Fall of Legs Diamond.* He is survived by his fourth wife.

**ROY BOULTING, 87,** British film director-producer-writer who collaborated with his twin brother John on several notable films in the 1950s and '60s, died of cancer on Nov. 5, 2001 in London. Among his films as producer were *Brighton Rock, Seven Days to Noon, The Magic Box, Private's Progress* (also co-writer), *I'm All Right Jack* (also co-writer), *Heaven's Above!* (also co-writer), and *Rotten to the Core,* while his credits as director include *High Treason* (also co-writer), *Run for the Sun* (also co-writer), *Carlton Browne of the F.O.* (*Man in a Cocked Hat*; also co-writer), *The Family Way* (also co-writer), and *There's a Girl in My Soup.* Survivors include his son from his marriage to actress Hayley Mills.

**FOSTER BROOKS, 89,** Kentucky-born comedian, known for his drunk act, died of natural causes at his home in Encino, CA, on Dec. 20, 2001. His handful of film appearances include *The Villain, Cracking Up* (*Smorgasbord*), and *Cannonball Run II.* Survived by his wife, two daughters, and three grandchildren.

**JULES BUCK, 83,** St. Louis-born cameraman-turned-producer died in Paris on July 19, 2001 of complications from Alzheimer's disease. With actor Peter O'Toole he formed Keep Films, resulting in the collaborations *Lord Jim, Great Catherine, The Ruling Class,* and *Under Milk Wood.* His other credits as producer include *Love Nest, Fixed Bayonets, The Day They Robbed the Bank of England,* and *Operation Snatch.* Survived by his daughter.

**RALPH BURNS, 79,** motion picture arranger-composer, who won Academy Awards for his work on the Bob Fosse films *Cabaret* and *All That Jazz,* died on Nov. 21, 2001 in Los Angeles of pneumonia and complications from a stroke. He also worked on such other movies as *Bananas, Mame, Lenny, New York New York, Annie, My Favorite Year, The Muppets Take Manhattan, Perfect, In the Mood,* and *Bert Rigby You're a Fool.* No immediate survivors.

Roy Boutling          Corinne Calvet

**CORINNE CALVET (Corinne Dibois), 75,** French screen and television actress died of a cerebral hemorrhage on June 23, 2001 in Los Angeles. After coming to the U.S. in 1949 she appeared in movies such as *Rope of Sand, When Willie Comes Marching Home, My Friend Irma Goes West, Quebec, On the Riviera, Peking Express, Sailor Beware, What Price Glory?* (1952), *Flight to Tangier, The Far Country, So This Is Paris, The Plunderers of Painted Flats, Bluebeard's Ten Honeymoons, Hemingway's Adventures of a Young Man,* and *Apache Uprising.* She is survived by a son.

**JOHN CHAMBERS, 78,** screen and television makeup artist, who won a special Academy Award in 1968 for his work on the film *Planet of the Apes*, died on Aug. 25, 2001 in Woodland Hills, CA. His other movies include *The List of Adrian Messenger* and *The Island of Dr. Moreau* (1977). No reported survivors.

Imogene Coca          Perry Como

**IMOGENE COCA, 92,** Philadelphia-born actress-comedian, best known for her Emmy Award-winning pairing opposite Sid Caesar on the television series "Your Show of Shows," died on June 2, 2001 at her home in Westport, CT. She appeared in such movies as *Under the Yum Yum Tree*, *Rabbit Test*, and *National Lampoon's Vacation*. No survivors.

**CHARLOTTE COLEMAN, 33,** British actress, best known for playing Hugh Grant's roommate in the 1994 comedy hit *Four Weddings and a Funeral*, died at her London home on Nov. 14, 2001 following an asthma attack. Survived by her father, mother, and sister.

**PERRY COMO (Pierino Como), 88,** Pittsburgh-born singer, who became one of the top recording artists of the 1950s with such songs as "Hot Diggity," "Don't Let the Stars Get in Your Eyes," "Round and Round," and "Catch a Falling Star," died in his sleep at his home in Jupiter, FL, on May 12, 2001. In addition to his long-running television series, he showed up in movies such as *Something for the Boys*, *Doll Face*, and *Words and Music*. He is survived by two sons, a daughter, thirteen grandchildren, and four great-grandchildren.

**PEGGY CONVERSE, 95,** Oregon-born screen, stage, and television actress, died on March 2, 2001 in her Los Angeles home. She could be seen in films such as *Girl of the Limberlost*, *The Brute Man*, *Day of the Bad Man*, *Father Is a Bachelor*, *Miss Sadie Thompson*, and *The Accidental Tourist*. She is survived by her daughter, actress-singer Melissa Converse, a son, three grandchildren, and three great-grandchildren.

**ROSEMARY DeCAMP, 90,** Arizona-born screen, stage, and television actress, died at her home in Torrance, CA, on Feb. 20, 2001. Following her 1941 debut in *Cheers for Miss Bishop* she appeared in such motion pictures as *Hold Back the Dawn*, *Yankee Doodle Dandy* (as James Cagney's mother), *Commandos Strike at Dawn*, *This Is the Army*, *The Merry Monahans*, *Pride of the Marines*, *Rhapsody in Blue*, *Week-End at the Waldorf*, *Blood on the Sun*, *Two Guys From Milwaukee*, *Nora Prentiss*, *Look for the Silver Lining*, *The Story of Seabiscuit*, *On Moonlight Bay*, *By the Light of the Silvery Moon*, *Many Rivers to Cross*, *Strategic Air Command*, and *13 Ghosts*. On television she appeared on the series "The Life of Riley" (she had appeared in a film version as well), "The Bob Cummings Show," and "That Girl." Survived by four daughters.

Rosemary DeCamp          Anthony Dexter

**FRED DeCORDOVA, 90,** New York City-born film and television producer-director, best known as the long-running producer of "The Tonight Show Starring Johnny Carson," died in Los Angeles, CA, on Sept. 15, 2001. His film credits as director include *Too Young to Know*, *That Way With Women*, *The Countess of Monte Cristo*, *Peggy*, *Bedtime for Bonzo*, *Katie Did It*, *Little Egypt*, *Here Come the Nelsons*, *Bonzo Goes to College*, *I'll Take Sweden*, and *Frankie and Johnny*. Survived by his wife.

**ANTHONY DEXTER (Walter Reinhold Alfred Fleischmann), 82,** Nebraska-born screen actor, best known for playing the title role in the 1952 film biography *Valentino*, died on Mar. 27, 2001, in Greeley, CO. His other movies included *The Brigand*, *Captain John Smith and Pocahontas*, *Fire Maidens From Outer Space*, *The Story of Mankind* (as Christopher Columbus), *The Parson and the Outlaw*, *12 to the Moon*, and *Thoroughly Modern Millie*. He eventually left show business and became a teacher. No reported survivors.

**DANILO DONATI, 75,** Italian costume and set designer, who won Academy Awards for his costume designs for *Romeo and Juliet* and *Fellini's Casanova*, died at his home in Rome on Dec. 1, 2001. His other film credits include *The Gospel According to St. Matthew*, *Ginger and Fred*, and *Life Is Beautiful*. No reported survivors.

Gloria Foster

Arlene Francis

Troy Donahue

Dale Evans

**TROY DONAHUE (Merle Johnson, Jr.), 65,** New York City-born screen and television actor, best known for starring in the 1959 romance *A Summer Place*, died of a heart attack in Los Angeles, on Sept. 2, 2001. Following his 1957 film debut in *Man Afraid*, he was seen in such pictures as *The Tarnished Angels*, *The Voice in the Mirror*, *Summer Love*, *Monster on the Campus*, *Imitation of Life* (1959), *The Crowded Sky*, *Parrish*, *Susan Slade*, *Rome Adventure*, *Palm Springs Weekend*, *A Distant Trumpet*, *My Blood Runs Cold*, *Blast Off!* (*Those Fantastic Flying Fools*), *Seizure*, *Cockfighter*, *The Godfather Part II*, *Omega Cop*, and *Cry-Baby*. One of his four wives was actress Suzanne Pleshette. Survived by his sister and two children.

**DALE EVANS (Frances Octavia Smith), 88,** Texas-born film and television actress, who became famous for the many westerns she starred in opposite husband Roy Rogers, died on Feb. 7, 2001 at her home in Apple Valley, CA. A few years after her 1940 motion picture debut in *The East Side Kids*, she was hired by Republic Pictures. That company made her a leading lady in westerns, including her first with Rogers, *The Cowboy and the Senorita*, in 1944. They married in 1948, continuing to co-star in such features as *The Man From Oklahoma*, *Rainbow Over Texas*, *My Pal Trigger*, *Out California Way*, *Under Nevada Skies*, *Helldorado*, *Susanna Pass*, *Trigger Jr.*, and *Pals of the Golden West*, her last acting credit, in 1952. Rogers died in 1998.

**A. D. FLOWERS, 84,** special effects coordinator who won Academy Awards for his work on the films *Tora! Tora! Tora!* and *The Poseidon Adventure*, died on July 5, 2001 in Fullerton, CA. His other credits include *The Godfather*, *The Towering Inferno*, and *Apocalypse Now*. No reported survivors.

**GLORIA FOSTER, 64,** Chicago-born screen, stage, and television actress died from diabetes on Sept. 29, 2001 at her Manhattan home. She was seen in films such as *Nothing but a Man*, *The Angel Levine*, *Man and Boy*, *Leonard Part 6*, and *The Matrix*. No survivors.

**ARLENE FRANCIS (Arlene Francis Kazanjian), 93,** Boston-born screen, stage, and television actress, better known for appearing as a panelist on the quiz show "What's My Line?" for 25 years, died of complications of cancer and Alzheimer's disease in San Francisco on May 31, 2001. She was seen in films such as *All My Sons, One Two Three,* and *The Thrill of It All.* She is survived by her son from her marriage to actor Martin Gabel (who died in 1986).

**KATHLEEN FREEMAN, 78,** Chicago-born screen, stage, and television character actress, who played vocal coach Phoebe Dinsmore in the classic musical *Singin' in the Rain* and made eleven movies opposite Jerry Lewis, died of lung cancer on Aug. 23, 2001 in New York City. She was appearing in the Broadway musical *The Full Monty,* for which she received a Theatre World Award, at the time of her death. Her many other movies include *The Naked City, A Life of Her Own, A Place in the Sun, Love Is Better Than Ever, Wait Till the Sun Shines Nellie, The Bad and the Beautiful, Bonzo Goes to College, Three Ring Circus* (her first with Lewis), *The Far Country, Houseboat, The Fly, Don't Give Up the Ship, North to Alaska, The Ladies Man, The Errand Boy, The Nutty Professor* (1963), *The Disorderly Orderly, The Rounders, Point Blank, Support Your Local Sheriff!, Myra Breckinridge, The Blues Brothers, Dragnet* (1987), *In the Mood, Naked Gun 33 1/3: The Final Insult,* and *I'll Be Home for Christmas.* No reported survivors.

Kathleen Freeman

Jane Greer

**RUTH GOETZ (Ruth Goodman), 93,** Philadelphia-born writer, who collaborated with her husband Augustus Goetz on the 1947 play *The Heiress* and adapted it to the screen two years later, died in Englewood, NJ, on Oct. 12, 2001. The Goetzes also wrote screenplays such as *Carrie* (1952) and *Stage Struck.* Augustus died in 1957. She is survived by her daughter and a granddaughter.

**SALLY GRACIE, 80,** screen, stage, and television actress died on Aug. 13, 2001 at her home in Manhattan. Her films include *Patterns, Stage Struck, The Fugitive Kind, The Rain People,* and *Passed Away.* She was the first wife of actor Rod Steiger. She is survived by a son from her second marriage, a stepdaughter, a stepson, and six grandchildren.

**JANE GREER (Bettejane Greer), 76,** Washington-born screen and television actress, perhaps best known for her femme fatale role in the 1947 noir *Out of the Past,* died from complications of cancer on Aug. 24, 2001 in Los Angeles. A former big band singer, she was briefly married to crooner-actor Rudy Vallee, shortly before embarking on her film career, in 1945, with *Pan American,* billed under her real name. Her other credits included *Dick Tracy* (1945), *Sunset Pass, Sinbad the Sailor, They Won't Believe Me, The Big Steal, You're in the Navy Now* (U.S.S. Teakettle), *I Married a Communist, The Company She Keeps, The Prisoner of Zenda* (1952), *You for Me, The Clown, Down Among the Sheltering Palms, Run for the Sun, Man of a Thousand Faces, Where Love Has Gone, Billie, Against All Odds* (the 1984 remake of *Out of the Past*), *Just Between Friends,* and *Immediate Family.* Survived by three sons, a twin brother, and two grandchildren.

**JACK GWILLIM, 91,** British character player died on July 2, 2001 in Los Angeles. Among his many film appearances are *Solomon and Sheba, Flame Over India, Sink the Bismarck!, Circus of Horror, Lawrence of Arabia, Lisa* (The Inspector), *In Search of the Castaways, Jason and the Argonauts, A Boy Ten Feet Tall* (Sammy Going South), *A Man for All Seasons, Battle of Britain, Patton, Cromwell, Clash of the Titans,* and *The Monster Squad.* Survived by his wife, three children, two grandchildren, and a brother.

**JACK HALEY, JR., 67,** Los Angeles-born producer, director, and documentarian, best known for the 1974 tribute to MGM musicals *That's Entertainment!*, died of respiratory failure on Apr. 21, 2001 in Santa Monica, CA. His other films include *The Love Machine* and *That's Dancing!* On television he won an Emmy for directing the special "Movin' With Nancy." He was the son of actor Jack Haley and had been married in the 1970s to actress-singer Liza Minnelli. Survived by his sister.

Minister," the bulk of his film credits did not come until late in his life. His motion pictures include *Young Winston*, *The Hiding Place*, *History of the World Part 1*, *Gandhi*, *Turtle Diary*, *Demolition Man*, *Richard III* (as Clarence), *Twelfth Night* (as Malvolio), *Amistad*, *The Object of My Affection*, *Madeleine*, and *The Winslow Boy* (1999). He won a Tony Award for his performance in *Shadowlands*. Survived by his companion, Trevor Bentham.

| Jack Haley, Jr. | George Harrison | Nigel Hawthorne | Eileen Heckart |

**GEORGE HARRISON, 58,** Liverpool-born singer-songwriter-film producer-actor-guitarist, who helped revolutionize the rock music scene as one of the members of the Beatles, died of cancer in Los Angeles on Nov. 29, 2001. With the Beatles he performed his own compositions such as "Taxman," "While My Guitar Gently Weeps," "Here Comes the Sun," and "Something," and appeared with them in the films *A Hard Day's Night*, *Help!*, *Yellow Submarine*, and *Let It Be* (sharing the Academy Award for Best Music Score). As a solo performer, he went on to write and record such hit songs as "My Sweet Lord" and "All Those Years Ago." As a film producer and head of his own company, Handmade Films, he was responsible for such movies as *Life of Brian*, *Time Bandits*, *The Long Good Friday*, *Mona Lisa*, and *Withnail and I*. Survived by his second wife, their son, two brothers, and a sister.

**NIGEL HAWTHORNE, 72,** British screen, stage, and television actor, who received an Oscar nomination for his performance in *The Madness of King George*, died of a heart attack at his home in Baldock, Hertfordshire, England, on Dec. 26, 2001. Well-known in theater, and on television for his series "Yes,

**EILEEN HECKART (Anna Eileen Heckart), 82,** Columbus-born screen, stage, and television character actress, who won an Academy Award as Best Supporting Actress for repeating her stage role as the protective mother of a young blind man in *Butterflies Are Free*, died of cancer on Dec. 31, 2001 at her home in Norwalk, CT. In addition to her countless appearances on the New York stage, she was seen in such other films as *Miracle in the Rain*, *Somebody Up There Likes Me*, *The Bad Seed* (for which she received an Oscar nomination), *Hot Spell*, *Up the Down Staircase*, *No Way to Treat a Lady*, *The Hiding Place*, *Burnt Offerings*, *Heartbreak Ridge*, and *The First Wives Club*. In 2000 she was awarded a special Tony Award for her lifetime of work in the theater. She is survived by three sons, two half-sisters, and two grandchildren.

**CHRISTOPHER HEWETT, 80,** British screen, stage, and television character actor, who played the flamboyant director Roger DeBris in the classic comedy *The Producers*, died on Aug. 3, 2001 in Los Angeles. He appeared in only three other theatrical features: *Pool of London*, *The Lavender Hill Mob*, and *Ratboy*. On television he was best known for starring in the series "Mr. Belvedere." No reported survivors.

Christopher Hewett          Ken Hughes

**KEN HUGHES, 79,** Liverpool-born director-writer of such films as *Chitty Chitty Bang Bang* and *Cromwell*, died in Los Angeles on Apr. 28, 2001. He had been suffering from Alzheimer's disease. Among his other films as director and writer are *The House Across the Lake*, *The Trials of Oscar Wilde*, *Jazz Boat*, *The Small World of Sammy Lee*, *Arrivederci Baby! (Drop Dead Darling)*, and *Alfie Darling*. He is survived by his wife and a daughter.

**EUGENE JACKSON, 84,** Buffalo-born screen and television actor, who had appeared as "Pineapple" in six silent Our Gang shorts, died of a heart attack at his home in Compton, CA, on Oct. 26, 2001. He could also be seen in such feature films as *Cimarron* (1931), *Dixiana*, *Tumbling Tumbleweeds*, *Thoroughbreds Don't Cry*, *Arrest Bulldog Drummond*, *Reap the Wild Wind*, *Reveille With Beverly*, *Jeanne Eagles*, and *Cleopatra Jones*. He is survived by his wife, two daughters, and a son.

**BURT KENNEDY, 78,** Michigan-born director-writer of westerns such as *The War Wagon* and *Support Your Local Sheriff!*, died at his home in Sherman Oaks, CA, on Feb. 15, 2001. His other credits include *The Rounders*, *Welcome to Hard Times*, *The Good Guys and the Bad Guys*, *Dirty Dingus Magee*, *Hannie Caulder*, and *The Train Robbers*. Survived by his companion, Nancy Pendleton, two daughters, and five grandchildren.

**STANLEY KRAMER, 87,** New York City-born director-producer, noted for such socially conscious commercial entertainments as *The Defiant Ones*, *Judgment at Nuremberg*, and *Guess Who's Coming to Dinner* (each of which earned him dual Oscar nominations as producer and director), died of complications from pneumonia in Woodland Hills, CA, on Feb. 19, 2001. His films as a producer include *Champion*, *Home of the Brave*, *The Men*, *Cyrano de Bergerac* (1950), *Death of a Salesman*, *High Noon* (Oscar nomination), *The Member of the Wedding*, *The 5000 Fingers of Dr. T*, *The Wild One*, and *The Caine Mutiny* (Oscar nomination). He made his debut as director in 1955 with *Not as a Stranger*, followed by such titles (most of which found him also serving as producer) as *The Pride and the Passion*, *On the Beach*, *Inherit the Wind*, *It's a Mad Mad Mad Mad World*, *Ship of Fools* (Oscar nomination as producer), *The Secret of Santa Vittoria*, *Bless the Beasts and Children*, and his last, *The Runner Stumbles*, in 1979. In 1962 he was given the Irving G. Thalberg Award by the Academy of Motion Picture Arts and Sciences. Survived by his wife, a son, three daughters.

Stanley Kramer

Jack Lemmon

**JACK LEMMON (John Uhler Lemmon 3rd), 76,** Boston-born screen, stage, and television actor, who became one of America's most popular and beloved performers in his nearly 50-year career in movies, died on June 27, 2001 in Los Angeles of complications from cancer. Following work in theater and on live television, he made his motion picture debut in 1954 in *It Should Happen to You.* He went on to win Academy Awards for Best Supporting Actor for *Mister Roberts,* in 1955, and as Best Actor for *Save the Tiger,* in 1973. There were additional nominations for *Some Like It Hot, The Apartment, Days of Wine and Roses, The China Syndrome, Tribute,* and *Missing.* His other films are *Phffft, Three for the Show, My Sister Eileen* (1955), *You Can't Run Away from It, Fire Down Below, Operation Mad Ball, Cowboy, Bell Book and Candle, It Happened to Jane, The Wackiest Ship in the Army, Pepe, The Notorious Landlady, Irma La Duce, Under the Yum Yum Tree, Good Neighbor Sam, How to Murder Your Wife, The Great Race, The Fortune Cookie, Luv, The Odd Couple, The April Fools, The Out-of-Towners, Kotch* (which he also directed), *The War Between Men and Women, Avanti!, The Front Page* (1974), *The Prisoner of Second Avenue, Alex and the Gypsy, Airport '77, Buddy Buddy, Mass Appeal, Macaroni, That's Life!, Dad, JFK, The Player, Glengarry Glen Ross, Short Cuts, Grumpy Old Men, Grumpier Old Men, Getting Away With Murder, The Grass Harp, Hamlet* (1996), *My Fellow Americans, Out to Sea, The Odd Couple 2,* and *The Legend of Bagger Vance.* He was the recipient of such awards as the Kennedy Center Honors and the American Film Institute Life Achievement Award. Survived by his second wife, actress Felicia Farr; their daughter; a son from his first marriage, actor Chris Lemmon; and three grandchildren.

**JAY LIVINGSTON, 86,** Pennsylvania-born composer-lyricist who, with his collaborator Ray Evans, won Academy Awards for the songs "Buttons and Bows" (from *The Paleface*), "Mona Lisa" (from *Captain Carey, U.S.A.*), and "Que Sera Sera/Whatever Will Be Will Be" (from *The Man Who Knew Too Much*), died from pneumonia in Los Angeles on Oct. 17, 2001. He received additional nominations for "The Cat and the Canary" (from *Why Girls Leave Home*), "Tammy" (from *Tammy and the Bachelor*), "Almost in Your Arms" (from *Houseboat*), and the title song from *Dear Heart.* Two of his most famous songs were the title tune written for but not used in *To Each His Own,* and "Silver Bells," composed for *The Lemon Drop Kid.* He is survived by his second wife; his daughter; his brother, Alan Livingston, president of Capitol Records; a granddaughter; and three great-grandchildren.

**TED MANN, 84,** North Dakota-born theater entrepreneur and movie producer, died of complications from a stroke on Jan. 15, 2001, in Los Angeles. He ran the Mann Theatres company and, later, National General Theaters, before turning to film production with such films as *The Illustrated Man, Buster and Billie, Lifeguard, The Nude Bomb,* and *Krull.* He is survived by his wife, actress Rhonda Fleming, two daughters, a sister, and four grandchildren.

Dorothy McGuire

**LAWRENCE B. MARCUS, 84,** Utah-born screenwriter, who received an Oscar nomination in collaboration with Richard Rush for adapting the script for *The Stunt Man,* died in Los Angeles on Aug. 28, 2001 due to complications from Parkinson's disease. His other credits include *Petulia, Justine, Going Home,* and *Alex & the Gypsy.* Survived by his wife, son, sister, and a grandchild.

**WHITMAN MAYO, 70,** New York City-born screen and television character actor, best known for playing "Grady Wilson" on the series "Sanford and Son," died of a heart attack on May 22, 2001 in Atlanta, GA. He was seen in films such as *The Main Event, D.C. Cab, The Seventh Coin,* and *Boyz N the Hood.* No reported survivors.

**DOROTHY McGUIRE, 83,** Omaha-born screen, stage, and television actress, who starred in such notable films as *A Tree Grows in Brooklyn, Gentleman's Agreement* (for which she earned an Oscar nomination), and *Swiss Family Robinson,* died on Sept. 14, 2001 in Santa Monica, CA. She had broken her leg three weeks prior and had developed an arrhythmia. She came to Hollywood in 1943 to repeat her stage role in *Claudia,* and thereafter was seen in such movies as *The Enchanted Cottage, The Spiral Staircase* (1946), *Till the End of Time, Mr. 880, I Want You, Three Coins in the Fountain, Trial, Friendly Persuasion, Old Yeller, This Earth Is Mine, A Summer Place, The Dark at the Top of the Stairs, Summer Magic, The Greatest Story Ever Told,* and *Flight of the Doves.* She is survived by her daughter and a son.

**JASON MILLER, 62,** New York-born actor-playwright, who earned an Academy Award nomination for playing the title role in the 1973 horror hit *The Exorcist,* died of a heart attack on May 13, 2001 in Scranton, PA. He first came to prominence as the Pulitzer Prize-winning author of the Broadway success *That Championship Season,* which he later adapted into a film, also serving as director. His other movie credits as an actor include *The Nickel Ride, Twinkle Twinkle Killer Kane (The Ninth Configuration), Light of Day,* and *Rudy.* Survived by three sons, including actor Jason Patric, and a daughter.

**JOHN MITCHUM, 82,** Connecticut-born character actor, and younger brother of Robert Mitchum, died in Los Angeles on Nov. 28, 2001. Among his movie credits are *Flying Leathernecks, The Lusty Men, Johnny Rocco, El Dorado, Paint Your Wagon, Chisum, Dirty Harry, Magnum Force,* and *The Outlaw Josey Wales.* Survived by his wife, two daughters, and several grandchildren.

**PAULINE MOORE, 87,** Pennsylvania-born film actress died of amyotrophic lateral sclerosis on Dec. 7, 2001 in Sequim, WA. In addition to starring in the serial *King of the Texas Rangers,* she was seen in features such as *Love Is News, Heidi* (1937), *The Three Musketeers* (1939; as Constance), *Charlie Chan at Treasure Island, Young Mr. Lincoln,* and *Trail Blazers.* Survived by her two daughters and a son.

**PEGGY MOUNT, 85,** British character actress, best known to American audiences for playing Mrs. Bumble in the Oscar-winning musical *Oliver!,* died in London on Nov. 13, 2001. Her other films include *Panic in the Parlor (Sailor Beware), The Embezzler, Ladies Who Do, One Way Pendulum,* and *Hotel Paradiso.* No immediate survivors.

Jason Miller    Virginia O'Brien

**PORTIA NELSON (Betty Mae Nelson), 80,** Utah-born actress and nightclub singer, died at her home in Manhattan on March 6, 2001. In addition to appearing on Broadway in *The Golden Apple* and acting in the soap opera "All My Children," she was seen in movies such as *The Sound of Music* (as Sister Berthe). Survived by a brother.

**VIRGINIA O'BRIEN, 81,** Los Angeles-born screen and stage actress-singer, famous for her deadpan comical specialty numbers in several MGM musicals, died on Jan. 16, 2001 in Woodland Hills, CA. She made her film debut in 1940 in *Hullabaloo,* which was followed by such films as *The Big Store, Lady Be Good, Ship Ahoy, Panama Hattie, Du Barry Was a Lady, Thousands Cheer, Two Girls and a Sailor, Meet the People, Ziegfeld Follies, The Harvey Girls, The Show-Off, Till the Clouds Roll By, Francis in the Navy,* and *Gus.* She is survived by three daughters, a son, several grandchildren, and two great-grandchildren.

**CARROLL O'CONNOR**, 76, New York City-born screen, television, and stage actor, best known for his Emmy Award-winning characterization of Archie Bunker on the classic television series "All in the Family," died on June 21, 2001 in Culver City, CA, of a heart attack brought on by complications from diabetes. He was seen in such motion pictures as *Parrish, By Love Possessed, Lonely Are the Brave, Cleopatra* (1963), *In Harm's Way, Hawaii, Not With My Wife You Don't, What Did You Do in the War Daddy?, Waterhole #3, Point Blank, The Devil's Brigade, Marlowe, Law and Disorder,* and *Return to Me.* Survived by his wife.

**JOHN PHILLIPS**, 65, South Carolina-born singer-songwriter, a member of the 1960s pop group the Mamas and the Papas, died of heart failure on March 18, 2001 in Los Angeles. He wrote such hit songs as "Monday, Monday," "San Francisco," and "California Dreamin'." The Mamas and the Papas were seen in the concert documentary *Monterey Pop,* and Phillips supplied songs for the film *Brewster McCloud* and the hit "Kokomo," featured in *Cocktail.* Survived by his fourth wife; three daughters, actresses Mackenzie and Bijou Phillips and singer Chynna Phillips; two sons; and two stepdaughters.

Carroll O'Connor      Francisco Rabal

**ANTHONY QUINN**, 86, Mexican-born screen, stage, and television actor, who, during a career spanning more than 60 years, won Academy Awards for his performances in *Viva Zapata!* and *Lust for Life,* died of respiratory failure in Boston, MA, on June 3, 2001. After making his film debut in 1936 in *Parole,* he went on to appear in more than 100 motion pictures including *The Plainsman* (1936), *Swing High Swing Low, Waikiki Wedding, The Buccaneer* (1938; he also directed the 1958 remake), *Union Pacific, Road to Singapore, The Ghost Breakers, City for Conquest, Blood and Sand* (1941), *They Died With Their Boots On, Larceny Inc., Road to Morocco, Irish Eyes Are Smiling, California, Sinbad the Sailor, The Brave Bulls, The World in His Arms, Against All Flags, Ride Vacquero!, Blowing Wild, Ulysses* (1954), *La Strada, Seven Cities of Gold, Man From Del Rio, The Hunchback of Notre Dame* (1957), *Wild Is the Wind* (Oscar nomination), *Hot Spell, Last Train From Gun Hill, Warlock, Portrait in Black, The Savage Innocents, The Guns of Navarone, Lawrence of Arabia, Requiem for a Heavyweight, Behold a Pale Horse, The Visit, Zorba the Greek* (receiving another Oscar nomination, for perhaps his most famous role), *High Wind in Jamaica, The Happening, The Shoes of the Fisherman, The Secret of Santa Vittoria, A Dream of Kings, A Walk in the Spring Rain, Flap, R.P.M., Across 110th Street, The Don Is Dead, The Greek Tycoon, The Passage, Lion of the Desert, Jungle Fever, Mobsters, Only the Lonely, Last Action Hero,* and *A Walk in the Clouds.* He is survived by his companion, Kathy Benvin, their two children, seven other sons, and three other daughters.

**FRANCISCO RABAL**, 75, Spanish film actor died of compensatory dilating emphysema during a flight between Montreal and Madrid on Aug. 29, 2001. His many credits include *The Wide Blue Road, Nazarin, The Witches* (1966), *Belle de Jour, Stay As You Are, The Holy Innocents, A Time of Destiny, Tie Me Up! Tie Me Down!,* and *Goya in Bordeaux.* Survived by his wife, a daughter, and a son.

**ALAN RAFKIN**, 73, New York City-born Emmy Award-winning television and motion picture director, died of heart disease on Aug. 6, 2001 in Los Angeles. Although he principally directed for television, he also helmed the movies *Ski Party, The Ghost and Mr. Chicken, Nobody's Perfect* (1968), *The Shakiest Gun in the West, Angel in My Pocket,* and *How to Frame a Figg.* No reported survivors.

Anthony Quinn

**WALTER REED, 85,** Washington-born character actor, died of kidney failure on Aug. 20, 2001 at his home in Santa Cruz, CA. His film appearances include *Mexican Spitfire's Elephant*, *Bombardier*, *Fighter Squadron*, *Return of the Bad Men*, *Young Man With a Horn*, *The Clown*, *Submarine Command*, *Horizons West*, *The High and the Mighty*, *Forever Female*, *The Horse Soldiers*, and *Where Love Has Gone*. Survived by his three children and a brother.

**MICHAEL RITCHIE, 62,** Wisconsin-born motion picture director of such films as *The Candidate*, *The Bad News Bears*, and *Semi-Tough*, died of complications from prostate cancer on Apr. 16, 2001 in Manhattan. Following some work in television, he made his theatrical directorial debut in 1969 with *Downhill Racer*, followed by such other pictures as *Smile*, *An Almost Perfect Affair*, *Divine Madness*, *The Survivors*, *Fletch*, *Wildcats*, *Diggstown*, *Cops and Robbersons*, and *The Fantasticks*. He is survived by his wife, a son, four daughters, two stepchildren, a brother, and a sister.

serving as producer as well) as *The Owl and the Pussycat*, *Play It Again Sam*, *The Last of Sheila*, *Funny Lady*, *The Sunshine Boys*, *The Seven Percent Solution*, *The Goodbye Girl*, *California Suite*, *Nijinsky*, *Pennies From Heaven* (1981), *Max Dugan Returns*, *Footloose*, *Protocol*, *The Secret of My Success*, *Steel Magnolias*, *My Blue Heaven*, *True Colors*, and *Boys on the Side*. He is survived by his sister, a niece, and a nephew.

**HARRY SECOMBE, 79,** British actor, comedian, and singer, best known as one of the stars (along with Peter Sellers and Spike Milligan) of Britain's pioneering humor series "The Goon Show," died of cancer on Apr. 11, 2001 in Guildford, England. In America he was perhaps most known by movie audiences for playing Mr. Bumble in the Oscar-winning *Oliver!*, in 1968. His other films include *Down Among the Z Men*, *Penny Points to Paradise*, *Davy*, *Jet Storm*, *The Bed Sitting Room*, *Song of Norway*, and *The Magnificent Seven Deadly Sins*. Survived by his wife of 53 years, four children, and five grandchildren.

Michael Ritchie     Herbert Ross     Harry Secombe     Kim Stanley

**NORMAN RODWAY, 72,** British actor and noted member of the Royal Shakespeare Company, died in Banbury, England on Mar. 13, 2001, following a stroke. He was seen in such motion pictures as *Chimes at Midnight*, *I'll Never Forget What's 'is Name*, *The Penthouse*, *Tai Pan*, *Mother Night*, and *The Empty Mirror*. Survived by his fourth wife and a daughter.

**HERBERT ROSS, 74,** Brooklyn-born choreographer-turned-film director, who earned dual Oscar nominations for helming and producing the 1977 film *The Turning Point*, died of heart failure on Oct. 9, 2001 in New York City. Following his stage work he came to Hollywood to choreograph the films *Inside Daisy Clover*, *Doctor Dolittle*, and *Funny Girl*. He became a film director starting in 1969 with the musical remake of *Goodbye Mr. Chips* and followed it with such other pictures (sometimes

**ANTHONY SHAFFER, 75,** British playwright, who won a Tony Award for *Sleuth*, which he later adapted into a film starring Laurence Olivier and Michael Caine, died of a heart attack on Nov. 6, 2001 in London. After his stage success he went on to write screenplays for such films as *Frenzy*, *The Wicker Man*, *Death on the Nile*, and *Absolution*. Survived by his third wife, actress Diane Cilento; his twin brother, writer Peter Shaffer; and two daughters from his second marriage.

**ANN SOTHERN (Harriette Lake), 92,** North Dakota-born screen and television actress, whose films ranged from "B's" like *Maisie* to "A" films like *A Letter to Three Wives*, died of heart failure at her home in Ketchum, ID, on March 15, 2001. Following her 1927 film debut in *Broadway Nights*, she was seen in such movies as *The Show of Shows, Broadway Thru a Keyhole, Kid Millions, Folies Bergere, My American Wife, Hell Ship Morgan, The Smartest Girl in Town, There Goes My Girl, Danger—Love at Work, Trade Winds, Joe and Ethel Turp Call on the President, Elsa Maxwell's Hotel for Women, Congo Maisie, Brother Orchid, Maisie Was a Lady, Lady Be Good, Panama Hattie, Cry Havoc, Thousands Cheer, Three Hearts for Julia, Undercover Maisie, Words and Music, Nancy Goes to Rio, The Blue Gardenia, Lady in a Cage, The Best Man* (1964), *Sylvia, The Killing Kind, Crazy Mama,* and *The Whales of August*, for which she received an Oscar nomination. Survived by her daughter, actress Tisha Sterling, from her marriage to actor Robert Sterling; a sister; and a granddaughter.

**KIM STANLEY (Patricia Reid), 76,** New Mexico-born screen, stage, and television actress, one of the leading Broadway stars of the 1950s, who appeared in the original productions of *Picnic* and *Bus Stop*, died in Santa Fe, NM, on Aug. 20, 2001 of uterine cancer. She appeared in only five motion pictures: *The Goddess, Seance on a Wet Afternoon* (Oscar nomination), *The Three Sisters, Frances* (Oscar nomination), and *The Right Stuff*, in addition to narrating *To Kill a Mockingbird*. She is survived by a son, two daughters, three grandchildren, and a brother.

Anthony Steel          Beatrice Straight

**ANTHONY STEEL, 80,** British screen and television actor, died on March 21, 2001 in London. Among his films are *The Mudlark, The Wooden Horse, Malta Story, Outpost in Malaya, Anzio,* and *The Mirror Crack'd*. Survived by a son and two daughters.

**BEATRICE STRAIGHT, 86,** New York-born screen, stage, and television actress, who won an Academy Award for playing William Holden's neglected wife in *Network*, died on Apr. 7, 2001 in North Ridge, CA. Principally a stage actress in productions such as *The Crucible* and *The Innocents*, she was seen in such films as *Phone Call From a Stranger, Patterns, The Nun's Story, Bloodline, The Formula, Endless Love, Poltergeist,* and *Power*. She is survived by two sons, two stepchildren, seven grandchildren, and three great-grandchildren.

Ann Sothern

**DAVID SWIFT, 82,** Minnesota-born director-writer responsible for films such as *Pollyanna* and *How to Succeed in Business Without Really Trying*, died of a heart attack in Santa Monica, CA, on Dec. 31, 2001. A former animator for Disney Studios, he went on to create the television series "Mr. Peepers" and then to direct and write other movies such as *The Parent Trap* (1961), *The Interns, Under the Yum Yum Tree, Good Neighbor Sam*, and *Candleshoe*. He is survived by his wife, two daughters, and two grandchildren.

**RALPH TABAKIN, 79,** Texas-born screen character actor, who received a tiny role in director Barry Levinson's 1982 film *Diner* and then went on to appear in all of his films up to *Liberty Heights,* in 1999, died of heart disease on May 13, 2001 in Rockville, MD. Other Levinson movies include *Young Sherlock Holmes, Good Morning Vietnam, Rain Man, Avalon, Bugsy, Disclosure*, and *Wag the Dog*. Survived by two daughters, two sisters, and a granddaughter.

Dorothy Tutin    Deborah Walley

**RALPH THOMAS, 85,** British film director, best known for helming *Doctor in the House* and several of its sequels, died in London on March 17, 2001. His other credits include *The Clouded Yellow, Appointment With Venus, The Wind Cannot Read, Conspiracy of Hearts, The Iron Petticoat, Campbell's Kingdom, A Tale of Two Cities* (1958), *The Thirty-Nine Steps* (1959), *Hot Enough for June*, and *Percy*. He is survived by his wife; his son, producer Jeremy Thomas; and a daughter.

**HARRY TOWNES, 86,** Alabama-born character actor, died at his home in Huntsville, AL, on May 23, 2001. Among his films are *The Mountain, Screaming Mimi, The Brother Karamazov, Sanctuary, Fitzwilly*, and *The Hawaiians*. In 1970 he became an Episcopalian minister. No reported survivors.

Ray Walston    Edward Winter

**LARRY TUCKER, 67,** Philadelphia-born writer-producer, who, in collaboration with Paul Mazursky, created the series "The Monkees" and earned an Oscar nomination for the script for *Bob & Carol & Ted & Alice*, died on Apr. 1, 2001 in Los Angeles due to complications from multiple sclerosis and cancer. He also worked with Mazursky on the films *I Love You Alice B. Toklas* and *Alice in Wonderland*. No reported survivors.

**DOROTHY TUTIN, 71,** London-born screen, stage, and television actress, who played Cecily in the 1952 film version of *The Importance of Being Earnest*, died of leukemia on Aug. 6, 2001 in London. Although principally a theater performer she was seen in other movies such as *The Beggar's Opera, A Tale of Two Cities* (1958), *Cromwell, Savage Messiah*, and *The Shooting Party*. She is survived by her husband, actor Derek Waring; a daughter; and a son.

**DIANA VAN DER VLIS, 66,** Toronto-born actress died from a pulmonary embolism on Oct . 22, 2001 in Missoula, MT. Her films include *The Girl in Black Stockings, X: The Man With the X-Ray Eyes, The Incident*, and *The Swimmer*, among others. Survived by her husband, a son, and a daughter.

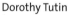

**DEBORAH WALLEY, 57,** Connecticut-born screen, stage, and television actress, who appeared in such teen-oriented sixties fare as *Gidget Goes Hawaiian* and *Beach Blanket Bingo*, died of esophageal cancer on May 10, 2001 at her home in Sedona, AZ. Her other movie credits include *Bon Voyage!*, *Summer Magic*, *The Young Lovers*, *Sergeant Deadhead*, *Ski Party*, *Dr. Goldfoot and the Bikini Machine*, *It's a Bikini World*, and *Benji*. Survived by two sons.

**RAY WALSTON, 86,** New Orleans-born screen, stage, and television actor, best known for his star-making, Tony Award-winning performance as the Devil in the musical *Damn Yankees*, which he then recreated for film, died after a long battle with lupus on Jan. 1, 2001 at his home in Beverly Hills, CA. He was seen in such other films as *Kiss Them for Me*, *South Pacific*, *The Apartment*, *Portrait in Black*, *Tall Story*, *Who's Minding the Store?*, *Kiss Me Stupid*, *Caprice*, *Paint Your Wagon*, *The Sting*, *Silver Streak*, *Popeye*, *Fast Times at Ridgemont High*, *Johnny Dangerously*, *From the Hip*, *Popcorn*, *Of Mice and Men* (1992), and *My Favorite Martian* (based on the television series on which he had starred). Also on television he received an Emmy Award for "Picket Fences." He is survived by his wife, a daughter, and two grandchildren.

**EDWARD WINTER, 63,** California-born screen, stage, and television actor, died of Parkinson's disease on March 8, 2001 in Los Angeles. He was seen in movies such as *The Parallax View*, *A Change of Seasons*, *The Buddy System*, and *From the Hip*. No reported survivors.

**VICTOR WONG, 74,** San Francisco-born character actor who made his way from journalism to acting with the Asian-American Theatre Group, died of heart failure on Sept. 12, 2001 at his home near Locke, CA. His movies include *Dim Sum: A Little Bit of Heart*, *Year of the Dragon*, *Big Trouble in Little China*, *The Golden Child*, *The Last Emperor*, *Tremors*, *3 Ninjas*, *The Joy Luck Club*, *Jade*, and *Seven Years in Tibet*. Survived by his wife, two daughters, a brother, three sisters, and five grandchildren.

Victor Wong       Otis Young

**OTIS YOUNG, 69,** Providence-born screen and television actor, best known for appearing opposite Jack Nicholson in the 1973 film *The Last Detail*, died on October 11, 2001. His few other movie roles include *Don't Just Stand There*, *The Hollywood Knights*, and *Blood Beach*. He later served as a pastor and as a college professor. Survived by his wife and four children.

# INDEX

Dunk, Bert, 195
Dunk, Jim, 237
Dunlap, Dave, 19
Dunlap, Doreen, 105
Dunlap, Pamela, 166
Dunn, Andrew, 18, 160, 243, 275
Dunn, Andrew T., 200
Dunn, Beverly, 238
Dunn, Henry, 206
Dunn, John, 303
Dunn, Nora, 29, 56, 107, 198
Dunn, Robert, 29
Dunn, Steve, 208
Dunn, Wally, 204
Dunn, Will, 89
Dunnam, Bill, 128
Dunne, Griffin, 92, 145, 329
Dunne, John Gregory, 171
Dunnock, Patricia, 170
Dunphy, Catherine, 89
Dunst, Kirsten, 24, 67, 329
Dunster, Delena, 276
Dunsworth, John, 159
Duperey, Anny, 329
Duplaix, Daphne, 311
Duplessis, Craig, 200
Duppin, Andy, 187
Dupré, Clément, 307
Durá, Pau, 232
Duran, Dan, 17, 44
Durand, Marie-Claire, 258
Durbin, Deanna, 329
Durell, R. J., 190
Duret, Marc, 287
Durke, Delta, 183
Durkin, Shevonne, 191
Durning, Charles, 39, 329
Dürrenmatt, Friedrich, 10
Durst, Debi, 18
Durst, Eric, 128
Durst, Fred, 107
Dury, Ken, 237
Dusek, Jaroslav, 255
Dushku, Eliza, 94, 191, 329
Dushku, Nate, 9
Dussart, Catherine, 273
Dusseldorp, Marta, 270
Dussollier, André, 284, 317, 329
Dutcher, Ethan, 177
Dutcher, Richard, 177
Duteil, Arnaud, 73
Duthie, Michael, 19
Dutton, Charles, 329
Duva, Lou, 172
Duval, Dean Rader, 57
Duval, James, 123
Duvall, Clea, 95
Duvall, Robert, 329
Duvall, Shelley, 329
Duvall, Wayne, 62

Duvauchelle, Nicolas, 320
Duveau, Jean-Rene, 282
Dvorak, Jan, 296
Dwan, Lisa, 33
Dwyer, Justin "Juddy," 304
Dwyer, Mark, 293
Dye, Dale, 135
Dyer, Clint, 301
Dyer, Danny, 266, 318
Dyer, James R., 129
Dyer, Karen, 95
Dykeman, Erin-Marie, 169
Dykstra, Russell, 293
Dylan, Alice, 185
Dylan, Jesse, 153
Dylan, Todd, 181
Dymally, Amentha, 66
Dyrholm, Trine, 299
Dysart, Richard, 329
Dysart, Tommy, 304
Dysinger, Elaine, 26
Dytman, Wendy, 56
Dzumber, Srecko, 224
Dzundza, George, 329

**E**

Eads, Paul, 8
Eads, Robert, 173
Eagle Cover Entertainment, 176
Eagles, Bill, 243
Earl, Jim, 187
Earl, Shaun, 202
Earnest, Randal P., 196
East, Guy, 11, 25, 291, 307
East, Ian, 266
Easter, Ben, 54
Easter Rock Church, 172
Eastman, Rodney, 20
Easton, Anthony, 214
Easton, Robert, 329
Eastside, Lori, 311
Eastwood, Clint, 329
*Eat Drink Man Woman,* 95
Eaton, Jamia, 194
Eaton, Shirley, 329
*Eban and Charley,* 210
Eben, Al, 112
Ebenbauer, Erwin, 254
Eberl, Luke, 82, 209
Ebeyer, Lisa, 18
Ebony Jo-Ann, 158, 187
Ebouaney, Eriq, 309
Ebsen, Buddy, 329
Eccleston, Christopher, 171, 269
Echard, Jim, 183
Echarri, Pablo, 280
Echavarria, Hector, 167
Echevarría, Emilio, 241
Echevarría, Lourdes, 241
Echo Lake Productions, 199
Echols, Jennifer, 8
Eckemyr, Agneta, 329

Ecker, Ryan, 139
Eckert, John M., 28
Eckhart, Aaron, 10
Eckhouse, James, 197
Ecklund, Peter, 93
Economy, Melissa, 139
Ecosse Films, 295
*Ed Gein,* 182
Eddy, Rev. Norm, 171
Edelman, Gregg, 329
Edelman, Pierre, 277
Edelman, Randy, 89, 112, 136, 169
Edelman, Shane, 42
Edelson, Kenneth, 93
Edelstein, Neal, 277
Edelstein, Rick, 95
Eden, Barbara, 329
Edery, Simon, 303
Edge, Michael, 51
Edis, Steve, 291
Edmond, Jennifer, 100
Edmond, Valerie, 237
Edmonds, Kenneth, 37
Edmonds, Kenneth "Babyface," 202
Edmonds, Tracey E., 37, 202
Edson, Richard, 205, 233
Edwards, Anthony, 188, 329
Edwards, Cheryl, 8
Edwards, Craig Alan, 189
Edwards, Dennis, 89
Edwards, Derek, 201
Edwards, Elizabeth, 210
Edwards, Jean Daniel, 200
Edwards, Johnny, 19
Edwards, Lee Ann, 196
Edwards, Luke, 88, 329
Edwards, Maribeth, 197
Edwards, Megan, 151
Edwards, Neville, 28
Edwards, Novie, 194
Edwards, Sally, 266
Edwards, Sean, 104
Edwards, Stacy, 44
Eftekhar, Kirt, 208, 254
Efve Film, 260
Egan, Angela Sue, 192
Egan, James, 188
Egan, Jennifer, 171
Egan, Martha Heather, 192
Egan, Michael, 194
Egers, "Dawn" Mitchell, 167
Eggar, Samantha, 329
Eggers, Sien, 261
Eggleston, Ralph, 126
Eglington, Holly, 207
Eguchi, Hisashi, 315
Ehrlich, Jodi, 16
Ehrlich Kalfus, Renée, 159
Eichberg Film (Monaco), 306
Eichelberger, Rick, 175

Eichholtz, Coralie, 51
Eichhorn, Lisa, 329
Eichling, Ike, 178
Eidel, Philippe, 299
Eidelman, Cliff, 87
Eidos Interactive Limited, 63
Eigenberg, Helen, 197
8X Entertainment, 173, 195
Eikenberry, Jill, 329
Eilber, Janet, 329
Eimers, Brenda, 57
Ein, Jon, 25
Einbinder, Scott, 181
Einstürzende Neubauten, 315
Eirik, Sten, 170
Eisen, Andrew, 196
Eisenberg, Ned, 185
Ejogo, Carmen, 56
Ekberg, Anita, 329
Ekblad, Stina, 230
Ekdahl, Lisa, 43
Ekins, Susan, 143
Ekland, Britt, 329
Ekoku, AJ, 32
Ekulona, Sadiah Arrika, 96, 148
El Cheli, Jose Ramirez, 312
El Deseo, SA, 285
El Ewaly, Rahab, 115
El Katsha, Sherief, 47
El Moror, 312
Elbaum, Diana, 312
Elbert, Chris, 169
Eldard, Ron, 165, 329
Eldon, Kevin, 318
Eldred, Judi, 51
Electra, Carmen, 24
Eleftheriou, Irini, 90
*Elegy for Iris,* 291
Eleni, Kaliopi, 16
Elephant Ears, 186
Elfman, Danny, 29, 31, 82
Elfman, Jenna, 43, 329
Elfont, Harry, 37
Elias, Arye, 179
Elias, Blas, 100
Elias, Jeannie, 152
Elias, Rahael, 207
Eliot, Jonathan, 263
Eliott, Tim, 51
Elizabeth, Shannon, 88, 94, 120, 176
Elizondo, Hector, 83, 95, 153, 329
Elizondo, Juliet, 83
Elkaïm, Jérémie, 258
Ellero, Maria Micol, 314
Elliot, Fran, 170
Elliot, Shan, 83
Elliot, Shannon, 191
Elliott, Alison, 329
Elliott, Chris, 89, 187, 329
Elliott, David, 156

Elliott, Jeremy, 177
Elliott, Missy, 187
Elliott, Patricia, 329
Elliott, Peter, 297
Elliott, Sam, 329
Elliott, Shawn, 9
Elliott, Ted, 48
Elliott, William, 95
Ellis, A. Delon, Jr., 103
Ellis, Aunjanue, 20, 211
Ellis, Chris, 82, 129
Ellis, David, 199
Ellis, James, 153
Ellis, Mark, 96, 103
Ellis, Mark Robert, 96, 103
Ellis, Michael, 11
Ellis, Mike, 181
Ellis, Ronald, 108
Ellis, Tom, 318
Ellwood, Kip, 86
Eloy, Alain, 224
Elswit, Robert, 130
Elsworth, Michael, 151
Elton, Ben, 270
Eluau, Sylvain, 235
Elwes, Cary, 209, 329
Elwood, Chris, 153
Ely, Ron, 329
Embarek, Ouassini, 248
Embry, Carey, 180
Embry, Ethan, 208, 329
E+MC2 Digital, 98
Emerson, Chloe, 234
Emerson, Todd, 209
Emmanuel, Heather, 33
Emmanuelli, François, 233
Emmerich, Toby, 84
Emmett, Bert, 181
Emmett, Jonathan, 279
Emmett, Randall, 191
Empire Pictures, 113, 279
Emtsis, Annalise, 243
Enberg, Alex, 80
Encore Entertainment, 95
*End of the Road, The,* 181
Endelman, Stephen, 254
Enden, Jeff, 196
Endewardt, Andrea Hecht, 39
Endie, Bruce, 199
Endô, Kôji, 268
Endou, Kouri, 307
Endre, Lena, 230
*Endurance, The: Shackleton's Legendary Antarctic Adventure,* 200
*Enemy at the Gates,* 227, 239–40
Engel, David, 192
Engelman, Jeremy, 304
Engemann, Shannon, 177
England, Joseph, 237
Engle, Melissa, 182
English, Rick, 298
English, William, 108
Englund, Robert, 329

Golden, Annie, 199, 332
*Golden Bowl, The,* 247
Golden Harvest, 279
Goldenberg, William, 156
Goldenring, Jane, 114
Goldenthal, Elliot, 70
Goldfield, Cindy, 113
Goldfiem, Frédéric de, 273
Goldhaber, Mickey, 188
Goldheart Production, 204
Goldman, Alain, 309
Goldman, Bernie, 13
Goldman, Beth, 189
Goldman, Dina, 97, 144
Goldman, Henrique, 320
Goldman, William, 104
Gold-Miller, 187
Goldpaugh, Kathleen, 204
Goldring, Danny, 178
Goldschmidt, Ernst, 270
Goldsman, Akiva, 214
Goldsmith, Aeja, 37
Goldsmith, David, 205
Goldsmith, Jerry, 36, 117
Goldsmith, Merwin, 25
Goldstein, Al, 167
Goldstein, Brett, 187, 312
Goldstein, Jenette, 332
Goldstein, Julie, 110, 236
Goldstein, Libby, 80, 85, 95
Goldstein, Limor, 179
Goldstein, Lionel, 320
Goldstein, Steven, 298
Goldthwait, Bob, 332
Goldthwait, Bobcat, 34
Goldwater, Richard, 37
Goldwyn, 230, 316
Goldwyn, Samuel, Jr., 95
Goldwyn, Tony, 32, 87, 332
Goletz, Erinn Seaghda Rice, 166
Golia, David, 167
Golijov, Osvaldo, 253
Golino, Valeria, 332
Gomelsky, Giorgio, 188
Gomes, D. Luzia, 234
Gomes, Isabel, 194
Gomes, Larissa, 24
Gómez, Andrés Vicente, 287
Gomez, Carlos, 209
Gómez, Eduardo, 28
Gomez, Ian, 42
Gomez, Jaime, 174
Gomez, Jaime P., 108
Gómez, Juan, 192
Gómez, Marco, 287
Gómez, Matteo, 25
Gómez, Octavio, 25
Gomez, Panchito, 145
Gomez, Terri, 19
Goncalves, Oscar, 13
Gonder, Matthew, 48
Gonneau, Jackie, 89
Gonneau, Pierre, 29
Gonzales, Julio R., 205
Gonzales, Louie, 174
Gonzales-Gonzalez, Pedro, 332
González Compeán, Francisco, 241
Gonzalez, Cordelia, 332
González, Eduardo, 232
Gonzalez, Homero, 276
González Iñárritu, Alejandro, 241
Gonzalez, Javier, 285
Gonzalez, Nicholas, 320
Gonzalez, Quinn, 173
Gonzalez, Richard, 172
Gonzalez, Rick, 180
González Sinde, Andrés, 287
Gonzalo, Estevan, 54
Good Machine, 139
Good Machine International, 251
Goodall, Caroline, 83, 332
Goodall, Louise, 268
Goode, Christopher, 158
Goode, Conrad, 106, 176
Gooding, Cuba, Jr., 54, 91, 107, 331–332
Gooding, Omar, 66
Goodman, Barak, 168
Goodman, Brian, 34, 117
Goodman, Dody, 332
Goodman, Fredrick B., 97
Goodman, Hazelle, 14
Goodman, Jennifer, 8
Goodman, Joe, 170
Goodman, Joel, 193
Goodman, John, 42, 114, 126, 332
Goodman, John B., 173
Goodman, Lisa, 198
Goodman-Hill, Tom, 295
Goodspeed, Margie, 87
Goodwin, Danny, 196
Goodwin, Jamie, 110
Goodwin, Michael, 64
Goore, Ziablé Honoré, 310
Goossen, Greg, 148
Goossen, Gregory B., 140
Goossen, Gregory Bryant, 130
Goossen, Joe, 71
Gordey, Keith, 192
Gordon, Chad, 209
Gordon, Dennie, 39
Gordon, George, 179
Gordon, Jade, 199
Gordon, Jamie, 145
Gordon, Jonathan, 94
Gordon, Keith, 332
Gordon, Lawrence, 63, 121
Gordon, Lori, 39
Gordon, Lucy, 110
Gordon, Madison, 177
Gordon, Molly, 166
Gordon, Pamela, 203
Gordon, Stuart, 250
Gordon-Levitt, Joseph, 332
Gorela, Darjan, 224
Gorelik, Olga, 250
Gorham, Christopher, 210
Gorham, Mel, 42
Goritsas, Demetri, 135
Gorman, Breon, 207
Gorman, Cliff, 204, 332
Gorman, Jen, 184
Gorme, Eydie, 143
Gorovaia, Irene, 148
Gorris, Marleen, 246
Gorshin, Frank, 332
Gortner, Marjoe, 332
Goryl, Stacey, 175
Gosch, Chris, 195
*Gosford Park,* 160–61, 223, 228
*Gospel According to Philip K. Dick, The,* 173
Gosset, Pascal, 304
Gossett, Louis, Jr., 332
Goti, Luis A., 33
Götting, Manfred, 257
Gottlieb, Meyer, 95
Gottlieb, Steve "Simcha," 312
Goude, Jean-Philippe, 273
Goudie, Peter, 9
Gould, Dana, 208
Gould, Elliott, 142–143, 332
Gould, Harold, 332
Gould, Jack, 92
Gould, Jason, 332
Gould, Lisa, 88
Goulder, Ann, 199
Goulet, Robert, 16, 332
Goumane, Dembo, 305
Goumane, Goundo, 305
Goumane, Halimatou, 305
Goumane, Mustapha, 305
Goumane, Myriam, 305
Goupil, Romain, 278
Gourary, Manuela, 282
Gourson, Jeff, 56
Goux, Monica, 310
Gowan, Peter, 304
Gowdy, Curt, 96
GQ, 56, 202
Grabianski, Greg, 187
Grabowsky, Paul, 270, 288
Grace, April, 69
Grace, Francey, 42
Grace, Nickolas, 247
Grace, Steven, 51
Grace, Topher, 143
Grace, Wayne, 277
Grace, Yvonne, 19
Gracia, Ana, 232
Gracie Family, 197
Gracie Films, 118
Gracie, Sally, 355
Gradilone, Michael, 54, 175
Graf, Allan, 46
Graf, David, 332
Graff, Todd, 332
Graham, Heather, 119, 137, 175, 331–332
Graham, Isla, 237
Graham, Kenny, 243
Graham, Lauren, 16
Graham, Marcus, 277
Graham, Nathan Lee, 107
Graham, Sophie, 178
Graham, Stephen, 236
Graham, Zoë, 131
Grail, Gil, 207
Grainger, Andrew, 135
Grammer, Kelsey, 23
Granada Film, 78
Granat, Cary, 31, 207
Granath, Björn, 230
Grande, Sean, 154
Grande, Sonia, 269
Grandidier, Didier, 310
Grandpierre, Richard, 299
Grangé, Jean-Christophe, 309
Granger, Farley, 332
Grano, Andrea, 82
Grant, Beth, 54, 100, 123, 183
Grant, David Marshall, 332
Grant, Derick Karlton, 32
Grant, Hugh, 40–41, 332
Grant, James, 304
Grant, "J.G." Jimmy, 19
Grant, Kathryn, 332
Grant, Lee, 168, 277, 332
Grant, Richard E., 160–161, 309, 332
Grant, Rodney A., 95
Grant, Tiffany, 315
Granville, Hollis, 17
Grapey, Marc, 156
Grassl, Carolyn, 169
*Grateful Dawg,* 197
Grateful Dead, The, 181, 197
Gratton, Bill, 155
Grauer, Kelly, 51
Graves, Daniel, 78
Graves, Douglas, 186
Graves, Peter, 332
Graves, Rupert, 332
Graves, Sara, 129
Graves, William, 22
Graves-Bartolini, Lori, 196
Gravier, 93
Gravity Entertainment, 73
Gray, Allan, 179
Gray, Coleen, 332
Gray, Devin, 53
Gray, Dylan, 289
Gray, Ernie, 243
Gray, Glyn, 51
Gray, Jacque, 177
Gray, James "Mala," 312
Gray, Jennifer, 184
Gray, Jim, 156
Gray, Leah, 137
Gray, Linda, 332
Gray, Macy, 108–109, 178
Gray, Rothaford, 28
Gray, Sim, 304
Gray, Spalding, 153, 158, 332
Grayhm, Steven, 39
Grayson, Kathryn, 332
Gray-Stanford, Jason, 214
Grazer, Brian, 214
Graziani, Christophe, 278
Grdevich, Sabrina, 69
Greaney, Patti, 105
Greatrex, Richard, 46
Greaves, Gail, 23
Greco, Carlo, 246
Greco, Joe, 168
Greco, Marco, 14
Greco, Massimo, 286
Green, Al, 178, 202
Green, Alex, 175
Green, Brent, 115
Green, Bruce, 83
Green, Chris, 206
Green, Dan, 300
Green, Dannon, 66
Green, George Dawes, 20
Green, Gerald, 114, 254
Green, Josh, 54
Green, Kerri, 332
Green, Lester "Bettlejuice," 187
Green, Marian, 197
Green, Michael, 136
Green Moon Productions, 179
Green, Raymond, 247
Green, Richard, 277
Green, Seth, 37, 80, 91, 183, 332
*Green Tambourine,* 16
Green, Tom, 179–180
Green, Vince, 8, 103
Green, Whitney, 42
Greenberg, Jerry, 47, 52
Greenberg, Jonathan, 16
Greenberg, Julie, 8
Greenberg, Paul, 152
Greenberg, Robbie, 8
Greenberg-Goldman, Bonnie, 91
Greenbury, Christopher, 110, 131
Green-Dove, Abigail, 83
Greene, Brian, 178, 204
Greene, Daniel, 131
Greene, Ellen, 332
Greene, Graham, 263, 332
Greene, James, 119
Greene, Rodney, 205
GreeneStreet Films, 25, 92, 139, 145
Greenfield, Luke, 56

Karyo, Tchéky, 262
Karz, Mike, 198
Karzis, Alex, 20
Kas, Najat, 282
Kasbian, Hossein, 300
Kasch, Dylan, 182
Kaschock, Taryn, 8
Kash, Daniel, 28, 106, 159
Kashana, Vikram, 107
Kashima, Kenn, 174
Kaspar, Caroline, 51
Kass, Carmen, 107
Kassai, Csongor, 255
Kassovitz, Mathieu, 283–284, 309, 335
Kastein, Franca, 229
Kastner, Elliott, 16
Katala, Anthony, 11
Katalifos, Dimitris, 298
Katanga, Richard, 156
Katase, Rino, 264
Katdare, Deep, 174
*Kate & Leopold,* 158, 228
Kates, Brian A., 199
Katic, Branka, 289
Katims, Robert, 277
Kato, Hiroyuki, 311
Kato, Masaya, 264
Katt, Nicky, 115
Katt, William, 336
Kattan, Chris, 18, 112, 336
Katz, Loulou, 304
Katz, Ross, 139
Katz, Susan, 80
Katzenberg, Jeffrey, 48
Kaufman, Amy, 110
Kaufman, Avy, 8, 34, 69, 97, 106, 130
Kaufman, David, 54
Kaufman, Lloyd, 188, 203
Kaufmann, Christine, 336
Kava, Caroline, 208
Kavanagh, John, 306
Kavner, Julie, 336
Kavovit, Andrew, 91
Kawaguchi, Takashi, 300
Kawajiri, Yoshiaki, 313
Kawalkowski, Daru, 83
Kawano, Osami, 85
Kawasaki, Hirotsuge, 315
Kawasaki, Peter, 207
Kay, Billy, 101
Kay, Lisa, 41
Kay, Peter, 236
Kay, Roger, 300
Kay, Stephen Thomas, 52
Kaycheck, Michael, 22
Kaye, David, 19
Kaye, Norman, 51, 270
Kayser, Eberhard, 98
Kayser, Karen, 92
Kaz Entertainment, 198
Kazan, Lainie, 335–336
Kazanjian, Howard, 167, 196

Kazantzidis, Stavros, 308
Kaznelson, Ayelet, 200
Kazurinsky, Tim, 336
Kazzazi, Behzad, 290
KBK Entertainment, 204
Ke, 206
Keach, Stacy, 336
Kean, Greg, 175
Kearney, Joseph, 277
Kearsley, Harlin, 17
Keaton, Diane, 43, 336
Keaton, Michael, 336
Keats, David, 128
Keaveney, Anna, 307
Kedar, 17
Kedwani, Maged, 297
Kee, Bettina, 276
Keegan, Andrew, 97, 336
Keehn, Dorka, 171
Keel, Howard, 336
Keena, Monica, 206
Keenan, Caroline, 166
Keenan, Dane, 298
Keenan, Joe, 117
Keenan, Will, 188
Keene, Lisa, 61
Keener, Catherine, 336
Keenleyside, Eric, 9, 179
Keenon, Jean Paul, 201
*Keep The River on Your Right: A Modern Cannibal Tale,* 176–177
*Keeping It Real,* 204
*Keeping It Real: The Adventures of Greg Walloch,* 205
Keeslar, Matt, 207, 336
Kehela, Karen, 214
Kehela, Steve, 62
Kehler, Jack, 184
Kehoe, Michael, 146
Keibler, Stacy, 190
Keiffer, Dennis, 112
Keim, Claire, 301
Keir, Andy, 189, 208
Keische, Tom, 56
Keitel, Harvey, 336
Keith, David, 140, 336
Keith, Gregory, 202
Keith, Kevin, 194
Keith, Paul, 78
Keith, Warren, 193
Keleghan, Peter, 317
Kelemer, Dov, 196
Keller, Catherine, 281
Keller, Duncan, 19
Keller, George, 299
Keller, Hiram, 306
Keller, Marthe, 336
Keller, Stacy Joy, 8
Kellerman, Sally, 336
Kelley, Jennifer Marie, 146
Kelley, Sheila, 201
Kellner, Catherine, 54–55
Kellog, Ann, 12

Kellogg, Jeff, 96
Kelly, Brett, 192, 207
Kelly, Daragh, 302
Kelly, David, 266
Kelly, David Patrick, 64, 121
Kelly, Dean Lennox, 301
Kelly, Frank, 302
Kelly, Ian "Blaze," 99
Kelly, Jessica, 110
Kelly, Joe, 54
Kelly, Katie, 12
Kelly, Kristen Lee, 183
Kelly, Moira, 336
Kelly, Monroe, 162
Kelly, Nuala, 237
Kelly, Patrick Smith, 106
Kelly, Paul, 293
Kelly, Que, 39
Kelly, Richard, 123
Kelly, Tim, 188
Kelsch, Ken, 311
Kelsey, Mary, 204
Kelso, Steve, 44
Keltie, Luke, 238
Kemp, Jeremy, 336
Kemp, Lance Fabian, 151
Kemp, Sacha, 153
Kempster, Victor, 113
Kempter, Karl, 169
Ken Mandel Films, 168
Kendall, Cavan, 256
Kendra, Christopher, 184
Kendrick, Christopher E., 177
Keneally, Laura, 316
Kener, David, 32
Keneshea, Ellen, 61
Kenley-Letts, Ruth, 309
Kennar, Larry, 99
Kennard, Malcolm, 230
Kenne, Brock, 96
Kennedy, Annie, 311
Kennedy, Bobby, Jr., 169
Kennedy, Burt, 357
Kennedy, Carrie, 238
Kennedy, Dwayne, 153
Kennedy, George, 336
Kennedy, Jamie, 64, 94, 198
Kennedy, Jane, 238
Kennedy, Joey, 270
Kennedy, Kathleen, 69, 75
Kennedy, Kerri, 188
Kennedy, Leon Isaac, 336
Kennedy, Lora, 57
Kennedy, Matthew, 207
Kennedy, Merle, 190
Kennedy, Miles, 100
Kennedy, Sandra, 81
Kennedy, Tufford, 170
Kenny, Coco, 237
Kenny, Francis, 38, 153
Kenny, JC, 194
Kensei, Ken, 43
Kensit, Patsy, 191, 199, 336

Kent, Alan, 83
Kent, Allegra, 169
Kent, Gary, 62
Kent, Graham, 119
Kent, Karol, 134
Kent, Melissa, 67
Kent, Peter, 19, 180
Kent, Rolfe, 32, 43, 74, 158
Kentaro, 262
Kenworthy, Duncan, 309
Kenyon, Katisha, 270
Keogh, Danny, 182
Keogh, Doreen, 306
Keogh, Garrett, 306
Keogh, Jeff, 238
Kepley, John, 146
Kepniss, Stephen A., 97
Kepros, Nicholas, 173
Keramidas, Harry, 176
Kerbel, Diane, 28
Kerber, Randy, 98
Kerdaffrec, Réjane, 258
Keresztúri, Bori, 87
Kergoat, Yannick, 245
Kerman, Ken, 128
Kermit Ruffins & His Barbecue Swingers, 172
Kerner, Jordan, 209
Kerner, Norberto, 25
Kerns, Joanna, 189
Kerns, Linda, 91
Kerr, Catherine, 295
Kerr, Deborah, 336
Kerr, E. Katherine, 64
Kerr, John, 336
Kerr, Rowland, 174
Kerry, Roy, 208
Kershen, Ed, 184
Kerwin, Brian, 336
Kerwin, Jim, 197
Kerzner, D. J., 189
Kesmodel, Maximillian, 198
Kessel, Brandon, 122
Kessel, Sam, 271
Kessler, Henri M., 312
Kessler, Stephen, 208
Kestner, Boyd, 14, 165
Ketcham, Tony, 78
Kettler, Mark W., 182
Key, Jeff, 209
Keyes, Eric, 16
Keyes, Evelyn, 336
Keyfilms Roma, 271
Keystone, 297
Keyzer, Bruno de, 249
Khajuria, Ravi Steve, 24
Khalil, Caroline, 297
Khalili, Mahbobeh, 312
Khan, Shah Rukh, 318
Khanjian, Arsinée, 278, 287
Khatib, Kastro, 268
Khazai, Malek Jahan, 290
Khoury, Makhram J., 179

Kianian, Reza, 300
Kiarostami, Abbas, 176
Kibbe, Gary B., 95
Kibbe, Kyle, 186
Kicked Down Prods., 199
Kid Rock, 39, 178
Kidd, David, 169
Kidd, Tom, 196
Kidder, Margot, 203, 336
Kidman, Nicole, 6, 50–51, 221, 227, 269, 336
Kidney, Ric, 74
*Kids World,* 209
Kiebranz, Johannes, 14
Kiel, Richard, 336
Kiem, Geoffrey, 51
Kier, Udo, 195, 336
Kiernan, Paul, 172
Kiesewetter, Ina, 257
Kightlinger, Laura, 131, 187, 208
Kihal, Husky, 282
Kikuchi, Hideyuki, 313
Kikumura, Takusho, 311
Kilar, Cedomir, 224
Kilbane, Pat, 18, 62
Kilbride, Kerry, 56, 113
Kilgariff, Karen, 58
Kilgore, Alex, 170
*Kill Me Later,* 192
Killebrew, K.A., 169
Killer Films, 22, 77
*Killings,* 139
Kilmek, Johnny, 257
Kilmer, Val, 336
Kilner, Kevin, 88
Kilpatrick, Tracy, 64
Kilvert, Lilly, 29
Kim, Bryan, 190
Kim Eun-jung, 313
Kim, Jacqueline, 199
Kim, James "Tiger Twins," 28
Kim Sang-bum, 313
Kim, Simon "Tiger Twins," 28
Kim Sung-bok, 313
Kim, Tanya, 194
Kimball, Kristen, 47
Kimbro, Art, 89
Kimbrough, Charles, 11, 16
Kimbrough, John, 263
Kimbrough, Matthew, 111, 180
Kimes, Patricia, 74
Kimiai, Masud, 176
Kimmel, Adam, 184
Kimmel, Sidney, 43, 92
Kimsey, Todd, 82
Kimstim, 287
Kimura, Hideo, 264
Kina, 107
Kincaid, Aron, 336
Kincaid, Jamaica, 186
Kinchen, Arif S., 205

Morris, Jacob, 237
Morris, Jane, 83
Morris, Jonathan, 250
Morris, Joshua, 237
Morris, Kathryn, 69
Morris, Phil, 61
Morris, Redmond, 141
Morris, Tom, 57, 277
Morrisette, Alanis, 94
Morrison, Daver, 168
Morrison, James, 128
Morrison, Lisa, 182
Morrissey, David, 90, 276
Morrissey, John, 38, 56
Morrissey, Mary, 189
Morrow, Andy, 69, 198
Morrow, Carrie, 11
Morrow, Kirby, 120
Morrow, Rob, 204, 340
Morse, David, 104, 340
Morse, Laila, 298
Morse, Robert, 340
Morse, Wayne, 102
Morshower, Glenn, 54, 165
Mortensen, Viggo, 150–151, 340
Mortimer, Mark, 92
Mortley, Ben, 293
Morton, Billy, 207
Morton, Joe, 156, 340
Morton, Rebecca, 190
Morton, Samantha, 261, 340
Mortorff, Lawrence, 173, 195
Mos Def, 162, 213
Mosby, Josh, 22
Moscato, Vincent, 260
Moscovitch, Ilan, 299
Moscow, David, 118
Moscrop, Liz, 119
Moseley, Marion, 67
Moses, Evan, 104
Moses, William, 340
Mosher, Susan, 11
Mosier, Scott, 94
Moss, Carrie-Anne, 26–27, 340
Moss, Jesse, 317
Moss, Marc, 36
Moss, Paige, 184
Moss-Bacharach, Ebon, 148
Mosso, Joe, 158
Mosso, Joe J., 32
Mostel, Josh, 340
Motevali, Morteza, 244
Mothersbaugh, Mark, 12, 148
Motion Picture Corporation of America, 197
Motiwala, Chetan, 318
Motley, Alexa, 195
Motu, Rangi, 298

Mouchet, Catherine, 340
Mouhibian, Araksi, 289
Moulay, Moustapha, 135
Moulévrier, Gérard, 273
*Moulin Rouge,* 50–51, 221, 227
Mount, Michael, 253
Mount, Peggy, 360
*Mountain King, The,* 175
Moura, Wagner, 294
Moussazadeh, Ahmad, 312
Moustaki, Leticia, 90
Mouthoub, Nadéra, 299
Mower, Mark, 73
Moyer, Mike, 56
Moyer, Stephen, 209
Moynahan, Bridget, 110
Moynihan, Mary, 302
Moynihan, Sean, 131
MP Film Management, 239
M.P. Productions, 299
Mr. Mudd, 78
Mr. T, 147, 347
MRI Inc., 319
M6 Films, 245
MTV Films, 8, 187
Mu Qi, 242
Mueller, Carl, 197
Mueller, Cookie, 188
Mueller, Weston, 175
Muellerleile, Marianne, 26
Mueller-Stahl, Armin, 340
Muenter, Leilani, 80
Mugge, Robert, 172
Mug-Shot Production, 172
Mühlhahn, Stefanie, 257
Muir, Rory, 298
Muirhead, Peter, 51
Mulat, Mena, 186
Mulcahy, Jerry, 298
Mulcahy, Lara, 50–51
Muldaur, Diana, 340
Mulder, Mark, 156
Mulgrew, Kate, 340
Mulhall, Lauren, 302
Mulheren, Michael, 56, 93
Mulhern, Ciaran, 99
Mulhern, Matt, 340
*Mulholland Dr.,* 213, 277
Mulholland, Mark, 306
Mulholland, Ross, 147
Mulkey, Randy, 34
Mull, Martin, 340
Mullally, Megan, 18, 180, 203
Mullan, Carrie, 99
Mullan, Kathleen, 34
Mullan, Mark, 171
Mullan, Peter, 87
Mullane, Liz, 151
Mullen, John, 186
Mullen, Kimberly, 98
Mullen, M. David, 188
Mullen, Marie, 237
Muller, Eddie, 178

Muller, Elizabeth, 173
Müller, Marco, 224
Muller, Stephen, 193
Mulqueen, Tracey, 23
Mulroney, Dermot, 340
*Mummy Returns, The,* 45, 227
Mumy, Bill, 340
Mundell, Gary, 70
Mundy, Kevin, 19
Mune, Ian, 151
Mung Ling Tsui, 17
Mungo, Domenico, 286
Mungo, Howard, 54
Muniz, Frankie, 64
Munn, Jack "Jay," 97
Muñoz, David, 285
Muñoz, Gustavo, 241
Munro, Lochlyn, 192
Munroe, Odessa, 13, 207
Munson, Camden, 139
Munter, Pam, 210
Murakami, Ren, 264
Murakami, Ryû, 268
Murase, Shuko, 70
Murbach, Eliza, 13
Murciano, Enrique, 165
Murdoch, Alex, 147
Murdoch, Jessica, 37
Murdoch, Laurie, 179
Murdock, Charles, 115
Murdock, Colin, 308
Murgea, Catalina, 289
Murphy, Bill, 230
Murphy, Brittany, 96, 106, 118, 137, 340
Murphy, Dan, 175
Murphy, Danny, 89, 131
Murphy, David, 165
Murphy, Don, 73, 119
Murphy, Donna, 340
Murphy, D-Taylor, 202
Murphy, Eddie, 48, 64, 340
Murphy, Erin, 39
Murphy, Fred, 191
Murphy, Jamie, 309
Murphy, John, 275
Murphy, Martin, 237, 302
Murphy, Michael, 340
Murphy, Pat, 302
Murphy, Tab, 61
Murphy, Tracey, 288
Murray, Bill, 89, 148–149, 340
Murray, Chad Michael, 195
Murray, Daniella, 19
Murray, Devon, 132
Murray, Don, 340
Murray, Jeff, 78
Murray, Martin Glyn, 90
Murray, Melanee, 121
Murray, Rodrigo, 241
Murray, Susan, 178, 237
Murray, W. Clapham, 139

Murrell, Linda, 187
Murtagh, John, 243
Murtaugh, Jim, 146
Musaka, Naomasa, 264
Musante, Tony, 340
Musca, Tom, 95
Muscal, Michael, 182
Muse, 73
Muser, Wolf, 195
Mushroom Pictures, 243
Musiban, Ashwin, 276
*Musketeer, The,* 99, 228
Musky, Jane, 25
Musnicki, Robert, 169
Mussenden, Isis, 94
Mussenden, Roger, 22, 39, 56, 112
Must, Miriam, 12
Musto, Michael, 180, 205
Mutambirwa, Garikayi, 120
Muth, Ellen, 182
Mutual Film Company, 63
Mwale, Judith, 156
Mwinga, Stephen, 263
*My First Mister,* 114
*My Voyage to Italy (Il Mio Viaggio in Italia),* 316
MYA, 61
Myers, Chris, 91
Myers, Jake, 263
Myers, Johann, 165
Myers, Lou, 11
Myers, Margo, 189
Myers, Mark Robert, 16
Myers, Mike, 48, 340
Myers, Ruth, 25, 291
Myerscough, Damian, 295
Myhre, John, 156
Myles, Lynda, 237
Myles, Sophia, 119
Mylius, Wade, 118
Mylonas, Alexandros, 298
Mylrea, David, 13
Myra, 198
Myriad Entertainment, 169
Myrin, Arden, 190
*Mysterious Object At Noon,* 318

# N
Nabokov, Vladimir, 246
Nabors, Jim, 340
Nabozny, Barbara J., 83
Nadarevic, Mustafa, 224
Nader, George, 340
Nader, Michael, 340
Nagasawa, Takayuki, 313
Naghavi, Fatemeh, 244
Nagle, Rob, 153
Nagler, Morgan, 62, 88
Nagy, Christine, 184
Nagy, Wes, 203
Nahas, Fouad, 290
Nahlous, Caroline, 51
Nahon, Chris, 262

Nahon, Philippe, 309
Nahoum, Simon, 248
Nai Yuan Hu, 158
Naidu, Ajay, 14, 105, 121
Naji, Mohammad Reza, 290
Najimy, Kathy, 11, 91
Nakagawa, Anna, 311
Nakagawa, Joy, 264
Nakahara, Sanaye, 310
Nakamura, Kanemon, 310
Nakanishi, Masayasu, 43
Nakauchi, Brian, 99
Nakazawa, Kazunori, 70
Nall, Frank, 135
Nall, Rashaan, 205
Namath, Joe, 340
Namesake Entertainment, 170
Nancy Boy, 180
Nandi, Swapan, 307
Nankou, Dah, 176
Nanty, Isabelle, 284
Napal, Jackie, 67
Napes, Boris, 235
Napier, Charles, 169
Naples, Carly, 123
Napolitano, Ted, 100
Napper, Sian, 302
Naranjo, Victor, 186
Narbey, Leon, 298
Narohna, Ajay, 205
Narong, Kannikar, 318
Nasar, Sylvia, 214
Nascarella, Arthur, 93, 158
Nash, Shawn Patrick, 92
Nashel, Peter, 86
Nashville Bluegrass Band, The, 186
Nathan & the Zydeco Cha Chas, 172
Nathan, Robert H., 86, 144, 210
Nathanson, Jeff, 84
Nathanson, Julie, 183
National Asian American Telecommunications Association, 174
Native Pictures, 153
Natividad, Kitten, 167
Natural Nylon Entertainment, 302
Natwick, Myron, 70
Naude, Nicky, 309
Naughton, David, 340
Naughton, James, 340
Navarrete, Javier, 285
Navarro, Berta, 285
Navarro, Demetrius, 205
Navarro, Guillermo, 31, 285
Navarro, Lolo, 21
Navedo, Andrea, 9
Navrot, Ada, 287
Nayar, Deepak, 233
Nayci, Errol, 261

Salvay, Bennet, 98
Salvitore, Gene, 167
Salvo, Brian de, 306
Samaha, Elie, 10, 19–20,
    44, 52, 130, 184
Samaroo, Dennison, 153
Sambora, Richie, 202
Samian, Inna, 239
Samie, Céline, 320
Samir, Sami, 179
Samkao, Kroi, 273
Sammarco, Charles, 145
Sammel, Richard, 253
Samms, Emma, 345
Sampietro, Mercedes, 287
Samra, Narinder, 128
Samson, Dil, 61
Samson, Vanessa, 276
Samuel Goldwyn Films,
    95, 266
Samuel, Marc, 278
Samuel, Martin, 194
Samuels, Jeremiah, 184,
    205
Samuels, Terry, 170
Samuels, Thea, 277
Samuelson, Hymie, 115
Samuelsson, Emma, 271
San Bao, 252
San Giacomo, Laura, 345
San Juan, Olga, 345
Sánchez Berlanga, Manuel,
    256
Sanchez, Jaime, 145
Sánchez, Jordi, 232
Sanchez, Marisol Padilla,
    170
Sanchez, Oscar Ortega, 99
Sanchez, Roselyn, 84
Sanchez, Salvador, 21
Sanchez, Virginia, 67
Sanda, Dominique, 309
Sandberg, Per, 267
Sandcastle 5, 160
Sandell, William, 64
Sandells, Richard, 270
Sanders, Amanda, 187
Sanders, Andrew, 247
Sanders, Cynthena, 147
Sanders, Ivin, 70
Sanders, Jay O., 36, 345
Sanders, Lowell, 154
Sanders, Tim, 151, 298
Sanderson, Martyn, 151
Sandfort, Stephen, 117
Sanditz, Stephanie, 158
Sandke, Randy, 93
Sandler, Adam, 39, 56, 345
Sandler, Ethan, 83
Sandler, Jana, 39
Sandler, Mallory, 91
Sandmel, Ben, 172
Sandoval Chavez, Jesus
    Gabriel, 172
Sandoval, Hermila, 172
Sandoval, Jesus, 172

Sandoval, Jimmy, 172
Sandoval, Lidia, 172
Sandoval, Miguel, 34
Sandoval, Rosario, 172
Sandow, Nick, 192
Sandquist, Greg, 103
Sandrich, Cathy, 9, 52, 114
Sands, Aislinn, 288
Sands, Julian, 233, 345
Sands, Roland, 188
Sands, Tommy, 345
Sandston, Pat, 165
Sandstorm Films, 181
Sandys, Eric, 87
Sanford, A. Alexandra, 207
Sanford, Jesse, 201
Sanford, John, 61
Sanford, Kate, 97, 204
Sanford, William, 158
Sangare, Bakary, 320
Sangari, Giuseppe, 286
Sanger, Jonathan, 146
Sangmo Gurung, 242
Sanjur, Cesar, 33
Sanoussi-Bliss, Pierre, 306
Sans, Jacques, 248
Sansalone, Paolo, 286
Santana, Carlos, 178
Santaolalla, Gustavo, 241
Santelli, Heidi, 64
Santiago, Luis B., 287
Santiago, Ray, 145
Santiago, Renoly, 202
Santiago-Hudson, Ruben,
    129
Santibanez, Roberto, 31
Santillana, Fernando, 186
Santoni, Reni, 64
Santopietro, Michele, 200
Santoro, Rodrigo, 294
Santos, Amanda, 131
Santos, Encar, 195
Santos, Joe, 184
Santy, Charles, 145
Sanz, Carmen, 312
Sanz, Horatio, 176
Sapir, Richard Ben, 179
Sapp, Alem Brhan, 187
Sapp, David Greenlaw, 177
Sapsford, Beau, 178
Sara, Mia, 345
Sarabia, Ric, 42, 178
Saracen Street, 309
Sarafian, Richard C., 64
Sarandon, Chris, 345
Sarandon, Susan, 70, 345
Sarchielli, Massimo, 246
Sarchielli, Sacha, 209
Sarde, Alain, 277, 287, 297
Sarin, Vic, 170
Sarkar, Samir, 318
Sarkissian, Arthur, 84
Sarossy, Paul, 39
Sarr, Awa Sène, 300
Sarra, Eduardo, 235
Sarrazin, Michael, 345

Sarri, Olle, 271
Sarsgaard, Peter, 42
Sartain, Gailard, 156
Sartor, Fabio, 246
Sarubbi, Pedro, 90
Sasia, Bernard, 281
Sassone, Michael, 191
Sata, Yugo, 319
Sætervoll, Einar, 315
Sather, Drake, 107
Sato, Don, 264
Sato, Garret T., 54
Satterthwaite, McKenzie,
    111
Sattler, Bob, 67
*Saudade Do Futuro*, 308
Sauer, Dorit, 23
Saul, Louis, 305
Saunders, Emily, 316
Saunders, Julie, 266
Saunders, Kendall, 171, 207
Saunders, Merl, 181
Saunders Triplets, 132
Saunders, Warner, 156
Sautelet, Pascal, 236
Savage, Fred, 345
Savage, John, 345
Savage, Martin, 33, 276
Savage, Red, 202
Savage, Tom, 171
Savante, Stelio, 214
*Save the Last Dance*, 8, 227
Savenkoff, Elizabeth Carol,
    9
Savidge, Jennifer, 62
Savin, Eric, 258
*Saving Silverman*, 13
Saviola, Camille, 345
Savoy, Teresa Ann, 345
Sawaki, Tetsu, 268
Sawitz, "Reb," 167
Sawyer, Tom, 198
Saxon, John, 345
Saxon, Kelly, 185
Saxton, Richard, 56
*Say It Isn't So*, 175
Sayeed, Malik, 186
Sayyed, Nafisah Tahirah,
    191
Sbaraglia, Leonardo, 280
Sbarge, Raphael, 54, 345
Sbragia, Mattia, 247
Sburlan, Suzana, 186
Scacchi, Greta, 345
Scahel, Bernard, 180
Scala Productions, 288
Scales, Crystal, 152
Scalia, Jack, 345
Scalia, Pietro, 14, 165
ScanBox, 299
Scanlon, Pat, 206
Scanlon, Patricia, 193
Scantlebury, Glen, 63, 111
Scarabelli, Ricardo, 9
Scarborough, Adrian, 160,
    234

Scarborough, Victoria, 295
Scardifield, Simon, 318
Scarpa, David, 117
Scarry, Rick, 125
Scarwid, Diana, 345
*Scary Movie 2*, 187, 227
Scattini, Monica, 302
Schaal, Jayson, 174
Schaal, Kristen, 158
Schad, Brenda, 169
Schaech, Johnathon, 181
Schaefer, Bob, 16
Schaefer, Eric, 208
Schaefer, Roberto, 162,
    203
Schaeffer, Eric, 42
Schaffer, Perry, 267
Schaffer, Stephen R., 89
Schamus, James, 95
Scharf, Helga, 305
Scheck, Olivia Morgan,
    118
Schedwill, Jacqueline, 257
Scheelar, Darryl, 36
Scheider, Roy, 345
Schein, Justin, 190
Scheine, Raynor, 345
Scheinman, Greg, 168
Scheinmann, Danny, 253
Schell, Johnny Lee, 181
Schell, Maria, 345
Schell, Maximilian, 345
Schenk, Michael, 239
Schenkenberg, Marcus,
    105
Schenker, Wendy, 80
Schepisi, Fred, 288
Scheuer, Walter, 189
Schick, Clemans, 239
Schiff, Paul, 136
Schiff, Richard, 56, 166
Schiffbauer, Sascha, 99
Schiffer, Claudia, 107, 311
Schifrin, Lalo, 84
Schill, Trish, 70
Schily, Jenny, 229
Schimenti, Vincent, 309
Schimmel, Robert, 187
Schipper, Sebastian, 257
Schirripa, Steve, 191
Schirripa, Steven, 39
Schirripa, Steven R., 22
Schirrmacher, Leslie, 34
Schlaich, Anne, 319
Schlaich, Frieder, 319
Schlansky-Hoch, Lynn,
    199
Schlatter, Charlie, 345
Schlegel, Alex, 191
Schlegel, Sam, 191
Schlesinger, Katharine, 237
Schlöndorf, Volker, 229
Schlosser, Jens, 251
Schmidt, Eddie, 186
Schmidt, John, 172
Schmidt, Lenny, 39

Schmidt, Lucy, 10
Schmidt, Wayne, 319
Schmidt-Ohen, Katja, 319
Schmit, Anthony, 305
Schmitt, Irma, 257
Schmölzer, August, 254
Schmolzer, Jonathan, 51
Schneebaum, Tobias,
    176–177
Schneid, Hervé, 253, 284
Schneider, Charles, 78
Schneider, David, 46
Schneider, John, 56, 345
Schneider, Kelley, 88
Schneider, Maria, 345
Schneider, Pilar, 56
Schneider, Rob, 56
Schneider, Stephanie, 203
Schnell, Jurgen, 289
Schoen, Jessie, 12
Schoeny, Jeff, 208
Schoeny, Jeffrey, 183
Schofield, Andrew, 275
Schofield, David, 99, 119,
    304
Schofield, John D., 239
Schooley, Mark, 70
Schooley, Randy, 120
Schoonmaker, Thelma, 316
Schramek, Géza, 135
Schreiber, Catherine, 91
Schreiber, Liev, 158, 345
Schreiber, Nancy, 242
Schreiber, Pablo, 190
Schreier, Deborah, 207
Schrock, Melissa, 185
Schröder, Jana, 257
Schroder, Rick, 345
Schroeder, Adam, 107
Schroeder, Barbet, 274
Schroeder, David, 277
Schroeder, Romain, 99
Schrott, 229
Schubarth, Marischka, 239
Schubert, Stephan, 289
Schuck, John, 93, 345
Schuckett, Ralph, 300
Schulberg Productions, 242
Schulberg, Sandra, 242
Schuler, Julia Anne, 146
Schulman, Cathy, 137
Schulman, Felicia, 263
Schulman, Roger S. H., 48
Schult, Staffen, 257
Schultz, Armand, 146
Schultz, Dwight, 313, 345
Schultz, Julia, 84, 176, 181
Schultz, Philip Jon, 176
Schulze, Matt, 65
Schulze, Paul, 106
Schumate, Rachel, 97
Schurmann, Francis, 237
Schuster, Tom, 92
Schutze, Jim, 73
Schutzhofer, Josef, 254
Schwab, Eric, 197